EVERYMAN'S LIBRARY

EVERYMAN'S LIBRARY

EVERYMAN,
I WILL GO WITH THEE,
AND BE THY GUIDE,
IN THY MOST NEED
TO GO BY THY SIDE

WILLIAM SHAKESPEARE

Tragedies

with an Introduction by Tony Tanner
General Editor – Sylvan Barnet

VOLUME 2

EVERYMAN'S LIBRARY

(LLSS
80837

bra Mc
C6052

This book is one of 250 volumes in Everyman's Library
which have been distributed to 4500 state schools
throughout the United Kingdom.
The project has been supported by a grant of £4 million
from the Millennium Commission.

First included in Everyman's Library, 1906
These plays are published by arrangement with New American
Library, a division of Penguin Books USA Inc.
Titus Andronicus: Copyright © 1963, 1964, 1989 by Sylvan Barnet.
Troilus and Cressida: Copyright © 1963 by Daniel Seltzer.
Copyright © 1963, 1988 by Sylvan Barnet.
Julius Caesar: Copyright © 1963, 1986 by William and Barbara Rosen.
Copyright © 1963, 1987 by Sylvan Barnet.
Antony and Cleopatra: Copyright © 1964, 1988 by Barbara Everett.
Copyright © 1963, 1988 by Sylvan Barnet.
Timon of Athens: Copyright © 1965, 1989 by Maurice Charney.
Copyright © 1963, 1989 by Sylvan Barnet.
Coriolanus: Copyright © 1966, 1988 by Reuben Brower.
Copyright © 1963, 1988 by Sylvan Barnet.
Introduction © Tony Tanner, 1993
Bibliography and Chronology © David Campbell Publishers Ltd.,
1993
Typography by Peter B. Willberg

ISBN 1-85715-164-X

A CIP catalogue record for this book is available from the
British Library

Published by David Campbell Publishers Ltd., 79 Berwick Street,
London W1V 3PF

Distributed by Random House (UK) Ltd.,
20 Vauxhall Bridge Road, London SW1V 2SA

TRAGEDIES

TRAGEDIES

CONTENTS

CONTENTS

SHAKESPEARE:
THE GREEK AND ROMAN PLAYS

Thou art a Roman, be not barbarous ...
(Titus Andronicus, I, i, 379)

dost thou not perceive
That Rome is but a wilderness of tigers?
(ibid., III, i, 53–4)

When Shakespeare perused North's translation of Plutarch's
Lives (1579) – which he did most carefully; the main source for
the last four plays in this volume is North's translation – he
would have read this:

To be short, it may be truly sayd, that the reading of histories, is
the schole of wisedome, to facion mens understanding, by considering
advisedly the state of the world that is past, and by marking diligently
by what lawes, maners and discipline, Empires, Kingdomes and
dominions, have in old time bene stablished and afterward main-
tayned and increased: or contrariwise changed, diminished and
overthrown.

Just why the history of Rome was so important to the
Elizabethans, and how and to what ends Shakespeare imagi-
natively deployed that history, will, I hope, be made a little
clearer in the course of this introduction. But, from the outset,
it is important to remember that although the following six
plays are conventionally, and correctly, classified as tragedies,
they are also histories. Indeed, to describe them, we can
scarcely do better than avail ourselves of one of Polonius'
felicitous, and too often wrongly mocked, compounds. These
plays are 'tragical-historical'.

*

TITUS ANDRONICUS (1592–4)
Rome, Roman, Romans – the name of the imperial city echoes
and re-echoes throughout the long opening scene (in varying
forms, it occurs at least sixty times by my count). The play is

certainly 'The most Lamentable Romaine Tragedie of Titus Andronicus', as the quarto has it, but it is also, and inextricably, a play about Rome itself. More will emerge concerning this Elizabethan preoccupation with Rome, but at this point it will be helpful to have an authoritative statement from T. J. B. Spencer, who made a special study of the Roman plays.

> Roman history was used as the material for political lessons, because it was one of the few bodies of consistent and continuous historical material available. English national history, in spite of patriotic sentiment, was much more limited in scope and interest, and the historians were not nearly so good as the ancient Latin writers ... When Shakespeare turned from English history to Roman history as the subject of plays, he was touching upon grave and provocative problems of political morality ... Rome loomed much larger in the history of the world than it does to modern historians and writers; and the Roman Empire was much more important than the Roman Republic. The potentates elected as heads of the Holy Roman Empire were still numbered from Julius Caesar by Shakespeare's contemporaries. There were very few republics in sixteenth-century Europe, but there were plenty of aspiring Roman emperors; and it was therefore from the history of the growth of monarchical rule in Rome (the political events which allowed the rise and led to the fall of Julius Caesar and the conflict between Octavian and Mark Antony) that the most useful and relevant lessons could be learnt.
>
> (*Shakespeare: The Roman Plays*, p.9)

The Rome of the opening scene displays all the panoply and adjuncts of a proud, imperial city. In the first speech we hear of 'noble patricians', 'the justice of my cause', 'the imperial diadem', 'my father's honors'. We hear of 'the gods of Rome', there are vows to heaven, priests with holy water, sacrificial rites, sacred monuments to the dead. There is a triumphal entry of the returning victorious general (Titus) along with his prisoners and spoils. We seem to be witnessing the confident ceremonies of the – very patriarchal – power of invincible Rome. But the scene starts with ferocious dispute about the imperial succession, and moves on to a brutal human sacrifice. This is followed by a disastrous mistake when Titus rejects election as Emperor and, being a believer in hereditary monarchy, bestows the title on the manifestly unscrupulous

INTRODUCTION

and ignoble Saturninus. Worse is to come when Titus kills one
of his own sons who is courageously, and correctly, defending
the rights of his sister; then the new Emperor Saturninus
impulsively – and one infers lustfully – marries the captive
Gothic Queen, Tamora. It was her son whom Titus had
sacrificed, so when she murmurs in an aside to her new
husband – 'I'll find a day to massacre them all' (I, i, 451) –
meaning Titus and his family – it is clear that there is trouble
ahead. Almost her last words in this scene are

> Titus, I am incorporate in Rome,
> A Roman now adopted happily ...
>
> (I, i, 463–4)

The Goth, the vengeful woman, is now '*incorporate*' in patriarchal Rome. Whatever condition the 'body' of the state of
Rome was in – and despite the litany of 'just', 'noble', 'virtue',
etc., it seems far from stable – that body is now going to be
threatened from within by an alien, savage, female agent.

'Kind Rome' (I, i, 165) says Titus at one point. But this
Rome is visibly far from 'kind'. The matter of the human
sacrifice is particularly pertinent here:

> Give us the proudest prisoner of the Goths,
> That we may hew his limbs, and on a pile
> *Ad manes fratrum* sacrifice his flesh ...
>
> (I, i, 96–8)

Rome was a singularly brutal state, but it did *not* practise
human sacrifice. Spencer makes the point that, although
Shakespeare's depiction of Rome can be rather confused (at
times it seems to be 'a free commonwealth, with the characteristic mixture of patrician and plebeian institutions'), he does
seem to be trying to get Roman history 'right'. But then he
deliberately inserts this archaic barbarity. As the 'barbarian'
Goths note – 'Was never Scythia half so barbarous' (I, i, 131).
It is as if, *from the very beginning*, Shakespeare wants to suggest
that the conventional opposition of Rome–Barbarian simply
will not hold. And we may note the words of Tamora, mother
of the sacrificed Goth, as she pleads that her son be spared:

xiii

> O, if to fight for king and commonweal
> Were piety in thine, it is in these.
> Andronicus, stain not thy tomb with blood.
> Wilt thou draw near the nature of the gods?
> Draw near them then in being merciful;
> Sweet mercy is nobility's true badge.
>
> (I, i, 114–19)

We may recall what Portia says of mercy in *The Merchant of Venice* – 'it becomes/The throned monarch better than his crown' (IV, i, 189) – and feel that from every conceivable perspective Tamora is, here, humanly in the right of it. And Titus in the wrong. Tamora's comment, as the sacrifice is taking place – 'O cruel, irreligious piety!' (I, i, 130) – inevitably becomes a comment on all the 'pieties' which noble, just, kind Rome regards as the distinguishing mark of its civilized state.

Titus is surely as equally in the wrong when he stabs his son Mutius who is honourably defending his sister Lavinia. As his brother Marcus – one of the few wise and temperate figures in the play – says to Titus, he has 'In a bad quarrel slain a virtuous son' (I, i, 343). The insensate rage of Titus at this point, his fury at any sign of filial insubordination, his willingness to destroy his own child, have suggested to a number of critics, rightly I think, that we can already detect here the early signs of a King Lear – a proleptic similarity enhanced when, as he is buffeted with grief after grief and atrocity after atrocity, it seems he must go mad ('my heart all mad with misery', 'no man should be mad but I' – III, ii, 9, 24). Like Lear, in this opening scene, Titus gets everything – the succession, the sacrifice, the treatment of his children – terribly, and as it will prove disastrously, wrong. (It might be added that some have also seen adumbrations of the figure of Othello in Titus – the great soldier living by a naive, martial code, who proves to be hopelessly vulnerable to the machinations of evil plotters when he moves from the battlefield to the city. In fact, in his courage, almost maniacal bravery, stubbornness, hardness, intemperate anger, and – yes – stupidity, the old warrior, an almost archaic pre-political figure, looks straight forward to Shakespeare's last Roman tragic hero,

Coriolanus – whose desire to be revenged on Rome is referred
to in this play – IV, iv, 69.)

Titus kills his son because he claims he has 'dishonored all
our family' (I, i, 346). When his other sons plead that, since
Mutius 'died in honor', he should be allowed a place in the
family tomb, Titus most grudgingly allows it, but comments
'To be dishonored by my sons in Rome!' (I, i, 386). When the
decent Bassianus attempts to defend Titus to the evil Saturninus, Titus stops him:

> leave to plead my deeds;
> 'Tis thou and those that have dishonored me.
> Rome and the righteous heavens be my judge,
> How I have loved and honored Saturnine!
>
> (I, i, 425–8)

Saturninus, hypocritically pretending that he has been robbed
of Lavinia, has the gall to protest to Tamora:

> What, madam! Be dishonored openly,
> And basely put it up without revenge?

These Romans are everywhere and continuously invoking
'honor' (the word occurs at least seventeen times), not least
when they are committing some cruel and ruthless deed.
Contrariwise, any attempt at a decent or just deed is said by
one man or other to 'dishonor' him. Clearly something has
gone hopelessly wrong with the very concept of 'honor'; not
only has it been devalued and emptied out of any positive
value or meaning – it has been perverted, indeed at times
inverted. It will not be long before Falstaff is famously asking
'what is this honor?' and we will be hearing much about
'honor' in later plays by Shakespeare. But, from the start,
Roman honour is made to seem a twisted, deviant thing.

Act II starts with a shock – the black Aaron standing alone
in front of the palace in Rome. We have seen the northern
barbarian – the Goth – made 'incorporate' in Rome, and now
here is the southern barbarian – the Moor – in the same city.
He immediately announces his determination to 'wanton'
with Tamora, the new queen of Rome, and cause the 'shipwrack' of the whole state. Aaron, of course, is *the* villain –

lustful, infinitely sadistic, delighting in the cruellest tricks and stratagems (for example, persuading Titus to cut off his hand in the deluded belief it will save the life of his son), incapable of remorse and completely committed to evil. Characteristically, he says such things as 'Aaron will have his soul black like his face' (III, i, 205) and:

> But, I have done a thousand dreadful things
> As willingly as one would kill a fly,
> And nothing grieves me heartily indeed,
> But that I cannot do ten thousand more.
>
> (V, i, 141–4)

and

> If one good deed in all my life I did,
> I do repent it from my very soul ...
>
> (V, iii, 189–90)

We may find the racist implications disturbing, but Aaron's soul is meant to seem of the same 'hue' as his body – 'Spotted, detested, and abominable' (II, iii, 74). He takes such a ghoulish pleasure in committing or arranging atrocities that some people have claimed to find him a comic figure – and indeed, faced with the horrors he contrives, that may be the more comfortable strategy. But I doubt that was how it struck the Elizabethan audience, and I'm not sure it should us. Certainly, he is an extreme and in some ways crudely outlined figure (probably owing something to Marlowe's Barabas), but as Titus is an early Lear, so Aaron foreshadows Iago (there is a premonitory hint of this when on one occasion he threatens 'I'll speak no more but "Vengeance rot you all!"' – V, i, 58). He is an embodiment of that phenomenon, awesome to Shakespeare, of almost motiveless and utterly uncontainable evil, though Shakespeare does add one rather surprising touch – Aaron's devotion to his illegitimate child by Tamora. There is no such blurring of the figure of Iago.

After the solo appearance of Aaron at the start of Act II, we move to 'A forest near Rome'. Shakespeare was to make much of the juxtaposition of the different realms of court and forest (or city and country), and in this play, where Rome was undoubtedly dominated by men and 'law' and ceremony, the forest offers the release of the barbarous – it is dominated by Tamora and Aaron, the woman and the savage, and is the place of lustful sexuality and the hunting of animals, literal and metaphorical. The occasion is a supposedly celebratory panther hunt. And here again, Shakespeare seems to be adding a deliberate anachronism, or non-historical incongruity, for his own purposes – there was no panther-hunting in ancient Rome. But it enables him to relate the literal pursuit of animals to all the sexual pursuit going on ('as if a double hunt were heard at once,' as Tamora says), and have them converge horribly on the 'doe', Lavinia, who is first ravished, then hideously mutilated. The forest is the ideal realm for Aaron's operations. As he says:

> The Emperor's court is like the House of Fame,
> The palace full of tongues, of eyes, and ears:
> The woods are ruthless, dreadful, deaf, and dull ...
>
> (II, 1, 126–8)

It is there he can 'wanton' with Tamora, and it is there he digs the pit which will fatally trap Quintus and Marcus. That pit itself becomes the image of frightening female sexuality, as is made tolerably explicit:

> What subtle hole is this,
> Whose mouth is covered with rude-growing briers,
> Upon whose leaves are drops of new-shed blood ...
>
> (II, iii, 198–200)

It is also described as 'this detested, dark, blood-drinking pit' and 'this fell devouring receptacle' (II, 111, 224, 235); and while one part of the forest is full of animal life, in the dark part where there is the 'abhorred pit', as sexual and fecund Tamora says – 'here nothing breeds' (II, iii, 96). That Shakespeare felt a nausea, a fear, at certain aspects of female sexuality becomes clear in later plays. But here, thus early, he identifies or equates this kind of ravenous, negative female sexuality – it 'devours' rather then 'breeds' – with treachery, murder, death.

Thus the forest is made to appear the complete opposite of

the city. And yet, perhaps not quite so, either. The Capitol has its murders, and the palace has its 'wantonness' and irrational cruelties, as we have seen. Limbs are 'lopped' in Rome as they are, less 'ceremoniously', in the 'ruthless, vast, and gloomy woods', as Titus describes the forest (IV, i, 53). Confronted with the appalling spectacle of the tongueless, handless Lavinia, ravished and maimed in the dark part of the forest, the good Marcus asks:

> O, why should nature build so foul a den,
> Unless the gods delight in tragedies?
>
> (IV, i, 59–60)

But you cannot blame tragedy on terrain, and, as in *King Lear*, the invoked 'gods' are not remotely in evidence. It is *men* who 'foul' the den.

The remainder of the play takes in Rome, mainly in or near the house of Titus – though there is a scene on 'a plain near Rome'. We watch the intensification and acceleration of the horrors visited on Titus and his family (through the devices of Aaron and Tamora and the willing participation of Saturninus). We witness the apparent madness of Titus as the multiplication of atrocities passes way beyond the bearable. When he is confronted with his mutilated daughter, Lavinia, he reacts with powerful tropes:

> What fool hath added water to the sea,
> Or brought a faggot to bright-burning Troy?
> My grief was at the height before thou cam'st,
> And now like Nilus it disdaineth bounds.
>
> (III, i, 68–71)

It is all, simply and literally, *too much* – Titus' grief is as uncontainable as Aaron's evil. Shakespeare was always drawn to the study of what 'disdaineth bounds' – excess of all kinds – and with the image of the rampant, overflowing Nile, we already have an adumbration of his greatest drama of excess – *Antony and Cleopatra*. Marcus, the balanced humane Marcus, laments that 'These miseries are more than may be borne!' (III, i, 243), and Titus' son Lucius refers to his father as 'The woefull'st man that ever lived in Rome!' (III, i, 289). Here again, this is where the tragedy prefigures *King Lear*. But another play, too, when Titus seems to go mad. He shoots arrows to the gods with letters attached, asking for justice and revenge ('There's not a god left unsolicited'). But there is method in his madness for, of course, the arrows and letters fall in Rome, as Saturninus recognizes, 'blazoning our unjustice everywhere ... As who would say, in Rome no justice were' (IV, iv, 18–20). That is exactly what Titus is saying – he has already called Rome 'a wilderness of lions', definitively confounding the conventional culture–nature distinctions. But if he is mad – deranged with grief – he is also steely sane. During Tamora's final, grotesque, attempt to trick him (pretending she is 'Revenge, sent from below'), in an aside Titus says:

> I knew them all, though they supposed me mad;
> And will o'erreach them in their own devices ...
>
> (V, ii, 142–3)

This anticipates Shakespeare's most famous character. *Titus Andronicus* is a 'revenge' play and shows some of the crudities of that genre, but by the time Shakespeare has finished transforming that genre, we will have *Hamlet*.

The final Act depicts Titus' revenge, as, in the last ghoulish incident in the play, he serves up to Tamora her sons baked in a pie ('Eating the flesh that she herself hath bred' – V, iii, 62) – a feast, incidentally, described by the unwitting Marcus as 'ordained to an honorable end,/For peace, for love, for league, and good to Rome' (V, iii, 22–3). Honorific terms are by now taking a hiding. The play ends in a rout of deaths and killings (but so does *Hamlet* – 'This quarry cries on havoc,' exclaims Fortinbras). More interesting, perhaps, is the spectacle of what we may call the radical shift, or inversion, of allegiance. The great defender and saviour of Rome becomes its most implacable enemy as Titus' son, Lucius, goes off to raise an army of Goths to attack Rome. This, of course, is to be the great theme of Shakespeare's last Roman play, *Coriolanus*. But here it is, from the start. When Lucius is banished, Titus says:

> How happy art thou then,
> From these devourers to be banished!
>
> (III, i, 57)

Lucius himself has some rather Coriolanus-like lines:

> Lastly, myself unkindly banished,
> The gates shut on me, and turned weeping out,
> To beg relief among Rome's enemies ...
> I am the turned-forth ...
>
> (V, iii, 104–9)

What does it mean, what does it portend, when Rome 'turns-forth' its bravest and most illustrious defender-heroes? When a Goth can say:

> the great Andronicus,
> Whose name was once our terror, now our comfort,
> Whose high exploits and honorable deeds
> Ingrateful Rome requites with foul contempt ...
>
> (V, i, 9–12)

Where is the authoritative voice now? With the Goths rather than the Romans? Can a 'terror' so quickly become a 'comfort' – and, presumably, *vice versa*? Here are problems of inversion, reversibility, even inter-changeability, to which Shakespeare was clearly extraordinarily well attuned. Now a Roman, now a Goth – handy-dandy, which is which?

This is not to say that Shakespeare erases all differences between the Romans and Goths, between the city and the forest. There is always the possibility – in patriarchal, cruel, and – yes – 'barbarous' Rome – of law, order, stability, degree. Though if Saturninus is Emperor, one feels that Romans might as well head for the forest. But the forest offers *no* possibility of law. The emergence of the ravished and muti-lated Lavinia from the forest is an apt image of what the realm encourages and permits. The continuous presence of Marcus – just, rational, decent, humane – is a reminder of what Rome can produce and what it might stand for. If – *if* – it can get the words right, it can, could, be the place and source of honour, virtue, nobility. *If*. At the end, Lucius is the new Emperor of Rome and seems to bespeak or promise a restoration of true justice and order:

INTRODUCTION

> may I govern so,
> To heal Rome's harms and wipe away her woe!
>
> (V, iii, 147–8)

But the actual, and dramatic, ending has Rome disgorging itself of the body of the female Goth, Tamora, which had been so disastrously 'incorporated' into the city. Rome's ceremony ends here – there are to be no commemorative, funereal rites:

> But throw her forth to beasts and birds of prey.
> Her life was beastly and devoid of pity,
> And being dead, let birds on her take pity.
>
> (V, iii, 198–200)

But Rome has been shown to be 'devoid of pity' – where was 'mercy' in scene one? The issues are not clear cut, and Shakespeare makes very sure that we see that.

So what of the play as a whole? Famously, Edward Ravenscroft in 1687 described it as 'a heap of rubbish'. It has been described as black comedy, Grand Guignol, and melodrama (by H. B. Charlton, who found in the play no 'inner world' of the characters). Because the particularly horrifying episodes are quite explicitly 'quotations', as it were, from Ovid (Lavinia's mutilation repeats the story of Tereus and Philomena) and Seneca (the children in the pie comes from *Thyestes* out of Aeschylus), Muriel Bradbrook offered the opinion that '*Titus Andronicus* is a Senecal exercise; the horrors are all classical and quite unfelt, so that the violent tragedy is contradicted by the decorous imagery. The tone is cool and cultured in its effect.' I can understand this response, but do not share it. Modern readers will, of course, make up their own minds; but, while the play is marked by harsh oratory rather than the sinuous and subtle speech of psychological revelation, it seems to me to touch on issues of great moment – for the Elizabethans and for us. Not least – what does our Roman heritage – and we in the West are all inheritors of Rome – really comprise and stand for? And – is it possible, ever, to delimit and demarcate the 'barbarous'?

*

TROILUS AND CRESSIDA (1601–2)

In *Titus Andronicus* 'our Troy, our Rome', are elided; Titus himself is referred to as the 'Roman Hector'. It was easy for Shakespeare to move from Rome to Troy as the two great cities – and their fates – were closely linked in the European imagination. Troy had a particular significance for western Europe since it traced its ancestry back to the Trojans, through Aeneas and Ascanius. According to the legend as recounted by Geoffrey of Monmouth, Brute, the great-grandson of Aeneas, founded London, which was New Troy. The legend of Troy was well known to Elizabethans: eight translations of Homer were available; there was plenty of Trojan material in Ovid's *Metamorphoses*, Chaucer's epic poem *Troilus and Criseyde* was well known, and Shakespeare would also almost certainly have known Henryson's *The Testament of Cresseid*, which offers itself as a sequel to Chaucer and traces out her pitiful life – and death – as a whore after Diomed has tired of her. Before considering the kind of drama Shakespeare made out of this familiar legend, it is important to bear in mind that the many medieval re-tellings of the legend of the Trojan war invariably debased it and degraded the participants. As Phillips puts it: 'the history of Troy in the middle ages is a history of degeneration and debasement' (*The State in Shakespeare*, p. 114). The Greeks in particular were invariably shown in a bad light – 'merry Greek' was a pejorative, disparaging term. It is what Helen is called in Shakespeare's play. So it is perhaps not surprising that Shakespeare should choose to dramatize a moment in the war when demoralization and social disintegration – not to say corruption and rottenness – are heavy in the air. There are 'heroes', but heroism degenerates into squalid thuggery. There are 'lovers', but love deliquesces into lubricious promiscuity. The positive graces should be valour and devotion – but 'war and lechery confound all!' (II, iii, 77). Values are everywhere degraded – 'soiled' in the language of the play. The root cause of the war is 'the soil of [Helen's] fair rape' (II, ii, 148), and this early oxymoron discolours the whole play, in which what seems fair invariably turns out to be soiled. The 'soilure' (IV, i, 56) of Helen permeates the play, so that even when Troilus maintains that it is a matter of honour for Troy to keep Helen, his metaphor partakes of the general contamination. 'We turn not back the silks upon the merchant/When we have soiled them' (II, ii, 69–70).

The play starts, rather unusually, with an 'armed Prologue'. His last words are distinctly casual, nonchalant to the point of indifference:

> Like or find fault; do as your pleasures are;
> Now good or bad, 'tis but the chance of war.

In a way, this sets the tone of the play. In the first Act, Pandarus and Cressida are discussing whether or not Troilus has a 'brown' – dark – complexion:

Pandarus. Faith, to say truth, brown and not brown.
Cressida. To say the truth, true and not true.

(I, ii, 97–8)

What it is to 'say the truth', and whether it is still possible, become matters of some moment. We seem to be tending, sliding, towards a situation, a world, in which things are indifferently 'good or bad', 'true and not true'. When Cressida asks Pandarus if Helenus can fight, his answer perfectly expresses this mood. 'No. Yes, he'll fight indifferent well' (I, ii, 228). A positive compounded with a negative producing – indifference. Good, bad; true, not true; yes, no. 'Tis but the chance of war.

The first scene in the Greek camp opens with Agamemnon summarizing and describing the current state of the army:

> Checks and disasters
> Grow in the veins of actions highest reared,
> As knots, by the conflux of meeting sap,
> Infects the sound pine and diverts his grain
> Tortive and errant from his course of growth.

(I, iii, 5–9)

I will simply note that 'knots' is a word which occurs quite frequently – things, people, are constantly being blocked from following what might seem their natural course; but 'tortive and errant' – twisted and wandering in wrong directions – is a phrase that might fairly be said to apply to the whole play. When, shortly after, in his 'Degree' speech, Ulysses depicts the chaos that follows 'when the planets/In evil mixture to disorder wander', he says that the resultant 'commotion' serves to 'deracinate/The unity and married calm of states/Quite from their fixture' (I, iii, 94–5, 99–101). Troilus thinks that 'Never did young man fancy/With so eternal and so fixed a soul' (V, ii, 163). But there is no 'married calm' in the vortex, or wasteland, stemming from Helen's 'soilure', and nothing is 'fixed' any more in this world. At the very start of the play, we hear this. 'Hector, whose patience/Is as a virtue fixed, today was moved' (I, ii, 4–5). Even Hector. All are 'deracinated' in one way or another – Cressida most visibly, as she is brutally shifted from the Trojan to the Greek camp; but Hector as notably, as he suddenly shifts from one side to the other in the vital debate concerning the keeping or giving up of Helen. Too much of the movement (and thinking and feeling) in this play is 'tortive and errant'.

To return to Agamemnon's opening speech. He says that things have gone wrong ('bias and thwart') since the start of the siege, but that we should regard all these failures as:

> But the protractive trials of great Jove
> To find persistive constancy in men ...
>
> (I, iii, 21–2)

Here indeed is a question raised by the play – is it possible to find any 'persistive constancy' in men? A constancy that would help to create and ensure stability and continuity – 'unity and married calm' – both in individual relationships and the state? It is not to be found in this play, in which there is more discontinuity and instability of character than anywhere else in Shakespeare. Inconstancy is the norm. The one character who shows 'persistive constancy' is Thersites, and it is the constancy of virulent and scabrous negation. Agamemnon likens true constancy to a fine, rare metal. You will not find it if you leave it to Fortune – Fortune, he says, conflates and confounds all values. You need – it is an unusual personification – Distinction.

> Distinction, with a broad and powerful fan,
> Puffing at all, winnows the light away,
> And what hath mass or matter by itself
> Lies rich in virtue and unmingled.

(I, iii, 27–30)

Winnowing and straining or distilling are processes referred to more than once, and are connected to one of the great motivating questions of the play. If, in the name of 'Distinction', all the 'light' stuff, the chaff, the rubbish, is blown and winnowed away, will you be left with something solid and of unquestionable value – 'rich in virtue and unmingled'? The question applies particularly to people, and one of the disquieting or dismaying – or displeasing – features of this play is the sense one has at the end of the main characters having been winnowed away to nothingness, as though none of them had the requisite 'mass or matter' to persist as on-goingly authentic, reliable human beings throughout the wasting and debilitating travails of the war. Thersites and Pandarus alone retain their original shape, remain what they were – 'unmingled' perhaps, but hardly 'rich in virtue'.

Distinction – 'distinguishableness', if I may gloss with an ugly but useful word – is visibly, audibly being lost. In his 'Degree' speech, Ulysses maintains:

> Take but degree away, untune that string,
> And hark what discord follows. Each thing meets
> In mere oppugnancy.

(I, iii, 109–11)

In the Quarto, 'meets' reads as 'melts' (to be a crucial word in *Antony and Cleopatra*) – I have no wish, and certainly no competence, to adjudicate between the readings. Indeed, ideally one would hear both words, for there is a sense in this play in which 'meeting' in oppugnancy becomes tantamount to 'melting' – it becomes hard to tell one thing from the other. Ulysses continues his vision of a world bereft of degree:

xxv

> Force should be right, or rather right and wrong –
> Between whose endless jar justice resides –
> Should lose their names, and so should justice too.
> Then everything include itself in power,
> Power into will, will into appetite,
> And appetite, an universal wolf,
> So doubly seconded with will and power,
> Must make perforce an universal prey
> And last eat up himself.
>
> (I, iii, 116–24)

Right and wrong and justice should lose their names ('Now good or bad, 'tis but the chance of war'), and everything be resolved, dissolved (melted) into the single matter of force, power, will, and self-devouring appetite. And not only ethical categories – most of the main characters effectively 'lose their names' as well, winnowed away by the long attritions of the war. Hector makes a comparable point in the Trojan camp when he answers the impetuous arguments offered by Troilus and Paris for continuing the war:

> The reasons you allege do more conduce
> To the hot passion of distempered blood
> Than to make up a free determination
> 'Twixt right and wrong; for pleasure and revenge
> Have ears more deaf than adders to the voice
> Of any true decision.
>
> (II, ii, 168–73)

In the atmosphere of this war, it no longer seems possible to make a true decision – 'a free determination' – between right and wrong. And if this 'distinction' is gone, then clearly all distinctions are at risk.

Of course, differences remain. The Trojans – Hector certainly – seem to retain a vestige of the old heroic code and traces and shreds of a chivalric ideal; they are more courtly and courteous than their adversaries. As Thersites says – 'the Grecians begin to proclaim barbarism, and policy grows into an ill opinion' (V, iv, 16–18). When Achilles calls on his gang of Myrmidons to fall on the unarmed Hector, we witness the ultimate debasement, or rather abandonment, of any and every code of conduct – martial or otherwise. Achilles' relish in the foulness of his act is sickening:

> Look, Hector, how the sun begins to set,
> How ugly night comes breathing at his heels.
> Even with the vail and dark'ning of the sun,
> To close the day up, Hector's life is done ...
> The dragon wing of night o'erspreads the earth ...
>
> (V, viii, 5–8, 17)

It is as though night is falling – the curtain coming down (the play is nearly over) – on whatever values might have operated – in war, in love, in politics and government – in the pre-Christian classical world. Although Hector's magnanimity in sparing Greeks at his mercy – including Achilles – seems like the cherishable remnant of an older and better code, in the current atmosphere it is disparaged as a foolish anachronism. ''Tis fair play,' he says to his brother Troilus, who replies – 'Fool's play, by heaven, Hector'. Fair is soiled, fair is foolish – it has come to this.

In this great melt-down of distinctions and values, which the play both portends and enacts, questions of value and valuation become of paramount importance. What is this worth? How do you esteem that? What are your grounds for attributing this value, this worth, this price? Is it intrinsic, or in the eye of the beholder, the appraiser, the attributor, the reflector? Here, of course, the debate among the Trojans as to whether to send Helen back to the Greeks is central. Hector is very clear in his own mind – 'Let Helen go'. He gives his reasons, and unanswerably good reasons they are. But Troilus invokes 'honor' and pours metaphoric contempt on 'reason'.

> You fur your gloves with reason ...
> ... Nay, if we talk of reason,
> Let's shut our gates and sleep! Manhood and honor
> Should have hare-hearts, would they but fat their thoughts
> With this crammed reason.
>
> (II, ii, 38, 46–9)

Hector is too intelligent to be rebuffed and beclouded by metaphors, and simply, cogently replies:

> Brother, she is not worth what she doth cost
> The keeping.
>
> (II, ii, 51–2)

At which point, Troilus articulates the central question of the play: 'What's aught but as 'tis valued?' The question implies an extreme relativism in the realm of values (and we may remember that in *Hamlet*, written perhaps one year earlier, Hamlet had delivered himself of the opinion that 'There is nothing good or bad but thinking makes it so'). Troilus is saying, or implying, that there are no intrinsic values, only attributed ones. Coming from a young man who regards himself as exemplifying, as incorporating, an absolute standard of fidelity, this is somewhat inconsistent – but inconsistency prevails in this play. However, at this point, Hector deals firmly with his younger brother's casuistry:

> But value dwells not in particular will.
> It holds his estimate and dignity
> As well wherein 'tis precious of itself
> As in the prizer. 'Tis mad idolatry
> To make the service greater than the god;
> And the will dotes that is attributive
> To what infectiously itself affects,
> Without some image of th' affected merit.
>
> (II, ii, 53–60)

Difficult words (as so often in this tortive and errant play), but Hector is saying that many Trojans, like Troilus, have made 'the service' (of keeping Helen) 'greater than the god' (Helen's own worth). There is, he says, a lot of doting 'attributive' will around, which ascribes value without any objective sense of the thing or person thus evaluated. Mainly Hector wants to assert that something, someone, can be 'precious of itself/As in the prizer'. Simply, there are intrinsic, non-contingent values – values not dependent on the eye of the 'prizer' or appraiser. Things are *not* simply as they are valued. Hector is still capable of making a 'free determination' between right and wrong. Of course Helen should be given back to the Greeks:

INTRODUCTION

> There is a law in each well-ordered nation
> To curb those raging appetites that are
> Most disobedient and refractory.
> If Helen, then, be wife to Sparta's king,
> As it is known she is, these moral laws
> Of nature and of nations speak aloud
> To have her back returned. Thus to persist
> In doing wrong extenuates not wrong,
> But makes it much more heavy. Hector's opinion
> Is this in way of truth.
>
> (II, ii, 180–89)

In way of truth. This is the absolutely crucial moment in the play – is it still possible to think, and speak, and winnow your way down and along to 'truth'? Or is everything now merely a matter of 'opinion'? This is a word which keeps occurring in the play, as if to mock the unitary pretensions of 'truth', until we realize the aptness and accuracy of Thersites' outburst – 'A plague of opinion! A man may wear it on both sides like a leather jerkin' (III, iii, 265–6). There is opinion – lots of it – but so far from leading to the 'way of truth', it seems to lead, scatteringly, away from it. You can turn it this way and that way, inside and out; good–bad; right–wrong; true–false – either way, a reversible leather jerkin. Hector is still speaking out for the stabilities of truth against the unpredictable sways and surges of the errant tides of 'opinion'. But if we think we now have a 'fixed' point, we are about to be monumentally disappointed. Hector is about to reverse himself.

Following his statement that 'Hector's opinion/Is this in way of truth' – where for just one moment in the play opinion and truth are at one, identical – he announces:

> Yet ne'ertheless,
> My spritely brethren, I propend to you
> In resolution to keep Helen still ...
>
> (II, ii, 189–91)

Having clearly perceived and delineated the 'way of truth', Hector suddenly abandons it, swerves away – he 'propends' to the others, a strange word meaning leans or inclines, a tortive and errant movement and moment indeed. Cressida's rapid metamorphosis from chaste lover to one of the 'daughters of the game' – under gruesome Grecian mass male pressure, be it said – is not more swift or surprising than Hector's defection from the 'way of truth'. Of course, Shakespeare had made things impossibly difficult for himself. He can write against the grain of history, as he often, dazzlingly, does. But even he could not rewrite history. Helen was not given back, and Troy fell. No way round that. Hector's arguments cannot prevail if the play is to remain within the plausible limits of the legend. What Shakespeare can show in this extraordinary moment in which, for one last time, truth is unanswerably articulated and asserted, and then haplessly abandoned, is that truth, and a free determination of right and wrong, are prime casualties of the war.

After this putting aside of 'truth' it is perhaps not surprising that things and people are no longer regarded as 'precious of themselves' but only in the eye of the 'prizer' or appraiser. There is much discussion – centred on Achilles who hopes to keep his fame while refusing to fight – as to the extent to which fame and value are essentially reflective. A man, says Ulysses:

> Cannot make boast to have that which he hath
> Nor feels not what he owes but by reflection ...

> (III, iii, 98–9)

Achilles takes the point:

> What the declined is
> He shall as soon read in the eyes of others
> As feel in his own fall ...

> (III, iii, 76–8)

This means, of course, a complete externalization of value – it is completely in the eye of the beholder, and for that eye to confer or withhold. And, indeed, an ephemeralization of value – 'The present eye praises the present object' (III, iii, 179). It is as if nothing (no one) can any longer be something (someone) in and for itself. Through time. No wonder they are all winnowed away. Ulysses comments to Achilles:

> Nature, what things there are
> Most abject in regard and dear in use!

INTRODUCTION

> What things again most dear in the esteem
> And poor in worth ...
>
> (III, iii, 127–30)

Abject, poor, dear – worth, esteem, use: this is the shifting
value-lexicon of the play. At one end of the spectrum there is a
lot of merchant talk (particularly among the Greeks) using
terms concerned with prices, weights, measures – scruples,
little characters, ounces, counters, spans, inches, fractions,
orts, etc. At the other end, there is a more metaphysical
language of truth and honour, but that language is as terribly
under siege as Troy itself, and even sooner to be undermined.
When Cressida is handed over to the Greeks, Troilus urges
and warns Diomedes to value her in absolute, soaring terms.
Diomedes replies: 'I'll answer to my lust ... To her own worth/
She shall be prized' (IV, iv, 133–4). Once she is surrounded
and serially kissed by the merchant-macho Greek 'prizers'
(hints of a gang rape there), we can imagine what that 'worth'
will be, and how it will be esteemed. Diomedes will answer to
his lust. Ominous.

Troy–Greece; chivalry–barbarism; it looks, at the beginning, as if some such simple dualism and polarity is to be
envisaged – and to an extent something of that remains. The
Greeks, certainly, are the real bastards of the play. But there is,
throughout, too much 'commixtion' to sustain any sense of
simple divisions and oppositions. When, as the result of the
rather foolish challenge to single combat, Hector is to confront
Ajax, Trojan Aeneas says:

> This Ajax is half made of Hector's blood,
> In love whereof half Hector stays at home;
> Half heart, half hand, half Hector comes to seek
> This blended knight, half Troyan, and half Greek ...
>
> (IV, v, 83–6)

– blended, melted, it is difficult to sort things out into stable
oppositional – Troy–Greece – categories. As Hector himself
recognizes (speaking to Ajax):

> The obligation of our blood forbids
> A gory emulation 'twixt us twain.
> Were thy commixtion Greek and Troyan so

> That thou couldst say, 'This hand is Grecian all,
> And this is Troyan; the sinews of this leg
> All Greek, and this all Troy; my mother's blood
> Runs on the dexter cheek, and this sinister
> Bounds in my father's,' by Jove multipotent,
> Thou shouldst not bear from me a Greekish member
> Wherein my sword had not impressure made
> Of our rank feud.
>
> (IV, v, 121–31)

But it cannot be done. You cannot say of a person's body – or temperament, or being – that's the Trojan bit and that's the Greek bit. I'll reject this, save that. We are all, put it this way, Trojan–Greek compounds or 'commixtions', and, going by this play, not the much better off for it.

All of this makes the question of 'identity' a troubling matter (you may be as much of a Trojan as a Greek, but you have to take sides). People seem endlessly uncertain as to other people's identities. Who are you? Who is that? Is that so-and-so? Are you so-and so? Such questions are asked more in this play than in any other of Shakespeare's works. Even self-identity is in doubt. An early exchange:

Pandarus. Well, I say Troilus is Troilus
Cressida. Then you say as I say, for I am sure he is not Hector.
Pandarus. No, nor Hector is not Troilus in some degrees.
Cressida. 'Tis just to each of them; he is himself.
Pandarus. Himself? Alas, poor Troilus, I would he were.
Cressida. So he is.
Pandarus. Condition, I had gone barefoot to India.
Cressida. He is not Hector.
Pandarus. Himself? No, he's not himself. Would 'a were himself.

(I, ii, 66–78)

There is a good deal of splitting of the self in the play – these days we would, of course, refer to the divided self. A simple example is provided by warriors meeting during a truce. Aeneas greets Diomedes very courteously, but says – when we meet on the field, I will inflict all possible damage on you. That is absolutely all right by Diomedes:

> The one and other Diomed embraces.
> Our bloods are now in calm, and, so long, health!

INTRODUCTION

> But when contention and occasion meet,
> By Jove, I'll play the hunter for thy life
> With all my force, pursuit, and policy.
>
> (IV, i, 14–18)

Which encounter prompts Paris to comment:

> This is the most despiteful gentle greeting,
> The noblest hateful love, that e'er I heard of.
>
> (IV, i, 32–4)

These are the oxymorons of war, and in the event it is the
gentleness and nobleness that go under, while spite and hate
triumph. But it is the splitting occasioned by this war – 'the
one and other' – I want briefly to stay with. And while all the
main characters are split – divided, fractured, fragmented – in
various ways, the crucial figure is Cressida.

This play is one of three by Shakespeare which has for its
title the names of a pair of lovers (*Romeo and Juliet* and *Antony
and Cleopatra* are the others). In fact, by the most generous
estimate, barely one third of the play directly concerns the
doomed lovers – and perhaps Shakespeare has not quite
managed to make the private erotic affair fruitfully and
illuminatingly coalesce with the public matters of the war –
though clearly he wants to show love and war, or the erotic
and martial, as inseparably intertwined. This is a play about
the Trojan war, but still, the tragically split Cressida is central
to the play, and she is aware of latent instabilities and divisions
within herself, almost from the start:

> I have a kind of self resides with you;
> But an unkind self, that itself will leave
> To be another's fool. I would be gone.
> Where is my wit? I know not what I speak.
>
> (III, ii, 149–52)

There is a kind of hapless honesty about Cressida. Secure in
Troy, there is no reason to doubt that she would have been
sincerely faithful to Troilus; but in a new, alien, context, with
new pressures, fears, needs, importunities, other aspects of her
self, or other selves, emerge (for which of us would that not be

the case?). Troilus seems to have some intimation of possible danger ahead:

> But something may be done that we will not;
> And sometimes we are devils to ourselves
> When we will tempt the frailty of our powers,
> Presuming on their changeful potency.
>
> (IV, iv, 94-7)

All this leads up to the crucial speech by Troilus when he actually witnesses Cressida being unfaithful with Diomedes:

> This she? No, this is Diomed's Cressida.
> If beauty have a soul, this is not she;
> If souls guide vows, if vows be sanctimonies ...
> If there be rule in unity itself,
> This was not she. O madness of discourse,
> That cause sets up with and against itself:
> Bifold authority, where reason can revolt
> Without perdition, and loss assume all reason
> Without revolt. This is, and is not, Cressid.
> Within my soul there doth conduce a fight
> Of this strange nature that a thing inseparate
> Divides more wider than the sky and earth;
> And yet the spacious breadth of this division
> Admits no orifex for a point as subtle
> As Ariachne's broken woof to enter.
> Instance, O instance, strong as Pluto's gates;
> Cressid is mine, tied with the bonds of heaven.
> Instance, O instance, strong as heaven itself;
> The bonds of heaven are slipped, dissolved, and loosed,
> And with another knot, five-finger-tied,
> The fractions of her faith, orts of her love,
> The fragments, scraps, the bits, and greasy relics
> Of her o'ereaten faith, are given to Diomed.
>
> (V, ii, 134-57)

There should be one Cressida – 'a thing inseparate' – but she seems to have 'divided' into Troilus' Cressida and Diomedes' Cressida. There should be 'rule in unity' (i.e. one cannot equal two) but in the case of Cressida one has become two. Hence Troilus finds himself pushed to the ontologically impossible conclusion – 'This is, and is not, Cressid.' As he experiences it, there is a madness seeping into language itself: 'O madness of discourse,/That cause sets up with and against itself: Bifold authority'. Language seems to be going in opposite directions at the same time – with and against itself; bifold authority – an authority which upholds and refutes at the same time. Such is the double, self-contradictory, authority operative in this play.

It is particularly horrifying and unacceptable to Troilus that the bonds which tied Cressida to him and which should be absolute – 'strong as heaven itself' – 'are slipped, dissolved, and loosed'. Bonds were holy things for Shakespeare, too 'intrince t'unloose' (*Lear* II, ii, 77). If they do not hold, nothing else holds. And in this play, nothing else does. It is notable that Troilus, in his understandable nausea, thinks of Cressida's 'love' with Diomedes in terms of unpleasant leftovers – 'greasy relics of her o'ereaten faith'. In a play in which rampant appetite is allowed free rein, it is hardly surprising that so many of the activities and processes are likened to eating, with taste constantly sickening over into distaste. From the start, love, or rather sex, is made a kitchen matter – 'He that will have a cake out of the wheat must tarry the grinding' (I, i, 15). Reputation in war is, likewise, a table matter: 'For here the Troyans taste our dear'st repute/With their fin'st palate' (I, iii, 337–8). War is a ravenous glutton – 'what else dear that is consumed/In hot digestion of this cormorant war' (II, ii, 5–6). So is Time – 'A great-sized monster of ingratitudes./Those scraps are good deeds past, which are devoured/As fast as they are made' (III, iii, 147–9). (In this play, time is only and always 'injurious' – in other plays, 'mature' or 'ripe' time can be an agent of restoration, regeneration, renewed continuities. It is what always defeats evil when it seems that nothing else can. But in this play – it is part of its bleakness – time is only a gobbler-up, a destroyer. 'What's past and what's to come is strewed with husks/And formless ruin of oblivion;/But in this extant moment ...' (IV, v, 165–7). These Trojans and Greeks live only in the 'extant moment' – and it is desolating.) Agamemnon tells Achilles that virtues left unused 'like fair fruit in an unwholesome dish,/Are like to rot untasted' (II, iii, 122–3). But perhaps the most important food is honey, associated from the first with Helen, and by implication with the lubricious pleasures of sex. There is one scene in Priam's palace in which Helen ('honey-sweet'), Paris and Pandarus bandy innuendoes and the word 'sweet' is used seven times (II, i). By which time it has come to sound, and feel, distinctly sickly, sickening. One rather sympathizes with a later, spitting comment from Thersites – ' "Sweet," quoth 'a! Sweet sink, sweet sewer' (V, i, 79). In the epilogue by Pandarus, added later, he refers to the time when a bee loses 'his honey and his sting' and 'Sweet honey and sweet notes together fail' (V, x, 45). As they have failed in this play. The play was to have ended with Troilus' line – 'Hector is dead; there is no more to say' (V, x, 22). But Shakespeare decided there was just a little more to say, and he lets Pandarus say it. It is a speech about brothels, prostitution, venereal disease, and his own imminent death. No other play ends with such an unpleasant gesture to the audience:

> Till then I'll sweat and seek about for eases,
> And at that time bequeath you my diseases.

(V, x, 55–6)

*

It is a strange play, and in many ways a sour and abrasive one. Any intimations of grace and a return to normal human life are ruthlessly excluded. It is easy to agree with Brockbank that there is 'no sense of betrayal of an heroic and chivalric tradition, for of that there were no glimpses', and his summing up seems apt: 'Love's infinity, heroic glory, and universal harmonies of state have only a transient visionary and verbal validity in a world that has lost touch with the values by which it pretends to live' (*On Shakespeare*, p. 10). There is little physical action in the play – Cressida goes to bed with Troilus, Hector is murdered. Most of the time, in both camps, is taken up with debate. Some scholars see this as supporting the theory that it was written for the Inns of Court, with its forensically sophisticated audience in mind. Certainly a lot of the rhetoric is strangely formal, intricate, hyperbolic. At the height of his anguish, Troilus uses words like 'recordation', 'esperance', 'deceptious' (V, ii, 113–21); wooing Cressida intensely he says things like – 'What makes this pretty abruption? What too curious dreg espies my sweet lady in the fountain of our love?' (III, ii, 65–7) – which is oddly elaborate, to say the least. The language usage ranges from the smooth political orations of Ulysses (often founded on banalities, clichés, and tautologies), to the snarling, splenetic invective of Thersites – 'all the argument is a whore and a cuckold' (II, iii, 75); ' – nothing but lechery! All incontinent varlets!' (V, i, 103). We must allow Thersites the validity and consistency of his perspective, but he is too biliously predictable to merge as the reliable voice of the play. There is no such voice. Interestingly, Thersites and Ulysses never meet and confront each other. Perhaps these are two discourses which can just run on, uninterruptedly, forever. Perhaps too there is a sense in which the play is an experiment in language and its possibilities – certainly, the characters seem to stand a long way from us, and hardly engage us as characters in Shakespeare's other plays do. Nevertheless it is a disturbing and disconsolating experience as Shakespeare shows us, as only Shakespeare could, how war devours everything.

*

JULIUS CAESAR (1599)

Plutarch's *Parallel Lives* of twenty-three Romans and twenty-three Greeks (as translated by North in 1579 from Amyot's French) was probably the most important book Shakespeare read from the point of view of his play-writing. (Terence Spencer reminds us that it was no easy undertaking – he would have had to pore over more than a thousand pages in a very large and heavy folio volume.) No play owes as much to Plutarch's *Lives* (*Life of Caesar*, *Life of Brutus*, *Life of Antonius*) as *Julius Caesar* – all the matters of substance, most of the events, many of the details, and indeed quite a number of lines, are transcribed directly from Plutarch. Of course, Shakespeare made additions, modifications, amplifications, and crucial shifts in interpretative emphasis, and in the event this play is one of his most searching dramatic explorations of the nature and processes of politics and power. But so close does the play seem to Plutarch that I want to start by quoting a number of passages from his work, as a prelude, perhaps, to appreciating what Shakespeare did with his source material.

Plutarch was a Greek philosopher, writing in the latter half of the first century AD. His preference was for republican ideals. In Spencer's words: 'The triumph of the monarchical principle was something that Plutarch, a Greek philosopher who looked back on the past of his own country and its brilliant small city-states with admiration and a kind of sentimental regret, detested although he saw its inevitability.' He regarded Caesar as the cause of the downfall of the Roman republic. And yet, many positive features emerge from his account of Caesar:

the Romans, inclining to Caesar's prosperity and taking the bit in the mouth, supposing that to be ruled by one man alone, it would be a good mean for them *to take breath a little, after so many troubles and miseries as they had abidden in these civil wars, they chose him perpetual dictator* ... And now for himself, after he had ended his civil wars, he did so honorably behave himself, that there was no fault to be found in him ...

The italicized words apply exactly to the Elizabethans, worn out after the Wars of the Roses and the power-struggles of Catholics and Protestants under Edward VI and Mary, and glad to be 'ruled by one *woman* alone'. And we should remember that Brutus finds no actual fault with Caesar. Furthermore, Caesar treated the people with paternalistic fondness and respect:

Now Caesar immediately won many men's good wills at Rome, through his eloquence in pleading of their causes, and the people loved him marvellously also, because of the courteous manner he had to speak to every man, and to use them gently, being more *ceremonius* therein than was looked for in one of his years. Furthermore, he ever kept a good board ...

Almost Caesar's first words are 'Set on, and leave no ceremony out' (I, ii, 11) and I shall be returning to the word I have italicized. We shall also catch a very significant glimpse of Caesar keeping that 'good board'.

So wherein did he offend? Well, there was the nature of his

last 'triumph into Rome' (with which the play begins). A reminder of a little actual history might help here. Caesar had defeated Pompey at Pharsalus in 48 BC, and now he has returned from his final triumph over Pompey's sons in Spain in 45 BC. This made him sole dictator; more beneficially, it ended the factional strife which had marred and disturbed civil life under the Republic. But is it true that, with this victory and consolidation of Caesar as dictator, the citizens lost all their power and the Senatorial party lost much of its? Plutarch sees this as a bad moment. 'But the triumph he made into Rome for the same did as much offend the Romans, and more, than any thing that ever he had done before: because he had not overcome captains that were strangers, nor barbarous kings, but had destroyed the sons of the noblest man of Rome, whom fortune had overthrown.' But – for Plutarch – there was worse. 'But the chiefest cause that made him mortally hated was the covetous desire he had to be called king: which first gave the people just cause, and next his secret enemies honest colour, to bear him ill will ... they could not abide the name of a king, detesting it as the utter destruction of their liberty.' Given his republican sympathies, Plutarch seems more on the side of Brutus, to whom he gives all the Roman virtues – he was noble minded, lowly, virtuous, valiant, and so on. He ascribes to him only the purest and highest of motives for killing Caesar. Yet Plutarch also gives us a troubled Brutus: 'when he was out of his house, he did so frame and *fashion* his countenance and looks that no man could discern he had anything to trouble his mind. But when night came that he was in his own house, then he was clean changed: for either care did wake him against his will when he would have slept, or else oftentimes of himself he fell into such deep thoughts of his enterprise, casting in his mind all the dangers that might happen: that his wife, lying by him, found that there was some marvellous great matter that troubled his mind ...' (my italics). This is all Shakespeare needs to dramatize a crucial split in Brutus between the public and the private man – between the noble, idealistic, Roman, performer; and the tormented, introspecting, insomniac, individual. And he will make devastating use of that word 'fashion'. Plutarch

certainly lends no nobility to the actual killing of Caesar –
quite the reverse: 'Caesar ... was hacked and mangled among
them, as a wild beast taken of hunters.' In the play Brutus tries
to make a 'sacrifice' out of the deed, but Plutarch's description
is definitive. And after the assassination, in Plutarch's description, Caesar's 'great prosperity and good fortune that
favoured him all his lifetime, did continue afterwards in the
revenge of his death, pursuing the murtherers both by sea and
land, till they had not left a man more to be executed, all of
them that were actors or counsellors in the conspiracy of his
death'. Only, in Shakespeare, it is not Caesar's 'good fortune'
which 'did continue afterward' – but his 'spirit'.

It has also to be remembered that, by Shakespeare's time,
Caesar and Brutus had acquired symbolic identities in the
popular imagination; they were seen as representative world-
historical figures who embodied respectively – I simplify – the
monarchical (and imperial) principle, and the republican
ideal. It is undeniable that the numerous references to Caesar
in Shakespeare's other plays treat him almost without exception with admiration, if not with something more. We may
take one example, from *Hamlet* which refers to

> the most high and palmy state of Rome,
> A little ere the mightiest Julius fell ...
>
> (I, i, 113–14)

– as if the time of Julius Caesar was regarded as the high point
of Roman history. According to Spencer, 'Shakespeare's
audience seem to have regarded Caesar's death as one of the
great crimes of history' (idem, p. 20). This is in line with
Ernest Schanzer's contention in his essay on the play that 'a
large part of the audience were in sympathy with the mediae-
val apotheosis of Caesar'. (And, of course, Dante put Brutus at
the bottom of his Inferno.) In the same article however,
Schanzer reminds us that during the Renaissance there were
also divided and ambivalent readings of the two men – Caesar
as boastful tyrant, Brutus as liberator and patriot. As we have
seen, there are detectable ambivalences in Plutarch himself. It
is certainly true that by the sixteenth century a number of
writers openly admired Brutus, and his reputation seems to

INTRODUCTION

have increased after Shakespeare's time – understandable,
perhaps, as the monarchical principle faded and waned. The
period of Roman history from Julius Caesar to Augustus was
of particular importance for a number of Elizabethan and
Renaissance political thinkers to confirm the argument in
favour of monarchy. As Phillips puts it: 'In the stability which
Caesar achieved under his dictatorship, in the civil strife
which followed his assassination, and in the peace which
returned under the imperial rule of Augustus, Tudor theorists
found proof that under monarchy states flourish, under
divided authority they decline' (op. cit., pp. 172–3). I hope all
this gives some slight idea of the wealth and weight of
material, and contradictoriness of opinion and interpretation,
which Shakespeare could draw on when he turned to write the
play he decided to call *Julius Caesar*.

I put it that way because, over the years, some commentators have questioned the appropriateness of naming a play
after a character who has such a small part (some 130 lines out
of 2,500), and who dies in the middle of the action. We may
start from a consideration of this – quite accurate – point.
Visibly, audibly, Caesar appears on stage for a shorter period
than any other major Shakespearian protagonist. Yet his *name*
occurs, re-echoes, throughout the play on *more* occasions than
that of any other major protagonist: 211 times to Brutus' 130.
This is a non-trivial point. The body goes: the name lives on.
Caesar and Brutus both refer to themselves in the third person,
as though it were possible to distinguish between, and separate, the self and the name (e.g. Caesar: 'I fear him not./Yet if
my name were liable to fear ...' – I, ii, 198–9). In the final
battle at Philippi, for the defeated allies of Brutus it seems as
though their names are all that remain to them – Cato: 'I will
proclaim my name about the field' (V, iv, 4). Lucilius, to
protect his leader, announces to the enemy soldiers – 'And I
am Brutus, Marcus Brutus, I;/Brutus, my country's friend;
know me for Brutus!' (V, iv, 8–9). And, imprisoning the
'name', they think they have caught the man. Perhaps the
most important speech in this connection comes from Cassius
early on, when he is trying to 'seduce' Brutus to his murderous
cause:

> Brutus and Caesar: what should be in that 'Caesar'?
> Why should that name be sounded more than yours?
> Write them together, yours is as fair a name;
> Sound them, it doth become the mouth as well;
> Weigh them, it is as heavy; conjure with 'em,
> 'Brutus' will start a spirit as soon as 'Caesar'.

> (I, ii, 142–7)

Cassius is a materialist (at this point) – there is nothing in a name. But the mistake articulated in that last line is absolutely central to the play. 'Brutus' does *not* 'start' (raise) 'a spirit' – 'Caesar' does. The possible divorce and discrepancy between the 'name' (the concept, the ideal, the image) and the actual thing (person, behaviour, event) is constantly coming to the fore. How lethal this divorce can be is vividly brought out in the short scene in which the plebeians kill Cinna the poet:

Cinna. I am not Cinna the conspirator.
Fourth Plebeian. It is no matter, his name's Cinna; pluck but his name out of his heart, and turn him going.

> (III, iii, 32–5)

Can you pluck out the name without plucking out the heart? No – says the play. The name of 'Rome' and 'Romans' are as constantly heard (seventy-two times) as in *Titus Andronicus*, and I will not try to better the comment of Foakes: 'There is a contrast between the Roman ideal and Romans in action, as is seen in the behaviour of the conspirators and the plebeians, similar to that between the ideal and the living person represented in Caesar and Brutus.' Perhaps the most telling and central dramatized illustration of this split between the bodily self and name (reputation, image) is provided by Antony's vivid evocation of the death of Caesar – of Caesar the man, that is:

> Then burst his mighty heart;
> And, in his mantle muffling up his face,
> Even at the base of Pompey's statue
> (Which all the while ran blood) great Caesar fell.
> O, what a fall was there, my countrymen!
> Then I, and you, and all of us fell down,
> Whilst bloody treason flourished over us.

> (III, ii, 188–94)

INTRODUCTION

The bodily Caesar can fall – we have already had intimations
of this in his 'falling sickness'. But while the body falls, the
statues of previous great men (here Pompey the Great) stand
erect after the death of those they commemorate. Monument,
reputation, image, name – spirit – these are phenomena which
can outlast corporeal terminations.

What do we gather of the living, speaking Caesar of the first
two Acts and from his last speeches before the Capitol? Hazlitt
– always a commentator to attend to – found the depiction
disappointing. 'We do not much admire the representation
here given of Julius Caesar, nor do we think it answers to the
portrait given of him in his Commentaries. He makes several
vapouring and rather pedantic speeches, and does nothing.'
There is some vapour and pedantry in his speeches, but
whether he 'does nothing' depends on your sense of action and
agency. From one point of view, Caesar, or rather 'Caesar',
does almost everything. The play opens with a street festival –
Lupercal, a fertility festival which Shakespeare conflates with
Caesar's triumph (which actually took place some five months
earlier – there are numerous compressions and compactions in
this play, a lot of history sometimes being dramatically
squeezed into a single day). Apart from giving us our first
glimpse of the people or 'commoners' – here quite effervescent
and holiday-merry (later to turn mutinous and murderous) –
this first scene is most important for the behaviour of the
tribunes (representatives of the people and thus on guard
against the Senate, never mind 'kings') – Flavius and Marullus. The people have festooned the images of Caesar in the city
with 'trophies' (i.e. ornaments in honour of Caesar, not – here
– spoils of war), and the tribunes go around stripping them:

> Disrobe the images,
> If you do find them decked with ceremonies.
> ... let no images
> Be hung with Caesar's trophies.

(I, i, 67–8, 71–2)

I have mentioned that almost Caesar's first words are 'leave
no ceremony out', and after his death Brutus says 'we are
contented Caesar shall/Have all true rites and lawful ceremonies' (III, i, 240–1). In these three uses of the word, it

xliii

means, variously and not mutually exclusively, symbols of state and ritual observances. But the word is used on two other occasions with a different meaning. (The original Latin word – *caeromonia* – means reverence or dread, and in the plural form came to refer to the rituals by which people express or cope with these feelings; also it came to refer to the respect felt for dread-ful portents.) When Cassius expresses his doubt as to whether Caesar will go to the Capitol he says:

> For he is superstitious grown of late,
> Quite from the main opinion he held once
> Of fantasy, of dreams, and ceremonies.

Here the word means portents or omens. It is used in this sense in the next scene when Caesar's wife, Calphurnia, tries to persuade Caesar to remain at home because of her ominous dreams and the terrible prodigies seen in the city the previous night. 'Caesar, I never stood on ceremonies,/Yet now they fright me' (II, ii, 13–14). It is an important part of the movement and atmosphere of the play that Cassius himself, an extreme materialist in the Epicurus line, grows 'superstitious' as his end approaches:

> You know that I held Epicurus strong,
> And his opinion; now I change my mind,
> And partly credit things that do presage.
>
> (V, i, 76–8)

The play is full of superstition of all kinds – soothsayers, prophets or fortune-tellers, augurers, omens and portents and 'things that do presage' – the 'prodigies' seen during the storm on the night preceding the assassination which seem to show 'a civil strife in heaven', presaging, indeed, a civil strife on earth (most of the prodigies are from Plutarch, be it said), and of course the ghost of Caesar. In respect of this atmosphere of gathering portentousness, one may adopt the sharp, dismissive sanity of Cicero:

> Indeed, it is a strange-disposed time:
> But men may construe things after their fashion,
> Clean from the purpose of the things themselves.
>
> (I, iii, 33–5)

xliv

Or one may hover, awed and respectful, between belief and unbelief. After all, if Caesar had not defied augury and overcome his superstition with some rather bombastic self-grandiloquizing ('Danger knows full well/That Caesar is more dangerous than he ... Caesar shall go forth' – II, ii, 45, 48) he might well have lived to fight – *and* be crowned – another day. Whether or not Shakespeare believed in ghosts, auguries, prodigies and so on, is nothing to the point. What he unerr-ingly understood was that at a time when some crisis or catastrophic breakdown of the known social order seems or feels imminent, superstition floods the streets. We have seen it in our era in times of war, and it can be seen in California (in suitably ersatz form) any day of the week. That there *are* 'things that do presage' – straws in the wind, hints in the air, signs of things to come – Shakespeare, of course, knew was simply true.

From the start, then, Caesar is associated with 'ceremony' – rituals (with the troubling shadow-meaning of portents), images, symbols, trophies. These, indeed, can all be part of the panoply and mystique of power and hierarchy, but they can also help to maintain and reinforce order, civic regularity, peace – 'after so many troubles and miseries as they had abidden in these civil wars'. Caesar is, in the exact Plutarch–North word – 'ceremonious'. All these adornments and appur-tenances can serve to make Caesar seem almost god-like, and there is no question but that Caesar is approaching this status at the start of the play. The ambiguous cheers of the crowd (reported in scene two) as Caesar is both offered and refuses the crown (*three* times is too loaded to pass unnoticed in a Christian culture), reveals something of Shakespeare's insight into mob psychology. It likes to create heroes, or kings, or gods – but, as we later see, it is as equally willing to tear them down.

The tribunes want to do away with ceremony, symbol, image, and strip Caesar down to the poor, forked, fallible, physical body he undoubtedly is. This is the republican–reductive drive at its crudest – no great men, please. (For their pains, they are 'put to silence' – in view of the brutal eliminations to come, it is worth noting that this may simply mean they lost their jobs as spokesmen for the people.) But we cannot – or at least should not – take the tribunes' view of Caesar. If you strip away *all* the 'ceremonies', it is not clear what might be left to hold the city – the state – together and in order. That Caesar is physically vulnerable even when he is at his most masterful – god-like and imperial – Shakespeare brings out in a little touch which, for once, he did not find in Plutarch. At the end of his wonderfully penetrating and acutely accurate analysis of Cassius, there is a sudden lapse into intimations of mortality:

> Such men as he be never at heart's ease
> Whiles they behold a greater than themselves,
> And therefore are they very dangerous.
> I rather tell thee what is to be feared
> Than what I fear; for always I am Caesar.
> Come on my right hand, for this ear is deaf ...
>
> (I, ii, 208–13)

The deafness is provided by Shakespeare – at our most potent and resplendent, we are already beginning to deteriorate and decay (as the Sonnets everywhere insist). But this is not a matter for contempt – the sort of contempt which Cassius expresses when he describes Caesar shaking like 'a sick girl' when he had a fever in Spain. It is hardly to Caesar's discredit that, whatever else he may be, he is unavoidably corporal and human. Just *what* Caesar is remains, perhaps, something of an enigma. There are various versions of Caesar, ranging from that of the mean and envious Cassius ('he doth bestride the narrow world/Like a Colossus' – I, ii, 135–6) to that of the loyal and loving Antony ('Thou art the ruins of the noblest man/That ever lived in the tide of times' – III, i, 256–7). And there is Caesar's version of himself, not to mention the crowd's Caesar. We only see him as he is constructed – *fashioned*, but I'll come back to that – by others, and by himself. In this connection, it is pertinent to acknowledge that a good deal of his speech (little enough though we hear of it), is self-aggrandizing and self-inflating, somewhat thrasonical and given to self-hyperbolizing. But to suggest that the arrogance of his last speech –

> Yet in the number I do know but one
> That unassailable holds on his rank,
> Unshaked of motion; and that I am he ...
>
> (III, i, 68–70)

is sufficient justification for his assassination, as some critics
have, seems to me to submit to conspiratorial homicidal
intoxication, and identification with Cassius, that 'hot, choleric, and cruel man' (Plutarch). There is one little scene in
Caesar's house on the morning of the murder which seems to
me crucial – and here we come to what Plutarch called
Caesar's 'good board'. Caesar is surrounded with, supposedly
his good friends, actually those who will kill him. Before they
set out for the Capitol, Caesar says:

> Good friends, go in and taste some wine with me,
> And we (like friends) will straightway go together.

To which, Brutus adds a concluding aside:

> That every like is not the same, O Caesar,
> The heart of Brutus earns to think upon.
>
> (II, ii, 126–9)

Shortly afterwards, in front of the Capitol, Brutus who, as
these lines reveal, knows he is only a dissembling friend, says to
Caesar – 'I kiss thy hand, but not in flattery, Caesar' (III, i,
52). No, not in flattery – in betrayal. After the ceremonial
communal wine of the Last Supper, the Judas kiss. At this
point, the Elizabethans would surely have known what they
were witnessing.

Brutus is a more complex figure. One reading sees him as a
noble, idealistic, exemplary Roman who is 'seduced' into the
conspiracy by the envious and bloody-minded Cassius (who
knows very well that the 'work' he has 'in hand' is 'Most
bloody, fiery, and most terrible' – I, iii, 130). Certainly he
hopes that 'the great opinion/That Rome holds of his name'
(I, ii, 319–20) will give honour and respectability to their
enterprise. Just as Casca hopes that:

> that which would appear offense in us,
> His countenance, like richest alchemy,
> Will change to virtue and to worthiness ...
>
> (I, iii, 158-60)

(In the event, Brutus proves to be a failed alchemist – he cannot transform 'butchery' into 'sacrifice', betrayal into virtue, murder into worthiness.) This view of Brutus was fostered by Plutarch, and Shakespeare is happy enough to take a Plutarchian line for Antony's panegyric over the dead Brutus:

> All the conspirators save only he
> Did that they did in envy of great Caesar;
> He, only in a general honest thought
> And common good to all, made one of them.
>
> (V, v, 69-71)

Did he, now? All Romans seemingly become 'noble' at their death. Brutus calls the vicious Cassius 'the last of all the Romans'; Antony dubs betrayer-murderer Brutus 'the noblest Roman of them all'; Octavius Caesar, in a later play, casts around for some appropriately respectful things to say about Antony whom he always regarded as a hopelessly debauched defector, but, as we shall see, he cannot even be bothered to finish. These encomiastic elegies are formulaic, Roman prescriptions which are, to all intents and purposes, interchangeable. Death can certainly bring dignity in Shakespeare, and it is appropriate at such a moment to let remembered virtues shine while flaws fade. But do not look for the truth of a man – and that includes Brutus – in these conventional orations and exequies.

From the very start, Brutus, by his own account, is 'with himself at war' (I, ii, 46). Cassius offers to be his 'glass', a mirror which:

> Will modestly discover to yourself
> That of yourself which you yet know not of.
>
> (I, ii, 69-70)

He *does* know it, as we shall see, but he does not want to know that he knows it. Shakespeare is nowhere more brilliant in this play than in showing the operations and stratagems of self-deception. At the end of the scene, Cassius is content with his work:

> Well Brutus, thou art noble; yet I see
> Thy honorable *mettle* may be *wrought*
> From that it is disposed . . .
> For who so firm that cannot be seduced?
>
> (I, ii, 308–10, 312: my italics)

There are a number of references to 'mettle' in the play (the people, not surprisingly, are regarded as 'the basest mettle') and there is always an implicit play on 'mettle' (disposition) and 'metal' (a material which can be 'wrought'). In this play, people can be sharp or blunt or dull, but, more importantly, they can be 'wrought'. The dictionary glosses that as meaning 'fashioned or formed'. It is the past participle of 'work' – another important word in the play. Crowds, of course, can be 'wrought' – now this shape, now that. And so can individuals, as when Brutus says of Caius Ligarius – 'Send him but hither, and I'll fashion him' (II, i, 220). The vocabulary bespeaks a manipulative and instrumental – not to say materialistic – view of people, at the least. Perhaps Shakespeare thought this was very 'Roman' – though what price 'honour' and 'nobility' in such metallic people? But there is an even more insidious form of 'fashioning', as emerges in Brutus' first soliloquy. His first words to himself are – 'It must be by his death'. That is, deep inside him the decision has been taken – Caesar, his best friend, is to be killed. Make no mistake, this Brutus is a murderer, though not the usual ambitious regicide of other Tudor plays. Now he has to find some reasons for the deed – political imperatives to mask the personal compulsion. Has to find them because – 'for my part/I know no personal cause to spurn at him' and 'to speak truth of Caesar,/I have not known when his affections swayed/More than his reason' (II, 1, 10–11, 19–21). So he moves from the indicative tense – Caesar as he *is* – to the subjunctive and conditional, drawing hypothetical scenarios. *If* Caesar is crowned, he '*may* do danger' – 'So Caesar *may*' (my italics). Always 'may' is allowed to supplant 'is'. Then this, which is decisive:

>   And, since the quarrel
> Will bear no color for the thing he *is*,
> *Fashion* it thus: that what he is, augmented,
> *Would* run to these and these extremities;
> And therefore *think him as* a serpent's egg
> Which hatched, *would* as his kind grow mischievous,
> And kill him in the shell.

(II, i, 28–34: my italics)

Fashion it thus – words and arguments are like people, as far as Brutus is concerned; you can mould and shape them to suit, and justify, any ulterior intention. But this perverse substitution of the possible for the actual, is a step into anarchy – of self, and then of state. His own internal anarchy is revealed in a following soliloquy which starts: 'Since Cassius first did whet me against Caesar,/I have not slept' (II, i, 61–2). Note 'whet' – by which Brutus depicts himself as a tool which has been sharpened. He goes on – in a speech which anticipates Macbeth – to describe the 'phantasma' and nightmare inner world he is living in:

>   The genius and the mortal instruments
>   Are then in council, and the state of a man,
>   Like to a little kingdom, suffers then
>   The nature of an insurrection.

(II, i, 66–9)

Brutus has been 'at war' with himself since the beginning, and what he effectively does is to extend that inner 'insurrection' to the state at large.

As the conspirators come in with their heads cloaked and concealed – as Portia says, they 'hide their faces/Even from darkness' (II, i, 277–8) – Brutus reveals, by his words, that he is well aware of the evil nature of the deed they are premeditating:

>   O conspiracy
> Sham'st thou to show thy dang'rous brow by night,
> When evils are most free? O, then by day
> Where wilt thou find a cavern dark enough
> To mask thy monstrous visage? Seek none, conspiracy;
> Hide it in smiles and affability ...

(II, i, 77–82)

1

INTRODUCTION

'Monstrous' is an important word for Shakespeare, indicating something which is in nature, since it is undeniably *there*, but also horribly *un*natural as well. Nature against itself. Brutus could hardly have chosen a more self-incriminating, self-damning, word. He also reveals a Machiavellian streak as he indicates the need for concealment, simulation and dissembling:

> And let our hearts, as subtle masters do,
> Stir up their servants to an act of rage,
> And after seem to chide 'em.
>
> (II, i, 175–7)

Calculated self-manipulation and strategic self-deception – let our hearts goad our hands to the act of murder, then afterwards, 'seem' to reproach them for doing it. What a splitting of the self! No wonder he can't sleep. But perhaps the key metaphor comes from the stage. As the conspirators are dispersing, Cassius says 'show yourselves true Romans', immediately followed by this exhortation from Brutus:

> Good gentlemen, look fresh and merrily.
> Let not our looks put on our purposes,
> But bear it as our Roman actors do,
> With untired spirits and formal constancy.
>
> (II, 1, 224–7)

'False face must hide what the false heart doth know,' as Macbeth will say. We have had the stage mentioned before – while Caesar was dallying with the crown, the people, according to Casca, did 'clap him and hiss him, according as he pleased and displeased them, as they use to do the players in the theater' (I, ii, 259–60). After the assassination, in a strange self-conscious moment, Cassius says:

> How many ages hence
> Shall this our lofty scene be acted over
> In states unborn and accents yet unknown ...

and Brutus: 'How many times shall Caesar bleed in sport' (III, i, 111–14). It seems as if 'true Romans' have to be 'Roman actors' and that public Rome – street, Capitol,

Forum – is akin to theatre (Brutus, indeed, refers to 'our performance').

At this moment, in the theatre of Rome, Caesar is bleeding in dead earnest (although of course in the Globe Theatre he is even now bleeding 'in sport'). As the blood 'streams forth' from Caesar's 'wounds' – 'rushing out of doors, to be resolved/ If Brutus so unkindly knocked, or no,' as Antony remarkably puts it, stirring up the people (III, ii, 181–2) – we seem to have entered a blood storm: 'bloody men' with 'bloody hands' at their 'bleeding business', reducing Caesar to a 'bleeding piece of earth':

> Pardon me, Julius! Here wast thou bayed, brave hart;
> Here didst thou fall, and here thy hunters stand,
> Signed in thy spoil and crimsoned in thy lethe ...
>
> (III, i, 204–6)

and 'all the while' Pompey's statue 'ran blood'.

In the 'play' as Brutus plans it he will act the role of high priest and doctor of the republic – 'Let's be sacrificers, but not butchers ... purgers, not murderers' (II, i, 166, 180) – but Shakespeare knew that Plutarch's hunting image was the right one. Hunters and butchers. In the event, the conspirators fall on Caesar and 'hew him as a carcass fit for hounds' (II, i, 174). There will be blood everywhere – as if still streaming from Caesar's wounds – until the end of the ensuing civil war. As foretold by Antony:

> Over thy wounds now do I prophesy ...
> Domestic fury and fierce civil strife
> Shall cumber all the parts of Italy;
> Blood and destruction shall be so in use ...
> And Caesar's spirit, ranging for revenge,
> With Ate by his side come hot from hell,
> Shall in these confines with a monarch's voice
> Cry 'Havoc,' and let slip the dogs of war,
> That this foul deed shall smell above the earth
> With carrion men, groaning for burial.
>
> (III, i, 259–75)

This pretty exactly describes the rest of the play, which will be dominated by Caesar's 'spirit', and in which Antony will

INTRODUCTION

prove to be one of the fiercest of the 'dogs of war' (his opening
words in Act IV – 'These many then shall die' – are as, if not
more, ominous as Brutus' 'It must be by his death'. By the end,
Brutus is more than justified in his comment – 'Slaying is the
word;/It is a deed in fashion' (V, v, 4–5).

Naively (to be generous), Brutus seems to think that after
the assassination, it will be enough if they go into the streets
and 'cry "Peace, freedom, and liberty!"' (III, i, 110), as if the
republic would somehow run itself, without any structured
authority. (However idealistic he may be, Brutus is a disastrously bad practical politician: he does not dispatch Antony;
he lets Antony address the people; he insists on the wrong
military tactics at Philippi – in all these matters, from a purely
political point of view, Cassius is right. That they should
quarrel after the assassination, and thus weaken their cause,
seems almost inevitable – a case, as I see it, of rogues falling
out.) Caesar kept, and represented, a central control of power.
In killing him – as a 'tyrant' – Brutus merely releases chaos,
anarchy, and civil war as different factions struggle for the
masterless power let loose. Brutus has not purged the republic,
but destroyed *all* government, and helped to usher in the new
tyranny of the triumvirate, which will prove to be far more
cruel, oppressive, and terrible than anything associated with
the rule (if not reign) of Caesar. (The triumvirate, at first
dominated by Antony, kill one hundred senators, including
Cicero, and deliberately – nastily – including a number of
each others' relatives – thus eliminating the senatorial party.
Antony also tries to fiddle Caesar's will. Before Caesar's death,
Antony appeared headstrong and passionately loyal – though
Cassius knows him for a 'shrewd contriver'. Afterwards he
becomes both greedy and barbarous. A dog of war indeed.)

Before the assassination, Brutus says to his fellow
conspirators:

> We all stand up against the spirit of Caesar,
> And in the spirit of men there is no blood.
> O, that we then could come by Caesar's spirit,
> And not dismember Caesar! But, alas,
> Caesar must bleed for it.

(II, i, 167–71)

liii

They do dismember Caesar, and he certainly bleeds: but they do not 'come by' his spirit, which escapes and returns to haunt and hunt them – 'ranging for revenge' as Antony predicts. Caesar seems to have a terrible posthumous power. Cassius and Brutus both commit suicide with his name on their lips, and Brutus comes to recognize that, indeed, they never did 'come by' his spirit:

> O Julius Caesar, thou art mighty yet!
> Thy spirit walks abroad, and turns our swords
> In our own proper entrails.
>
> (V, iii, 94–6)

'Spirit' is closely associated with 'fire' in this play:

> You are dull, Casca, and those sparks of life
> That should be in a Roman you do want ...
>
> (I, iii, 57–8)

Cicero, on the other hand, has 'fiery eyes'. Cassius is glad 'That my weak words have struck but thus much show/Of fire from Brutus' (I, ii, 176–7).

During the night of prodigies there is 'a tempest dropping fire' and 'Men, all in fire, walk up and down the streets' (I, iii, 10, 25). It seems as if there is fire, flickering or flaming, all over the place. There are fires of portent; there is literal fire – the plebeians, incited by Antony, go for 'firebrands' crying 'Burn all', while Portia, who eats coals in Plutarch, here simply 'swallowed fire' (IV, iii, 155); and there is inner fire – 'new-fired' hearts, the 'hasty spark' of anger, fiery spirits. Clearly, it is preferable to be 'fiery' with Cicero than 'dull' with Casca. But fire is the most dangerous element, spreading rapidly in unpredictable directions, and in this play there is a sense that it has become lethally out of control. And this loss of control is associated with the death of Caesar. After that, the fire rages and 'ranges' along with Caesar's spirit.

The source of fire is, ultimately the sun. There is an odd moment during the night-time meeting of the conspirators when three of them argue just where the sun is rising – 'doth not the day break here?' No, there; both wrong, over there is where he 'first presents his fire' (II, i, 101, 110). It is as if they sense that they are standing on the threshold of a new dawn in Roman history, but are not quite sure, as it were, where the fire will be coming from. Nor, by the same token, the direction it will take. At the end, Titinius laments over dead Cassius:

> O setting sun,
> As in thy red rays thou dost sink to night,
> So in his red blood Cassius' day is set.
> The sun of Rome is set. Our day is gone ...
>
> (V, iii, 60–63)

The bloody, fiery day of Roman history initiated by Brutus and his followers is over. But another sun is rising.

Octavius Caesar has very few lines in the play – about forty – and comes across as passionless, cold, detached. (It might be mentioned that much of the language in this play is cool, sparing of images, formal – perhaps because the play is dominated by Roman males.) But it is extraordinary how he makes his presence felt. Shakespeare did something very interesting here. In Plutarch, Octavius is sick and does not take part in the battle of Philippi. In Shakespeare, of course, he does; and there is this curiously telling exchange:

Antony. Octavius, lead your battle softly on
  Upon the left hand of the even field.
Octavius. Upon the right hand I; keep thou the left.
Antony. Why do you cross me in this exigent?
Octavius. I do not cross you; but I will do so.

> (V, i, 16–20)

This calm assertive confidence, at once emotionless and assured, is rather chilling. You begin to realize, as perhaps Antony does – this man is going to run *everything!* Not for nothing does he, literally, have the last word of the play. Shakespeare will show Octavius' sun reach its zenith in his next Roman play. But the atmosphere in that play will be very different. For there we will have Egypt – and Cleopatra.

*

lv

ANTONY AND CLEOPATRA (1607)

This, from North's translation of Plutarch's *Life of Antonius*: 'For they [Antony and Cleopatra] made an order between them, which they called AMIMETOBION (as much as to say, no life comparable and matcheable with it). Later, they invented another word – SYNAPOTHANUMENON (signifying the order and agreement of those that will die together).' They invented words. That is, from what was available they put together special terms which would apply to them alone – using language as a repository of possibilities, trying to transcend the limitations of the available formulations, re-rehearsing reality by stretching language in new directions and combinations. Shakespeare gloriously takes the hint. His Antony and Cleopatra seem intent on pre-empting language to establish new words to describe their love. New words, new worlds – this is the linguistic atmosphere of the play; ordinary language must be 'melted' (a key word) and reconstituted, so that new propositions and descriptions can be articulated to project and express their emotions. In their speech, everything tends towards hyperbole – i.e. 'excess, exaggeration'. Rhetorically this is related to *Superlatio*, which a dictionary of rhetorical terms glosses as 'exaggerated or extravagant terms used for emphasis and not intended to be understood literally'. Of course, Antony and Cleopatra do not want to be understood 'literally' – they do not work, or play, or love, or live, by the 'letter'. It is precisely the 'letter', and all fixed alphabetical restrictions, that they talk, and love, to dissolve, so that, as it were, they can live and speak in a 'higher' language of their own inventing. For Antony, to burst his armour and his alphabet are, alike, related modes of energy moving towards transcendence.

In his introductory *Lectures on Philosophy*, Hegel wrote that 'alphabetic writing is in itself and for itself the most intelligent'; he also wrote 'everything oriental must be excluded from the history of philosophy'. Alphabetic writing is transparent, an instrument of clarity, it maintains the unity of consciousness; the oriental thus becomes an opaque script, another, more iconic, language altogether, another mode of writing and thus of being-in-the-world, which threatens to disturb and disrupt, even destroy, the alphabetic clarity of consciousness. We can apply this opposition to the play. Caesar is nothing if not 'alphabetic'. He instructs Taurus and his army as he hands out his written orders before the battle of Actium – 'Do not exceed/The prescript of this scroll' (III, viii, 4–5). He never deviates from exact 'pre-scriptions' – the already written – and lives by and from within the orderings of his· 'scroll'. Cleopatra, on the other hand, is quintessentially oriental – in Hegel's terms: her actions, like her temperament, are impossible to 'read' in any alphabetic way. She is, from Caesar's point of view, illegible; hardly to be 'read' in his Roman language. She is an ultimate opacity – from Rome's point of view – confounding all customary alphabetic descriptions and decodings. She is in no way 'prescribed' or prescribable, and can no more be held within Caesar's 'scroll' than she can be trapped by his plots and policies.

But first, let me turn to the question of armour, the steel second skin of the man, the soldier, the Roman. As so often in Shakespeare, the opening lines set up terms and problems which will reverberate throughout the play. Philo, a Roman soldier with Antony in Egypt, opens:

> Nay, but this dotage of our general's
> O'erflows the measure.
>
> (I, i, 1–2)

The play, unlike any other by Shakespeare, opens with a negative. It thus implies the denial of a previous assertion – perhaps more affirmative – and his speech goes on to negate, or attempt to degrade and belittle, Antony's behaviour since he has been in Egypt. 'Overflowing the measure' immediately opposes the flooding Nile of Egypt to the concept of 'measure' – control, constraint, containment – which is the very language of Rome. The contest of the play is to be between overflow (excess) and measure (boundaries). Philo goes on to describe the transformation – or rather, in his terms, the deformation – of Antony the soldier into Antony the 'strumpet's fool', the victim of 'lust'. Philo always chooses the diminishing, pejorative word when referring to anything to do with Cleopatra and Egypt, anything which is not connected with Rome, Mars, and the 'office and devotion' of the warrior's code. Thus it is that he goes on to recall the great *soldier* Antony, to contrast him with the man who now serves Eros and Venus–Cleopatra. Again, his terms anticipate much that is to follow:

> His captain's heart
> Which in the scuffles of great fights hath burst
> The buckles on his breast, reneges all temper
> And is become the bellows and the fan
> To cool a gypsy's lust.
>
> (I, i, 6–10)

In battle, then, Antony could not be confined within his own armour; such was his force and energy that it broke out of his soldier's attire – it burst the buckles. Now his great heart 'reneges all temper' – renounces all restraint – but it is clear that it is not finally possible for Antony to be held within any 'temper', any restraints, or, indeed, any bonds. To be sure, he occasionally tries to stay within Roman rules; but in whatever he does – in war, in love – he is driven to burst whatever is 'buckling' him.

In Act IV, Antony is preparing for battle and calls for his armour. The aptly named Eros (as in Plutarch) brings it; but Cleopatra wants to help. She thus becomes, in Antony's words, 'the armourer of my heart' as she fastens the buckles and asks – 'Is this not buckled well?' Antony:

> Rarely, rarely:
> He that unbuckles this, till we do please
> To daff't for our repose, shall hear a storm.
> Thou fumblest, Eros, and my queen's a squire
> More tight at this than thou.
>
> (IV, iv, 11–15)

Armour – amour: there is no etymological connection, but phonetically the words are close. And what we see here, with Cleopatra buckling Antony's armour, almost while they are still in bed, is an overlaying of amour onto armour, so that the armour is eroticized and sensualized – the *business* of war (often referred to) here subsumed into the more all-embracing game of love. (By contrast, we may say that any sensuality and physicality of love and play is 'armoured' by Caesar and

Rome: there the policy of war tries to subsume love's body, making marriage and mating into mere instruments of policy.) Antony's armour, erotically saturated by the hands of Cleopatra, will not be taken off, he says, 'till we do please to daff't for our repose'. This anticipates his death.

As he moves towards that death, Antony says to Eros:

> Sometime we see a cloud that's dragonish,
> A vapor sometime like a bear or lion ...
> ... Thou hast seen these signs:
> They are black vesper's pageants ...
> That which is now a horse, even with a thought
> The rack dislimns, and makes it indistinct
> As water is in water.
>
> (IV, xiv, 2–11)

'Dis-limn' – that is, un-paint, efface – is Shakespeare's own invention; it is part of the 'reversal' which is happening to Antony, whose role in the 'pageant' (which also meant a mobile play or stage) is nearly over. He is moving towards 'indistinctness' – he, the man of the greatest 'distinction' in the world: he is being physically 'dis-limned' (which sounds the homophone 'dislimbed'), effaced by Caesar, by nature, by himself. (Cleopatra will 'paint' him again after his death, but we will come to that dazzling act of retrieval and recuperation.) Antony continues:

> My good knave Eros, now thy captain is
> Even such a body: here I am Antony,
> Yet cannot hold this visible shape ...
>
> (IV, xiv, 12–14)

He is in fact moving towards physical invisibility, because Antony, the name, the individual, the specific and world-famous identity, can no longer 'hold' onto his bodily shape. He is moving out, moving through, moving beyond; melting, but also transcending the final barrier – the body itself. And so *he* takes his armour off, since he is indeed ready for 'repose':

> Unarm Eros. The long day's task is done,
> And we must sleep ...

> Off, pluck off:
> The sevenfold shield of Ajax cannot keep
> The battery from my heart. O, cleave, my sides!
> Heart, once be stronger than thy continent,
> Crack thy frail case! Apace, Eros, apace.
> No more a soldier. Bruised pieces, go;
> You have been nobly borne ...
>
> (IV, xiv, 35–43)

The armour is not broken or burst, but discarded; it is almost as though he is taking his body to pieces and throwing it away – 'Bruised pieces, go' does seem almost to refer to the body as well, for it is that 'frail case' which he now wishes to burst free from. The body is the final boundary.

Boundary; bounty; bound; bond; band – these are words of varying importance in the play, but they all serve to set up a crucial series of echoes, half-echoes, indeed anti-echoes, if one can imagine such a thing. Rome is the place of bonds (Caesar: 'I know it for my bond'); and bounds ('He's bound unto Octavia,' the luckless messenger tells Cleopatra); and bands (Caesar says to Octavia – 'prove such a wife ... as my farthest band/Shall pass on thy aproof'). It is also the place of 'hoops' and 'knots' (in relation to the problem of what can bind Caesar and Antony together), and of 'squares', 'rules', and 'measures'. Antony tries to make a return to this Roman world, but no matter what 'bonds' he enters into, no matter how much he intends to try to live 'by the rule', it is, for him, finally not possible. This is not because he is a traitorous man, making and breaking promises for devious purposes. He simply cannot, as we say, be held 'within bounds'. When he is in Rome, in Caesar's house – in the heart of the heart of Rome, as it were – he seems to lose his natural strength and spirit and fortune. As his soothsayer tells him: 'If thou dost play with him at any game,/Thou art sure to lose; and of that natural luck/He beats thee 'gainst the odds' (II, iii, 26–8). And Antony recalls that this is indeed true; whatever game they play, with dice, cocks, quail etc., Caesar always wins. These details are all in Plutarch, but note the word that Shakespeare gives to Antony – 'and his quails ever/Beat mine, inhooped, at odds' (II, iii, 38–9). 'Inhooped' refers to the game of putting the

quails within a hoop so that they could not avoid fighting
(apparently a very ancient sport, going back to China). But of
course it is really Antony who is 'inhooped' in Rome, and
within the hoop he cannot be himself, rendered almost im-
potent within the 'bounds' of Caesar's domain. Antony is most
remarkable for his 'bounty', with all that that word suggests of
generosity, an endless spending and giving of a superabundant nature. In North's Plutarch, this 'liberality' is often
referred to – and with admiration, even when Plutarch is
criticizing Antony for his riotous feasting and wasteful negli-
gence. Antony, whatever else, is an example of '*magnanimitas*'.

In the play, this 'bounty' is constantly referred to and made
manifest. I shall single out three notable occasions. On the
night before the critical battle of Actium, Antony reasserts
himself as 'Antony'. 'Come,/Let's have one other gaudy night:
call to me/All my sad captains; fill our bowls once more', and
Cleopatra joins in the spirit of the occasion, reasserting the *role*
which in this case is the *reality*, of both of them: 'But since my
lord/Is Antony again, I will be Cleopatra' (III, xiii, 182–7).
They are most themselves when playing themselves. They are
out-playing history, as I shall suggest later. But we then
immediately go over to Caesar's camp and hear Caesar give
his instructions on this important night: 'And feast the army;
we have store to do't,/And they have earned the waste. Poor
Antony!' (IV, i, 15–16). Then we are back in Cleopatra's
palace, and hear Antony saying – 'Be bounteous at our meal
...' (IV, ii, 10). In the context and frame of Antony's 'bounty',
Caesar's arid, quantifying speech seems like the utterance of a
very small soul indeed – the epitome of cynical parsimony, so
that 'feast' is translated into 'store', and then further degraded
into 'waste'. Here is another absolutely basic opposition in the
play, a confrontation and contestation of vocabularies so that
what is 'feast' in one, is regarded as 'waste' in the other.
Antony gives from bounty; Caesar works from inventories.
'Poor Antony!' – yes, from one point of view; from another he
is rich Antony, since he gives unthinkingly from his spirit,
while Caesar – poor Caesar – distributes carefully from his
'store'. 'Feast' celebrates excess: 'waste' defers to boundaries.

In North's Plutarch (and Shakespeare took almost as much

from Plutarch for this play as he did for *Julius Caesar*) there is a
little incident during the battle of Actium recorded thus:

Furthermore, he dealt very friendly and courteously with Domitius,
and against Cleopatra's mind. For, he being sick of an ague when he
went and took a little boat to go to Caesar's camp, Antonius was very
sorry for it, but yet he sent after him all his carriage, train, and men;
and the same Domitius, as though he gave him to understand that he
repented his open treason, he died immediately after.

Shakespeare amplifies this in his account of the defection and
death of Enobarbus. Enobarbus, a good though cynical
soldier, begins to feel that it is foolish to remain loyal to
Antony in his visible decline:

> Mine honesty and I begin to square.
> The loyalty well held to fools does make
> Our faith mere folly: yet he that can endure
> To follow with allegiance a fall'n lord
> Does conquer him that did his master conquer,
> And earns a place 'i th' story.

> (III, xiii, 41–6)

But shortly thereafter he leaves Antony and goes over to
Caesar. Antony's reaction is immediate. He sends 'gentle
adieus, and greetings', and soon a Roman soldier is telling
Enobarbas:

> Antony
> Hath after thee sent all thy treasure, with
> *His bounty overplus*.

> (IV, vi, 20–23: my italics)

Bounty *overplus* – superabundant abundance, excessive excess.
This is the mark of Antony. Enobarbus has no ague; but this
act of bounty effectively kills him. His reaction:

> I am alone the villain of the earth,
> And feel I am so most. O Antony,
> Thou mine of bounty, how wouldst thou have paid
> My better service, when my turpitude
> Thou dost so crown with gold! This blows my heart ...
> I fight against thee! No, I will go seek

> Some ditch wherein to die: the foul'st best fits
> My latter part of life.

(IV, vi, 30–39)

His last words are:

> O, Antony,
> Nobler than my revolt is infamous,
> Forgive me in thine own particular,
> But let the world rank me in register
> A master-leaver and a fugitive.
> O, Antony! O, Antony!

(IV, ix, 18–23)

Thus Enobarbus dies in a ditch – the lowest earth– untranscended; unlike Antony and Cleopatra, who move towards fire and air from the mud of the Nile. To be 'politic' with Caesar after being loyal to Antony, is a degenerative deformation which cannot be endured. And Enobarbus effectively 'loses his place in the story' – he cancels himself, writes himself out of the poetic termination of Antony's life, annihilates himself in a ditch. And his parting word is – not 'Poor Antony!'; but the far more expressive 'O, Antony!' This Antony is the measureless measure of all that Enobarbus has deserted. After such bounty – what forgiveness?

My third reference is to Cleopatra's imaginative re-creation and recuperation of Antony after his death. It takes place in the presence of Dolabella, and leads to one of the most crucial exchanges in the play. Cleopatra has her own oriental bounty, and she now speaks with an overflowing super-abundance of language which makes her final speeches perhaps the most poetically powerful and coruscating in the whole of Shakespeare. Her re-creation of Antony concludes:

> For his bounty,
> There was no winter in't: an autumn 'twas
> That grew the more by reaping. His delights
> Were dolphinlike, they show'd his back above
> The element they lived in. In his livery
> Walked crowns and crownets: realms and islands were
> As plates dropped from his pocket.

(V, ii, 86–93)

Such a way of speaking, which goes beyond hyperbole into

another realm of 'truth', is too much for the Roman-practical-empirical Dolabella, who interrupts her – 'Cleopatra –'. To which she says:

> Think you there was or might be such a man
> As this I dreamt of?

Dolabella is sure – 'Gentle madam, no.'

> You lie, up to the hearing of the gods.
> But if there be nor ever were one such,
> It's past the size of dreaming; nature wants stuff
> To vie strange forms with fancy, yet t'imagine
> An Antony were nature's piece 'gainst fancy,
> Condemning shadows quite.

(V, ii, 93–100)

Cleopatra's image of Antony out-imagines the imagination, out-dreams dream. If you agree with Dolabella's Roman negative, the Roman deflationary perspective – the 'nay' which starts the play, then you deny Cleopatra's poetry and its power; deny Antony's bounty and *its* power. And you are well in danger of 'losing a place in the story'. But that is hardly possible; for by this stage, the soaring bounty of the imagination has passed beyond the boundaries and circumscriptions of nature itself. This is the awesome, magical excess which makes the world itself but a place of limits and limitations. Recall Antony and Cleopatra's opening words:

Cleopatra. If it be love indeed, tell me how much.
Antony. There's beggary in the love that can be reckoned.
Cleopatra. I'll set a bourn how far to be beloved.
Antony. Then must thou needs find out new heaven, new earth.

(I, i, 14–17)

Philo's 'lust' is immediately rephrased as 'love'. Cleopatra, playing, speaks temporarily in Roman terms – how much? (quantifying), and wanting to set a 'bourn' (boundary) on being loved. But Antony already points out the direction in which the play will move. For they do have to find out 'new heaven, new earth', a whole new world beyond quantifications and boundaries, until the 'truth' engendered by their love, their imagination, their dreaming, goes far beyond the restricted and impoverished realism of the Roman eye. By which point it simply *is* 'paltry to be Caesar'.

There is a great stress on 'time' in *Julius Caesar*, and it is well to remember that this is a history play. The outcome of the events it dramatized was the so-called 'Augustan peace', during which Christ was born and the pagan Empire – which Virgil called the Empire without end – was established, according to later writers, as a divine preparation for the Christian Empire. Octavius Caesar, himself a pagan, unknowingly laid the way for the True City, so in Christian terms the struggles and battles in the play affect, not merely his society, but all human society, the *orbis terrae* of Augustine. The events of the play are indeed of 'world' importance – world-shattering, world-remaking (the word 'world' occurs at least forty-five times in the play). By the same token, an earlier pagan world is being silenced, extinguished, and history – as the audience would know – is on Caesar's side. He is in time with Time. Antony and Cleopatra are out of time, in more than one sense. Thus, at the beginning, when Antony decides that he must return to Rome, Cleopatra silences his apologies, referring to the time-out-of-time when they were together – 'Eternity was in our lips and eyes' – while Antony, thinking Romanly for the moment, refers to 'the strong necessity of time'. Egypt, in this play, is a timeless present, which is to say an Eternity.

It can hardly escape our attention that the play is full of messengers from the start – two in the first scene, some thirty-five in all, with nearly every scene having a messenger of some kind. The play itself is extremely episodic, with some forty-two scenes (no scene breaks at all in the Folio), which makes for a very rapid sequence of change of place. There are nearly two hundred entrances and exits, all contributing to what Dr Johnson called the 'continual hurry' and 'quick succession' of events, which 'call the mind forward without intermission'. This can all be interpreted in different ways, but it certainly depicts a world in constant movement, in which time and place move and change so quickly that the whole world seems in a 'hurry' and in a state of flux – fluid, melting, re-forming. Messengers and messages bring information from the outside –

they are interruptions, irruptions, precipitants of change. History is going on, and on, and at an ever accelerating pace. Yet the remarkable thing is that time seems somehow to stand still in Egypt – both within and without the reach of 'messages'; both vulnerable to history yet outside it. When Antony is away, Cleopatra simply wants to 'sleep out this great gap of time' (I, v, 6). (When she first approaches Antony in her 'barge', the city goes out to see her, leaving Antony alone 'Whistling to th' air; which, but for vacancy,/Had gone to gaze on Cleopatra too,/And made a gap in nature' – II, ii, 222–4. It is as if Cleopatra creates 'gaps' – gaps of time, gaps of nature.) For Rome, Egypt represents a great waste of time while the 'business' of history is going on. The word 'business', more often than not, carries pejorative connotations in Shakespeare. It is notable that Caesar interrupts his formulaic (as I hear it), elegiac 'praise' of the dead Antony because of – a messenger: 'The *business* of this man looks out of him;/We'll hear him what he says' (V, i, 50: my italics). He never completes the speech. Conversely, Cleopatra interrupts history to complete her poetic re-creation of Antony – from which no 'business' can distract her. From the Egyptian perspective, history itself is a 'gap of time', and Cleopatra, though growing physically older ('wrinkled deep in time'), seems to linger in Eternity, waiting for Antony to return from the trivial – though world-shattering – distractions of history.

As well as being a history play, *Antony and Cleopatra* contains within it traces of the outlines of a morality play – for by the early Renaissance the 'moral' of the story of the illustrious lovers was well established. We can find it in Spenser's *Fairie Queene*, Book V, Canto VIII:

> Nought under heaven so strongly doth allure
> The sence of man, and all his minde possesse,
> As beauties lovely baite, that doth procure,
> Great warriours oft their rigour to represse,
> And mighty hands forget their manlinesse ...
> So also did that great Oetean Knight
> For his loves sake his Lions skin undight:

and

> so did warlike Antony neglect
> The worlds whole rule for Cleopatra's sight.
> Such wondrous powre hath womens fair aspect,
> To captive men, and make them all the world reject.

This 'moral' reading is there in Plutarch's version, in which Antony becomes 'effeminate' and made 'subject to a woman's will'. He is particularly critical of Antony's behaviour at the battle of Actium (when he followed the fleeing Cleopatra). 'There Antonius showed plainly, that he had not only lost the courage and heart of an Emperor, but also of a valiant man, and that he was not his own man ... he has so carried away with the vain love of this woman, as if he had been glued unto her, and that she could not have removed without moving of him also.' In Spenser's terms, Antony 'rejected' the world for the mere love of a woman. Whether he found or made a better world is not, of course, considered. But, while Shakespeare's play does include these historical–morality elements (unquestionably, his glue-like relationship with Cleopatra ruins him as a politician and spoils him as a soldier, and, in worldly terms, she does – as he recognizes – lead him 'to the very heart of loss' – IV, xii, 29) – it complicates any ethical 'reading' of the story, so there can be no question of seeing it simply as another version of a good soldier losing his empire because of a bad woman. To understand this more clearly, we have to take into account another figure. For, if Octavius Caesar is related to the onward and inexorable movement of History, Antony is related to a god, Hercules.

This relationship is suggested in Plutarch who, however, relates Antony more closely to Bacchus. Shakespeare strengthens the association with Hercules. Hercules was famous for his anger, and so is Antony. As his anger begins to rise, Cleopatra says: 'Look, prithee, Charmian,/How this Herculean Roman does become/The carriage of his chafe' (I, iii, 84–5). Reacting in fury to Cleopatra's flight from the battle and what ensues, he cries out:

> The shirt of Nessus is upon me; teach me,
> Alcides, thou mine ancestor, thy rage.

> (IV, xii, 44–5)

Plutarch refers to Antony being deserted by a god: 'it is said that suddenly they heard a marvellous sweet harmony of sundry sorts of instruments of music ... as they use in Bacchus feasts ... Now, such as in reason sought the depth of the interpretation of this wonder, thought it was the god unto whom Antonius bare singular devotion to counterfeit and resemble him, that did forsake them.' Shakespeare takes the scene, and the interpretation, but makes one telling change. Late in the play, some soldiers hear 'Music i' th' air' and decide "Tis the god Hercules, whom Antony loved,/Now leaves him' (IV, iii, 15–16). Where his Antony is concerned – despite his manifest taste for wine – Shakespeare wants us to think more of Hercules, less of Bacchus. Hercules was of course *the* hero – hero turned god – *par excellence*. There were many allegories concerning Hercules current by the Middle Ages. One (apparently from the Sophist, Prodicus), has Hercules as a young man arriving at a place where the road branches into two paths, one leading up a steep hill, the other into a pleasant glade. At the dividing point, two fair women meet him: one, modest and sober, urges him to take the steep path; the other, seductive if meretricious, uses her arts in an attempt to attract him into the glade. The hero, of course chooses the steep hill of Virtue over the beckoning glades of Pleasure. There were many medieval and Renaissance depictions of this struggle of Virtue and Pleasure over Hercules (there is a famous Dürer engraving of it – *Der Hercules*), with Pleasure, *hedone, voluptas*, sometimes associated with Venus. The implications, for us, are quite clear: if Antony is related to Hercules, Cleopatra is related to Venus. The key difference, of course, is that Hercules–Antony chooses Pleasure, pays heed to the solicitations of Venus – thus inverting the traditional moral of this allegory. According then to the accumulated traditional lore which had grown up around the much metamorphosed and allegorized figure of Hercules, Antony is indeed a version of Hercules, but one who, as it were, decided to take the wrong road – not up the steep hill of (Roman) virtue, but off the track into the (oriental) glades of pleasure.

There are other divinities in the play, and if Hercules deserts Antony, he in turn goes on to play Osiris to Cleopatra's Isis.

The union of these divinities assures the fertility of Egypt: in Plutarch's study of the myth (well known in Shakespeare's time), Osiris is the Nile which floods and makes fertile the land – he is form, the seminal principle, and Isis is matter. From their union are bred not only crops, but animals, such as the serpents of the Nile. Typhon the crocodile, born of Nile mud, represents for Plutarch the irrational, bestial part of the soul by which Osiris is deceived and torn to pieces. There are, of course, numerous references to the Nile, its floods, its serpents, and so on, in the play, and Shakespeare clearly has this myth actively in mind. But it is not a stable or fixed incorporation. Cleopatra is Isis but also Antony's 'serpent of old Nile', and by a serpent of Nile will she die – a serpent by a serpent 'valiantly vanquished', as Antony–Osiris is 'a Roman by a Roman valiantly vanquished' (the second Roman is more Antony than Caesar – as Cleopatra says: 'Not Caesar's valor hath o'erthrown Antony,/But Antony's hath triumphed on itself' – IV, xv, 14–15). The monster-crocodile who destroys Antony is, in this play, Octavius Caesar – though he is hardly seen in those terms. He is a disguised Typhon for Antony and Cleopatra, who are playing at being Osiris and Isis – but, really, he is not in their self-mythologizing act, not in their 'play' at all. I use the word 'play' advisedly and deliberately. Cleopatra is, of course, above all a great actress. She can play with Antony to beguile him; she can play at being Isis, thus anticipating her own move towards transcendence; and she can 'play' at her death, easily outplaying Caesar's crafty political deviousness. In this way, she completely transforms her desolate state, not submitting to the downward turn of Fortune, but inverting it into the occasion of her own triumph of the imagination:

> My desolation does begin to make
> A better life. 'Tis paltry to be Caesar:
> Not being Fortune, he's but Fortune's knave,
> A minister of her will ...
>
> (V, ii, 1–4)

Cleopatra will be her *own* Fortune – a triumph of the 'will'.
    She is aware that Caesar will display her in Rome, and that

her life with Antony will be 'staged' in a degraded form, in keeping with that tendency of Roman rhetoric to devalue and translate downwards the life associated with Egypt:

> The quick comedians
> Extemporally will stage us, and present
> Our Alexandrian revels: Antony
> Shall be brought drunken forth, and I shall see
> Some squeaking Cleopatra boy my greatness
> I' th' posture of a whore.

(V, ii, 216–21)

(Which, of course, exactly describes what is going on in the Elizabethan theatre at that moment, with some boy 'squeaking' Cleopatra. This is not Nabokovian self-reflexivity. Rather, it is effectively as if the drama is so incandescent that it is scorning its own resources, shedding the very medium which has served to put its poetry into flight. It is as though 'representation' is scorching itself away to reveal the thing itself – an electrifying moment of astonishing histrionic audacity and magic.) So – Cleopatra puts on her own play, on her own stage, with her own costume, speeches, and gestures:

> Now, Charmian!
> Show me, my women, like a queen: go fetch
> My best attires. I am again for Cydnus,
> To meet Mark Antony. Sirrah Iras, go …
> And when thou hast done this chare, I'll give thee leave
> To play till doomsday. – Bring our crown and all.

(V, ii, 227–32)

> My resolution's placed, and I have nothing
> Of woman in me: now from head to foot
> I am marble-constant: now the fleeting moon
> No planet is of mine.

(V, ii, 238–41)

She is moving beyond the body, beyond time, beyond the whole world of transience and decay, beyond her own planet the moon, with all that it implies of tidal periodicity. The clown enters with his figs, which contain the serpent she will use for her suicide (at the beginning, Charmian says 'I love long life better than figs' – I, ii, 32 – by the end this, like so much else, is reversed: Cleopatra likes figs better than long life). We move to her final self-apotheosis, played with great dignity and ceremony, at which Cleopatra is at once her own directress and her own priestess:

> Give me my robe, put on my crown, I have
> Immortal longings in me ...
> ... Husband, I come:
> Now to that name my courage prove my title!
> I am fire, and air; my other elements
> I give to baser life ...
>
> (V, ii, 280–90)

Out of the earth, mud, dung, water associated with the Nile and its fertility, she has distilled an essence composed only of the higher elements, air and fire. She is 'marble' for the duration of the performance; she is also, like Antony, 'melting', dissolving, but melting into a higher atmosphere. She gives a farewell kiss to Iras who falls down dead – perhaps from poison, perhaps from grief – and Cleopatra comments:

> Dost thou lie still?
> If thus thou vanishest, thou tell'st the world
> It is not worth leave-taking.
>
> (V, ii, 296–8)

To the snake she says:

> O, couldst thou speak,
> That I might hear thee call great Caesar ass
> Unpolicied!
>
> (V, ii, 306–8)

She has seen through Caesar's tricks and stratagems – 'He words me, girls, he words me, that I should not/Be noble to myself' (V, ii, 191–2); she knows, too, that he uses language instrumentally, merely for devious political ends. And when Proculeus refers to Caesar's 'bounty', she knows that it is but a pitiful and transparent travesty of the real bounty of Antony. In her superbly performed death, we see the triumph of the 'oriental' imagination over the 'alphabetic' utilitarianism of Caesar. The world will indeed be his, and another kind of Empire inaugurated; but from the perspective of Cleopatra, and *just for the duration of the play*, it seems a world 'not worth leave-taking'. So her last words are an incomplete question: 'What should I stay – ' as she passes out of language, body, world, altogether. There is no *staying* her now. Charmian completes her question with her own final speech:

> In this wild world? So, fare thee well.
> Now boast thee, death, in thy possession lies
> A lass unparalleled. Downy windows, close;
> And golden Phoebus never be beheld
> Of eyes again so royal! Your crown's awry;
> I'll mend it, and then play –

> (V, ii, 314–19)

Thus Cleopatra, and her girls, play their way out of the reach of history, with an intensity of self-sustaining, self-validating poetry which does indeed eclipse the policies and purposes of Caesar. (There are some recent readings which see Antony and Cleopatra as failed politicians who turn to aesthetics to gloss over their mistakes and cheer themselves up with poetry. I can imagine such a play, but this one is not it.) Cleopatra was 'confined' in her monument, a prisoner of Caesar's force – apparently secure within the boundaries of his soldiers and his 'scroll'. It is by the unforgettable excess and bounty/beauty of her last 'Act' that she triumphs over all that would confine her, and turns death into 'play', *the* play that will take her into Eternity.

Let me return to the opposition between feast and waste. Feast derives from *festa* – holiday – and in one sense, Antony and Cleopatra turn life in Egypt into a perpetual holiday. 'Waste' is more interesting. Just as 'dirt' has been defined as 'matter out of place', so the idea of 'waste' presupposes a boundary or classification mark which enables one to draw a distinction between what is necessary, valuable, usable in some way, and what lies outside these categories – 'waste'. Antony, we may say, recognizes no such boundary. Indeed, he 'wastes' himself, in the sense that he is endlessly prodigal of all he has and does not count the cost. From Antony's point of view, all life in Egypt can be seen as a feast; in Caesar's eyes – the Roman perspective – it is all 'waste'. From the etymology of the word (*uacare*, to be empty or vacant; *uanus*, hollow, vain; *uastus*, desolated, desert, vast; up to Old English *weste* – see Eric Partridge's *Origins*), we can say that there is a connection between vastness, vacancy, vanity, and waste. Antony is inhabiting a realm of vastness, vanity, vacancy – the 'great gap' named by Cleopatra (Caesar, indeed, refers to Antony's 'vacancy'). From Caesar's point of view, and those who see with the Roman eye, Antony is indeed 'empty' while Caesar is referred to as 'the fullest man'. Thus Enobarbus, commenting on Antony's challenge to Caesar to meet him in single battle: 'that he should dream,/Knowing all measures, the full Caesar will/Answer his emptiness!' Caesar is, from one point of view, *full* – full of history, of Fortune, of time. Antony is 'empty' – committed to vacancy, vanity, waste. The question implicitly posed is whether he and Cleopatra, and their way of life, are not 'full' of something quite outside of Caesar's discourse and his measurements, something which makes *him* the empty man. Caesar is full of politics, empty of poetry: Antony and Cleopatra reach a point where they are empty of politics, but full of poetry. Which is the real 'vacancy'? It depends where you are standing, how you are looking. But there is nothing 'vast' about Caesar: even if he conquers the whole world, everything is done with 'measure' and 'temper' (temperance). If Antony and Cleopatra melt and dissolve, it is into a 'vastness' which is the necessary space for their exceeding, their excess – 'beyond the size of dreaming'. In this play, Shakespeare compels a complete revaluation of 'waste'. Historically, it was *not* paltry to be Caesar, certainly not this Caesar, who is insured of, and will ensure, a 'temperate' imperial future, during which time Christ would be born. This Caesar certainly has his place in the story of history. But in this play, his conquest is registered as a gradual diminishment as he – alphabetically – takes over the Orient, but in doing so merely imposes Roman 'prescriptions' on a vast world of pagan fecundity, spilled plenty, and an oriental magnificence which transforms 'waste' into 'bounty', and makes Caesar seem like the 'merchant' he is, a calculating Machiavel – an ass unpolicied.

Boundaries are, of course, of central importance for civilization. For Vico, in *The New Science*, civilized man is precisely one who creates and guards 'confines' – 'for it was necessary to set up boundaries to the field in order to put a stop to the infamous promiscuity of things in the bestial state. On these boundaries were to be fixed the confines first of families, then of gentes or houses, later of peoples, and finally of nations.' There is much in Shakespeare which honours and defends the importance of recognizing the need for boundaries. But in this play, writing against the recorded, inexorable grain and movement of history, Shakespeare makes us re-value what might have been lost in the triumph of Caesar:

> O, see, my women,
> The crown o' th' earth doth melt. My lord!
> O, withered is the garland of the war,
> The soldier's pole is fall'n: young boys and girls
> Are level now with men. The odds is gone,
> And there is nothing left remarkable
> Beneath the visiting moon.
>
> (IV, xv, 62–8)

This is 'waste'? Rather, the fecundity, plenitude and bounty associated with Egypt, and Antony in Egypt, have fed into and nourished Cleopatra's speech, until she is speaking a kind of language of pure poetry about which alphabetic man can have nothing to say. A whole pagan age is over; the future belongs to Caesar – and Christ. But confronted with this kind of transcendent poetry, which is indeed all 'excess', that future seems merely trivial, temporal, temperate. 'The road of excess leads to the Palace of Wisdom,' wrote Blake. In this play, the poetry of excess leads to the unbounded, unboundaried, spaces of infinity. Saving leads to earthly empire: squandering opens an avenue to Eternity. All air and fire – and poetry. Bounty overplus.

*

TIMON OF ATHENS (1607–8?)
'Bounty' figures prominently and plays a large role in what may, or may not, be Shakespeare's next play – *Timon of Athens*. (It first finds print in the Folio of 1623 where it occupies the

place intended for *Troilus and Cressida*, which had to be withdrawn because of copyright difficulties. On internal evidence, it belongs to the 1605–9 period of Shakespeare's plays. But it seems unfinished and could conceivably have been written later. I give the conventionally agreed-on date.) Bounty, bounteous, bounteousness – the words occur at least seventeen times by my count. But something has taken a turn. This is the wrong kind of bounty, bounty gone wrong. We hear, in the opening lines as the Poet, Painter, Jeweler, and Merchant enter Timon's house (bent on hypocritical sycophancy and cynical exploitation): 'See,/Magic of bounty, all these spirits thy power/Hath conjured to attend' (I, i, 5–7). But the 'magic' is irresponsible, discreative, ruinous, and all the 'spirits' it 'conjures to attend' turn out to be venal, heartless, 'monstrous'. As well as the continuous acclaiming of Timon's 'bounty', there are some warning lines:

> 'Tis pity bounty had not eyes behind,
> That man might ne'er be wretched for his mind.
>
> (I, ii, 166–7)

'for his mind' – on account of his inclinations: this from Flavius, the loyal and honest steward.

> No villainous bounty yet hath passed my heart;
> Unwisely, not ignobly, have I given.
>
> (II, ii, 183–4)

Thus Timon defends himself against the 'sermon' of his despairing steward. And it is the steward who, in response to Timon's expression of confidence that his friends will not let him 'sink', comments sadly:

> I would I could not think it; that thought is bounty's foe.
> Being free itself, it thinks all others so.
>
> (II, ii, 242–3)

Of course, Timon's friends are no friends at all – and first he 'sinks', and then he dives.

> Strange, unusual blood,
> When man's worst sin is, he does too much good.

> Who then dares to be half so kind again?
> For bounty, that makes gods, do still mar men.
>
> (IV, ii, 38–41)

It is something of a question whether Timon is truly 'kind' – and how much *good* he actually does. Dr Johnson maintained that the play 'is a warning against that ostentatious liberality which scatters bounty but confers no benefits and buys flattery but no friendship'. Another eighteenth-century writer, William Richardson, also judges Timon adversely. In this play, he says, Shakespeare 'illustrates the consequences of that inconsiderate profusion which has the appearance of liberality and is supposed even by the inconsiderate person himself to proceed from a generous principle, but which, in reality, has its chief origin in the love of distinction'. As Richardson trenchantly points out, Timon 'is not so solicitous of alleviating the distress of obscure affliction ... He is not represented as visiting the cottage of the fatherless and widow, but is wonderfully generous to men of high rank and character.' It would only be a little overstating the case to say that Timon's idea of 'bounty' is to lay on drunken orgies for his posh acquaintances. Witness Flavius:

> When all our offices have been oppressed
> With riotous feeders, when our vaults have wept
> With drunken spilth of wine, when every room
> Hath blazed with lights and brayed with minstrelsy,
> I have retired me to a wasteful cock,
> And set mine eyes at flow.
>
> (II, ii, 168–73)

('blazed with lights and brayed with minstrelsy' – this is Shakespeare at his most powerful). Aristotle states; 'he is liberal who spends according to his substance *and on the right objects*; and he who exceeds is prodigal' (my italics). Timon is not liberal: he is prodigal, culpably prodigal.

But certainly, his flatterers treat him, and possibly he regards himself, as a god. One of them says of his 'bounty':

> He pours it out. Plutus, the god of gold,
> Is but his steward ...
>
> (I, i, 283–4)

INTRODUCTION

We will come back to gods – and gold. Here it will serve to note that Timon's kind of 'bounty' – blind, indiscriminate, proud, self-deceiving, and terribly vulnerable – certainly 'mars the man'. Indeed, it could be said that Timon is never seen as a 'man' at all. When he can no longer go on playing 'god', he insists on being 'beast' – the two words recur, often in close proximity as if squeezing out, or foreclosing on, possible intermediate states. This is a play about extremes.

The main point about Timon's munificence is that it is as reckless, indiscriminate, and all-embracing, as his later invectives and denunciations are to be. All motives come mixed, but there is something distinctly impure in Timon's generosity. As the honest Flavius tells him:

> Great Timon, noble, worthy, royal Timon!
> Ah, when the means are gone that buy this praise,
> The breath is gone whereof this praise is made.
> Feast-won, fast-lost . . .

(II, ii, 178–81)

Proud, ostentatious Timon has been buying praise and adulation – but, as Flavius well knows, all he purchases is empty words. He is indeed often called 'noble' and worthy', just as his 'bounty' is consistently referred to. But the words undergo what is sometimes referred to as devaluation through repetition (something similar happens to the word 'honourable' in Antony's famous speech over Caesar's body). When Flaminius goes to Lucullus to ask for money to help Timon, Lucullus, expecting another gift, asks him what he has under his cloak. 'Faith, nothing but an empty box, sir, which in my lord's behalf I come to entreat your honor to supply' (III, i, 16–19). But Lucullus has no 'honour' to 'supply' (fill) the box, so it remains empty. This is what happens to the honorific terms in the play. There is no longer anything to fill them; they are emptied out, and by the end, words like 'bounty' and 'noble' have a hollow ring. As with the key words, so with the main characters in this Athens – they are hollow, all 'outside', no inside. Timon commends painting because 'These penciled figures are/Even such as they give out' (I, i, 159–60). What you see is all there is. This is true of the characters who may, indeed, be said to be 'penciled' – outlined, sketched. They are just as hypocritical, mean, ungrateful as they appear. Most unusually for Shakespeare, they have no interiority (this very definitely includes Timon himself). Indeed, the play itself may be said to have no 'inside' and is, itself, something of an empty box.

Coleridge called this play an 'after vibration' of *King Lear*, and there are certainly distinctive echoes. These include the horror of ingratitude ('O see the monstrousness of man/When he looks out in an ungrateful shape' – III, ii, 77–8); Timon's denudation and reduction to an 'unhoused' condition in the wilderness outside the city walls; and the ominous reiteration of the word 'nothing' ('For these my present friends, as they are to me nothing, so in nothing bless them, and to nothing are they welcome' – III, vi, 82–5). But there is a very definite 'after vibration' of *Antony and Cleopatra* as well, an after-echo which has a distressing or displeasing tendency towards satire and even travesty, of a rather bleak kind. There is good reason to think that Shakespeare wrote the two plays closely together (but no point in speculating as to the possible explanations for such a drastic change of mood and tone). At times, Timon speaks lines reminiscent of Antony (e.g. 'Methinks I could deal kingdoms to my friends' – I, ii, 228), but it is somehow not the same. As in *Antony and Cleopatra* we have the regular use of the words 'bind', 'bond', 'bound'; but not only is 'bounty' revalued, or rather devalued, but 'feast' is rather horribly degraded, even, I shall suggest, to the point of sacrilegious parody. In *Antony and Cleopatra*, 'feast' was opposed to 'waste'; in *Timon of Athens* 'feast' *is* 'waste'. The first feast in the play is a veritable debauch, exemplifying Flavius' description of Timon's habitual prodigal entertainment – amply justifying the question to Timon, 'What needs these feasts, pomps, and vainglories?' (I, ii, 253–4). This is spoiled ceremony, hospitality vulgarized, wasteful bounty. As a Senator comments: 'Still in motion/Of raging waste? It cannot hold, it will not' (II, i, 3–4). Timon's bounty starts out as a flow of gold ('He pours it out' – I, i, 283); it manifests itself as a 'flow of riot' (II, ii, 3); and soon becomes a 'flow of debts' (II, ii, 152). Uncontrolled spillage. 'Feast-won, fast-lost,' as Flavius succinctly puts it.

Trying to 'win' people with this kind of feasting, ensures that you will lose them. Timon's second 'feast', at which he serves water to his ungrateful 'friends' ('Uncover, dogs, and lap'), is a sort of anti-feast, a complete negation at the opposite extreme from the earlier squandering. These are Timon's two, Timon's *only*, positions. 'One day he gives us diamonds, next day stones' (III, vi, 121), says one of the lords as they are driven away from the anti-feast. Diamonds or stones: nothing in between.

But something worse. At the first feast, there is the following exchange:

Timon. You had rather be at a breakfast of enemies than a dinner of friends.

Alcibiades. So they were bleeding new, my lord, there's no meat like 'em; I could wish my best friends at such a feast.

(I, ii, 76–80)

The exaggeration or jesting of a military man, perhaps. But there is more than a hint of cannibalism in this play in which flatterers are said to 'drink' men, and ladies to 'eat' lords. Timon, in his glory days, 'had the world as my confectionary' (IV, iii, 261), which suggests a too sickly-sweet meal, luxurious rather than nourishing. When, at the height of his hysterical revulsion, he scrabbles around in the wilds and finds a root, he says:

> That the whole life of Athens were in this!
> Thus would I eat it.

(IV, iii, 282–3)

Sweets, roots, Athenians – it is all 'eating'. This is a society in which, to the very edges of metaphor, people variously 'devour' each other. Feast as waste; feast as cannibalism. It is no wonder that, in this play, feasting leads to 'vomit' and what should be nourishment turns to 'poison'. And there is one more turn to this particular screw. Here is Apemantus, the scourge at the feast:

O you gods! What a number of men eats Timon, and he sees 'em not! It grieves me to see so many dip their meat in one man's blood, and all the madness is, he cheers them up too.

I wonder men dare trust themselves with men.
Methinks they should invite them without knives:
Good for their meat, and safer for their lives.
There's much example for't; the fellow that sits next him, now parts
bread with him, pledges the breath of him in a divided draught, is the
readiest man to kill him.

(I, ii, 38–49)

Much example indeed – Jesus and Judas providing the most
famous example of all. And here is the First Stranger – from
outside Athens and revealed to be both dispassionate and
compassionate:

Who can call him his friend
That dips in the same dish?

(III, ii, 70–71)

Honest Flavius refers to the 'glutt'nous maws' of the 'false
masters [who] ate of my lord's meat' (III, iv, 50). And when
Timon is set upon by the servants of ruthless creditors, he cries
out: 'Tell out my blood . . . Tear me, take me, and the gods fall
upon you' (III, iv, 94, 99). As you (his well-feasted 'friends')
fall upon the god, taking and tearing his meat, his bread, his
blood, his body. Of course, there are here deliberate echoes of
the Last Supper, and Christian communion (and the eating of
gods in general); it would be impossible to miss them. But to
argue from this, as some have done (most famously Wilson
Knight), that this makes of Timon something of a Christ
figure, seems to me badly to misread, misapprehend, the tone
and atmosphere of the play. Certainly, Timon disports himself
as a god, and is willing to be treated (or addressed) as one by
his flatterers, who readily comply as long as his 'grace' and
beneficence is flowing their way. Tear, take, eat: this is my
blood, this is my body. And so they do. But this is no *sparagmos*
and *omophagia*, in the ancient sense; or, to the extent that it is, it
has been sordidly translated into financial terms. Nor is it even
analogous to the Christian communion. There is no hint of the
sacred here; not a touch of ritual observance. What we *do* have
is a blasphemous, empty, parody or travesty of sacrificial rites
which have elsewhere and at other times been dignifying,

meaningful, perhaps redeeming. But not here, not now – not in *this* Athens.

Timon of Athens is a very schematic play. It is composed of two starkly contrasting halves (the first half clearly more finished than the second). It is very static, the second half consisting of a series of interviews. Characterization is cursory, 'penciled', thin to the point of impersonality and abstraction. It seems more like an allegory or morality play (or even a folk tale – three false friends, loyal servant, etc.) than a fully developed drama. For the first ninety-four lines none of the speakers is named – they are types. (At line ninety-four, Timon enters and his first word is 'Imprisoned' – anticipating his own imprisonment, in his own house, his debts, but most of all in his temperament – for he, too, proves to be a fixed 'type'.) The play has been seen as more of a bitter satire than a tragedy, and certainly there is none of the dramatic conflict and sense of inexorable progress (or development and move- ment) that we experience in Shakespeare's great tragedies (just compare *Macbeth*). Perhaps more to the point, there is no development in the 'characters', particularly of Timon. There is no halting but growing self-awareness, no bruising stum- bling to an initially resisted self-knowledge. In his soliloquies, Timon exhibits none of the meditative inwardness and deepening self-exploration of Hamlet. When he stops giving, he starts cursing. Having postured and dispensed like a god, he turns to crawling and snarling like a beast. Where Hamlet really thinks, Timon mainly rants. This is not to deny the undoubted power of some of his furious and nauseated out- bursts (see, for example, the speech beginning 'O blessed breeding sun, draw from the earth/Rotten humidity' – IV, iii, 1 *et seq*.; or his address to the bandits starting 'I'll example you with thievery' – IV, iii, 442 *et seq*.; both worthy of Lear himself). But like his 'generosity', his hatred is indiscriminate, all-inclusive. At times, he is reduced – if that is the word – to lists:

> Piety, and fear,
> Religion to the gods, peace, justice, truth,
> Domestic awe, night-rest, and neighborhood,

> Instruction, manners, mysteries, and trades,
> Degrees, observances, customs, and laws,
> Decline to your confounding contraries,
> And let confusion live.
>
> (IV, i, 15–21)

In other words, *everything* that makes human, civilized life possible – damn and confound the lot. Having instantly arrived at, jumped or inverted to, this state of terminal misanthropic nihilism, there is no way in which Timon can change or develop – he can only reiterate, and die. The dramatic possibilities of such a figure are strictly limited, and perhaps that is why Shakespeare left the play unfinished and moved on to more fruitful fields.

Apemantus, the Cynic (i.e. 'dog' – the word re-echoes through the play), has some cogent insights into Timon during their climactic exchange in Act IV:

> Thou'dst courtier be again
> Wert thou not beggar.
>
> (IV, iii, 242–3)

The middle of humanity thou never knewest, but the extremity of both ends.

> (IV, iii, 301–2)

God, or beast – this extremism was familiar to the Elizabethans from the well-known saying of Aristotle that 'that man which cannot live in civil company either he is a god or a beast, seeing only God is sufficient of himself, and a solitary life agreeth with a beast' (this is, of course, very relevant for *Coriolanus* as well). Whatever we think of Apemantus, a descendant of Jacques and Thersites, we may take William Richardson's felicitous formulation – 'his invectives are bitter, but his remarks are true'.

The god who really *does* rule and dominate in the play is – gold:

> What a god's gold, that he is worshiped
> In a baser temple than where swine feed!
>
> (V, i, 49–50)

Thus Timon, as people come flocking to him in the wilderness, trying to ease, or flatter, out of him his new-found gold. As a 'god' himself, he had 'poured' out gold in Athens; now he distributes it freely again, with, of course, a directly opposite motive:

> Thou visible god,
> That sold'rest close impossibilities
> And mak'st them kiss; that speak'st with every tongue
> To every purpose. O thou touch of hearts,
> Think thy slave man rebels, and by thy virtue
> Set them into confounding odds, that beasts
> May have the world in empire.
>
> (IV, iii, 391-7)

May the god gold turn all humans to beasts (again, the words appear in close proximity as if to occlude intermediary possibilities). And if the announced position of the two prostitutes is anything to go by – 'we'll do anything for gold' (IV, iii, 151) – his hope may well be realized. Perhaps it has been realized already, given Apemantus' declaration – 'The commonwealth of Athens is become a forest of beasts.' (Incidentally, the Greek word *time* or *timos* means both honour and price, thus pointing to the equivocal nature of true 'value'. Timon's initial belief in the 'honour' of his friends, switches to an unshakable conviction that money rules all. He carries his fate in his name.)

But the Athenians are not, not quite, *all* beasts. Lowly figures often play a vital role in Shakespeare – for instance the unnamed servant who turns on his master, Cornwall, and kills him – refusing to stand and watch his cruelty – and it is a very important part of this play that Timon's steward, Flavius, also unnamed in the early part of the folio version, is truly loyal and loving to his master, Timon. (Flaminius and Timon's other servants are also loyal, and disgusted at the base and cruel rapacity of their so-called 'betters'.) In the first half of the play, Flavius agonizes over the irresponsible waste he is helpless to prevent – 'I bleed inwardly for my lord' (I, ii, 210). And when the impoverished Timon takes to the wilds, Flavius seeks him out, loyal as ever:

> O you gods!
> Is yond despised and ruinous man my lord?

> Full of decay and failing? ...
> ... I will present
> My honest grief unto him, and as my lord
> Still serve him with my life. My dearest master.
>
> (IV, iii, 467–9, 477–9)

In the face of Timon's suspicions as to his motives for seeking him out – having trusted everyone he will, of course, henceforth trust no one – Flavius protests:

> That which I show, heaven knows, is merely love,
> Duty and zeal to your unmatched mind ...
>
> (IV, iii, 524–5)

We may blink at that 'unmatched mind', of which we have seen precious little evidence (similarly it strains credulity when the Senators come and beg him to take over the captaincy of the city as being the only man who can save Athens from the threatened attack of Alcibiades – one senses Timon would be hardly a better strategist than he is an economist); but – 'only love'. With the crucial exception of Flavius' unwavering devotion, this non-commercial 'commodity' is *entirely* absent from the play. And this is, certainly, intimately connected to another absence – the absence of women, apart from two prostitutes (who, like the Athenian men, will 'do anything for gold') and the Amazons in the masque (hardly representative of 'the female'). When Flavius announces himself to the misanthrope Timon as 'an honest poor servant of yours', Timon feigns non-recognition:

> Then I know thee not.
> I never had honest man about me, I; *all*
> I kept were knaves ...
>
> (IV, iii, 485–7: my italics)

As he had cried out at the end of his 'anti-feast' – 'henceforth hated be/Of Timon man and *all* humanity' (III, vi, 105–6). Given Timon's particular mentality and temperament, it always has to be 'all' – or 'nothing', of course. But with 'humanity', you never can say 'all', whether in this direction or that. With tears, Flavius protests the genuineness of his honest compassion – 'Nev'r did poor steward wear a truer grief/For his undone lord than mine eyes for you' (IV, iii, 489–90). What follows is a key speech by Timon:

> What, dost thou weep? Come nearer. Then I love thee
> Because thou art a woman, and disclaim'st
> Flinty mankind, whose eyes do never give
> But thorough lust and laughter. Pity's sleeping.
>
> (IV, iii, 491–4)

No one who remembers Cordelia's tears will need reminding of the importance of weeping in Shakespeare. It is associated – certainly not exclusively, but predominantly – with women, and true compassion and devotion. Pity is certainly sleeping among the Athenian men in this play (Flavius and other servants apart). And it is a powerful reminder of the absence of 'true women' from this play that Timon should identify Flavius as 'a woman' simply on account of his manifesting 'pity' – as though that makes him an anomaly among men. Timon continues:

> Had I a steward
> So true, so just, and now so comfortable?
> It almost turns my dangerous nature mild.
> ...
> Forgive my general and exceptless rashness,
> You perpetual-sober gods. I do proclaim
> One honest man. Mistake me not, *but one*.
> No more I pray – and he's a steward.
> How fain would I have hated *all* mankind,
> And thou redeem'st thyself. But *all* save thee
> I fell with curses.
>
> (IV, iii, 499–510: my italics)

'and he's a steward' – so he *almost* doesn't count. But of course he does. Enormously. Because once an exception is admitted to a totalizing generalization, once absolutism is punctured, the protective shell of '*all*' is broken. One, two – who *knows* how many there may be? Potentially, Timon would not be able to staunch a leak of his own conceding.

Perhaps this is the point of including Alcibiades and his story in the play (a point that has been queried by some commentators). He, too, is most ungratefully treated by an

THE GREEK AND ROMAN PLAYS

Athens which he has valiantly defended. The Senate is
determined to execute a brave fellow-soldier who has been
involved in some civic violence. In a speech reminiscent of the
'mercy' speeches of Portia (*The Merchant of Venice*), and
Isabella (*Measure for Measure*), and, come to that, Tamora
(*Titus Andronicus*), Alcibiades pleads for his friends:

> For pity is the virtue of the law,
> And none but tyrants use it cruelly.
>
> (III, v, 8–9)

The Senators abjure 'mercy' and, unmoved and unmovable,
identify with the supreme rigour of the 'law'. 'We are for law.
He dies' (III, v, 86). As the admirably humane 'First
Stranger' comments: 'But I perceive/Men must learn now
with pity to dispense,/For policy sits above conscience' (III, ii,
91–3). Alcibiades vows revenge against Athens (which is why,
in Plutarch, Timon makes much of him; and why, in the play,
he gives him gold). At the end of the play, he is indeed
marching on Athens. Having failed to secure Timon's apparently indispensable help, the Senators can only plead with
Alcibiades who is approaching their city 'like a boar too
savage' (V, i, 166 – it would be otiose to point out how often
men are referred to as animals in this 'beastly' play). And their
case is, to a rational person, unassailable:

> We were not all unkind, nor all deserve
> The common stroke of war.
>
> (V, iv, 21–2)

> All have not offended.
> For those that were, it is not square to take
> On those that are, revenge.
>
> (V, iv, 35–7)

We were not *all* unkind ... *all* have not offended ... those that
are, are not the same as those that were. Times change; one
generation yields to another; it is not an absolute world.
Unlike Timon, Alcibiades accepts this, and exchanges vengeance for that mercy which he himself had once pleaded for.
In a rather perfunctory conclusion, he takes on the role of a

Richmond, a Malcolm, a Fortinbras, restoring peace and order to the city-state:

> And I will use the olive with my sword,
> Make war breed peace ...
>
> (V, iv, 82–3)

This is the sort of change or modification of attitude which is impossible for Timon, who can only live in, and by, extremes. The only 'action' he is capable of in the second half is negative speech, and when he gives that up – 'Lips, let four words go by and language end' (V, i, 221) – he can only die, under two – just to make sure – characteristically venomous and nihilistic epitaphs. Arguably, death has been his real aim:

> My long sickness
> Of health and living now begins to mend,
> And nothing brings me all things.
>
> (V, i, 187–9)

And all things bring him nothing. These lines offer a curious, distant echo of Cleopatra's 'My desolation does begin to make/A better life'; yet, as is fitting in a play in which, indeed, 'all's obliquy' – twisted, crooked, awry – they are utterly unlike them as well, Again, Shakespeare seems to be exploring, experimenting with, a completely negative version of some of the drives and values, and poetic achievements, of *Antony and Cleopatra*. In that play, I suggested, we could appreciate the meaning of Blake's assertion that 'the road of excess leads to the palace of wisdom'. In *Timon of Athens*, the road of excess leads to nothing – nothing at all. Shortly after writing his most glorious play, it seems that Shakespeare wrote his bitterest. Who knows why?

*

CORIOLANUS (1608)
Timon was *first* a god – or 'godded' by his sycophantic friends (to use an apt and striking noun-verb from *Coriolanus*) – and *then* a beast. Coriolanus, in what appears to be the last of Shakespeare's Roman plays (and thus, arguably, his last

tragedy), seems to move inexorably towards becoming both at the same time. Both, and more besides. More and less. But here again, as, once more and for the last time, Shakespeare turns to Plutarch for the main outlines of his hero and the events of his play, it signally helps to have some of North's version of Plutarch before us:

Caius Martius, whose life we intend now to write, ... was brought up under his mother a widow ... This man also is a good proof to confirm men's opinions, that a rare and excellent wit, untaught, doth bring forth many good and evil things together ... For this Martius' natural wit and great heart did marvelously stir up his courage to do and attempt notable acts. But on the other side, for lack of education, he was so choleric and impatient, that he would yield to no living creature, which made him churlish, uncivil, and altogether unfit for any man's conversation. Yet men marveling much at his constancy, that he was never overcome with pleasure nor money and how he would endure easily all manner of pains and travails, thereupon they well liked and commended his stoutness and temperancy. But for all that, they could not be acquainted with him, as one citizen useth to be with another in the city. His behaviour was so unpleasant to them by reason of a certain insolent and stern manner he had, which, because he was too lordly, was disliked. And to say truly, the greatest benefit that learning bringeth unto men is this: that it teachest men that be rude and rough of nature, by compass and rule of reason, to be civil and courteous, and to like better the mean state than the higher. Now in those days, valiantness was honored in Rome above all other virtues, which they call *virtus*, by the name of virtue itself, as including in that general name all other special virtues besides. So that *virtus* in the Latin was as much as valiantness. But Martius, being more inclined to the wars than any other gentleman of his time, began from his childhood to give himself to handle weapons ...

As we shall see, 'handle weapons' is what Shakespeare's Coriolanus does from very first to very last. But first, one more amplification of his character from Plutarch:

For he was a man too full of passion and choler, and too much given over to self-will and opinion, as one of a high mind and great courage that lacked the gravity and affability that is gotten with judgment of learning and reason, which only is to be looked for in a *governor of state*: and that remembered not how willfulness is the thing of the world, which a *governor of a commonwealth*, for pleasing should shun, being that which Plato called 'solitariness,' as in the end, all men that are willfully given to a self-opinion and obstinate mind, and who will never yield to others' reason but to their own, remain without company and forsaken of all men.

(My italics)

During the Renaissance there was much discussion concerning the proper education, duties, and responsibilities of the good prince or governor – what qualified a person to exercise 'the speciality of rule'. As Plutarch stresses, it is precisely these qualifications which Coriolanus so signally lacks: he is a prime example of what Renaissance thinkers regarded as the ill-educated prince, a man from the governing classes who is, by nature, temperament, and upbringing, unfitted and unfit to rule. Magnificent as a soldier, he is disastrous as a politician. Shakespeare takes the latent tensions between martial and civic (and domestic) values, between the battlefield and the city, between – in the play's terms – the 'casque' (a helmet) and the 'cushion' (indicating a seat in the Senate), and screws these tensions up to breaking point, dramatically exposing, in the process, not just their perennially potential incompatibility, but – *in extremis* – their very actual and active explosive oppugnancy. The problem – a permanent one – baldly stated is as simple as this. You certainly could not found, much less renew and prolong, any form of civil society on such figures as Coriolanus. But it is debatable whether you could defend and thus preserve any such society *without* such men. (Having banished Coriolanus, the tribunes complacently say 'Rome/ sits safe and still without him' – IV, vi, 37. They could not be more wrong, nor was Rome ever more vulnerable.) Society cannot do *without* the sort of '*virtus*-valiantness' embodied in Coriolanus; but, given its uncontainable explosiveness, it cannot very well do *with* it either. Shakespeare never took hold of a more enduring and intractable social problem. This is one of the most violent of Shakespeare's plays, with tremendous and terrible powers released to do their 'mammocking' and 'mangling' work (two apt words – from the play – for the wrecking forces let loose). And, when Coriolanus is savagely cut down, we feel awed at what Bradley eloquently called 'the instantaneous cessation of enormous energy'.

The legendary history of Coriolanus dates from the fifth century BC, and refers to the creation of the tribunate of 494 BC and the corn riots three years later (Shakespeare, for more urgent impact, conflates these events). Phillips summarizes the importance of this period of Roman history for the Eliza-bethans. 'The consular government which had supplanted the earlier monarchy underwent further modification in the direc-tion of popular rule when economic unrest forced the Senate to grant political representation to citizens of Rome. One result of this concession was conflict between the democratic and aristocratic elements within the republic. In the turbulent history of Rome in this period Tudor theorists who argued in defence of monarchy and the hierarchy of degrees found a convincing demonstration of the dangers of democratic government' (op. cit., p. 147). There was no previous play about Coriolanus, and his story was only occasionally referred to by political writers as illustrative of the dangers of popular riot, or of civic ingratitude. Shakespeare certainly uses Plu-tarch, but the play is all his own. He makes it a very 'Roman'-feeling play. Four of the early Roman kings are referred to (Numa, Tullus, Ancus Martius, and Tarquin), and there are references to political and religious customs and the Roman mythology and pantheon. Dryden thought that there was something in the play 'that is truly great and truly Roman' – though, as always in Shakespeare, Rome and the Romans appear in a far from unequivocal light. But there are also Greek, Homeric, echoes. Hector is twice named in connection with Coriolanus (and Virgilia is 'another Penelope'). Plutarch mentions Homer as well, and he also names Achilles. Cur-iously, that name is absent from Shakespeare's play; yet, given the well-known epic theme of the wrath of Achilles, this would seem a more appropriate name to invoke than that of the more moderate, temperate Hector – for Coriolanus is nothing if not 'choleric'. Perhaps, by withholding the obvious name, but reminding us of Greek heroes, Shakespeare is prompting us to see Coriolanus as an Achilles in a Roman context. (Achilles also had a mother, Thetis, who made him almost, but not quite, invulnerable – a point certainly not lost on Shakes-peare.) Certainly, Coriolanus is another of Shakespeare's great warriors, embodying an almost archaic heroic code, who gets hopelessly, disastrously confused when he is removed from the relative simplicities of the battlefield, and forced to negotiate the more complicated political world of the *polis* (I am thinking of, in particular, Titus Andronicus and Othello). Coriolanus cannot, or will not, see that words and conduct which are most fitting and efficacious on the battlefield might be ruinously inappropriate in the city. The fearless and undefeatable soldier may, using the same code, sound politically like an intolerant and unacceptable tyrant. You can't, in this case, make a cushion out of a casque.

The god invoked by Coriolanus himself is, understandably enough, Mars – 'Now, Mars, I prithee, make us quick in work' (I, iv, 10). Then, effectively, he *becomes* Mars – 'thou Mars' (IV, v, 122) – thus Aufidius addresses him when he goes over to the Volscians. Indeed, as Cominius says, 'He is their god' (IV, vi, 91). But this is not a god of mercy ('there is no more mercy in him than there is milk in a male tiger' – V, iv, 28–30), but an angry god:

> You speak o' th' people,
> As if you were a god, to punish, not
> A man of their infirmity.
>
> (III, i, 80–82)

By the end, his harsh and uncompromising demeanour moves Menenius to declare: 'He wants nothing of a god but eternity and a heaven to throne in' (V, iv, 24–5). (A Volscian soldier gives the not very different opinion that 'He's the devil' – I, x, 17.) But, if a god, also a beast, and a very particular beast. He is once an eagle, once a tiger, once a horse, but three times a 'dragon'. First, by his own designation, after being banished – 'I go alone,/Like to a lonely dragon, that his fen/Makes feared and talked of more than seen' (IV, i, 29–31). For the Volscians, he fights 'dragon-like' (IV, vii, 23). After he has switched his allegiance, his old Roman friend Menenius comments:

There is a difference between a grub and a butterfly; yet your butterfly was a grub. This Marcius is grown from man to dragon: he has wings; he's more than a creeping thing.

> (V, iv, 11–14)

In post St-George times, knights are obliged to kill dragons; this ancient pre-Christian, and decidedly *un*Christian, proto-knight is metamorphosing *into* a dragon. (This late reference to butterflies of course echoes the early account of Coriolanus' son's characteristic conduct: 'I saw him run after a gilded butterfly; and when he caught it, he let it go again ... catched it again; or whether his fall enraged him, or how 'twas, he did so set his teeth, and tear it. O, I warrant, how he mammocked it!'. Volumnia's comment 'One on's father's moods' – I, iii, 63–70 – might well prepare us for Coriolanus' subsequent behaviour. Butterflies for boys: dragons, or dragonish behaviour, for men.)

God, and beast, he is also described as a 'planet' and an 'engine'. Always more or less than human. And perhaps the most decisive pointer to his inhumanity, non-humanity, is the number of times he is referred to simply as a 'thing':

> from face to foot
> He was a thing of blood, whose every motion
> Was timed with dying cries.
>
> (II, ii, 110–11)

> He sits in his state as a thing made for Alexander.
>
> (V, iv, 22)

He also becomes 'a kind of *nothing*' (V, i, 13: my italics). Talk of reification, or self-reification, is perhaps superegatory; we all know, more or less, what it implies to call a person a 'thing'. Whether, and how, we can witness the 'tragedy' of a 'thing' – or a 'no-thing' – is a matter to which we will have to return.

More specifically, Coriolanus is closely identified with his sword. It is often referred to, usually 'smoking' with slaughter. One comes to feel that he is seldom happy, or quite at ease with himself, when it is out of his hand. Like his little son, he 'had rather see the swords and hear a drum than look upon his schoolmaster' (I, iii, 58–9). His ambitions are entirely military and not, indeed, remotely 'scholastic', nor even – in truth – political. He is happy with, and perhaps only with, the casque.

And the sword. One of his earliest interventions in the row precipitated by the 'mutinous citizens' is:

> And let me use my sword, I'd make a quarry
> With thousands of these quartered slaves ...
>
> (I, i, 199–200)

His very last words are 'To use my lawful sword' (V, vi, 129) – his sword is full of law, *is* the law as far as he is concerned. But civic society depends on having laws *instead* of swords. In his younger days he 'lurched all swords of the garland' (II, ii, 102), and at Corioles 'His sword, death's stamp,/Where it did mark, it took' (II, ii, 108–9). Lartius pays him a rather curious compliment:

> O noble fellow!
> Who sensibly outdares his senseless sword,
> And when it bows stand'st up!
>
> (I, iv, 53–5)

This seems to suggest that Coriolanus himself remains erect, even when his sword droops. I think there is an entirely appropriate phallic hint there. Effectively, *all* his energy and appetite and drive – in sum, a colossal force – have been directed (displaced, if you will) into his fearful, 'smoking', instrument of death – Eros 'bowing' to the stand-up work of Thanatos. When his soldiers lift him up in their arms (presumably carrying him on their shoulders), after his exploits at Corioles, Coriolanus cries out, not unhappily one feels – 'Make you a sword of me?' (I, vi, 76). He is, indeed, to all intents and purposes, *the* sword of the city. The deeper truth is that he has made a sword out of himself.

This engine, this thing, this sword, this man of steel (let us say) – it is hard to see what could break or bend, deflect or deter, him. Yet that, of course, is just what happens at the climax of the play. After his victory at Corioles, Marcius (soon to be named 'Coriolanus'), in a speech refusing praise and flattery, says:

> When steel grows soft as the parasite's silk,
> Let him be made a coverture for th' wars!
>
> (I, ix, 45–6)

This is a much disputed and debated passage, marked by that
harsh, over-compacted meaning so characteristic of the play.
Take one possible meaning as – when the army turns soft, use
silk for armour. The power of the image lies, of course, in the
idea of steel growing soft as silk. Impossible. Yet steel Coriolanus does turn, briefly, fatally, as soft as silk, when he capitulates to the intercessionary pleas to spare Rome. Aufidius picks
up the image for us, after the capitulation:

> Breaking his oath and resolution, like
> A twist of rotten silk; never admitting
> Counsel o' th' war; but at his nurse's tears
> He whined and roared away your victory ...
>
> (V, vi, 95–8)

Man of steel to man of silk (rotten silk to the critical) – part of
the tragic power of the play surely lies in this sudden
transformation, and we must inquire a little as to how it comes
about.

The crucial factor, or influence, is of course his mother,
Volumnia. Plutarch–North has this to say concerning the
relationship between Marcius (later Coriolanus) and his
mother:

the only thing that made him to love honor was the joy he saw his
mother did take of him. For he thought nothing made him so happy
and honorable, as that his mother might hear everybody praise and
commend him, that she might always see him return with a crown
upon his head ... thinking all due to his mother ... at her desire [he]
took a wife also, by whom he had two young children, and yet *never
left his mother's house therefore.*

(My italics)

There is not much more concerning Volumnia in Plutarch,
apart from the crucial intercessionary scene when she dis-
suades her son from sacking his native city, Rome. All the
other scenes involving Volumnia in the play are Shakespeare's
invention, and, with powerful dramatic economy, they serve
to reveal how – psychologically and emotionally – Coriolanus,
indeed, never leaves 'his mother's house'. Whatever else he is
or becomes – sword, engine, dragon, planet, god – he remains,

ineradicably, a *mother's-boy*. These two words are central and crucial to the play.

Volumnia embodies, and articulates, the martial values of Rome. In her first speech, she celebrates that shift of affect, and affection, from the cushion to the casque – or rather, from the bed to the battlefield – we have already noted as a 'Roman' predisposition:

If my son were my husband, I should freelier rejoice in that absence wherein he won honor than in the embracements of his bed where he would show most love.

(I, iii, 3–5)

Better an absent honour than a present embrace – that's Rome. Or, at least, Volumnia's Rome. Virgilia, the wife of Coriolanus, is given no words by Plutarch, though he makes nothing of the fact. Shakespeare's Virgilia is, as it were, audibly silent. 'My gracious silence, hail! (II, i, 181) is about as amorous as Coriolanus gets in exchanges with his wife – but though she is almost entirely effaced and displaced by the extremely vociferous Volumnia, there *is* grace in Virgilia's silence. Ruskin found her 'perhaps the loveliest of Shakespeare's female characters', and, while that doubtless tells us something about Ruskin, as always he has a point. Most of the speech in this play is, one way or another, pretty unpleasant. In the circumstances, there is, as it were, much to be said for not speaking. Such *very* few words as she does speak (Desdemona and Cordelia are loquacious by comparison), are either modestly decorous, or right against the Roman grain. For example, when Volumnia voluptuously wallows in the thought of her son's 'bloody brow' in battle, Virgilia's involuntary interjection is 'O Jupiter, no blood!' (I, iii, 41). Virgilia is, in Volumnia's terms, very distinctly *not* a 'Roman' woman – and more power to her!

*

Having made him what he is – 'Thy valiantness was mine, thou suck'st it from me' (III, ii, 129) – Volumnia, on two crucial occasions, uses her influence to persuade him, against his better judgement (or steely, intransigent resolve), to go right against the rigid martial inclinations and instincts which she herself nurtured in him. It is she who launches the idea that he should stand for consulship – 'There's one thing wanting, which I doubt not but/Our Rome will cast upon thee.' Knowing that that will involve having to ingratiate himself with the common people, whom he quite intemperately and viscerally loathes, Coriolanus, rightly, senses immediately that such a role is not for him – 'Know, good mother,/I had rather be their servant in my way/Than sway with them in theirs' (II, i, 207–10). In particular, he shrinks in aversion from the prospect of having to put off his armour and don the 'vesture of humility' and then going to stand in the market-place, showing his wounds and begging for votes. Such a parade of pseudo-humility ill becomes a man who is uncorruptibly a total soldier – a butcher-soldier perhaps, but with his martial integrity intact. Quite simply, he won't do it:

> I do beseech you
> Let me o'erleap that custom, for I cannot
> Put on the gown, stand naked, and entreat them,
> For my wounds' sake, to give their suffrage. Please you
> That I may pass this doing.

(II, ii, 136–40)

More pertinently – 'It is a part/That I shall blush in acting' (II, ii, 145–6). Coriolanus is a soldier who can, emphatically, do *deeds* (there is much stress on this), but who cannot act parts. But Volumnia is a mother who always gets her way. So he tries, though not without some heavy irony concerning the self-falsification it involves. 'I will practice the insinuating nod, and be off to them most counterfeitly; that is, sir, I will counterfeit the bewitchment of some popular man' (II, iii, 103–6). Though his instinct is all the other way. 'Rather than fool it so,/Let the high office and the honor go' (II, iii, 126–7). After his session in the market-place, he cannot wait to 'change these garments' – thereby 'knowing myself again' (II, iii, 153). He seems to have the people's 'voice', but then the tribunes agitate the crowd and it turns against Coriolanus. Coriolanus lets the tribunes know what he thinks of 'the mutable, rank-scented meiny [crowd]' (III, i, 66), and as his anger mounts his words concerning the people (Hydra-headed mob etc.) become more bilious and choleric, until the tribunes can say he has 'spoken like a traitor' (III, i, 162) and urge his execution. Coriolanus draws his sword – knowing himself again – and the people are beaten back. He intends to be uncompromisingly defiant, uncompromisingly himself, come what may – 'yet will I still/Be thus to them' (III, ii, 5–6). But he has reckoned without his mother – and her maternal desires and ambitions. She wants to be able to say 'my son the consul' as well as 'my son the soldier'. Coriolanus is confused. His mother had taught him *always* to despise the people:

> I muse my mother
> Does not approve me further, who was wont
> To call them woolen vassals, things created
> To buy and sell with groats ...
> [Volumnia enters]
>   I talk of you:
> Why did you wish me milder – Would you have me
> False to my nature? Rather say I play
> The man I am.
>
> (III, ii, 7–16)

But she, with some clever if partly specious arguments, urges him to play the man he is *not*:

>   You are too absolute;
> Though therein you can never be too noble
> But when extremities speak. I have heard you say,
> Honor and policy, like unsevered friends,
> I' th' war do grow together. Grant that, and tell me
> In peace what each of them by th' other lose
> That they combine not there.
>
> (III, ii, 39–45)

Coriolanus' response is a rather helpless 'Tush, tush!', as well it might be, since the point is a tricky one, though one that touches on the problem at the centre of the play. All's fair, certainly in war, and there it is not incompatible with 'honour' to outwit your enemy with 'politic' stratagems. So why not in peacetime? Why not trick the plebeians, for the honour of a consulship? Coriolanus knows, or rather *feels*, that there is an

important difference, but he is quite unable to argue it
through. No man is less a sophist than Coriolanus. Just what
his 'nature' is, and what being true or false to it might entail,
we must consider later. Here, his mother – 'I would dissemble
with my nature ... I should do so in honor' – asserts herself as
his instructor-director:

> speak
> To th' people, not by your own instruction,
> Nor by th' matter which your heart prompts you,
> But with such words that are but roted in
> Your tongue, though but bastards and syllables
> Of no allowance to your bosom's truth.
>
> (III, ii, 52–7)

We have only recently heard Coriolanus' old friend Menenius
say of him – 'His heart's his mouth:/What his breast forges,
that his tongue must vent' (III, i, 256–7), and we should
recognize that, with their theatrical instructions – 'perform a
part', 'come, we'll prompt you' (Cominius) – his mother and
the supporting Roman nobles are making an impossible
demand of Coriolanus. Cornered, the intellectually
unresourceful Coriolanus can only capitulate, though not
without a good deal of foot-dragging and something like a
tantrum of protest at the self-division, self-dispersal, indeed
self-dissolution, which is being asked of him:

> Well, I will do't ...
> You have put me now to such a part which never
> I shall discharge to th' life.
>
> (III, ii, 101–6)

Be like a harlot, eunuch, virgin, knave, schoolboy, beggar? –
why can't I just be a soldier? Why should I make my mind and
body play false to each other? No, damn it, I *won't* go through
with it! At which, his mother turns from him, as if giving up on
a child in a particularly fretful and tiresome mood. 'At thy
choice then.' As much as to say – well, if you are going to be
that difficult! And Coriolanus wilts back into her scolded,
remorseful little boy.

> Pray, be content:
> Mother, I am going to the marketplace;
> Chide me no more ...
>
> (III, ii, 130–32)

And, though we do not know it yet, there will indeed be some 'boy's tears' to follow. This mother will be the death of him.

Coriolanus leaves for the market-place, attended by the hopeless injunction – 'mildly' (repeated five times). 'Well, mildly be it then – mildly' (III, ii, 145). 'Mildness' is certainly *not* in his nature, whatever that nature might be; and, as the tribunes well know, it will take little to make him 'play the man I am':

> Being once chafed, he cannot
> Be reined again to temperance; then he speaks
> What's in his heart, and that is there which looks
> With us to break his neck.
>
> (III, iii, 27–30)

Coriolanus is nothing if not honest, and once the tribunes have 'chafed' him by calling him 'traitor' (the word is not in Plutarch), he lets fly at the people with such vitriolic fury that by communal (or rather, mob) agreement, he is banished. His response is, we may say, predictable:

> You common cry of curs, whose breath I hate
> As reek o' th' rotten fens, whose loves I prize
> As the dead carcasses of unburied men
> That do corrupt my air, I banish you.
> ... Despising
> For you the city, thus I turn my back.
> There is a world elsewhere.
>
> (III, iii, 120–35)

Brave and powerful talk; and we can surely still respond to a something heroic in Coriolanus' 'absolute' and unyielding refusal of compromise, his furious and contemptuous rejection of the mass, the masses, the world *here*. The question the remainder of the play will explore is whether it is finally possible for Coriolanus to 'banish' Rome – his city, his class, his friends, his family, his *mother*. Or – put it another way – can there finally be, for a Roman, 'a world elsewhere'?

Coriolanus has always appeared as single, singular; sharply outlined and standing out against the rest. He is 'constant', 'absolute', *adamant* we might say. During the war against the Volscians, he is locked, trapped, within the enemy's gates on his own – as a soldier says: 'He is himself alone,/To answer all the city' (I, iv, 52–3). This description holds good whether the city is Corioli or Rome. 'O me alone!' he cries, after his one-man victory (I, vii, 76) – and the cry reverberates throughout the play. After his banishment from Rome, he goes – instantly – over to the enemy. As in the case of Timon, it seems that 'absolutists' are either rigidly 'constant', or must *totally* invert their commitments. As we have seen, Shakespeare is very interested in these sudden switches of allegiance whereby a passionate Roman becomes a virulent anti-Roman (I am thinking of Lucius in *Titus Andronicus* and Alcibiades in *Timon of Athens*) – on the spot, as it were. In what is arguably his only soliloquy (as with Timon, there is no inwardness in the depiction of Coriolanus, none of the wracked, intelligent, conscience-searching of a Macbeth: Coriolanus is all outside, all deed, all sword), Coriolanus says:

> O world, thy slippery turns! Friends now fast sworn ...
> On a dissension of a doit, break out
> To bitterest enmity ...
> ... So with me:
> My birthplace hate I, and my love's upon
> This enemy town.
>
> (IV, iv, 12–24)

Well, it might be – and Shakespeare could be exploring the unstable and changeable foundations of what we fondly take to be our our most immovably fixed commitments, allegiances, and loyalties. But Coriolanus might not be so rid of his 'birthplace', so cleanly and hatefully disengaged from Rome, as he thinks. It is notable that, after his banishment, he is seen entering the enemy town of Actium 'in mean apparel, disguised and muffled'. This detail, unremarked, is in Plutarch.

But Shakespeare would surely have seen an added irony in Coriolanus having recourse to almost the same 'dissembling' strategies he had so furiously repudiated in Rome. Has he learnt theatricals in spite of himself? Is he going to 'play' the dragon, 'act' the vengeful god, 'counterfeit' the ireful anti-Roman? If so, he may well not prove as impregnable as he has hitherto seemed, for a time could come when the 'acting' has to stop. Not that he gives signs of dissembling. His determined disavowal and rejection of Rome seems absolutely resolute and total. His single imperative to his old friend, Menenius, who comes to plead with him on Rome's behalf, summarizes the stance of denial and dismissal he has adopted – 'Away!' He spells it out:

> Wife, mother, child, I know not. My affairs
> Are servanted to others ...
> Therefore be gone.

(V, ii, 83–4, 88)

Away *every* Roman; away even his own Roman self. Cominius receives as much of a brush-off as Menenius:

> Coriolanus
> He would not answer to; forbad all names;
> He was a kind of nothing, titleless,
> Till he had forged himself a name o' th' fire
> Of burning Rome.

(V, i, 11–15)

I will come to the importance of 'names' in the play. Here we may note his attempt entirely to erase and disown all traces of his Roman identity, rendering himself – certainly from the Roman point of view – 'a kind of nothing'. Just as swords are 'forged', so he will forge a new name in the fire of burning Rome.

To my knowledge, it was Bradley who first pointed out how references to fire and burning Rome (not mentioned in Plutarch), suddenly start and then proliferate in Acts IV and V, as the not-Coriolanus, the anonymous, titleless 'nothing', starts to move inexorably – all engine-beast-god now – against the city of his birth. This dragon is breathing fire. Territories

ci

are being 'consumed with fire'; there is terrified talk of burned temples and houses put to 'the brand'. Menenius gives his opinion:

> If he could burn us all into one coal,
> We have deserved it.
>
> (IV, vi, 138–9)

Volscian soldiers, talking to downcast Romans, refer gleefully to 'the intended fire your city is ready to flame in' (V, ii, 47), and Menenius, trying to get through to the alienated and no-longer Coriolanus, haplessly recognizes – 'Thou art preparing fire for us' (V, ii, 72). It is all summed up in Cominius' description of the oncoming avenger:

> I tell you he does sit in gold, his eye
> Red as 'twould burn Rome, and his injury
> The jailer to his pity.
>
> (V, i, 63–5)

Fire consumes everything and leaves, effectively, nothing. A total razing and cleansing. This is not so much revenge as an intended eradication, obliteration, annihilation. This unnamable and omnipotent figure is, indeed, absolute – 'too absolute'.

The nightmare prospect behind all this, is the destruction, the 'unbuilding', the 'unroofing', or the 'melting', of the city – THE city. Rome. When things come to crisis point between the plebeians and the tribunes, and Coriolanus and the nobles, Cominius cries out:

> That is the way to lay the city flat,
> To bring the roof to the foundation,
> And bury all which yet distinctly ranges,
> In heaps and piles of ruin.
>
> (III, i, 203–6)

For Rome, the 'city' simply *was* the available civilization (no matter what its internal impairments might be), and whatever was outside the city was uncontainable and unformulable (out of language, out of bounds), potentially 'monstrous' – dragons clawing their way towards the city walls. But there was a nightmare within the nightmare – pointed to when, in the internal crisis, Menenius beseechingly cries out:

> Proceed by process [i.e. by law, the cement of the city];
> Lest parties (as he is beloved) break out,
> *And sack great Rome with Romans*.

> (III, i, 312–14: my italics)

From the start of Shakespeare's Roman plays, we have seen that Rome could be 'barbarous', Romans barbarians (as in this play the plebeians are to Coriolanus – 'I would they were barbarians, as they are,/Though in Rome littered' – III, i, 237–8 – though no one, on his day, more 'barbaric' than Coriolanus). That could be handled, contained, perhaps worked out. The city would still stand. But if Rome should self-destructively turn on itself; not just a Roman by a Roman 'valiantly' vanquished, but *Rome* by Romans ... if the city tears *itself* to pieces, what price *any* hope for civilization and order then? We must be clear about this. Shakespeare is very far, *very* far, from being an uncritical admirer of the Roman world as he conceived it, or at least as he dramatized his version of it. It is a hard, brutal, militarized, legalistic, excessively male world, with women and domestic values and virtues – procreative eroticism, love, gentleness, mildness, pity – marginalized to the point of near-extinction. But Rome – arid, unimaginative, unbounteous, politic and cruel Rome – was the alternative to chaos, the (badly faulted) prototype of civilized (problematic, question-begging word, as Shakespeare well knew) societies in the western world. Shakespeare being Shakespeare, he lent some of his finest poetry to a final elegiac efflorescent flaring of an Egyptian world that was inevitably superseded. For good or bad, good *and* bad, Rome was the future, and the future was to be – *mutatis, mutandis* – Roman.

The Rome of *Coriolanus* is a noisy place; more specifically it is a city of 'voices'. Since most plays are comprised of speakers, I must attempt to avoid a fatuity here. But the word 'voice' (or 'voices') occurs over forty times, far more often than in any other Shakespeare play. And the voices are, pre-eminently, the voices of the people. In this play, the people (or mob, or rabble, or children, or slaves – according to their behaviour and your point of view) are, certainly, volatile, fickle, too – easily swayable, and, when pressed too hard or deprived too far, dangerously dissentious and mutinous. (They are probably 'stinking' too – the working classes are the sweating classes, and doubtless, their food is none of the best either.) But the play makes clear that many of their grievances are justified, while the behaviour of the supposedly responsible, 'paternalistic' patricians, leaves a lot to be desired. Coriolanus is only the *most* obscenely contemptuous of the common people among his class – it is a matter of degree, not kind. Menenius is as willing to call them 'rats' as Coriolanus is determined to call them 'curs'. The use by Menenius of the tired allegory of the body politic to placate the mob in the first scene, is really a piece of gross effrontery. Smugly and complacently, he allows the Belly (= the Senators) to explain to the 'mutinous members' (= the people) that they 'From me receive that natural competency/Whereby they live'. A 'natural competency' is just exactly what these famished citizens–plebeians lack, and, indeed, all they ask for. Later in the play, Menenius says how 'supple' we are 'when we have stuffed/These pipes and these conveyances of our blood/With wine and feeding' (V, i, 53–5). Clearly, he speaks from experience, and the earlier, hostile case against the Belly–Senate –

> it did remain
> I' th' midst o' th' body, idle and unactive,
> Still cupboarding the viand, never bearing
> Like labor with the rest ...

(I, i, 99–102)

– would seem to fit him, and who knows how many other Senators, perfectly. The voice and 'voices' of the people, then; to which we should add the unusually large number of references to mouth(s), tongue(s), breath(s). There is the heroic-martial Coriolanian world of swordly doings and deeds; and the people's world of voices, or mouthly deeds. Coriolanus is an 'engine', but the voice of the people is an instrument, too. Voices are votes (as in some Elizabethan elections, during this period in Rome the elected where chosen

by vocal acclaim, or 'shouting'), and it is having to supplicate
for the people's 'voices' in the market-place which is anathema
to Coriolanus. But – 'the people/Must have their voices' (II, ii,
140–41), and if Coriolanus cannot finally bring himself to ask
for them 'kindly', the voices will turn on him. In the event, he
will be 'Whooped out of Rome' by, as he sees it, 'th' voice of
slaves' (IV, v, 81–2). (For all his gnashing vituperations,
Coriolanus is not really at ease using tongue, mouth, voice.
When Cominius describes how Coriolanus dismissed him
'with his speechless hand' – V, i, 67 – we have the essential
man in all his silent physicality.) But the voices which 'did
hoot him out o' th' city' might well 'roar him in again' (IV, vi,
124–5). When it is learned that Coriolanus will spare Rome, a
Senator exhorts the city, impossibly as it sounds, to 'Unshout
the noise that banished Marcius' (V, v, 4). Shouting, whoop-
ing, hooting, roaring – this civic noise sounds ugly. And there
is not much to redeem it in the rhetoric of the patrician, either.
Gordon would seem to be justified in his pessimistic summing
up of the play (in his essay 'Name to Fame'; see bibliography):

It is a show of civil life. The city must stand and continue, for outside
it there is the monstrous, or the nothing. But within the walls
absolutes turn out to be instrumental; the words that identify and
bind become words that debase and destroy: whoops, or hoots,
curses, lies, flatteries, voices, stinking breath . . . In this city to speak is
to be guilty.

No wonder Virgilia prefers to remain silent.

'Voices' are also intimately connected with 'fame' and
'name' – two more words which often recur. Gordon again:
'Name is Fame, is Honour, and is won by deeds – in Rome, by
deeds in war' (ibid. p. 60). Fame depends on 'praise',
'renown', 'applause and clamor', 'good report' – all more or
less dependent on 'voice'. Volumnia, explaining to Virgilia
how she brought up her son, says: 'I, considering how honor
would become such a person – that it was no better than
picture-like to hang by th' wall, if *renown made it not stir* – was
pleased to let him seek danger where he was like to find *fame*'
(I, iii, 10–14: my italics). To acquire 'name' and 'fame',
Coriolanus will need 'voices' in a more than electoral sense.

(In ancient Greece, the word for 'truth' – '*aletheia*' – meant, literally, *not* forgetting, or forgotten. The epic singers and reciters were so important just because they prevented the silent deeds of heroic warriors from falling into an eternal, soundless, oblivion. They preserved and perpetuated the 'renown', exactly by *re*knowing, *re*naming. This keeps the honour 'stirring'.) Caius Marcus of course wins fame and name after his exploits at Corioli:

> from this time,
> For what he did before Corioles, call him,
> With all th' applause and clamor of the host,
> Caius Marcius Coriolanus.
> Bear th' addition nobly ever!
>
> (I, ix, 62–6)

Or, as the Herald announces it:

> he hath won,
> With fame, a name to Caius Marcius; these
> In honor follows Coriolanus.
>
> (II, i, 169–71)

As his mother proudly says – he is 'By deed-achieving honor newly named' (II, i, 179).

But if name and fame depend upon voice, mouth, breath, their possible persistingness is always vulnerable, precarious. Voices can be withheld, or – just like that – shout the other way. (It is notable that only once does Coriolanus think of *writing* as possibly a proper preservative of fame – and I will come to that moment.) Of course, when Coriolanus leaves Rome to join the Volscians, he makes a point of trying to shed and disown all his previous names, both family-given and war-won ('forbad all names'). This attempt by Coriolanus to reject or leave behind his names is highlighted by Shakespeare (but not Plutarch) when the disguised and prevaricating Coriolanus first arrives in Antium, and Aufidius has to ask him *five times* – 'what is thy name?' At last, Coriolanus has to answer. His attempt at an act of willed dis-nomination proves finally to be impossible. And when Aufidius at the end refuses to call his Roman ally by 'thy stol'n name/Coriolanus' (V, vi, 89), it is, to be exact, the last but one straw. Perhaps the most poignant episode illustrating both the cardinal importance and the ephemeral forgettability of names, occurs after the first battle with the Volscians. Victorious Coriolanus asks a modest, and indeed honourable, favour of his commander Cominius:

> I sometimes lay here in Corioles
> At a poor man's house; he used me kindly.
> He cried to me; I saw him prisoner;
> . . . I request you
> To give my poor host freedom.
>
> (I, ix, 82–7)

Cominius is more than happy to comply. All they need is 'his name'.

> By Jupiter, forgot!
> I am weary; yea, my memory is tired.
> Have we no wine here?
>
> (I, ix, 90–92)

So easily can a 'name' be 'lost'. In Plutarch, the kindly 'enemy' host is wealthy, and there is no mention of his name having been forgotten by Coriolanus. You can decide what kind of a point Shakespeare was making with his changes. But, clearly, some amnesias are lethal, and the forgetting of a person's name may cost the forgotten one not less than everything. Coriolanus himself will effectively give up his life in one last desperate attempt to secure fitting and appropriate remembrance.

When his mother and family approach, to plead for Rome, he tries to stiffen his resolve:

> But out, affection!
> All bond and privilege of nature, break!
> Let it be virtuous to be obstinate.
>
> (V, iii, 24–6)

But, even at the sight of them (particularly his mother), he is beginning to crack (he is too brittle, too 'forged', to bend):

cvii

> I melt, and am not
> Of stronger earth than others. My mother bows,
> ... and my young boy
> Hath an aspect of intercession which
> Great Nature cries 'Deny not.' Let the Volsces
> Plough Rome, and harrow Italy! I'll never
> Be such a gosling to obey instinct, but stand
> As if a man were author of himself
> And knew no other kin.
>
> (V, iii, 28–37)

He is trying to hold on to his inflexible intransigence, regain that unshakable, immovable erectness he so admires – 'Like a great sea-mark, standing every flaw' (V, iii, 74). But he is wobbling, 'melting' (he even speaks of kissing his wife), slipping from steel to silk. Coriolanus is discovering that he cannot 'stand' as if he were 'author of himself', some 'unnatural' parthenogenetic freak; discovering that there are some bonds of nature which cannot be broken, some imperatives of 'Great Nature' which cannot be refused. He *will* be a 'gosling' and 'obey instinct', before reasserting his lost identity as an 'eagle'. But, even as he is capitulating to nature, he feels he is also being untrue to his *own* nature. Coriolanus is being torn apart by contradictions in nature, contradictions *of* nature. We have heard much of his nature – he cannot help his nature, his nature is too noble for this world, 'his nature/In that's no changeling' (IV, vii, 10–11), and so on. Aufidius has the most searching speech about Coriolanus, when explaining to his lieutenant why Rome banished him:

> Whether 'twas pride,
> Which out of daily fortune ever taints
> The happy man; whether defect of judgment,
> To fail in the disposing of those chances
> Which he was lord of; or whether *nature*,
> *Not to be other than one thing, not moving*
> *From th' casque to th' cushion*, but commanding peace
> Even with the same austerity and garb
> As he controlled the war; but one of these –
> As he hath spices of them all ...
> ... made him feared,
> So hated, and so banished.
>
> (IV, vii, 37–48: my italics)

cviii

INTRODUCTION

The tragedy which Coriolanus experiences and enacts is the discovered impossibility for a man 'not to be other than one thing'. He tries, more ferociously than any other of Shakespeare's heroes. He can certainly dispense with the 'cushion' – never wanted it, anyway. But he cannot defy or deny his mother. It is not, finally, in his 'nature'. Whatever that nature is. We hear and see quite a lot of his *un*nature, too, best summed up in Cominius' description of him as he marches on Rome with the Volscians:

> he leads them like a thing
> Made by some other deity than Nature,
> That shapes men better ...
>
> (IV, vi, 91–3)

To his mother, in the final scene, still trying to stave off her influence, he cries out:

> Tell me not
> Wherein I seem unnatural. Desire not
> T' allay my rages and revenges with
> Your colder reasons.
>
> (V, iii, 83–6)

It is perhaps his truest nature to *be* unnatural? In which case, when he capitulates and obeys 'Great Nature', is he finally maturing into a new, recognized, and accepted humanity (as some have thought)? Or is he succumbing to an internal splitting which will destroy whatever integrity of identity he may have – helplessly regressing to the enfeebled status of 'mother's boy'? You can see it in either way; though I think it is better, somehow, to try to see it as both.

As he feels his resolve slipping in front of his family, he says:

> Like a dull actor now,
> I have forgot my part and I am out,
> Even to a full disgrace.
>
> (V, iii, 40–43)

When he was asked to stop being a soldier and at least pretend he was a politician, he discovered it just wasn't in him to act a part. But this speech seems to imply that he is being discomfited out of his 'part' of the adamantine warrior. Or does he just mean that being confronted with his mother again gives him the equivalent of stage-fright? Is he losing his grip on what, exactly, he is as a man? The arguments and appeals with which his mother works on him need not be summarized here. He is effectively lost when she kneels to him – 'What's this?/Your knees to me? To your corrected son?' (V, iii, 55–6); it horrifies him as if it were some chaotic inversion in nature. She inevitably has her way with her 'corrected son'. But there is a barb in the words that recognize her triumph:

> O mother, mother!
> What have you done? Behold, the heavens do ope,
> The gods look down, and this unnatural scene
> They laugh at. O my mother, mother! O!
> You have won a happy victory to Rome;
> But, for your son – believe it, O, believe it! –
> Most dangerously you have with him prevailed,
> If not most mortal to him. But let it come.
>
> (V, iii, 182–9)

What *has* she done? She has saved Rome: but in the case of her son, she has both made and marred him; taught him immutability and made him change; 'manned' him and unmanned him. Made him steel, turned him silk. As Aufidius says:

> He bowed his nature, never known before
> But to be rough, unswayable, and free
>
> (V, vi, 25–6)

For Plutarch, the moment when Coriolanus gives in is all 'nature'. 'And nature so wrought with him that the tears fell from his eyes and ... [he] yielded to the affection of his blood.' It is Shakespeare who makes Coriolanus deem it an '*unnatural* scene'. At the very least, we can say that one 'nature' has been undermined by another, and while that is undoubtedly good for Rome (and perhaps humanity), Coriolanus is clearly right in sensing that it will prove disastrous for him. Much of the rest of his speech is in Plutarch – but not those last four words. 'But let it come.' This, as Brockbank remarked, is directly reminiscent of Hamlet's 'Let be.' It is as if he recognizes that, by what had just happened, an inexorable process has been set in train, the outcome of which is at once unforeseeable and ineluctable. It amounts to a recognition and acceptance of the tragic workings of nature.

After this, it is easy for Aufidius to goad Coriolanus to a self-destructive fury. He calls him 'traitor' – as Rome did; denies him his 'stol'n' name; and, when Coriolanus invokes Mars, delivers the final taunt which he knows will drive him completely out of control: 'Name not the god, thou boy of tears!' (V, vi, 101). This makes Coriolanus explode:

> Measureless liar, thou hast made my heart
> Too great for what contains it.
>
> (V, vi, 103–4)

and he calls down the knives:

> Cut me to pieces, Volsces, men and lads,
> Stain all your edges on me. 'Boy'! False hound!
> If you have writ your annals true, 'tis there,
> That, like an eagle in a dovecote, I
> Fluttered your Volscians in Corioles.
> Alone I did it. 'Boy'?

In a sense, Aufidius is absolutely correct (sometimes, nothing wounds like the truth) – Coriolanus *did* regress to being a 'boy of tears' in front of his mother. (Though, of course, there could be a less denigrating, more generous way of describing his transformation.) But if he goes down as 'Boy', he wants once more to assert his old martial-eagle identity of the matchless warrior who could take a city 'alone'. And he wants to think of this identity and exploit set down and preserved in the immutability of writing (not trusting to the vagaries of voice). 'Annals' are the distinctively Roman form of history, primarily associated with Tacitus (it is the only time Shakespeare used the word). Having employed the heroized Coriolanus, banished and then besought him, Rome will continue without him, finding other soldiers for other wars. That is why Coriolanus wants what he has been and done to be written '*true*' and written '*there*'. So ends the last great tragedy written for the English stage.

King's College, Cambridge   Tony Tanner

SELECT BIBLIOGRAPHY

BIOGRAPHY

The standard biography is now Samuel Schoenbaum, *William Shake-speare: A Documentary Life*, Oxford University Press, Oxford, 1975. A shortened version of this excellent volume was published in 1977. For those interested in Shakespearian mythology, Schoenbaum has also produced *Shakespeare's Lives*, Clarendon Press, Oxford, 1970, a witty dissection of the myriad theories concerning the playwright's identity and the authorship of the plays. Rather in the same vein is Anthony Burgess, *Shakespeare*, Penguin, London, 1972, a lively intro-duction to the presumed facts of the poet's life, enhanced by novelistic licence.

BIBLIOGRAPHY

Among the vast quantity of Shakespeare criticism it is probably only useful to list texts which are both outstanding and easily available. This I do below. For further information the serious student may consult the bibliographies of works listed. There are also three major journals which record the flow of critical work: the *Shakespeare Quarterly*; and the *Shakespeare Survey* and *Shakespeare Studies* which are published annually.

CRITICISM

The two indispensable Shakespearian critics are Johnson and Coleridge. Their dispersed comments are collected in *Samuel Johnson on Shakespeare*, ed., H. R. Woodhuysen, Penguin, London, 1989, and S. T. Coleridge, *Shakespearian Criticism*, two vols., Everyman's Library, London, 1960.

Among distinguished older commentaries which still have a great deal to offer are A. C. Bradley, *Shakespearian Tragedy*, Macmillan, London, 1904; Lily B. Campbell, *Shakespeare's Tragic Heroes: Slaves of Passion*, Cambridge University Press, Cambridge, 1930; H. B. Charlton, *Shakespearian Tragedy*, Cambridge University Press, Cam-bridge, 1948; G. W. Knight, *The Wheel of Fire*, Methuen, London, 1930; and Harley Granville-Barker, *Prefaces to Shakespeare*, two vols., Batsford, London, 1958. All contain detailed commentary on individual plays and discussion of Shakespeare's theatrical art, though Bradley concentrates on character study and Barker on dramaturgy, while the others pay more attention to themes, imagery and structure. All five grapple in different ways with the perplexing question of whether Shakespeare can be said to have a consistent practice and an implicit theory of tragedy – issues also addressed by more recent commentators, including Kenneth Muir, *Shakespeare and the Tragic Pattern*, Longman, London, 1958, and *William Shakespeare: The Great Tragedies*, Longman, London, 1961; Ruth Nevgo, *Tragic Form in Shakespeare*, Princeton University Press, Princeton, N.J., 1972; J. V. Cunningham, *Woe or Wonder: The Emotional Effect of Shakespearian Tragedy*, University of Denver Press, Denver, 1951; Maynard Mack, *Killing the King: Three Studies in Shakespeare's Tragic Structure*, Yale University Press, New Haven, 1973; and Irving Ribner, *Patterns in Shakespearian Tragedy*, Methuen, London, 1960.

John Holloway, *The Story of the Night: Studies in Shakespearian Tragedy*, Routledge, London, 1967; and John Lawlor, *The Tragic Sense in Shakespeare*, Chatto & Windus, London, 1960, both comment on the plays severally and together. N. M. Proser, *The Heroic Image in Five Shakespearian Tragedies*, Princeton University Press, Princeton, N.J., 1965, pursues the evolution of a single crucial image; P. N. Siegel considers the political context in *Shakespearian Tragedy and the Elizabethan Compromise*, New York University Press, New York, 1957; while William Rosen, *Shakespeare and the Craft of Tragedy*, Harvard University Press, Cambridge, Mass., 1960, and V. K. Whitaker, *The Mirror Up To Nature: The Technique of Shakespeare's Tragedies*, Huntingdon Library, San Marino, California, 1965, offer detailed examinations of the playwright's artistry with reference to contemporary writers.

Three innovative views can be found in Northrop Frye, *Fools of Time: Studies in Shakespearian Tragedy*, University of Toronto Press, Toronto, 1967; Jonathon Dollimore, *Radical Tragedy*, Harvester, Brighton, 1984; and Stephen Greenblatt, *Shakespearian Negotiations*, Clarendon, Oxford, 1988. Dollimore is a Cultural Materialist who wants to situate Shakespeare in the economic and political circumstances of his time; Greenblatt is a New Historicist who weaves the plays into a complex tapestry of contemporary texts and events; while Frye writes against the background of his own theory of Archetypes.

As their titles indicate, the following commentaries all provide an overview of the Greek and Roman plays or discuss crucial aspects of their political, historical or literary context:

BROCKBANK, J. P., *On Shakespeare*, 1989.

SELECT BIBLIOGRAPHY

BROWER, REUBEN, *Shakespeare and the Graeco-Roman Heroic Tradition*, 1971.

CHARNEY, MAURICE, *Shakespeare's Roman Plays: The Function of Imagery in the Drama*, 1961.

CHARNEY, MAURICE, ed., *Discussions of Shakespeare's Roman Plays*, 1964.

HONIGMAN, E. A. J., *Shakespeare: Seven Tragedies*, 1976.

KNIGHT, G. W., *The Imperial Theme*, 1931.

MACCULLUM, M. W., *Shakespeare's Roman Plays and Their Background*, 1910.

MIOLA, ROBERT S., *Shakespeare's Rome*, 1983.

PALMER, JOHN, *Political Characters of Shakespeare*, 1945.

PHILLIPS, J. E., *The State in Shakespeare's Greek and Roman Plays*, 1940.

RICHMOND, HUGH M., *Shakespeare's Political Plays*, 1967.

SHAKESPEARE SURVEY (10), 1957 (mainly on the Roman plays).

SPENCER, T. J. B., *Shakespeare: The Roman Plays*, 1963.

STAMPFER, JUDITH, *The Tragic Engagement: A Study of Shakespeare's Classical Tragedies*, 1963.

TRAVERSI, DEREK, *Shakespeare: The Roman Plays*, 1963.

WAITH, EUGENE, *The Herculean Hero*, 1962.

WHITAKER, VIRGIL K., *Shakespeare's Use of Learning*, 1953.

On particular plays the following texts may be found useful:

Titus Andronicus

BAKER, HOWARD, *Induction to Tragedy*, 1939.

HAMILTON, A. C., '*Titus Andronicus*: The Form of Shakespearian Tragedy', *Shakespeare Survey* 10, 1963.

HUNTER, G. K., 'Sources and Meanings in *Titus Andronicus*' in *The Mirror Up To Nature*, ed. J. C. Gray, 1983.

ROBERTS, JEANNE ANDERSON, *The Shakespearian Wild*, 1991.

SOMMERS, ALAN, ' "Wilderness of Tigers": Structure and Symbolism in *Titus Andronicus*', *Essays in Criticism* 10, 1960.

TRICOMI, ALBERT H., 'The Mutilated Garden in *Titus Andronicus*', *Shakespeare Studies* 9, 1976.

Troilus and Cressida

ADELMAN, JANET, ' "This Is and Is Not Cressid": The Characterization of Cressida' in *The M(o)ther Tongue*, ed. Shirley Nelson Garner, 1985.

BAYLEY, JOHN, 'Time and the Trojans', *Essays in Criticism* 25, 1975.

BRADBROOK, MURIEL C., 'What Shakespeare Did to Chaucer's *Troilus and Criseyde*', *Shakespeare Quarterly* 9, 1958.

EMPSON, WILLIAM, *Some Versions of Pastoral*, 1935.

GIRARD, RENE, 'The Politics of Desire in *Troilus and Cressida*' in *Shakespeare and the Question of Theory*, ed. Patricia Parker and Geoffrey Hartman, 1985.

HUNTER, G. K., '*Troilus and Cressida*: A Tragic Satire', *Shakespeare Studies* 13, 1974-5.

KERMODE, FRANK, '"Opinion" in *Troilus and Cressida*' in *Teaching the Text*, ed. Susanne Kappeler and Norman Bryson, 1983.

KIMBROUGH, ROBERT, *Shakespeare's Troilus and Cressida and Its Setting*, 1964.

PRESSON, R. K., *Shakespeare's Troilus and Cressida and the Legends of Troy*, 1953.

RABKIN, NORMAN, '*Troilus and Cressida*: The Uses of the Double Plot', *Shakespeare Studies* 1, 1965.

SOUTHALL, RAYMOND, 'Troilus and Cressida and the Spirit of Capitalism' in *Shakespeare in the Changing World*, ed. Arnold Kettle, 1964.

STEIN, ARNOLD, '*Troilus and Cressida*: The Disjunctive Imagination', *ELH* 36, 1969.

Julius Caesar

BARTON, ANNE, '*Julius Caesar* and *Coriolanus*: Shakespeare's Roman World of Words' in *Shakespeare's Craft*, ed. Philip H. Highfill, 1982.

BONJOUR, ADRIEN, *The Structure of Julius Caesar*, 1958.

FOAKES, R. A., 'An Approach to *Julius Caesar*', *Shakespeare Quarterly* V, 1954.

HEILMAN, ROBERT, 'To Know Himself: An Aspect of Tragic Structure', *Review of English Literature* 4, 1964.

LEVITSKY, RUTH M., '"The Elements Were So Mix'd . . ."', *PMLA* 88, 1973.

SCHANZER, ERNEST, 'The Problem of *Julius Caesar*', *Shakespeare Quarterly* VI, 1955.

SMITH, GORDON ROSS, 'Brutus, Virtue, and Will', *Shakespeare Quarterly* 10, 1959.

STEWART, J. I. M., *Character and Motive in Shakespeare*, 1949.

Antony and Cleopatra

ADELMAN, JANET, *The Common Liar: An Essay on Antony and Cleopatra*, 1973.

BARROLL, J. LEEDS, *Shakespearean Tragedy: Genre, Tradition, and Change in Antony and Cleopatra*, 1984.

BAYLEY, JOHN, *Shakespeare and Tragedy*, 1981.

COATES, JOHN, '"The Choice of Hercules" in *Antony and Cleopatra*', *Shakespeare Survey* 31, 1978.

SELECT BIBLIOGRAPHY

DANBY, JOHN F., *Poets on Fortune's Hill*, 1952.

FARNHAM, WILLARD, *Shakespeare's Tragic Frontier*, 1950.

LEAVIS, F. R., '*Antony and Cleopatra* and *All For Love*: A Critical Exercise', *Scrutiny* 5, 1936–7.

LLOYD, MICHAEL, 'Cleopatra as Isis', *Shakespeare Survey* 12, 1959.

MARKELS, JULIAN, *The Pillar of the World: Antony and Cleopatra in Shakespeare's Development*, 1968.

Timon of Athens

BRILL, LESLEY W., 'Truth and *Timon of Athens*', *Modern Language Quarterly* 40, 1979.

BUTLER, FRANCILIA, *The Strange Critical Fortunes of Shakespeare's Timon of Athens*, 1966.

CAMPBELL, OSCAR JAMES, *Shakespeare's Satire*, 1943.

ELLIS-FERMOR, UNA, '*Timon of Athens*: An Unfinished Play', *Review of English Studies* 18, 1942.

HANDELMAN, SUSAN, 'The Rise of Disillusion', *American Image* 36, 1979.

HONIGMAN, E. A. J., '*Timon of Athens*', *Shakespeare Quarterly* 12, 1961.

KNIGHT, G. WILSON, *The Wheel of Fire*, 1930.

SLIGHTS, WILLIAM W. E., '*Genera mixta* and *Timon of Athens*', *Studies in Philology* 74, 1977.

SOELLNER, ROLF, *Timon of Athens: Shakespeare's Pessimistic Tragedy*, 1979.

SPENCER, T. J. B., 'Shakespeare Learns the Value of Money: The Dramatist at Work on *Timon of Athens*', *Shakespeare Survey* 6, 1953.

Coriolanus

BROCKBANK, J. P., *Coriolanus*, The Arden Edition, 1976.

BROWNING, I. R., 'Coriolanus – "Boy of Tears" ', *Essays in Criticism* 5, 1955.

FRYE, DEAN, 'Commentary in Shakespeare: The Case of Coriolanus', *Shakespeare Studies* 1, ed. J. Leeds Barroll, 1965.

GORDON, D. J., 'Name and Fame: Shakespeare's Coriolanus' in *Papers Mainly Shakespearian*, ed. G. L. Duthie, 1964.

HEUER, HERMAN, 'From Plutarch to Shakespeare: A Study of *Coriolanus*', *Shakespeare Survey* 10, 1957.

MAXWELL, J. C., 'Animal Imagery in *Coriolanus*', *Modern Language Review* 42, 1947.

RABKIN, NORMAN, '*Coriolanus*: The Tragedy of Politics', *Shakespeare Quarterly* 37, 1987.

SICHERMAN, CAROL, '*Coriolanus*: The Failure of Words', *ELH* 39, 1972.

VAN DYKE, JOYCE, 'Making a Scene: Language and Gesture in *Coriolanus*', *Shakespeare Survey* 30, 1977.
WATSON, ROBERT N., *Shakespeare and the Hazards of Ambition*, 1984.

BACKGROUND AND SOURCES

Shakespeare scholarship is massive and exhaustive, covering every imaginable aspect of the writer's work, life and times. Most editions of the text, including the Everyman Shakespeare, are now supplied with notes which are more than adequate for all normal purposes. However, those who wish to explore questions of Shakespearian language further may care to consult John Bartlett, *A New and Complete Concordance to Shakespeare*, Macmillan, New York, 1894, and C. T. Onions, *A Shakespeare Glossary*, Oxford University Press, London, 1911 (and frequently reprinted). Between them, these texts define and explain every single word Shakespeare uses, citing the places where they appear and exploring obsolete usages.

The thorny questions of textual transmission are covered in W. W. Greg's *The Shakespeare First Folio*, Oxford University Press, New York and London, 1955. This gives a detailed history of the first collected edition of the plays which appeared in 1623.

Finally, a word on sources. Most individual editions of the plays include a note on particular sources, together with extensive quotation. The most readily available and accessible general book on this matter is Kenneth Muir's *Shakespeare's Sources*, Methuen, London, 1957. Muir was one of the most distinguished scholar-critics of his time and his book throws fascinating light on the whole field of Shakespeare studies.

Even more comprehensive – though considerably more daunting – are the eight volumes of Geoffrey Bullough's *Narrative and Dramatic Sources of Shakespeare*, Routledge & Kegan Paul, London, and Columbia University Press, New York, 1957–75.

CHRONOLOGY

DATE	AUTHOR'S LIFE	LITERARY CONTEXT
1564	Born in Stratford, Warwickshire, the eldest surviving son of John Shakespeare, glover and occasional dealer in wool, and Mary Arden, daughter of a prosperous farmer.	Birth of Christopher Marlowe.
1565	John Shakespeare elected Alderman of Stratford.	Clinthio: *Hecatommithi*. Edwards: *Damon and Pythias*.
1566	Birth of Shakespeare's brother Gilbert.	Gascoigne: *Supposes*.
1567		Udall: *Roister Doister*. Golding: *The Stories of Venus and Adonis and of Hermaphroditus and Salamcis*.
1568	His father is elected bailiff.	Gascoigne: *Jocasta*. Wilmot: *Tancred and Gismunda*. Second Edition of Vasari's *Lives of the Artists*.
1569	Probably starts attending the petty school attached to the King's New School in Stratford. Birth of his sister Joan.	
1570	His father involved in money-lending.	
1571	John Shakespeare is elected Chief Alderman and deputy to the new bailiff.	
1572		Whitgift's *Answer* to the 'Admonition' receives Cartwright's *Reply*, beginning the first literary debate between Anglicans and Puritans. Tasso: *Aminta*.
1573		
1574	Probably enters the Upper School (where studies include rhetoric, logic, the Latin poets, and a little Greek). Birth of his brother Richard.	

HISTORICAL EVENTS

Death of Michelangelo. Birth of Galileo.

Rebellion against Spain in the Netherlands. Birth of the actor Edward Alleyn.
Birth of the actor Richard Burbage.

Mary Stuart flees to England from Scotland.

Northern Rebellion.

Excommunication of Elizabeth. *Baïf's* Academy founded in Paris to promote poetry, music and dance.
Ridolfi Plot. Puritan 'Admonition' to Parliament.

Dutch rebels conquer Holland and Zeeland. Massacre of St Bartholomew's Day in Paris.

Accession of Henry III and new outbreak of civil war in France. First Catholic missionaries arrive in England from Douai. Earl of Leicester's Men obtain licence to perform within the City of London.

DATE	AUTHOR'S LIFE	LITERARY CONTEXT
1575		*Gammer Gurton's Needle* is printed.
1576		Castiglione's *The Book of the Courtier* banned by the Spanish Inquisition. George Gascoigne: *The Steel Glass.*
1577		John Northbrooke's attack in *Treatise wherein Dicing, Dancing, Vain Plays etc are reproved.*
1578	Shakespeare family fortunes are in decline, and John is having to sell off property to pay off his increasing debts.	Sidney writes *The Lady of May* and begins the 'Old' *Arcadia.* George Whetstone: *Promos and Cassandra.* John Lyly: *Euphues, the Anatomy of Wit.* Pierre de Ronsard, leader of the Pléiade, publishes his *Sonnets pour Hélène.* He is said to have exercised a considerable influence on the English sonnet-writers of the sixteenth century.
1579		Spenser: *The Shepherd's Calendar.* North: translation of Plutarch. Gossen: *The School of Abuse, and Pleasant Invective against Poets, Pipers, Players etc.*
1580	Birth of Shakespeare's brother Edmund.	
1581		John Newton's translation of Seneca's *Ten Tragedies.* Barnaby Rich: *Apolonius and Silla.*
1582	Shakespeare marries Anne Hathaway, a local farmer's daughter, 7 or 8 years his senior, who is already pregnant with their first child.	Tasso: *Gerusalemme Liberata.* Watson: *Hekatompathia* (First sonnet sequence published in England). Whetstone: *Heptameron of Civil Discourses.* Sidney begins *Astrophel and Stella* and the 'New' *Arcadia.* Lope de Vega writing for the Corrals in Madrid.

CHRONOLOGY

HISTORICAL EVENTS

Kenilworth Revels.

Restricted by the City of London's order that no plays be performed within the City boundaries, James Burbage of The Earl of Leicester's Men builds The Theatre only just outside the boundaries in Shoreditch. The Blackfriars Theatre is built. End of civil war in France. Observatory of Uraniborg built for the Danish astronomer, Tycho Brahe. Death of Titian.

Drake's circumnavigation of the world. The Curtain Theatre built. Birth of Rubens.

First visit to England of the duc d'Alençon as a suitor to Elizabeth, provoking much opposition to a French match. The Corral de la Cruz built in Madrid.

Spanish conquest of Portugal. Jesuit mission arrives in England from Rome led by Edmund Campion and Parsons.

Stricter enforcement of treason laws and increased penalties on recusants. Campion captured and executed. Northern provinces of the Netherlands renounce their allegiance to Phillip II, and invite the duc d'Alençon to be their sovereign.

Sir Walter Ralegh established in the Queen's favour. The Corral del Principe built in Madrid.

DATE	AUTHOR'S LIFE	LITERARY CONTEXT
1583	Birth of their daughter Susanna.	
1583–4	The players' companies of the Earls of Essex, Oxford and Leicester perform in Stratford.	Giordarno Bruno visits England.
1584		Bruno publishes *La cena de le Ceneri* and *Spaccio della bestia trionfante*. Reginald Scott: *The Discovery of Witchcraft*.
1585	Birth of Shakespeare's twins Hamnet and Judith. The following years until 1592 are the 'Lost Years' for which no documentary records of his life survive, only legends such as the one of deer-stealing and flight from prosecution, and conjectures such as ones that he became a schoolmaster, travelled in Europe, or went to London to be an actor as early as the mid 1580s.	Death of Pierre de Ronsard. Bruno: *De gli eroici furori*, dedicated to Sidney.
1586		Timothy Bright: *A Treatise of Melancholy*.
1586–7	Five players' companies visit Stratford, including the Queen's, Essex's, Leicester's and Stafford's.	
1587		Holinshed: *Chronicles of England Scotland and Ireland*. Marlowe: First part of *Tamburlaine the Great* acted. New edition of *The Mirror for Magistrates*.
1588		Marlowe: Second part of *Tamburlaine*. Thomas Kyd: *The Spanish Tragedy*. Lope de Vega, serving with the Armada, writes some of *The Beauty of Angelica*.

CHRONOLOGY

HISTORICAL EVENTS

First meeting of the Durham House Set led by Ralegh, Northumberland
and Harriot, to promote mathematics, astronomy and navigation.
Archbishop Whitgift leads more extreme anti-Puritan policy.
Throckmorton plot, involving the Spanish ambassador.

Death of d'Alençon. Assassination of William of Orange. The Teatro
Olimpico, Vicenza, built by Palladio.

England sends military aid to the Dutch rebels under the command of
Leicester. Ralegh organizes the colonization of Virginia.

Babington plot. Death of Sir Philip Sidney. Rise of the Earl of Essex.
Colonization of Munster.

Execution of Mary Stuart. Drake's raid on Cadiz.

Defeat of the Armada. Death of the Earl of Leicester. The first of the
Puritan Marprelate Tracts published.

DATE	AUTHOR'S LIFE	LITERARY CONTEXT
1589	The earliest likely date at which Shakespeare began composition of his first plays (1 *Henry VI*, *The Taming of the Shrew*) when he would have been working as an actor at The Theatre, with Burbage's company.	Marlowe: *The Jew of Malta*. Thomas Nashe: *The Anatomy of Absurdity*. Richard Hakluyt: *Principal Navigations, Voyages and Discoveries of the English nation*.
1590	2 *Henry VI*, 3 *Henry VI*.	Spenser: first 3 books of *The Faerie Queen*. Publication of Sidney's 'New' *Arcadia*. Nashe: *An Almond for a Parrot*, one of the Marprelate Tracts. Greene: *Menaphon*. Guarina: *The Faithful Shepherd*.
1590–91	*King John* written.	
1590–92	Performances of *Henry VI*, parts 2 and 3, *Titus* and *The Shrew* by the Earl of Pembroke's Men.	
1591	*Richard III* and *The Comedy of Errors* written.	Spenser's *Complaints* which includes his translation of fifteen of Joachim du Bellay's sonnets – du Bellay was a member of the Pléiade and responsible for its manifesto. Sir John Harington's translation of *Orlando Furioso*. Publication of Sidney's *Astrophel and Stella*.
1592	First recorded reference to Shakespeare as an actor and playwright in Greene's attack in *The Groatsworth of Wit* describing him as 'an upstart crow'.	Samuel Daniel: *Delia*. Marlowe's *Edward II* and *Doctor Faustus* performed. *Arden of Feversham* printed. Nashe: *Strange News*.
1592–4	*Titus Andronicus* written.	
1593	Publication of *Venus and Adonis*, dedicated to the Earl of Southampton. The *Sonnets* probably begun.	Marlowe: *Massacre of Paris*. *The Phoenix Nest*, miscellany of poems including ones by Ralegh, Lodge and Breton. Barnabe Barnes: *Parthenophil and Parthenope*. George Peele: *The Honour of the Garter*. Lodge: *Phillis*. Nashe: *Christ's Tears over Jerusalem*.

CHRONOLOGY

HISTORICAL EVENTS

Failure of the Portugal expedition. Henry III of France assassinated.
English military aid sent to Henry of Navarre. Marlowe's tutor, Francis
Ket, burned at the stake for atheism.

English government discovers and suppresses the Puritan printing press.

Earl of Essex given command of the English army in France. The last fight
of the *Revenge* under Spanish attack.

Capture of Madre de Dios. Split in the main players' company.
Shakespeare and Burbage's group remain at The Theatre, Alleyn's move to
the Rose on Bankside. Plague in London: the theatres closed.

Marlowe arrested on blasphemy charges and murdered two weeks later.
Kyd arrested for libel. Henry of Navarre converts to Catholicism in order
to unite France.

DATE	AUTHOR'S LIFE	LITERARY CONTEXT
1593–4	*The Two Gentlemen of Verona.*	
1593–6		John Donne writing his early poems, the Satires and Elegies.
1594	*The Rape of Lucrece* dedicated to his patron Southampton. *The Comedy of Errors* and *Titus Andronicus* performed at the Rose. Shakespeare established as one of the shareholders in his company, The Chamberlain's Men, which performs before the Queen during the Christmas festivities.	Daniel: *Cleopatra.* Spenser: *Amoretti* and *Epithalamion.* Drayton: *Idea's Mirror.* Nashe: *The Terrors of the Night, The Unfortunate Traveller.* Greene: *Friar Bacon and Friar Bungay.*
1594–5	*Love's Labour's Lost* and *Romeo and Juliet* written.	
1595	*Richard II.*	Daniel: *The First Four Books of the Civil Wars between the two houses of Lancaster and York.* Sidney: *Defence of Poesy* published. Ralegh: *The Discovery of the Empire of Guiana.*
1595–6	*A Midsummer Night's Dream.*	
1596	Death of his son, Hamnet. *The Merchant of Venice.* Shakespeare living in Bishopsgate ward. His father, John, is granted a coat of arms.	Lodge: *Wits Miserie.* First complete edition of Spenser's *Faerie Queen.*
1597	*Henry IV* Part 1. First performance of *The Merry Wives of Windsor.* Shakespeare's company now under the patronage of the new Lord Chamberlain, Hunsdon. In Stratford, Shakespeare buys New Place, the second largest house in the town, with its own orchards and vines.	John Donne writes 'The Storme' and 'The Calme'. Francis Bacon: first edition of *Essays.* Jonson and Nashe imprisoned for writing *The Isle of Dogs.*
1597–8	*Henry IV* Part 2.	
1598	Shakespeare one of the 'principal comedians' with Richard Burbage, Heminge and Cordell in Jonson's *Every Man in his Humour.* For the second year, Shakespeare is listed as having failed to pay tax levied on all householders.	Publication of Sidney's *Works* and of Marlowe's *Hero and Leander* (together with Chapman's continuation). *Seven Books of the Iliads* (first of Chapman's Homeric translations). Meres: *Palladia Tamia.*

CHRONOLOGY

HISTORICAL EVENTS

Henry of Navarre accepted as King in Paris. Rebellion in Ireland. The London theatres re-open. The Swan Theatre is built. Ralegh accused of blasphemy.

France declares war on Spain. Failure of the Indies voyage and death of Hawkins. Ralegh's expedition to Guiana.

England joins France in the war against Spain. Death of Drake. Raid on Cadiz led by Essex. In long-standing power struggle with Essex, Robert Cecil is appointed Secretary of State.

Islands Voyage led by Essex and Ralegh. The government suppresses the *Isle of Dogs* at the Swan and closes the theatres. Despite the continued hostility of the City of London, they soon re-open. James Burbage builds the second Blackfriars Theatre. Death of James Burbage.

Peace between France and Spain. Death of Philip II. Tyrone defeats the English at Armagh. Essex appointed Lord Deputy of Ireland.

cxxix

DATE	AUTHOR'S LIFE	LITERARY CONTEXT
1598 cont.		New edition of Lodge's *Rosalynde*. Lope de Vega: *La Arcadia*. James VI of Scotland: *The True Law of Free Monarchies*.
1598–9	*As You Like It*.	
1598–1600	*Much Ado About Nothing*.	
1599	*Henry V, Julius Caesar*. Shakespeare one of the shareholders in the Globe Theatre. He moves lodgings to Bankside. Publication of *The Passionate Pilgrim*, a miscellany of 20 poems, at least 5 by Shakespeare.	Jonson: *Every Man out of his Humour*. Dekker: *The Shoemaker's Holiday*. Sir John Hayward: *The First Part of the Life and Reign of King Henry IV*. Greene's translation of *Orlando Furioso*.
1600		'England's Helicon'.
1600–1	*Hamlet* (performed with Burbage as the Prince and Shakespeare as the Ghost).	
1601	*The Phoenix and the Turtle*. The Lord Chamberlain's Men paid by one of Essex's followers to perform *Richard II* on the day before the rebellion. Death of John Shakespeare.	
1601–2	*Troilus and Cressida*.	
1602	Shakespeare buys more property in Stratford.	
1602–4	*Alls Well That Ends Well*.	
1603	Shakespeare's company now under the patronage of King James. Shakespeare is one of the principal tragedians in Jonson's *Sejanus*.	Montaigne's *Essays* translated into English. Thomas Heywood: *A Woman Killed with Kindness*.
1604	Shakespeare known to be lodging in Silver Street with a Huguenot family called Mountjoy. *Othello*; first performance of *Measure for Measure*.	Chapman: *Bussy d'Ambois*. Marston: *The Malcontent*.
1604–5	Ten of his plays performed at court by the King's Men.	

CHRONOLOGY

The Burbage brothers, Richard and Cuthbert, pull down The Theatre and, with its timbers, build the Globe on Bankside. Essex's campaign fails in Ireland, and after returning without permission to court he is arrested. The government suppresses satirical writings, and burns pamphlets by Nashe and Harvey.

Essex released but still in disgrace. The Fortune Theatre built by Alleyn and Henslowe. Bruno executed for heresy by the Inquisition in Rome.

Essex's Rebellion. Essex and Southampton arrested, and the former executed. Spanish invasion of Ireland. Monopolies debates in Parliament.

Spanish troops defeated in Ireland.

Death of Elizabeth, and accession of James I. Ralegh imprisoned in the Tower. Plague in London. Sir Thomas Bodley re-founds the library of Oxford University.

Peace with Spain. Hampton Court Conference.

DATE	AUTHOR'S LIFE	LITERARY CONTEXT
1605	First performance of *King Lear* at the Globe, with Burbage as the King, and Robert Armin as the Fool. Shakespeare makes further investments in Stratford, buying a half interest in a lease of tithes.	Cervantes: *Don Quixote* (part one). Bacon: *The Proficience and Advancement of Learning*. Jonson and Inigo Jones: *The Masque of Blackness*. Jonson and co-authors imprisoned for libellous references to the court in *Eastward Ho*.
1605–6		Jonson: *Volpone*.
1606	First performance of *Macbeth*.	John Ford's masque *Honour Triumphant*.
1607	*Antony and Cleopatra*. Susanna marries John Hall, a physician. Death of Shakespeare's brother Edmund, an actor.	Tourneur's *The Revenger's Tragedy* printed. Barnes: *The Devil's Charter*.
1607–8	*Timon of Athens*, *Coriolanus*, *Pericles*.	
1608	Shakespeare one of the shareholders in the Blackfriars Theatre. Death of his mother.	Lope de Vega: *Peribanez*. Beaumont and Fletcher: *Philaster*. Jonson and Jones: *The Masque of Beauty*. Donne writes *La Corona*. Twelve books of Homer's *Iliad* (Chapman's translation).
1609	Publication, probably unauthorized, of the quarto edition of the *Sonnets* and *A Lover's Complaint*.	Jonson and Jones: *The Masque of Queens*. Donne's 'The Expiration' printed; 'Liturgie' and 'On the Annunciation' written. Bacon: *De Sapientia Veterum*. Lope de Vega: *New Art of Writing Plays for the Theatre*.
1609–10	*Cymbeline*.	
1610		Donne: *Pseudo-Martyr* printed and *The First Anniversarie* written. Jonson: *The Alchemist*. Beaumont and Fletcher: *The Maid's Tragedy*.
1610–11	*The Winter's Tale*.	
1611	*The Tempest* performed in the Banqueting House, Whitehall. Simon Forman records seeing performances of *Macbeth*, *The Winter's Tale* and *Cymbeline*.	Beaumont and Fletcher: *A King and No King*, *The Knight of the Burning Pestle*. Tourneur: *The Atheist's Tragedy*.

CHRONOLOGY

DATE	AUTHOR'S LIFE	LITERARY CONTEXT
1611 *cont.*		Jonson and Jones: *Masque of Oberon.* Authorized Version of the Bible. Sir John Davies: *The Scourge of Folly.* Donne writes the *The Second Anniversarie* and a 'A Valediction: forbidding mourning'.
1612	Shakespeare appears as a witness in a Court of Requests case involving a dispute over a dowry owed by his former landlord, Mountjoy, to his son-in-law, Belott. Death of his brother Gilbert.	Webster: *The White Devil* printed. Tourneur: *The Nobleman.* Lope de Vega: *Fuente Ovejuna.*
1613	At a performance of his last play, *Henry VIII*, the Globe Theatre catches fire and is destroyed. As part of the court celebrations for the marriage of Princess Elizabeth, The King's Men perform 14 plays, including *Much Ado, Othello, The Winter's Tale* and *The Tempest.* Death of his brother Richard.	Sir Thomas Overbury: *The Wife.* Donne: 'Good Friday' and 'Epithalamion' on Princess Elizabeth's marriage. Cervantes: *Novelas ejemplares* – a collection of short stories.
1614	In Stratford, Shakespeare protects his property interests during a controversy over a threat to enclose the common fields.	Jonson: *Bartholomew Fair.* Webster: *The Duchess of Malfi.* Ralegh: *The History of the World.*
1615	The Warwick Assizes issue an order to prevent enclosures, which ends the dispute in Stratford.	Cervantes publishes 8 plays and *Don Quixote* (part two).
1616	Marriage of his daughter Judith to Thomas Quincy, a vintner, who a month later is tried for fornication with another woman whom he had made pregnant. Death of Shakespeare (23 April).	Jonson: *The Devil is an Ass.* Jonson publishes his *Works.*
1623	The players Heminge and Condell publish the plays of the First Folio.	

CHRONOLOGY

Death of Henry, Prince of Wales.

Marriage of Princess Elizabeth to Frederick, Elector Palatine. Bacon appointed Attorney-General.

The second Globe and the Hope Theatre built.

Inquiry into the murder of Sir Thomas Overbury in the Tower implicates the wife of the King's favourite, Somerset.

Ralegh released from the Tower to lead an expedition to Guiana; on his return he is executed.

HISTORICAL EVENTS

WILLIAM SHAKESPEARE

THE MOST LAMENTABLE ROMAN TRAGEDY OF TITUS ANDRONICUS

Edited by *Sylvan Barnet*

[*Dramatis Personae*

SATURNINUS, son to the late Emperor of Rome, afterward
    Emperor
BASSIANUS, brother to Saturninus
TITUS ANDRONICUS, a noble Roman
MARCUS ANDRONICUS, Tribune, and brother to Titus
LUCIUS ⎫
QUINTUS ⎬ sons to Titus Andronicus
MARTIUS ⎪
MUTIUS ⎭
YOUNG LUCIUS, a boy, son to Lucius
PUBLIUS, son to Marcus Andronicus
SEMPRONIUS ⎫
CAIUS ⎬ kinsmen to Titus Andronicus
VALENTINE ⎭
AEMILIUS, a noble Roman
ALARBUS ⎫
DEMETRIUS ⎬ sons to Tamora
CHIRON ⎭
AARON, a Moor, beloved by Tamora
A CAPTAIN
A MESSENGER
A CLOWN
TAMORA, Queen of the Goths
LAVINIA, daughter to Titus Andronicus
NURSE, and a blackamoor Infant
ROMANS, GOTHS, SENATORS, TRIBUNES, OFFICERS, SOLDIERS,
    and ATTENDANTS

    Scene: Rome, and the countryside near it]

2

THE MOST LAMENTABLE
ROMAN TRAGEDY OF
TITUS ANDRONICUS

[ACT I

Scene I. *Rome. Before the Capitol.*]

[*Flourish.*[1]] *Enter the Tribunes and Senators aloft; and then
enter Saturninus and his followers at one door, and Bassianus
and his followers [at the other,] with drums and trumpets.*

SATURNINUS Noble patricians, patrons of my right,
Defend the justice of my cause with arms;
And, countrymen, my loving followers,
Plead my successive title with your swords.
I am his first-born son that was the last   5
That ware the imperial diadem of Rome;
Then let my father's honors live in me,
Nor wrong mine age with this indignity.

BASSIANUS Romans, friends, followers, favorers of my
    right,
If ever Bassianus, Caesar's son,   10

---

1. Text references are printed in **bold** type; the annotation follows in roman type.
I.i.s.d. **Flourish** trumpet fanfare   4 **successive title** right to the succession
8 **age** i.e., seniority

3

Were gracious in the eyes of royal Rome,
Keep then this passage to the Capitol,
And suffer not dishonor to approach
The imperial seat, to virtue consecrate,
15 To justice, continence, and nobility;
But let desert in pure election shine,
And, Romans, fight for freedom in your choice.

MARCUS (*With the crown*) Princes, that strive by factions
     and by friends
Ambitiously for rule and empery,
20 Know that the people of Rome, for whom we stand
A special party, have by common voice,
In election for the Roman empery,
Chosen Andronicus, surnamèd Pius
For many good and great deserts to Rome.
25 A nobler man, a braver warrior,
Lives not this day within the city walls.
He by the senate is accited home
From weary wars against the barbarous Goths;
That with his sons, a terror to our foes,
30 Hath yoked a nation strong, trained up in arms.
Ten years are spent since first he undertook
This cause of Rome, and chastisèd with arms
Our enemies' pride: five times he hath returned
Bleeding to Rome, bearing his valiant sons
35 In coffins from the field.
And now at last, laden with honor's spoils,
Returns the good Andronicus to Rome,
Renownèd Titus, flourishing in arms.
Let us entreat, by honor of his name,
40 Whom worthily you would have now succeed,

11 **gracious** acceptable   12 **Keep** guard   15 **continence** restraint   19 **empery** dominion (but in line 22 **empery** = emperor)   27 **accited** summoned   30 **yoked** subjugated   35 **field** (this word is followed by: "and at this day/To the monument of that Andronici/Done sacrifice of expiation,/And slain the noblest prisoner of the Goths." These lines, omitted from the second and third quartos and from the Folio, are inconsistent with the ensuing action, in which Alarbus is sacrificed. Perhaps Shakespeare neglected to cancel them in the manuscript after deciding to make Alarbus' execution part of the action)

And in the Capitol and Senate's right,
Whom you pretend to honor and adore,
That you withdraw you and abate your strength,
Dismiss your followers, and, as suitors should,
Plead your deserts in peace and humbleness.   45

SATURNINUS How fair the tribune speaks to calm my
    thoughts!

BASSIANUS Marcus Andronicus, so I do affy
In thy uprightness and integrity,
And so I love and honor thee and thine,
Thy noble brother Titus and his sons,   50
And her to whom my thoughts are humbled all,
Gracious Lavinia, Rome's rich ornament,
That I will here dismiss my loving friends;
And to my fortunes and the people's favor
Commit my cause in balance to be weighed.   55
                        Exit [his] soldiers.

SATURNINUS Friends, that have been thus forward in
    my right,
I thank you all, and here dismiss you all,
And to the love and favor of my country
Commit myself, my person, and the cause.
                        [Exeunt his followers.]
Rome, be as just and gracious unto me   60
As I am confident and kind to thee.
Open the gates and let me in.

BASSIANUS Tribunes, and me, a poor competitor.
    [Flourish.] They go up into the Senate house.
            Enter a Captain.

CAPTAIN Romans, make way! The good Andronicus,
Patron of virtue, Rome's best champion,   65
Successful in the battles that he fights,
With honor and with fortune is returned
From where he circumscribèd with his sword

41 the Capitol and Senate's right the right of the Capitol and the Senate
42 pretend claim 46 fair courteously 47 affy trust 59 cause affair
61 confident and kind trusting and natural(ly devoted) 63 competitor
candidate 65 Patron representative

5

And brought to yoke the enemies of Rome.

*Sound drums and trumpets, and then enter two of Titus'
sons, and then two men bearing a coffin covered with
black, then two other sons, then Titus Andronicus, and
then Tamora, the Queen of Goths, and her three sons,
[Alarbus,] Chiron, and Demetrius, with Aaron the Moor,
and others as many as can be; then set down the coffin,
and Titus speaks.*

70   TITUS Hail, Rome, victorious in thy mourning weeds!
Lo, as the bark that hath discharged his fraught
Returns with precious lading to the bay
From whence at first she weighed her anchorage,
Cometh Andronicus, bound with laurel boughs,
75   To re-salute his country with his tears,
Tears of true joy for his return to Rome.
Thou great defender of this Capitol,
Stand gracious to the rites that we intend!
Romans, of five and twenty valiant sons,
80   Half of the number that King Priam had,
Behold the poor remains, alive and dead!
These that survive let Rome reward with love;
These that I bring unto their latest home,
With burial amongst their ancestors.
Here Goths have given me leave to sheathe my
85   sword.
Titus, unkind and careless of thine own,
Why suffer'st thou thy sons, unburied yet,
To hover on the dreadful shore of Styx?
Make way to lay them by their brethren.
                              They open the tomb.
90   There greet in silence, as the dead are wont,
And sleep in peace, slain in your country's wars!
O sacred receptacle of my joys,
Sweet cell of virtue and nobility,

70 **weeds** apparel   71 **his fraught** its freight   73 **anchorage** anchors   77 **Thou**
i.e., Jupiter   83 **latest** last   86 **unkind** unnatural   88 **Styx** river surrounding
Hades   89 **brethren** (trisyllabic here and occasionally elsewhere: "breth-e-rin")

How many sons hast thou of mine in store,
That thou wilt never render to me more!   95

LUCIUS Give us the proudest prisoner of the Goths,
That we may hew his limbs, and on a pile
Ad manes fratrum sacrifice his flesh,
Before this earthy prison of their bones,
That so the shadows be not unappeased,   100
Nor we disturbed with prodigies on earth.

TITUS I give him you, the noblest that survives,
The eldest son of this distressèd queen.

TAMORA Stay, Roman brethren! Gracious conqueror,
Victorious Titus, rue the tears I shed,   105
A mother's tears in passion for her son:
And if thy sons were ever dear to thee,
O, think my son to be as dear to me!
Sufficeth not that we are brought to Rome,
To beautify thy triumphs and return,   110
Captive to thee and to thy Roman yoke,
But must my sons be slaughtered in the streets,
For valiant doings in their country's cause?
O, if to fight for king and commonweal
Were piety in thine, it is in these.   115
Andronicus, stain not thy tomb with blood.
Wilt thou draw near the nature of the gods?
Draw near them then in being merciful;
Sweet mercy is nobility's true badge.
Thrice-noble Titus, spare my first-born son.   120

TITUS Patient yourself, madam, and pardon me.
These are their brethren, whom your Goths beheld
Alive and dead, and for their brethren slain
Religiously they ask a sacrifice.
To this your son is marked, and die he must,   125
T' appease their groaning shadows that are gone.

LUCIUS Away with him! And make a fire straight,

98 **Ad manes fratrum** to the ghosts of our brothers (Latin) 101 **prodigies**
ominous disturbances 106 **passion** violent emotion 110 **triumphs** triumphal
processions 121 **Patient** calm

7

And with our swords, upon a pile of wood,
Let's hew his limbs till they be clean consumed.

Exit Titus' sons with Alarbus.

130 TAMORA O cruel, irreligious piety!

CHIRON Was never Scythia half so barbarous.

DEMETRIUS Oppose not Scythia to ambitious Rome.
Alarbus goes to rest, and we survive
To tremble under Titus' threat'ning look.
135 Then, madam, stand resolved, but hope withal
The selfsame gods that armed the Queen of Troy
With opportunity of sharp revenge
Upon the Thracian tyrant in his tent
May favor Tamora, the Queen of Goths,
140 (When Goths were Goths and Tamora was queen)
To quit the bloody wrongs upon her foes.

Enter the sons of Andronicus again.

LUCIUS See, lord and father, how we have performed
Our Roman rites! Alarbus' limbs are lopped,
And entrails feed the sacrificing fire,
145 Whose smoke like incense doth perfume the sky.
Remaineth naught but to inter our brethren,
And with loud 'larums welcome them to Rome.

TITUS Let it be so, and let Andronicus
Make this his latest farewell to their souls.

*Sound trumpets, and lay the coffin
in the tomb.*

150 In peace and honor rest you here, my sons,
Rome's readiest champions, repose you here in rest,
Secure from worldly chances and mishaps!
Here lurks no treason, here no envy swells,
Here grow no damnèd drugs, here are no storms,

---

131 **Scythia** a region in southern Russia noted for its savage inhabitants
132 **Oppose** compare   135 **withal** with this   136 **Queen of Troy** Hecuba (who murdered the sons of Polymnestor—the Thracian tyrant of line 138—in revenge for his murder of her son)   141 **quit** requite, repay   147 **'larums** alarms, calls to arms   153 **envy** malice   154 **drugs** poisonous plants

8

No noise, but silence and eternal sleep: 155
In peace and honor rest you here, my sons!

Enter Lavinia.

LAVINIA In peace and honor live Lord Titus long,
My noble lord and father, live in fame!
Lo, at this tomb my tributary tears
I render for my brethren's obsequies,   160
And at thy feet I kneel, with tears of joy
Shed on this earth for thy return to Rome.
O, bless me here with thy victorious hand,
Whose fortunes Rome's best citizens applaud.

TITUS Kind Rome, that hast thus lovingly reserved   165
The cordial of mine age to glad my heart!
Lavinia, live, outlive thy father's days
And fame's eternal date, for virtue's praise!

[*Enter above Marcus Andronicus, Saturninus,
Bassianus, and others.*]

MARCUS Long live Lord Titus, my belovèd brother,
Gracious triumpher in the eyes of Rome!   170

TITUS Thanks, gentle tribune, noble brother Marcus.

MARCUS And welcome, nephews, from successful wars,
You that survive, and you that sleep in fame!
Fair lords, your fortunes are alike in all,
That in your country's service drew your swords,   175
But safer triumph is this funeral pomp,
That hath aspired to Solon's happiness
And triumphs over chance in honor's bed.
Titus Andronicus, the people of Rome,
Whose friend in justice thou hast ever been,   180
Send thee by me, their tribune and their trust,
This palliament of white and spotless hue,
And name thee in election for the empire
With these our late-deceasèd emperor's sons:

159 **tributary** given as tribute 166 **cordial** comfort (literally: stimulant to the heart) 168 **date** duration 177 **aspired** risen 177 **Solon's happiness** (Solon said: "Call no man happy until he is dead") 182 **palliament** robe

9

185   Be *candidatus* then, and put it on,
       And help to set a head on headless Rome.

       TITUS A better head her glorious body fits
       Than his that shakes for age and feebleness:
       What should I don this robe and trouble you?
190   Be chosen with proclamations today,
       Tomorrow yield up rule, resign my life,
       And set abroad new business for you all?
       Rome, I have been thy soldier forty years,
       And led my country's strength successfully,
195   And buried one and twenty valiant sons,
       Knighted in field, slain manfully in arms,
       In right and service of their noble country:
       Give me a staff of honor for mine age,
       But not a scepter to control the world.
200   Upright he held it, lords, that held it last.

       MARCUS Titus, thou shalt obtain and ask the empery.

       SATURNINUS Proud and ambitious tribune, canst thou
          tell?

       TITUS Patience, Prince Saturninus.

       SATURNINUS   Romans, do me right.
       Patricians, draw your swords and sheathe them not
205   Till Saturninus be Rome's emperor.
       Andronicus, would thou were shipped to hell
       Rather than rob me of the people's hearts.

       LUCIUS Proud Saturnine, interrupter of the good
       That noble-minded Titus means to thee!

210   TITUS Content thee, Prince, I will restore to thee
       The people's hearts, and wean them from
          themselves.

       BASSIANUS Andronicus, I do not flatter thee,
       But honor thee, and will do till I die.
       My faction if thou strengthen with thy friends,

185 **candidatus** candidate (Latin; literally: clad in white) 189 **What** why
201 **obtain and ask** i.e., obtain if you ask for

10

I will most thankful be, and thanks to men   215
Of noble minds is honorable meed.

TITUS People of Rome, and people's tribunes here,
I ask your voices and your suffrages:
Will ye bestow them friendly on Andronicus?

TRIBUNES To gratify the good Andronicus,   220
And gratulate his safe return to Rome,
The people will accept whom he admits.

TITUS Tribunes, I thank you, and this suit I make,
That you create our emperor's eldest son,
Lord Saturnine; whose virtues will, I hope,   225
Reflect on Rome as Titan's rays on earth,
And ripen justice in this commonweal:
Then, if you will elect by my advice,
Crown him and say, "Long live our emperor!"

MARCUS With voices and applause of every sort,   230
Patricians and plebeians, we create
Lord Saturninus Rome's great emperor,
And say "Long live our Emperor Saturnine!"
                    [*A long flourish till they come down.*]

SATURNINUS Titus Andronicus, for thy favors done
To us in our election this day,   235
I give thee thanks in part of thy deserts,
And will with deeds requite thy gentleness:
And for an onset, Titus, to advance
Thy name and honorable family,
Lavinia will I make my empress,   240
Rome's royal mistress, mistress of my heart,
And in the sacred Pantheon her espouse.
Tell me, Andronicus, doth this motion please thee?

TITUS It doth, my worthy lord, and in this match

216 **meed** reward 221 **gratulate** rejoice at 222 **admits** approves
226 **Titan's** the sun god's 235 **election** (here, as often in Shakespeare, **-ion** is
disyllabic) 236 **in** as 237 **gentleness** nobility 238 **onset** beginning
240 **empress** (here, and often elsewhere in *Titus*, trisyllabic: "em-per-es")
242 **Pantheon** temple dedicated to all the gods 243 **motion** proposal

245   I hold me highly honored of your grace,
       And here in sight of Rome to Saturnine,
       King and commander of our commonweal,
       The wide world's emperor, do I consecrate
       My sword, my chariot, and my prisoners,
250   Presents well worthy Rome's imperious lord.
       Receive them then, the tribute that I owe,
       Mine honor's ensigns humbled at thy feet.

       SATURNINUS Thanks, noble Titus, father of my life!
       How proud I am of thee and of thy gifts
255   Rome shall record, and when I do forget
       The least of these unspeakable deserts,
       Romans, forget your fealty to me.

       TITUS [To Tamora] Now, madam, are you prisoner to
           an emperor,
       To him that, for your honor and your state,
260   Will use you nobly and your followers.

       SATURNINUS [Aside] A goodly lady, trust me, of the
           hue
       That I would choose, were I to choose anew.
       [Aloud] Clear up, fair Queen, that cloudy
           countenance.
       Though chance of war hath wrought this change of
           cheer,
265   Thou com'st not to be made a scorn in Rome.
       Princely shall be thy usage every way.
       Rest on my word, and let not discontent
       Daunt all your hopes. Madam, he comforts you
       Can make you greater than the Queen of Goths.
270   Lavinia, you are not displeased with this?

       LAVINIA Not I, my lord, sith true nobility
       Warrants these words in princely courtesy.

       SATURNINUS Thanks, sweet Lavinia. Romans, let us go.

250 **imperious** imperial   252 **ensigns** tokens   257 **fealty** loyalty   264 **cheer**
countenance   268 **he** he who   271 **sith** since   272 **Warrants** justifies

12

Ransomless here we set our prisoners free.
Proclaim our honors, lords, with trump and drum. 275

BASSIANUS Lord Titus, by your leave, this maid is
mine.

TITUS How, sir! Are you in earnest then, my lord?

BASSIANUS Ay, noble Titus, and resolved withal
To do myself this reason and this right.

MARCUS *Suum cuique* is our Roman justice. 280
This prince in justice seizeth but his own.

LUCIUS And that he will, and shall, if Lucius live.

TITUS Traitors, avaunt! Where is the Emperor's
guard?
Treason, my lord! Lavinia is surprised!

SATURNINUS Surprised! By whom?

BASSIANUS   By him that justly may 285
Bear his betrothed from all the world away.
        [Exeunt Marcus and Bassianus, with Lavinia.]

MUTIUS Brothers, help to convey her hence away,
And with my sword I'll keep this door safe.
        [Exeunt Lucius, Quintus, and Martius.]

TITUS Follow, my lord, and I'll soon bring her back.
        *[During the fray, exeunt Saturninus, Tamora,
        Demetrius, Chiron, and Aaron.]*

MUTIUS My lord, you pass not here. 290

TITUS What, villain boy! Barr'st me my way in Rome?
        [He stabs Mutius.]

MUTIUS *[Dying]* Help, Lucius, help!

        [Enter Lucius.]

LUCIUS My lord, you are unjust; and more than so,

280 Suum cuique to each his own (Latin) 283 avaunt be gone 284 surprised
suddenly taken 288 door (disyllabic)

In wrongful quarrel you have slain your son.

295 TITUS Nor thou, nor he, are any sons of mine:
My sons would never so dishonor me.
Traitor, restore Lavinia to the Emperor.

LUCIUS Dead if you will, but not to be his wife
That is another's lawful promised love.   [*Exit.*]

*Enter aloft the Emperor with Tamora and her
two sons and Aaron the Moor.*

300 SATURNINUS No, Titus, no; the Emperor needs her not,
Nor her, nor thee, nor any of thy stock:
I'll trust by leisure him that mocks me once;
Thee never, nor thy traitorous haughty sons,
Confederates all thus to dishonor me.
305 Was none in Rome to make a stale
But Saturnine? Full well, Andronicus,
Agree these deeds with that proud brag of thine,
That saidst I begged the empire at thy hands.

TITUS O monstrous! What reproachful words are
these?

SATURNINUS But go thy ways, go, give that changing
310 piece
To him that flourished for her with his sword:
A valiant son-in-law thou shalt enjoy,
One fit to bandy with thy lawless sons,
To ruffle in the commonwealth of Rome.

315 TITUS These words are razors to my wounded heart.

SATURNINUS And therefore, lovely Tamora, Queen of
Goths,
That like the stately Phoebe 'mongst her nymphs
Dost overshine the gallant'st dames of Rome,
If thou be pleased with this my sudden choice,
320 Behold, I choose thee, Tamora, for my bride,

302 **by leisure** slowly   305 **stale** laughingstock   310 **changing piece** fickle
wench   313 **bandy** contend, bicker   314 **ruffle** brawl   317 **Phoebe** Diana,
goddess of the moon

And will create thee Empress of Rome.
Speak, Queen of Goths, dost thou applaud my
    choice?
And here I swear by all the Roman gods,
Sith priest and holy water are so near,
And tapers burn so bright, and everything   325
In readiness for Hymenaeus stand,
I will not re-salute the streets of Rome,
Or climb my palace, till from forth this place
I lead espoused my bride along with me.

TAMORA And here in sight of heaven to Rome
        I swear,
If Saturnine advance the Queen of Goths,   330
She will a handmaid be to his desires,
A loving nurse, a mother to his youth.

SATURNINUS Ascend, fair Queen, Pantheon. Lords,
        accompany
Your noble emperor and his lovely bride,   335
Sent by the heavens for Prince Saturnine,
Whose wisdom hath her fortune conquerèd.
There shall we consummate our spousal rites.
                        Exeunt omnes [except Titus].

TITUS I am not bid to wait upon this bride.
Titus, when wert thou wont to walk alone,   340
Dishonored thus and challengèd of wrongs?

        *Enter Marcus and Titus' sons [Lucius, Quintus,
                and Martius].*

MARCUS O Titus, see, O, see, what thou hast done!
In a bad quarrel slain a virtuous son.

TITUS No, foolish tribune, no; no son of mine,
Nor thou, not these, confederates in the deed   345
That hath dishonored all our family,
Unworthy brother, and unworthy sons!

326 **Hymenaeus** god of marriage 338 s.d. **omnes** all (Latin) 339 **bid**
asked 341 **challengèd** accused

LUCIUS But let us give him burial as becomes;
Give Mutius burial with our brethren.

350 TITUS Traitors, away! He rests not in this tomb:
This monument five hundred years hath stood,
Which I have sumptuously re-edified:
Here none but soldiers and Rome's servitors
Repose in fame; none basely slain in brawls.
355 Bury him where you can, he comes not here.

MARCUS My lord, this is impiety in you.
My nephew Mutius' deeds do plead for him;
He must be buried with his brethren.

Titus' two sons speak:

[QUINTUS, MARTIUS] And shall, or him we will
accompany.

360 TITUS And shall? What villain was it spake that word?

Titus' son speaks.

[QUINTUS.] He that would vouch it in any place but
here.

TITUS What, would you bury him in my despite?

MARCUS No, noble Titus, but entreat of thee
To pardon Mutius and to bury him.

365 TITUS Marcus, even thou hast stroke upon my crest,
And with these boys mine honor thou hast wounded.
My foes I do repute you every one,
So trouble me no more, but get you gone.

MARTIUS He is not with himself; let us withdraw.

370 QUINTUS Not I, till Mutius' bones be buried.
                       The brother and the sons kneel.

MARCUS Brother, for in that name doth nature plead—

QUINTUS Father, and in that name doth nature speak—

348 **becomes** is fitting   352 **re-edified** rebuilt   362 **in my despite** in spite of
me   367 **repute** consider

TITUS Speak thou no more, if all the rest will speed.

MARCUS Renownèd Titus, more than half my soul——

LUCIUS Dear father, soul and substance of us all—— 375

MARCUS Suffer thy brother Marcus to inter
His noble nephew here in virtue's nest,
That died in honor and Lavinia's cause.
Thou art a Roman, be not barbarous:
The Greeks upon advice did bury Ajax 380
That slew himself; and wise Laertes' son
Did graciously plead for his funerals:
Let not young Mutius then, that was thy joy,
Be barred his entrance here.

TITUS   Rise, Marcus, rise.
The dismal'st day is this that e'er I saw, 385
To be dishonored by my sons in Rome!
Well, bury him, and bury me the next.

                              They put him in the tomb.

LUCIUS There lie thy bones, sweet Mutius, with thy
    friends,
Till we with trophies do adorn thy tomb.

                They all kneel and say:

[ALL] No man shed tears for noble Mutius,
He lives in fame that died in virtue's cause. 390

MARCUS My lord, to step out of these dreary dumps,
How comes it that the subtle Queen of Goths
Is of a sudden thus advanced in Rome?

TITUS I know not, Marcus, but I know it is; 395
(Whether by device or no, the heavens can tell.)
Is she not then beholding to the man
That brought her for this high good turn so far?
Yes, and will nobly him remunerate.

373 **if all the rest will speed** if the rest is to go well (?) if the rest of you wish
to live (?) 376 **Suffer** allow 380 **advice** deliberation 380 **Ajax** (when Achilles'
arms were given to Odysseus, Ajax in a fury stabbed himself) 381 **Laertes' son**
Odysseus 392 **dumps** blues, melancholy state 396 **Whether** (probably pronounced "where") 396 **device** plot 397 **beholding** beholden, indebted

Enter the Emperor, Tamora and her two sons, with the Moor at one door. Enter at the other door Bassianus and Lavinia, with others.

400 SATURNINUS So Bassianus, you have played your
      prize: God give you joy, sir, of your gallant bride!

BASSIANUS And you of yours, my lord! I say no more,
      Nor wish no less, and so I take my leave.

SATURNINUS Traitor, if Rome have law, or we have
      power,
405   Thou and thy faction shall repent this rape.

BASSIANUS Rape, call you it, my lord, to seize my own,
      My true-betrothèd love, and now my wife?
      But let the laws of Rome determine all;
      Meanwhile am I possessed of that is mine.

410 SATURNINUS 'Tis good, sir; you are very short with us,
      But if we live we'll be as sharp with you.

BASSIANUS My lord, what I have done, as best I may
      Answer I must, and shall do with my life.
      Only thus much I give your grace to know—
415   By all the duties that I owe to Rome,
      This noble gentleman, Lord Titus here,
      Is in opinion and in honor wronged,
      That, in the rescue of Lavinia,
      With his own hand did slay his youngest son,
420   In zeal to you, and highly moved to wrath
      To be controlled in that he frankly gave.
      Receive him then to favor, Saturnine,
      That hath expressed himself in all his deeds
      A father and a friend to thee and Rome.

425 TITUS Prince Bassianus, leave to plead my deeds;
      'Tis thou and those that have dishonored me.
      Rome and the righteous heavens be my judge,
      How I have loved and honored Saturnine!

---

400 **played your prize** won your contest   417 **opinion** reputation   421 **controlled** opposed   421 **frankly** generously   425 **leave to plead** cease pleading

TAMORA My worthy lord, if ever Tamora
  Were gracious in those princely eyes of thine, 430
  Then hear me speak indifferently for all;
  And at my suit, sweet, pardon what is past.

SATURNINUS What, madam! Be dishonored openly,
  And basely put it up without revenge?

TAMORA Not so, my lord, the gods of Rome forfend 435
  I should be author to dishonor you!
  But on mine honor dare I undertake
  For good Lord Titus' innocence in all,
  Whose fury not dissembled speaks his griefs:
  Then at my suit look graciously on him; 440
  Lose not so noble a friend on vain suppose,
  Nor with sour looks afflict his gentle heart.
  [Aside] My lord, be ruled by me, be won at last,
  Dissemble all your griefs and discontents—
  You are but newly planted in your throne— 445
  Lest then the people, and patricians too,
  Upon a just survey, take Titus' part,
  And so supplant you for ingratitude,
  Which Rome reputes to be a heinous sin.
  Yield at entreats: and then let me alone. 450
  I'll find a day to massacre them all,
  And race their faction and their family,
  The cruel father and his traitorous sons,
  To whom I suèd for my dear son's life;
  And make them know what 'tis to let a queen 455
  Kneel in the streets and beg for grace in vain.
  [Aloud] Come, come, sweet Emperor—come,
    Andronicus—
  Take up this good old man, and cheer the heart
  That dies in tempest of thy angry frown.

SATURNINUS Rise, Titus, rise, my empress hath
    prevailed.
460

431 **indifferently** impartially 434 **put it up** (the figure is of putting up, or
sheathing, a sword) 435 **forfend** forbid 436 **author** agent 437 **undertake**
assert 441 **vain suppose** empty supposition 450 **at entreats** to entreaties
450 **let me alone** i.e., leave it to me 452 **race** root out

TITUS I thank your Majesty, and her, my lord.
These words, these looks, infuse new life in me.

TAMORA Titus, I am incorporate in Rome,
A Roman now adopted happily,
465 And must advise the Emperor for his good.
This day all quarrels die, Andronicus.
And let it be mine honor, good my lord,
That I have reconciled your friends and you.
For you, Prince Bassianus, I have passed
470 My word and promise to the Emperor
That you will be more mild and tractable.
And fear not, lords, and you, Lavinia;
By my advice, all humbled on your knees,
You shall ask pardon of his Majesty.

[LUCIUS.] We do, and vow to heaven, and to his
475 highness,
That what we did was mildly as we might,
Tend'ring our sister's honor and our own.

MARCUS That on mine honor here do I protest.

SATURNINUS Away, and talk not, trouble us no more.

TAMORA Nay, nay, sweet Emperor, we must all be
480 friends.
The tribune and his nephews kneel for grace.
I will not be denied. Sweet heart, look back.

SATURNINUS Marcus, for thy sake, and thy brother's
here,
And at my lovely Tamora's entreats,
485 I do remit these young men's heinous faults.
Stand up.
Lavinia, though you left me like a churl,
I found a friend, and sure as death I swore
I would not part a bachelor from the priest.
490 Come, if the Emperor's court can feast two brides,
You are my guest, Lavinia, and your friends.

476 mildly as we might as mild as we might do   477 Tend'ring having regard
for   489 part depart

20

This day shall be a love-day, Tamora.

TITUS Tomorrow, and it please your Majesty
To hunt the panther and the hart with me,
With horn and hound we'll give your Grace bonjour.   495

SATURNINUS Be it so, Titus, and gramercy too.

Exeunt.

Sound trumpets. Manet [Aaron the] Moor.

492 **love-day** day appointed to settle disputes (with a pun on day for love)
493 **and if**   495 **bonjour** good morning (French)   496 **gramercy** thanks
496 s.d. **Manet** remains (Latin. Clearly this and the next scene are continuous; the Folio's incorrect division into acts is retained merely to facilitate reference)

[ACT II]

Scene I. *Rome. Before the palace.*
Aaron alone.]

AARON Now climbeth Tamora Olympus' top,
Safe out of fortune's shot, and sits aloft,
Secure of thunder's crack or lightning flash,
Advanced above pale envy's threat'ning reach.
As when the golden sun salutes the morn,   5
And having gilt the ocean with his beams,
Gallops the zodiac in his glistering coach,
And overlooks the highest-peering hills;
So Tamora:
Upon her wit doth earthly honor wait,   10
And virtue stoops and trembles at her frown.
Then, Aaron, arm thy heart, and fit thy thoughts
To mount aloft with thy imperial mistress,
And mount her pitch, whom thou in triumph long
Hast prisoner held, fettered in amorous chains,   15
And faster bound to Aaron's charming eyes
Than is Prometheus tied to Caucasus.
Away with slavish weeds and servile thoughts!
I will be bright and shine in pearl and gold
To wait upon this new-made empress.   20
To wait, said I? To wanton with this queen,

II.i.1 **Olympus** Mount Olympus (reputed home of the gods) 3 **of** from 4 **envy's** hate's 7 **Gallops** gallops through 8 **overlooks** looks down upon 14 **mount her pitch** rise to the highest point of her flight (a term from falconry) 16 **charming** spellbinding 17 **Prometheus** a Titan fettered to a rock in the Caucasus because he stole fire from heaven 18 **weeds** apparel

22

This goddess, this Semiramis, this nymph,
This siren, that will charm Rome's Saturnine
And see his shipwrack and his commonweal's.
Hollo! What storm is this?   25

Enter Chiron and Demetrius, braving.

DEMETRIUS Chiron, thy years wants wit, thy wits
    wants edge,
And manners, to intrude where I am graced,
And may for aught thou knowest affected be.

CHIRON Demetrius, thou dost overween in all,
And so in this, to bear me down with braves.   30
'Tis not the difference of a year or two
Makes me less gracious, or thee more fortunate;
I am as able and as fit as thou
To serve, and to deserve my mistress' grace;
And that my sword upon thee shall approve,   35
And plead my passions for Lavinia's love.

AARON Clubs, clubs! These lovers will not keep the
    peace.

DEMETRIUS Why, boy, although our mother,
    unadvised,
Gave you a dancing-rapier by your side,
Are you so desperate grown, to threat your friends?   40
Go to; have your lath glued within your sheath,
Till you know better how to handle it.

CHIRON Meanwhile, sir, with the little skill I have,
Full well shalt thou perceive how much I dare.
                                                    They draw.

DEMETRIUS Ay, boy, grow ye so brave?

AARON   Why, how now, lords!   45

22 **Semiramis** legendary Assyrian queen, noted for her lust and beauty
25 s.d. **braving** challenging 26 **wants** (the ending -s is frequently found with a
plural subject) 27 **graced** favored 28 **affected** loved 29 **overween** arrogantly
presume 30 **braves** threats 32 **gracious** acceptable 35 **approve** prove
37 **Clubs, clubs** (the cry raised to call the watch to separate brawlers in
London) 38 **unadvised** unwisely 39 **dancing-rapier** ornamental light
sword 41 **lath** wooden (stage) sword

So near the Emperor's palace dare ye draw,
And maintain such a quarrel openly?
Full well I wot the ground of all this grudge.
I would not for a million of gold
50   The cause were known to them it most concerns,
Nor would your noble mother for much more
Be so dishonored in the court of Rome.
For shame, put up.

DEMETRIUS   Not I, till I have sheathed
My rapier in his bosom, and withal
55   Thrust those reproachful speeches down his throat,
That he hath breathed in my dishonor here.

CHIRON For that I am prepared and full resolved,
Foul-spoken coward, that thund'rest with thy tongue
And with thy weapon nothing dar'st perform.

60 AARON Away, I say!
Now, by the gods that warlike Goths adore,
This petty brabble will undo us all.
Why, lords, and think you not how dangerous
It is to jet upon a prince's right?
65   What, is Lavinia then become so loose,
Or Bassianus so degenerate,
That for her love such quarrels may be broached
Without controlment, justice, or revenge?
Young lords, beware! And should the Empress know
70   This discord's ground, the music would not please.

CHIRON I care not, I, knew she and all the world:
I love Lavinia more than all the world.

DEMETRIUS Youngling, learn thou to make some
         meaner choice.
Lavinia is thine elder brother's hope.

75 AARON Why, are ye mad? Or know ye not, in Rome
How furious and impatient they be,

48 wot know 53 put up sheathe your weapons 62 brabble brawl 64 jet
encroach 70 ground reason (with a pun on the musical meaning: bass to a
descant) 73 meaner lower

And cannot brook competitors in love?
I tell you, lords, you do but plot your deaths
By this device.

CHIRON   Aaron, a thousand deaths
Would I propose to achieve her whom I love.   80

AARON To achieve her how?

DEMETRIUS   Why makes thou it so strange?
She is a woman, therefore may be wooed;
She is a woman, therefore may be won;
She is Lavinia, therefore must be loved.
What, man! More water glideth by the mill   85
Than wots the miller of, and easy it is
Of a cut loaf to steal a shive, we know:
Though Bassianus be the Emperor's brother,
Better than he have worn Vulcan's badge.

AARON [Aside] Ay, and as good as Saturninus may.   90

DEMETRIUS Then why should he despair that knows to
    court it
With words, fair looks, and liberality?
What, hast not thou full often stroke a doe,
And borne her cleanly by the keeper's nose?

AARON Why then, it seems, some certain snatch or so   95
Would serve your turns.

CHIRON   Ay, so the turn were served.

DEMETRIUS Aaron, thou hast hit it.

AARON   Would you had hit it too,
Then should not we be tired with this ado.
Why, hark ye, hark ye! And are you such fools
To square for this? Would it offend you then   100
That both should speed?

---

80 **propose** be willing to meet   81 **Why makes thou it so strange** why do you
seem surprised   87 **shive** slice   89 **Vulcan's badge** i.e., the horns of cuckoldry
(Vulcan's wife, Venus, deceived him with Mars)   95 **snatch** catch (the likelihood
that there is also a sexual meaning here is increased by **turns** in the next line, a
word often denoting sexual acts)   100 **square** quarrel   101 **speed** prosper

CHIRON   Faith, not me.

DEMETRIUS Nor me, so I were one.

AARON For shame, be friends, and join for that you jar.
       'Tis policy and stratagem must do
105   That you affect, and so must you resolve,
       That what you cannot as you would achieve,
       You must perforce accomplish as you may.
       Take this of me, Lucrece was not more chaste
       Than this Lavinia, Bassianus' love.
110   A speedier course than ling'ring languishment
       Must we pursue, and I have found the path.
       My lords, a solemn hunting is in hand.
       There will the lovely Roman ladies troop:
       The forest walks are wide and spacious,
115   And many unfrequented plots there are
       Fitted by kind for rape and villainy.
       Single you thither then this dainty doe,
       And strike her home by force, if not by words:
       This way, or not at all, stand you in hope.
120   Come, come, our empress, with her sacred wit
       To villainy and vengeance consecrate,
       Will we acquaint withal what we intend,
       And she shall file our engines with advice,
       That will not suffer you to square yourselves,
125   But to your wishes' height advance you both.
       The Emperor's court is like the House of Fame,
       The palace full of tongues, of eyes, and ears:
       The woods are ruthless, dreadful, deaf, and dull;
       There speak, and strike, brave boys, and take your
            turns,
130   There serve your lust shadowed from heaven's eye,
       And revel in Lavinia's treasury.

103 for that you jar to get what you quarrel over   104 policy cunning   105 affect
desire   107 perforce necessarily   108 Lucrece Roman lady noted for her
chastity; she killed herself when Sextus Tarquinius raped her   112 solemn
ceremonious   115 unfrequented plots unvisited areas   116 kind nature
117 Single single out (a hunting term)   123 file our engines sharpen our
minds   126 House of Fame (Ovid and Chaucer have notable poems on it;
Fame = Rumor, and the House of Fame is full of gossip)   128 ruthless pitiless

26

CHIRON Thy counsel, lad, smells of no cowardice.

DEMETRIUS *Sit fas aut nefas*, till I find the stream
　To cool this heat, a charm to calm these fits,
　Per Stygia, per manes vehor.　　　　　*Exeunt*. 135

[Scene II. *A forest near Rome*.]

*Enter Titus Andronicus and his three sons [and Marcus],
making a noise with hounds and horns.*

TITUS The hunt is up, the morn is bright and gray,
　The fields are fragrant, and the woods are green:
　Uncouple here, and let us make a bay,
　And wake the Emperor and his lovely bride,
　And rouse the Prince, and ring a hunter's peal,　　5
　That all the court may echo with the noise.
　Sons, let it be your charge, as it is ours,
　To atttend the Emperor's person carefully:
　I have been troubled in my sleep this night,
　But dawning day new comfort hath inspired.　　10

*Here a cry of hounds, and wind horns in a peal: then
enter Saturninus, Tamora, Bassianus, Lavinia, Chiron,
Demetrius, and their attendants.*

Many good morrows to your Majesty!
Madam, to you as many and as good!
I promisèd your Grace a hunter's peal.

SATURNINUS And you have rung it lustily, my lords,
　Somewhat too early for new-married ladies.　　15

BASSIANUS Lavinia, how say you?

133 Sit fas aut nefas be it right or wrong (Latin)　135 Per Stygia, per manes
vehor I am carried through Stygian (infernal) regions, through ghosts (Latin,
derived from Seneca's *Hippolytus*, line 1177) II.ii.1 gray sky blue (?)
3 Uncouple unleash the hounds　3 make a bay keep up the cry of the hounds
10 s.d. cry deep barking

LAVINIA   I say, no;
I have been broad awake two hours and more.

SATURNINUS Come on then, horse and chariots let us
    have,
And to our sport. [*To Tamora*] Madam, now shall
    ye see
Our Roman hunting.

20 MARCUS   I have dogs, my lord,
Will rouse the proudest panther in the chase,
And climb the highest promontory top.

TITUS And I have horse will follow where the game
Makes way and runs like swallows o'er the plain.

DEMETRIUS Chiron, we hunt not, we, with horse nor
25   hound,
But hope to pluck a dainty doe to ground. *Exeunt.*

[Scene III. *The forest*.]

Enter Aaron alone, [with a bag of gold].

AARON He that had wit would think that I had none,
To bury so much gold under a tree
And never after to inherit it.
Let him that thinks of me so abjectly
5 Know that this gold must coin a stratagem,
Which, cunningly effected, will beget
A very excellent piece of villainy.
And so repose, sweet gold, for their unrest,
That have their alms out of the Empress' chest.
                                    [*Hides the gold.*]

Enter Tamora alone to the Moor.

10 TAMORA My lovely Aaron, wherefore look'st thou sad

II.iii.3 inherit possess   4 abjectly contemptuously

28

When every thing doth make a gleeful boast?
The birds chaunt melody on every bush,
The snakes lies rollèd in the cheerful sun,
The green leaves quiver with the cooling wind,
And make a checkered shadow on the ground: 15
Under their sweet shade, Aaron, let us sit,
And whilst the babbling echo mocks the hounds,
Replying shrilly to the well-tuned horns
As if a double hunt were heard at once,
Let us sit down and mark their yellowing noise: 20
And after conflict such as was supposed
The wandering prince and Dido once enjoyed,
When with a happy storm they were surprised
And curtained with a counsel-keeping cave,
We may, each wreathèd in the other's arms,   25
(Our pastimes done) possess a golden slumber,
Whiles hounds and horns and sweet melodious birds
Be unto us as is a nurse's song
Of lullaby to bring her babe asleep.

AARON Madam, though Venus govern your desires,   30
Saturn is dominator over mine:
What signifies my deadly-standing eye,
My silence and my cloudy melancholy,
My fleece of woolly hair that now uncurls
Even as an adder when she doth unroll   35
To do some fatal execution?
No, madam, these are no venereal signs:
Vengeance is in my heart, death in my hand,
Blood and revenge are hammering in my head.
Hark, Tamora, the empress of my soul,   40
Which never hopes more heaven than rests in thee,
This is the day of doom for Bassianus:
His Philomel must lose her tongue today,

11 boast display   20 yellowing loudly calling   22 The wandering prince and
Dido Aeneas and the Queen of Carthage (see Virgil's *Aeneid* IV)   31 Saturn is
dominator the planet Saturn (whose influence allegedly caused sluggishness)
dominates   32 deadly-standing fixed in a deathlike stare (?)   37 venereal
erotic   43 Philomel (Philomela was ravished by Tereus, who then cut out her
tongue; later she communicated her plight by weaving the story into a tapestry.
See II.iv.26-27, 38-39; IV.i.47-48; V.ii.195-6)

Thy sons make pillage of her chastity,
45 And wash their hands in Bassianus' blood.
Seest thou this letter? Take it up, I pray thee,
And give the King this fatal-plotted scroll.
Now question me no more; we are espied.
Here comes a parcel of our hopeful booty,
50 Which dreads not yet their lives' destruction.

Enter Bassianus and Lavinia.

TAMORA Ah, my sweet Moor, sweeter to me than life!

AARON No more, great Empress, Bassianus comes.
Be cross with him, and I'll go fetch thy sons
To back thy quarrels whatso'er they be.   [*Exit.*]

55 BASSIANUS Who have we here? Rome's royal Empress,
Unfurnished of her well-beseeming troop?
Or is it Dian, habited like her,
Who hath abandonèd her holy groves
To see the general hunting in this forest?

60 TAMORA Saucy controller of my private steps!
Had I the power that some say Dian had,
Thy temples should be planted presently
With horns, as was Actaeon's, and the hounds
Should drive upon thy new-transformèd limbs,
65 Unmannerly intruder as thou art!

LAVINIA Under your patience, gentle Empress,
'Tis thought you have a goodly gift in horning,
And to be doubted that your Moor and you
Are singled forth to try experiments:
70 Jove shield your husband from his hounds today!
'Tis pity they should take him for a stag.

BASSIANUS Believe me, Queen, your swart Cimmerian

49 **parcel of our hopeful booty** part of the victims we hope for   56 **Unfurnished of** unaccompanied by   57 **habited** dressed   60 **controller** critic
62 **presently** immediately   63 **Actaeon** legendary hunter who spied on Diana bathing; she transformed him into a stag and his own hounds killed him
67 **horning** (an unfaithful wife was said to give her husband horns)   68 **doubted** suspected   72 **Cimmerian** dweller in darkness

Doth make your honor of his body's hue,
Spotted, detested, and abominable.
Why are you sequest'rèd from all your train,   75
Dismounted from your snow-white goodly steed,
And wand'red hither to an obscure plot,
Accompanied but with a barbarous Moor,
If foul desire had not conducted you?

LAVINIA And, being intercepted in your sport,   80
Great reason that my noble lord be rated
For sauciness. I pray you, let us hence,
And let her joy her raven-colored love;
This valley fits the purpose passing well.

BASSIANUS The King my brother shall have notice of
this.   85

LAVINIA Ay, for these slips have made him noted long.
Good king, to be so mightily abused!

TAMORA Why, I have patience to endure all this.

Enter Chiron and Demetrius.

DEMETRIUS How now, dear sovereign, and our
gracious mother,
Why doth your Highness look so pale and wan?   90

TAMORA Have I not reason, think you, to look pale?
These two have ticed me hither to this place,
A barren detested vale, you see it is;
The trees, though summer, yet forlorn and lean,
Overcome with moss and baleful mistletoe: 95
Here never shines the sun; here nothing breeds,
Unless the nightly owl or fatal raven:
And when they showed me this abhorrèd pit,
They told me, here, at dead time of the night
A thousand fiends, a thousand hissing snakes,   100
Ten thousand swelling toads, as many urchins,
Would make such fearful and confusèd cries,

74 **Spotted** infected 81 **rated** berated, rebuked 83 **joy** enjoy 85 **notice**
(monosyllabic, pronounced "notes") 86 **noted** notorious 92 **ticed**
enticed 101 **urchins** hedgehogs

As any mortal body hearing it
Should straight fall mad, or else die suddenly.
105 No sooner had they told this hellish tale,
But straight they told me they would bind me here
Unto the body of a dismal yew,
And leave me to this miserable death.
And then they called me foul adulteress,
110 Lascivious Goth, and all the bitterest terms
That ever ear did hear to such effect.
And, had you not by wondrous fortune come,
This vengeance on me had they executed:
Revenge it, as you love your mother's life,
115 Or be ye not henceforth called my children.

DEMETRIUS This is a witness that I am thy son.
                                        Stab[s] him.

CHIRON And this for me, struck home to show my
   strength.   [*Stabs Bassianus.*]

LAVINIA Ay come, Semiramis, nay, barbarous Tamora!
   For no name fits thy nature but thy own!

TAMORA Give me the poniard! You shall know, my
120   boys,
   Your mother's hand shall right your mother's
      wrong.

DEMETRIUS Stay, madam; here is more belongs to her.
   First thrash the corn, then after burn the straw.
   This minion stood upon her chastity,
125   Upon her nuptial vow, her loyalty,
   And with that painted hope she braves your
      mightiness:
   And shall she carry this unto her grave?

CHIRON And if she do, I would I were an eunuch.
   Drag hence her husband to some secret hole,
   And make his dead trunk pillow to our lust.   130

---

110 Goth (possibly a pun on "goat," an animal believed to be lascivious)
124 minion stood upon hussy made a fuss about   126 painted specious, unreal

TAMORA But when ye have the honey we desire,
  Let not this wasp outlive us both to sting.

CHIRON I warrant you, madam, we will make that sure.
  Come, mistress, now perforce we will enjoy
  That nice-preservèd honesty of yours.   135

LAVINIA O Tamora! Thou bearest a woman's face——

TAMORA I will not hear her speak; away with her.

LAVINIA Sweet lords, entreat her hear me but a word.

DEMETRIUS Listen, fair madam, let it be your glory
  To see her tears, but be your heart to them   140
  As unrelenting flint to drops of rain.

LAVINIA When did the tiger's young ones teach the
    dam?
  O, do not learn her wrath; she taught it thee.
  The milk thou suck'st from her did turn to marble;
  Even at thy teat thou hadst thy tyranny.   145
  Yet every mother breeds not sons alike,
  [*To Chiron*] Do thou entreat her show a woman's
    pity.

CHIRON What! Wouldst thou have me prove myself a
  bastard?

LAVINIA 'Tis true; the raven doth not hatch a lark:
  Yet have I heard—O could I find it now!—   150
  The lion, moved with pity, did endure
  To have his princely paws pared all away.
  Some say that ravens foster forlorn children,
  The whilst their own birds famish in their nests:
  O, be to me, though thy hard heart say no,   155
  Nothing so kind but something pitiful!

TAMORA I know not what it means; away with her!

---

135 **nice-preservèd honesty** fastidiously guarded chastity 142 **dam**
mother 143 **learn** teach 156 **Nothing so kind but something pitiful** i.e.,
not so kind as the raven, but somewhat pitying

LAVINIA O, let me teach thee for my father's sake,
That gave thee life when well he might have slain
thee.
160   Be not obdurate, open thy deaf ears.

TAMORA Hadst thou in person ne'er offended me,
Even for his sake am I pitiless.
Remember, boys, I poured forth tears in vain
To save your brother from the sacrifice,
165   But fierce Andronicus would not relent.
Therefore away with her, and use her as you will;
The worse to her, the better loved of me.

LAVINIA O Tamora, be called a gentle queen,
And with thine own hands kill me in this place!
170   For 'tis not life that I have begged so long;
Poor I was slain when Bassianus died.

TAMORA What begg'st thou then? Fond woman, let me
go.

LAVINIA 'Tis present death I beg, and one thing more
That womanhood denies my tongue to tell.
175   O, keep me from their worse than killing lust,
And tumble me into some loathsome pit,
Where never man's eye may behold my body.
Do this, and be a charitable murderer.

TAMORA So should I rob my sweet sons of their fee.
180   No, let them satisfy their lust on thee.

DEMETRIUS Away! For thou hast stayed us here too
long.

LAVINIA No grace? No womanhood? Ah beastly
creature!
The blot and enemy to our general name!
Confusion fall——

CHIRON Nay, then I'll stop your mouth. Bring thou
185   her husband.

172 **Fond** foolish 174 **denies** forbids 183 **our general name** i.e.,
womankind 184 **Confusion** destruction

34

This is the hole where Aaron bid us hide him.
[*Demetrius throws the corpse into a pit and then covers it
with branches. Exeunt Demetrius and Chiron, dragging
Lavinia.*]

TAMORA Farewell, my sons, see that you make her
    sure.
    Ne'er let my heart know merry cheer indeed
    Till all the Andronici be made away.
    Now will I hence to seek my lovely Moor,   190
    And let my spleenful sons this trull deflower. [*Exit.*]

    *Enter Aaron with two of Titus' sons [Quintus and
                Martius].*

[AARON] Come on, my lords, the better foot before!
    Straight will I bring you to the loathsome pit
    Where I espied the panther fast asleep.

QUINTUS My sight is very dull, whate'er it bodes.   195

MARTIUS And mine, I promise you. Were it not for
    shame,
    Well could I leave our sport to sleep awhile.
                            [*He falls into the pit.*]

QUINTUS What, art thou fallen? What subtle hole is
    this,
    Whose mouth is covered with rude-growing briers,
    Upon whose leaves are drops of new-shed blood   200
    As fresh as morning dew distilled on flowers?
    A very fatal place it seems to me.
    Speak, brother, hast thou hurt thee with the fall?

MARTIUS O, brother, with the dismal'st object hurt
    That ever eye with sight made heart lament.   205

AARON [*Aside*] Now will I fetch the King to find them
    here,
    That he thereby may have a likely guess
    How these were they that made away his brother.
                                  Exit.

189 **made away** killed   191 **spleenful** lustful   191 **trull** strumpet

MARTIUS Why dost not comfort me and help me out
210   From this unhallowed and bloodstainèd hole?

QUINTUS I am surprisèd with an uncouth fear,
          A chilling sweat o'erruns my trembling joints;
          My heart suspects more than mine eye can see.

MARTIUS To prove thou hast a true-divining heart,
215   Aaron and thou look down into this den
          And see a fearful sight of blood and death.

QUINTUS Aaron is gone, and my compassionate heart
          Will not permit mine eyes once to behold
          The thing whereat it trembles by surmise.
220   O, tell me who it is, for ne'er till now
          Was I a child to fear I know not what.

MARTIUS Lord Bassianus lies berayed in blood,
          All on a heap, like to a slaughtered lamb,
          In this detested, dark, blood-drinking pit.

225 QUINTUS If it be dark, how dost thou know 'tis he?

MARTIUS Upon his bloody finger he doth wear
          A precious ring that lightens all this hole,
          Which, like a taper in some monument,
          Doth shine upon the dead man's earthy cheeks,
230   And shows the ragged entrails of this pit:
          So pale did shine the moon on Pyramus,
          When he by night lay bathed in maiden blood.
          O brother, help me with thy fainting hand—
          If fear hath made thee faint, as me it hath—
235   Out of this fell devouring receptacle,
          As hateful as Cocytus' misty mouth.

QUINTUS Reach me thy hand, that I may help thee out;
          Or, wanting strength to do thee so much good,
          I may be plucked into the swallowing womb
240   Of this deep pit, poor Bassianus' grave.
          I have no strength to pluck thee to the brink.

211 **surprisèd** dumbfounded   211 **uncouth** strange   222 **berayed** defiled
230 **ragged entrails** rugged interior   235 **fell** savage   236 **Cocytus** river in
Hades   238 **wanting** lacking

MARTIUS Nor I no strength to climb without thy help.

QUINTUS Thy hand once more; I will not loose again
Till thou art here aloft or I below:
Thou canst not come to me; I come to thee.   245

[Falls in.]

Enter the Emperor and Aaron the Moor.

SATURNINUS Along with me! I'll see what hole is here,
And what he is that now is leaped into it.
Say, who are thou, that lately didst descend
Into this gaping hollow of the earth?

MARTIUS The unhappy sons of old Andronicus,   250
Brought hither in a most unlucky hour,
To find thy brother Bassianus dead.

SATURNINUS My brother dead! I know thou dost but
jest:
He and his lady both are at the lodge,
Upon the north side of this pleasant chase;   255
'Tis not an hour since I left them there.

MARTIUS We know not where you left them all alive,
But, out alas! Here have we found him dead.

Enter Tamora, Andronicus, and Lucius.

TAMORA Where is my lord the King?

SATURNINUS Here, Tamora, though grieved with
killing grief.   260

TAMORA Where is thy brother, Bassianus?

SATURNINUS Now to the bottom dost thou search my
wound;
Poor Bassianus here lies murderèd.

TAMORA Then all too late I bring this fatal writ,
The complot of this timeless tragedy;   265
And wonder greatly that man's face can fold

262 **search** probe   265 **complot** plot   265 **timeless** untimely   266 **fold** hide
(in the creases of a hypocritical smile)

37

In pleasing smiles such murderous tyranny.
> *She giveth Saturnine a letter.*

SATURNINUS (*Reads the letter.*) "And if we miss to meet
    him handsomely—
    Sweet huntsman, Bassianus 'tis we mean—
270   Do thou so much as dig the grave for him.
    Thou know'st our meaning. Look for thy reward
    Among the nettles at the elder tree
    Which overshades the mouth of that same pit
    Where we decreed to bury Bassianus.
275   Do this and purchase us thy lasting friends."
    O, Tamora! Was ever heard the like?
    This is the pit, and this the elder tree.
    Look, sirs, if you can find the huntsman out
    That should have murdered Bassianus here.

280 AARON My gracious lord, here is the bag of gold.

SATURNINUS [*To Titus*] Two of thy whelps, fell curs of
    bloody kind,
    Have here bereft my brother of his life.
    Sirs, drag them from the pit unto the prison,
    There let them bide until we have devised
285   Some never-heard-of torturing pain for them.

TAMORA What, are they in this pit? O wondrous thing!
    How easily murder is discoverèd!

TITUS High Emperor, upon my feeble knee
    I beg this boon, with tears not lightly shed,
290   That this fell fault of my accursèd sons,
    Accursèd, if the faults be proved in them——

SATURNINUS If it be proved! You see, it is apparent.
    Who found this letter? Tamora, was it you?

TAMORA Andronicus himself did take it up.

295 TITUS I did, my lord, yet let me be their bail,
    For by my father's reverend tomb I vow
    They shall be ready at your Highness' will

268 And if if 268 handsomely handily 279 should was to 281 fell
savage 281 kind nature 292 apparent obvious

To answer their suspicion with their lives.

SATURNINUS Thou shalt not bail them; see thou follow
    me.
    Some bring the murdered body, some the murderers.   300
    Let them not speak a word; the guilt is plain,
    For by my soul were there worse end than death,
    That end upon them should be executed.

TAMORA Andronicus, I will entreat the King.
    Fear not thy sons; they shall do well enough.   305

TITUS Come, Lucius, come, stay not to talk with them.
                          [*Exeunt.*]

[Scene IV. *The forest*.]

Enter the Empress' sons with Lavinia, her hands cut off,
and her tongue cut out, and ravished.

DEMETRIUS So, now go tell, and if thy tongue can
    speak,
    Who 'twas that cut thy tongue and ravished thee.

CHIRON Write down thy mind, bewray thy meaning so,
    And if thy stumps will let thee play the scribe.

DEMETRIUS See how with signs and tokens she can
    scrowl.   5

CHIRON Go home, call for sweet water, wash thy
    hands.

DEMETRIUS She hath no tongue to call nor hands to
    wash,
    And so let's leave her to her silent walks.

---

298 **their suspicion** i.e., the suspicion they are under   305 **Fear not** do not fear
for   II.iv.1 **and if** if (as in line 4)   3 **bewray** reveal   5 **scrowl** scrawl (with a
pun on "scroll"?)   6 **sweet** perfumed

CHIRON And 'twere my cause, I should go hang
      myself.

DEMETRIUS If thou hadst hands to help thee knit the
10   cord.   *Exeunt [Chiron and Demetrius].*

                Enter Marcus from hunting.

MARCUS Who is this? My niece, that flies away so fast!
      Cousin, a word, where is your husband?
      If I do dream, would all my wealth would wake me!
      If I do wake, some planet strike me down,
15   That I may slumber an eternal sleep!
      Speak, gentle niece, what stern ungentle hands
      Hath lopped and hewed and made thy body bare
      Of her two branches, those sweet ornaments,
      Whose circling shadows kings have sought to sleep
          in,
20   And might not gain so great a happiness
      As half thy love? Why dost not speak to me?
      Alas, a crimson river of warm blood,
      Like to a bubbling fountain stirred with wind,
      Doth rise and fall between thy rosèd lips,
25   Coming and going with thy honey breath.
      But, sure, some Tereus hath deflowered thee,
      And, lest thou shouldst detect him, cut thy tongue.
      Ah, now thou turn'st away thy face for shame!
      And, notwithstanding all this loss of blood,
30   As from a conduit with three issuing spouts,
      Yet do thy cheeks look red as Titan's face
      Blushing to be encount'red with a cloud.
      Shall I speak for thee? Shall I say 'tis so?
      O, that I knew thy heart, and knew the beast,
35   That I might rail at him to ease my mind!
      Sorrow concealèd, like an oven stopped,
      Doth burn the heart to cinders where it is.
      Fair Philomela, why she but lost her tongue,

9 **cause** case   12 **Cousin** (commonly used of any near relative other than a
parent, child, or sibling)   26 **Tereus** ravisher of Philomela (see note to
II.iii.43)   27 **detect** expose   31 **Titan's** the sun god's

And in a tedious sampler sewed her mind:
But lovely niece, that mean is cut from thee;   40
A craftier Tereus, cousin, hast thou met,
And he hath cut those pretty fingers off,
That could have better sewed than Philomel.
O, had the monster seen those lily hands
Tremble like aspen leaves upon a lute,   45
And make the silken strings delight to kiss them,
He would not then have touched them for his life!
Or, had he heard the heavenly harmony
Which that sweet tongue hath made,
He would have dropped his knife, and fell asleep   50
As Cerberus at the Thracian poet's feet.
Come, let us go and make thy father blind,
For such a sight will blind a father's eye.
One hour's storm will drown the fragrant meads;
What will whole months of tears thy father's eyes?   55
Do not draw back, for we will mourn with thee:
O, could our mourning ease thy misery!   *Exeunt*.

---

39 **tedious sampler** laboriously executed tapestry   51 **Cerberus** three-headed
dog who guarded the entrance to Hades; he was lulled by Orpheus, **the Thracian
poet**

[ACT III

Scene I. *Rome. A street.*]

*Enter the Judges and Senators with Titus' two sons
bound, passing on the stage to the place of execution,
and Titus going before, pleading.*

TITUS Hear me, grave fathers! Noble tribunes, stay!
For pity of mine age, whose youth was spent
In dangerous wars, whilst you securely slept;
For all my blood in Rome's great quarrel shed,
5 For all the frosty nights that I have watched,
And for these bitter tears, which now you see
Filling the agèd wrinkles in my cheeks,
Be pitiful to my condemnèd sons,
Whose souls are not corrupted as 'tis thought.
10 For two and twenty sons I never wept,
Because they died in honor's lofty bed;

Andronicus lieth down and the Judges pass by him.

For these, tribunes, in the dust I write
My heart's deep languor and my soul's sad tears:
Let my tears staunch the earth's dry appetite;
15 My sons' sweet blood will make it shame and blush.
O earth, I will befriend thee more with rain,
That shall distill from these two ancient ruins,
Than youthful April shall with all his show'rs:
In summer's drought I'll drop upon thee still,

III.i.11 s.d. **lieth down** i.e., prostrates himself 13 **languor** grief 14 **staunch**
satisfy, satiate 19 **still** continuously

In winter with warm tears I'll melt the snow,   20
And keep eternal springtime on thy face,
So thou refuse to drink my dear sons' blood.

Enter Lucius, with his weapon drawn.

O reverend tribunes! O gentle agèd men!
Unbind my sons, reverse the doom of death,
And let me say, that never wept before,   25
My tears are now prevailing orators.

LUCIUS O noble father, you lament in vain,
The tribunes hear you not, no man is by,
And you recount your sorrows to a stone.

TITUS Ah, Lucius, for thy brothers let me plead.   30
Grave tribunes, once more I entreat of you.

LUCIUS My gracious lord, no tribune hears you speak.

TITUS Why, 'tis no matter, man, if they did hear
They would not mark me, if they did mark
They would not pity me, yet plead I must,   35
And bootless unto them.
Therefore I tell my sorrows to the stones,
Who though they cannot answer my distress,
Yet in some sort they are better than the tribunes,
For that they will not intercept my tale: 40
When I do weep they humbly at my feet
Receive my tears and seem to weep with me;
And were they but attirèd in grave weeds,
Rome could afford no tribunes like to these.
A stone is soft as wax, tribunes more hard than stones: 45
A stone is silent and offendeth not,
And tribunes with their tongues doom men to death.
But wherefore stand'st thou with thy weapon drawn?

LUCIUS To rescue my two brothers from their death,
For which attempt the judges have pronounced   50
My everlasting doom of banishment.

22 So provided that   24 doom judgment   36 bootless in vain   40 intercept
interrupt   43 grave weeds solemn apparel

TITUS O happy man! They have befriended thee.
Why, foolish Lucius, dost thou not perceive
That Rome is but a wilderness of tigers?
55 Tigers must prey, and Rome affords no prey
But mine and mine. How happy art thou then,
From these devourers to be banishèd!
But who comes with our brother Marcus here?

Enter Marcus with Lavinia.

MARCUS Titus, prepare thy agèd eyes to weep,
60 Or if not so, thy noble heart to break.
I bring consuming sorrow to thine age.

TITUS Will it consume me? Let me see it then.

MARCUS This was thy daughter.

TITUS   Why, Marcus, so she is.

LUCIUS Ay me! This object kills me!

65 TITUS Faint-hearted boy, arise, and look upon her.
Speak, Lavinia, what accursèd hand
Hath made thee handless in thy father's sight?
What fool hath added water to the sea,
Or brought a faggot to bright-burning Troy?
70 My grief was at the height before thou cam'st,
And now like Nilus it disdaineth bounds.
Give me a sword, I'll chop off my hands too,
For they have fought for Rome, and all in vain;
And they have nursed this woe, in feeding life;
75 In bootless prayer have they been held up,
And they have served me to effectless use.
Now all the service I require of them
Is that the one will help to cut the other.
'Tis well, Lavinia, that thou hast no hands,
80 For hands to do Rome service is but vain.

LUCIUS Speak, gentle sister, who hath mart'red thee?

MARCUS O, that delightful engine of her thoughts,

64 **object** sight 71 **Nilus** the Nile 81 **mart'red** mutilated 82 **engine** instrument

44

That blabbed them with such pleasing eloquence,
Is torn from forth that pretty hollow cage,
Where like a sweet melodious bird it sung   85
Sweet varied notes, enchanting every ear!

LUCIUS O, say thou for her, who hath done this deed?

MARCUS O, thus I found her, straying in the park,
Seeking to hide herself, as doth the deer
That hath received some unrecuring wound.   90

TITUS It was my dear, and he that wounded her
Hath hurt me more than had he killed me dead:
For now I stand as one upon a rock,
Environed with a wilderness of sea,
Who marks the waxing tide grow wave by wave,   95
Expecting ever when some envious surge
Will in his brinish bowels swallow him.
This way to death my wretched sons are gone,
Here stands my other son, a banished man,
And here my brother weeping at my woes: 100
But that which gives my soul the greatest spurn
Is dear Lavinia, dearer than my soul.
Had I but seen thy picture in this plight,
It would have madded me: what shall I do
Now I behold thy lively body so?   105
Thou hast no hands to wipe away thy tears,
Nor tongue to tell me who hath mart'red thee.
Thy husband he is dead, and for his death
Thy brothers are condemned, and dead by this.
Look, Marcus! Ah, son Lucius, look on her!   110
When I did name her brothers, then fresh tears
Stood on her cheeks, as doth the honey-dew
Upon a gath'red lily almost withered.

MARCUS Perchance she weeps because they killed her
    husband,
Perchance because she knows them innocent.   115

---

83 blabbed freely spoke 90 unrecuring incurable 96 envious malicious
101 spurn thrust 105 lively living 109 by this by this time

45

TITUS If they did kill thy husband, then be joyful,
    Because the law hath ta'en revenge on them.
    No, no, they would not do so foul a deed;
    Witness the sorrow that their sister makes.
120   Gentle Lavinia, let me kiss thy lips,
    Or make some sign how I may do thee ease.
    Shall thy good uncle, and thy brother Lucius,
    And thou, and I, sit round about some fountain,
    Looking all downwards, to behold our cheeks
125   How they are stained, like meadows yet not dry
    With miry slime left on them by a flood?
    And in the fountain shall we gaze so long
    Till the fresh taste be taken from that clearness,
    And made a brine-pit with our bitter tears?
130   Or shall we cut away our hands, like thine?
    Or shall we bite our tongues, and in dumb shows
    Pass the remainder of our hateful days?
    What shall we do? Let us, that have our tongues,
    Plot some device of further misery,
135   To make us wondered at in time to come.

LUCIUS Sweet father, cease your tears, for at your grief
    See how my wretched sister sobs and weeps.

MARCUS Patience, dear niece. Good Titus, dry thine
    eyes.

TITUS Ah, Marcus, Marcus! Brother, well I wot
140   Thy napkin cannot drink a tear of mine,
    For thou, poor man, hast drowned it with thine own.

LUCIUS Ah, my Lavinia, I will wipe thy cheeks.

TITUS Mark, Marcus, mark! I understand her signs:
    Had she a tongue to speak, now would she say
145   That to her brother which I said to thee:
    His napkin, with his true tears all bewet,
    Can do no service on her sorrowful cheeks.
    O, what a sympathy of woe is this!

121 **do thee ease** bring you relief   128 **clearness** i.e., clear pool   131 **dumb shows** silent signs   140 **napkin** handkerchief   148 **sympathy** agreement

As far from help as Limbo is from bliss!

Enter Aaron the Moor alone.

AARON Titus Andronicus, my lord the Emperor   150
    Sends thee this word, that, if thou love thy sons,
    Let Marcus, Lucius, or thyself, old Titus,
    Or any one of you, chop off your hand
    And send it to the King: he for the same
    Will send thee hither both thy sons alive,   155
    And that shall be the ransom for their fault.

TITUS O, gracious Emperor! O, gentle Aaron!
    Did ever raven sing so like a lark,
    That gives sweet tidings of the sun's uprise?
    With all my heart, I'll send the Emperor my hand.   160
    Good Aaron, wilt thou help to chop it off?

LUCIUS Stay, father! For that noble hand of thine
    That hath thrown down so many enemies
    Shall not be sent; my hand will serve the turn.
    My youth can better spare my blood than you,   165
    And therefore mine shall save my brothers' lives.

MARCUS Which of your hands hath not defended Rome
    And reared aloft the bloody battle-ax,
    Writing destruction on the enemy's castle?
    O, none of both but are of high desert: 170
    My hand hath been but idle; let it serve
    To ransom my two nephews from their death,
    Then have I kept it to a worthy end.

AARON Nay, come, agree whose hand shall go along,
    For fear they die before their pardon come.   175

MARCUS My hand shall go.

LUCIUS   By heaven, it shall not go.

TITUS Sirs, strive no more; such with'red herbs as these
    Are meet for plucking up, and therefore mine.

LUCIUS Sweet father, if I shall be thought thy son,
    Let me redeem my brothers both from death.   180

178 meet fit

47

MARCUS And, for our father's sake and mother's care,
    Now let me show a brother's love to thee.

TITUS Agree between you; I will spare my hand.

LUCIUS Then I'll go fetch an ax.

185 MARCUS But I will use the ax.
                    Exeunt [Lucius and Marcus].

TITUS Come hither, Aaron. I'll deceive them both;
    Lend me thy hand, and I will give thee mine.

AARON [*Aside*] If that be called deceit, I will be honest,
    And never whilst I live deceive men so:
190   But I'll deceive you in another sort,
    And that you'll say, ere half an hour pass.
                    He cuts off Titus' hand.

Enter Lucius and Marcus again.

TITUS Now stay your strife, what shall be is
    dispatched.
    Good Aaron, give his Majesty my hand;
    Tell him it was a hand that warded him
195   From thousand dangers; bid him bury it;
    More hath it merited, that let it have.
    As for my sons, say I account of them
    As jewels purchased at an easy price,
    And yet dear too because I bought mine own.

200 AARON I go, Andronicus, and for thy hand
    Look by and by to have thy sons with thee.
    [*Aside*] Their heads, I mean. O, how this villainy
    Doth fat me with the very thoughts of it!
    Let fools do good, and fair men call for grace,
205   Aaron will have his soul black like his face.   *Exit.*

TITUS O, here I lift this one hand up to heaven,
    And bow this feeble ruin to the earth.
    If any power pities wretched tears,
    To that I call! [*To Lavinia*] What, wouldst thou kneel
    with me?

194 warded guarded   203 fat delight (literally: "nourish")

48

Do then, dear heart, for heaven shall hear our
   prayers,   210
Or with our sighs we'll breathe the welkin dim,
And stain the sun with fog, as sometime clouds
When they do hug him in their melting bosoms.

MARCUS O brother, speak with possibility,
  And do not break into these deep extremes.   215

TITUS Is not my sorrow deep, having no bottom?
  Then be my passions bottomless with them.

MARCUS But yet let reason govern thy lament.

TITUS If there were reason for these miseries,
  Then into limits could I bind my woes:
  When heaven doth weep, doth not the earth
    o'erflow?   220
  If the winds rage, doth not the sea wax mad,
  Threat'ning the welkin with his big-swoll'n face?
  And wilt thou have a reason for this coil?
  I am the sea; hark, how her sighs doth flow!   225
  She is the weeping welkin, I the earth:
  Then must my sea be movèd with her sighs,
  Then must my earth with her continual tears
  Become a deluge, overflowed and drowned,
  For why my bowels cannot hide her woes,   230
  But like a drunkard must I vomit them.
  Then give me leave, for losers will have leave
  To ease their stomachs with their bitter tongues.

Enter a Messenger, with two heads and a hand.

MESSENGER Worthy Andronicus, ill art thou repaid
  For that good hand thou sent'st the Emperor.   235
  Here are the heads of thy two noble sons,
  And here's thy hand in scorn to thee sent back;
  Thy griefs their sports, thy resolution mocked:

211 **breathe the welkin dim** becloud the heavens with our breath
217 **passions** outbursts 224 **coil** fuss 230 **For why** because 230 **bowels**
(thought to be the seat of compassion; akin to the modern use of "heart")
233 **stomachs** feeling

49

That woe is me to think upon thy woes,
240 More than remembrance of my father's death.
                                                    [*Exit*.]

MARCUS Now let hot Etna cool in Sicily,
    And be my heart an ever-burning hell!
    These miseries are more than may be borne!
    To weep with them that weep doth ease some deal,
245 But sorrow flouted at is double death.

LUCIUS Ah, that this sight should make so deep a
        wound,
    And yet detested life not shrink thereat!
    That ever death should let life bear his name,
    Where life hath no more interest but to breathe!
                                    [*Lavinia kisses Titus*.]

250 MARCUS Alas, poor heart, that kiss is comfortless
    As frozen water to a starvèd snake.

TITUS When will this fearful slumber have an end?

MARCUS Now, farewell, flatt'ry, die Andronicus,
    Thou dost not slumber: see thy two sons' heads,
255 Thy warlike hand, thy mangled daughter here,
    Thy other banished son with this dear sight
    Struck pale and bloodless, and thy brother, I,
    Even like a stony image cold and numb.
    Ah! Now no more will I control thy griefs:
260 Rend off thy silver hair, thy other hand
    Gnawing with thy teeth, and be this dismal sight
    The closing up of our most wretched eyes:
    Now is a time to storm; why art thou still?

TITUS Ha, ha, ha!

MARCUS Why dost thou laugh? It fits not with this
265 hour.

TITUS Why, I have not another tear to shed.
    Besides, this sorrow is an enemy,

239 **That** so that   244 **some deal** somewhat   247 **shrink** slip away   248 **bear his name** i.e., be called "life"   251 **starvèd** numbed   252 **fearful slumber** i.e., nightmare existence   256 **dear** heartfelt

And would usurp upon my wat'ry eyes
And make them blind with tributary tears;
Then which way shall I find Revenge's Cave?   270
For these two heads do seem to speak to me,
And threat me I shall never come to bliss
Till all these mischiefs be returned again,
Even in their throats that hath committed them.
Come, let me see what task I have to do.   275
You heavy people, circle me about,
That I may turn me to each one of you,
And swear unto my soul to right your wrongs.
The vow is made. Come, brother, take a head;
And in this hand the other will I bear.   280
And Lavinia, thou shalt be employed in these arms,
Bear thou my hand, sweet wench, between thy teeth:
As for thee, boy, go, get thee from my sight.
Thou art an exile, and thou must not stay.
Hie to the Goths, and raise an army there,   285
And, if ye love me, as I think you do,
Let's kiss and part, for we have much to do.

Exeunt [all but Lucius].

LUCIUS Farewell, Andronicus, my noble father,
The woefull'st man that ever lived in Rome!
Farewell, proud Rome, till Lucius come again;   290
He loves his pledges dearer than his life.
Farewell, Lavinia, my noble sister;
O, would thou wert as thou tofore hast been!
But now nor Lucius nor Lavinia lives
But in oblivion and hateful griefs.   295
If Lucius live, he will requite your wrongs,
And make proud Saturnine and his empress
Beg at the gates, like Tarquin and his queen.

269 tributary paid as tribute   276 heavy sad   282 teeth (possibly Shakespeare
intended to delete "teeth" from the manuscript, and substituted the less grotesque
"arms" above it; if so, the compositor mistakenly took "arms" to be part of the
previous line, and to make sense of it he perhaps altered something like "employed
in this" to "employed in these arms")   293 tofore formerly   294 nor ... nor
neither ... nor   298 Tarquin Roman king whose rule was overthrown when his
son (of the same name) raped Lucrece

Now will I to the Goths and raise a pow'r,
300 To be revenged on Rome and Saturnine.

Exit Lucius.

[Scene II. *Rome. Within Titus' house.*]

A banket. Enter Andronicus, Marcus, Lavinia,
and the boy [*Lucius*].

TITUS So, so, now sit, and look you eat no more
Than will preserve just so much strength in us
As will revenge these bitter woes of ours.
Marcus, unknit that sorrow-wreathen knot:
5   Thy niece and I, poor creatures, want our hands,
And cannot passionate our tenfold grief
With folded arms. This poor right hand of mine
Is left to tyrannize upon my breast;
Who, when my heart all mad with misery
10   Beats in this hollow prison of my flesh,
Then thus I thump it down.
[*To Lavinia*] Thou map of woe, that thus dost talk in
        signs,
When thy poor heart beats with outrageous beating,
Thou canst not strike it thus to make it still.
15   Wound it with sighing, girl, kill it with groans;
Or get some little knife between thy teeth,
And just against thy heart make thou a hole,
That all the tears that thy poor eyes let fall
May run into that sink, and soaking in
20   Drown the lamenting fool in sea-salt tears.

MARCUS Fie, brother, fie! Teach her not thus to lay
Such violent hands upon her tender life.

III.ii.s.d. banket light meal 4 knot i.e., Marcus' folded arms, a sign of heavy
thoughts 6 passionate passionately express 12 map picture 15 wound it
with sighing (sighing was believed to shorten life) 19 sink sewer 20 fool
(here, as often, implying affection and pity)

TITUS How now! Has sorrow made thee dote already?
    Why, Marcus, no man should be mad but I.
    What violent hands can she lay on her life!   25
    Ah, wherefore dost thou urge the name of hands,
    To bid Aeneas tell the tale twice o'er,
    How Troy was burnt and he made miserable?
    O, handle not the theme, to talk of hands,
    Lest we remember still that we have none.   30
    Fie, fie, how franticly I square my talk,
    As if we should forget we had no hands,
    If Marcus did not name the word of hands!
    Come, let's fall to; and, gentle girl, eat this.
    Here is no drink? Hark, Marcus, what she says—   35
    I can interpret all her martyred signs—
    She says she drinks no other drink but tears,
    Brewed with her sorrow, meshed upon her cheeks.
    Speechless complainer, I will learn thy thought;
    In thy dumb action will I be as perfect   40
    As begging hermits in their holy prayers:
    Thou shalt not sigh, nor hold thy stumps to heaven,
    Nor wink, nor nod, nor kneel, nor make a sign,
    But I of these will wrest an alphabet,
    And by still practice learn to know thy meaning.   45

BOY Good grandsire, leave these bitter deep laments.
    Make my aunt merry with some pleasing tale.

MARCUS Alas, the tender boy, in passion moved,
    Doth weep to see his grandsire's heaviness.

TITUS Peace, tender sapling, thou art made of tears,   50
    And tears will quickly melt thy life away.
                Marcus strikes the dish with a knife.
    What dost thou strike at, Marcus, with thy knife?

MARCUS At that that I have killed, my lord—a fly.

TITUS Out on thee, murderer! Thou kill'st my heart;
    Mine eyes are cloyed with view of tyranny: 55
    A deed of death done on the innocent

27 Aeneas (see Virgil's *Aeneid* II.2)   31 square shape   38 meshed mashed, brewed   40 perfect fully knowing   43 wink shut the eyes   45 still constant

Becomes not Titus' brother. Get thee gone;
I see thou art not for my company.

MARCUS Alas, my lord, I have but killed a fly.

60 TITUS "But!" How, if that fly had a father and mother?
How would he hang his slender gilded wings,
And buzz lamenting doings in the air!
Poor harmless fly,
That, with his pretty buzzing melody,
Came here to make us merry! And thou has killed
65   him.

MARCUS Pardon me, sir; it was a black ill-favored fly,
Like to the Empress' Moor. Therefore I killed him.

TITUS O, O, O,
Then pardon me for reprehending thee,
70 For thou hast done a charitable deed.
Give me thy knife, I will insult on him,
Flattering myself, as if it were the Moor,
Come hither purposely to poison me.
                              [He strikes at it.]
There's for thyself, and that's for Tamora.
75 Ah, sirrah!
Yet I think we are not brought so low
But that between us we can kill a fly
That comes in likeness of a coal-black Moor.

MARCUS Alas, poor man! Grief has so wrought on him,
80 He takes false shadows for true substances.

TITUS Come, take away. Lavinia, go with me:
I'll to thy closet, and go read with thee
Sad stories chancèd in the times of old.
Come, boy, and go with me; thy sight is young,
85 And thou shalt read when mine begin to dazzle.
                                        Exeunt.

66 ill-favored ugly 71 insult on exult over 75 sirrah (common term of
address to an inferior) 81 take away clear the table 82 closet private
room 83 chancèd that happened

[ACT IV

Scene I. *Rome. Before Titus' house.*]

Enter Lucius' son and Lavinia running after him; and
the boy flies from her with his books under his arm.
Enter Titus and Marcus.

BOY Help, grandsire, help! My aunt Lavinia
Follows me everywhere, I know not why.
Good uncle Marcus, see how swift she comes.
Alas, sweet aunt, I know not what you mean.

MARCUS Stand by me, Lucius, do not fear thine aunt.   5

TITUS She loves thee, boy, too well to do thee harm.

BOY Ay, when my father was in Rome she did.

MARCUS What means my niece Lavinia by these signs?

TITUS Fear her not, Lucius. Somewhat doth she mean.
See, Lucius, see, how much she makes of thee: 10
Somewhither would she have thee go with her.
Ah, boy, Cornelia never with more care
Read to her sons than she hath read to thee
Sweet poetry and Tully's *Orator*.
Canst thou not guess wherefore she plies thee thus?   15

BOY My lord, I know not, I, nor can I guess,
Unless some fit or frenzy do possess her:
For I have heard my grandsire say full oft,

IV.i.12 **Cornelia** mother of the Gracchi, two famous tribunes 14 **Tully's**
Orator Cicero's *De oratore* (or his *Orator ad M. Brutum*)

Extremity of griefs would make men mad;
20 And I have read that Hecuba of Troy
Ran mad for sorrow. That made me to fear,
Although, my lord, I know my noble aunt
Loves me as dear as e'er my mother did,
And would not, but in fury, fright my youth,
25 Which made me down to throw my books and fly,
Causeless perhaps. But pardon me, sweet aunt:
And, madam, if my uncle Marcus go,
I will most willingly attend your ladyship.

MARCUS Lucius, I will.

30 TITUS How now, Lavinia? Marcus, what means this?
Some book there is that she desires to see.
Which is it, girl, of these? Open them, boy.
But thou art deeper read, and better skilled.
Come, and take choice of all my library,
35 And so beguile thy sorrow, till the heavens
Reveal the damned contriver of this deed.
Why lifts she up her arms in sequence thus?

MARCUS I think she means that there were more than
one
Confederate in the fact. Ay, more there was,
40 Or else to heaven she heaves them for revenge.

TITUS Lucius, what book is that she tosseth so?

BOY Grandsire, 'tis Ovid's *Metamorphosis*;
My mother gave it me.

MARCUS　　　　　　　　For love of her that's gone,
Perhaps she culled it from among the rest.

45 TITUS Soft! So busily she turns the leaves!
Help her! What would she find? Lavinia, shall I
read?
This is the tragic tale of Philomel,
And treats of Tereus' treason and his rape;

24 but in fury except in madness　28 attend wait on　39 fact crime
41 tosseth turns the pages of　42 Metamorphosis (so spelled in the title of an
Elizabethan translation by Golding, with which Shakespeare was familiar; properly
Metamorphoses)

56

And rape, I fear, was root of thy annoy.

MARCUS See, brother, see, note how she quotes the
    leaves.   50

TITUS Lavinia, wert thou thus surprised, sweet girl,
    Ravished and wronged, as Philomela was,
    Forced in the ruthless, vast, and gloomy woods?
    See, see!
    Ay, such a place there is, where we did hunt—   55
    O, had we never, never hunted there—
    Patterned by that the poet here describes,
    By nature made for murders and for rapes.

MARCUS O, why should nature build so foul a den,
    Unless the gods delight in tragedies?   60

TITUS Give signs, sweet girl, for here are none but
    friends,
    What Roman lord it was durst do the deed:
    Or slunk not Saturnine, as Tarquin erst,
    That left the camp to sin in Lucrece' bed?

MARCUS Sit down, sweet niece: brother, sit down by
    me.   65
    Apollo, Pallas, Jove, or Mercury,
    Inspire me, that I may this treason find!
    My lord, look here: look here, Lavinia.
            He writes his name with his staff,
            and guides it with feet and mouth.
    This sandy plot is plain; guide if thou canst,
    This after me. I have writ my name   70
    Without the help of any hand at all.
    Cursed be that heart that forced us to this shift!
    Write thou, good niece, and here display at last
    What God will have discovered for revenge.
    Heaven guide thy pen to print thy sorrows plain,   75
    That we may know the traitors and the truth!
            She takes the staff in her mouth and
            guides it with her stumps and writes.

50 **quotes** examines 53 **vast** desolate 57 **Patterned by** after the pattern
63 **erst** once 69 **plain** flat 70 **after me** as I do 72 **shift** device
74 **discovered** revealed

O, do ye read, my lord, what she hath writ?

[TITUS] "*Stuprum*. Chiron. Demetrius."

MARCUS What, what! The lustful sons of Tamora
80   Performers of this heinous, bloody deed?

TITUS *Magni Dominator poli,*
       Tam lentus audis scelera? tam lentus vides?

MARCUS O, calm thee, gentle lord! Although I know
       There is enough written upon this earth
85   To stir a mutiny in the mildest thoughts,
       And arm the minds of infants to exclaims.
       My lord, kneel down with me; Lavinia, kneel;
       And kneel, sweet boy, the Roman Hector's hope;
       And swear with me, as, with the woeful fere
90   And father of that chaste dishonored dame,
       Lord Junius Brutus sware for Lucrece' rape,
       That we will prosecute by good advice
       Mortal revenge upon these traitorous Goths,
       And see their blood, or die with this reproach.

95 TITUS 'Tis sure enough, and you knew how,
       But if you hunt these bear-whelps, then beware:
       The dam will wake; and if she wind ye once,
       She's with the lion deeply still in league,
       And lulls him whilst she playeth on her back,
100   And when he sleeps will she do what she list.
       You are a young huntsman, Marcus, let alone;
       And, come, I will go get a leaf of brass,
       And with a gad of steel will write these words,
       And lay it by. The angry northern wind
105   Will blow these sands like Sibyl's leaves abroad,
       And where's our lesson then? Boy, what say you?

---

78 **Stuprum** rape (Latin)   81–82 **Magni Dominator ... lentus vides?** ruler of
the great heavens, are you so slow to hear and to see crimes? (Latin; derived from
Seneca's *Hippolytus*, lines 668–69)   86 **exclaims** exclamations   88 **the Roman
Hector's** i.e., Andronicus (Titus is compared to Hector, Troy's champion)
89 **fere** spouse   91 **Junius Brutus** chief of those who drove the Tarquins from
Rome   92 **by good advice** after careful deliberation   97 **and if she wind ye** if
she get wind of (smell) you   100 **list** please   103 **gad** spike, stylus   105 **Sibyl's
leaves** leaves on which the Sibyl wrote prophecies

BOY I say, my lord, that if I were a man,
Their mother's bedchamber should not be safe
For these base bondmen to the yoke of Rome.

MARCUS Ay, that's my boy! Thy father hath full oft   110
For his ungrateful country done the like.

BOY And, uncle, so will I, and if I live.

TITUS Come, go with me into mine armory:
Lucius, I'll fit thee, and withal my boy
Shall carry from me to the Empress' sons   115
Presents that I intend to send them both.
Come, come; thou'lt do my message, wilt thou not?

BOY Ay, with my dagger in their bosoms, grandsire.

TITUS No, boy, not so; I'll teach thee another course.
Lavinia, come. Marcus, look to my house.   120
Lucius and I'll go brave it at the court;
Ay, marry, will we, sir; and we'll be waited on.
                                        Exeunt.

MARCUS O heavens, can you hear a good man groan,
And not relent, or not compassion him?
Marcus, attend him in his ecstasy,   125
That hath more scars of sorrow in his heart
Than foemen's marks upon his batt'red shield,
But yet so just that he will not revenge.
Revenge the heavens for old Andronicus!   *Exit.*

121 brave it behave defiantly   122 marry (an interjection, from "By the Virgin
Mary")   122 be waited on i.e., not be ignored   125 ecstasy fit of madness
129 Revenge the heavens may the heavens take revenge

[Scene II. *Rome. Within the palace.*]

Enter Aaron, Chiron, and Demetrius, at one door, and at the other door young Lucius and another, with a bundle of weapons and verses writ upon them.

CHIRON Demetrius, here's the son of Lucius,
He hath some message to deliver us.

AARON Ay, some mad message from his mad grand-
father.

BOY My lords, with all the humbleness I may,
5   I greet your honors from Andronicus.
[*Aside*] And pray the Roman gods confound you
both.

DEMETRIUS Gramercy, lovely Lucius, what's the news?

BOY [*Aside*] That you are both deciphered, that's the
news,
For villains marked with rape. [*Aloud*] May it please
you,
10   My grandsire, well-advised, hath sent by me
The goodliest weapons of his armory
To gratify your honorable youth,
The hope of Rome; for so he bid me say;
And so I do, and with his gifts present
15   Your lordships; whenever you have need,
You may be armèd and appointed well.
And so I leave you both, [*aside*] like bloody villains.
                                                     Exit.

DEMETRIUS What's here? A scroll, and written round
about?

IV.ii.6 confound destroy 7 Gramercy thanks 10 well-advised in sound
mind 16 appointed equipped

60

Let's see:

    Integer vitae, scelerisque purus,   20
    Non eget Mauri jaculis, nec arcu.

CHIRON O, 'tis a verse in Horace; I know it well:
  I read it in the grammar long ago.

AARON Ay, just; a verse in Horace; right, you have it.
  [*Aside*] Now, what a thing it is to be an ass!   25
  Here's no sound jest! The old man hath found their
    guilt,
  And sends them weapons wrapped about with lines
  That wound, beyond their feeling, to the quick.
  But were our witty empress well afoot,
  She would applaud Andronicus' conceit.   30
  But let her rest in her unrest awhile.
  [*Aloud*] And now, young lords, was't not a happy
    star
  Led us to Rome, strangers, and more than so,
  Captives, to be advancèd to this height?
  It did me good, before the palace gate   35
  To brave the tribune in his brother's hearing.

DEMETRIUS But me more good, to see so great a lord
  Basely insinuate and send us gifts.

AARON Had he not reason, Lord Demetrius?
  Did you not use his daughter very friendly?   40

DEMETRIUS I would we had a thousand Roman dames
  At such a bay, by turn to serve our lust.

CHIRON A charitable wish and full of love.

AARON Here lacks but your mother for to say amen.

CHIRON And that would she for twenty thousand more.   45

DEMETRIUS Come, let us go, and pray to all the gods
  For our belovèd mother in her pains.

20-21 Integer vitae ... nec arcu the man of upright life and free from crime has
no need of a Moor's javelins or bow (Latin; from Horace, *Odes*, I.xxii.1-2)
29 witty wise 30 conceit idea, design 38 insinuate curry favor 42 At such
a bay thus cornered

AARON [*Aside*] Pray to the devils, the gods have given
    us over.

Trumpets sound.

DEMETRIUS Why do the Emperor's trumpets flourish
    thus?

50 CHIRON Belike, for joy the Emperor hath a son.

DEMETRIUS Soft! Who comes here?

Enter Nurse with a blackamoor child.

NURSE   God morrow, lords.
    O, tell me, did you see Aaron the Moor?

AARON Well, more or less, or ne'er a whit at all,
    Here Aaron is; and what with Aaron now?

55 NURSE O gentle Aaron, we are all undone!
    Now help, or woe betide thee evermore!

AARON Why, what a caterwauling dost thou keep!
    What dost thou wrap and fumble in thy arms?

NURSE O, that which I would hide from heaven's eye,
60   Our empress' shame and stately Rome's disgrace!
    She is delivered, lords, she is delivered.

AARON To whom?

NURSE   I mean, she is brought abed.

AARON Well, God give her good rest! What hath he
    sent her?

NURSE A devil.

AARON   Why, then she is the devil's dam;
65   A joyful issue.

NURSE A joyless, dismal, black, and sorrowful issue!
    Here is the babe, as loathsome as a toad
    Amongst the fair-faced breeders of our clime.
    The Empress sends it thee, thy stamp, thy seal,

50 **Belike** probably 58 **fumble** clumsily bundle up 64 **dam** mother

And bids thee christen it with thy dagger's point.   70

AARON Zounds, ye whore! Is black so base a hue?
  Sweet blowse, you are a beauteous blossom, sure.

DEMETRIUS Villain, what hast thou done?

AARON That which thou canst not undo.

CHIRON Thou has undone our mother.   75

AARON Villain, I have done thy mother.

DEMETRIUS And therein, hellish dog, thou hast undone
    her.
  Woe to her chance, and damned her loathèd choice!
  Accursed the offspring of so foul a fiend!

CHIRON It shall not live.   80

AARON It shall not die.

NURSE Aaron, it must; the mother wills it so.

AARON What, must it, nurse? Then let no man but I
  Do execution on my flesh and blood.

DEMETRIUS I'll broach the tadpole on my rapier's
    point.   85
  Nurse, give it me; my sword shall soon dispatch it.

AARON Sooner this sword shall plow thy bowels up.
  Stay, murderous villains! Will you kill your brother?
  Now, by the burning tapers of the sky,
  That shone so brightly when this boy was got,   90
  He dies upon my scimitar's sharp point
  That touches this my first-born son and heir!
  I tell you, younglings, not Enceladus,
  With all his threat'ning band of Typhon's brood,
  Nor great Alcides, nor the god of war,   95
  Shall seize this prey out of his father's hands.

71 Zounds (an interjection, from "By God's wounds")   72 blowse ruddy wench
(here, ironic)   76 done had sexual intercourse with   78 chance luck
85 broach impale   90 got begat   93 Enceladus one of the Titans (sons of
Typhon) who fought the Olympians   95 Alcides Hercules

What, what, ye sanguine, shallow-hearted boys!
Ye white-limed walls! Ye alehouse painted signs!
Coal-black is better than another hue,
100   In that it scorns to bear another hue;
For all the water in the ocean
Can never turn the swan's black legs to white,
Although she lave them hourly in the flood.
Tell the Empress from me, I am of age
105   To keep mine own, excuse it how she can.

DEMETRIUS Wilt thou betray thy noble mistress thus?

AARON My mistress is my mistress, this my self,
The vigor and the picture of my youth:
This before all the world do I prefer;
110   This mauger all the world will I keep safe,
Or some of you shall smoke for it in Rome.

DEMETRIUS By this our mother is forever shamed.

CHIRON Rome will despise her for this foul escape.

NURSE The Emperor in his rage will doom her death.

115 CHIRON I blush to think upon this ignomy.

AARON Why, there's the privilege your beauty bears:
Fie, treacherous hue, that will betray with blushing
The close enacts and counsels of thy heart!
Here's a young lad framed of another leer:
120   Look, how the black slave smiles upon the father,
As who should say, "Old lad, I am thine own."
He is your brother, lords, sensibly fed
Of that self blood that first gave life to you,
And from your womb where you imprisoned were
125   He is enfranchisèd and come to light:
Nay, he is your brother by the surer side,
Although my seal be stampèd in his face.

97 **sanguine** pink-cheeked 98 **white-limed walls** (perhaps a reference to
the "whited sepulchers" of Matthew 23:27) 103 **lave** wash 110 **mauger** in
spite of 111 **smoke** suffer 113 **escape** escapade 115 **ignomy** ignominy
118 **close enacts** secret resolutions 119 **leer** complexion 122–23 **sensibly
fed/Of that self blood** i.e., his body draws on the same blood 126 **the surer
side** i.e., the mother's side

NURSE Aaron, what shall I say unto the Empress?

DEMETRIUS Advise thee, Aaron, what is to be done,
And we will all subscribe to thy advice: 130
Save thou the child, so we may all be safe.

AARON Then sit we down and let us all consult.
My son and I will have the wind of you:
Keep there; now talk at pleasure of your safety.

DEMETRIUS How many women saw this child of his?   135

AARON Why, so, brave lords! When we join in league,
I am a lamb: but if you brave the Moor,
The chafèd boar, the mountain lioness,
The ocean swells not so as Aaron storms.
But say again, how many saw the child?   140

NURSE Cornelia the midwife, and myself,
And no one else but the delivered Empress.

AARON The Empress, the midwife, and yourself:
Two may keep counsel when the third's away.
Go to the Empress, tell her this I said.   145

He kills her.

Wheak, wheak!
So cries a pig preparèd to the spit.

DEMETRIUS What mean'st thou, Aaron? Wherefore
did's't thou this?

AARON O, lord, sir, 'tis a deed of policy!
Shall she live to betray this guilt of ours?   150
A long-tongued babbling gossip? No, lords, no.
And now be it known to you my full intent.
Not far one Muliteus my countryman
His wife but yesternight was brought to bed;
His child is like to her, fair as you are.   155
Go pack with him, and give the mother gold,
And tell them both the circumstance of all,

130 **subscribe** agree 131 **so** provided that 133 **have the wind of you** i.e.,
keep you safely in our view (as game is watched, down wind) 138 **chafèd**
enraged 149 **policy** cunning 153-54 **countryman/His** countryman's
156 **pack** conspire 157 **circumstance of all** all the details

And how by this their child shall be advanced,
And be receivèd for the Emperor's heir,
160   And substituted in the place of mine,
To calm this tempest whirling in the court;
And let the Emperor dandle him for his own.
Hark ye, lords; you see I have given her physic,
And you must needs bestow her funeral;
165   The fields are near, and you are gallant grooms.
This done, see that you take no longer days,
But send the midwife presently to me.
The midwife and the nurse well made away,
Then let the ladies tattle what they please.

170   CHIRON Aaron, I see, thou wilt not trust the air
With secrets.

DEMETRIUS   For this care of Tamora,
Herself and hers are highly bound to thee.   *Exeunt.*

AARON Now to the Goths, as swift as swallow flies,
There to dispose this treasure in mine arms,
175   And secretly to greet the Empress' friends.
Come on, you thick-lipped slave, I'll bear you hence;
For it is you that puts us to our shifts.
I'll make you feed on berries and on roots,
And feed on curds and whey, and suck the goat,
180   And cabin in a cave, and bring you up
To be a warrior and command a camp.   *Exit.*

---

163 physic medicine   166 days time   177 puts us to our shifts causes us to
use stratagems   180 cabin dwell

[Scene III. *Rome. A street.*]

Enter Titus, old Marcus, [his son Publius,] young Lucius,
and other gentlemen, with bows; and Titus bears the arrows
with letters on the ends of them.

TITUS Come, Marcus, come; kinsmen, this is the way.
　　　Sir boy, let me see your archery;
　　　Look ye draw home enough, and 'tis there straight.
　　　Terras Astraea reliquit.
　　　Be you rememb'red, Marcus: she's gone, she's fled.　　5
　　　Sirs, take you to your tools. You, cousins, shall
　　　Go sound the ocean, and cast your nets;
　　　Happily you may catch her in the sea;
　　　Yet there's as little justice as at land:
　　　No, Publius and Sempronius, you must do it;　　　10
　　　'Tis you must dig with mattock and with spade,
　　　And pierce the inmost center of the earth:
　　　Then, when you come to Pluto's region,
　　　I pray you deliver him this petition:
　　　Tell him, it is for justice and for aid,　　　15
　　　And that it comes from old Andronicus,
　　　Shaken with sorrows in ungrateful Rome.
　　　Ah, Rome! Well, well; I made thee miserable
　　　What time I threw the people's suffrages
　　　On him that thus doth tyrannize o'er me.　　　20
　　　Go, get you gone, and pray be careful all,
　　　And leave you not a man of war unsearched:
　　　This wicked emperor may have shipped her hence,
　　　And, kinsmen, then we may go pipe for justice.

MARCUS O, Publius, is not this a heavy case,　　　25

IV.iii.3 **home** fully 4 **Terras Astraea reliquit** Astraea (goddess of justice) has
left the earth (Latin; from Ovid, *Metamorphoses*, I.150) 5 **Be you rememb'red**
remember 8 **Happily** perhaps 13 **Pluto's region** Hades 19 **What time**
when 24 **pipe for** i.e., whistle vainly for

To see thy noble uncle thus distract?

PUBLIUS Therefore, my lords, it highly us concerns
By day and night t' attend him carefully,
And feed his humor kindly as we may,
30   Till time beget some careful remedy.

MARCUS Kinsmen, his sorrows are past remedy.
But . . .
Join with the Goths, and with revengeful war
Take wreak on Rome for this ingratitude,
35   And vengeance on the traitor Saturnine.

TITUS Publius, how now! How now, my masters!
What, have you met with her?

PUBLIUS No, my good lord, but Pluto sends you word,
If you will have revenge from hell, you shall:
40   Marry, for Justice, she is so employed,
He thinks, with Jove in heaven, or somewhere else,
So that perforce you must needs stay a time.

TITUS He doth me wrong to feed me with delays.
I'll dive into the burning lake below,
45   And pull her out of Acheron by the heels.
Marcus, we are but shrubs, no cedars we,
No big-boned men framed of the Cyclops' size;
But metal, Marcus, steel to the very back,
Yet wrung with wrongs more than our backs can
       bear:
50   And sith there's no justice in earth nor hell,
We will solicit heaven, and move the gods
To send down Justice for to wreak our wrongs.
Come, to this gear. You are a good archer, Marcus.
                              He gives them the arrows.
Ad Jovem, that's for you: here, *Ad Apollinem*:
55   *Ad Martem*, that's for myself:

29 **humor** mood, caprice 32 **But** (a catchword indicates that the line begins
"But," though the line itself was omitted) 34 **wreak** vengeance 45 **Acheron**
river in Hades 47 **Cyclops** giants (in Homer's *Odyssey*) 50 **sith** since
52 **wreak** avenge 53 **gear** affair 54–55 **Ad Jovem** . . . **Ad Apollinem/Ad
Martem** to Jove . . . to Apollo; to Mars (Latin)

68

Here, boy, to Pallas: here, to Mercury:
To Saturn, Caius, not to Saturnine;
You were as good to shoot against the wind.
To it, boy! Marcus, loose when I bid.
Of my word, I have written to effect;   60
There's not a god left unsolicited.

MARCUS Kinsmen, shoot all your shafts into the court:
We will afflict the Emperor in his pride.

TITUS Now, masters, draw. O, well said, Lucius!
Good boy, in Virgo's lap; give it Pallas.   65

MARCUS My lord, I aim a mile beyond the moon;
Your letter is with Jupiter by this.

TITUS Ha, ha!
Publius, Publius, what hast thou done!
See, see, thou hast shot off one of Taurus' horns.   70

MARCUS This was the sport, my lord: when Publius
  shot,
The bull being galled, gave Aries such a knock
That down fell both the Ram's horns in the court,
And who should find them but the Empress' villain?
She laughed, and told the Moor he should not
  choose   75
But give them to his master for a present.

TITUS Why, there it goes! God give his lordship joy!

Enter the Clown, with a basket and two pigeons in it.

News, news from heaven! Marcus, the post is come.
Sirrah, what tidings? Have you any letters?
Shall I have justice? What says Jupiter?   80

CLOWN Ho, the gibbet maker! He says that he hath

---

58 **You were as good to shoot** you would do as much good by shooting
65 **Virgo's** the Virgin's (sign of the zodiac, as are **Taurus**—the bull—in line 70,
and **Aries**—the ram—in line 72) 77 s.d. **Clown** rustic fellow 81 **gibbet
maker** (apparently "Jupiter"—which in the original text is spelled "Jubiter"—
was pronounced rather like "gibbeter," i.e., gibbet maker)

taken them down again, for the man must not be
hanged till the next week.

TITUS But what says Jupiter, I ask thee?

85 CLOWN Alas, sir, I know not Jupiter; I never drank
with him in all my life.

TITUS Why, villain, art not thou the carrier?

CLOWN Ay, of my pigeons, sir, nothing else.

TITUS Why, didst thou not come from heaven?

90 CLOWN From heaven? Alas, sir, I never came there!
God forbid, I should be so bold to press to heaven
in my young days. Why, I am going with my pigeons
to the tribunal plebs, to take up a matter of
brawl betwixt my uncle and one of the Emperal's
95 men.

MARCUS Why, sir, that is as fit as can be to serve for
your oration; and let him deliver the pigeons to the
Emperor from you.

TITUS Tell me, can you deliver an oration to the
100 Emperor with a grace?

CLOWN Nay, truly, sir, I could never say grace in all
my life.

TITUS Sirrah, come hither: make no more ado,
But give your pigeons to the Emperor:
105 By me thou shalt have justice at his hands.
Hold, hold, meanwhile, here's money for thy
charges.
Give me pen and ink. Sirrah, can you with a grace
deliver up a supplication?

CLOWN Ay, sir.

110 TITUS Then here is a supplication for you. And when
you come to him, at the first approach you must

93 **tribunal plebs** (malaprop for *tribunus plebis*, "Tribune of the plebs"; **Emperal**, later in the sentence, is another malaprop)   106 **charges** i.e., pigeons

kneel, then kiss his foot, then deliver up your
pigeons, and then look for your reward. I'll be at
hand, sir! See you do it bravely.

CLOWN I warrant you, sir, let me alone.   115

TITUS Sirrah, has thou a knife? Come, let me see it.
Here, Marcus, fold it in the oration,
For thou hast made it like an humble suppliant.
And when thou hast given it to the Emperor,
Knock at my door, and tell me what he says.   120

CLOWN God be with you, sir; I will.   *Exit.*

TITUS Come, Marcus, let us go. Publius, follow me.
                                                                 Exeunt.

[Scene IV. *Rome. Before the palace.*]

*Enter Emperor and Empress and her two sons. The
Emperor brings the arrows in his hand that Titus shot
at him.*

SATURNINUS Why, lords, what wrongs are these! Was
      ever seen
An emperor in Rome thus overborne,
Troubled, confronted thus, and for the extent
Of egal justice used in such contempt?
My lords, you know, as know the mightful gods,   5
However these disturbers of our peace
Buzz in the people's ears, there naught hath passed
But even with law against the willful sons
Of old Andronicus. And what and if
His sorrows have so overwhelmed his wits,   10
Shall we be thus afflicted in his wreaks,
His fits, his frenzy, and his bitterness?

114 **bravely** well   IV.iv.3 **extent** exercise   4 **egal** equal   8 **even** agreeing
11 **wreaks** vengeful acts

And now he writes to heaven for his redress!
See, here's to Jove, and this to Mercury,
15   This to Apollo, this to the god of war.
Sweet scrolls to fly about the streets of Rome!
What's this but libeling against the Senate,
And blazoning our unjustice everywhere?
A goodly humor, is it not, my lords?
20   As who would say, in Rome no justice were.
But if I live, his feignèd ecstasies
Shall be no shelter to these outrages,
But he and his shall know that justice lives
In Saturninus' health; whom, if he sleep,
25   He'll so awake, as he in fury shall
Cut off the proud'st conspirator that lives.

TAMORA My gracious lord, my lovely Saturnine,
Lord of my life, commander of my thoughts,
Calm thee, and bear the faults of Titus' age,
30   Th' effects of sorrow for his valiant sons,
Whose loss hath pierced him deep and scarred his
       heart,
And rather comfort his distressèd plight
Than prosecute the meanest or the best
For these contempts. [*Aside*] Why, thus it shall
       become
35   High-witted Tamora to gloze with all.
But, Titus, I have touched thee to the quick,
Thy lifeblood out: if Aaron now be wise,
Then is all safe, the anchor in the port.

Enter Clown.

How now, good fellow? Wouldst thou speak with us?

40   CLOWN Yea, forsooth, and your mistress-ship be
       emperial.

TAMORA Empress I am, but yonder sits the Emperor.

CLOWN 'Tis he. God and Saint Stephen give you

---

18 blazoning proclaiming   21 ecstasies fits of madness   35 gloze use specious
words   37 Thy lifeblood out when your blood is out

72

godden. I have brought you a letter and a couple of
pigeons here.   45

        He [i.e., Saturninus] reads the letter.

SATURNINUS Go, take him away, and hang him
  presently.

CLOWN How much money must I have?

TAMORA Come, sirrah, you must be hanged.

CLOWN Hanged! By lady, then I have brought up a neck
  to a fair end.   *Exit [with guards].*   50

SATURNINUS Despiteful and intolerable wrongs!
  Shall I endure this monstrous villainy?
  I know from whence this same device proceeds.
  May this be borne as if his traitorous sons,
  That died by law for murder of our brother,
  Have by my means been butchered wrongfully.   55
  Go, drag the villain hither by the hair,
  Nor age nor honor shall shape privilege:
  For this proud mock I'll be thy slaughter-man—
  Sly frantic wretch, that holp'st to make me great,   60
  In hope thyself should govern Rome and me.

        Enter nuntius, Aemilius.

What news with thee, Aemilius?

AEMILIUS Arm, my lords. Rome never had more cause.
  The Goths have gathered head, and with a power
  Of high-resolvèd men, bent to the spoil,   65
  They hither march amain, under conduct
  Of Lucius, son to old Andronicus;
  Who threats, in course of this revenge, to do
  As much as ever Coriolanus did.

44 **godden** good evening 49 **By lady** (an interjection, from "By Our Lady")
50 **neck** (possibly with a pun on "knack," which means "deceitful trick")
58 **shape privilege** provide immunity 61 s.d. **nuntius** messenger (Latin)
64 **gathered head** raised an army 64 **power** army 66 **conduct** leadership
69 **Coriolanus** (this Roman hero who became Rome's enemy is the protagonist in
Shakespeare's last tragedy)

70 SATURNINUS Is warlike Lucius general of the Goths?
        These tidings nip me, and I hang the head
        As flowers with frost or grass beat down with
            storms.
        Ay, now begins our sorrows to approach:
        'Tis he the common people love so much;
75   Myself hath often heard them say,
        When I have walkèd like a private man,
        That Lucius' banishment was wrongfully,
        And they have wished that Lucius were their
            emperor.

    TAMORA Why should you fear? Is not your city strong?

80 SATURNINUS Ay, but the citizens favor Lucius,
        And will revolt from me to succor him.

    TAMORA King, be thy thoughts imperious, like thy
            name.
        Is the sun dimmed, that gnats do fly in it?
        The eagle suffers little birds to sing
85   And is not careful what they mean thereby,
        Knowing that with the shadow of his wings
        He can at pleasure stint their melody:
        Even so mayst thou the giddy men of Rome.
        Then cheer thy spirit: for know, thou Emperor,
90   I will enchant the old Andronicus
        With words more sweet, and yet more dangerous,
        Than baits to fish, or honey-stalks to sheep;
        Whenas the one is wounded with the bait,
        The other rotted with delicious feed.

95 SATURNINUS But he will not entreat his son for us.

    TAMORA If Tamora entreat him, then he will:
        For I can smooth, and fill his agèd ears
        With golden promises, that, were his heart
        Almost impregnable, his old ears deaf,
100   Yet should both ear and heart obey my tongue.

85 careful worried   87 stint stop   92 honey-stalks clover

74

[*To Aemilius*] Go thou before to be our ambassador:
Say that the Emperor requests a parley
Of warlike Lucius, and appoint the meeting
Even at his father's house, the old Andronicus.

SATURNINUS Aemilius, do this message honorably,   105
  And if he stand in hostage for his safety,
  Bid him demand what pledge will please him best.

AEMILIUS Your bidding shall I do effectually.   *Exit*.

TAMORA Now will I to that old Andronicus,
  And temper him with all the art I have,   110
  To pluck proud Lucius from the warlike Goths.
  And now, sweet Emperor, be blithe again,
  And bury all thy fear in my devices.

SATURNINUS Then go successantly, and plead to him.

                        Exeunt.

---

106 **stand in** insist upon   110 **temper** work upon   114 **successantly** one after the other (?)

[ACT V

Scene I. *A plain near Rome.*]

*Enter Lucius, with an army of Goths, with drums
and soldiers.*

LUCIUS Approvèd warriors, and my faithful friends,
I have receivèd letters from great Rome,
Which signifies what hate they bear their emperor,
And how desirous of our sight they are.
5 Therefore, great lords, be, as your titles witness,
Imperious, and impatient of your wrongs;
And wherein Rome hath done you any scath,
Let him make treble satisfaction.

GOTH Brave slip, sprung from the great Andronicus,
10 Whose name was once our terror, now our comfort,
Whose high exploits and honorable deeds
Ingrateful Rome requites with foul contempt,
Be bold in us: we'll follow where thou lead'st,
Like stinging bees in hottest summer's day,
15 Led by their master to the flow'red fields,
And be avenged on cursèd Tamora.

[OTHER GOTHS] And as he saith, so say we all with him.

LUCIUS I humbly thank him, and I thank you all.
But who comes here, led by a lusty Goth?

V.i.1 **Approvèd** tested   7 **scath** harm   9 **slip** offshoot   13 **bold** confident

Enter a Goth, leading of Aaron with his child in his arms.

GOTH Renownèd Lucius, from our troops I strayed   20
    To gaze upon a ruinous monastery,
    And, as I earnestly did fix mine eye
    Upon the wasted building, suddenly
    I heard a child cry underneath a wall.
    I made unto the noise, when soon I heard   25
    The crying babe controlled with this discourse:
    "Peace, tawny slave, half me and half thy dame.
    Did not thy hue bewray whose brat thou art,
    Had nature lent thee but thy mother's look,
    Villain, thou mightst have been an emperor: 30
    But where the bull and cow are both milk-white,
    They never do beget a coal-black calf.
    Peace, villain, peace!" Even thus he rates the babe,
    "For I must bear thee to a trusty Goth,
    Who, when he knows thou art the Empress' babe,   35
    Will hold thee dearly for thy mother's sake."
    With this, my weapon drawn, I rushed upon him,
    Surprised him suddenly, and brought him hither,
    To use as you think needful of the man.

LUCIUS O worthy Goth, this is the incarnate devil   40
    That robbed Andronicus of his good hand.
    This is the pearl that pleased your empress' eye,
    And here's the base fruit of her burning lust.
    Say, wall-eyed slave, whither wouldst thou convey
    This growing image of thy fiendlike face?   45
    Why dost not speak? What, deaf? Not a word?
    A halter, soldiers! Hang him on this tree,
    And by his side his fruit of bastardy.

AARON Touch not the boy; he is of royal blood.

LUCIUS Too like the sire for ever being good.   50
    First hang the child, that he may see it sprawl—
    A sight to vex the father's soul withal.

23 **wasted** ruined   27 **tawny** black   27 **dame** mother   28 **bewray** reveal
28 **brat** young offspring   33 **rates** berates   44 **wall-eyed** glaring (literally: having a whitish iris)

AARON Get me a ladder. Lucius, save the child,
   And bear it from me to the Empress.
55   If thou do this, I'll show thee wondrous things
   That highly may advantage thee to hear.
   If thou wilt not, befall what may befall,
   I'll speak no more but "Vengeance rot you all!"

LUCIUS Say on, and if it please me which thou
    speak'st,
60   Thy child shall live, and I will see it nourished.

AARON And if it please thee! Why, assure thee, Lucius,
   'Twill vex thy soul to hear what I shall speak;
   For I must talk of murders, rapes, and massacres,
   Acts of black night, abominable deeds,
65   Complots of mischief, treason, villainies
   Ruthful to hear, yet piteously performed:
   And this shall all be buried in my death,
   Unless thou swear to me my child shall live.

LUCIUS Tell on thy mind, I say thy child shall live.

70 AARON Swear that he shall, and then I will begin.

LUCIUS Who should I swear by? Thou believest no
    god:
   That granted, how canst thou believe an oath?

AARON What if I do not? As indeed I do not;
   Yet, for I know thou art religious,
75   And hast a thing within thee callèd conscience,
   With twenty popish tricks and ceremonies,
   Which I have seen thee careful to observe,
   Therefore I urge thy oath; for that I know
   An idiot holds his bauble for a god,
80   And keeps the oath which by that god he swears,
   To that I'll urge him: therefore thou shalt vow
   By that same god, what god soe'er it be,
   That thou adorest and hast in reverence,

53 **Get me a ladder** i.e., hang me rather than the child 66 **Ruthful** pitiful
66 **piteously performed** i.e., performed, which excites pity 79 **bauble** carved
head at the end of a court fool's stick

To save my boy, to nourish and bring him up;
Or else I will discover naught to thee.   85

LUCIUS Even by my god I swear to thee I will.

AARON First know thou, I begot him on the Empress.

LUCIUS O most insatiate and luxurious woman!

AARON Tut, Lucius, this was but a deed of charity
To that which thou shalt hear of me anon.   90
'Twas her two sons that murdered Bassianus;
They cut thy sister's tongue and ravished her,
And cut her hands, and trimmed her as thou sawest.

LUCIUS O detestable villain! Call'st thou that
    trimming?

AARON Why, she was washed, and cut, and trimmed,
    and 'twas   95
Trim sport for them which had the doing of it.

LUCIUS O barbarous, beastly villains, like thyself!

AARON Indeed, I was their tutor to instruct them.
That codding spirit had they from their mother,
As sure a card as ever won the set.   100
That bloody mind, I think, they learned of me,
As true a dog as ever fought at head.
Well, let my deeds be witness of my worth.
I trained thy brethren to that guileful hole,
Where the dead corpse of Bassianus lay;   105
I wrote the letter that thy father found,
And hid the gold within that letter mentioned,
Confederate with the Queen and her two sons;
And what not done, that thou hast cause to rue,
Wherein I had no stroke of mischief in it?   110
I played the cheater for thy father's hand,
And when I had it drew myself apart,

---

88 **luxurious** lustful   90 **To** in comparison with   99 **codding** lustful   100 **set** game   102 **at head** (a courageous bulldog went for the bull's nose)   104 **trained** lured   111 **cheater** officer appointed to look after escheats or property forfeited to the Crown

And almost broke my heart with extreme laughter.
I pried me through the crevice of a wall,
115   When for his hand he had his two sons' heads;
Beheld his tears and laughed so heartily
That both mine eyes were rainy like to his:
And when I told the Empress of this sport,
She sounded almost at my pleasing tale,
120   And for my tidings gave me twenty kisses.

GOTH What, canst thou say all this and never blush?

AARON Ay, like a black dog, as the saying is.

LUCIUS Art thou not sorry for these heinous deeds?

AARON Ay, that I had not done a thousand more.
125   Even now I curse the day—and yet, I think,
Few come within the compass of my curse—
Wherein I did not some notorious ill:
As kill a man or else devise his death,
Ravish a maid or plot the way to do it,
130   Accuse some innocent and forswear myself,
Set deadly enmity between two friends,
Make poor men's cattle break their necks,
Set fire on barns and haystalks in the night,
And bid the owners quench them with their tears.
135   Oft have I digged up dead men from their graves
And set them upright at their dear friends' door,
Even when their sorrows almost was forgot,
And on their skins, as on the bark of trees,
Have with my knife carvèd in Roman letters,
140   "Let not your sorrow die, though I am dead."
But, I have done a thousand dreadful things
As willingly as one would kill a fly,
And nothing grieves me heartily indeed,
But that I cannot do ten thousand more.

145 LUCIUS Bring down the devil, for he must not die
So sweet a death as hanging presently.

AARON If there be devils, would I were a devil,
To live and burn in everlasting fire,

119 **sounded** swooned 130 **forswear** perjure

80

So I might have your company in hell,
But to torment you with my bitter tongue!   150

LUCIUS Sirs, stop his mouth, and let him speak no
more.

Enter Aemilius.

GOTH My lord, there is a messenger from Rome
Desires to be admitted to your presence.

LUCIUS Let him come near.
Welcome, Aemilius, what's the news from Rome?   155

AEMILIUS Lord Lucius, and you princes of the Goths,
The Roman Emperor greets you all by me;
And, for he understands you are in arms,
He craves a parley at your father's house,
Willing you to demand your hostages,   160
And they shall be immediately delivered.

GOTH What says our general?

LUCIUS Aemilius, let the Emperor give his pledges
Unto my father and my uncle Marcus,
And we will come. March away.   [*Exeunt.*]   165

[Scene II. *Rome. Before Titus' house.*]

Enter Tamora and her two sons, disguised
[*as Revenge attended by Rape and Murder*].

TAMORA Thus, in this strange and sad habiliment,
I will encounter with Andronicus,
And say I am Revenge, sent from below
To join with him and right his heinous wrongs.
Knock at his study, where, they say, he keeps   5
To ruminate strange plots of dire revenge;
Tell him Revenge is come to join with him,
And work confusion on his enemies.

V.ii.1 **sad habiliment** dismal apparel   5 **keeps** dwells   8 **confusion** destruction

They knock, and Titus [above] opens his study door.

TITUS Who doth molest my contemplation?
10   Is it your trick to make me ope the door,
         That so my sad decrees may fly away,
         And all my study be to no effect?
         You are deceived: for what I mean to do
         See here in bloody lines I have set down.
15   And what is written shall be executed.

TAMORA Titus, I am come to talk with thee.

TITUS No, not a word. How can I grace my talk,
        Wanting a hand to give that accord?
        Thou hast the odds of me, therefore no more.

TAMORA If thou didst know me, thou wouldst talk
20   with me.

TITUS I am not mad, I know thee well enough.
        Witness this wretched stump, witness these crimson
            lines,
        Witness these trenches made by grief and care,
        Witness the tiring day and heavy night,
25   Witness all sorrow, that I know thee well
         For our proud empress, mighty Tamora:
         Is not thy coming for my other hand?

TAMORA Know thou, sad man, I am not Tamora;
        She is thy enemy, and I thy friend.
30   I am Revenge, sent from th' infernal kingdom
         To ease the gnawing vulture of thy mind,
         By working wreakful vengeance on thy foes.
         Come down and welcome me to this world's light;
         Confer with me of murder and of death:
35   There's not a hollow cave or lurking place,
         No vast obscurity or misty vale,
         Where bloody murder or detested rape
         Can couch for fear, but I will find them out,

18 **give that accord** i.e., provide appropriate gestures   19 **odds** of advantage
over   32 **wreakful** avenging   38 **couch** lie hidden

82

And in their ears tell them my dreadful name,
Revenge, which makes the foul offender quake.   40

TITUS Art thou Revenge? And art thou sent to me,
To be a torment to mine enemies?

TAMORA I am, therefore come down and welcome me.

TITUS Do me some service ere I come to thee.
Lo, by thy side where Rape and Murder stands;   45
Now give some surance that thou art Revenge;
Stab them, or tear them on thy chariot wheels;
And then I'll come and be thy wagoner,
And whirl along with thee about the globes.
Provide thee two proper palfreys, black as jet,   50
To hale thy vengeful wagon swift away,
And find out murder in their guilty caves:
And when thy car is loaden with their heads,
I will dismount, and by thy wagon wheel
Trot like a servile footman all day long,   55
Even from Hyperion's rising in the east,
Until his very downfall in the sea.
And day by day I'll do this heavy task,
So thou destroy Rapine and Murder there.

TAMORA These are my ministers and come with me.   60

TITUS Are them thy ministers? What are they called?

TAMORA Rape and Murder; therefore callèd so,
'Cause they take vengeance of such kind of men.

TITUS Good Lord, how like the Empress' sons they are!
And you the Empress! But we worldly men   65
Have miserable, mad, mistaking eyes.
O sweet Revenge, now do I come to thee:
And, if one arm's embracement will content thee,
I will embrace thee in it by and by.   [*Exit above.*]

TAMORA This closing with him fits his lunacy.   70

46 **surance** assurance   50 **proper palfreys** excellent horses   53 **car** chariot
56 **Hyperion's** the sun god's   59 **So** provided that   59 **Rapine** rape   65 **worldly**
mortal, of this world   70 **closing** agreement

Whate'er I forge to feed his brainsick humors,
Do you uphold and maintain in your speeches,
For now he firmly takes me for Revenge,
And, being credulous in this mad thought,
75 I'll make him send for Lucius his son;
And, whilst I at a banket hold him sure,
I'll find some cunning practice out of hand,
To scatter and disperse the giddy Goths,
Or at the least make them his enemies.
80 See, here he comes, and I must ply my theme.

[Enter Titus.]

TITUS Long have I been forlorn, and all for thee.
Welcome, dread Fury, to my woeful house:
Rapine and Murder, you are welcome too:
How like the Empress and her sons you are!
85 Well are you fitted, had you but a Moor:
Could not all hell afford you such a devil?
For well I wot the Empress never wags
But in her company there is a Moor;
And, would you represent our queen aright,
90 It were convenient you had such a devil:
But welcome, as you are. What shall we do?

TAMORA What wouldst thou have us do, Andronicus?

DEMETRIUS Show me a murderer, I'll deal with him.

CHIRON Show me a villain that hath done a rape,
95 And I am sent to be revenged on him.

TAMORA Show me a thousand that hath done thee
wrong,
And I will be revengèd on them all.

TITUS Look round about the wicked streets of Rome,
And when thou find'st a man that's like thyself,
100 Good Murder, stab him; he's a murderer.
Go thou with him, and when it is thy hap
To find another that is like to thee,

71 **forge** invent 77 **practice** scheme 77 **out of hand** on the spur of the
moment 87 **wags** moves 90 **convenient** fitting 101 **hap** chance

Good Rapine, stab him; he is a ravisher.
Go thou with them, and in the Emperor's court
There is a queen attended by a Moor;   105
Well shalt thou know her by thine own proportion,
For up and down she doth resemble thee;
I pray thee, do on them some violent death;
They have been violent to me and mine.

TAMORA Well hast thou lessoned us; this shall we do.   110
But would it please thee, good Andronicus,
To send for Lucius, thy thrice valiant son,
Who leads towards Rome a band of warlike Goths,
And bid him come and banquet at thy house:
When he is here, even at thy solemn feast,   115
I will bring in the Empress and her sons,
The Emperor himself, and all thy foes,
And at thy mercy shall they stoop and kneel,
And on them shalt thou ease thy angry heart.
What says Andronicus to this device?   120

TITUS Marcus, my brother! 'Tis sad Titus calls.

Enter Marcus.

Go, gentle Marcus, to thy nephew Lucius;
Thou shalt inquire him out among the Goths.
Bid him repair to me and bring with him
Some of the chiefest princes of the Goths: 125
Bid him encamp his soldiers where they are;
Tell him the Emperor and the Empress too
Feast at my house, and he shall feast with them.
This do thou for my love, and so let him,
As he regards his agèd father's life.   130

MARCUS This will I do, and soon return again. [*Exit.*]

TAMORA Now will I hence about thy business,
And take my ministers along with me.

TITUS Nay, nay, let Rape and Murder stay with me,
Or else I'll call my brother back again,   135
And cleave to no revenge but Lucius.

115 solemn ceremonious   124 repair come

85

TAMORA [*Aside to her sons*] What say you, boys? Will
   you abide with him,
   Whiles I go tell my lord the Emperor
   How I have governed our determined jest?
140 Yield to his humor, smooth and speak him fair,
   And tarry with him till I turn again.

TITUS [*Aside*] I knew them all, though they supposed
   me mad;
   And will o'erreach them in their own devices,
   A pair of cursèd hellhounds and their dame.

145 DEMETRIUS Madam, depart at pleasure, leave us here.

TAMORA Farewell, Andronicus: Revenge now goes
   To lay a complot to betray thy foes.

TITUS I know thou dost; and, sweet Revenge, farewell.
                    [*Exit Tamora.*]

CHIRON Tell us, old man, how shall we be employed?

150 TITUS Tut, I have work enough for you to do.
   Publius, come hither, Caius, and Valentine!

         [*Enter Publius and others.*]

PUBLIUS What is your will?

TITUS Know you these two?

PUBLIUS The Empress' sons, I take them: Chiron,
155 Demetrius.

TITUS Fie, Publius, fie! Thou art too much deceived;
   The one is Murder, and Rape is the other's name:
   And therefore bind them, gentle Publius:
   Caius and Valentine, lay hands on them:
160 Oft have you heard me wish for such an hour,
   And now I find it: therefore bind them sure;
   And stop their mouths if they begin to cry.   [*Exit.*]

139 governed our determined jest managed the jest we agreed ("determined")
upon   140 smooth and speak him fair flatter and speak courteously to
him   147 complot plot

CHIRON Villains, forbear! We are the Empress' sons.

PUBLIUS And therefore do we what we are
          commanded.
     Stop close their mouths, let them not speak a word: 165
     Is he sure bound? Look that you bind them fast.

          Enter Titus Andronicus with a knife,
          and Lavinia with a basin.

TITUS Come, come, Lavinia; look, thy foes are bound.
     Sirs, stop their mouths, let them not speak to me,
     But let them hear what fearful words I utter.
     O villains, Chiron and Demetrius!   170
     Here stands the spring whom you have stained with
          mud,
     This goodly summer with your winter mixed.
     You killed her husband, and, for that vile fault
     Two of her brothers were condemned to death,
     My hand cut off and made a merry jest: 175
     Both her sweet hands, her tongue, and that more dear
     Than hands or tongue, her spotless chastity,
     Inhuman traitors, you constrained and forced.
     What would you say if I should let you speak?
     Villains, for shame you could not beg for grace.   180
     Hark, wretches, how I mean to martyr you.
     This one hand yet is left to cut your throats,
     Whiles that Lavinia 'tween her stumps doth hold
     The basin that receives your guilty blood.
     You know your mother means to feast with me,   185
     And calls herself Revenge, and thinks me mad:
     Hark, villains, I will grind your bones to dust,
     And with your blood and it I'll make a paste,
     And of the paste a coffin I will rear,
     And make two pasties of your shameful heads,   190
     And bid that strumpet, your unhallowed dam,
     Like to the earth, swallow her own increase.
     This is the feast that I have bid her to,
     And this the banket she shall surfeit on;
     For worse than Philomel you used my daughter,   195

189 coffin pie crust   192 increase offspring

87

And worse than Progne I will be revenged.
And now prepare your throats. Lavinia, come,
Receive the blood; and when that they are dead,
Let me go grind their bones to powder small,
200   And with this hateful liquor temper it,
And in that paste let their vile heads be baked.
Come, come, be every one officious
To make this banket, which I wish may prove
More stern and bloody than the Centaurs' feast.

He cuts their throats.

205   So, now bring them in, for I'll play the cook,
And see them ready against their mother comes.

Exeunt.

[Scene III. *Rome. Within Titus' house.*]

*Enter Lucius, Marcus, and the Goths [with Aaron
a prisoner, and an Attendant bearing Aaron's child].*

LUCIUS   Uncle Marcus, since 'tis my father's mind
That I repair to Rome, I am content.

GOTH   And ours with thine, befall what fortune will.

LUCIUS   Good uncle, take you in this barbarous Moor,
5   This ravenous tiger, this accursèd devil;
Let him receive no sust'nance, fetter him,
Till he be brought unto the Empress' face
For testimony of her foul proceedings:
And see the ambush of our friends be strong;
10   I fear the Emperor means no good to us.

196 **Progne** wife of Tereus (Tereus raped and mutilated Progne's sister, Philomela, and in revenge Progne slaughtered Tereus'—and her own—son and served him to Tereus)   200 **temper** mix   202 **officious** busy   204 **Centaurs' feast** (a battle followed the marriage feast to which the Lapiths invited the Centaurs) 206 **against** in preparation for the time when   V.iii.2 **repair** return

88

AARON Some devil whisper curses in my ear,
  And prompt me, that my tongue may utter forth
  The venomous malice of my swelling heart!

LUCIUS Away, inhuman dog! Unhallowed slave!
  Sirs, help our uncle to convey him in.   15
          [Goths lead Aaron in. Trumpets sound.]
  The trumpets show the Emperor is at hand.

          Sound trumpets. Enter Emperor and Empress,
               with Tribunes and others.

SATURNINUS What, hath the firmament mo suns than
  one?

LUCIUS What boots it thee to call thyself a sun?

MARCUS Rome's Emperor, and nephew, break the
  parle;
  These quarrels must be quietly debated.   20
  The feast is ready, which the careful Titus
  Hath ordained to an honorable end,
  For peace, for love, for league, and good to Rome.
  Please you, therefore, draw nigh, and take your
  places.

SATURNINUS Marcus, we will.   25

          Trumpets sounding, enter Titus, like a cook, placing
          the dishes, and Lavinia with a veil over her face,
          [young Lucius, and others].

TITUS Welcome, my lord; welcome, dread Queen;
  Welcome, ye warlike Goths; welcome, Lucius;
  And welcome, all: although the cheer be poor,
  'Twill fill your stomachs; please you eat of it.

SATURNINUS Why art thou thus attired, Andronicus?   30

TITUS Because I would be sure to have all well,
  To entertain your Highness and your empress.

TAMORA We are beholding to you, good Andronicus.

17 mo more   18 boots avails   19 break the parle interrupt the talk (i.e., cease
quarreling)   21 careful full of sorrow   28 cheer hospitality

TITUS And if your Highness knew my heart, you were.
35   My lord the Emperor, resolve me this:
    Was it well done of rash Virginius
    To slay his daughter with his own right hand,
    Because she was enforced, stained, and deflow'r'd?

SATURNINUS It was, Andronicus.

40 TITUS Your reason, mighty lord!

SATURNINUS Because the girl should not survive her
    shame,
    And by her presence still renew his sorrows.

TITUS A reason mighty, strong, and effectual,
    A pattern, precedent, and lively warrant,
45   For me, most wretched, to perform the like.
    Die, die, Lavinia, and thy shame with thee,
    And with thy shame thy father's sorrow die!
                          [He kills her.]

SATURNINUS What has thou done, unnatural and
    unkind?

TITUS Killed her for whom my tears have made me
    blind.
50   I am as woeful as Virginius was,
    And have a thousand times more cause than he
    To do this outrage, and it now is done.

SATURNINUS What, was she ravished? Tell who did the
    deed.

TITUS Will't please you eat? Will't please your Highness
    feed?

55 TAMORA Why hast thou slain thine only daughter thus?

TITUS Not I; 'twas Chiron and Demetrius:
    They ravished her and cut away her tongue;
    And they, 'twas they, that did her all this wrong.

SATURNINUS Go, fetch them hither to us presently.

35 resolve answer 38 enforced forced, raped 48 unkind (1) unnatural
(2) cruel

TITUS Why, there they are, both bakèd in this pie,   60
  Whereof their mother daintily hath fed,
  Eating the flesh that she herself hath bred.
  'Tis true, 'tis true; witness my knife's sharp point.
                               He stabs the Empress.

SATURNINUS Die, frantic wretch, for this accursèd deed.
                               [*Kills Titus.*]

LUCIUS Can the son's eye behold his father bleed?   65
  There's meed for meed, death for a deadly deed.
                               [*Kills Saturninus.*]

MARCUS You sad-faced men, people and sons of Rome,
  By uproars severed, as a flight of fowl
  Scattered by winds and high tempestuous gusts,
  O, let me teach you how to knit again   70
  This scattered corn into one mutual sheaf,
  These broken limbs again into one body.

ROMAN LORD Let Rome herself be bane unto herself,
  And she whom mighty kingdoms curtsy to,
  Like a forlorn and desperate castaway,   75
  Do shameful execution on herself,
  But if my frosty signs and chaps of age,
  Grave witnesses of true experience,
  Cannot induce you to attend my words.
  [*To Lucius*] Speak, Rome's dear friend, as erst our
       ancestor,   80
  When with his solemn tongue he did discourse
  To lovesick Dido's sad attending ear
  The story of that baleful burning night,
  When subtle Greeks surprised King Priam's Troy;
  Tell us what Sinon hath bewitched our ears,   85
  Or who hath brought the fatal engine in
  That gives our Troy, our Rome, the civil wound.
  My heart is not compact of flint nor steel;

66 **meed for meed** measure for measure 73 **bane** destruction 77 **But if** unless 77 **frosty signs and chaps of age** i.e., white hair and cracked (wrinkled) skin 80 **erst** formerly 80 **our ancestor** i.e., Aeneas 82 **sad attending** seriously listening 83 **baleful** injurious 85 **Sinon** Greek who persuaded the Trojans to admit the wooden horse 88 **compact** composed

Nor can I utter all our bitter grief,
90 But floods of tears will drown my oratory
And break my utt'rance, even in the time
When it should move ye to attend me most,
And force you to commiseration.
Here's Rome's young captain, let him tell the tale,
95 While I stand by and weep to hear him speak.

LUCIUS Then, gracious auditory, be it known to you
That Chiron and the damned Demetrius
Were they that murd'red our emperor's brother;
And they it were that ravishèd our sister.
100 For their fell faults our brothers were beheaded,
Our father's tears despised, and basely cozened
Of that true hand that fought Rome's quarrel out
And sent her enemies unto the grave.
Lastly, myself unkindly banishèd,
105 The gates shut on me, and turned weeping out,
To beg relief among Rome's enemies,
Who drowned their enmity in my true tears
And oped their arms to embrace me as a friend:
I am the turned-forth, be it known to you,
110 That have preserved her welfare in my blood,
And from her bosom took the enemy's point,
Sheathing the steel in my advent'rous body.
Alas, you know I am no vaunter, I;
My scars can witness, dumb although they are,
115 That my report is just and full of truth.
But, soft! Methinks, I do digress too much,
Citing my worthless praise. O, pardon me,
For when no friends are by, men praise themselves.

MARCUS Now is my turn to speak. Behold the child:
120 Of this was Tamora deliverèd,
The issue of an irreligious Moor,
Chief architect and plotter of these woes:
The villain is alive in Titus' house,

---

100 fell savage   101 cozened cheated   113 vaunter braggart   116 soft hold (a common interjection)

And as he is to witness, this is true.
Now judge what cause had Titus to revenge   125
These wrongs, unspeakable, past patience,
Or more than any living man could bear.
Now have you heard the truth. What say you,
    Romans?
Have we done aught amiss, show us wherein,
And, from the place where you behold us pleading,   130
The poor remainder of Andronici
Will, hand in hand, all headlong hurl ourselves
And on the ragged stones beat forth our souls,
And make a mutual closure of our house.
Speak, Romans, speak, and if you say we shall,   135
Lo, hand in hand, Lucius and I will fall.

AEMILIUS Come, come, thou reverend man of Rome,
And bring our emperor gently in thy hand,
Lucius our emperor; for well I know
The common voice do cry it shall be so.   140

MARCUS Lucius, all hail, Rome's royal Emperor!
[To soldiers] Go, go into old Titus' sorrowful house,
And hither hale that misbelieving Moor,
To be adjudged some direful slaught'ring death,
As punishment for his most wicked life.   145
                            [Exeunt Attendants.]
Lucius, all hail, Rome's gracious governor!
                            [Cries of approval.]

LUCIUS Thanks, gentle Romans: may I govern so,
To heal Rome's harms and wipe away her woe!
But, gentle people, give me aim awhile,
For nature puts me to a heavy task.   150
Stand all aloof; but, uncle, draw you near
To shed obsequious tears upon this trunk.
O, take this warm kiss on thy pale cold lips,
These sorrowful drops upon thy bloodstained face,
The last true duties of thy noble son!   155

133 ragged rugged   134 mutual closure common end   149 give me aim
assist me   152 obsequious mourning

MARCUS　Tear for tear and loving kiss for kiss
　　Thy brother Marcus tenders on thy lips:
　　O, were the sum of these that I should pay
　　Countless and infinite, yet would I pay them!

160　LUCIUS　Come hither, boy; come, come, and learn of us
　　To melt in showers. Thy grandsire loved thee well;
　　Many a time he danced thee on his knee,
　　Sung thee asleep, his loving breast thy pillow;
　　Many a story hath he told to thee,
165　　And bid thee bear his pretty tales in mind,
　　And talk of them when he was dead and gone.

MARCUS　How many thousand times hath these poor
　　　lips,
　　When they were living, warmed themselves on thine!
　　O, now, sweet boy, give them their latest kiss.
170　　Bid him farewell; commit him to the grave;
　　Do them that kindness, and take leave of them.

BOY　O, grandsire, grandsire! Ev'n with all my heart
　　Would I were dead, so you did live again!
　　O Lord, I cannot speak to him for weeping;
175　　My tears will choke me if I ope my mouth.

[*Enter Attendants with Aaron.*]

ROMAN　You sad Andronici, have done with woes;
　　Give sentence on this execrable wretch
　　That hath been breeder of these dire events.

LUCIUS　Set him breast-deep in earth and famish him;
180　　There let him stand and rave and cry for food:
　　If anyone relieves or pities him,
　　For the offense he dies. This is our doom.
　　Some stay, to see him fast'ned in the earth.

AARON　Ah, why should wrath be mute, and fury dumb?
185　　I am no baby, I, that with base prayers
　　I should repent the evils I have done:

169 **latest** last　171 **them** i.e., "these poor lips" of line 167　182 **doom**
sentence

Ten thousand worse than ever yet I did
Would I perform, if I might have my will:
If one good deed in all my life I did,
I do repent it from my very soul.   190

LUCIUS Some loving friends convey the Emperor hence,
And give him burial in his father's grave:
My father and Lavinia shall forthwith
Be closèd in our household's monument.
As for that ravenous tiger, Tamora,   195
No funeral rite, nor man in mourning weed,
No mournful bell shall ring her burial;
But throw her forth to beasts and birds of prey.
Her life was beastly and devoid of pity,
And being dead, let birds on her take pity.   *Exeunt.* 200

FINIS

95

Textual Note

THERE is an allusion to a Roman hero named Titus in *A Knack to Know a Knave*, acted in June 1592. Though the allusion may, of course, be to an earlier play on the subject rather than to Shakespeare's play, there is no need to multiply entities; Shakespeare's *Titus Andronicus* may have been on the stage before 1592. The next bit of evidence is a reference of 23 January 1594 in Henslowe's *Diary* to the effect that Sussex's men acted a new piece, "titus & ondronicus." If the allusion in *A Knave* is not to Shakespeare's play, quite possibly *Titus Andronicus* was indeed new in 1594, but it is equally possible that it was "new" only to Sussex's company, or that it had been newly revised. On 6 February 1594 the Stationers' Register entered "a book intituled a Noble Roman Historye of Titus Andronicus." Perhaps this entry alludes to the play, which indeed was published in 1594, though possibly the entry is to some other piece on the same subject. In 1614 Ben Jonson, in the Induction to *Bartholomew Fair*, mentions that Andronicus was seen on the stage as long ago as "fiue and twentie or thirtie yeeres"; strictly, Jonson's reference would date the play 1584–89, though probably he is speaking loosely and his evidence surely does not prohibit a date in the early nineties. The date widely favored is 1592–94, but there is no compelling reason to believe that *Titus* could not have been written in the late eighties.

Only one copy of the first quarto (1594) is known to be extant. Apparently Q1 (i.e., the first quarto) was printed from Shakespeare's manuscript or from a copy of it; a number of stage directions—such as "Enter ... as many as can be"—suggest an author's hand. In 1600 a second quarto (Q2) was issued. It omits a few lines, adds some, and alters a good deal of punctuation. There is no reason to believe that the alterations represent Shakespeare's revisions; probably all the revisions are a compositor's tamperings. Q3, issued in 1611, was set up from Q2 and therefore has no authority. The version in the First Folio

(F) is based on Q3 but makes numerous small alterations (especially in stage directions) and adds the entire scene (III.ii). The new scene is of sufficient excellence to be Shakespeare's, and though the other changes in F do not suggest that great effort was made to give the play in a version much different from that of Q3, the new scene shows that the editors had access to some unpublished material. The present edition is based on Q1, except for III.ii, which is, of course, based on F. It regularizes speech prefixes (for example, Q1's "Saturnine," "Saturninus," "King," "Satur," are all given here as "Saturninus"); it slightly alters the position of a few stage directions, and it modernizes spelling and punctuation. The act divisions were first established by F; the scene divisions are the work of later editors and though of no authenticity they provide a convenient device for reference. Departures from Q1, other than those mentioned above and corrections of obvious typographical errors, are listed below, the adopted reading first, in bold type, followed by the original reading in roman. If the adopted reading is from Q2, Q3, or F, that fact is indicated in a bracket following the reading. If there is no such indication, the adopted reading is an editor's conjecture.

I.i.35 [for the three and a half lines that follow these words in Q1 see footnote to the line] 69 s.d. **her three sons** her two sonnes 98 **manes** manus 226 **Titan's** [Q2] Tytus 242 **Pantheon** Pathan 264 **chance** [Q2] change 280 **cuique** cuiqum 317 **Phoebe** Thebe 358 s.d. **speak** speakes 369 **Martius** 3. Sonne 370 **Quintus** 2. Sonne 372 **Quintus** 2. sonne 391 [Q1 follows with s.d.: "Exit all but Marcus and Titus," and the other early texts also indicate an exit] 399 **Yes ... remunerate** [F; omitted in the quartos]

II.i.110 **than** this

II.ii.1 **morn** [F] Moone

II.iii.69 **try** [Q2] trie thy 72 **swart** swartie 160 **ears** [Q3] yeares 210 **unhallowed** [F] vnhollow 222 **berayed** bereaud 231 **Pyramus** [Q2] Priamus 236 **Cocytus** Ocitus

II.iv.27 **him** them 30 **three** their

97

TEXTUAL NOTE

III.i.146 **his true** her true

III.ii [this scene is found only in F]   39 **complainer** complayne   52 **thy knife** knife   53 **fly** Flys   55 **are cloyed** cloi'd   72 **myself** my selfes

IV.i.50 **quotes** [Q2] coates   88 **hope** [Q2] hop [or "I op"]

IV.ii.95 **Alcides** [Q2] Alciades

IV.iii.57 **Saturn** Saturnine   78 **News** [Q2] Clowne. Newes

IV.iv.5 **know, as** know know   49 **By** be   99 **ears** [F] yeares

V.ii.52 **caves** cares   56 **Hyperion's** Epeons   65 **worldly** [Q2] wordlie

V.iii.125 **cause** course   144 **adjudged** [F] adiudge   154 **bloodstained** blood slaine   163 **Sung** [Q2] Song

WILLIAM SHAKESPEARE

THE HISTORY OF TROILUS AND CRESSIDA

Edited by Daniel Seltzer

A NEVER WRITER,
TO AN EVER READER.
NEWS.

Eternal reader, you have here a new play, never staled
with the stage, never clapperclawed with the palms of
the vulgar, and yet passing full of the palm comical;
for it is a birth of your brain[1] that never undertook
anything comical vainly. And were but the vain names
of comedies changed for the titles of commodities, or of
plays for pleas, you should see all those grand censors,
that now style them such vanities, flock to them for the
main grace of their gravities—especially this author's
comedies, that are so framed to the life that they serve
for the most common commentaries of all the actions of
our lives, showing such a dexterity and power of wit
that the most displeased with plays are pleased with his
comedies. And all such dull and heavy-witted world-
lings as were never capable of the wit of a comedy,
coming by report of them to his representations, have
found that wit there that they never found in themselves and have parted better witted than they came,
feeling an edge of wit set upon them more than ever
they dreamed they had brain to grind it on. So much
and such savored salt of wit is in his comedies that they
seem, for their height of pleasure, to be born in that sea
that brought forth Venus. Amongst all there is none
more witty than this; and had I time I would comment
upon it, though I know it needs not, for so much as
will make you think your testern well bestowed, but
for so much worth as even poor I know to be stuffed in
it. It deserves such a labor as well as the best comedy

---

1. Footnotes are keyed to the text by line number. Text references are printed in
bold type; the annotation follows in roman type.   **4 your brain** i.e., Shakespeare's
brain   **23 Venus** (the Greek goddess Aphrodite, who, according to Hesiod, was
born in ocean foam)   **26 testern** sixpence (slang)

in Terence or Plautus. And believe this, that when he
is gone and his comedies out of sale, you will scramble   30
for them and set up a new English Inquisition. Take
this for a warning, and at the peril of your pleasure's
loss, and judgment's, refuse not, nor like this the less
for not being sullied with the smoky breath of the
multitude; but thank fortune for the 'scape it hath   35
made amongst you, since by the grand possessors' wills
I believe you should have prayed for them rather
than been prayed. And so I leave all such to be prayed
for, for the state of their wits' healths, that will not
praise it. *Vale*.   40

---

36 **grand possessors** (presumably, the actor-sharers of the King's Men, who may
have tried to stop publication)

PRIAM, King of Troy

HECTOR
TROILUS
PARIS } his sons
DEIPHOBUS
HELENUS

MARGARELON, a bastard son of Priam

AENEAS } Trojan commanders
ANTENOR

CALCHAS, a Trojan priest, taking part with the Greeks

PANDARUS, uncle to Cressida

AGAMEMNON, the Greek general

MENELAUS, his brother

ACHILLES
AJAX
ULYSSES } Greek commanders
NESTOR
DIOMEDES
PATROCLUS

THERSITES, a deformed and scurrilous Greek

ALEXANDER, servant to Cressida

SERVANT TO TROILUS

SERVANT TO PARIS

SERVANT TO DIOMEDES

HELEN, wife to Menelaus

ANDROMACHE, wife to Hector

CASSANDRA, daughter to Priam; a prophetess

CRESSIDA, daughter to Calchas

TROJAN and GREEK SOLDIERS and ATTENDANTS

Scene: Troy, and the Greek camp before it]

THE HISTORY OF
TROILUS AND
CRESSIDA

THE PROLOGUE

[Enter the Prologue, armed for battle.]

In Troy there lies the scene. From isles of Greece
The princes orgulous, their high blood chafed,
Have to the port of Athens sent their ships,
Fraught with the ministers and instruments
Of cruel war. Sixty and nine, that wore   5
Their crownets regal, from th' Athenian bay
Put forth toward Phrygia; and their vow is made
To ransack Troy, within whose strong immures
The ravished Helen, Menelaus' queen,
With wanton Paris sleeps—and that's the quarrel.   10
To Tenedos they come,
And the deep-drawing barks do there disgorge
Their warlike fraughtage. Now on Dardan plains
The fresh and yet unbruisèd Greeks do pitch

Prologue 2 **orgulous** proud   7 **Phrygia** western Asia Minor   8 **immures** walls
11 **Tenedos** the port of Troy 13 **fraughtage** freight, i.e., soldiers
13 **Dardan** Trojan (after Dardanus, son of Zeus and the Pleiad Electra, and
ancestor of Priam)

15 Their brave pavilions. Priam's six-gated city,
    Dardan, and Timbria, Helias, Chetas, Troien,
    And Antenonidus, with massy staples
    And corresponsive and fulfilling bolts,
    Sperr up the sons of Troy.

20 Now expectation, tickling skittish spirits,
    On one and other side, Troyan and Greek,
    Sets all on hazard. And hither am I come,
    A prologue armed, but not in confidence
    Of author's pen or actor's voice, but suited

25 In like conditions as our argument,
    To tell you, fair beholders, that our play
    Leaps o'er the vaunt and firstlings of those broils,
    Beginning in the middle, starting thence away
    To what may be digested in a play.

30 Like or find fault; do as your pleasures are;
    Now good or bad, 'tis but the chance of war.

16-17 **Dardan ... Antenonidus** (names of the gates of Troy) 18 **fulfilling**
filling tightly 19 **Sperr up** shut up 20 **skittish** nervous 23 **armed** equipped
for fight 24 **suited** dressed 25 **argument** subject 27 **vaunt** beginning

[ACT I

Scene I. *Within Troy.*]

Enter Pandarus and Troilus.

TROILUS Call here my varlet, I'll unarm again.
   Why should I war without the walls of Troy
   That find such cruel battle here within?
   Each Troyan that is master of his heart,
   Let him to field; Troilus, alas, hath none.   5

PANDARUS Will this gear ne'er be mended?

TROILUS The Greeks are strong, and skillful to their
      strength,
   Fierce to their skill, and to their fierceness valiant;
   But I am weaker than a woman's tear,
   Tamer than sleep, fonder than ignorance,   10
   Less valiant than the virgin in the night,
   And skilless as unpracticed infancy.

PANDARUS Well, I have told you enough of this. For
   my part, I'll not meddle nor make no farther. He
   that will have a cake out of the wheat must tarry   15
   the grinding.

I.i.1 **varlet** servant   2 **without** outside   6 **gear** business   7 **to** in addition to, in
proportion to   10 **fonder** more unsophisticated, simpler   12 **skilless** inept, naïve

TROILUS Have I not tarried?

PANDARUS Ay, the grinding; but you must tarry the
bolting.

20 TROILUS Have I not tarried?

PANDARUS Ay, the bolting; but you must tarry the
leavening.

TROILUS Still have I tarried.

PANDARUS Ay, to the leavening; but here's yet in the
25 word "hereafter" the kneading, the making of the
cake, the heating the oven, and the baking. Nay,
you must stay the cooling too, or ye may chance
burn your lips.

TROILUS Patience herself, what goddess e'er she be,
30 Doth lesser blench at suff'rance than I do.
At Priam's royal table do I sit,
And when fair Cressid comes into my thoughts—
So, traitor, then she comes when she is thence.

PANDARUS Well, she looked yesternight fairer than ever
35 I saw her look, or any woman else.

TROILUS I was about to tell thee, when my heart,
As wedgèd with a sigh, would rive in twain,
Lest Hector or my father should perceive me—
I have, as when the sun doth light a-scorn,
40 Buried this sigh in wrinkle of a smile;
But sorrow, that is couched in seeming gladness,
Is like that mirth fate turns to sudden sadness.

PANDARUS An her hair were not somewhat darker
than Helen's—well, go to—there were no more
45 comparison between the women; but, for my part,
she is my kinswoman: I would not, as they term it,
praise her, but I would somebody had heard her talk

19 **bolting** sifting   30 **blench** flinch   33 **traitor** (a self-rebuke, for suggesting
that she is sometimes absent)   33 **then she comes when she is thence**
i.e., she returns immediately whenever she is absent   37 **rive** split   39 **a-scorn**
mockingly (?), grudgingly (?)   43 **An if**

yesterday, as I did. I will not dispraise your sister
Cassandra's wit, but——

TROILUS O Pandarus! I tell thee, Pandarus,   50
When I do tell thee, there my hopes lie drowned,
Reply not in how many fathoms deep
They lie indrenched. I tell thee I am mad
In Cressid's love; thou answer'st she is fair,
Pour'st in the open ulcer of my heart   55
Her eyes, her hair, her cheek, her gait, her voice;
Handlest in thy discourse, O, that her hand
In whose comparison all whites are ink,
Writing their own reproach; to whose soft seizure
The cygnet's down is harsh, and spirit of sense   60
Hard as the palm of plowman. This thou tell'st me,
As true thou tell'st me, when I say I love her;
But, saying thus, instead of oil and balm,
Thou lay'st in every gash that love hath given me
The knife that made it.   65

PANDARUS I speak no more than truth.

TROILUS Thou dost not speak so much.

PANDARUS Faith, I'll not meddle in it; let her be as she
is. If she be fair, 'tis the better for her; and she be
not, she has the mends in her own hands.   70

TROILUS Good Pandarus, how now, Pandarus?

PANDARUS I have had my labor for my travail; ill
thought on of her, and ill thought of you; gone
between and between, but small thanks for my labor.

TROILUS What, art thou angry, Pandarus? What, with   75
me?

PANDARUS Because she's kin to me, therefore she's
not so fair as Helen. An she were not kin to me,

---

57 **that her hand** that hand of hers 59 **seizure** grasp 60 **cygnet's** young
swan's 60 **spirit** (the thin bodily substance believed to transmit sense impres-
sions through the nerves) 70 **mends** (1) remedies (2) cosmetics 72 **travail**
(punning on "travel" ["gone between and between"])

she would be as fair a' Friday as Helen is on Sunday.
80   But what care I? I care not an she were a blackamoor; 'tis all one to me.

TROILUS Say I she is not fair?

PANDARUS I do not care whether you do or no. She's a
fool to stay behind her father. Let her to the Greeks,
85   and so I'll tell her the next time I see her. For my
part, I'll meddle nor make no more i' th' matter.

TROILUS Pandarus——

PANDARUS Not I.

TROILUS Sweet Pandarus——

90   PANDARUS Pray you, speak no more to me. I will leave
all as I found it, and there an end.

Exit. Sound alarum.

TROILUS Peace, you ungracious clamors! Peace, rude
sounds!
Fools on both sides! Helen must needs be fair,
When with your blood you daily paint her thus.
95   I cannot fight upon this argument;
It is too starved a subject for my sword.
But Pandarus—O gods, how do you plague me!
I cannot come to Cressid but by Pandar;
And he's as tetchy to be wooed to woo
100   As she is stubborn, chaste, against all suit.
Tell me, Apollo, for thy Daphne's love,
What Cressid is, what Pandar, and what we.
Her bed is India; there she lies, a pearl.
Between our Ilium and where she resides
105   Let it be called the wild and wand'ring flood,
Ourself the merchant, and this sailing Pandar

79 a' on   79-80 on Sunday i.e., in her Sunday best   84 father (Calchas, who
had deserted to the Greeks)   95 argument theme   99 tetchy peevish
101 Daphne (the nymph who was changed into a bay tree as she ran to escape
Apollo)   104 Ilium (here, Priam's palace; generally, Troy [for Ilus, founder of the
city, Priam's grandfather])

Our doubtful hope, our convoy and our bark.

Alarum. Enter Aeneas.

AENEAS How now, Prince Troilus, wherefore not
   afield?

TROILUS Because not there. This woman's answer
   sorts,
   For womanish it is to be from thence.   110
   What news, Aeneas, from the field today?

AENEAS That Paris is returnèd home, and hurt.

TROILUS By whom, Aeneas?

AENEAS   Troilus, by Menelaus.

TROILUS Let Paris bleed; 'tis but a scar to scorn:
   Paris is gored with Menelaus' horn.   *Alarum.*   115

AENEAS Hark what good sport is out of town today!

TROILUS Better at home, if "would I might" were
   "may."
   But to the sport abroad; are you bound thither?

AENEAS In all swift haste.

TROILUS   Come, go we then together.
                                           Exeunt.

---

109 **sorts** is appropriate   114 **but a scar to scorn** i.e., considering its source, the
kind of scar to be scorned   115 **horn** (of a cuckold)

[Scene II. *Within Troy.*]

Enter Cressida and [Alexander,] her man.

CRESSIDA Who were those went by?

MAN   Queen Hecuba and Helen.

CRESSIDA And whither go they?

MAN   Up to the eastern tower,
Whose height commands as subject all the vale,
To see the battle. Hector, whose patience
5   Is as a virtue fixed, today was moved.
He chid Andromache, and struck his armorer,
And, like as there were husbandry in war,
Before the sun rose he was harnessed light,
And to the field goes he, where every flower
10   Did, as a prophet, weep what it foresaw
In Hector's wrath.

CRESSIDA   What was his cause of anger?

MAN The noise goes, this: there is among the Greeks
A lord of Troyan blood, nephew to Hector;
They call him Ajax.

CRESSIDA   Good; and what of him?

15   MAN They say he is a very man per se
And stands alone.

CRESSIDA So do all men unless they are drunk, sick, or
have no legs.

MAN This man, lady, hath robbed many beasts of
20   their particular additions. He is as valiant as the

I.ii.7 **husbandry** good management, thrift 8 **harnessed** armored 20 **additions**
distinctive qualities, characteristics

lion, churlish as the bear, slow as the elephant; a man
into whom nature hath so crowded humors that his
valor is crushed into folly, his folly sauced with
discretion. There is no man hath a virtue that he
hath not a glimpse of, nor any man an attaint but he   25
carries some stain of it. He is melancholy without
cause and merry against the hair. He hath the joints
of everything, but everything so out of joint that he
is a gouty Briareus, many hands and no use, or
purblind Argus, all eyes and no sight.   30

CRESSIDA But how should this man that makes me
 smile make Hector angry?

MAN They say he yesterday coped Hector in the
 battle and struck him down, the disdain and shame
 whereof hath ever since kept Hector fasting and   35
 waking.

Enter Pandarus.

CRESSIDA Who comes here?

MAN Madam, your uncle Pandarus.

CRESSIDA Hector's a gallant man.

MAN As may be in the world, lady.   40

PANDARUS What's that? What's that?

CRESSIDA Good morrow, uncle Pandarus.

PANDARUS Good morrow, cousin Cressid. What do you
 talk of? Good morrow, Alexander. How do you,
 cousin? When were you at Ilium?   45

CRESSIDA This morning, uncle.

---

22 **humors** (bodily fluids which, in excess, were thought to cause emotional
disorder) 25 **glimpse** momentary shining 25 **attaint** imputation of dishonor
27 **against the hair** contrary to natural tendency (cf. "against the grain")
29 **Briareus** (a hundred-handed giant) 30 **Argus** (a herdsman with eyes covering
his body) 33 **coped** engaged, encountered 43 **cousin** (a term of familiarity;
here, niece)

PANDARUS What were you talking of when I came? Was Hector armed and gone ere ye came to Ilium? Helen was not up, was she?

50 CRESSIDA Hector was gone, but Helen was not up.

PANDARUS E'en so, Hector was stirring early.

CRESSIDA That were we talking of, and of his anger.

PANDARUS Was he angry?

CRESSIDA So he says here.

55 PANDARUS True, he was so; I know the cause too. He'll lay about him today, I can tell them that; and there's Troilus will not come far behind him. Let them take heed of Troilus, I can tell them that too.

CRESSIDA What, is he angry too?

60 PANDARUS Who, Troilus? Troilus is the better man of the two.

CRESSIDA O Jupiter! There's no comparison.

PANDARUS What, not between Troilus and Hector? Do you know a man if you see him?

65 CRESSIDA Ay, if I ever saw him before and knew him.

PANDARUS Well, I say Troilus is Troilus.

CRESSIDA Then you say as I say, for I am sure he is not Hector.

PANDARUS No, nor Hector is not Troilus in some
70 degrees.

CRESSIDA 'Tis just to each of them; he is himself.

PANDARUS Himself? Alas, poor Troilus, I would he were.

69-70 in some degrees by some distance; in some (specific) ways (?)
72-73 I would he were i.e., I wish he were himself, and not in love

CRESSIDA So he is.

PANDARUS Condition, I had gone barefoot to India.   75

CRESSIDA He is not Hector.

PANDARUS Himself? No, he's not himself. Would 'a
were himself. Well, the gods are above; time must
friend or end. Well, Troilus, well, I would my heart
were in her body. No, Hector is not a better man   80
than Troilus.

CRESSIDA Excuse me.

PANDARUS He is elder.

CRESSIDA Pardon me, pardon me.

PANDARUS Th' other's not come to't; you shall tell me   85
another tale when th' other's come to't. Hector shall
not have his will this year.

CRESSIDA He shall not need it if he have his own.

PANDARUS Nor his qualities.

CRESSIDA No matter.   90

PANDARUS Nor his beauty.

CRESSIDA 'Twould not become him. His own's better.

PANDARUS You have no judgment, niece. Helen herself
swore th' other day that Troilus, for a brown favor—
for so 'tis, I must confess—not brown neither——   95

CRESSIDA No, but brown.

PANDARUS Faith, to say truth, brown and not brown.

CRESSIDA To say the truth, true and not true.

PANDARUS She praised his complexion above Paris.

CRESSIDA Why, Paris hath color enough.   100

75 **Condition** i.e., even if to bring that about   77 **'a** he   86 **come to't** reached
manhood   87 **will** (some editors emend to wit, i.e., intelligence)   94 **brown
favor** dark complexion

113

PANDARUS So he has.

CRESSIDA Then Troilus should have too much. If she praised him above, his complexion is higher than his. He having color enough, and the other higher, is too
105 flaming a praise for a good complexion. I had as lief Helen's golden tongue had commended Troilus for a copper nose.

PANDARUS I swear to you, I think Helen loves him better than Paris.

110 CRESSIDA Then she's a merry Greek indeed.

PANDARUS Nay, I am sure she does. She came to him th' other day into the compassed window—and, you know, he has not past three or four hairs on his chin——

115 CRESSIDA Indeed, a tapster's arithmetic may soon bring his particulars therein to a total.

PANDARUS Why, he is very young; and yet will he, within three pound, lift as much as his brother Hector.

120 CRESSIDA Is he so young a man, and so old a lifter?

PANDARUS But to prove to you that Helen loves him, she came and puts me her white hand to his cloven chin——

CRESSIDA Juno have mercy; how came it cloven?

125 PANDARUS Why, you know 'tis dimpled; I think his smiling becomes him better than any man in all Phrygia.

CRESSIDA O, he smiles valiantly.

PANDARUS Does he not?

130 CRESSIDA O, yes, an 'twere a cloud in autumn.

---

110 a merry Greek i.e., one of frivolous or loose behavior (slang)   112 compassed bay   120 so old a lifter so experienced a thief (cf. "shoplifter")

PANDARUS Why, go to then. But to prove to you that
  Helen loves Troilus——

CRESSIDA Troilus will stand to the proof if you'll
  prove it so.

PANDARUS Troilus? Why, he esteems her no more than   135
  I esteem an addle egg.

CRESSIDA If you love an addle egg as well as you love
  an idle head, you would eat chickens i' the shell.

PANDARUS I cannot choose but laugh to think how she
  tickled his chin. Indeed, she has a marvel's white   140
  hand, I must needs confess.

CRESSIDA Without the rack.

PANDARUS And she takes upon her to spy a white hair
  on his chin.

CRESSIDA Alas poor chin, many a wart is richer.   145

PANDARUS But there was such laughing. Queen Hecuba
  laughed that her eyes ran o'er.

CRESSIDA With millstones.

PANDARUS And Cassandra laughed.

CRESSIDA But there was a more temperate fire under   150
  the pot of her eyes. Did her eyes run o'er too?

PANDARUS And Hector laughed.

CRESSIDA At what was all this laughing?

PANDARUS Marry, at the white hair that Helen spied on
  Troilus' chin.   155

CRESSIDA An't had been a green hair, I should have
  laughed too.

PANDARUS They laughed not so much at the hair as at
  his pretty answer.

133 **stand** (a bawdy pun; cf. Sonnet 151) 136 **addle** rotten 140 **marvel's**
marvelous 142 **rack** torture 154 **Marry** (an interjection, from the oath, "By
the Virgin Mary")

160 CRESSIDA What was his answer?

PANDARUS Quoth she, "Here's but two-and-fifty hairs on your chin, and one of them is white."

CRESSIDA This is her question.

PANDARUS That's true, make no question of that. 165 "Two-and-fifty hairs," quoth he, "and one white. That white hair is my father, and all the rest are his sons." "Jupiter!" quoth she, "which of these hairs is Paris, my husband?" "The forked one," quoth he; "pluck't out, and give it him." But there was such 170 laughing, and Helen so blushed, and Paris so chafed, and all the rest so laughed, that it passed.

CRESSIDA So let it now, for it has been a great while going by.

PANDARUS Well, cousin, I told you a thing yesterday; 175 think on't.

CRESSIDA So I do.

PANDARUS I'll be sworn 'tis true; he will weep you, an 'twere a man born in April.   *Sound a retreat.*

CRESSIDA And I'll spring up in his tears, an 'twere a 180 nettle against May.

PANDARUS Hark, they are coming from the field. Shall we stand up here and see them as they pass toward Ilium? Good niece, do; sweet niece, Cressida.

CRESSIDA At your pleasure.

185 PANDARUS Here, here, here's an excellent place; here we may see most bravely. I'll tell you them all by their names as they pass by, but mark Troilus above the rest.

Enter Aeneas [and passes across the stage].

168 forked (resembling a cuckold's horns [?])   178 an as if   180 against in advance of   186 bravely excellently

116

CRESSIDA Speak not so loud.

PANDARUS That's Aeneas. Is not that a brave man? 190
He's one of the flowers of Troy, I can tell you. But
mark Troilus; you shall see anon.

Enter Antenor [and passes across the stage].

CRESSIDA Who's that?

PANDARUS That's Antenor. He has a shrewd wit, I can
tell you; and he's man good enough—he's one o' the 195
soundest judgments in Troy whosoever, and a
proper man of person. When comes Troilus? I'll
show you Troilus anon. If he see me, you shall see
him nod at me.

CRESSIDA Will he give you the nod? 200

PANDARUS You shall see.

CRESSIDA If he do, the rich shall have more.

Enter Hector [and passes across the stage].

PANDARUS That's Hector, that, that, look you, that;
there's a fellow! Go thy way, Hector! There's a brave
man, niece. O brave Hector! Look how he looks; 205
there's a countenance! Is't not a brave man?

CRESSIDA O, a brave man.

PANDARUS Is 'a not? It does a man's heart good. Look
you what hacks are on his helmet. Look you yonder,
do you see? Look you there. There's no jesting; 210
there's laying on, take't off who will, as they say.
There be hacks!

CRESSIDA Be those with swords?

---

190 **brave** fine 197 **proper** handsome 200 **nod** (play on "noddy,"
simpleton) 202 **the rich shall have more** i.e., the fool shall become more
foolish 211 **take't off who will** i.e., whoever cares to say otherwise (to "lay on"
and "take off" were common colloquial tags)

PANDARUS Swords, anything, he cares not; an the devil
215   come to him, it's all one. By God's lid, it does one's
heart good.

Enter Paris [and passes across the stage].

Yonder comes Paris, yonder comes Paris. Look ye
yonder, niece. Is't not a gallant man too, is't not?
Why, this is brave now. Who said he came hurt
220   home today? He's not hurt. Why, this will do
Helen's heart good now, ha? Would I could see
Troilus now. You shall see Troilus anon.

CRESSIDA Who's that?

Enter Helenus [and passes across the stage].

PANDARUS That's Helenus. I marvel where Troilus is.
225   That's Helenus. I think he went not forth today.
That's Helenus.

CRESSIDA Can Helenus fight, uncle?

PANDARUS Helenus? No. Yes, he'll fight indifferent
well. I marvel where Troilus is. Hark, do you not
230   hear the people cry "Troilus"? Helenus is a priest.

CRESSIDA What sneaking fellow comes yonder?

Enter Troilus [and passes across the stage].

PANDARUS Where? Yonder? That's Deiphobus. 'Tis
Troilus! There's a man, niece, hem? Brave Troilus,
the prince of chivalry!

235 CRESSIDA Peace, for shame, peace!

PANDARUS Mark him, note him. O brave Troilus! Look
well upon him, niece. Look you how his sword is
bloodied, and his helm more hacked than Hector's—
and how he looks, and how he goes. O

---

218 gallant (general term of praise, as "brave')

admirable youth! He never saw three-and-twenty. 240
Go thy way, Troilus, go thy way! Had I a sister
were a grace, or a daughter a goddess, he should take
his choice. O admirable man! Paris? Paris is dirt to
him; and I warrant Helen, to change, would give an
eye to boot.   245

Enter Common Soldiers.

CRESSIDA Here comes more.

PANDARUS Asses, fools, dolts; chaff and bran, chaff and
bran; porridge after meat. I could live and die in the
eyes of Troilus. Ne'er look, ne'er look. The eagles
are gone; crows and daws, crows and daws. 250
I had rather be such a man as Troilus than Agamemnon and all Greece.

CRESSIDA There is amongst the Greeks Achilles, a
better man than Troilus.

PANDARUS Achilles? A drayman, a porter, a very camel. 255

CRESSIDA Well, well.

PANDARUS "Well, well"? Why, have you any discretion, have you any eyes, do you know what a man
is? Is not birth, beauty, good shape, discourse,
manhood, learning, gentleness, virtue, youth, lib- 260
erality, and such like, the spice and salt that season
a man?

CRESSIDA Ay, a minced man; and then to be baked
with no date in the pie, for then the man's date is
out.   265

---

242 grace attendant goddess   255 drayman one who draws a cart   255 camel
i.e., beast of burden   263 minced (1) mincing, affected (2) overspiced (3) divided
into parts beyond recognition   263-65 then to be baked ... out (dates were a
common ingredient in most pastries; Cressida's pun implies that Troilus, as
Pandarus compounds hm, could contain no substance and be of no interest, out
of date)

PANDARUS You are such a woman a man knows not at what ward you lie.

CRESSIDA Upon my back, to defend my belly; upon my wit, to defend my wiles; upon my secrecy, to defend
270 mine honesty; my mask, to defend my beauty; and you, to defend all these. And at all these wards I lie, at a thousand watches.

PANDARUS Say one of your watches.

CRESSIDA Nay, I'll watch you for that; and that's one
275 of the chiefest of them too. If I cannot ward what I would not have hit, I can watch you for telling how I took the blow; unless it swell past hiding, and then it's past watching.

PANDARUS You are such another!

Enter [Troilus'] Boy.

280 BOY Sir, my lord would instantly speak with you.

PANDARUS Where?

BOY At your own house. There he unarms him.

PANDARUS Good boy, tell him I come.   [*Exit Boy.*]
I doubt he be hurt. Fare ye well, good niece.

285 CRESSIDA Adieu, uncle.

PANDARUS I will be with you, niece, by and by.

CRESSIDA To bring, uncle.

PANDARUS Ay, a token from Troilus.

---

267 **ward** position of defense in swordplay   270 **honesty** chastity   272 **watches** periods of the night   276 **watch you for telling** i.e., to make certain you do not tell   277 **swell past hiding** (Cressida thus completes her ribald play on words)   284 **doubt** suspect that, fear that   287 **To bring** (an idiomatic intensifier, now obsolete, meaning roughly, "indeed" or "with a vengeance"; Cressida says, with mild sarcasm, "yes, I am sure you will," although Pandarus picks up the word in its normal verbal sense)

CRESSIDA By the same token, you are a bawd.

Exit Pandarus.

Words, vows, gifts, tears, and love's full sacrifice   290
He offers in another's enterprise;
But more in Troilus thousandfold I see
Than in the glass of Pandar's praise may be.
Yet hold I off. Women are angels, wooing;
Things won are done, joy's soul lies in the doing.   295
That she beloved knows nought that knows not this:
Men prize the thing ungained more than it is;
That she was never yet, that ever knew
Love got so sweet as when desire did sue.
Therefore this maxim out of love I teach: 300
Achievement is command; ungained, beseech.
Then, though my heart's content firm love
     doth bear,
Nothing of that shall from mine eyes appear.   *Exit.*

[Scene III. *The Greek camp.*]

Sennet. Enter Agamemnon, Nestor, Ulysses, Diomedes,
Menelaus, with others.

AGAMEMNON Princes,
What grief hath set these jaundies o'er your cheeks?
The ample proposition that hope makes
In all designs begun on earth below
Fails in the promised largeness. Checks and disasters   5

---

294 wooing while being wooed 296 That she that woman 297 it is its
value 299 got i.e., by men 300 out of love from love's teaching
301 Achievement ... beseech when men achieve love, they command; while still
trying to gain it, they will beg I.iii.s.d. Sennet (a trumpet call announcing
specific personages in a procession) 2 jaundies jaundice (an obsolete plural)

Grow in the veins of actions highest reared,
As knots, by the conflux of meeting sap,
Infects the sound pine and diverts his grain
Tortive and errant from his course of growth.
10 Nor, princes, is it matter new to us
That we come short of our suppose so far
That after seven years' siege yet Troy walls stand;
Sith every action that hath gone before,
Whereof we have record, trial did draw
15 Bias and thwart, not answering the aim
And that unbodied figure of the thought
That gave't surmisèd shape. Why then, you princes,
Do you with cheeks abashed behold our works
And call them shames, which are indeed nought
        else
20 But the protractive trials of great Jove
To find persistive constancy in men?
The fineness of which metal is not found
In Fortune's love; for then, the bold and coward,
The wise and fool, the artist and unread,
25 The hard and soft, seem all affined and kin.
But, in the wind and tempest of her frown,
Distinction, with a broad and powerful fan,
Puffing at all, winnows the light away,
And what hath mass or matter by itself
30 Lies rich in virtue and unmingled.

NESTOR With due observance of thy godlike seat,
Great Agamemnon, Nestor shall apply
Thy latest words. In the reproof of chance
Lies the true proof of men. The sea being smooth,
35 How many shallow bauble boats dare sail
Upon her patient breast, making their way
With those of nobler bulk?

---

7 conflux flowing together 9 Tortive and errant twisted and wandering
11 suppose anticipation 15 Bias and thwart to one side and crosswise
18 cheeks abashed i.e., faces turned aside in confusion and shame 20 protractive extended 24 artist scholar 25 affined in affinity, related 30 unmingled
unmixed with other essences 32 apply show examples of (as in a rhetorical
exercise) 33 reproof rebuff

But let the ruffian Boreas once enrage
The gentle Thetis, and anon behold
The strong-ribbed bark through liquid mountains
    cut,   40
Bounding between the two moist elements
Like Perseus' horse, where's then the saucy boat,
Whose weak untimbered sides but even now
Corrivaled greatness? Either to harbor fled,
Or made a toast for Neptune. Even so   45
Doth valor's show and valor's worth divide
In storms of fortune. For in her ray and brightness
The herd hath more annoyance by the breese
Than by the tiger; but when the splitting wind
Makes flexible the knees of knotted oaks,   50
And flies fled under shade, why then the thing of
    courage,
As roused with rage, with rage doth sympathize,
And with an accent tuned in selfsame key
Returns to chiding fortune.

ULYSSES   Agamemnon,
Thou great commander, nerves and bone of Greece,   55
Heart of our numbers, soul and only sprite,
In whom the tempers and the minds of all
Should be shut up, hear what Ulysses speaks.
Besides th' applause and approbation
The which [to Agamemnon], most mighty for thy
    place and sway,   60
[to Nestor] And thou most reverend for thy
    stretched-out life,
I give to both your speeches—which were such
As Agamemnon and the hand of Greece
Should hold up high in brass; and such again

---

38 **Boreas** (the north wind)   39 **Thetis** (a sea maiden, Achilles' mother, but here personifying the sea)   42 **Perseus' horse** (Pegasus, the winged horse)   45 **toast** (a piece of toast was usually soaked in wine)   46 **show** outward appearance 48 **breese** gadfly   52 **sympathize** becomes similar to   54 **Returns** replies 55 **nerves** sinews   56 **sprite** spirit   58 **shut up** gathered in

65   As venerable Nestor, hatched in silver,
Should with a bond of air, strong as the axletree
On which heaven rides, knit all the Greekish ears
To his experienced tongue—yet let it please both,
Thou great, and wise, to hear Ulysses speak.

70   AGAMEMNON Speak, Prince of Ithaca; and be't of less
     expect
That matter needless, of importless burden,
Divide thy lips than we are confident,
When rank Thersites opes his mastic jaws,
We shall hear music, wit, and oracle.

75   ULYSSES Troy, yet upon his basis, had been down,
And the great Hector's sword had lacked a master,
But for these instances.
The specialty of rule hath been neglected;
And look, how many Grecian tents do stand
80   Hollow upon this plain, so many hollow factions.
When that the general is not like the hive
To whom the foragers shall all repair,
What honey is expected? Degree being vizarded,
Th' unworthiest shows as fairly in the mask.
85   The heavens themselves, the planets, and this center
Observe degree, priority, and place,
Insisture, course, proportion, season, form,
Office, and custom, in all line of order.
And therefore is the glorious planet Sol
90   In noble eminence enthroned and sphered
Amidst the other; whose med'cinable eye
Corrects the influence of evil planets,

---

65 **hatched in silver** (referring to the silver lines in his hair)   73 **mastic** abusive, scourging (sometimes emended to "mastiff")   77 **instances** reasons   78 **The specialty of rule** the particular organization of ruling, the distinction of rights in a chain of authority   81–83 **When ... expected** i.e., when the endeavors of the general populace are not similar to those of the agent which rules them, and to which they are responsible, what profit can be expected? (?); when the ruling general is dissimilar in kind to the soldiers in his army, what profit, etc. (?)   83 **Degree being vizarded** the hierarchy of authority being hidden   87 **Insisture** regularity of position   89 **Sol** the sun   91 **other** others   92 **influence** astrological effect

And posts, like the commandment of a king,
Sans check, to good and bad. But when the planets
In evil mixture to disorder wander,   95
What plagues, and what portents, what mutiny,
What raging of the sea, shaking of earth,
Commotion in the winds, frights, changes, horrors,
Divert and crack, rend and deracinate
The unity and married calm of states   100
Quite from their fixure? O, when degree is shaked,
Which is the ladder of all high designs,
The enterprise is sick. How could communities,
Degrees in schools, and brotherhoods in cities,
Peaceful commerce from dividable shores,   105
The primogenity and due of birth,
Prerogative of age, crowns, scepters, laurels,
But by degree, stand in authentic place?
Take but degree away, untune that string,
And hark what discord follows. Each thing meets   110
In mere oppugnancy. The bounded waters
Should lift their bosoms higher than the shores
And make a sop of all this solid globe;
Strength should be lord of imbecility,
And the rude son should strike his father dead;   115
Force should be right, or rather right and wrong—
Between whose endless jar justice resides—
Should lose their names, and so should justice too.
Then everything include itself in power,
Power into will, will into appetite,   120
And appetite, an universal wolf,
So doubly seconded with will and power,
Must make perforce an universal prey
And last eat up himself. Great Agamemnon,
This chaos, when degree is suffocate,   125
Follows the choking.
And this neglection of degree it is

95 **evil mixture** unlucky or malignant relationship (astrological)   99 **deracinate** uproot   106 **primogenity** right of the eldest son to succeed to his father's estate   111 **mere oppugnancy** total strife   113 **sop** pulp   114 **imbecility** i.e., weakness   117 **jar** discord   119 **include itself in power** enclose itself within power, i.e., become power

That by a pace goes backward with a purpose
It hath to climb. The general's disdained
130   By him one step below, he by the next,
That next by him beneath; so every step,
Exampled by the first pace that is sick
Of his superior, grows to an envious fever
Of pale and bloodless emulation;
135   And 'tis this fever that keeps Troy on foot,
Not her own sinews. To end a tale of length,
Troy in our weakness stands, not in her strength.

NESTOR   Most wisely hath Ulysses here discovered
The fever whereof all our power is sick.

AGAMEMNON   The nature of the sickness found,
140   Ulysses,
What is the remedy?

ULYSSES   The great Achilles, whom opinion crowns
The sinew and the forehand of our host,
Having his ear full of his airy fame,
145   Grows dainty of his worth, and in his tent
Lies mocking our designs. With him Patroclus
Upon a lazy bed the livelong day
Breaks scurril jests,
And with ridiculous and silly action
150   (Which, slanderer, he imitation calls)
He pageants us. Sometimes, great Agamemnon,
Thy topless deputation he puts on,
And, like a strutting player, whose conceit
Lies in his hamstring, and doth think it rich
155   To hear the wooden dialogue and sound
'Twixt his stretched footing and the scaffoldage,

127-29 **And this neglection ... climb** this neglect of hierarchy causes a step toward disintegration each time an attempt is made to climb upward 134 **emulation** rivalry 145 **dainty of** finicky about 149-50 **silly action ... imitation** (Ulysses contrasts such charades with true imitation to the life, presumably the goal of the excellent actor) 151 **pageants** mimics 152 **topless deputation** unlimited office 153-54 **conceit Lies in his hamstring** imagination lies in the tendon of his leg 155 **wooden dialogue** i.e., the thumps of heavy footfalls on the wooden stage floor 156 **stretched footing** absurdly long strides 156 **scaffoldage** scaffold, stage

Such to-be-pitied and o'erwrested seeming
He acts thy greatness in; and when he speaks,
'Tis like a chime a-mending, with terms unsquared,
Which, from the tongue of roaring Typhon dropped,   160
Would seem hyperboles. At this fusty stuff
The large Achilles, on his pressed bed lolling,
From his deep chest laughs out a loud applause,
Cries, "Excellent! 'tis Agamemnon right.
Now play me Nestor; hem, and stroke thy beard,   165
As he being drest to some oration."
That's done, as near as the extremest ends
Of parallels, as like as Vulcan and his wife,
Yet god Achilles still cries, "Excellent!
'Tis Nestor right. Now play him me, Patroclus,   170
Arming to answer in a night alarm."
And then, forsooth, the faint defects of age
Must be the scene of mirth; to cough and spit,
And with a palsy fumbling on his gorget,
Shake in and out the rivet. And at this sport   175
Sir Valor dies; cries, "O, enough, Patroclus,
Or give me ribs of steel; I shall split all
In pleasure of my spleen!" And in this fashion
All our abilities, gifts, natures, shapes,
Severals and generals of grace exact,   180
Achievements, plots, orders, preventions,
Excitements to the field or speech for truce,
Success or loss, what is or is not, serves
As stuff for these two to make paradoxes.

---

157 **o'erwrested seeming** overstrained impersonation 159 **chime a-mending** (1) chime being repaired (2) dissonant combination of sounds just following the ringing of many chimes (?) 159 **unsquared** inappropriate 160 **roaring Typhon** (a monster with serpents' heads and a tremendous voice) 161 **fusty** stale, second-rate 166 **drest** carefully prepared for, addressed 168 **Vulcan and his wife** (Vulcan, god of the smithy and forge, was depicted as sooty, and was lame besides; his "wife" was Venus, who cuckolded him with Mars) 170 **me** i.e., for me 174 **gorget** throat armor 178 **spleen** (supposed the seat of the emotions of anger and hilarity) 180 **Severals and generals** individual and general qualities 184 **paradoxes** absurdities

185 NESTOR And in the imitation of these twain,
         Who, as Ulysses says, opinion crowns
         With an imperial voice, many are infect.
         Ajax is grown self-willed, and bears his head
         In such a rein, in full as proud a place
190   As broad Achilles; keeps his tent like him;
         Makes factious feasts; rails on our state of war,
         Bold as an oracle, and sets Thersites,
         A slave whose gall coins slanders like a mint,
         To match us in comparisons with dirt,
195   To weaken and discredit our exposure,
         How rank soever rounded in with danger.

    ULYSSES They tax our policy and call it cowardice,
         Count wisdom as no member of the war,
         Forestall prescience, and esteem no act
200   But that of hand. The still and mental parts
         That do contrive how many hands shall strike
         When fitness calls them on, and know by measure
         Of their observant toil the enemies' weight—
         Why, this hath not a finger's dignity.
205   They call this bed-work, mapp'ry, closet war;
         So that the ram that batters down the wall,
         For the great swinge and rudeness of his poise,
         They place before his hand that made the engine,
         Or those that with the fineness of their souls
210   By reason guide his execution.

    NESTOR Let this be granted, and Achilles' horse
         Makes many Thetis' sons.   *Tucket.*

    AGAMEMNON What trumpet? Look, Menelaus.

    MENELAUS From Troy.

---

189 **In such a rein** i.e., so high   193 **gall** (the source of bile, which was thought
to produce rancor and abuse)   196 **rank** densely, abundantly   197 **tax**
criticize   199 **Forestall prescience** discount foresight   202 **fitness** readiness
205 **mapp'ry** map work   207 **swinge** impetus, whirling force   211 **Achilles'
horse** (either literally, or collectively, for his soldiers, the Myrmidons)
212 s.d. **Tucket** trumpet call

Enter Aeneas.

AGAMEMNON What would you 'fore our tent?   215

AENEAS Is this great Agamemnon's tent, I pray you?

AGAMEMNON Even this.

AENEAS May one that is a herald and a prince
    Do a fair message to his kingly eyes?

AGAMEMNON With surety stronger than Achilles' arm   220
    'Fore all the Greekish heads, which with one voice
    Call Agamemnon head and general.

AENEAS Fair leave and large security. How may
    A stranger to those most imperial looks
    Know them from eyes of other mortals?

AGAMEMNON   How?   225

AENEAS Ay.
    I ask, that I might waken reverence,
    And bid the cheek be ready with a blush
    Modest as morning when she coldly eyes
    The youthful Phoebus.   230
    Which is that god in office, guiding men?
    Which is the high and mighty Agamemnon?

AGAMEMNON This Troyan scorns us, or the men of
        Troy
    Are ceremonious courtiers.

AENEAS Courtiers as free, as debonair, unarmed,   235
    As bending angels; that's their fame in peace.
    But when they would seem soldiers, they have galls,
    Good arms, strong joints, true swords—and, great
        Jove's accord,
    Nothing so full of heart. But peace, Aeneas;
    Peace, Troyan; lay thy finger on thy lips.   240
    The worthiness of praise distains his worth,

219 **to his kingly eyes** i.e., in his presence   230 **Phoebus** Phoebus Apollo (the sun god)   236 **bending** bowing   238 **Jove's accord** i.e., with Jove on their side   241 **distains** sullies

If that the praised himself bring the praise forth.
But what the repining enemy commends,
That breath fame blows; that praise, sole pure, transcends.

AGAMEMNON Sir, you of Troy, call you yourself
245   Aeneas?

AENEAS Ay, Greek, that is my name.

AGAMEMNON What's your affair, I pray you?

AENEAS Sir, pardon; 'tis for Agamemnon's ears.

AGAMEMNON He hears nought privately that comes
from Troy.

250 AENEAS Nor I from Troy come not to whisper him.
I bring a trumpet to awake his ear,
To set his seat on the attentive bent,
And then to speak.

AGAMEMNON   Speak frankly as the wind;
It is not Agamemnon's sleeping hour.
255 That thou shalt know, Troyan, he is awake,
He tells thee so himself.

AENEAS   Trumpet, blow loud,
Send thy brass voice through all these lazy tents;
And every Greek of mettle, let him know,
What Troy means fairly shall be spoke aloud.

Sound trumpet.

260 We have, great Agamemnon, here in Troy
A prince called Hector—Priam is his father—
Who in this dull and long-continued truce
Is rusty grown. He bade me take a trumpet,
And to this purpose speak: kings, princes, lords,
265 If there be one among the fair'st of Greece
That holds his honor higher than his ease,
That seeks his praise more than he fears his peril,
That knows his valor and knows not his fear,
That loves his mistress more than in confession

252 To ... bent i.e., to make him, and his place of government, pay
attention   263 trumpet i.e., a trumpeter in attendance

With truant vows to her own lips he loves, 270
And dare avow her beauty and her worth
In other arms than hers—to him this challenge;
Hector, in view of Troyans and of Greeks,
Shall make it good, or do his best to do it;
He hath a lady wiser, fairer, truer, 275
Than ever Greek did compass in his arms;
And will tomorrow with his trumpet call,
Midway between your tents and walls of Troy,
To rouse a Grecian that is true in love.
If any come, Hector shall honor him; 280
If none, he'll say in Troy when he retires,
The Grecian dames are sunburnt and not worth
The splinter of a lance. Even so much.

AGAMEMNON This shall be told our lovers, Lord
Aeneas;
If none of them have soul in such a kind, 285
We left them all at home. But we are soldiers;
And may that soldier a mere recreant prove,
That means not, hath not, or is not in love!
If then one is, or hath, or means to be,
That one meets Hector; if none else, I am he. 290

NESTOR Tell him of Nestor, one that was a man
When Hector's grandsire sucked. He is old now,
But if there be not in our Grecian host
A nobleman that hath one spark of fire
To answer for his love, tell him from me, 295
I'll hide my silver beard in a gold beaver,
And in my vantbrace put my withered brawns,
And, meeting him, will tell him that my lady
Was fairer than his grandam, and as chaste
As may be in the world. His youth in flood, 300
I'll prove this truth with my three drops of blood.

269-70 **That loves … lips he loves,** i.e., one that loves his mistress even more than the false oaths of lip service (?); more than enough to swear false vows that he loves her (?) 272 **In other arms than hers** i.e., with weapons 282 **sunburnt** dark (for the Elizabethans, ugly) 296 **beaver** movable face-guard of a helmet 297 **vantbrace** armor fitting the forearm 297 **brawns** arm (or leg) muscles (an obsolete plural)

AENEAS Now heavens forfend such scarcity of youth!

ULYSSES Amen.

[AGAMEMNON] Fair Lord Aeneas, let me touch your
        hand;
305   To our pavilion shall I lead you first.
    Achilles shall have word of this intent;
    So shall each lord of Greece, from tent to tent.
    Yourself shall feast with us before you go,
    And find the welcome of a noble foe.

                    Exeunt. Manent Ulysses and Nestor.

310 ULYSSES Nestor.

NESTOR What says Ulysses?

ULYSSES I have a young conception in my brain;
    Be you my time to bring it to some shape.

NESTOR What is't?

315 ULYSSES This 'tis:
    Blunt wedges rive hard knots; the seeded pride
    That hath to this maturity blown up
    In rank Achilles, must or now be cropped
    Or, shedding, breed a nursery of like evil
320   To overbulk us all.

NESTOR   Well, and how?

ULYSSES This challenge that the gallant Hector sends,
    However it is spread in general name,
    Relates in purpose only to Achilles.

NESTOR True, the purpose is perspicuous as substance
325   Whose grossness little characters sum up;
    And, in the publication, make no strain
    But that Achilles, were his brain as barren
    As banks of Libya—though, Apollo knows,
    'Tis dry enough—will with great speed of judgment,

---

309 s.d. **Manent** (they) remain   312-13 **I have ... some shape** i.e., I have the
beginning of an idea; let me develop it as you listen   319 **shedding** i.e., scattering
seed   325 **Whose grossness ... sum up** whose large size can be defined by small
figures   326 **make no strain** you may be sure

Ay with celerity, find Hector's purpose   330
Pointing on him.

ULYSSES And wake him to the answer, think you?

NESTOR Why, 'tis most meet. Who may you else
      oppose
    That can from Hector bring his honor off,
    If not Achilles? Though't be a sportful combat,   335
    Yet in the trial much opinion dwells;
    For here the Troyans taste our dear'st repute
    With their fin'st palate; and trust to me, Ulysses,
    Our imputation shall be oddly poised
    In this vild action. For the success,   340
    Although particular, shall give a scantling
    Of good or bad unto the general;
    And in such indexes, although small pricks
    To their subsequent volumes, there is seen
    The baby figure of the giant mass   345
    Of things to come at large. It is supposed
    He that meets Hector issues from our choice;
    And choice, being mutual act of all our souls,
    Makes merit her election, and doth boil,
    As 'twere from forth us all, a man distilled   350
    Out of our virtues—who miscarrying,
    What heart receives from hence a conquering part,
    To steel a strong opinion to themselves;
    Which entertained, limbs are his instruments,
    In no less working than are swords and bows   355
    Directive by the limbs.

ULYSSES Give pardon to my speech. Therefore 'tis
      meet
    Achilles meet not Hector. Let us, like merchants,
    First show foul wares, and think perchance they'll
      sell;

336 **opinion** reputation   337-38 **taste ... palate** put our most valued reputation
to the test of their most careful, sensitive observation   339-40 **Our ... action** our
reputation shall be unequally balanced in this trivial action   341 **scantling**
sample   342 **general** (1) general view (2) entire army   343-44 **small ...
volumes** small markings compared to the great significance to follow
349 **election** criteria for choice   354 **his** i.e., of the strong opinion

360 If not, the luster of the better shall exceed
     By showing the worse first. Do not consent
     That ever Hector and Achilles meet;
     For both our honor and our shame in this
     Are dogged with two strange followers.

NESTOR I see them not with my old eyes; what are
365   they?

ULYSSES What glory our Achilles shares from Hector,
     Were he not proud, we all should share with him.
     But he already is too insolent,
     And it were better parch in Afric sun
370 Than in the pride and salt scorn of his eyes,
     Should he 'scape Hector fair. If he were foiled,
     Why then we do our main opinion crush
     In taint of our best man. No, make a lott'ry;
     And by device let blockish Ajax draw
375 The sort to fight with Hector; among ourselves
     Give him allowance for the better man,
     For that will physic the great Myrmidon
     Who broils in loud applause, and make him fall
     His crest that prouder than blue Iris bends.
380 If the dull brainless Ajax comes safe off,
     We'll dress him up in voices; if he fail,
     Yet go we under our opinion still
     That we have better men. But, hit or miss,
     Our project's life this shape of sense assumes:
385 Ajax employed plucks down Achilles' plumes.

NESTOR Now, Ulysses, I begin to relish thy advice,
     And I will give a taste thereof forthwith
     To Agamemnon. Go we to him straight.
     Two curs shall tame each other; pride alone
390 Must tarre the mastiffs on, as 'twere a bone.
                                    Exeunt.

364 **followers** consequences   370 **salt** bitter   372 **our main opinion** the
mainstay of our reputation   373 **In taint of** to the loss of, with the shame
of   375 **sort** lot   377 **the great** Myrmidon (Achilles, whose father, Peleus, had
subjects called Myrmidons)   387 **broils** bakes; i.e., suns himself   379 **Iris** (the
rainbow)   390 **tarre** incite, provoke

[ACT II

Scene I. *The Greek camp.*]

Enter Ajax and Thersites.

AJAX Thersites!

THERSITES Agamemnon, how if he had boils—full, all over, generally?

AJAX Thersites!

THERSITES And those boils did run?—say so—did not   5
the general run then? Were not that a botchy core?

AJAX Dog!

THERSITES Then would come some matter from him. I see none now.

AJAX Thou bitch-wolf's son, canst thou not hear?   10
Feel then.   *Strikes him.*

THERSITES The plague of Greece upon thee, thou mongrel beef-witted lord!

AJAX Speak then, thou vinewed'st leaven, speak. I will beat thee into handsomeness.   15

II.i.6 **botchy core** erupted boil   14 **vinewed'st leaven** most mildewed dough

THERSITES I shall sooner rail thee into wit and holiness; but I think thy horse will sooner con an oration than thou learn a prayer without book. Thou canst strike, canst thou? A red murrain o' thy jade's tricks!

AJAX Toadstool, learn me the proclamation.

THERSITES Dost thou think I have no sense, thou strikest me thus?

AJAX The proclamation!

THERSITES Thou art proclaimed fool, I think.

AJAX Do not, porpentine, do not; my fingers itch.

THERSITES I would thou didst itch from head to foot; an I had the scratching of thee, I would make thee the loathsomest scab in Greece. When thou art forth in the incursions, thou strikest as slow as another.

AJAX I say, the proclamation!

THERSITES Thou grumblest and railest every hour on Achilles, and thou art as full of envy at his greatness as Cerberus is at Proserpina's beauty, ay, that thou bark'st at him.

AJAX Mistress Thersites!

THERSITES Thou shouldst strike him.

AJAX Cobloaf!

THERSITES He would pun thee into shivers with his fist, as a sailor breaks a biscuit.

AJAX You whoreson cur!   [*Beating him.*]

---

17 **con** memorize 18 **without book** by heart 19 **red murrain** (form of plague manifested in red skin eruptions) 20 **jade's** nag's 21 **learn me** find out for me 26 **porpentine** porcupine 30 **incursions** battle raids, attacks 35 **Cerberus** (the monstrous watchdog of Hades) 35 **Proserpina** (a beautiful goddess carried off by Pluto to the underworld) 39 **Cobloaf** a badly baked, crusty loaf of bread 40 **pun** pound

THERSITES Do, do.

AJAX Thou stool for a witch!

THERSITES Ay, do, do, thou sodden-witted lord! thou   45
hast no more brain than I have in mine elbows; an
asinico may tutor thee. Thou scurvy-valiant ass,
thou art here but to thrash Troyans, and thou art
bought and sold among those of any wit like a
barbarian slave. If thou use to beat me, I will begin   50
at thy heel, and tell what thou art by inches, thou
thing of no bowels, thou!

AJAX You dog!

THERSITES You scurvy lord!

AJAX You cur!   [*Beating him.*]   55

THERSITES Mars his idiot! Do, rudeness; do, camel; do,
do.

Enter Achilles and Patroclus.

ACHILLES Why, how now, Ajax, wherefore do you
thus? How now, Thersites, what's the matter, man?

THERSITES You see him there? Do you?   60

ACHILLES Ay, what's the matter?

THERSITES Nay, look upon him.

ACHILLES So I do. What's the matter?

THERSITES Nay, but regard him well.

ACHILLES "Well"—why so I do.   65

THERSITES But yet you look not well upon him; for,
whosomever you take him to be, he is Ajax.

ACHILLES I know that, fool.

---

47 asinico ass, simpleton 49 bought and sold i.e., made fun of   52 bowels
mercy (the bowels were thought to be the source of compassion) 56 Mars his
Mars's 67 whosomever whomsoever

THERSITES Ay, but that fool knows not himself.

70 AJAX Therefore I beat thee.

THERSITES Lo, lo, lo, lo, what modicums of wit he
utters! His evasions have ears thus long. I have
bobbed his brain more than he has beat my bones.
I will buy nine sparrows for a penny, and his pia
75 mater is not worth the ninth part of a sparrow.
This lord, Achilles, Ajax, who wears his wit in his
belly and his guts in his head, I'll tell you what I
say of him.

ACHILLES What?

80 THERSITES I say, this Ajax——
                                    [*Ajax threatens to strike him.*]

ACHILLES Nay, good Ajax.

THERSITES Has not so much wit——
                                    [*Ajax threatens again to strike him.*]

ACHILLES Nay, I must hold you.

THERSITES As will stop the eye of Helen's needle, for
85 whom he comes to fight.

ACHILLES Peace, fool!

THERSITES I would have peace and quietness, but the
fool will not—he there, that he. Look you there.

AJAX O thou damned cur, I shall——

90 ACHILLES Will you set your wit to a fool's?

THERSITES No, I warrant you; the fool's will shame it.

PATROCLUS Good words, Thersites.

ACHILLES What's the quarrel?

---

69 **that fool** (as though Achilles had said "I know that fool")   72 **thus long** i.e.,
as long as those of an ass   74–75 **pia mater** i.e., brain (literally, the membrane
covering the brain)   90 **set** match

AJAX I bade the vile owl go learn me the tenor of the
proclamation, and he rails upon me.   95

THERSITES I serve thee not.

AJAX Well, go to, go to.

THERSITES I serve here voluntary.

ACHILLES Your last service was suff'rance, 'twas
not voluntary; no man is beaten voluntary. Ajax was   100
here the voluntary, and you as under an impress.

THERSITES E'en so. A great deal of your wit, too, lies
in your sinews, or else there be liars. Hector shall
have a great catch if he knock out either of your
brains. 'A were as good crack a fusty nut with no   105
kernel.

ACHILLES What, with me too, Thersites?

THERSITES There's Ulysses and old Nestor, whose wit
was moldy ere your grandsires had nails on their
toes, yoke you like draft oxen and make you plow up   110
the wars.

ACHILLES What, what?

THERSITES Yes, good sooth. To, Achilles! To, Ajax!
To——

AJAX I shall cut out your tongue.   115

THERSITES 'Tis no matter, I shall speak as much as
thou afterwards.

PATROCLUS No more words, Thersites; peace!

THERSITES I will hold my peace when Achilles' brach
bids me, shall I?   120

ACHILLES There's for you, Patroclus.

THERSITES I will see you hanged like clotpoles, ere

101 impress (pun on impressment, compulsory military service) 113–114 To,
Achilles! To, Ajax! To (imitation of the shouts of a driver, urging on his
horses) 119 brach bitch 122 clotpoles blockheads

I come any more to your tents. I will keep where
there is wit stirring and leave the faction of fools.

Exit.

125   PATROCLUS A good riddance.

ACHILLES Marry, this, sir, is proclaimed through all
        our host:
    That Hector, by the fifth hour of the sun,
    Will, with a trumpet, 'twixt our tents and Troy
    Tomorrow morning call some knight to arms
130   That hath a stomach, and such a one that dare
    Maintain—I know not what; 'tis trash. Farewell.

AJAX Farewell? Who shall answer him?

ACHILLES I know not. 'Tis put to lott'ry. Otherwise,
    He knew his man.

        [Exeunt Achilles and Patroclus.]

135   AJAX O, meaning you? I will go learn more of it.

Exit.

[Scene II. *Troy; Priam's palace.*]

Enter Priam, Hector, Troilus, Paris, and Helenus.

PRIAM After so many hours, lives, speeches spent,
    Thus once again says Nestor from the Greeks:
    "Deliver Helen, and all damage else,
    As honor, loss of time, travail, expense,
    Wounds, friends, and what else dear that is
        consumed
5   In hot digestion of this cormorant war,
    Shall be struck off." Hector, what say you to't?

127 **fifth hour** i.e., eleven in the morning   130 **stomach** temperament or relish
(here, for chivalric achievement)   II.ii.6 **cormorant** ravenous, rapacious

HECTOR Though no man lesser fears the Greeks than I,
As far as toucheth my particular,
Yet, dread Priam,   10
There is no lady of more softer bowels,
More spongy to suck in the sense of fear,
More ready to cry out, "Who knows what follows?"
Than Hector is. The wound of peace is surety,
Surety secure; but modest doubt is called   15
The beacon of the wise, the tent that searches
To the bottom of the worst. Let Helen go.
Since the first sword was drawn about this question,
Every tithe soul, 'mongst many thousand dismes,
Hath been as dear as Helen. I mean, of ours.   20
If we have lost so many tenths of ours
To guard a thing not ours nor worth to us,
Had it our name, the value of one ten,
What merit's in that reason which denies
The yielding of her up?

TROILUS   Fie, fie, my brother!   25
Weigh you the worth and honor of a king
So great as our dread father in a scale
Of common ounces? Will you with counters sum
The past proportion of his infinite,
And buckle in a waist most fathomless   30
With spans and inches so diminutive
As fears and reasons? Fie, for godly shame!

HELENUS No marvel, though you bite so sharp at
reasons,
You are so empty of them. Should not our father

---

9 my particular me, personally   11 of more softer bowels more averse to
violence   14 The wound of peace is surety peace is endangered by a sense of
safety   16 tent (roll of absorbent material, for cleaning or probing wounds)
19 Every ... dismes every tenth soul, among many thousand tens (?); every soul
taken by war as its tenth among many thousand such tenths (?)   23 one ten i.e.,
one in ten   28 counters pieces of worthless metal used for computation   29 The
past ... infinite i.e., his infinite greatness which is past all measurement
30 fathomless i.e., immeasurable   31 spans (units of measure averaging nine
inches)

35   Bear the great sway of his affairs with reason,
      Because your speech hath none that tell him so?

      TROILUS You are for dreams and slumbers, brother
         priest;
         You fur your gloves with reason. Here are your
            reasons:
         You know an enemy intends you harm;
40   You know a sword employed is perilous,
         And reason flies the object of all harm.
         Who marvels then, when Helenus beholds
         A Grecian and his sword, if he do set
         The very wings of reason to his heels
45   And fly like chidden Mercury from Jove,
         Or like a star disorbed? Nay, if we talk of reason,
         Let's shut our gates and sleep! Manhood and honor
         Should have hare-hearts, would they but fat their
            thoughts
         With this crammed reason. Reason and respect
50   Make livers pale and lustihood deject.

      HECTOR Brother, she is not worth what she doth cost
         The keeping.

      TROILUS   What's aught but as 'tis valued?

      HECTOR But value dwells not in particular will.
         It holds his estimate and dignity
55   As well wherein 'tis precious of itself
         As in the prizer. 'Tis mad idolatry
         To make the service greater than the god;
         And the will dotes that is attributive
         To what infectiously itself affects,
60   Without some image of th' affected merit.

---

38 **You fur your gloves with reason** i.e., you use reason as a comfortable word with which to decorate your speech, much as fur lines gloves 41 **object** (here, presentation, sight) 46 **disorbed** thrown from its sphere 49 **crammed** filled to excess, doughy 50 **livers** (thought to be the seats of passions) 53 **particular will** the individual's inclination 54 **his** its 54 **dignity** value 56 **prizer** appraiser 58 **attributive** dependent, subservient 59–60 **To what ... merit** to what it, to its own infection, desires, with no objective perception of the worth of the thing desired

TROILUS I take today a wife, and my election
  Is led on in the conduct of my will—
  My will enkindled by mine eyes and ears,
  Two traded pilots 'twixt the dangerous shores
  Of will and judgment. How may I avoid,   65
  Although my will distaste what it elected,
  The wife I chose? There can be no evasion
  To blench from this and to stand firm by honor.
  We turn not back the silks upon the merchant
  When we have soiled them, nor the remainder
    viands   70
  We do not throw in unrespective sieve
  Because we now are full. It was thought meet
  Paris should do some vengeance on the Greeks.
  Your breath with full consent bellied his sails;
  The seas and winds, old wranglers, took a truce   75
  And did him service; he touched the ports desired,
  And for an old aunt whom the Greeks held captive
  He brought a Grecian queen, whose youth and
    freshness
  Wrinkles Apollo's and makes pale the morning.
  Why keep we her? The Grecians keep our aunt.   80
  Is she worth keeping? Why, she is a pearl
  Whose price hath launched above a thousand ships
  And turned crowned kings to merchants.
  If you'll avouch 'twas wisdom Paris went—
  As you must needs, for you all cried, "Go, go"—   85
  If you'll confess he brought home worthy prize—
  As you must needs, for you all clapped your hands
  And cried, "Inestimable!"—why do you now
  The issue of your proper wisdoms rate,
  And do a deed that never Fortune did: 90
  Beggar the estimation which you prized

61-62 **I take ... my will—** (Troilus is setting forth, rhetorically, an example to prove his point; whatever he may be thinking, he is not announcing, of course, his approaching liaison with Cressida) 64 **traded** experienced 68 **blench** shrink 71 **unrespective sieve** common receptacle 77 **aunt** (Hesione, Priam's sister and Ajax's mother, married to Telamon; another son was Teucer, greatest archer among the Greeks) 89 **The issue ... rate** condemn the result of your own judgments 91 **estimation** thing esteemed

Richer than sea and land? O theft most base,
That we have stol'n what we do fear to keep!
But thieves unworthy of a thing so stol'n,
95   That in their country did them that disgrace
We fear to warrant in our native place.

Enter Cassandra raving with her hair about her ears.

CASSANDRA Cry, Troyans, cry!

PRIAM   What noise? What shriek is this?

TROILUS 'Tis our mad sister. I do know her voice.

CASSANDRA Cry, Troyans!

100   HECTOR It is Cassandra.

CASSANDRA Cry, Troyans, cry! Lend me ten thousand
eyes,
And I will fill them with prophetic tears!

HECTOR Peace, sister, peace!

CASSANDRA Virgins and boys, mid-age and wrinkled
eld,
105   Soft infancy, that nothing canst but cry,
Add to my clamors! Let us pay betimes
A moiety of that mass of moan to come.
Cry, Troyans, cry! Practice your eyes with tears!
Troy must not be, nor goodly Ilion stand;
110   Our firebrand brother, Paris, burns us all.
Cry, Troyans, cry! A Helen and a woe!
Cry, cry! Troy burns, or else let Helen go.   *Exit.*

HECTOR Now, youthful Troilus, do not these high
strains
Of divination in our sister work
115   Some touches of remorse? Or is your blood

95 **disgrace** i.e., the abduction of Helen 96 **warrant** justify by defense
98 **our mad sister** (when Cassandra refused Apollo's love, he destroyed his
former gift of prophecy by causing her never to be believed) 107 **moiety** part
110 **firebrand** (Hecuba dreamed she was delivered of a firebrand when Paris was
born)

144

So madly hot that no discourse of reason,
Nor fear of bad success in a bad cause,
Can qualify the same?

TROILUS   Why, brother Hector,
We may not think the justness of each act
Such and no other than event doth form it,   120
Nor once deject the courage of our minds
Because Cassandra's mad. Her brainsick raptures
Cannot distaste the goodness of a quarrel
Which hath our several honors all engaged
To make it gracious. For my private part,   125
I am no more touched than all Priam's sons;
And Jove forbid there should be done amongst us
Such things as might offend the weakest spleen
To fight for and maintain.

PARIS Else might the world convince of levity   130
As well my undertakings as your counsels;
But I attest the gods, your full consent
Gave wings to my propension and cut off
All fears attending on so dire a project.
For what, alas, can these my single arms?   135
What propugnation is in one man's valor
To stand the push and enmity of those
This quarrel would excite? Yet, I protest,
Were I alone to pass the difficulties,
And had as ample power as I have will,   140
Paris should ne'er retract what he hath done
Nor faint in the pursuit.

PRIAM   Paris, you speak
Like one besotted on your sweet delights.
You have the honey still, but these the gall;
So to be valiant is no praise at all.   145

PARIS Sir, I propose not merely to myself

118 qualify moderate   120 event outcome   122 brainsick raptures fits of
prophecy   123 distaste make distasteful   128 spleen temper, temperament
130 convince convict   133 propension inclination   136 propugnation defense
139 pass suffer, undergo

The pleasure such a beauty brings with it;
But I would have the soil of her fair rape
Wiped off in honorable keeping her.
150 What treason were it to the ransacked queen,
Disgrace to your great worths, and shame to me,
Now to deliver her possession up
On terms of base compulsion! Can it be
That so degenerate a strain as this
155 Should once set footing in your generous bosoms?
There's not the meanest spirit on our party
Without a heart to dare or sword to draw
When Helen is defended, nor none so noble
Whose life were ill bestowed or death unfamed
160 Where Helen is the subject. Then, I say,
Well may we fight for her whom we know well
The world's large spaces cannot parallel.

HECTOR Paris and Troilus, you have both said well,
And on the cause and question now in hand
165 Have glozed—but superficially: not much
Unlike young men, whom Aristotle thought
Unfit to hear moral philosophy.
The reasons you allege do more conduce
To the hot passion of distempered blood
170 Than to make up a free determination
'Twixt right and wrong; for pleasure and revenge
Have ears more deaf than adders to the voice
Of any true decision. Nature craves
All dues be rendered to their owners. Now,
175 What nearer debt in all humanity
Than wife is to the husband? If this law
Of nature be corrupted through affection,
And that great minds, of partial indulgence

---

148 **rape** carrying off   150 **ransacked** carried off   155 **generous** nobly born
(therefore magnanimous)   165 **glozed** commented, glossed   167 **moral** (Aristotle wrote "political" [*Nicomachean Ethics*, I.3], but the use of "moral" here is
paralleled in Erasmus, Bacon, and many other contemporary translations and
commentaries; the two words were roughly interchangeable in sixteenth-century
terminology)   172 **more deaf than adders** (cf. Psalm 58:4-5)   177 **affection**
appetite   178 **partial** biased, favoring

To their benumbèd wills, resist the same,
There is a law in each well-ordered nation   180
To curb those raging appetites that are
Most disobedient and refractory.
If Helen, then, be wife to Sparta's king,
As it is known she is, these moral laws
Of nature and of nations speak aloud   185
To have her back returned. Thus to persist
In doing wrong extenuates not wrong,
But makes it much more heavy. Hector's opinion
Is this in way of truth. Yet ne'ertheless,
My spritely brethren, I propend to you   190
In resolution to keep Helen still;
For 'tis a cause that hath no mean dependence
Upon our joint and several dignities.

TROILUS Why, there you touched the life of our design!
Were it not glory that we more affected   195
Than the performance of our heaving spleens,
I would not wish a drop of Troyan blood
Spent more in her defense. But, worthy Hector,
She is a theme of honor and renown,
A spur to valiant and magnanimous deeds,   200
Whose present courage may beat down our foes
And fame in time to come canonize us;
For I presume brave Hector would not lose
So rich advantage of a promised glory
As smiles upon the forehead of this action   205
For the wide world's revenue.

HECTOR   I am yours,
You valiant offspring of great Priamus.
I have a roisting challenge sent amongst
The dull and factious nobles of the Greeks
Will strike amazement to their drowsy spirits.   210
I was advertised their great general slept

179 **benumbèd** paralyzed (by affection and appetite) 187 **extenuates**
lessens 190 **spritely** spirited 190 **propend** incline 193 **joint and several**
collective and individual 196 **heaving spleens** angry passions 208 **roisting**
noisy, clamorous 211 **advertised** informed

147

Whilst emulation in the army crept;
This, I presume, will wake him.   *Exeunt.*

[Scene III. *The Greek camp; near Achilles' tent.*]

Enter Thersites solus.

THERSITES How now, Thersites? What, lost in the
labyrinth of thy fury? Shall the elephant Ajax carry
it thus? He beats me, and I rail at him. O worthy
satisfaction! Would it were otherwise—that I could
beat him, whilst he railed at me. 'Sfoot, I'll learn to
conjure and raise devils, but I'll see some issue of my
spiteful execrations. Then there's Achilles, a rare
enginer. If Troy be not taken till these two under-
mine it, the walls will stand till they fall of themselves. O thou great thunder-darter of Olympus,
forget that thou art Jove, the king of gods; and,
Mercury, lose all the serpentine craft of thy
caduceus, if ye take not that little, little, less than
little wit from them that they have; which short-
armed ignorance itself knows is so abundant scarce
it will not in circumvention deliver a fly from a
spider, without drawing their massy irons and
cutting the web. After this, the vengeance on the
whole camp! Or, rather, the Neapolitan bone-ache,
for that, methinks, is the curse depending on those
that war for a placket. I have said my prayers,
and devil Envy say "Amen." What ho, my Lord
Achilles!

---

212 **emulation** envious rivalry (see I.iii.134) II.iii.2-3 **carry it** carry it off,
come out on top 5 **'Sfoot** (an oath; "God's foot") 6 **but I'll see** rather than not
see 8 **enginer** (a soldier in a company used for ditch digging, tunneling, and
otherwise undermining the battlements of an enemy camp) 13 **caduceus** (Mercury's staff, twined with serpents) 19 **Neapolitan bone-ache** syphilis
21 **placket** opening in a petticoat (used obscenely, with anatomical suggestion)

Enter Patroclus.

PATROCLUS Who's there? Thersites? Good Thersites, come in and rail.   25

THERSITES If I could 'a' rememb'red a gilt counterfeit, thou wouldst not have slipped out of my contemplation. But it is no matter; thyself upon thyself! The common curse of mankind, folly and ignorance, be thine in great revenue. Heaven bless thee from a   30 tutor, and discipline come not near thee. Let thy blood be thy direction till thy death. Then, if she that lays thee out says thou art a fair corse, I'll be sworn and sworn upon't she never shrouded any but lazars. Amen. Where's Achilles?   35

PATROCLUS What, art thou devout? Wast thou in prayer?

THERSITES Ay, the heavens hear me!

PATROCLUS Amen.

Enter Achilles.

ACHILLES Who's there?   40

PATROCLUS Thersites, my lord.

ACHILLES Where? Where? O, where? Art thou come? Why, my cheese, my digestion, why hast thou not served thyself in to my table so many meals? Come, what's Agamemnon?   45

THERSITES Thy commander, Achilles. Then tell me, Patroclus, what's Achilles?

PATROCLUS Thy lord, Thersites. Then tell me, I pray thee, what's thyself?

---

27 **slipped** (pun on "slip," a counterfeit coin of brass, covered with silver or gold)   30 **bless** i.e., save   32 **blood** passion   33 **corse** corpse   35 **lazars** lepers (with decayed bodies)   43 **my cheese, my digestion** (cheese served as the final course of a meal was thought to aid digestion)

50 THERSITES Thy knower, Patroclus. Then tell me,
       Patroclus, what art thou?

    PATROCLUS Thou must tell that knowest.

    ACHILLES O tell, tell.

    THERSITES I'll decline the whole question. Agamem-
55   non commands Achilles, Achilles is my lord, I am
       Patroclus' knower, and Patroclus is a fool.

    PATROCLUS You rascal!

    THERSITES Peace, fool! I have not done.

    ACHILLES He is a privileged man. Proceed, Thersites.

60 THERSITES Agamemnon is a fool, Achilles is a fool,
       Thersites is a fool, and, as aforesaid, Patroclus is a
       fool.

    ACHILLES Derive this; come.

    THERSITES Agamemnon is a fool to offer to command
65   Achilles, Achilles is a fool to be commanded of
       Agamemnon, Thersites is a fool to serve such a fool,
       and this Patroclus is a fool positive.

    PATROCLUS Why am I a fool?

    THERSITES Make that demand of the Creator; it suf-
70   fices me thou art. Look you, who comes here?

            Enter Agamemnon, Ulysses, Nestor,
               Diomedes, Ajax, and Calchas.

    ACHILLES Patroclus, I'll speak with nobody. Come in
       with me, Thersites.   *Exit.*

    THERSITES Here is such patchery, such juggling, and
       such knavery. All the argument is a whore and a
75   cuckold, a good quarrel to draw emulous factions

---

54 **decline** run through (in the grammatical sense, as to decline a noun)   59 **He is
a privileged man** (in the sense that the railing of a professional jester or fool was
"allowed")   64 **offer** attempt   73 **patchery** roguery   75 **emulous** jealous

and bleed to death upon. Now, the dry serpigo on
the subject, and war and lechery confound all!

                                             [Exit.]

AGAMEMNON Where is Achilles?

PATROCLUS Within his tent, but ill-disposed, my lord.

AGAMEMNON Let it be known to him that we are here.   80
He shent our messengers, and we lay by
Our appertainments, visiting of him.
Let him be told so, lest perchance he think
We dare not move the question of our place
Or know not what we are.   85

PATROCLUS   I shall so say to him.

                                             [Exit.]

ULYSSES We saw him at the opening of his tent. He is
not sick.

AJAX Yes, lion-sick, sick of proud heart. You may call it
melancholy if you will favor the man; but, by my
head, 'tis pride. But why, why? Let him show us   90
a cause. A word, my lord.

                           [Takes Agamemnon aside.]

NESTOR What moves Ajax thus to bay at him?

ULYSSES Achilles hath inveigled his fool from him.

NESTOR Who, Thersites?

ULYSSES He.   95

NESTOR Then will Ajax lack matter, if he have lost his
argument.

ULYSSES No, you see, he is his argument that has his
argument, Achilles.

NESTOR All the better. Their fraction is more our   100

---

76 **serpigo** a quickly spreading skin disease, with eruptions   81 **shent** rebuked
82 **appertainments** rights of rank   84 **move** raise   97 **argument** subject
matter   100 **fraction** fracture, break

wish than their faction. But it was a strong composure a fool could disunite.

ULYSSES The amity that wisdom knits not, folly may
easily untie.

Enter Patroclus.

105   Here comes Patroclus.

NESTOR No Achilles with him?

ULYSSES The elephant hath joints, but none for courtesy. His legs are legs for necessity, not for flexure.

PATROCLUS Achilles bids me say he is much sorry
110   If anything more than your sport and pleasure
Did move your greatness and this noble state
To call upon him. He hopes it is no other
But, for your health and your digestion sake,
An after-dinner's breath.

AGAMEMNON   Hear you, Patroclus.
115   We are too well acquainted with these answers;
But his evasion, winged thus swift with scorn,
Cannot outfly our apprehensions.
Much attribute he hath, and much the reason
Why we ascribe it to him; yet all his virtues,
120   Not virtuously on his own part beheld,
Do in our eyes begin to lose their gloss—
Yea, like fair fruit in an unwholesome dish,
Are like to rot untasted. Go and tell him
We come to speak with him; and you shall not sin
125   If you do say we think him overproud
And underhonest, in self-assumption greater
Than in the note of judgment, and worthier than
       himself

---

101 **faction** union 101-02 **composure** union 108 **flexure** bending
111 **noble state** assemblage of noblemen 114 **breath** exercise 117 **apprehensions** perceptions 120 **Not ... beheld** not carried with modesty 126 **underhonest** calculating, not open 127 **the note of judgment** the opinion of men of
judgment

Here tend the savage strangeness he puts on,
Disguise the holy strength of their command,
And underwrite in an observing kind   130
His humorous predominance; yea, watch
His pettish lunes, his ebbs and flows, as if
The passage and whole carriage of this action
Rode on his tide. Go tell him this; and add
That, if he overhold his price so much,   135
We'll none of him; but let him, like an engine
Not portable, lie under this report:
"Bring action hither, this cannot go to war."
A stirring dwarf we do allowance give
Before a sleeping giant. Tell him so.   140

PATROCLUS I shall, and bring his answer presently.
                                          [*Exit.*]

AGAMEMNON In second voice we'll not be satisfied;
We come to speak with him. Ulysses, enter you.
                                      Exit Ulysses.

AJAX What is he more than another?

AGAMEMNON No more than what he thinks he is.   145

AJAX Is he so much? Do you not think he thinks
himself a better man than I am?

AGAMEMNON No question.

AJAX Will you subscribe his thought, and say he is?

AGAMEMNON No, noble Ajax; you are as strong, as   150
valiant, as wise, no less noble, much more gentle,
and altogether more tractable.

AJAX Why should a man be proud? How doth pride
grow? I know not what pride is.

---

128 **tend the savage strangeness** wait upon the rude aloofness   129-31 **Disguise ... predominance** allow to be hidden the divine authority of their command, and, in a form of acquiescence, subscribe to his eccentric notion of superiority   132 **pettish lunes** capricious variations (like the changes of the moon)   135 **overhold** overvalue   136 **engine** mechanical contrivance (here, military)   139 **allowance** praise

155 AGAMEMNON Your mind is the clearer and your virtues
      the fairer. He that is proud eats up himself. Pride is
      his own glass, his own trumpet, his own chronicle;
      and whatever praises itself but in the deed, devours
      the deed in the praise.

Enter Ulysses.

160 AJAX I do hate a proud man as I hate the engend'ring
      of toads.

      NESTOR [*Aside*] And yet he loves himself. Is't not
      strange?

      ULYSSES Achilles will not to the field tomorrow.

      AGAMEMNON What's his excuse?

165 ULYSSES   He doth rely on none,
      But carries on the stream of his dispose
      Without observance or respect of any,
      In will peculiar and in self-admission.

      AGAMEMNON Why will he not upon our fair request
170   Untent his person and share th'air with us?

      ULYSSES Things small as nothing, for request's sake
      only,
      He makes important. Possessed he is with greatness,
      And speaks not to himself but with a pride
      That quarrels at self-breath. Imagined worth
175   Holds in his blood such swoln and hot discourse
      That 'twixt his mental and his active parts
      Kingdomed Achilles in commotion rages
      And batters down himself. What should I say?

---

157 **glass** mirror   166 **dispose** inclination   168 **In ... self-admission** i.e., with
will exclusively his own and with self-approval   171 **for request's sake
only** only because requested   174 **That quarrels at self-breath** that quarrels with
speech itself   177 **Kingdomed** i.e., as though Achilles were himself a kingdom
engaged in civil strife

He is so plaguy proud that the death-tokens of it
Cry "No recovery."

AGAMEMNON   Let Ajax go to him.   180
  Dear lord, go you and greet him in his tent;
  'Tis said he holds you well, and will be led
  At your request a little from himself.

ULYSSES O Agamemnon, let it not be so!
  We'll consecrate the steps that Ajax makes   185
  When they go from Achilles. Shall the proud lord
  That bastes his arrogance with his own seam
  And never suffers matter of the world
  Enter his thoughts, save such as doth revolve
  And ruminate himself—shall he be worshiped   190
  Of that we hold an idol more than he?
  No, this thrice-worthy and right valiant lord
  Shall not so stale his palm, nobly acquired,
  Nor, by my will, assubjugate his merit,
  As amply titled as Achilles' is,   195
  By going to Achilles.
  That were to enlard his fat-already pride,
  And add more coals to Cancer when he burns
  With entertaining great Hyperion.
  This lord go to him! Jupiter forbid,   200
  And say in thunder, "Achilles, go to him."

NESTOR [Aside] O, this is well. He rubs the vein of him.

DIOMEDES [Aside] And how his silence drinks up his
  applause!

AJAX If I go to him, with my armèd fist
  I'll pash him o'er the face.   205

AGAMEMNON O, no! You shall not go.

---

179 **death-tokens** external symptoms of the plague preceding death   187 **seam**
grease, fat   193 **stale his palm** detract from his glory   194 **assubjugate** debase
198 **Cancer** i.e., summer, which begins under this sign of the zodiac
199 **Hyperion** the sun   202 **vein** mood   205 **pash** bash

AJAX An he be proud with me, I'll pheese his pride. Let me go to him.

ULYSSES Not for the worth that hangs upon our quarrel.

210 AJAX A paltry, insolent fellow!

NESTOR [*Aside*] How he describes himself!

AJAX Can he not be sociable?

ULYSSES [*Aside*] The raven chides blackness.

AJAX I'll let his humor's blood.

215 AGAMEMNON [*Aside*] He will be the physician that should be the patient.

AJAX An all men were of my mind——

ULYSSES [*Aside*] Wit would be out of fashion.

AJAX 'A should not bear it so, 'a should eat swords
220 first! Shall pride carry it?

NESTOR [*Aside*] An 'twould, you'd carry half.

ULYSSES [*Aside*] 'A would have ten shares.

AJAX I will knead him; I'll make him supple.

NESTOR [*Aside*] He's not yet through warm. Force
225 him with praises; pour in, pour, his ambition is dry.

ULYSSES [*To Agamemnon*] My lord, you feed too much
on this dislike.

NESTOR Our noble general, do not do so.

DIOMEDES You must prepare to fight without Achilles.

ULYSSES Why, 'tis this naming of him does him harm.
230 Here is a man—but 'tis before his face;
I will be silent.

207 **pheese** settle the business of   214 **let his humor's blood** i.e., cure him by
letting blood, thus decreasing the strength of Achilles' humor, his mood of
pride   219 **'A** he   224 **through** thoroughly   224 **Force** stuff

NESTOR   Wherefore should you so?
He is not emulous, as Achilles is.

ULYSSES Know the whole world, he is as valiant——

AJAX A whoreson dog, that shall palter with us thus!
Would he were a Troyan!   235

NESTOR What a vice were it in Ajax now——

ULYSSES If he were proud——

DIOMEDES Or covetous of praise——

ULYSSES Ay, or surly borne——

DIOMEDES Or strange, or self-affected!   240

ULYSSES Thank the heavens, lord, thou art of sweet
     composure;
  Praise him that gat thee, she that gave thee suck;
  Famed be thy tutor, and thy parts of nature
  Thrice-famed beyond, beyond all erudition;
  But he that disciplined thine arms to fight,   245
  Let Mars divide eternity in twain
  And give him half; and, for thy vigor,
  Bull-bearing Milo his addition yield
  To sinewy Ajax. I will not praise thy wisdom,
  Which, like a bourn, a pale, a shore, confines   250
  Thy spacious and dilated parts. Here's Nestor,
  Instructed by the antiquary times,
  He must, he is, he cannot but be wise;
  But pardon, father Nestor, were your days
  As green as Ajax, and your brain so tempered,   255
  You should not have the eminence of him,
  But be as Ajax.

232 **emulous** jealously competitive   234 **palter** play shifty games, dodge
240 **strange, or self-affected** haughty, or self-centered   242 **gat** begat
243-44 **thy parts ... erudition** your natural attributes three times more famous
(i.e., than your tutor), even more famous than all learning itself   248 **Milo** (a
famous Greek athlete, said to have carried a bull upon his shoulders for forty
yards)   248 **addition** title, i.e., "Bull-bearing"   250 **a bourn, a pale** a boundary, a fence   252 **Instructed by the antiquary times** i.e., his wisdom learned
from olden times, all the years of his old age

AJAX   Shall I call you father?

NESTOR Ay, my good son.

DIOMEDES   Be ruled by him, Lord Ajax.

ULYSSES There is no tarrying here; the hart Achilles
260   Keeps thicket. Please it our great general
         To call together all his state of war;
         Fresh kings are come to Troy. Tomorrow,
         We must with all our main of power stand fast.
         And here's a lord—come knights from east to west,
265   And cull their flower, Ajax shall cope the best.

AGAMEMNON Go we to council. Let Achilles sleep;
         Light boats sail swift, though greater hulks draw
         deep.   *Exeunt*.

261 **state** noblemen in council   263 **main** might

[ACT III

Scene I. *Troy; Priam's palace.*]

Music sounds within. Enter Pandarus and a Servant.

PANDARUS Friend you, pray you a word. Do you not follow the young Lord Paris?

SERVANT Ay, sir, when he goes before me.

PANDARUS You depend upon him, I mean.

SERVANT Sir, I do depend upon the Lord.   5

PANDARUS You depend upon a notable gentleman; I must needs praise him.

SERVANT The Lord be praised!

PANDARUS You know me, do you not?

SERVANT Faith, sir, superficially.   10

PANDARUS Friend, know me better. I am the Lord Pandarus.

SERVANT I hope I shall know your honor better.

PANDARUS I do desire it.

III.i.4 **depend** i.e., serve, in a position of dependence

15 SERVANT You are in the state of grace.

PANDARUS Grace? Not so, friend. Honor and lordship
are my titles. What music is this?

SERVANT I do but partly know, sir. It is music in
parts.

20 PANDARUS Know you the musicians?

SERVANT Wholly, sir.

PANDARUS Who play they to?

SERVANT To the hearers, sir.

PANDARUS At whose pleasure, friend?

25 SERVANT At mine, sir, and theirs that love music.

PANDARUS Command, I mean, friend.

SERVANT Who shall I command, sir?

PANDARUS Friend, we understand not one another. I
am too courtly, and thou too cunning. At whose
30   request do these men play?

SERVANT That's to't, indeed, sir. Marry, sir, at the
request of Paris, my lord, who is there in person;
with him the mortal Venus, the heartblood of
beauty, love's invisible soul.

35 PANDARUS Who? My cousin Cressida?

SERVANT No, sir, Helen. Could not you find out that
by her attributes?

PANDARUS It should seem, fellow, that thou hast not
seen the Lady Cressid. I come to speak with
40   Paris from the Prince Troilus. I will make a

---

15 **You ... grace** (pretending that Pandarus meant that he desired his own honor
to be better; also, perhaps, the servant is hinting for a gratuity)   16 **Grace** (the
courtly title of a duke, etc.)   18–19 **music in parts** music containing several
vocal or instrumental parts in counterpoint

complimental assault upon him, for my business
seethes.

SERVANT Sodden business! There's a stewed phrase,
indeed.

Enter Paris and Helen [with courtiers].

PANDARUS Fair be to you, my lord, and to all this fair   45
company. Fair desires in all fair measure fairly guide
them. Especially to you, fair queen, fair thoughts be
your fair pillow.

HELEN Dear lord, you are full of fair words.

PANDARUS You speak your fair pleasure, sweet queen.   50
Fair prince, here is good broken music.

PARIS You have broke it, cousin; and, by my life, you
shall make it whole again; you shall piece it out with
a piece of your performance. Nell, he is full of
harmony.
                                                          55

PANDARUS Truly, lady, no.

HELEN O, sir!

PANDARUS Rude, in sooth; in good sooth, very rude.

PARIS Well said, my lord. Well, you say so in fits.

PANDARUS I have business to my lord, dear queen. My   60
lord, will you vouchsafe me a word?

HELEN Nay, this shall not hedge us out. We'll hear you
sing, certainly.

PANDARUS Well, sweet queen, you are pleasant with
me. But, marry, thus, my lord: my dear lord and   65
most esteemed friend, your brother Troilus——

---

42 **seethes** boils, i.e., demands immediate attention 43 **stewed** (1) boiled
(2) pertaining to stews, or brothels (?) 51 **broken music** music the parts of
which are written for different solo instruments, or groups of different instruments
58 **Rude** unpolished, rough 59 **fits** sections or divisions of a song (perhaps Paris
means, "you say so only at times")

HELEN My Lord Pandarus, honey-sweet lord——

PANDARUS Go to, sweet queen, go to—commends himself most affectionately to you.

70 HELEN You shall not bob us out of our melody. If you do, our melancholy upon your head!

PANDARUS Sweet queen, sweet queen, that's a sweet queen, i' faith.

HELEN And to make a sweet lady sad is a sour offense.

75 PANDARUS Nay, that shall not serve your turn; that shall it not, in truth, la. Nay, I care not for such words; no, no. And, my lord, he desires you that, if the king call for him at supper, you will make his excuse.

80 HELEN My Lord Pandarus——

PANDARUS What says my sweet queen, my very, very sweet queen?

PARIS What exploit's in hand? Where sups he tonight?

HELEN Nay, but my Lord——

85 PANDARUS What says my sweet queen? My cousin will fall out with you.

HELEN You must not know where he sups.

PARIS I'll lay my life, with my disposer Cressida.

PANDARUS No, no; no such matter; you are wide. Come
90 your disposer is sick.

PARIS Well, I'll make excuse.

PANDARUS Ay, good my lord. Why should you say Cressida? No, your poor disposer's sick.

PARIS I spy.

70 bob cheat   85–86 My cousin … you (Pandarus lightly pretends that Paris, his "cousin," will become jealous if Helen continues to flirt with him, Pandarus) 88 disposer i.e., she who rules him (Paris jokingly uses an excessively gallant term)   89 wide wide of the mark

PANDARUS You spy? What do you spy? Come, give me   95
an instrument now, sweet queen.

HELEN Why, this is kindly done.

PANDARUS My niece is horribly in love with a thing
you have, sweet queen.

HELEN She shall have it, my lord, if it be not my Lord   100
Paris.

PANDARUS He? No, she'll none of him; they two are
twain.

HELEN Falling in, after falling out, may make them
three.   105

PANDARUS Come, come, I'll hear no more of this. I'll
sing you a song now.

HELEN Ay, ay, prithee. Now by my troth, sweet lord,
thou hast a fine forehead.

PANDARUS Ay, you may, you may.   110

HELEN Let thy song be love. This love will undo us all.
O Cupid, Cupid, Cupid!

PANDARUS Love! Ay, that it shall, i' faith.

PARIS Ay, good now, "Love, love, nothing but love."

PANDARUS In good troth, it begins so: [Sings.]   115
Love, love, nothing but love, still love still more!
For, O, love's bow shoots buck and doe.
The shaft confounds not that it wounds,
But tickles still the sore.
These lovers cry, O ho! they die!   120
Yet that which seems the wound to kill

98-99 My niece is ... sweet queen i.e., Cressida loves, or would love to have, a
sexual partner such as Paris is to Helen   103 twain at odds, having nothing in
common   104-05 Falling in ... them three (Helen's bawdy joke picks up the
train of thought begun by Pandarus)   110 you may, i.e., have your joke
118 confounds not that does not distress because   119 sore wound (perhaps a
pun on the term for a buck in his fourth year)

Doth turn O ho! to Ha, ha, he!
So dying love lives still.
O ho! a while, but Ha, ha, ha!
125   O ho! groans out for Ha, ha, ha!—Heigh ho!

HELEN In love, i' faith, to the very tip of the nose.

PARIS He eats nothing but doves, love, and that breeds
hot blood, and hot blood begets hot thoughts, and
hot thoughts beget hot deeds, and hot deeds is love.

130   PANDARUS Is this the generation of love—hot blood,
hot thoughts, and hot deeds? Why, they are vipers.
Is love a generation of vipers? Sweet lord, who's
a-field today?

PARIS Hector, Deiphobus, Helenus, Antenor, and all
135   the gallantry of Troy. I would fain have armed
today, but my Nell would not have it so. How
chance my brother Troilus went not?

HELEN He hangs the lip at something. You know all,
Lord Pandarus.

140   PANDARUS Not I, honey-sweet queen. I long to hear
how they sped today. You'll remember your
brother's excuse?

PARIS To a hair.

PANDARUS Farewell, sweet queen.

145   HELEN Commend me to your niece.

PANDARUS I will, sweet queen. [*Exit.*] *Sound a retreat.*

PARIS They're come from the field. Let us to Priam's
hall
To greet the warriors. Sweet Helen, I must woo you
To help unarm our Hector. His stubborn buckles,
150   With these your white enchanting fingers touched,

132 a generation of vipers (cf. Matthew 3:7) 141 how they sped i.e., the
results of their action 143 To a hair (does Paris jokingly recall Troilus' "pretty
answer" about the hairs on his chin [see I.ii.167–69]?)

Shall more obey than to the edge of steel
Or force of Greekish sinews. You shall do more
Than all the island kings—disarm great Hector.

HELEN 'Twill make us proud to be his servant, Paris;
Yea, what he shall receive of us in duty   155
Gives us more palm in beauty than we have,
Yea, overshines ourself.

PARIS Sweet, above thought I love thee.   *Exeunt.*

[Scene II. *Within Troy.*]

Enter Pandarus and Troilus' Man.

PANDARUS How now, where's thy master? At my
cousin Cressida's?

MAN No, sir; he stays for you to conduct him thither.

Enter Troilus.

PANDARUS O, here he comes. How now, how now?

TROILUS Sirrah, walk off.   [*Exit Man.*]   5

PANDARUS Have you seen my cousin?

TROILUS No, Pandarus. I stalk about her door
Like a strange soul upon the Stygian banks
Staying for waftage. O, be thou my Charon,
And give me swift transportance to those fields   10
Where I may wallow in the lily beds
Proposed for the deserver. O gentle Pandar,
From Cupid's shoulder pluck his painted wings,
And fly with me to Cressid.

---

153 **island kings** i.e., kings of the Grecian islands   III.ii.8 **Stygian** (from Styx,
the principal river of the underworld) 9 **waftage** passage across water
9 **Charon** (ferryman of the dead, across the Styx to Hades) 12 **Proposed**
promised

15 PANDARUS Walk here i' th' orchard. I'll bring her
    straight.   *Exit Pandarus.*

    TROILUS I am giddy; expectation whirls me round.
    Th' imaginary relish is so sweet
    That it enchants my sense. What will it be
20 When that the wat'ry palates taste indeed
    Love's thrice-repurèd nectar? Death, I fear me,
    Sounding destruction, or some joy too fine,
    Too subtle, potent, tuned too sharp in sweetness
    For the capacity of my ruder powers.
25 I fear it much; and I do fear besides
    That I shall lose distinction in my joys,
    As doth a battle, when they charge on heaps
    The enemy flying.

                    Enter Pandarus.

    PANDARUS She's making her ready; she'll come
30 straight; you must be witty now. She does so blush,
    and fetches her wind so short as if she were frayed
    with a spirit. I'll fetch her. It is the prettiest
    villain; she fetches her breath as short as a
    new-ta'en sparrow.   *Exit Pandarus.*

35 TROILUS Even such a passion doth embrace my bosom.
    My heart beats thicker than a feverous pulse,
    And all my powers do their bestowing lose,
    Like vassalage at unawares encount'ring
    The eye of majesty.

                    Enter Pandarus and Cressida.

40 PANDARUS Come, come, what need you blush? Shame's
    a baby. Here she is now; swear the oaths now to

---

20 **wat'ry** watering (cf. mouth "watering" with appetite)   21 **thrice-repurèd**
distilled again and again (i.e., to extract the purest essence)   22 **Sounding**
swooning   24 **ruder** physical   26 **distinction** ability to distinguish   30 **be**
witty be alert, have your wits about you   31–32 **frayed with a spirit** frightened
by a ghost   33 **villain** (here a term of endearment)   37 **bestowing** proper
use   38 **vassalage** vassals

her that you have sworn to me. What! Are you
gone again? You must be watched ere you be made
tame, must you? Come your ways, come your
ways; an you draw backward, we'll put you i' the   45
fills. Why do you not speak to her? Come, draw
this curtain, and let's see your picture. Alas the
day, how loath you are to offend daylight! An
'twere dark, you'd close sooner. So, so; rub on,
and kiss the mistress. How now, a kiss in fee-   50
farm! Build there, carpenter; the air is sweet. Nay,
you shall fight your hearts out ere I part you. The
falcon as the tercel, for all the ducks i' the river. Go
to, go to.

TROILUS You have bereft me of all words, lady.   55

PANDARUS Words pay no debts, give her deeds; but
she'll bereave you o' the deeds too if she call your
activity in question. What, billing again? Here's
"In witness whereof the parties interchangeably"—
Come in, come in. I'll go get a fire.   [*Exit.*]   60

CRESSIDA Will you walk in, my lord?

TROILUS O Cressid, how often have I wished me thus!

CRESSIDA Wished, my lord? The gods grant—O my
lord!

TROILUS What should they grant? What makes this   65
pretty abruption? What too curious dreg espies my
sweet lady in the fountain of our love?

43-44 **watched ere you be made tame** i.e., prodded on until made submissive
(a hawk was tamed by "watching" it, i.e., keeping it constantly awake) 46 **fills**
shafts (of a cart) 47 **curtain** i.e., her veil 49 **close** move together 49-50 **rub
... mistress** (terms from bowling, where "to rub" was to meet obstacles in the
way of the small object-ball, called the "mistress"; bowls are still said "to kiss"
when they touch gently) 50-51 **a kiss in fee-farm** i.e., a long kiss (a fee-farm
was a grant of lands in perpetuity) 52-53 **The falcon ... river** i.e., I will bet on
the falcon (the term applied only to the female of the species) against the tercel (the
male) to bring down any game 59 **"In witness ... interchangeably"** (a legal
formula, usually ending with the words "have set their hands and seals")
66 **abruption** breaking off 66 **too curious** overly cautious, anxious, or
inquisitive

CRESSIDA More dregs than water, if my fears have
eyes.

70 TROILUS Fears make devils of cherubins; they never
see truly.

CRESSIDA Blind fear, that seeing reason leads, finds
safer footing than blind reason stumbling without
fear. To fear the worst oft cures the worse.

75 TROILUS O, let my lady apprehend no fear; in all
Cupid's pageant there is presented no monster.

CRESSIDA Nor nothing monstrous neither?

TROILUS Nothing but our undertakings when we vow
to weep seas, live in fire, eat rocks, tame tigers,
80 thinking it harder for our mistress to devise imposi-
tion enough than for us to undergo any difficulty
imposed. This is the monstruosity in love, lady, that
the will is infinite and the execution confined; that
the desire is boundless and the act a slave to
85 limit.

CRESSIDA They say all lovers swear more performance
than they are able, and yet reserve an ability that
they never perform, vowing more than the perfection
of ten and discharging less than the tenth part of
90 one. They that have the voice of lions and the act of
hares—are they not monsters?

TROILUS Are there such? Such are not we. Praise us
as we are tasted, allow us as we prove; our head
shall go bare till merit crown it. No perfection in
95 reversion shall have a praise in present; we will
not name desert before his birth, and, being born,
his addition shall be humble. Few words to fair
faith. Troilus shall be such to Cressid, as what envy

75-76 **apprehend ... no monster** (Troilus refers to some type of dramatic
allegory such as Cupid might be depicted as "presenting," or the emblematic
characters, such as Fear, in pageants or court masques)   93 **tasted** tested
95 **reversion** right or anticipation of future possession   97 **his addition shall be
humble** it shall be given no high or pompous titles

can say worst shall be a mock for his truth, and
what truth can speak truest not truer than Troilus.   100

CRESSIDA Will you walk in, my lord?

Enter Pandarus.

PANDARUS What, blushing still? Have you not done
talking yet?

CRESSIDA Well, uncle, what folly I commit, I dedicate
to you.   105

PANDARUS I thank you for that. If my lord get a boy of
you, you'll give him me. Be true to my lord; if he
flinch, chide me for it.

TROILUS You know now your hostages: your uncle's
word and my firm faith.   110

PANDARUS Nay, I'll give my word for her too. Our
kindred, though they be long ere they be wooed,
they are constant being won. They are burrs, I can
tell you; they'll stick where they are thrown.

CRESSIDA Boldness comes to me now and brings me
heart.   115
Prince Troilus, I have loved you night and day
For many weary months.

TROILUS Why was my Cressid then so hard to win?

CRESSIDA Hard to seem won; but I was won, my lord,
With the first glance that ever—pardon me;   120
If I confess much you will play the tyrant.
I love you now, but, till now, not so much
But I might master it. In faith, I lie;
My thoughts were like unbridled children grown
Too headstrong for their mother. See, we fools!   125
Why have I blabbed? Who shall be true to us
When we are so unsecret to ourselves?

98-100 **as what envy … Troilus** so that the worst malice can do is sneer at his
constancy, and even the best truth that truth can speak will not be truer than
Troilus

But, though I loved you well, I wooed you not;
And yet, good faith, I wished myself a man,
130   Or that we women had men's privilege
Of speaking first. Sweet, bid me hold my tongue,
For in this rapture I shall surely speak
The thing I shall repent. See, see! Your silence,
Cunning in dumbness, from my weakness draws
135   My very soul of counsel. Stop my mouth.

TROILUS And shall, albeit sweet music issues thence.

PANDARUS Pretty, i'faith.

CRESSIDA My lord, I do beseech you, pardon me;
'Twas not my purpose thus to beg a kiss.
140   I am ashamed. O heavens, what have I done?
For this time will I take my leave, my lord.

TROILUS Your leave, sweet Cressid?

PANDARUS Leave! An you take leave till tomorrow
morning——

CRESSIDA Pray you, content you.

145   TROILUS   What offends you, lady?

CRESSIDA Sir, mine own company.

TROILUS You cannot shun yourself.

CRESSIDA Let me go and try.
I have a kind of self resides with you;
150   But an unkind self, that itself will leave
To be another's fool. I would be gone.
Where is my wit? I know not what I speak.

TROILUS Well know they what they speak that speak so
wisely.

CRESSIDA Perchance, my lord, I show more craft than
love,
155   And fell so roundly to a large confession

135 very soul of counsel inmost thoughts and secrets   151 fool dupe
155 roundly frankly, openly   155 large unrestrained

170

To angle for your thoughts. But you are wise,
Or else you love not, for to be wise and love
Exceeds man's might; that dwells with gods above.

TROILUS O that I thought it could be in a woman—
As, if it can, I will presume in you—   160
To feed for aye her lamp and flames of love;
To keep her constancy in plight and youth,
Outliving beauty's outward, with a mind
That doth renew swifter than blood decays;
Or that persuasion could but thus convince me   165
That my integrity and truth to you
Might be affronted with the match and weight
Of such a winnowed purity in love;
How were I then uplifted! But, alas,
I am as true as truth's simplicity,   170
And simpler than the infancy of truth.

CRESSIDA In that I'll war with you.

TROILUS   O virtuous fight,
When right with right wars who shall be most right!
True swains in love shall in the world to come
Approve their truth by Troilus. When their rhymes,   175
Full of protest, of oath and big compare,
Wants similes, truth tired with iteration,
"As true as steel, as plantage to the moon,
As sun to day, as turtle to her mate,
As iron to adamant, as earth to the center,"   180
Yet, after all comparisons of truth,
As truth's authentic author to be cited,
"As true as Troilus" shall crown up the verse
And sanctify the numbers.

156–58 But you are wise ... man's might i.e., you are reasonable, which means
you are not in love, for no man can follow reason and love at the same time
162 in plight and youth as it was when it was plighted, and as fresh
163 beauty's outward external, transitory beauty 167 affronted confronted,
i.e., equaled 168 winnowed i.e., distilled 175 Approve attest 178 plantage
to the moon (the moon was thought to influence plantage, or vegetation)
179 turtle turtledove (an emblem of eternally faithful love) 180 adamant the
loadstone (magnetic) 184 numbers metrical verses

CRESSIDA   Prophet may you be!
185   If I be false or swerve a hair from truth,
When time is old and hath forgot itself,
When waterdrops have worn the stones of Troy,
And blind oblivion swallowed cities up,
And mighty states characterless are grated
190   To dusty nothing, yet let memory,
From false to false among false maids in love,
Upbraid my falsehood! When they've said, "As false
As air, as water, wind or sandy earth,
As fox to lamb, as wolf to heifer's calf,
195   Pard to the hind, or stepdame to her son,"
Yea, let them say, to stick the heart of falsehood,
"As false as Cressid."

PANDARUS Go to, a bargain made. Seal it, seal it; I'll
be the witness. Here I hold your hand, here my
200   cousin's. If ever you prove false one to another,
since I have taken such pains to bring you together, let all pitiful goers-between be called to the
world's end after my name; call them all Pandars.
Let all constant men be Troiluses, all false women
205   Cressids, and all brokers-between Pandars! Say,
"Amen."

TROILUS Amen.

CRESSIDA Amen.

PANDARUS Amen. Whereupon I will show you a cham-
210   ber which bed, because it shall not speak of your
pretty encounters, press it to death. Away!
                              Exeunt [Troilus and Cressida].
And Cupid grant all tongue-tied maidens here
Bed, chamber, Pandar to provide this gear!   *Exit*.

---

189 **characterless** without an identifying mark   195 **Pard to the hind** leopard to
the doe   210 **which bed** the bed in which   210 **because** (1) for the reason that
(normal usage) (2) in order that (?)

[Scene III. *The Greek camp*.]

Enter Ulysses, Diomedes, Nestor, Agamemnon,
[Menelaus, Ajax, and] Calchas. Flourish [of trumpets.]

CALCHAS Now, princes, for the service I have done,
  Th' advantage of the time prompts me aloud
  To call for recompense. Appear it to mind
  That through the sight I bear in things to come,
  I have abandoned Troy, left my possession,   5
  Incurred a traitor's name, exposed myself,
  From certain and possessed conveniences,
  To doubtful fortunes, sequest'ring from me all
  That time, acquaintance, custom, and condition
  Made tame and most familiar to my nature;   10
  And here, to do you service, am become
  As new into the world, strange, unacquainted.
  I do beseech you, as in way of taste,
  To give me now a little benefit
  Out of those many registered in promise,   15
  Which, you say, live to come in my behalf.

AGAMEMNON What wouldst thou of us, Troyan? Make
  demand.

CALCHAS You have a Troyan prisoner, called Antenor,
  Yesterday took; Troy holds him very dear.
  Oft have you—often have you thanks therefor—   20
  Desired my Cressid in right great exchange,
  Whom Troy hath still denied; but this Antenor

III.iii.4 **sight** i.e., foresight   8 **sequest'ring** putting aside   10 **tame** familiar,
comfortable   13 **taste** foretaste   21 **right great exchange** exchange for someone
sufficiently great   22 **still** always

I know is such a wrest in their affairs
That their negotiations all must slack,
25 Wanting his manage; and they will almost
Give us a prince of blood, a son of Priam,
In change of him. Let him be sent, great princes,
And he shall buy my daughter; and her presence
Shall quite strike off all service I have done
In most accepted pain.

30 AGAMEMNON   Let Diomedes bear him,
And bring us Cressid hither; Calchas shall have
What he requests of us. Good Diomed,
Furnish you fairly, for this interchange.
Withal bring word if Hector will tomorrow
35 Be answered in his challenge. Ajax is ready.

DIOMEDES This shall I undertake, and 'tis a burden
Which I am proud to bear.   *Exit* [*with Calchas*].

Achilles and Patroclus stand in their tent.

ULYSSES Achilles stands i' th' entrance of his tent.
Please it our general pass strangely by him,
40 As if he were forgot; and, princes all,
Lay negligent and loose regard upon him.
I will come last. 'Tis like he'll question me
Why such unplausive eyes are bent, why turned, on
    him.
If so, I have derision medicinable
45 To use between your strangeness and his pride,
Which his own will shall have desire to drink.
It may do good; pride hath no other glass
To show itself but pride, for supple knees
Feed arrogance and are the proud man's fees.

50 AGAMEMNON We'll execute your purpose, and put on
A form of strangeness as we pass along.
So do each lord, and either greet him not

---

23 **wrest** a key used for tuning stringed instruments (i.e., the influence of harmony in Trojan discussions) 30 **accepted** cheerfully endured 37 s.d. **stand in their tent** i.e., appear and stand in the entrance of their tent 39 **strangely** aloofly 43 **unplausive** disapproving 48 **show** mirror

Or else disdainfully, which shall shake him more
Than if not looked on. I will lead the way.

ACHILLES What comes the general to speak with me?   55
You know my mind; I'll fight no more 'gainst Troy.

AGAMEMNON What says Achilles? Would he aught with
us?

NESTOR Would you, my lord, aught with the general?

ACHILLES No.

NESTOR Nothing, my lord.   60

AGAMEMNON The better.

ACHILLES Good day, good day.

MENELAUS How do you? How do you?

ACHILLES What, does the cuckold scorn me?

AJAX How now, Patroclus?   65

ACHILLES Good morrow, Ajax.

AJAX Ha?

ACHILLES Good morrow.

AJAX Ay, and good next day too.

Exeunt.

ACHILLES What mean these fellows? Know they not
Achilles?   70

PATROCLUS They pass by strangely. They were used to
bend,
To send their smiles before them to Achilles,
To come as humbly as they used to creep
To holy altars.

ACHILLES   What, am I poor of late?
'Tis certain, greatness, once fall'n out with fortune,   75
Must fall out with men too. What the declined is
He shall as soon read in the eyes of others
As feel in his own fall; for men, like butterflies,

Show not their mealy wings but to the summer,
80 And not a man, for being simply man,
Hath any honor, but honor for those honors
That are without him, as place, riches, and favor,
Prizes of accident as oft as merit;
Which when they fall, as being slippery standers,
85 The love that leaned on them as slippery too,
Doth one pluck down another, and together
Die in the fall. But 'tis not so with me;
Fortune and I are friends. I do enjoy
At ample point all that I did possess,
90 Save these men's looks—who do, methinks, find out
Something not worth in me such rich beholding
As they have often given. Here is Ulysses;
I'll interrupt his reading.
How now, Ulysses.

ULYSSES   Now, great Thetis' son.

ACHILLES What are you reading?

95 ULYSSES   A strange fellow here
Writes me that man, how dearly ever parted,
How much in having, or without or in,
Cannot make boast to have that which he hath,
Nor feels not what he owes but by reflection;
100 As when his virtues aiming upon others
Heat them, and they retort that heat again
To the first giver.

ACHILLES   This is not strange, Ulysses.
The beauty that is borne here in the face
The bearer knows not, but commends itself
105 To others' eyes; nor doth the eye itself,
That most pure spirit of sense, behold itself,
Not going from itself; but eye to eye opposed

---

79 mealy powdery 82 without external to 89 At ample point in full
measure, in every way   96 how dearly ever parted however excellently endowed
by nature 97 How much ... or in however much in possession, whether
externally or internally 99 Nor feels ... by reflection and understands what he
himself possesses (owes = "owns") only as it is reflected

Salutes each other with each other's form;
For speculation turns not to itself
Till it hath traveled and is married there   110
Where it may see itself. This is not strange at all.

ULYSSES I do not strain at the position—
It is familiar—but at the author's drift;
Who in his circumstance expressly proves
That no man is the lord of anything—   115
Though in and of him there be much consisting—
Till he communicate his parts to others.
Nor doth he of himself know them for aught
Till he behold them formèd in th' applause
Where they're extended; who, like an arch, reverb'rate   120
The voice again, or, like a gate of steel
Fronting the sun, receives and renders back
His figure and his heat. I was much rapt in this,
And apprehended here immediately
Th' unknown Ajax.   125
Heavens, what a man is there! A very horse,
That has he knows not what. Nature, what things there are
Most abject in regard and dear in use!
What things again most dear in the esteem
And poor in worth! Now shall we see tomorrow,   130
An act that very chance doth throw upon him:
Ajax renowned. O heavens, what some men do,
While some men leave to do!
How some men creep in skittish Fortune's hall,
While others play the idiots in her eyes!   135
How one man eats into another's pride,
While pride is fasting in his wantonness!
To see these Grecian lords—why, even already

---

109 speculation power of sight   112 position i.e., that of the writer whom
Ulysses paraphrases above   114 circumstance detailed discussion   116 Though
... consisting although much exists in him and also because of him
120 Where they're extended in which his natural attributes are noised abroad
120 who which   128 Most ... use most despised and yet invaluable   134 in into
134 skittish i.e., unreliable   137 his wantonness its own self-satisfaction

They clap the lubber Ajax on the shoulder,
140   As if his foot were on brave Hector's breast,
And great Troy shrinking.

ACHILLES I do believe it; for they passed by me
As misers do by beggars, neither gave to me
Good word nor look. What, are my deeds forgot?

145 ULYSSES Time hath, my lord, a wallet at his back,
Wherein he puts alms for oblivion,
A great-sized monster of ingratitudes.
Those scraps are good deeds past, which are
devoured
As fast as they are made, forgot as soon
150   As done. Perseverance, dear my lord,
Keeps honor bright. To have done, is to hang
Quite out of fashion, like a rusty mail
In monumental mock'ry. Take the instant way;
For honor travels in a strait so narrow
155   Where one but goes abreast. Keep, then, the path;
For emulation hath a thousand sons
That one by one pursue. If you give way,
Or hedge aside from the direct forthright,
Like to an ent'red tide they all rush by
160   And leave you hindmost;
Or, like a gallant horse fall'n in first rank,
Lie there for pavement to the abject rear,
O'errun and trampled on. Then what they do in
present,
Though less than yours in past, must o'ertop yours.
165   For time is like a fashionable host,
That slightly shakes his parting guest by the hand,
And with his arms outstretched, as he would fly,
Grasps in the comer. The welcome ever smiles,
And farewell goes out sighing. Let not virtue seek
170   Remuneration for the thing it was. For beauty, wit,
High birth, vigor of bone, desert in service,

152 mail piece of armor   153 instant most immediate   158 direct forthright
course of action clearly at hand, the path straight ahead   162 the abject rear the
miserable, degraded members of the rear (as in a military charge or parade)

Love, friendship, charity, are subjects all
To envious and calumniating time.
One touch of nature makes the whole world kin,
That all with one consent praise newborn gauds,   175
Though they are made and molded of things past,
And give to dust that is a little gilt
More laud than gilt o'erdusted.
The present eye praises the present object.
Then marvel not, thou great and complete man,   180
That all the Greeks begin to worship Ajax;
Since things in motion sooner catch the eye
Than what stirs not. The cry went once on thee,
And still it might, and yet it may again,
If thou wouldst not entomb thyself alive   185
And case thy reputation in thy tent;
Whose glorious deeds, but in these fields of late,
Made emulous missions 'mongst the gods themselves
And drave great Mars to faction.

ACHILLES   Of this my privacy
I have strong reasons.

ULYSSES   But 'gainst your privacy   190
The reasons are more potent and heroical.
'Tis known, Achilles, that you are in love
With one of Priam's daughters.

ACHILLES Ha! Known!

ULYSSES Is that a wonder?   195
The providence that's in a watchful state
Knows almost every grain of Pluto's gold
Finds bottom in th' uncomprehensive deeps,

174 **One touch of nature** a natural inclination, common to all men (to praise
according to superficial values)   175 **gauds** toys, trifles   178 **More laud than
gilt o'erdusted** more praise than gold covered with dust   183 **cry** public
opinion   186 **case** encase   188 **emulous missions** competitive and jealous
warfare (the gods took sides in the Trojan war, fighting among themselves)
189 **to faction** to become a partisan   193 **one of Priam's daughters**
(Polyxena)   196 **providence** careful and timely understanding   197 **Pluto's**
(Shakespeare's error for Plutus, god of wealth; Pluto was god of the underworld)   198 **uncomprehensive** unfathomable

Keeps place with thought, and almost, like the
gods,
200   Do thoughts unveil in their dumb cradles.
There is a mystery—with whom relation
Durst never meddle—in the soul of state,
Which hath an operation more divine
Than breath or pen can give expressure to.
205   All the commerce that you have had with Troy
As perfectly is ours as yours, my lord;
And better would it fit Achilles much
To throw down Hector than Polyxena.
But it must grieve young Pyrrhus now at home,
210   When fame shall in our islands sound her trump,
And all the Greekish girls shall tripping sing,
"Great Hector's sister did Achilles win,
But our great Ajax bravely beat down him."
Farewell, my lord; I as your lover speak;
215   The fool slides o'er the ice that you should break.

                                        [*Exit.*]

PATROCLUS To this effect, Achilles, have I moved you.
A woman impudent and mannish grown
Is not more loathed than an effeminate man
In time of action. I stand condemned for this;
220   They think my little stomach to the war
And your great love to me restrains you thus.
Sweet, rouse yourself; and the weak wanton Cupid
Shall from your neck unloose his amorous fold
And, like a dewdrop from the lion's mane,
Be shook to air.

225   ACHILLES   Shall Ajax fight with Hector?

PATROCLUS Ay, and perhaps receive much honor by
him.

ACHILLES I see my reputation is at stake.
My fame is shrewdly gored.

199 **Keeps place** keeps up, runs parallel   201 **relation** open statement
209 **Pyrrhus** (Achilles' son, also called Neoptolemus)   228 **shrewdly gored**
sorely wounded

PATROCLUS   O, then, beware!
　Those wounds heal ill that men do give themselves.
　Omission to do what is necessary   230
　Seals a commision to a blank of danger;
　And danger, like an ague, subtly taints
　Even then when they sit idly in the sun.

ACHILLES Go call Thersites hither, sweet Patroclus.
　I'll send the fool to Ajax and desire him   235
　T' invite the Troyan lords after the combat
　To see us here unarmed. I have a woman's longing,
　An appetite that I am sick withal,
　To see great Hector in his weeds of peace,
　To talk with him and to behold his visage,   240
　Even to my full of view.

                        Enter Thersites.

                        A labor saved!

THERSITES A wonder!

ACHILLES What?

THERSITES Ajax goes up and down the field, asking for
　himself.   245

ACHILLES How so?

THERSITES He must fight singly tomorrow with Hec-
　tor, and is so prophetically proud of an heroical
　cudgeling that he raves in saying nothing.

ACHILLES How can that be?   250

THERSITES Why, he stalks up and down like a
　peacock—a stride and a stand; ruminates like an

___

231 Seals ... danger i.e., binds one to confront unnamed danger (royal officers
sometimes carried blank warrants for arrest, already bearing the commissioning
seal of authority, which could be filled in as necessary) 232 taints infects
237 woman's i.e., pregnant woman's (?) 239 weeds apparel 240-41 to
behold ... view (since in full armor Hector's face would have been hidden behind
the closed beaver of his helmet) 244-45 asking for himself (here "Ajax" is
probably a pun on a jakes, i.e., a privy)

hostess that hath no arithmetic but her brain to set
down her reckoning; bites his lip with a politic
255   regard, as who should say, "There were wit in
his head an 'twould out"; and so there is, but it
lies as coldly in him as fire in a flint, which will not
show without knocking. The man's undone forever, for if Hector break not his neck i' the combat,
260   he'll break't himself in vainglory. He knows not me.
I said, "Good morrow, Ajax"; and he replies,
"Thanks, Agamemnon." What think you of this man
that takes me for the general? He's grown a
very land-fish, languageless, a monster. A plague of
265   opinion! A man may wear it on both sides like a
leather jerkin.

ACHILLES Thou must be my ambassador to him,
Thersites.

THERSITES Who, I? Why, he'll answer nobody. He pro-
270   fesses not answering. Speaking is for beggars; he
wears his tongue in's arms. I will put on his presence; let Patroclus make demands to me, you shall
see the pageant of Ajax.

ACHILLES To him, Patroclus. Tell him I humbly desire
275   the valiant Ajax to invite the most valorous Hector to
come unarmed to my tent, and to procure safe-
conduct for his person of the magnanimous and
most illustrious, six-or-seven-times-honored cap-
tain-general of the Grecian army, Agamemnon, et
280   cetera. Do this.

PATROCLUS Jove bless great Ajax!

THERSITES Hum.

PATROCLUS I come from the worthy Achilles——

THERSITES Ha!

285   PATROCLUS Who most humbly desires you to invite
Hector to his tent——

254-55 **politic regard** expression of shrewd judgment   266 **jerkin** close-fitting
jacket   271 **put on** imitate

THERSITES Hum!

PATROCLUS And to procure safe-conduct from Agamemnon.

THERSITES Agamemnon?   290

PATROCLUS Ay, my lord.

THERSITES Ha!

PATROCLUS What say you to't?

THERSITES God b'wi'you, with all my heart.

PATROCLUS Your answer, sir.   295

THERSITES If tomorrow be a fair day, by eleven of the
clock it will go one way or other; howsoever, he shall
pay for me ere he has me.

PATROCLUS Your answer, sir.

THERSITES Fare ye well, with all my heart.   300

ACHILLES Why, but he is not in this tune, is he?

THERSITES No, but out of tune thus. What music will
be in him when Hector has knocked out his brains, I
know not; but I am sure none, unless the fiddler
Apollo get his sinews to make catlings on.   305

ACHILLES Come, thou shalt bear a letter to him
straight.

THERSITES Let me bear another to his horse, for that's
the more capable creature.

ACHILLES My mind is troubled, like a fountain stirred,   310
And I myself see not the bottom of it.
                             [*Exeunt Achilles and Patroclus.*]

THERSITES Would the fountain of your mind were clear
again, that I might water an ass at it! I had rather
be a tick in a sheep than such a valiant ignorance.
                                                    [*Exit.*]

305 **catlings** strings of catgut   309 **capable** intelligent

[ACT IV

Scene I. *Within Troy*.]

Enter, at one door, Aeneas [with a torch;] at another, Paris, Deiphobus, Antenor, Diomed the Grecian, [and others,] with torches.

PARIS See, ho! Who is that there?

DEIPHOBUS   It is the Lord Aeneas.

AENEAS Is the prince there in person?
  Had I so good occasion to lie long
  As you, Prince Paris, nothing but heavenly business
5 Should rob my bedmate of my company.

DIOMEDES That's my mind too. Good morrow, Lord
  Aeneas.

PARIS A valiant Greek, Aeneas; take his hand.
  Witness the process of your speech, wherein
  You told how Diomed, a whole week by days,
  Did haunt you in the field.

10 AENEAS   Health to you, valiant sir,
  During all question of the gentle truce;

IV.i.8 **process** gist, drift   9 **by days** day by day   11 **question of the gentle truce** i.e., intercourse made possible by the truce

184

But when I meet you armed, as black defiance
As heart can think or courage execute.

DIOMEDES The one and other Diomed embraces.
Our bloods are now in calm, and, so long, health!   15
But when contention and occasion meet,
By Jove, I'll play the hunter for thy life
With all my force, pursuit, and policy.

AENEAS And thou shalt hunt a lion that will fly
With his face backward. In humane gentleness,   20
Welcome to Troy. Now, by Anchises' life,
Welcome indeed! By Venus' hand I swear,
No man alive can love in such a sort
The thing he means to kill more excellently.

DIOMEDES We sympathize. Jove, let Aeneas live,   25
If to my sword his fate be not the glory,
A thousand complete courses of the sun!
But, in mine emulous honor, let him die
With every joint a wound, and that tomorrow!

AENEAS We know each other well.   30

DIOMEDES We do, and long to know each other worse.

PARIS This is the most despiteful gentle greeting,
The noblest hateful love, that e'er I heard of.
What business, lord, so early?

AENEAS I was sent for to the king; but why, I know not. 35

PARIS His purpose meets you; it was to bring this
    Greek
To Calchas' house, and there to render him,
For the enfreed Antenor, the fair Cressid.
Let's have your company; or, if you please,
Haste there before us. I constantly do think—   40
Or rather call my thought a certain knowledge—
My brother Troilus lodges there tonight.

16 occasion opportunity 18 policy cunning 21 Anchises (Aeneas'
father) 22 Venus' hand (Diomedes was supposed to have wounded Venus,
Aeneas' mother, in the hand) 25 sympathize have the same feeling
40 constantly firmly

Rouse him and give him note of our approach,
With the whole quality wherefore. I fear
We shall be much unwelcome.

45 AENEAS   That I assure you.
Troilus had rather Troy were borne to Greece
Than Cressid borne from Troy.

PARIS   There is no help.
The bitter disposition of the time
Will have it so. On, lord; we'll follow you.

50 AENEAS Good morrow, all.   *Exit Aeneas.*

PARIS And tell me, noble Diomed; faith, tell me true,
Even in the soul of sound good-fellowship,
Who, in your thoughts, deserves fair Helen best,
Myself or Menelaus?

DIOMEDES   Both alike.
55 He merits well to have her that doth seek her,
Not making any scruple of her soilure,
With such a hell of pain and world of charge;
And you as well to keep her that defend her,
Not palating the taste of her dishonor,
60 With such a costly loss of wealth and friends.
He, like a puling cuckold, would drink up
The lees and dregs of a flat tamèd piece;
You, like a lecher, out of whorish loins
Are pleased to breed out your inheritors.
65 Both merits poised, each weighs nor less nor more;
But he as he, the heavier for a whore.

PARIS You are too bitter to your countrywoman.

DIOMEDES She's bitter to her country! Hear me,
          Paris—

44 **quality** occasion, explanation   57 **charge** cost   59 **Not palating** insensible
to   62 **flat tamèd piece** (1) cask of wine opened so long that the wine has gone
flat (2) woman so promiscuous that she can no longer excite or be excited
sexually   65 **poised** weighed   66 **But he ... a whore** (1) but he, i.e., Menelaus,
as heavy as his small merit may be, plus the weight of the whore who is, after all,
his legal possession (?); (2) but he, whoever wins her, heavier only by the weight of
a whore (to be "light" was to be morally loose) (?)

For every false drop in her bawdy veins
A Grecian's life hath sunk; for every scruple   70
Of her contaminated carrion weight
A Troyan hath been slain. Since she could speak,
She hath not given so many good words breath
As for her Greeks and Troyans suffered death.

PARIS Fair Diomed, you do as chapmen do,   75
    Dispraise the thing that you desire to buy;
    But we in silence hold this virtue well,
    We'll not commend what we intend to sell.
    Here lies our way.   *Exeunt.*

[Scene II. *Within Troy; Calchas' house.*]

Enter Troilus and Cressida.

TROILUS Dear, trouble not yourself; the morn is cold.

CRESSIDA Then, sweet my lord, I'll call mine uncle
    down;
    He shall unbolt the gates.

TROILUS   Trouble him not;
    To bed, to bed. Sleep kill those pretty eyes,
    And give as soft attachment to thy senses   5
    As infants' empty of all thought!

CRESSIDA   Good morrow then.

TROILUS I prithee now, to bed.

CRESSIDA   Are you aweary of me?

TROILUS O Cressida! But that the busy day,

70 **scruple** (the smallest possible unit of weight)   75 **chapmen** hawkers of cheap
wares   78 **We'll not ... to sell** i.e., we'll not practice the seller's tricks although
you practice the buyer's (Paris does not imply that Helen is for sale)   IV.ii.4 **kill**
overpower   5 **attachment** seizure

Waked by the lark, hath roused the ribald crows,
10   And dreaming night will hide our joys no longer,
I would not from thee.

CRESSIDA   Night hath been too brief.

TROILUS Beshrew the witch! With venomous wights
    she stays
As tediously as hell, but flies the grasps of love
With wings more momentary-swift than thought.
You will catch cold and curse me.

15 CRESSIDA   Prithee, tarry;
You men will never tarry.
O foolish Cressid! I might have still held off,
And then you would have tarried. Hark, there's one
    up.

PANDARUS (*Within*) What's all the doors open here?

20 TROILUS It is your uncle.

CRESSIDA A pestilence on him! Now will he be
    mocking.
I shall have such a life.

Enter Pandarus.

PANDARUS How now, how now! How go maidenheads?
Here, you maid, where's my cousin Cressid?

CRESSIDA Go hang yourself, you naughty mocking
25   uncle.
You bring me to do—and then you flout me too.

PANDARUS To do what? To do what? Let her say what.
What have I brought you to do?

CRESSIDA Come come; beshrew your heart! You'll
    ne'er be good,
30   Nor suffer others.

PANDARUS Ha, ha! Alas, poor wretch! A poor capocchia!

---

12 **venomous weights** malignant witches (or, simply, evil creatures) 26 **do**
(used sometimes in obscene sense) 31 **capocchia** simpleton

Hast not slept tonight? Would he not, a naughty
man, let it sleep? A bugbear take him!

CRESSIDA Did not I tell you? Would he were knocked i'
the head!   *One knocks.*
Who's that at door? Good uncle, go and see.   35
My lord, come you again into my chamber.
You smile and mock me, as if I meant naughtily.

TROILUS Ha, ha!

CRESSIDA Come, you are deceived, I think of no such
thing.   *Knock.*
How earnestly they knock! Pray you, come in.   40
I would not for half Troy have you seen here.
                        Exeunt [Troilus and Cressida].

PANDARUS Who's there? What's the matter? Will you
beat down the door? How now, what's the matter?

[*Enter Aeneas.*]

AENEAS Good morrow, lord, good morrow.

PANDARUS Who's there? My Lord Aeneas! By my
troth,
I knew you not. What news with you so early?   45

AENEAS Is not Prince Troilus here?

PANDARUS Here? What should he do here?

AENEAS Come, he is here, my lord. Do not deny him.
It doth import him much to speak with me.   50

PANDARUS Is he here, say you? 'Tis more than I know,
I'll be sworn. For my own part, I came in late. What
should he do here?

AENEAS Who! Nay, then. Come, come, you'll do him
wrong ere you are ware. You'll be so true to him, to   55

---

33 bugbear hobgoblin   50 doth import is important to   54 Who! (an exclamation of impatience; sometimes as to call "stop!" to a horse)

be false to him. Do not you know of him, but yet go
fetch him hither; go.

Enter Troilus.

TROILUS How now, what's the matter?

AENEAS My lord, I scarce have leisure to salute you,
60   My matter is so rash. There is at hand
      Paris your brother, and Deiphobus,
      The Grecian Diomed, and our Antenor
      Delivered to us; and for him forthwith,
      Ere the first sacrifice, within this hour,
65   We must give up to Diomedes' hand
      The Lady Cressida.

TROILUS   Is it so concluded?

AENEAS By Priam, and the general state of Troy.
      They are at hand and ready to effect it.

TROILUS How my achievements mock me!
70   I will go meet them. And, my Lord Aeneas,
      We met by chance; you did not find me here.

AENEAS Good, good, my lord; the secrets of nature
      Have not more gift in taciturnity.
                              Exeunt [Troilus and Aeneas].

PANDARUS Is't possible? No sooner got but lost? The
75   devil take Antenor! The young prince will go mad.
      A plague upon Antenor! I would they had broke 's
      neck!

Enter Cressida.

CRESSIDA How now? What's the matter? Who was
      here?

80 PANDARUS Ah, ah!

CRESSIDA Why sigh you so profoundly? Where's my

---

60 **rash** urgent 67 **general state** noblemen in council 72 **secrets** most
unknown parts

lord? Gone? Tell me, sweet uncle, what's the matter?

PANDARUS Would I were as deep under the earth as I
am above! 85

CRESSIDA O the gods! What's the matter?

PANDARUS Pray thee, get thee in. Would thou hadst
ne'er been born! I knew thou wouldst be his death.
O poor gentleman! A plague upon Antenor!

CRESSIDA Good uncle, I beseech you on my knees, 90
what's the matter?

PANDARUS Thou must be gone, wench, thou must be
gone; thou art changed for Antenor. Thou must to
thy father and be gone from Troilus. 'Twill be his
death; 'twill be his bane; he cannot bear it. 95

CRESSIDA O you immortal gods! I will not go.

PANDARUS Thou must.

CRESSIDA I will not, uncle. I have forgot my father;
I know no touch of consanguinity—
No kin, no love, no blood, no soul so near me 100
As the sweet Troilus. O you gods divine,
Make Cressid's name the very crown of falsehood
If ever she leave Troilus! Time, force, and death,
Do to this body what extremes you can;
But the strong base and building of my love 105
Is as the very center of the earth,
Drawing all things to it. I will go in and weep——

PANDARUS Do, do.

CRESSIDA ——Tear my bright hair, and scratch my
praisèd cheeks,
Crack my clear voice with sobs, and break my 110
heart
With sounding Troilus. I will not go from Troy.
Exeunt.

93 **changed** exchanged 95 **bane** poison, destruction 99 **no touch of consan-**
guinity no sense of relationship

[Scene III. *Within Troy; near Calchas' house.*]

Enter Paris, Troilus, Aeneas, Deiphobus, Antenor, Diomedes.

PARIS It is great morning, and the hour prefixed
 For her delivery to this valiant Greek
 Comes fast upon. Good my brother Troilus,
 Tell you the lady what she is to do,
 And haste her to the purpose.

5 TROILUS   Walk into her house.
 I'll bring her to the Grecian presently;
 And to his hand when I deliver her,
 Think it an altar, and thy brother Troilus
 A priest there off'ring to it his own heart.

10 PARIS I know what 'tis to love;
 And would, as I shall pity, I could help.
 Please you walk in, my lords.   *Exeunt.*

[Scene IV. *Within Troy; Calchas' house.*]

Enter Pandarus and Cressida.

PANDARUS Be moderate, be moderate.

CRESSIDA Why tell you me of moderation?
 The grief is fine, full, perfect, that I taste,
 And violenteth in a sense as strong
5 As that which causeth it. How can I moderate it?
 If I could temporize with my affections,

IV.iii.1 **great morning** broad daylight   6 **presently** immediately   IV.iv.4 **vio-lenteth** rages

Or brew it to a weak and colder palate,
The like allayment could I give my grief.
My love admits no qualifying dross;
No more my grief, in such a precious loss.   10

Enter Troilus.

PANDARUS Here, here, here he comes. Ah, sweet
ducks!

CRESSIDA O Troilus! Troilus!

PANDARUS What a pair of spectacles is here! Let me
embrace too. "O heart," as the goodly saying is—   15
    O heart, heavy heart,
      Why sigh'st thou without breaking?
where he answers again,
    Because thou canst not ease thy smart
      By friendship nor by speaking.   20
There was never a truer rhyme. Let us cast away
nothing, for we may live to have need of such a
verse. We see it, we see it. How now, lambs!

TROILUS Cressid, I love thee in so strained a purity,
That the blest gods, as angry with my fancy,   25
More bright in zeal than the devotion which
Cold lips blow to their deities, take thee from me.

CRESSIDA Have the gods envy?

PANDARUS Ay, ay, ay, ay, 'tis too plain a case.

CRESSIDA And is it true that I must go from Troy?   30

TROILUS A hateful truth.

CRESSIDA   What, and from Troilus too?

TROILUS From Troy and Troilus.

CRESSIDA   Is't possible?

7 **palate** taste   9 **qualifying dross** moderating impurity   14 **spectacles** (a
pun)   24 **strained** distilled, filtered   25 **fancy** love

TROILUS And suddenly, where injury of chance
         Puts back leave-taking, justles roughly by
35   All time of pause, rudely beguiles our lips
         Of all rejoindure, forcibly prevents
         Our locked embrasures, strangles our dear vows
         Even in the birth of our own laboring breath.
         We two, that with so many thousand sighs
40   Did buy each other, must poorly sell ourselves
         With the rude brevity and discharge of one.
         Injurious time now with a robber's haste
         Crams his rich thievery up, he knows not how;
         As many farewells as be stars in heaven,
45   With distinct breath and consigned kisses to them,
         He fumbles up into a loose adieu,
         And scants us with a single famished kiss,
         Distasted with the salt of broken tears.

AENEAS (*Within*) My lord, is the lady ready?

50 TROILUS Hark! You are called. Some say the Genius
         Cries so to him that instantly must die.
         Bid them have patience; she shall come anon.

PANDARUS Where are my tears? Rain, to lay this wind,
         or my heart will be blown up by the root! [*Exit.*]

CRESSIDA I must, then, to the Grecians?

55 TROILUS   No remedy.

CRESSIDA A woeful Cressid 'mongst the merry Greeks!
         When shall we see again?

TROILUS Hear me, love. Be thou but true of heart——

CRESSIDA I true! How now! What wicked deem is this?

60 TROILUS Nay, we must use expostulation kindly,

---

33 injury of chance injurious accident 36 rejoindure reunion 45 With
distinct ... to them with the words of each farewell and the kisses which ratify
each of them 46 fumbles wraps clumsily 48 Distasted the taste (of the kiss)
ruined 50 Genius guardian spirit 59 deem thought

For it is parting from us.
I speak not "be thou true" as fearing thee,
For I will throw my glove to Death himself
That there's no maculation in thy heart;
But "be thou true," say I, to fashion in   65
My sequent protestation: be thou true,
And I will see thee.

CRESSIDA O, you shall be exposed, my lord, to dangers
As infinite as imminent; but I'll be true.

TROILUS And I'll grow friend with danger. Wear this
sleeve.   70

CRESSIDA And you this glove. When shall I see you?

TROILUS I will corrupt the Grecian sentinels,
To give thee nightly visitation.
But yet, be true.

CRESSIDA   O heavens! "Be true" again!

TROILUS Hear why I speak it, love.   75
The Grecian youths are full of quality;
They're loving, well composed with gift of nature,
And swelling o'er with arts and exercise.
How novelty may move, and parts with person,
Alas! A kind of godly jealousy—   80
Which, I beseech you, call a virtuous sin—
Makes me afeared.

CRESSIDA   O heavens, you love me not!

TROILUS Die I a villain then!
In this I do not call your faith in question
So mainly as my merit. I cannot sing,   85

60-61 Nay, we ... from us we must be gentle in all remonstrance, for we are now
saying good-bye   63 throw my glove give challenge   64 maculation taint,
blemish (i.e., disloyalty)   65-66 to fashion in ... sequent protestation as
introduction for my own promise to follow   76 quality qualities   77 loving
adept in the arts of love   78 arts and exercise talents both in theory and
practice   79 parts with person specific qualities and talents, combined with
personal charm

Nor heel the high lavolt, nor sweeten talk,
Nor play at subtle games—fair virtues all,
To which the Grecians are most prompt and
    pregnant;
But I can tell that in each grace of these
90 There lurks a still and dumb-discoursive devil
That tempts most cunningly. But be not tempted.

CRESSIDA Do you think I will?

TROILUS No!
But something may be done that we will not;
95 And sometimes we are devils to ourselves
When we will tempt the frailty of our powers,
Presuming on their changeful potency.

AENEAS (Within) Nay, good my lord!

TROILUS   Come, kiss; and
    let us part.

PARIS (Within) Brother Troilus!

TROILUS   Good brother, come
    you hither;
100 And bring Aeneas and the Grecian with you.

CRESSIDA My lord, will you be true?

TROILUS Who? I? Alas, it is my vice, my fault.
Whiles others fish with craft for great opinion,
I with great truth catch mere simplicity;
105 Whilst some with cunning gild their copper crowns,
With truth and plainness I do wear mine bare.
Fear not my truth; the moral of my wit
Is "plain and true"—there's all the reach of it.

[Enter Aeneas, Paris, Antenor, Deiphobus and Diomedes.]

Welcome, Sir Diomed. Here is the lady

86 **the high lavolt** (the lavolt was a dance for two persons, requiring many high steps and bounds) 88 **pregnant** ready, fully able 90 **dumb-discoursive** articulate even in silence 97 **changeful potency** power which may alter to failure 103 **opinion** reputation 104 **catch** achieve; i.e., achieve a reputation for 107 **moral** maxim

Which for Antenor we deliver you.   110
At the port, lord, I'll give her to thy hand,
And by the way possess thee what she is.
Entreat her fair; and, by my soul, fair Greek,
If e'er thou stand at mercy of my sword,
Name Cressid, and thy life shall be as safe   115
As Priam is in Ilion.

DIOMEDES   Fair Lady Cressid,
So please you, save the thanks this prince expects.
The luster in your eye, heaven in your cheek,
Pleads your fair usage; and to Diomed
You shall be mistress, and command him wholly.   120

TROILUS Grecian, thou dost not use me courteously,
To shame the seal of my petition to thee
In praising her. I tell thee, lord of Greece,
She is as far high-soaring o'er thy praises
As thou unworthy to be called her servant.   125
I charge thee use her well, even for my charge;
For, by the dreadful Pluto, if thou dost not,
Though the great bulk Achilles be thy guard,
I'll cut thy throat.

DIOMEDES   O, be not moved, Prince Troilus.
Let me be privileged by my place and message   130
To be a speaker free. When I am hence,
I'll answer to my lust; and know you, lord,
I'll nothing do on charge. To her own worth
She shall be prized; but that you say "be't so,"
I speak it in my spirit and honor, "no."   135

TROILUS Come, to the port. I'll tell thee, Diomed,
This brave shall oft make thee to hide thy head.
Lady, give me your hand, and, as we walk,
To our own selves bend we our needful talk.
                    [*Exeunt Troilus, Cressida, and Diomedes.*]
                                       Sound trumpet.

111 **port** gate (of the city)   112 **possess** inform   113 **Entreat** treat   122 **To
shame the seal of my petition** to disdain the worth of my charge and
promise   126 **even for my charge** simply because I say so   132 **answer to my
lust** do as I please   137 **brave** boast

PARIS Hark! Hector's trumpet.

AENEAS   How have we spent this
140   morning!
         The prince must think me tardy and remiss,
         That swore to ride before him to the field.

PARIS 'Tis Troilus' fault. Come, come, to field with
         him.

DEIPHOBUS Let us make ready straight.

145 AENEAS Yea, with a bridegroom's fresh alacrity,
         Let us address to tend on Hector's heels.
         The glory of our Troy doth this day lie
         On his fair worth and single chivalry.   *Exeunt.*

[Scene V. *The Greek camp.*]

*Enter Ajax, armed; Achilles, Patroclus, Agamemnon,
Menelaus, Ulysses, Nestor, Calchas, &c.*

AGAMEMNON Here art thou in appointment fresh and
         fair,
         Anticipating time. With starting courage,
         Give with thy trumpet a loud note to Troy,
         Thou dreadful Ajax, that the appallèd air
5   May pierce the head of the great combatant
         And hale him hither.

AJAX   Thou, trumpet, there's my
         purse.
         Now crack thy lungs, and split thy brazen pipe.
         Blow, villain, till thy spherèd bias cheek
         Outswell the colic of puffed Aquilon!

---

146 **address** prepare   IV.v.1 **appointment** equipment and apparel   2 **starting**
active, prompt   6 **trumpet** trumpeter   8 **bias** puffed-out   9 **the colic of**
puffed Aquilon the north wind, distended as if by colic

Come, stretch thy chest, and let thy eyes spout
   blood;   10
Thou blow'st for Hector.   [*Trumpet sounds.*]

ULYSSES No trumpet answers.

ACHILLES   'Tis but early days.

AGAMEMNON Is not yond Diomed with Calchas'
   daughter?

ULYSSES 'Tis he, I ken the manner of his gait;
He rises on the toe. That spirit of his   15
In aspiration lifts him from the earth.

        [*Enter Diomedes, with Cressida.*]

AGAMEMNON Is this the Lady Cressid?

DIOMEDES   Even she.

AGAMEMNON Most dearly welcome to the Greeks,
   sweet lady.

NESTOR Our general doth salute you with a kiss.

ULYSSES Yet is the kindness but particular.   20
'Twere better she were kissed in general.

NESTOR And very courtly counsel. I'll begin.
So much for Nestor.

ACHILLES I'll take that winter from your lips, fair
   lady.
Achilles bids you welcome.   25

MENELAUS I had good argument for kissing once.

PATROCLUS But that's no argument for kissing now;
For thus popped Paris in his hardiment,
And parted thus you and your argument.

ULYSSES O, deadly gall, and theme of all our scorns,   30

12 **days** in the day   20 **particular** single   21 **in general** (1) by the general
(2) universally   24 **that winter** i.e., Nestor's kiss (cold from old age)   28 **hardiment** boldness   29 **argument** i.e., Helen

For which we lose our heads to gild his horns.

PATROCLUS The first was Menelaus' kiss; this, mine.
Patroclus kisses you.

MENELAUS   O, this is trim.

PATROCLUS Paris and I kiss evermore for him.

35 MENELAUS I'll have my kiss, sir. Lady, by your leave.

CRESSIDA In kissing, do you render or receive?

PATROCLUS Both take and give.

CRESSIDA   I'll make my match to
live,
The kiss you take is better than you give;
Therefore no kiss.

MENELAUS I'll give you boot; I'll give you three for
40   one.

CRESSIDA You are an odd man; give even, or give none.

MENELAUS An odd man, lady? Every man is odd.

CRESSIDA No, Paris is not, for you know 'tis true
That you are odd and he is even with you.

MENELAUS You fillip me o' the head.

45 CRESSIDA   No, I'll be sworn.

ULYSSES It were no match, your nail against his
horn.
May I, sweet lady, beg a kiss of you?

CRESSIDA You may.

ULYSSES   I do desire it.

CRESSIDA   Why, beg then.

---

37 I'll ... match to live I'll bet my life   40 boot odds   41 odd i.e., single and
singular   45 fillip tap   46 It ... horn your nail, in tapping, would be no match
for his hard cuckold's horn

ULYSSES Why, then, for Venus' sake, give me a kiss,
  When Helen is a maid again, and his.   50

CRESSIDA I am your debtor; claim it when 'tis due.

ULYSSES Never's my day, and then a kiss of you.

DIOMEDES Lady, a word. I'll bring you to your father.
                          [*Exeunt Diomedes and Cressida.*]

NESTOR A woman of quick sense.

ULYSSES   Fie, fie upon her!
  There's language in her eye, her cheek, her lip;   55
  Nay, her foot speaks. Her wanton spirits look out
  At every joint and motive of her body.
  O, these encounterers, so glib of tongue,
  That give a coasting welcome ere it comes,
  And wide unclasp the tables of their thoughts   60
  To every ticklish reader, set them down
  For sluttish spoils of opportunity
  And daughters of the game.

Flourish. Enter all of Troy [*Hector, Paris, Aeneas, Helenus,*
              Troilus, and Attendants].

ALL The Troyans' trumpet.

AGAMEMNON   Yonder comes the troop.

AENEAS Hail, all the state of Greece. What shall be
    done   65
  To him that victory commands? Or do you purpose
  A victor shall be known? Will you the knights
  Shall to the edge of all extremity
  Pursue each other, or shall they be divided

---

54 **Fie, fie upon her!** (Ulysses' exclamation does not imply disagreement with
Nestor's observation; the following nine lines elaborate "quick sense")
57 **motive** moving part   59 **a coasting welcome ere it comes** a sidelong,
flirtatious greeting before being greeted   60 **tables** tablets   62 **sluttish spoils of
opportunity** harlots who yield at every opportunity   63 **daughters of the game**
whores   63 **The Troyans' trumpet** (in the theater, this line becomes a pun on
"strumpet")   69 **divided** i.e., separated during the fight

70   By any voice or order of the field?
       Hector bade ask.

AGAMEMNON   Which way would Hector have it?

AENEAS He cares not; he'll obey conditions.

ACHILLES 'Tis done like Hector; but securely done,
       A little proudly, and great deal misprising
       The knight opposed.

75 AENEAS   If not Achilles, sir.
       What is your name?

ACHILLES   If not Achilles, nothing.

AENEAS Therefore Achilles; but, whate'er, know this:
       In the extremity of great and little,
       Valor and pride excel themselves in Hector;
80   The one almost as infinite as all,
       The other blank as nothing. Weigh him well;
       And that which looks like pride is courtesy.
       This Ajax is half made of Hector's blood,
       In love whereof half Hector stays at home;
85   Half heart, half hand, half Hector comes to seek
       This blended knight, half Troyan, and half Greek.

ACHILLES A maiden battle, then? O, I perceive you.

                [*Enter Diomedes.*]

AGAMEMNON Here is Sir Diomed. Go, gentle knight,
       Stand by our Ajax. As you and Lord Aeneas
90   Consent upon the order of their fight,
       So be it; either to the uttermost,
       Or else a breath. The combatants being kin
       Half stints their strife before their strokes begin.
                [*Ajax and Hector enter the lists.*]

ULYSSES They are opposed already.

73 **securely** overconfidently 83 **Hector's blood** (see note to II.ii.77)
87 **maiden** bloodless (as of novices or men in training, who do not intend to kill)
92 **breath** exercise

AGAMEMNON What Troyan is that same that looks so
    heavy?   95

ULYSSES The youngest son of Priam, a true knight,
    Not yet mature, yet matchless; firm of word,
    Speaking in deeds and deedless in his tongue,
    Not soon provoked, nor being provoked soon
      calmed;
    His heart and hand both open and both free,   100
    For what he has he gives, what thinks he shows;
    Yet gives he not till judgment guide his bounty,
    Nor dignifies an impare thought with breath;
    Manly as Hector, but more dangerous;
    For Hector, in his blaze of wrath, subscribes   105
    To tender objects, but he in heat of action
    Is more vindicative than jealous love.
    They call him Troilus, and on him erect
    A second hope as fairly built as Hector.
    Thus says Aeneas, one that knows the youth   110
    Even to his inches, and with private soul
    Did in great Ilion thus translate him to me.
                  Alarum. [*Hector and Ajax fight.*]

AGAMEMNON They are in action.

NESTOR Now, Ajax, hold thine own!

TROILUS   Hector, thou
    sleep'st; awake thee!

AGAMEMNON His blows are well disposed. There, Ajax!   115

DIOMEDES You must no more.   *Trumpets cease.*

AENEAS   Princes, enough, so please
    you.

---

95 **heavy** heavyhearted   98 **deedless in his tongue** free of boasts   100 **free**
generous   103 **impare thought** (1) ill-considered thought (2) thought unequal to
the dignity of his character   105–06 **subscribes/To tender objects** grants
merciful terms to the defenseless   111 **Even to his inches** i.e., from head to
toe   111 **with private soul** in confidence   115 **well disposed** well aimed, well
placed

AJAX I am not warm yet; let us fight again.

DIOMEDES As Hector pleases.

HECTOR   Why, then will I no more.
    Thou art, great lord, my father's sister's son,
120   A cousin-german to great Priam's seed;
    The obligation of our blood forbids
    A gory emulation 'twixt us twain.
    Were thy commixtion Greek and Troyan so
    That thou couldst say, "This hand is Grecian all,
125   And this is Troyan; the sinews of this leg
    All Greek, and this all Troy; my mother's blood
    Runs on the dexter cheek, and this sinister
    Bounds in my father's," by Jove multipotent,
    Thou shouldst not bear from me a Greekish member
130   Wherein my sword had not impressure made
    Of our rank feud. But the just gods gainsay
    That any drop thou borrow'dst from thy mother,
    My sacred aunt, should by my mortal sword
    Be drained! Let me embrace thee, Ajax—
135   By him that thunders, thou hast lusty arms;
    Hector would have them fall upon him thus.
    Cousin, all honor to thee!

AJAX   I thank thee, Hector;
    Thou art too gentle and too free a man.
    I came to kill thee, cousin, and bear hence
140   A great addition earnèd in thy death.

HECTOR Not Neoptolemus so mirable,
    On whose bright crest Fame with her loud'st
      "Oyes"
    Cries, "This is he!" could promise to himself
    A thought of added honor torn from Hector.

---

123 **commixtion** composition   127 **dexter** right   127 **sinister** left   128 **multi-potent** of many powers   135 **him that thunders** i.e., Jove (Zeus)   136 **thus** i.e., embracing him   141 **Neoptolemus** (this name probably applies here to Achilles himself, and not to his son, Pyrrhus)   141 **mirable** wonderful 142 **Oyes** cries beginning the proclamations of heralds or sessions of a court

AENEAS There is expectance here from both the sides,   145
  What further you will do.

HECTOR   We'll answer it.
  The issue is embracement. Ajax, farewell.

AJAX If I might in entreaties find success—
  As seld I have the chance—I would desire
  My famous cousin to our Grecian tents.   150

DIOMEDES 'Tis Agamemnon's wish; and great Achilles
  Doth long to see unarmed the valiant Hector.

HECTOR Aeneas, call my brother Troilus to me,
  And signify this loving interview
  To the expecters of our Troyan part.   155
  Desire them home. Give me thy hand, my cousin;
  I will go eat with thee and see your knights.

    [*Agamemnon and the rest approach them.*]

AJAX Great Agamemnon comes to meet us here.

HECTOR The worthiest of them tell me name by name;
  But for Achilles, my own searching eyes   160
  Shall find him by his large and portly size.

AGAMEMNON Worthy all arms [*embraces him*], as
    welcome as to one
  That would be rid of such an enemy—
  But that's no welcome. Understand more clear,
  What's past and what's to come is strewed with
    husks   165
  And formless ruin of oblivion;
  But in this extant moment, faith and troth,
  Strained purely from all hollow bias-drawing,
  Bids thee, with most divine integrity,
  From heart of very heart, great Hector, welcome.   170

---

147 **issue** result, outcome 149 **seld** seldom 154 **signify** expound, explain
155 **the expecters of our Troyan part** those on our side, the Trojans, awaiting
news 156 **Desire them home** ask them to go home 167 **extant** present
168 **all hollow bias-drawing** all fruitless and tortuous dealings (in the course
of the war, as in the course given by the bias of a bowl in bowling)

HECTOR I thank thee, most imperious Agamemnon.

AGAMEMNON [*To Troilus*] My well-famed lord of Troy,
    no less to you.

MENELAUS Let me confirm my princely brother's
    greeting.
    You brace of warlike brothers, welcome hither.

HECTOR Who must we answer?

175 AENEAS   The noble Menelaus.

HECTOR O, you, my lord? By Mars his gauntlet,
    thanks!
    Mock not that I affect th' untraded oath;
    Your quondam wife swears still by Venus' glove.
    She's well, but bade me not commend her to you.

MENELAUS Name her not now, sir; she's a deadly
180   theme.

HECTOR O, pardon! I offend.

NESTOR I have, thou gallant Troyan, seen thee oft,
    Laboring for destiny, make cruel way
    Through ranks of Greekish youth; and I have seen
    thee,
185 As hot as Perseus, spur thy Phrygian steed,
    Despising many forfeits and subduements,
    When thou hast hung thy advancèd sword i' th' air,
    Not letting it decline on the declinèd,
    That I have said to some my standers-by,
190 "Lo, Jupiter is yonder, dealing life!"
    And I have seen thee pause and take thy breath,

---

177 **untraded** unusual, unfamiliar (Hector, apologizing for what might appear to
be an affected oath, gives his reason for using it in the following line, in which he
completes a satirical reference to Menelaus and Helen by alluding to the liaison
between Mars and Venus) 178 **quondam** former 183 **Laboring for destiny**
working in behalf of destiny, i.e., causing destined deaths 186 **Despising many
forfeits and subduements** ignoring or disdaining those already vanquished,
whose lives were forfeit 187 **hung** held suspended 190 **dealing life** dispensing
life (as a god might do by not causing death)

When that a ring of Greeks have shraped thee in,
Like an Olympian wrestling. This have I seen;
But this thy countenance, still locked in steel,
I never saw till now. I knew thy grandsire,   195
And once fought with him. He was a soldier good;
But, by great Mars, the captain of us all,
Never like thee. O, let an old man embrace thee;
And, worthy warrior, welcome to our tents.

AENEAS 'Tis the old Nestor.   200

HECTOR Let me embrace thee, good old chronicle,
That has so long walked hand in hand with time.
Most reverend Nestor, I am glad to clasp thee.

NESTOR I would my arms could match thee in conten-
    tion,
As they contend with thee in courtesy.   205

HECTOR I would they could.

NESTOR Ha,
By this white beard, I'd fight with thee tomorrow.
Well, welcome, welcome. I have seen the time——

ULYSSES I wonder now how yonder city stands,   210
When we have here her base and pillar by us.

HECTOR I know your favor, Lord Ulysses, well.
Ah, sir, there's many a Greek and Troyan dead,
Since first I saw yourself and Diomed
In Ilion, on your Greekish embassy.   215

ULYSSES Sir, I foretold you then what would ensue.
My prophecy is but half his journey yet;
For yonder walls, that pertly front your town,
Yon towers, whose wanton tops do buss the clouds,
Must kiss their own feet.

HECTOR   I must not believe you.   220
There they stand yet, and modestly I think,

192 **shraped** trapped   194 **still** always   195 **grandsire** (Laomedon, the builder
of Troy)   212 **favor** face, features   219 **buss** kiss

The fall of every Phrygian stone will cost
A drop of Grecian blood. The end crowns all,
And that old common arbitrator, Time,
Will one day end it.

225 ULYSSES   So to him we leave it.
Most gentle and most valiant Hector, welcome.
After the general, I beseech you next
To feast with me and see me at my tent.

ACHILLES I shall forestall thee, Lord Ulysses, thou!
230 Now, Hector, I have fed mine eyes on thee;
I have with exact view perused thee, Hector,
And quoted joint by joint.

HECTOR   Is this Achilles?

ACHILLES I am Achilles.

HECTOR Stand fair, I pray thee; let me look on thee.

ACHILLES Behold thy fill.

235 HECTOR   Nay, I have done already.

ACHILLES Thou art too brief. I will the second time,
As I would buy thee, view thee limb by limb.

HECTOR O, like a book of sport thou'lt read me o'er;
But there's more in me than thou understand'st.
240 Why dost thou so oppress me with thine eye?

ACHILLES Tell me, you heavens, in which part of his
body
Shall I destroy him, whether there, or there, or
there?
That I may give the local wound a name,
And make distinct the very breach whereout
245 Hector's great spirit flew. Answer me, heavens!

HECTOR It would discredit the blessed gods, proud man,
To answer such a question. Stand again.

232 **quoted** made exact mental note, scrutinized   234 **Stand fair** stand openly,
face me

Think'st thou to catch my life so pleasantly
As to prenominate in nice conjecture
Where thou wilt hit me dead?

ACHILLES   I tell thee, yea.   250

HECTOR Wert thou an oracle to tell me so,
    I'd not believe thee. Henceforth guard thee well,
    For I'll not kill thee there, nor there, nor there;
    But, by the forge that stithied Mars his helm,
    I'll kill thee everywhere, yea, o'er and o'er.   255
    You wisest Grecians, pardon me this brag.
    His insolence draws folly from my lips;
    But I'll endeavor deeds to match these words,
    Or may I never——

AJAX   Do not chafe thee, cousin;
    And you, Achilles, let these threats alone,   260
    Till accident or purpose bring you to't.
    You may have every day enough of Hector,
    If you have stomach. The general state, I fear,
    Can scarce entreat you to be odd with him.

HECTOR I pray you, let us see you in the field.   265
    We have had pelting wars since you refused
    The Grecians' cause.

ACHILLES   Dost thou entreat me, Hector?
    Tomorrow do I meet thee, fell as death;
    Tonight all friends.

HECTOR   Thy hand upon that match.

AGAMEMNON First, all you peers of Greece, go to my
        tent;   270
    There in the full convive we. Afterwards,
    As Hector's leisure and your bounties shall
    Concur together, severally entreat him

248 **pleasantly** casually, merrily   249 **prenominate in nice conjecture** name beforehand in detailed conjecture   254 **stithied** forged   263 **stomach** inclination, relish   263 **general state** commanders in council   264 **odd** at odds, engaged in combat   266 **pelting** paltry, petty   267 **entreat** invite   268 **fell** fierce   271 **convive** feast   273 **severally** individually

To taste your bounties. Let the trumpets blow,
275   That this great soldier may his welcome know.
                    Exeunt [all except Troilus and Ulysses].

TROILUS My Lord Ulysses, tell me, I beseech you,
In what place of the field doth Calchas keep?

ULYSSES At Menelaus' tent, most princely Troilus.
There Diomed doth feast with him tonight—
280   Who neither looks upon the heaven nor earth,
But gives all gaze and bent of amorous view
On the fair Cressid.

TROILUS Shall I, sweet lord, be bound to you so much,
After we part from Agamemnon's tent,
To bring me thither?

285 ULYSSES   You shall command me, sir.
But gentle tell me, of what honor was
This Cressida in Troy? Had she no lover there
That wails her absence?

TROILUS O, sir, to such as boasting show their scars
290   A mock is due. Will you walk on, my lord?
She was beloved, she loved; she is, and doth;
But still sweet love is food for fortune's tooth.
                                    Exeunt.

277 keep dwell

[ACT V

Scene I. *The Greek camp*.]

Enter Achilles and Patroclus.

ACHILLES I'll heat his blood with Greekish wine to-
night,
Which with my scimitar I'll cool tomorrow.
Patroclus, let us feast him to the height.

Enter Thersites.

PATROCLUS Here comes Thersites.

ACHILLES   How now, thou cur
of envy!
Thou crusty batch of nature, what's the news?   5

THERSITES Why, thou picture of what thou seemest,
and idol of idiot-worshipers, here's a letter for thee.

ACHILLES From whence, fragment?

THERSITES Why, thou full dish of fool, from Troy.

V.i.5 **batch** (a mass of anything baked together, or baked without reheating the oven) 6 **thou picture of what thou seemest** (i.e., who is nothing more than one glance sufficiently reveals)

10 PATROCLUS Who keeps the tent now?

THERSITES The surgeon's box or the patient's wound.

PATROCLUS Well said, adversity, and what needs these
tricks?

THERSITES Prithee, be silent, boy; I profit not by thy
15   talk. Thou art said to be Achilles' male varlet.

PATROCLUS Male varlet, you rogue! What's that?

THERSITES Why, his masculine whore. Now, the rotten
diseases of the south, the guts-griping ruptures,
catarrhs, loads o' gravel in the back, lethargies,
20   cold palsies, raw eyes, dirt-rotten livers, wheezing
lungs, bladders full of imposthume, sciaticas,
lime-kilns i'the palm, incurable bone-ache, and
the riveled fee-simple of the tetter, and the like,
take and take again such preposterous discoveries!

25 PATROCLUS Why, thou damnable box of envy, thou,
what means thou to curse thus?

THERSITES Do I curse thee?

PATROCLUS Why, no, you ruinous butt, you whoreson
indistinguishable cur, no.

30 THERSITES No? Why art thou then exasperate, thou
idle immaterial skein of sleave silk, thou green
sarcenet flap for a sore eye, thou tassel of a
prodigal's purse, thou? Ah, how the poor world is

---

10 **Who keeps the tent now?** (Thersites can no longer taunt Achilles for refusing to leave his tent) 11 **The surgeon's ... wound** (from the play on "tent," a surgeon's probe for wounds) 18 **diseases of the south** i.e., venereal diseases 19–20 **gravel ... palsies** kidney stones, apoplectic strokes, paralysis of the limbs 21 **imposthume** internal abscess 22 **lime-kilns** psoriasis (burning red patches covered with scales) 23 **riveled** wrinkled 23 **fee-simple of the tetter** chronic ringworm (?) ("fee-simple" implies unlimited possession) 24 **discoveries** (referring generally to—in Thersites' opinion—such absurd monstrosities as Patroclus) 28 **ruinous butt** dilapidated cask 29 **indistinguishable** shapeless (here suggesting mongrel) 31 **sleave silk** soft silk floss 32 **sarcenet** (a fine silk taffeta)

pestered with such water-flies, diminutives of na-
ture.   35

PATROCLUS Out, gall!

THERSITES Finch egg!

ACHILLES My sweet Patroclus, I am thwarted quite
From my great purpose in tomorrow's battle.
Here is a letter from Queen Hecuba,   40
A token from her daughter, my fair love,
Both taxing me and gaging me to keep
An oath that I have sworn. I will not break it.
Fall Greeks, fail fame, honor or go or stay,
My major vow lies here; this I'll obey.   45
Come, come, Thersites, help to trim my tent;
This night in banqueting must all be spent.
Away, Patroclus!   *Exit [with Patroclus].*

THERSITES With too much blood and too little brain,
these two may run mad; but if with too much brain   50
and too little blood they do, I'll be a curer of madmen. Here's Agamemnon, an honest fellow enough,
and one that loves quails, but he has not so much
brain as ear-wax; and the goodly transformation
of Jupiter there, his brother, the bull, the primi-   55
tive statue and oblique memorial of cuckolds—a
thrifty shoeing-horn in a chain, hanging at his
brother's leg—to what form but that he is should wit
larded with malice and malice forced with wit turn
him to? To an ass, were nothing; he is both   60
ass and ox. To an ox, were nothing; he is both ox
and ass. To be a dog, a mule, a cat, a fitchew,

42 **taxing** censuring   42 **gaging** engaging to a promise   44 **or go or** either go
or   53 **quails** prostitutes   54-55 **transformation of Jupiter** (i.e., into a bull, in
which shape he seduced Europa)   55-56 **the primitive statue ... of cuckolds**
(in having horns, the emblem or symbol of cuckoldry, although since Europa was
not married, the parallel to Paris' rape of Helen is "oblique")   57 **thrifty**
stingy   57-58 **hanging at his brother's leg** (1) as Agamemnon's tool, appropriately enough a "horn," his pretext for war (2) as being entirely dependent on
Agamemnon   59 **forced** stuffed, intermixed   62 **fitchew** polecat

a toad, a lizard, an owl, a puttock, or a herring
without a roe, I would not care; but to be Menelaus!
65　I would conspire against destiny. Ask me not what
I would be, if I were not Thersites, for I care not
to be the louse of a lazar, so I were not Menelaus.
Hey-day, sprites and fires!

Enter Agamemnon, Ulysses, Nestor, [Hector, Ajax, Troilus,
Menelaus,] and Diomedes, with lights.

AGAMEMNON　We go wrong, we go wrong.

AJAX　　　　　　　　　　　No, yonder 'tis;
There, where we see the lights.

70　HECTOR　　　　　　　　　　I trouble you.

AJAX　No, not a whit.

ULYSSES　　　　　Here comes himself to guide you.

Enter Achilles.

ACHILLES　Welcome, brave Hector; welcome, princes
all.

AGAMEMNON　So now, fair prince of Troy, I bid good
night.
Ajax commands the guard to tend on you.

75　HECTOR　Thanks and good night to the Greeks' general.

MENELAUS　Good night, my lord.

HECTOR　Good night, sweet Lord Menelaus.

THERSITES　Sweet draught! "Sweet," quoth 'a! Sweet
sink, sweet sewer.

ACHILLES　Good night and welcome both at once, to
80　　　those
That go or tarry.

---

63 **puttock** kite, a small hawk feeding on carrion　66-67 **I care not to be** I
wouldn't mind being　67 **lazar** leper　78 **draught** privy, cesspool

AGAMEMNON Good night.

Exeunt Agamemnon, Menelaus.

ACHILLES Old Nestor tarries, and you too, Diomed,
Keep Hector company an hour or two.

DIOMEDES I cannot, lord; I have important business,   85
The tide whereof is now. Good night, great Hector.

HECTOR Give me your hand.

ULYSSES [*Aside to Troilus*] Follow his torch; he goes to
Calchas' tent.
I'll keep you company.

TROILUS Sweet sir, you honor me.

HECTOR   And so, good night.   90
[*Exeunt Diomedes, then Ulysses and Troilus.*]

ACHILLES Come, come, enter my tent.
Exeunt [Achilles, Hector, Ajax, and Nestor].

THERSITES That same Diomed's a false-hearted rogue,
a most unjust knave; I will no more trust him when
he leers than I will a serpent when he hisses. He
will spend his mouth and promise like Brabbler   95
the hound; but when he performs, astronomers
foretell it. It is prodigious, there will come some
changes. The sun borrows of the moon when Diomed keeps his word. I will rather leave to see
Hector than not to dog him. They say he keeps a   100
Troyan drab, and uses the traitor Calchas' tent.
I'll after—nothing but lechery! All incontinent varlets!   [*Exit.*]

---

86 tide time   95–96 Brabbler the hound (a hunting hound who would "spend
his mouth" in barking while not on the scent would be called "babbler" or
"brabbler" by his master)   99 leave to see miss seeing

[Scene II. *The Greek camp.*]

Enter Diomed.

DIOMEDES What, are you up here, ho? Speak.

CALCHAS [*Within*] Who calls?

DIOMEDES Diomed. Calchas, I think. Where's your
    daughter?

CALCHAS [*Within*] She comes to you.

Enter Troilus and Ulysses; [after them Thersites.]

5 ULYSSES Stand where the torch may not discover us.

Enter Cressid.

TROILUS Cressid comes forth to him.

DIOMEDES   How now, my charge!

CRESSIDA Now, my sweet guardian! Hark, a word with
    you.   [*Whispers.*]

TROILUS Yea, so familiar!

ULYSSES She will sing any man at first sight.

10 THERSITES And any man may sing her, if he can take
    her cliff; she's noted.

DIOMEDES Will you remember?

CRESSIDA Remember? Yes.

DIOMEDES Nay, but do, then;
15 And let your mind be coupled with your words.

V.ii.11 **cliff** clef (signifying the musical key; with an obscene pun on "cleft")
11 **noted** reputed a loose woman (with a pun on musical notes)

TROILUS What shall she remember?

ULYSSES List!

CRESSIDA Sweet honey Greek, tempt me no more to
    folly.

THERSITES Roguery!

DIOMEDES Nay, then——

CRESSIDA   I'll tell you what——   20

DIOMEDES Foh, foh! Come, tell a pin. You are for-
    sworn.

CRESSIDA In faith, I cannot. What would you have me
    do?

THERSITES A juggling trick—to be secretly open.

DIOMEDES What did you swear you would bestow on
    me?

CRESSIDA I prithee, do not hold me to mine oath;   25
    Bid me do anything but that, sweet Greek.

DIOMEDES Good night.

TROILUS Hold, patience!

ULYSSES How now, Troyan?

CRESSIDA Diomed——   30

DIOMEDES No, no, good night; I'll be your fool no
    more

TROILUS Thy better must.

CRESSIDA   Hark, a word in your ear.

TROILUS O plague and madness!

ULYSSES You are moved, prince; let us depart, I pray,
    Lest your displeasure should enlarge itself   35

23 **secretly** privately, sexually

To wrathful terms. This place is dangerous;
The time right deadly. I beseech you, go.

TROILUS Behold, I pray you!

ULYSSES   Nay, good my lord, go off;
You flow to great distraction. Come, my lord.

TROILUS I prithee, stay.

40 ULYSSES   You have not patience; come.

TROILUS I pray you, stay! By hell, and all hell's tor-
ments,
I will not speak a word!

DIOMEDES   And so, good night.

CRESSIDA Nay, but you part in anger.

TROILUS   Doth that grieve thee?
O withered truth!

ULYSSES   How now, my lord!

TROILUS   By Jove,
I will be patient.

45 CRESSIDA   Guardian! Why, Greek!

DIOMEDES Foh, foh! Adieu; you palter.

CRESSIDA In faith, I do not. Come hither once again.

ULYSSES You shake, my lord, at something. Will you
go?
You will break out.

TROILUS   She strokes his cheek!

ULYSSES   Come, come.

50 TROILUS Nay, stay; by Jove, I will not speak a word.
There is between my will and all offenses
A guard of patience. Stay a little while.

THERSITES How the devil Luxury, with his fat rump

53 Luxury lechery

and potato finger, tickles these together. Fry, lechery,
fry!   55

DIOMEDES But will you, then?

CRESSIDA In faith, I will, la; never trust me else.

DIOMEDES Give me some token for the surety of it.

CRESSIDA I'll fetch you one.   *Exit.*

ULYSSES You have sworn patience.

TROILUS   Fear me not, my lord;   60
    I will not be myself, nor have cognition
    Of what I feel. I am all patience.

                    Enter Cressida.

THERSITES Now the pledge! Now, now now!

CRESSIDA Here, Diomed, keep this sleeve.

TROILUS O beauty, where is thy faith?

ULYSSES   My lord——   65

TROILUS I will be patient; outwardly I will.

CRESSIDA You look upon that sleeve; behold it well.
    He loved me—O false wench! Give't me again.

DIOMEDES Whose was't?

CRESSIDA   It is no matter, now I have't again.
    I will not meet with you tomorrow night.   70
    I prithee, Diomed, visit me no more.

THERSITES Now she sharpens. Well said, whetstone!

DIOMEDES I shall have it.

CRESSIDA   What, this?

DIOMEDES   Ay, that.

CRESSIDA O, all you gods! O pretty, pretty pledge!

54 **potato** (potatoes were thought to be aphrodisiac)   72 **sharpens** i.e., whets
Diomedes' desire

75 Thy master now lies thinking on his bed
Of thee and me, and sighs, and takes my glove,
And gives memorial dainty kisses to it,
As I kiss thee. Nay, do not snatch it from me;
He that takes that doth take my heart withal.

80 DIOMEDES I had your heart before; this follows it.

TROILUS I did swear patience.

CRESSIDA You shall not have it, Diomed; faith, you
shall not;
I'll give you something else.

DIOMEDES I will have this. Whose was it?

CRESSIDA   It is no matter.

85 DIOMEDES Come, tell me whose it was.

CRESSIDA 'Twas one's that loved me better than you
will.
But, now you have it, take it.

DIOMEDES   Whose was it?

CRESSIDA By all Diana's waiting-women yond,
And by herself, I will not tell you whose.

90 DIOMEDES Tomorrow will I wear it on my helm,
And grieve his spirit that dares not challenge it.

TROILUS Wert thou the devil, and wor'st it on thy horn,
It should be challenged.

CRESSIDA Well, well, 'tis done, 'tis past. And yet it is
not;
I will not keep my word.

95 DIOMEDES   Why then, farewell;
Thou never shalt mock Diomed again.

CRESSIDA You shall not go. One cannot speak a word
But it straight starts you.

77 memorial in remembrance 88 Diana's waiting-women i.e., the stars
clustered about the moon 98 straight starts you immediately makes you start
angrily away

DIOMEDES   I do not like this fooling.

THERSITES   Nor I, by Pluto; but that that likes not you
Pleases me best.   100

DIOMEDES   What, shall I come? The hour?

CRESSIDA   Ay, come—O Jove!—
Do come—I shall be plagued.

DIOMEDES   Farewell till then.

CRESSIDA   Good night. I prithee, come.
                                  Exit [Diomedes].
Troilus, farewell. One eye yet looks on thee,
But with my heart the other eye doth see.   105
Ah, poor our sex! This fault in us I find,
The error of our eye directs our mind.
What error leads must err. O, then conclude,
Minds swayed by eyes are full of turpitude.   *Exit*.

THERSITES   A proof of strength she could not publish more,   110
Unless she said, "My mind is now turned whore."

ULYSSES   All's done, my lord.

TROILUS   It is.

ULYSSES   Why stay we, then?

TROILUS   To make a recordation to my soul
Of every syllable that here was spoke.
But if I tell how these two did coact,   115
Shall I not lie in publishing a truth?
Sith yet there is a credence in my heart,
An esperance so obstinately strong,
That doth invert th' attest of eyes and ears,
As if those organs had deceptious functions,   120
Created only to calumniate.

---

99 **likes** pleases   102 **plagued** punished   106 **poor our sex** our poor sex
107 **error** wandering (here, physically and morally)   110 **proof of strength**
strong proof   110 **publish more** confess more clearly   118 **esperance**
hope   119 **attest** testimony   120 **deceptious** deceiving

Was Cressid here?

ULYSSES   I cannot conjure, Troyan.

TROILUS She was not, sure.

ULYSSES   Most sure she was.

TROILUS Why, my negation hath no taste of madness.

125 ULYSSES Nor mine, my lord. Cressid was here but now.

TROILUS Let it not be believed for womanhood!
        Think we had mothers; do not give advantage
        To stubborn critics, apt, without a theme,
        For depravation, to square the general sex
130   By Cressid's rule. Rather think this not Cressid.

ULYSSES What hath she done, prince, that can soil our
        mothers?

TROILUS Nothing at all, unless that this were she.

THERSITES Will 'a swagger himself out on's own eyes?

TROILUS This she? No, this is Diomed's Cressida.
135   If beauty have a soul, this is not she;
        If souls guide vows, if vows be sanctimonies,
        If sanctimony be the gods' delight,
        If there be rule in unity itself,
        This was not she. O madness of discourse,
140   That cause sets up with and against itself:
        Bifold authority, where reason can revolt

---

122 **conjure** raise spirits 124 **negation** denial 126 **for** for the sake of
128-29 **apt ... For depravation** ready and eager to claim the depravity of
women, but lacking examples 129-30 **square the ... Cressid's rule** take the
measure of womankind by Cressida's standard 133 **Will 'a ... on's own eyes?**
i.e., will he bluff himself out of trusting his own sight? 138 **If there ... unity
itself** i.e., if it is a true principle that one cannot be two (that Cressida may not
be divided into two persons) 139 **discourse** reasonable sequence of thought
140-41 **That cause ... Bifold authority** that case of principle wherein divided
authority both supports and confutes the question

Without perdition, and loss assume all reason
Without revolt. This is, and is not, Cressid.
Within my soul there doth conduce a fight
Of this strange nature that a thing inseparate   145
Divides more wider than the sky and earth;
And yet the spacious breadth of this division
Admits no orifex for a point as subtle
As Ariachne's broken woof to enter.
Instance, O instance, strong as Pluto's gates;   150
Cressid is mine, tied with the bonds of heaven.
Instance, O instance, strong as heaven itself;
The bonds of heaven are slipped, dissolved, and
    loosed,
And with another knot, five-finger-tied,
The fractions of her faith, orts of her love,   155
The fragments, scraps, the bits, and greasy relics
Of her o'ereaten faith, are given to Diomed.

ULYSSES May worthy Troilus be half attached
With that which here his passion doth express?

TROILUS Ay, Greek! And that shall be divulgèd well   160
In characters as red as Mars his heart
Inflamed with Venus. Never did young man fancy
With so eternal and so fixed a soul.
Hark, Greek. Much as I do Cressid love,
So much by weight hate I her Diomed;   165
That sleeve is mine that he'll bear on his helm;
Were it a casque composed by Vulcan's skill,
My sword should bite it. Not the dreadful spout

141–43 where reason ... Without revolt where reason can rebel without
subsequent chaos, and loss of understanding assume the appearance of reason
without reason itself objecting 144 conduce go on 145 thing inseparate that
which is indivisible; i.e., Cressida 148 orifex opening 148 subtle finely sharp
149 Ariachne's broken woof (Arachne was a Lydian woman who challenged
Athene to a weaving contest, but the goddess, angered, tore her work to shreds and
changed her to a spider) 150 Instance example, proof (here, in the sense of "for
instance") 154 five-finger-tied (1) so tied because Cressida's hand is now
Diomedes' (?) (2) i.e., impossible to untie (?) 155 orts scraps, pieces (as of
food) 157 o'ereaten eaten through, picked over (as a dog will eat the best pieces
first, the last scraps left over) 158 half attached i.e., half so much affected (as it
appears) 167 casque helmet

Which shipmen do the hurricano call,
170   Constringed in mass by the almighty sun,
Shall dizzy with more clamor Neptune's ear
In his descent than shall my prompted sword
Falling on Diomed.

THERSITES He'll tickle it for his concupy.

175 TROILUS O Cressid! O false Cressid! False, false, false!
Let all untruths stand by thy stainèd name,
And they'll seem glorious.

ULYSSES   O, contain yourself;
Your passion draws ears hither.

                    Enter Aeneas.

AENEAS I have been seeking you this hour, my lord.
180   Hector, by this, is arming him in Troy;
Ajax, your guard, stays to conduct you home.

TROILUS Have with you, prince. My courteous lord,
        adieu.
Farewell, revolted fair; and Diomed,
Stand fast, and wear a castle on thy head!

185 ULYSSES I'll bring you to the gates.

TROILUS Accept distracted thanks.
                    Exeunt Troilus, Aeneas, and Ulysses.

THERSITES Would I could meet that rogue Diomed. I
        would croak like a raven; I would bode, I would
        bode. Patroclus will give me anything for the intel-
190   ligence of this whore. The parrot will not do
        more for an almond than he for a commodious
        drab. Lechery, lechery; still wars and lechery;
        nothing else holds fashion. A burning devil take
        them!   *Exit.*

170 **Constringed** drawn together 172 **prompted** i.e., urged on, as having its
own motive 174 **He'll tickle it for his concupy** he'll be well tickled for his
concupiscence ("it" refers contemptuously to Diomedes) 180 **him** himself
182 **Have with you** let's go along 188 **bode** portend disaster 191-92 **com-
modious drab** serviceable whore 193 **burning devil** venereal disease

[Scene III. *Troy; Priam's palace.*]

Enter Hector and Andromache.

ANDROMACHE When was my lord so much ungently
    tempered,
  To stop his ears against admonishment?
  Unarm, unarm, and do not fight today.

HECTOR You train me to offend you; get you in.
  By all the everlasting gods, I'll go.   5

ANDROMACHE My dreams will, sure, prove ominous to
    the day.

HECTOR No more, I say.

Enter Cassandra.

CASSANDRA   Where is my brother Hector?

ANDROMACHE Here, sister; armed and bloody in intent.
  Consort with me in loud and dear petition;
  Pursue we him on knees, for I have dreamed   10
  Of bloody turbulence, and this whole night
  Hath nothing been but shapes and forms of
    slaughter.

CASSANDRA O, 'tis true.

HECTOR   Ho, bid my trumpet sound.

CASSANDRA No notes of sally, for the heavens, sweet
    brother.

HECTOR Be gone, I say; the gods have heard me swear.   15

V.iii.4 **train** tempt 4 **offend** injure, insult 6 **ominous to the day** omens
applicable to this day

CASSANDRA The gods are deaf to hot and peevish
      vows.
    They are polluted offerings, more abhorred
    Than spotted livers in the sacrifice.

ANDROMACHE O, be persuaded! Do not count it holy
20   To hurt by being just. It is as lawful,
    For we would give much, to use violent thefts,
    And rob in the behalf of charity.

CASSANDRA It is the purpose that makes strong the
      vow;
    But vows to every purpose must not hold.
    Unarm, sweet Hector.

25 HECTOR   Hold you still, I say.
    Mine honor keeps the weather of my fate.
    Life every man holds dear; but the dear man
    Holds honor far more precious-dear than life.

                    Enter Troilus.

    How now, young man; mean'st thou to fight today?

30 ANDROMACHE Cassandra, call my father to persuade.
                                Exit Cassandra.

HECTOR No, faith, young Troilus; doff thy harness,
      youth.
    I am today i' the vein of chivalry.
    Let grow thy sinews till their knots be strong,
    And tempt not yet the brushes of the war.
35   Unarm thee; go, and doubt thou not, brave boy,
    I'll stand today for thee and me and Troy.

TROILUS Brother, you have a vice of mercy in you,
    Which better fits a lion than a man.

---

16 peevish brash, perverse 18 spotted i.e., spoiled 21 For because 24 But
vows ... not hold i.e., vows sworn indiscriminately or to unlawful purpose should
not bind the swearer 26 keeps the weather i.e., maintains the position of
advantage 27 dear valuable, worthy 34 brushes encounters

HECTOR What vice is that? Good Troilus, chide me for
   it.

TROILUS When many times the captive Grecian falls,   40
   Even in the fan and wind of your fair sword,
   You bid them rise and live.

HECTOR O, 'tis fair play.

TROILUS   Fool's play, by heaven, Hector.

HECTOR How now? How now?

TROILUS   For the love of all the gods,
   Let's leave the hermit pity with our mother,　　　　45
   And when we have our armors buckled on,
   The venomed vengeance ride upon our swords,
   Spur them to ruthful work, rein them from ruth.

HECTOR Fie, savage, fie!

TROILUS   Hector, then 'tis wars.

HECTOR Troilus, I would not have you fight today.   50

TROILUS Who should withhold me?
   Not fate, obedience, nor the hand of Mars
   Beck'ning with fiery truncheon my retire;
   Not Priamus and Hecuba on knees,
   Their eyes o'ergallèd with recourse of tears;   55
   Nor you, my brother, with your true sword drawn,
   Opposed to hinder me, should stop my way,
   But by my ruin.

Enter Priam and Cassandra.

CASSANDRA Lay hold upon him, Priam, hold him fast;
   He is thy crutch. Now if thou lose thy stay,   60
   Thou on him leaning, and all Troy on thee,
   Fall all together.

---

48 **ruthful** i.e., to be pitied, woeful　48 **ruth** pity　49 **then 'tis wars** that's what war is　53 **truncheon** (a kind of baton used by the referee of a combat to signal the end of the fight)　55 **o'er-gallèd** inflamed　55 **recourse** repeated coursing down, constant flowing　60 **stay** support

PRIAM   Come, Hector, come; go back.
  Thy wife hath dreamt, thy mother hath had visions,
  Cassandra doth foresee, and I myself
65 Am like a prophet suddenly enrapt
  To tell thee that this day is ominous.
  Therefore, come back.

HECTOR   Aeneas is afield;
  And I do stand engaged to many Greeks,
  Even in the faith of valor, to appear
  This morning to them.

70 PRIAM   Ay, but thou shalt not go.

HECTOR I must not break my faith.
  You know me dutiful; therefore, dear sir,
  Let me not shame respect, but give me leave
  To take that course by your consent and voice,
75 Which you do here forbid me, royal Priam.

CASSANDRA O Priam, yield not to him!

ANDROMACHE   Do not, dear father.

HECTOR Andromache, I am offended with you.
  Upon the love you bear me, get you in.
                                        Exit Andromache.

TROILUS This foolish, dreaming, superstitious girl
  Makes all these bodements.

80 CASSANDRA   O farewell, dear Hector!
  Look, how thou diest; look, how thy eye turns pale;
  Look, how thy wounds do bleed at many vents!
  Hark, how Troy roars, how Hecuba cries out,
  How poor Andromache shrills her dolors forth!
85 Behold, distraction, frenzy, and amazement,
  Like witless antics, one another meet,
  And all cry Hector! Hector's dead! O Hector!

TROILUS Away! Away!

69 the faith of valor a brave man's promise   73 shame respect i.e., disgrace the
respect due to a parent   80 bodements evil omens   86 antics madmen

228

CASSANDRA Farewell. Yet, soft; Hector, I take my
    leave.
  Thou dost thyself and all our Troy deceive.   *Exit*.   90

HECTOR You are amazed, my liege, at her exclaim.
  Go in and cheer the town. We'll forth and fight;
  Do deeds worth praise and tell you them at night.

PRIAM Farewell. The gods with safety stand about
    thee.   *[Exeunt Priam and Hector.] Alarum.*

TROILUS They are at it, hark. Proud Diomed, believe,   95
  I come to lose my arm, or win my sleeve.

Enter Pandar.

PANDARUS Do you hear, my lord? Do you hear?

TROILUS What now?

PANDARUS Here's a letter come from yond poor girl.

TROILUS Let me read.   100

PANDARUS A whoreson tisick, a whoreson rascally
tisick so troubles me, and the foolish fortune of
this girl; and what one thing, what another, that I
shall leave you one o'th'se days; and I have a
rheum in mine eyes too, and such an ache in my   105
bones that, unless a man were cursed, I cannot tell
what to think on't. What says she there?

TROILUS Words, words, mere words, no matter from
    the heart;
  Th' effect doth operate another way.
                     [Tearing the letter.]
  Go, wind to wind, there turn and change together.   110
  My love with words and errors still she feeds,
  But edifies another with her deeds.   *Exeunt.*

---

101 **tisick** cough   111 **errors** meanderings, i.e., underhanded tricks (?)

[Scene IV. *The battlefield*.]

[*Alarum*.] *Enter Thersites. Excursions.*

THERSITES Now they are clapperclawing one another;
I'll go look on. That dissembling abominable varlet,
Diomed, has got that same scurvy doting foolish
young knave's sleeve of Troy there in his helm. I
5   would fain see them meet, that that same young
Troyan ass, that loves the whore there, might send
that Greekish whoremasterly villain with the sleeve
back to the dissembling luxurious drab, of a sleeveless errand. O' th' t'other side, the policy of those
10 crafty swearing rascals—that stale old mouse-
eaten dry cheese, Nestor, and that same dog-fox,
Ulysses—is not proved worth a blackberry. They
set me up, in policy, that mongrel cur, Ajax,
against that dog of as bad a kind, Achilles; and
15 now is the cur Ajax prouder than the cur Achilles,
and will not arm today. Whereupon the Grecians
begin to proclaim barbarism, and policy grows into
an ill opinion.

Enter Diomedes and Troilus.

Soft, here comes sleeve, and t'other.

20 TROILUS Fly not; for shouldst thou take the river Styx,
I would swim after.

DIOMEDES   Thou dost miscall retire.

V.iv.8–9 **sleeveless** futile, fruitless   10 **crafty swearing** craftily swearing, i.e.,
crafty to the extent of perjury   17 **proclaim barbarism** i.e., recognize the
authority of chaos (to replace policy)

I do not fly, but advantageous care
Withdrew me from the odds of multitude.
Have at thee!

THERSITES Hold thy whore, Grecian! Now for thy
  whore,   25
Troyan! Now the sleeve, now the sleeve!
          [*Exeunt Troilus and Diomedes, fighting.*]

          Enter Hector.

HECTOR What art thou, Greek? Art thou for Hector's
  match?
Art thou of blood and honor?

THERSITES No, no, I am a rascal, a scurvy railing
  knave, a very filthy rogue.   30

HECTOR I do believe thee; live.   [*Exit.*]

THERSITES God-a-mercy, that thou wilt believe me; but
  a plague break thy neck—for frighting me. What's
  become of the wenching rogues? I think they have
  swallowed one another. I would laugh at that mir-   35
  acle—yet, in a sort, lechery eats itself. I'll seek
  them.   *Exit.*

          [Scene V. *The battlefield.*]

          Enter Diomed and Servant.

DIOMEDES Go, go, my servant, take thou Troilus'
  horse;
Present the fair steed to my Lady Cressid.
Fellow, commend my service to her beauty;

22–23 but advantageous … of multitude care for my own advantage led me to
avoid facing absurdly heavy odds

Tell her I have chastised the amorous Troyan,
And am her knight by proof.

5   SERVANT   I go, my lord.   [*Exit.*]

Enter Agamemnon.

AGAMEMNON Renew, renew! The fierce Polydamas
Hath beat down Menon; bastard Margarelon
Hath Doreus prisoner,
And stands colossus-wise, waving his beam,
10   Upon the pashèd corses of the kings
Epistrophus and Cedius; Polyxenes is slain,
Amphimachus and Thoas deadly hurt,
Patroclus ta'en or slain, and Palamedes
Sore hurt and bruised. The dreadful Sagittary
15   Appals our numbers. Haste we, Diomed,
To reinforcement, or we perish all.

Enter Nestor.

NESTOR Go, bear Patroclus' body to Achilles,
And bid the snail-paced Ajax arm for shame.
There is a thousand Hectors in the field;
20   Now here he fights on Galathe his horse,
And there lacks work; anon he's there afoot,
And there they fly or die, like scalèd sculls
Before the belching whale; then is he yonder,
And there the strawy Greeks, ripe for his edge,
25   Fall down before him, like a mower's swath.
Here, there, and everywhere, he leaves and takes,
Dexterity so obeying appetite
That what he will he does, and does so much
That proof is called impossibility.

V.v.9 **beam** spear   10 **pashèd corses** battered corpses   14 **Sagittary** (a centaur
[half man, half horse], who was a splendid archer and aided the Trojans)
22 **scalèd sculls** scaly schools of fish   24 **strawy ... edge** i.e., Greeks who are
like straw, ripe for the edge of the scythe   29 **proof** visible fact

Enter Ulysses.

ULYSSES   O, courage, courage, princes! Great Achilles   30
   Is arming, weeping, cursing, vowing vengeance!
   Patroclus' wounds have roused his drowsy blood,
   Together with his mangled Myrmidons,
   That noseless, handless, hacked and chipped, come
     to him,
   Crying on Hector. Ajax hath lost a friend,   35
   And foams at mouth, and he is armed and at it,
   Roaring for Troilus, who hath done today
   Mad and fantastic execution,
   Engaging and redeeming of himself
   With such a careless force and forceless care   40
   As if that luck, in very spite of cunning,
   Bade him win all.

Enter Ajax.

AJAX   Troilus, thou coward Troilus!   *Exit.*

DIOMEDES   Ay, there, there.

NESTOR   So, so, we draw together.   *Exit.*

Enter Achilles.

ACHILLES   Where is this Hector?
   Come, come, thou boy-queller, show thy face;   45
   Know what it is to meet Achilles angry.
   Hector, where's Hector? I will none but Hector.
                       Exit.

40 **forceless** casual, reckless   45 **boy-queller** boy-killer

[Scene VI. *The battlefield*.]

Enter Ajax.

AJAX Troilus, thou coward Troilus, show thy head!

Enter Diomedes.

DIOMEDES Troilus, I say, where's Troilus?

AJAX   What wouldst thou?

DIOMEDES I would correct him.

AJAX Were I the general, thou shouldst have my office
5   Ere that correction. Troilus, I say! What, Troilus!

Enter Troilus.

TROILUS O traitor Diomed! Turn thy false face, thou
        traitor,
        And pay thy life thou owest me for my horse.

DIOMEDES Ha, art thou there?

AJAX I'll fight with him alone. Stand, Diomed.

10 DIOMEDES He is my prize; I will not look upon.

TROILUS Come, both you cogging Greeks; have at you
        both!   [*Exeunt, fighting*.]

[*Enter Hector*.]

HECTOR Yea, Troilus? O, well fought, my youngest
        brother!

V.vi.5 **correction** i.e., privilege to correct   7 **horse** (with a pun on whore?)
10 **look upon** stand by   11 **cogging** deceitful

Enter Achilles.

ACHILLES Now do I see thee, ha! Have at thee,
    Hector!   [*They fight; Achilles tires.*]

HECTOR Pause, if thou wilt.

ACHILLES I do disdain thy courtesy, proud Troyan;   15
    Be happy that my arms are out of use.
    My rest and negligence befriends thee now,
    But thou anon shalt hear of me again;
    Till when, go seek thy fortune.   *Exit.*

HECTOR   Fare thee well;
    I would have been much more a fresher man,   20
    Had I expected thee.

Enter Troilus

              How now, my brother!

TROILUS Ajax hath ta'en Aeneas! Shall it be?
    No, by the flame of yonder glorious heaven,
    He shall not carry him; I'll be ta'en too,
    Or bring him off. Fate, hear me what I say!   25
    I reck not though thou end my life today.   *Exit.*

Enter one in armor.

HECTOR Stand, stand, thou Greek; thou art a goodly
    mark.
    No? Wilt thou not? I like thy armor well;
    I'll frush it and unlock the rivets all,
    But I'll be master of it. Wilt thou not, beast, abide?   30
    Why then, fly on, I'll hunt thee for thy hide.
                         Exit [in pursuit].

22 ta'en taken captive   24 carry him prevail over him   29 frush smash

235

[Scene VII. *The battlefield*.]

Enter Achilles with Myrmidons.

ACHILLES Come here about me, you my Myrmidons;
Mark what I say. Attend me where I wheel.
Strike not a stroke, but keep yourselves in breath.
And when I have the bloody Hector found,
5   Empale him with your weapons round about;
In fellest manner execute your arms.
Follow me, sirs, and my proceedings eye;
It is decreed Hector the great must die.

Exit [with Myrmidons].

Enter Thersites, Menelaus, Paris [the last two fighting].

THERSITES The cuckold and the cuckold-maker are at
10   it. Now, bull! Now, dog! 'Loo, Paris, 'loo! Now, my
double-horned Spartan! 'Loo, Paris, 'loo! The bull
has the game; 'ware horns, ho!

Exeunt Paris and Menelaus.

Enter Bastard [Margarelon].

BASTARD Turn, slave, and fight.

THERSITES What art thou?

15 BASTARD A bastard son of Priam's.

THERSITES I am a bastard too; I love bastards. I am
bastard begot, bastard instructed, bastard in mind,
bastard in valor, in everything illegitimate. One bear
will not bite another, and wherefore should one bas-

V.vii.5 **Empale him** hem him in   6 **fellest** cruelest   6 **execute** use   10 **Now,
bull! Now, dog! 'Loo** (Thersites compares the combat of Menelaus and Paris to
the baiting of a bull by a dog, as it was done in such arenas as the Paris
Garden)   12 **has the game** wins

tard? Take heed, the quarrel's most ominous to us.   20
If the son of a whore fight for a whore, he tempts
judgment. Farewell, bastard.

BASTARD The devil take thee, coward!   *Exeunt.*

[Scene VIII. *The battlefield.*]

Enter Hector.

HECTOR Most putrefièd core, so fair without,
    Thy goodly armor thus hath cost thy life.
    Now is my day's work done; I'll take my breath.
    Rest, sword; thou hast thy fill of blood and death.
                        [*Puts off his helmet, and hangs
                        his shield behind him.*]

        Enter Achilles and Myrmidons.

ACHILLES Look, Hector, how the sun begins to set,   5
    How ugly night comes breathing at his heels.
    Even with the vail and dark'ning of the sun,
    To close the day up, Hector's life is done.

HECTOR I am unarmed; forgo this vantage, Greek.

ACHILLES Strike, fellows, strike. This is the man I seek.   10
                        [*Hector falls.*]
    So, Ilion, fall thou next! Come, Troy, sink down!
    Here lies thy heart, thy sinews, and thy bone.
    On, Myrmidons, and cry you all amain,
    "Achilles hath the mighty Hector slain!"   *Retreat.*
    Hark, a retire upon our Grecian part.   15

V.viii.7 **vail** sinking, going down

ONE GREEK The Troyans' trumpets sound the like, my
    lord.

ACHILLES The dragon wing of night o'erspreads the
    earth.
    And, sticklerlike, the armies separates.
    My half-supped sword, that frankly would have
      fed,
20   Pleased with this dainty bait, thus goes to bed.
                              [*Sheathes his sword.*]
    Come, tie his body to my horse's tail;
    Along the field I will the Troyan trail.   *Exeunt.*

[Scene IX. *The battlefield.*]

*Enter Agamemnon, Ajax, Menelaus, Nestor, Diomed,
  and the rest, marching.* [*Sound retreat. Shout.*]

AGAMEMNON Hark, hark, what shout is that?

NESTOR   Peace, drums!

SOLDIERS (*Within*)   Achilles!
    Achilles! Hector's slain! Achilles!

DIOMEDES The bruit is, Hector's slain, and by
    Achilles.

AJAX If it be so, yet bragless let it be;
5   Great Hector was as good a man as he.

AGAMEMNON March patiently along. Let one be sent
    To pray Achilles see us at our tent.
    If in his death the gods have us befriended,
    Great Troy is ours, and our sharp wars are ended.
                                   Exeunt.

---

18 **sticklerlike** like an umpire separating combatants, and ordering the field
19 **frankly** freely, abundantly   V.ix.3 **bruit** rumor

[Scene X. *The battlefield*.]

Enter Aeneas, Paris, Antenor, Deiphobus.

AENEAS Stand, ho! Yet are we masters of the field.
　Never go home; here starve we out the night.

Enter Troilus.

TROILUS Hector is slain.

ALL   Hector! The dogs forbid!

TROILUS He's dead and at the murderer's horse's tail,
　In beastly sort, dragged through the shameful field.   5
　Frown on, you heavens, effect your rage with speed;
　Sit, gods, upon your thrones, and smile at Troy.
　I say, at once let your brief plagues be mercy,
　And linger not our sure destructions on.

AENEAS My lord, you do discomfort all the host.   10

TROILUS You understand me not that tell me so.
　I do not speak of flight, of fear, of death,
　But dare all imminence that gods and men
　Address their dangers in. Hector is gone.
　Who shall tell Priam so, or Hecuba?   15
　Let him that will a screech-owl aye be called
　Go in to Troy, and say there Hector's dead.
　There is a word will Priam turn to stone,
　Make wells and Niobes of the maids and wives,

V.x.7 **smile** i.e., in derision   8 **let ... mercy** be merciful in letting the plagues
you send destroy us quickly   13-14 **But dare ... dangers in** but instead dare
whatever imminent dangers gods and men may be preparing   16 **screech-owl** (a
bearer of ill omen)   19 **Niobes** (Niobe wept for her slain children until she was
turned into a column of stone, from which tears continued to flow)

20   Cold statues of the youth, and in a word
        Scare Troy out of itself. But march away.
        Hector is dead; there is no more to say.
        Stay yet. You vile abominable tents,
        Thus proudly pitched upon our Phrygian plains,
25   Let Titan rise as early as he dare,
        I'll through and through you! And, thou great-sized
            coward,
        No space of earth shall sunder our two hates.
        I'll haunt thee like a wicked conscience still,
        That moldeth goblins swift as frenzy's thoughts.
30   Strike a free march to Troy. With comfort go;
        Hope of revenge shall hide our inward woe.

                        Enter Pandarus.

PANDARUS But hear you, hear you!

TROILUS Hence, broker, lackey! Ignominy and shame
        Pursue thy life, and live aye with thy name.
                        Exeunt all but Pandarus.

35   PANDARUS A goodly medicine for my aching bones! O
        world, world! Thus is the poor agent despised. O
        traders and bawds, how earnestly are you set awork,
        and how ill requited! Why should our en-
        deavor be so loved, and the performance so
40   loathed? What verse for it? What instance for it? Let
        me see.
            Full merrily the humble-bee doth sing,
            Till he hath lost his honey and his sting;
            And being once subdued in armèd tail,
45   Sweet honey and sweet notes together fail.
        Good traders in the flesh, set this in your painted
            cloths:
        "As many as be here of Pandar's hall,
        Your eyes, half out, weep out at Pandar's fall;
        Or if you cannot weep, yet give some groans,

25 Titan (Helios, the sun, one of the Titans) 26 coward i.e., Achilles
46 painted cloths painted cloth hangings, used in brothels, sometimes bearing
mottoes

Though not for me, yet for your aching bones." 50
Brethren and sisters of the hold-door trade,
Some two months hence my will shall here be made.
It should be now, but that my fear is this,
Some gallèd goose of Winchester would hiss.
Till then I'll sweat and seek about for eases, 55
And at that time bequeath you my diseases.

[*Exit.*]

FINIS

---

51 **hold-door trade** prostitution   54 **gallèd goose of Winchester** angry prostitute (the Bishop of Winchester had once held jurisdiction over the area of London
called Southwark, where many brothels stood; a prostitute—and sometimes a
venereal disease—was called a "Winchester goose")   55 **sweat** (a treatment for
gout or rheumatism, as well as for venereal disease)

Textual Note

IT IS NOW generally believed that the 1609 quarto of *Troilus and Cressida* was printed from a transcript made from Shakespeare's original draft of the play. It omits about forty-five lines, the Prologue, and many stage directions that appear in the Folio, but on the whole contains a text that stands closer to Shakespeare's original than does that of the Folio. Since the compositors of the Folio apparently worked not only from the Quarto but from Shakespeare's autograph manuscript, it is surprising that they did not produce the better text; their readings are mainly inferior to those of the Quarto.

The relative values of the two texts (both of them, in different ways, stemming from Shakespeare's manuscript, and both of them, therefore, authoritative) depend on the nature of the copy used by the compositors, and the care and intelligence with which they worked. It is possible that the Quarto represents the play as it was shortened for performance, but more likely that the transcriber of the original manuscript was confused by Shakespeare's own second thoughts and deletions and failed to record some revisions and added speeches. On the other hand, although the compositors of the Folio probably had for reference and collation not only the Quarto but the original manuscript itself, their goal was speed and not always accuracy. While they added many lines omitted in the Quarto, they also introduced many mistaken readings; one compositor in particular evidently suited himself in interpreting difficult words and phrases, and made hash of most of them. Other portions of the Folio text were printed with greater care, however, and since the manuscript at hand may have been used in the playhouse, these portions include more complete stage directions and speech heads than appear in the Quarto. The Folio, therefore, supplies the fuller text; it should be used occasionally to emend the Quarto, but the earlier edition remains the better text. Its readings are frequently superior to those of the Folio, although, naturally, where the Folio prints speeches entirely omitted in the Quarto, these must be considered authoritative. Similarly, those readings in the Folio which introduce corrections on the basis of copy which was either Shakespeare's or very close to his should be followed.

The present edition is based on the Quarto but adds passages from the Folio. (These additions are recorded in the list of departures printed below.) Act and scene divisions (none is given for this play in Quarto or Folio) have been added in square brackets, along with simple indications of locale. Abbreviations have been amplified, spelling and punctuation have been modernized, and "and" is printed "an" when it means "if." The position of a few stage directions has been slightly altered when necessary. Other departures from the Quarto are listed below, the adopted reading first in bold, and then the original reading in roman. The adopted reading is most often from the Folio; when it is not, it is followed by (ed) to indicate that it is an editor's conjecture rather than an authoritative reading.

Dedicatory address   39 **state** (ed) states

Prologue (Q omits)   12 **barks** (ed; F has "Barke")   19 Sperr (ed; F has "Stirre")

I.i.77 **she were not** she were   80 **what care I** what I

I.ii.17 **they** the   36 s.d. **Enter Pandarus** (Q omits)   183 **Ilium** Ilion   208 **man's heart** man heart   245 s.d. **Enter Common Soldiers** (Q omits)   289 s.d. **Exit Pandarus** (Q omits)

I.iii.i. s.d. **Sennet** (Q omits)   13 **every** euer   31 **thy** the   36 **patient** ancient   54 **Returns** (ed) Retires   61 **thy** the   70–74 **Agamemnon. Speak ... oracle** (Q omits)   75 **basis** bases   110 **meets** melts   159 **unsquared** vnsquare   195 **and discredit** our discredit   212 s.d. **Tucket** (Q omits)   214 s.d. **Enter Aeneas** (Q omits)   247 **affair** affaires   250 **whisper him** whisper with him   252 **the attentive** that attentiue   256 **loud** alowd   263 **rusty** restie   267 **That seeks** And feeds   276 **compass** couple   294 **one** no   298 **will tell** tell   302 **youth** men   305 **first** sir   309 s.d. **Exeunt. Manent Ulysses and Nestor** (Q omits)   315 **This 'tis** (Q omits)   334 **his honor** those honours   354–56 **which ... the limbs** (F emended from "in his" to "his"; Q omits)   390 **tarre** arre

243

II.i.11 s.d. **Strikes him** (Q omits)   14 **vinewed'st** (F: whinid'st)
vnsalted   18 **oration** oration without booke   18 **a prayer** praier
42-43 **Ajax ... Do, do** (Q assigns to Thersites as one speech)   47 **Thou
scurvy-valiant** you scuruy valiant   57 s.d. **Enter Achilles and Patroclus** (Q omits)   58 **do you** do yee   74 **I** It   77 **I'll** I   104 **if he knock
out** and knocke at   109 **your grandsires had nails on their toes** (F
emended from "their" to "your") their grandsiers had nailes   119 **brach**
(ed) brooch   127 **fifth** first   135 s.d. **Exit** (Q omits)

II.ii.14-15 **surety, Surety** surely Surely   27 **father** fathers   33 **at
reasons** of reasons   47 **Let's** Sets   64 **shores** shore   75 **truce**
ttuce   86 **he be**   96 s.d. **with her hair about her ears** (Q omits)
104 **eld** (ed; F has "old") elders   210 **strike** shrike

II.iii.23 s.d. **Enter Patroclus** (Q omits)   27 **wouldst** couldst   33 **art**
art not   49 **thyself** Thersites   57-62 **Patroclus. You ... a fool** (Q
omits)   65 **commanded of Agamemnon** commanded   69 **Creator**
Prouer   71 **Patroclus** Come Patroclus   72 s.d. **Exit** (Q omits)
76-77 **Now ... all** (Q omits)   81 **shent** (ed; F has "sent") sate
82 **appertainments** appertainings   91 **A word, my lord** (Q omits)
104 s.d. **Enter Patroclus** (Q omits)   132 **pettish lunes** (F emended
from "lines" to "lunes") course, and time   132 **as if** and if
133 **carriage of this action** streame of his commencement   143 **enter
you** entertaine   143 s.d. **Exit Ulysses** (Q omits)   160 **I do hate** I
hate   193 **stale** (ed) staule   195 **titled** liked   205 **pash** push   214 **let
his humor's** tell his humorous   222 **'A would ... shares** (Q gives to
Ajax)   224 **He's ... warm** (ed; Q and F give to Ajax)   225 **praises**
praiers   244 **beyond, beyond all erudition** beyond all thy
erudition   250 **bourn** boord   251 **Thy** This   265 **cull** call

III.i. s.d. **Music ... Servant** Enter Pandarus   24 **friend** (Q omits)
38 **that thou** thou   93 **your poor disposer's** your disposers   108 **lord**
lad   115 **In ... so** (Q omits)   118 **shaft confounds** shafts
confound   150 **these** this   158 **thee** her

III.ii.1 s.d. **and Troilus'** Troylus   3 **he stays** stayes   3 s.d. **Enter
Troilus** (Q omits)   8 **Like** like to   10 **those** these   16 s.d. **Exit
Pandarus** (Q omits)   28 s.d. **Enter Pandarus** (Q omits)   34 s.d. **Exit
Pandarus** (Q omits)   38 **unawares** vnwares   68 **fears** (ed) teares
82 **This is** This   94 **merit crown it. No perfection** merit louer part
no affection   101 s.d. **Enter Pandarus** (Q omits)   134 **Cunning** (ed)
Comming   161 **aye** age   181 **Yet, after** After   186 **and** or   194 **as
wolf** or Wolfe   201 **pains** paine

III.iii. s.d. **Flourish** (Q omits)   4 **come** (ed) loue   102 **giver** giuers
128 **abject** obiect   140 **on** one   141 **shrinking** shriking   155 **one
on**   158 **hedge** turne   160 **hindmost** him, most   161-63 **Or ... on**
(F emended from "neere" to "rear"; Q omits)   164 **past** passe
177 **give** (ed) goe   183 **Than** That   197 **every grain of Pluto's gold**
euery thing   198 **th' uncomprehensive deeps** the vncomprehensiue

TEXTUAL NOTE

depth   224 **a dewdrop** dew drop   251 **he** a   267 **ambassador to him**
Ambassador   275 **most valorous** valorous   279 **Grecian army**
armie   279–80 **Agamemnon, et cetera** Agamemnon   294 **God b'wi'**
you (ed) God buy you

IV.i.4 **you** your   16 **But Lul'd**   36 **it was** twas   40 **do think** beleeue
50 s.d. **Exit Aeneas** (Q omits)   52 **the soul** soule   56 **soilure**
soyle   76 **you** they

IV.ii.19 s.d. **Within** (Q omits)   22 s.d. **Enter Pandarus** (F places after
line 20; Q omits)   51 **'Tis** Its   57 s.d. **Enter Troilus** (Q omits)   63 **to**
us; and for him forthwith to him, and forth-with   72 **nature** neighbor
Pandar   107 **I will** Ile   112 s.d. **Exeunt** (Q omits)

IV.iv.54 **the root** my throate   64 **there's** there is   77 **They're ...**
nature (Q omits)   79 **person** portion   139 s.d. **Sound trumpet** (Q
omits)   144–48 **Deiphobus. Let us ... chivalry** (F, with 144 assigned
to Diomedes; Q omits)

IV.v.94 **Ulysses. They ... already** (Q omits)   95 **Agamemnon**
Vlises   98 **in deeds** deeds   131 **Of our rank feud** (Q omits)   132
drop day   164–69 **But that's ... integrity** (Q omits)   177 **that I**
affect th' untraded oath thy affect, the vntraded earth   187 **thy** th'
192 **shraped** (ed) shruped   205 **As they ... courtesy** (Q omits)
254 **stithied** stichied   291 **she loved my Lord**

V.i.12 **these** this   14 **boy** box   19 **catarrhs** (Q omits)   23 **and the**
like (Q omits)   48 s.d. **Exit** (Q omits)   55 **brother** be   57–58 **hang-**
ing at his brother's leg at his bare legge   59 **forced** faced   61 **he is**
her's   62 **dog, a mule** day, a Moyle   62 **fitchew** Fichooke   65 **Ask**
me not aske me   71 s.d. **Enter Achilles** (Q omits)   73 **good God**
79 **sewer** (ed) sure   80 **both at once** both

V.ii.4 s.d. **Enter ... Ulysses** (Q omits)   13 **Cressida** Cal   38 **Nay**
Now   39 **distraction** distruction   46 **Adieu** (Q omits)   54 **these**
together together   56 **But will** Will   57 **la** (ed) lo   66 **Troilus. I ...**
will (Q omits)   67 **Cressida** Troy   78 **Nay ... me** (Q, F assigned
to Diomedes   82 **Cressida** (Q omits)   88 **By** And by   103 s.d. **Exit** (Q
omits)   115 **coact** Court   120 **had deceptious** were deceptions
131 **soil** spoile   154 **five** finde   164 **Much as** as much

V.iii.14 **Cassandra** Cres   20–22 **To hurt ... charity** (F emended from
"would count" to "would," and from "as" to "use"; Q omits)   23–25 **It**
is ... sweet Hector (Q assigns to Andromache)   29 **mean'st**
meanest   58 **But by my ruin** (Q omits)   85 **distraction** destruction   90 **Exit** (Q omits)

V.iv.4 **young knave's** knaues   9 **errand** (F has "errant") arrant   9 **O'**
th' Ath   17 **begin** (ed) began   18 s.d. **Enter Diomedes and Troilus**
(Q omits)   27 **art thou** art

V.v. 22 **scalèd** scaling   41 **luck** lust

TEXTUAL NOTE

V.vii.11 **double-horned** (ed) double-hen'd   12 s.d. **Exeunt** (ed) Exit   23 **Exeunt** Exit

V.viii.16 **One Greek** (F has "Gree.") One

V.ix.1 **what shout is that** what is this

V.x.2 **Never ... night** (Q assigns to Troilus, and places his entrance before the line)   21-22 **But march away. Hector is dead** (Q omits)   23 **Vile** proud   32-34 **Pandarus. But hear you! ... aye with thy name** (in F these lines appear as well after V.iii.112, concluding that scene)   33 **Ignominy and** ignominy   37 **traders** (ed) traitors   50 **your aching** my aking   51 **hold-door** hold-ore

WILLIAM SHAKESPEARE

THE TRAGEDY OF JULIUS CAESAR

Edited by *William and Barbara Rosen*

THE TRAGEDY OF
JULIUS CAESAR

ACT I

Scene I. [*Rome. A street.*]

*Enter Flavius, Marullus,
and certain Commoners over the stage.*

FLAVIUS Hence! Home, you idle creatures, get you
　　home!
　Is this a holiday? What, know you not,
　Being mechanical,[1] you ought not walk
　Upon a laboring day without the sign
　Of your profession? Speak, what trade art thou?　　　5

CARPENTER Why, sir, a carpenter.

MARULLUS Where is thy leather apron and thy rule?
　What dost thou with thy best apparel on?
　You, sir, what trade are you?

COBBLER Truly, sir, in respect of a fine workman, I am　　10
　but, as you would say, a cobbler.

MARULLUS But what trade art thou? Answer me
　directly.

COBBLER A trade, sir, that, I hope, I may use with a

---

1. Text references are printed in **bold** type; the annotation follows in roman type.
I.i.3 **mechanical** of the working class　**4–5 sign/Of your profession** mark of
your trade, i.e., working clothes　10 **in respect of a fine** in comparison with a
skilled　11 **cobbler** (1) shoemaker (2) bungler　12 **directly** straightforwardly

15   safe conscience, which is indeed, sir, a mender of
          bad soles.

          FLAVIUS What trade, thou knave? Thou naughty knave,
          what trade?

          COBBLER Nay, I beseech you, sir, be not out with me:
          yet, if you be out, sir, I can mend you.

20   MARULLUS What mean'st thou by that? Mend me,
          thou saucy fellow?

          COBBLER Why, sir, cobble you.

          FLAVIUS Thou art a cobbler, art thou?

          COBBLER Truly, sir, all that I live by is with the awl: I
25   meddle with no tradesman's matters, nor women's
          matters; but withal, I am indeed, sir, a surgeon to
          old shoes: when they are in great danger, I recover
          them. As proper men as ever trod upon neat's
          leather have gone upon my handiwork.

30   FLAVIUS But wherefore art not in thy shop today?
          Why dost thou lead these men about the streets?

          COBBLER Truly, sir, to wear out their shoes, to get
          myself into more work. But indeed, sir, we make
          holiday to see Caesar and to rejoice in his triumph.

          MARULLUS Wherefore rejoice? What conquest brings he
35   home?
          What tributaries follow him to Rome,
          To grace in captive bonds his chariot wheels?
          You block, you stones, you worse than senseless
          things!
          O you hard hearts, you cruel men of Rome,
40   Knew you not Pompey? Many a time and oft
          Have you climbed up to walls and battlements,

15 soles (pun on "souls") 16 naughty worthless 18 out angry 19 be out
i.e., have worn-out shoes 19 mend you (1) mend your shoes (2) improve your
character 26 withal (1) nevertheless (2) with awl (3) with all 27 recover
(1) resole (2) cure 28-29 neat's leather cattle's hide 34 triumph triumphal
celebration 36 tributaries captives 40 Pompey (defeated by Caesar in 48 B.C.,
later murdered)

To tow'rs and windows, yea, to chimney tops,
Your infants in your arms, and there have sat
The livelong day, with patient expectation,
To see great Pompey pass the streets of Rome.   45
And when you saw his chariot but appear,
Have you not made an universal shout,
That Tiber trembled underneath her banks
To hear the replication of your sounds
Made in her concave shores?   50
And do you now put on your best attire?
And do you now cull out a holiday?
And do you now strew flowers in his way
That comes in triumph over Pompey's blood?
Be gone!   55
Run to your houses, fall upon your knees,
Pray to the gods to intermit the plague
That needs must light on this ingratitude.

FLAVIUS Go, go, good countrymen, and, for this fault,
Assemble all the poor men of your sort;   60
Draw them to Tiber banks and weep your tears
Into the channel, till the lowest stream
Do kiss the most exalted shores of all.
                              Exeunt all the Commoners.
See, whe'r their basest mettle be not moved;
They vanish tongue-tied in their guiltiness.   65
Go you down that way towards the Capitol;
This way will I. Disrobe the images,
If you do find them decked with ceremonies.

MARULLUS May we do so?
You know it is the feast of Lupercal.   70

FLAVIUS It is no matter; let no images
Be hung with Caesar's trophies. I'll about

49 **replication** echo   50 **concave shores** hollowed-out banks   54 **in triumph
over Pompey's blood** as the conqueror of Pompey's sons   57 **intermit** hold
back   63 **most exalted shores of all** highest water mark   64 **whe'r** whether
64 **mettle** (1) substance (2) disposition   68 **ceremonies** robes (or ornaments)
70 **Lupercal** (fertility festival held on February 15; Caesar's triumph really took
place in the preceding October, but Shakespeare combines events and shortens
time spans for dramatic effect)

And drive away the vulgar from the streets;
So do you too, where you perceive them thick.
75   These growing feathers plucked from Caesar's wing
Will make him fly an ordinary pitch,
Who else would soar above the view of men
And keep us all in servile fearfulness.   *Exeunt.*

[Scene II. *A public place.*]

Enter Caesar, Antony (for the course), Calphurnia,
Portia, Decius, Cicero, Brutus, Cassius, Casca, a
Soothsayer; after them, Marullus and Flavius.

CAESAR Calphurnia!

CASCA   Peace, ho! Caesar speaks.

CAESAR   Calphurnia!

CALPHURNIA Here, my lord.

CAESAR Stand you directly in Antonius' way
When he doth run his course. Antonius!

5   ANTONY Caesar, my lord?

CAESAR Forget not in your speed, Antonius,
To touch Calphurnia; for our elders say
The barren, touchèd in this holy chase,
Shake off their sterile curse.

ANTONY   I shall remember:
10   When Caesar says "Do this," it is performed.

CAESAR Set on, and leave no ceremony out.

SOOTHSAYER Caesar!

CAESAR Ha! Who calls?

73 **vulgar** common people   76 **pitch** height

252

CASCA Bid every noise be still; peace yet again!

CAESAR Who is it in the press that calls on me?   15
  I hear a tongue, shriller than all the music,
  Cry "Caesar." Speak; Caesar is turned to hear.

SOOTHSAYER Beware the ides of March.

CAESAR   What man is that?

BRUTUS A soothsayer bids you beware the ides of March.

CAESAR Set him before me; let me see his face.   20

CASSIUS Fellow, come from the throng; look upon
  Caesar.

CAESAR What say'st thou to me now? Speak once
  again.

SOOTHSAYER Beware the ides of March.

CAESAR He is a dreamer, let us leave him. Pass.
       Sennet. Exeunt. Mane[n]t Brutus and Cassius.

CASSIUS Will you go see the order of the course?   25

BRUTUS Not I.

CASSIUS I pray you do.

BRUTUS I am not gamesome: I do lack some part
  Of that quick spirit that is in Antony.
  Let me not hinder, Cassius, your desires;   30
  I'll leave you.

CASSIUS Brutus, I do observe you now of late;
  I have not from your eyes that gentleness
  And show of love as I was wont to have;
  You bear too stubborn and too strange a hand   35
  Over your friend that loves you.

I.ii.15 **press** crowd   18 **ides of March** March 15   24 s.d. **Sennet** flourish of
trumpets marking ceremonial entrance or exit   24 s.d. **Mane[n]t** (they)
remain   25 **order of the course** progress of the race   28 **gamesome** (1) fond of
sport (2) merry   29 **quick spirit** (1) lively nature (2) prompt obedience
34 **wont** accustomed   35 **bear ... hand** treat too haughtily and distantly, keep at
arm's length (the metaphor is from horsemanship)

BRUTUS   Cassius,
Be not deceived: if I have veiled my look,
I turn the trouble of my countenance
Merely upon myself. Vexèd I am
40   Of late with passions of some difference,
Conceptions only proper to myself,
Which give some soil, perhaps, to my behaviors;
But let not therefore my good friends be grieved
(Among which number, Cassius, be you one)
45   Nor construe any further my neglect
Than that poor Brutus, with himself at war,
Forgets the shows of love to other men.

CASSIUS Then, Brutus, I have much mistook your
        passion;
By means whereof this breast of mine hath buried
50   Thoughts of great value, worthy cogitations.
Tell me, good Brutus, can you see your face?

BRUTUS No, Cassius; for the eye sees not itself
But by reflection, by some other things.

CASSIUS 'Tis just:
55   And it is very much lamented, Brutus,
That you have no such mirrors as will turn
Your hidden worthiness into your eye,
That you might see your shadow. I have heard
Where many of the best respect in Rome
60   (Except immortal Caesar), speaking of Brutus,
And groaning underneath this age's yoke,
Have wished that noble Brutus had his eyes.

BRUTUS Into what dangers would you lead me, Cassius,
That you would have me seek into myself
65   For that which is not in me?

37-39 **if I have ... upon myself** i.e., if I have seemed withdrawn, it is because I am displeased with myself and no one else (**Merely**=wholly) 40 **passions of some difference** conflicting emotions 41 **Conceptions ... myself** ideas concerning me only 42 **soil** blemish 45 **construe** interpret 47 **shows** manifestations 48 **passion** feelings 49 **By means whereof** as a consequence of which 54 **just** true 58 **shadow** reflection, i.e., yourself as others see you 59 **best respect** highest reputation

CASSIUS Therefore, good Brutus, be prepared to hear;
    And since you know you cannot see yourself
    So well as by reflection, I, your glass
    Will modestly discover to yourself
    That of yourself which you yet know not of.   70
    And be not jealous on me, gentle Brutus:
    Were I a common laughter, or did use
    To stale with ordinary oaths my love
    To every new protester; if you know
    That I do fawn on men and hug them hard,   75
    And after scandal them; or if you know
    That I profess myself in banqueting
    To all the rout, then hold me dangerous.

                        Flourish and shout.

BRUTUS What means this shouting? I do fear the people
    Choose Caesar for their king.

CASSIUS   Aye, do you fear it?   80
    Then must I think you would not have it so.

BRUTUS I would not, Cassius, yet I love him well.
    But wherefore do you hold me here so long?
    What is it that you would impart to me?
    If it be aught toward the general good,   85
    Set honor in one eye and death i' th' other,
    And I will look on both indifferently;
    For let the gods so speed me, as I love
    The name of honor more than I fear death.

CASSIUS I know that virtue to be in you, Brutus,   90
    As well as I do know your outward favor.
    Well, honor is the subject of my story.
    I cannot tell what you and other men
    Think of this life, but for my single self,

---

68 **glass** mirror 71 **jealous on** suspicious of 72 **laughter** object of
mockery 72–74 **did use ... protester** were accustomed to make cheap with glib
and frequent avowals to every new promiser of friendship (**ordinary** = [1] tavern
[2] everyday) 76 **scandal** slander 77 **profess myself** declare my
friendship 78 **rout** vulgar crowd 78 s.d. **Flourish** ceremonial sounding of
trumpets 85 **general good** public welfare 87 **indifferently** impartially
88 **speed me** make me prosper 91 **favor** appearance

95   I had as lief not be, as live to be
     In awe of such a thing as I myself.
     I was born free as Caesar; so were you:
     We both have fed as well, and we can both
     Endure the winter's cold as well as he:
100 For once, upon a raw and gusty day,
     The troubled Tiber chafing with her shores,
     Caesar said to me "Dar'st thou, Cassius, now
     Leap in with me into this angry flood,
     And swim to yonder point?" Upon the word,
105 Accout'red as I was, I plungèd in
     And bade him follow: so indeed he did.
     The torrent roared, and we did buffet it
     With lusty sinews, throwing it aside
     And stemming it with hearts of controversy.
110 But ere we could arrive the point proposed,
     Caesar cried "Help me, Cassius, or I sink!"
     I, as Aeneas, our great ancestor,
     Did from the flames of Troy upon his shoulder
     The old Anchises bear, so from the waves of Tiber
115 Did I the tired Caesar. And this man
     Is now become a god, and Cassius is
     A wretched creature, and must bend his body
     If Caesar carelessly but nod on him.
     He had a fever when he was in Spain,
120 And when the fit was on him, I did mark
     How he did shake. 'Tis true, this god did shake.
     His coward lips did from their color fly,
     And that same eye whose bend doth awe the world
     Did lose his luster. I did hear him groan;
125 Ay, and that tongue of his, that bade the Romans
     Mark him and write his speeches in their books,
     Alas, it cried, "Give me some drink, Titinius,"

95 as lief not be just as soon not exist   96 such a thing as I myself i.e., another
human being (Caesar)   101 chafing with raging against   105 Accout'red fully
armed   109 stemming ... controversy moving forward against it (1) aggres-
sively (2) in rivalry   112 Aeneas (legendary founder of the Roman state and hero
of Virgil's *Aeneid*. Anchises was his feeble father)   122 His coward ... fly the
color fled from his lips like a deserter fleeing from his banner in battle (color = [1]
hue [2] banner)   123 bend glance   124 his its

As a sick girl. Ye gods! It doth amaze me,
A man of such a feeble temper should
So get the start of the majestic world,   130
And bear the palm alone.   *Shout. Flourish.*

BRUTUS Another general shout?
I do believe that these applauses are
For some new honors that are heaped on Caesar.

CASSIUS Why, man, he doth bestride the narrow world   135
Like a Colossus, and we petty men
Walk under his huge legs and peep about
To find ourselves dishonorable graves.
Men at some time are masters of their fates:
The fault, dear Brutus, is not in our stars,   140
But in ourselves, that we are underlings.
Brutus and Caesar: what should be in that "Caesar"?
Why should that name be sounded more than yours?
Write them together, yours is as fair a name;
Sound them, it doth become the mouth as well;   145
Weigh them, it is as heavy; conjure with 'em,
"Brutus" will start a spirit as soon as "Caesar."
Now, in the names of all the gods at once,
Upon what meat doth this our Caesar feed,
That he is grown so great? Age, thou art shamed!   150
Rome, thou hast lost the breed of noble bloods!
When went there by an age, since the great flood,
But it was famed with more than with one man?
When could they say (till now) that talked of Rome,
That her wide walks encompassed but one man?   155
Now is it Rome indeed, and room enough,

129 **feeble temper** weak constitution 130 **get the start** of outdistance
131 **bear the palm** carry off the victor's prize 136 **Colossus** (an immense statue
of Apollo, said to straddle the entrance to the harbor of Rhodes so that ships sailed
under its legs) 138 **dishonorable** (because we are dominated by Caesar)
140 **stars** destinies (in Shakespeare's day one's temperament and therefore one's
actions and course of life, were thought to be largely determined by the position
of the planets at one's birth) 143 **sounded** (1) spoken (2) proclaimed by
trumpet 147 **start** raise 152 **great flood** (classical story told of the drowning of
all mankind except Deucalion and his wife Pyrrha, spared by Zeus because of their
virtue) 153 **But it was famed with** without the age being made famous
by 156 **Rome ... room** (homonyms, hence a pun)

When there is in it but one only man.
O, you and I have heard our fathers say,
There was a Brutus once that would have brooked
160　Th' eternal devil to keep his state in Rome
As easily as a king.

BRUTUS That you do love me, I am nothing jealous;
What you would work me to, I have some aim;
How I have thought of this, and of these times,
165　I shall recount hereafter. For this present,
I would not so (with love I might entreat you)
Be any further moved. What you have said
I will consider; what you have to say
I will with patience hear, and find a time
170　Both meet to hear and answer such high things.
Till then, my noble friend, chew upon this:
Brutus had rather be a villager
Than to repute himself a son of Rome
Under these hard conditions as this time
Is like to lay upon us.

175　CASSIUS　　　　　　　I am glad
That my weak words have struck but thus much show
Of fire from Brutus.

Enter Caesar and his Train.

BRUTUS The games are done, and Caesar is returning.

CASSIUS As they pass by, pluck Casca by the sleeve,
180　And he will (after his sour fashion) tell you
What hath proceeded worthy note today.

BRUTUS I will do so. But look you, Cassius,
The angry spot doth glow on Caesar's brow,
And all the rest look like a chidden train:
185　Calphurnia's cheek is pale, and Cicero

---

159 a **Brutus** (Lucius Junius Brutus helped expel the Tarquins and found the
Republic in 509 B.C.) 159 **brooked** tolerated 162 **nothing jealous** not at all
doubtful 163 **work me to** persuade me of 163 **aim** idea 170 **meet**
suitable 171 **chew** reflect 177 s.d. **Train** retinue

Looks with such ferret and such fiery eyes
As we have seen him in the Capitol,
Being crossed in conference by some senators.

CASSIUS Casca will tell us what the matter is.

CAESAR Antonius.   190

ANTONY Caesar?

CAESAR Let me have men about me that are fat,
Sleek-headed men, and such as sleep a-nights.
Yond Cassius has a lean and hungry look;
He thinks too much: such men are dangerous.   195

ANTONY Fear him not, Caesar, he's not dangerous;
He is a noble Roman, and well given.

CAESAR Would he were fatter! But I fear him not.
Yet if my name were liable to fear,
I do not know the man I should avoid   200
So soon as that spare Cassius. He reads much,
He is a great observer, and he looks
Quite through the deeds of men. He loves no plays,
As thou dost, Antony; he hears no music;
Seldom he smiles, and smiles in such a sort   205
As if he mocked himself, and scorned his spirit
That could be moved to smile at anything.
Such men as he be never at heart's ease
Whiles they behold a greater than themselves,
And therefore are they very dangerous.   210
I rather tell thee what is to be feared
Than what I fear; for always I am Caesar.
Come on my right hand, for this ear is deaf,
And tell me truly what thou think'st of him.
                Sennet. Exeunt Caesar and his Train.

186 **ferret** ferretlike (a ferret is a vicious, weasel-like animal with red eyes)
188 **conference** debate   197 **given** disposed   199 **if my name ... to fear** i.e.,
if the idea of fear could ever be associated with me   203 **through the deeds** i.e.,
to the hidden motives of actions   204 **hears no music** (cf. *Merchant of Venice*,
V.i.83ff: "The man that hath no music in himself,/Nor is not moved with concord
of sweet sounds,/Is fit for treasons.... Let no such man be trusted")   205 **sort**
manner

CASCA You pulled me by the cloak; would you speak
215   with me?

BRUTUS Ay, Casca; tell us what hath chanced today,
     That Caesar looks so sad.

CASCA Why, you were with him, were you not?

BRUTUS I should not then ask Casca what had chanced.

220 CASCA Why, there was a crown offered him; and being
         offered him, he put it by with the back of his hand,
         thus; and then the people fell a-shouting.

BRUTUS What was the second noise for?

CASCA Why, for that too.

225 CASSIUS They shouted thrice; what was the last cry for?

CASCA Why, for that too.

BRUTUS Was the crown offered him thrice?

CASCA Ay, marry, was't, and he put it by thrice, every
         time gentler than other; and every putting-by mine
230   honest neighbors shouted.

CASSIUS Who offered him the crown?

CASCA Why, Antony.

BRUTUS Tell us the manner of it, gentle Casca.

CASCA I can as well be hanged as tell the manner of it:
235   it was mere foolery; I did not mark it. I saw Mark
         Antony offer him a crown—yet 'twas not a crown
         neither, 'twas one of these coronets—and, as I told
         you, he put it by once; but for all that, to my think-
         ing, he would fain have had it. Then he offered it to
240   him again; then he put it by again; but to my think-
         ing, he was very loath to lay his fingers off it. And

217 **sad** serious   221 **put it by** pushed it aside   228 **marry** truly (originally an
oath, "By the Virgin Mary")   237 **coronets** small crowns   239 **fain** gladly

then he offered it the third time. He put it the third
time by; and still as he refused it, the rabblement
hooted, and clapped their chopt hands, and threw
up their sweaty nightcaps, and uttered such a deal   245
of stinking breath because Caesar refused the crown,
that it had, almost, choked Caesar; for he swounded
and fell down at it. And for mine own part, I durst
not laugh, for fear of opening my lips and receiving
the bad air.   250

CASSIUS But, soft, I pray you; what, did Caesar
    swound?

CASCA He fell down in the market place, and foamed at
    mouth, and was speechless.

BRUTUS 'Tis very like he hath the falling-sickness.

CASSIUS No, Caesar hath it not; but you, and I,   255
    And honest Casca, we have the falling-sickness.

CASCA I know not what you mean by that, but I am
    sure Caesar fell down. If the tag-rag people did not
    clap him and hiss him, according as he pleased and
    displeased them, as they use to do the players in the   260
    theater, I am no true man.

BRUTUS What said he when he came unto himself?

CASCA Marry, before he fell down, when he perceived
    the common herd was glad he refused the crown, he
    plucked me ope his doublet and offered them his   265
    throat to cut. An I had been a man of any occupation,
    if I would not have taken him at a word, I would I
    might go to hell among the rogues. And so he fell.
    When he came to himself again, he said, if he had

---

243 still every time   244 chopt rough, chapped   245 nightcaps (contemptuous
term for workingmen's caps)   247 swounded fainted   251 soft slowly, "wait a
minute"   254 falling-sickness epilepsy   256 we have the falling-sickness
i.e., we are becoming powerless and are declining under Caesar's rule   258 tag-
rag people ragged mob   260 use are accustomed   265 ope his doublet open
his jacket   266 man of any occupation (1) workingman, i.e., one of those to
whom Caesar's speech was addressed (2) "man of action"

270   done or said anything amiss, he desired their worships to think it was his infirmity. Three or four
wenches, where I stood, cried "Alas, good soul!" and
forgave him with all their hearts; but there's no heed
to be taken of them; if Caesar had stabbed their
275   mothers, they would have done no less.

BRUTUS And after that, he came thus sad away?

CASCA Ay.

CASSIUS Did Cicero say anything?

CASCA Ay, he spoke Greek.

280 CASSIUS To what effect?

CASCA Nay, an I tell you that, I'll ne'er look you i' th'
face again. But those that understood him smiled at
one another and shook their heads; but for mine own
part, it was Greek to me. I could tell you more news
285   too: Marullus and Flavius, for pulling scarfs off
Caesar's images, are put to silence. Fare you well.
There was more foolery yet, if I could remember it.

CASSIUS Will you sup with me tonight, Casca?

CASCA No, I am promised forth.

290 CASSIUS Will you dine with me tomorrow?

CASCA Ay, if I be alive, and your mind hold, and your
dinner worth the eating.

CASSIUS Good; I will expect you.

CASCA Do so. Farewell, both.   *Exit.*

295 BRUTUS What a blunt fellow is this grown to be!
He was quick mettle when he went to school.

CASSIUS So is he now in execution
Of any bold or noble enterprise,

---

286 **put to silence** silenced (by being stripped of their tribuneships, and perhaps
exiled or executed) 289 **am promised forth** have a previous engagement
291 **hold** does not change 296 **quick mettle** of a lively disposition

However he puts on this tardy form.
This rudeness is a sauce to his good wit,   300
Which gives men stomach to disgest his words
With better appetite.

BRUTUS And so it is. For this time I will leave you.
Tomorrow, if you please to speak with me,
I will come home to you; or if you will,   305
Come home to me, and I will wait for you.

CASSIUS I will do so. Till then, think of the world.
                                        Exit Brutus.
Well, Brutus, thou art noble; yet I see
Thy honorable mettle may be wrought
From that it is disposed; therefore it is meet   310
That noble minds keep ever with their likes;
For who so firm that cannot be seduced?
Caesar doth bear me hard, but he loves Brutus.
If I were Brutus now, and he were Cassius,
He should not humor me. I will this night,   315
In several hands, in at his windows throw,
As if they came from several citizens,
Writings, all tending to the great opinion
That Rome holds of his name; wherein obscurely
Caesar's ambition shall be glancèd at.   320
And after this, let Caesar seat him sure;
For we will shake him, or worse days endure.   *Exit.*

---

299 **tardy form** sluggish appearance 300 **wit** intelligence 301 **stomach**
appetite 301 **disgest** digest 307 **the world** i.e., the current state of
affairs 309 **mettle** (1) disposition (2) metal 309-10 **wrought ... disposed**
shaped (like iron) contrary to its natural form 310 **meet** fitting 313 **bear me
hard** hold a grudge against me 315 **humor** cajole, influence by flattery
316 **several hands** different handwritings 318 **tending to** bearing on
320 **glancèd at** indirectly touched upon 321 **seat him sure** make his position
secure

[Scene III. *A street*.]

Thunder and lightning. Enter [from opposite sides,]
Casca and Cicero.

CICERO Good even, Casca; brought you Caesar home?
Why are you breathless? And why stare you so?

CASCA Are not you moved, when all the sway of earth
Shakes like a thing unfirm? O Cicero,
5 I have seen tempests, when the scolding winds
Have rived the knotty oaks, and I have seen
Th' ambitious ocean swell and rage and foam,
To be exalted with the threat'ning clouds;
But never till tonight, never till now,
10 Did I go through a tempest dropping fire.
Either there is a civil strife in heaven,
Or else the world, too saucy with the gods,
Incenses them to send destruction.

CICERO Why, saw you anything more wonderful?

15 CASCA A common slave—you know him well by sight—
Held up his left hand, which did flame and burn
Like twenty torches joined, and yet his hand,
Not sensible of fire, remained unscorched.
Besides—I ha' not since put up my sword—
20 Against the Capitol I met a lion,
Who glazed upon me and went surly by
Without annoying me. And there were drawn
Upon a heap a hundred ghastly women,

I.iii.3 **all the sway of earth** i.e., the whole scheme of things (sway: ruling
principle) 6 **rived** split 8 **exalted with** elevated to 12 **saucy** presumptuous
18 **sensible of** sensitive to 20 **Against** directly opposite (?) near (?) 21 **glazed**
stared 22-23 **drawn/Upon a heap** huddled together 23 **ghastly** white as
ghosts

Transformèd with their fear, who swore they saw
Men, all in fire, walk up and down the streets.   25
And yesterday the bird of night did sit
Even at noonday upon the market place,
Hooting and shrieking. When these prodigies
Do so conjointly meet, let not men say,
"These are their reasons, they are natural,"   30
For I believe they are portentous things
Unto the climate that they point upon.

CICERO Indeed, it is a strange-disposèd time:
But men may construe things after their fashion,
Clean from the purpose of the things themselves.   35
Comes Caesar to the Capitol tomorrow?

CASCA He doth; for he did bid Antonius
Send word to you he would be there tomorrow.

CICERO Good night then, Casca; this disturbèd sky
Is not to walk in.

CASCA   Farewell, Cicero.   *Exit Cicero.*   40

                    Enter Cassius.

CASSIUS Who's there?

CASCA   A Roman.

CASSIUS   Casca, by your voice.

CASCA Your ear is good. Cassius, what night is this?

CASSIUS A very pleasing night to honest men.

CASCA Who ever knew the heavens menace so?

CASSIUS Those that have known the earth so full of
    faults.   45
For my part, I have walked about the streets,
Submitting me unto the perilous night,

---

26 **bird of night** owl (a bird of ill omen) 28 **prodigies** unnatural events
29 **conjointly meet** coincide 32 **climate** region 33 **strange-disposèd**
abnormal 34 **after their fashion** in their own way 35 **Clean from the
purpose** quite contrary to the real meaning

And thus unbracèd, Casca, as you see,
Have bared my bosom to the thunder-stone;
50 And when the cross blue lightning seemed to open
The breast of heaven, I did present myself
Even in the aim and very flash of it.

CASCA But wherefore did you so much tempt the
heavens?
It is the part of men to fear and tremble
55 When the most mighty gods by tokens send
Such dreadful heralds to astonish us.

CASSIUS You are dull, Casca, and those sparks of life
That should be in a Roman you do want,
Or else you use not. You look pale, and gaze,
60 And put on fear, and cast yourself in wonder,
To see the strange impatience of the heavens;
But if you would consider the true cause
Why all these fires, why all these gliding ghosts,
Why birds and beasts from quality and kind,
65 Why old men, fools, and children calculate,
Why all these things change from their ordinance,
Their natures and preformèd faculties,
To monstrous quality, why, you shall find
That heaven hath infused them with these spirits
70 To make them instruments of fear and warning
Unto some monstrous state.
Now could I, Casca, name to thee a man
Most like this dreadful night,
That thunders, lightens, opens graves, and roars
75 As doth the lion in the Capitol;
A man no mightier than thyself, or me,

48 unbracèd with doublet unfastened 49 thunder-stone lightning bolt
50 cross jagged 54 part role 55 tokens prophetic signs 56 astonish stun
58 want lack 60 put on display 60 cast yourself in wonder are amazed
64 from quality and kind (act) against their natures 65 old men i.e., the
senile, in second childhood 65 calculate make predictions (cf. proverb, "Fools
and children often do prophesy") 66 ordinance natural order of behavior
67 preformèd faculties innate qualities 68 monstrous quality unnatural
condition 69 spirits supernatural powers 71 monstrous state abnormal state
of affairs

In personal action, yet prodigious grown
And fearful, as these strange eruptions are.

CASCA 'Tis Caesar that you mean, is it not, Cassius?

CASSIUS Let it be who it is; for Romans now   80
Have thews and limbs like to their ancestors;
But, woe the while! Our fathers' minds are dead,
And we are governed with our mothers' spirits;
Our yoke and sufferance show us womanish.

CASCA Indeed, they say the senators tomorrow   85
Mean to establish Caesar as a king;
And he shall wear his crown by sea and land,
In every place save here in Italy.

CASSIUS I know where I will wear this dagger then;
Cassius from bondage will deliver Cassius.   90
Therein, ye gods, you make the weak most strong;
Therein, ye gods, you tyrants do defeat.
Nor stony tower, nor walls of beaten brass,
Nor airless dungeon, nor strong links of iron,
Can be retentive to the strength of spirit;   95
But life, being weary of these worldly bars,
Never lacks power to dismiss itself.
If I know this, know all the world besides,
That part of tyranny that I do bear
I can shake off at pleasure.   *Thunder still.*

CASCA   So can I;   100
So every bondman in his own hand bears
The power to cancel his captivity.

CASSIUS And why should Caesar be a tyrant then?
Poor man, I know he would not be a wolf
But that he sees the Romans are but sheep;   105
He were no lion, were not Romans hinds.

---

77 **prodigious** ominous   78 **fearful** causing fear   78 **eruptions** disturbances of
nature   81 **thews** sinews   82 **woe the while** alas for the times   84 **yoke and
sufferance** servitude and the meek endurance of it   91 **Therein** i.e., in suicide
95 **be retentive** to hold in   106 **hinds** (1) female deer (2) peasants (3) servants

Those that with haste will make a mighty fire
Begin it with weak straws. What trash is Rome,
What rubbish and what offal, when it serves
110   For the base matter to illuminate
So vile a thing as Caesar! But, O grief,
Where hast thou led me? I, perhaps, speak this
Before a willing bondman; then I know
My answer must be made. But I am armed,
115   And dangers are to me indifferent.

CASCA   You speak to Casca, and to such a man
That is no fleering tell-tale. Hold, my hand.
Be factious for redress of all these griefs,
And I will set this foot of mine as far
As who goes farthest.   [*They clasp hands.*]

120 CASSIUS   There's a bargain made.
Now know you, Casca, I have moved already
Some certain of the noblest-minded Romans
To undergo with me an enterprise
Of honorable dangerous consequence;
125   And I do know, by this they stay for me
In Pompey's porch; for now, this fearful night,
There is no stir or walking in the streets,
And the complexion of the element
In favor's like the work we have in hand,
130   Most bloody, fiery, and most terrible.

Enter Cinna.

CASCA   Stand close awhile, for here comes one in haste.

CASSIUS   'Tis Cinna; I do know him by his gait;
He is a friend. Cinna, where haste you so?

114 **My answer must be made** I shall have to answer for my words
115 **indifferent** unimportant   117 **fleering** flattering   118 **factious** active in
forming a political party   123 **undergo** undertake   125 **by this** by this
time   126 **Pompey's porch** portico of Pompey's Theater   128 **complexion of
the element** condition of the sky   129 **In favor's like** in appearance is like
131 **close** hidden

CINNA To find out you. Who's that? Metellus Cimber?

CASSIUS No, it is Casca, one incorporate   135
  To our attempts. Am I not stayed for, Cinna?

CINNA I am glad on't. What a fearful night is this!
  There's two or three of us have seen strange sights.

CASSIUS Am I not stayed for? Tell me.

CINNA   Yes, you are.
  O Cassius, if you could   140
  But win the noble Brutus to our party——

CASSIUS Be you content. Good Cinna, take this paper,
  And look you lay it in the praetor's chair,
  Where Brutus may but find it; and throw this
  In at his window; set this up with wax   145
  Upon old Brutus' statue. All this done,
  Repair to Pompey's porch, where you shall find us.
  Is Decius Brutus and Trebonius there?

CINNA All but Metellus Cimber, and he's gone
  To seek you at your house. Well, I will hie,   150
  And so bestow these papers as you bade me.

CASSIUS That done, repair to Pompey's Theater.
                                        Exit Cinna.
  Come, Casca, you and I will yet ere day
  See Brutus at his house; three parts of him
  Is ours already, and the man entire   155
  Upon the next encounter yields him ours.

135-36 **incorporate/To** intimately bound up with   136 **stayed** waited
137 **on't** of it (i.e., that Casca has joined the conspiracy)   143 **praetor's chair**
official chair in which Brutus would sit as chief magistrate, an office next in rank
to consul   144 **Where Brutus may but find it** where only Brutus may find it
146 **old Brutus** (Lucius Junius Brutus, founder of the Roman Republic)
147 **Repair** go   148 **Decius** (actually Decimus, a kinsman of Marcus Brutus; the
error is found in North's Plutarch)   150 **hie** hurry

CASCA O, he sits high in all the people's hearts;
And that which would appear offense in us,
His countenance, like richest alchemy,
160   Will change to virtue and to worthiness.

CASSIUS Him, and his worth, and our great need of him,
You have right well conceited. Let us go,
For it is after midnight, and ere day
We will awake him and be sure of him.   *Exeunt*.

159 **countenance** support   159 **alchemy** (the "science" by which many experi-
menters tried to turn base metals into gold)   162 **conceited** (1) understood
(2) described in an elaborate simile

ACT II

[Scene I. *Rome*.]

Enter Brutus in his orchard.

BRUTUS What, Lucius, ho!
  I cannot, by the progress of the stars,
  Give guess how near to day. Lucius, I say!
  I would it were my fault to sleep so soundly.
  When, Lucius, when? Awake, I say! What, Lucius!   5

Enter Lucius.

LUCIUS Called you, my lord?

BRUTUS Get me a taper in my study, Lucius.
  When it is lighted, come and call me here.

LUCIUS I will, my lord.   *Exit*.

BRUTUS It must be by his death; and for my part,   10
  I know no personal cause to spurn at him,
  But for the general. He would be crowned.
  How that might change his nature, there's the
    question.
  It is the bright day that brings forth the adder,
  And that craves wary walking. Crown him that,   15
  And then I grant we put a sting in him

II.i.s.d. **orchard** garden   7 **taper** candle   11 **spurn at** rebel (literally "kick")
against   12 **general** public welfare   15 **craves** demands

That at his will he may do danger with.
Th' abuse of greatness is when it disjoins
Remorse from power; and, to speak truth of Caesar,
20   I have not known when his affections swayed
More than his reason. But 'tis a common proof
That lowliness is young ambition's ladder,
Whereto the climber upward turns his face;
But when he once attains the upmost round,
25   He then unto the ladder turns his back,
Looks in the clouds, scorning the base degrees
By which he did ascend. So Caesar may;
Then lest he may, prevent. And, since the quarrel
Will bear no color for the thing he is,
30   Fashion it thus: that what he is, augmented,
Would run to these and these extremities;
And therefore think him as a serpent's egg
Which hatched, would as his kind grow mischievous,
And kill him in the shell.

Enter Lucius.

35   LUCIUS The taper burneth in your closet, sir.
Searching the window for a flint, I found
This paper thus sealed up, and I am sure
It did not lie there when I went to bed.

                                          Gives him the letter.

   BRUTUS Get you to bed again; it is not day.
40   Is not tomorrow, boy, the ides of March?

   LUCIUS I know not, sir.

   BRUTUS Look in the calendar and bring me word.

   LUCIUS I will, sir.   *Exit.*

---

17 **danger** harm   18-19 **disjoins/Remorse** separates mercy   20 **affections swayed** emotions ruled   21 **common proof** matter of common experience   22 **lowliness** humility   24 **round** rung   26 **base degrees** (1) low steps of the ladder (2) less important grades of office (3) common people   28 **prevent** take action to forestall   28 **quarrel** cause of complaint   29 **bear no color** have no excuse   30 **Fashion it** construct the case   31 **these and these extremities** such and such extremes (of tyranny)   33 **as his kind** according to its nature   35 **closet** study

BRUTUS The exhalations whizzing in the air
　Give so much light that I may read by them.   45
　　　　　　　　　Opens the letter and reads.

　　"Brutus, thou sleep'st; awake, and see thyself.
　　Shall Rome, &c. Speak, strike, redress.
　　Brutus, thou sleep'st; awake."

　Such instigations have been often dropped
　Where I have took them up.   50
　"Shall Rome, &c." Thus must I piece it out:
　Shall Rome stand under one man's awe? What,
　　Rome?
　My ancestors did from the streets of Rome
　The Tarquin drive, when he was called a king.
　"Speak, strike, redress." Am I entreated   55
　To speak and strike? O Rome, I make thee promise,
　If the redress will follow, thou receivest
　Thy full petition at the hand of Brutus!

　　　　　　　　　Enter Lucius.

LUCIUS Sir, March is wasted fifteen days. *Knock within.*

BRUTUS 'Tis good. Go to the gate; somebody knocks.   60
　　　　　　　　　[*Exit Lucius.*]
　Since Cassius first did whet me against Caesar,
　I have not slept.
　Between the acting of a dreadful thing
　And the first motion, all the interim is
　Like a phantasma, or a hideous dream.   65
　The genius and the mortal instruments
　Are then in council, and the state of a man,
　Like to a little kingdom, suffers then
　The nature of an insurrection.

44 exhalations meteors　47, 51 &c. (read "et cetera")　51 piece it out develop
the meaning　52 under one man's awe in awe of one man　58 Thy full ...
hand of all you ask from　61 whet incite　64 motion prompting　65 phantasma hallucination　66 genius guardian spirit (?) reasoning spirit (?)
66 mortal instruments the emotions and physical powers (which should be ruled
and guided by reason)　69 nature of an insurrection a kind of insurrection

Enter Lucius.

70 LUCIUS Sir, 'tis your brother Cassius at the door,
        Who doth desire to see you.

    BRUTUS   Is he alone?

    LUCIUS No, sir, there are moe with him.

    BRUTUS   Do you know them?

    LUCIUS No, sir; their hats are plucked about their ears,
        And half their faces buried in their cloaks,
75   That by no means I may discover them
        By any mark of favor.

    BRUTUS   Let 'em enter.   [*Exit Lucius.*]
        They are the faction. O conspiracy,
        Sham'st thou to show thy dang'rous brow by night,
        When evils are most free? O, then by day
80   Where wilt thou find a cavern dark enough
        To mask thy monstrous visage? Seek none,
            conspiracy;
        Hide it in smiles and affability:
        For if thou path, thy native semblance on,
        Not Erebus itself were dim enough
85   To hide thee from prevention.

    Enter the conspirators, Cassius, Casca, Decius, Cinna,
        Metellus [Cimber], and Trebonius.

    CASSIUS I think we are too bold upon your rest.
        Good morrow, Brutus; do we trouble you?

    BRUTUS I have been up this hour, awake all night.
        Know I these men that come along with you?

90 CASSIUS Yes, every man of them; and no man here
        But honors you; and every one doth wish

70 **brother** i.e., brother-in-law (Cassius was married to Brutus' sister) 72 **moe**
more 75 **discover** recognize 76 **favor** appearance 79 **evils are most free**
evil things roam most freely 83 **path** walk (verb) 83 **native semblance** true
appearance 84 **Erebus** dark region between earth and Hades 85 **from prevention** from being forestalled and hindered 86 **upon** in intruding on

You had but that opinion of yourself
Which every noble Roman bears of you.
This is Trebonius.

BRUTUS   He is welcome hither.

CASSIUS This, Decius Brutus.

BRUTUS   He is welcome too.   95

CASSIUS This, Casca; this, Cinna; and this, Metellus
    Cimber.

BRUTUS They are all welcome.
    What watchful cares do interpose themselves
    Betwixt your eyes and night?

CASSIUS Shall I entreat a word?   *They whisper*.   100

DECIUS Here lies the east; doth not the day break here?

CASCA No.

CINNA O, pardon, sir, it doth; and yon gray lines
    That fret the clouds are messengers of day.

CASCA You shall confess that you are both deceived   105
    Here, as I point my sword, the sun arises,
    Which is a great way growing on the south,
    Weighing the youthful season of the year.
    Some two months hence, up higher toward the north
    He first presents his fire; and the high east   110
    Stands as the Capitol, directly here.

BRUTUS Give me your hands all over, one by one.

CASSIUS And let us swear our resolution.

BRUTUS No, not an oath. If not the face of men,
    The sufferance of our souls, the time's abuse—   115

98 **watchful cares** cares that keep you awake   104 **fret** pattern, interlace
107 **growing on** tending toward   108 **Weighing** considering   110 **high** due
114 **the face of men** i.e., the sincere and resolute appearance of the conspirators,
which should not be distrusted   115 **sufferance** patient endurance   115 **time's
abuse** corruption of the age (i.e., Caesar's assumption of unconstitutional powers)

If these be motives weak, break off betimes,
And every man hence to his idle bed.
So let high-sighted tyranny range on
Till each man drop by lottery. But if these
120   (As I am sure they do) bear fire enough
To kindle cowards and to steel with valor
The melting spirits of women, then, countrymen,
What need we any spur but our own cause
To prick us to redress? What other bond
125   Than secret Romans that have spoke the word,
And will not palter? And what other oath
Than honesty to honesty engaged
That this shall be, or we will fall for it?
Swear priests and cowards and men cautelous,
130   Old feeble carrions and such suffering souls
That welcome wrongs; unto bad causes swear
Such creatures as men doubt; but do not stain
The even virtue of our enterprise,
Nor th' insuppressive mettle of our spirits,
135   To think that or our cause or our performance
Did need an oath; when every drop of blood
That every Roman bears, and nobly bears,
Is guilty of a several bastardy
If he do break the smallest particle
140   Of any promise that hath passed from him.

CASSIUS But what of Cicero? Shall we sound him?
I think he will stand very strong with us.

CASCA Let us not leave him out.

CINNA   No, by no means.

METELLUS O, let us have him, for his silver hairs

116 **betimes** immediately   118 **high-sighted** arrogant (viewing widely from on
high, like a falcon ready to swoop on prey)   118 **range** rove or fly in search of
prey   119 **by lottery** by chance, i.e., at the tyrant's whim   124 **prick** urge
125 **secret Romans** the fact that we are Romans capable of maintaining secrecy
126 **palter** equivocate   127 **honesty** personal honor   127 **engaged** pledged
129 **Swear** bind by oath   129 **cautelous** deceitful   130 **carrions** wretches
almost dead and rotting   133 **even** unblemished, perfect   134 **insuppressive**
mettle indomitable temper   135 **or ... or** either ... or   138 **guilty ... bastardy**
i.e., guilty of an act not truly Roman

Will purchase us a good opinion, 145
And buy men's voices to commend our deeds.
It shall be said his judgment ruled our hands;
Our youths and wildness shall no whit appear,
But all be buried in his gravity.

BRUTUS O, name him not! Let us not break with him; 150
For he will never follow anything
That other men begin.

CASSIUS   Then leave him out.

CASCA Indeed, he is not fit.

DECIUS Shall no man else be touched but only Caesar?

CASSIUS Decius, well urged. I think it is not meet 155
Mark Antony, so well beloved of Caesar,
Should outlive Caesar; we shall find of him
A shrewd contriver; and you know, his means;
If he improve them, may well stretch so far
As to annoy us all; which to prevent, 160
Let Antony and Caesar fall together.

BRUTUS Our course will seem too bloody, Caius
Cassius,
To cut the head off and then hack the limbs,
Like wrath in death and envy afterwards;
For Antony is but a limb of Caesar. 165
Let's be sacrificers, but not butchers, Caius.
We all stand up against the spirit of Caesar,
And in the spirit of men there is no blood.
O, that we then could come by Caesar's spirit,
And not dismember Caesar! But, alas, 170
Caesar must bleed for it. And, gentle friends,
Let's kill him boldly, but not wrathfully;

145 opinion reputation   148 no whit not in the slightest   149 gravity sobriety
and stability (Latin *gravitas*)   150 break with him divulge our plan to him
155 urged suggested   157 of in   158 shrewd contriver cunning and malicious
plotter   159 improve make good use of   160 annoy harm   160 prevent
forestall   164 envy malice, i.e., as though we were killing Caesar for personal
spite and hatred   167 the spirit of Caesar the principles (of tyranny) for which
Caesar stands   169 come by get possession of   171 gentle noble

Let's carve him as a dish fit for the gods,
Not hew him as a carcass fit for hounds.
175　And let our hearts, as subtle masters do,
Stir up their servants to an act of rage,
And after seem to chide 'em. This shall make
Our purpose necessary, and not envious;
Which so appearing to the common eyes,
180　We shall be called purgers, not murderers.
And for Mark Antony, think not of him;
For he can do no more than Caesar's arm
When Caesar's head is off.

CASSIUS　　　　　　　　Yet I fear him;
For in the ingrafted love he bears to Caesar——

185　BRUTUS Alas, good Cassius, do not think of him.
If he love Caesar, all that he can do
Is to himself—take thought and die for Caesar.
And that were much he should, for he is given
To sports, to wildness, and much company.

190　TREBONIUS There is no fear in him; let him not die,
For he will live and laugh at this hereafter.
　　　　　　　　　　　　　　　　Clock strikes.

BRUTUS Peace! Count the clock.

CASSIUS　　　　　　The clock hath stricken three.

TREBONIUS 'Tis time to part.

CASSIUS　　　　　　　　But it is doubtful yet
Whether Caesar will come forth today or no;
195　For he is superstitious grown of late,
Quite from the main opinion he held once
Of fantasy, of dreams, and ceremonies.
It may be these apparent prodigies,
The unaccustomed terror of this night,

176 **servants** (1) the hands (2) the passions　178 **envious** malicious
180 **purgers** healers　184 **ingrafted** firmly rooted　187 **take thought** grow
melancholy with brooding　188 **that were much he should** that would be too
much to expect of him　190 **no fear** nothing to fear　196 **Quite from the main**
at variance with the strong　197 **ceremonies** omens　198 **apparent prodigies**
obvious signs of disaster

278

And the persuasion of his augurers   200
    May hold him from the Capitol today.

DECIUS Never fear that. If he be so resolved,
    I can o'ersway him; for he loves to hear
    That unicorns may be betrayed with trees,
    And bears with glasses, elephants with holes,   205
    Lions with toils, and men with flatterers;
    But when I tell him he hates flatterers,
    He says he does, being then most flatterèd.
    Let me work;
    For I can give his humor the true bent,   210
    And I will bring him to the Capitol.

CASSIUS Nay, we will all of us be there to fetch him.

BRUTUS By the eighth hour; is that the uttermost?

CINNA Be that the uttermost, and fail not then.

METELLUS Caius Ligarius doth bear Caesar hard,   215
    Who rated him for speaking well of Pompey.
    I wonder none of you have thought of him.

BRUTUS Now, good Metellus, go along by him.
    He loves me well, and I have given him reasons;
    Send him but hither, and I'll fashion him.   220

CASSIUS The morning comes upon 's; we'll leave you,
        Brutus.
    And, friends, disperse yourselves; but all remember
    What you have said, and show yourselves true
        Romans.

BRUTUS Good gentlemen, look fresh and merrily.
    Let not our looks put on our purposes,   225

---

200 **augurers** augurs (priests who foretold, from omens, the future)   203 **o'er-sway him** persuade him to change his mind   204 **betrayed with trees** i.e., tricked into running at a tree (at the last moment its prey steps aside so that the horn is deeply embedded and the unicorn is helpless)   205 **glasses** mirrors   205 **holes** pitfalls   206 **toils** nets, snares   210 **humor** temperament   210 **bent** direction   213 **uttermost** latest   215 **bear Caesar hard** has a grudge against Caesar   216 **rated** berated   218 **him** his house   220 **fashion** shape (to our designs)   225 **put on** display

But bear it as our Roman actors do,
With untired spirits and formal constancy.
And so good morrow to you every one.

Exeunt. Manet Brutus.

Boy! Lucius! Fast asleep? It is no matter;
230   Enjoy the honey-heavy dew of slumber.
Thou hast no figures nor no fantasies
Which busy care draws in the brains of men;
Therefore thou sleep'st so sound.

Enter Portia.

PORTIA   Brutus, my lord.

BRUTUS Portia, what mean you? Wherefore rise you now?
235   It is not for your health thus to commit
Your weak condition to the raw cold morning.

PORTIA Nor for yours neither. Y'have ungently, Brutus,
Stole from my bed; and yesternight at supper
You suddenly arose and walked about,
240   Musing and sighing, with your arms across;
And when I asked you what the matter was,
You stared upon me with ungentle looks.
I urged you further; then you scratched your head,
And too impatiently stamped with your foot.
245   Yet I insisted, yet you answered not,
But with an angry wafter of your hand
Gave sign for me to leave you. So I did,
Fearing to strengthen that impatience
Which seemed too much enkindled, and withal
250   Hoping it was but an effect of humor,
Which sometime hath his hour with every man.
It will not let you eat, nor talk, nor sleep,
And could it work so much upon your shape

---

226 **bear it** play our parts 227 **formal constancy** consistent decorum
228 s.d. **Manet** remains 230 **dew** i.e., refreshment 231 **figures ... fantasies**
(both words specify figments of the imagination) 237 **ungently** discourteously 240 **across** folded (a sign of melancholy) 246 **wafter** waving
249 **withal** also 250 **effect of humor** i.e., sign of a temporary mood
251 **his** its

As it hath much prevailed on your condition,
I should not know you Brutus. Dear my lord,   255
Make me acquainted with your cause of grief.

BRUTUS I am not well in health, and that is all.

PORTIA Brutus is wise and, were he not in health,
He would embrace the means to come by it.

BRUTUS Why, so I do. Good Portia, go to bed.   260

PORTIA Is Brutus sick, and is it physical
To walk unbracèd and suck up the humors
Of the dank morning? What, is Brutus sick,
And will he steal out of his wholesome bed,
To dare the vile contagion of the night,   265
And tempt the rheumy and unpurgèd air
To add unto his sickness? No, my Brutus;
You have some sick offense within your mind,
Which by the right and virtue of my place
I ought to know of; and upon my knees   270
I charm you, by my once commended beauty,
By all your vows of love, and that great vow
Which did incorporate and make us one,
That you unfold to me, your self, your half,
Why you are heavy, and what men tonight   275
Have had resort to you; for here have been
Some six or seven, who did hide their faces
Even from darkness.

BRUTUS   Kneel not, gentle Portia.

PORTIA I should not need, if you were gentle Brutus.
Within the bond of marriage, tell me, Brutus,   280
Is it excepted I should know no secrets
That appertain to you? Am I your self

---

254 **condition** disposition 255 **know you** recognize you as 261 **physical**
healthy 262 **unbracèd** with doublet unfastened 262 **humors** dampness,
mist 265 **night** (night air was thought to be harmful, even poisonous)
266 **tempt ... air** risk the damp and unpurified (by the sun) air 268 **sick
offense** sickness that harms 269 **place** situation (as wife) 271 **charm**
entreat 273 **incorporate** make us one flesh (cf. Matthew 19:5, "they twain shall
be one flesh") 275 **heavy** dejected 281 **excepted** made an exception that

But, as it were, in sort or limitation,
To keep with you at meals, comfort your bed,
And talk to you sometimes? Dwell I but in the
285   suburbs
Of your good pleasure? If it be no more,
Portia is Brutus' harlot, not his wife.

BRUTUS You are my true and honorable wife,
As dear to me as are the ruddy drops
290   That visit my sad heart.

PORTIA If this were true, then should I know this secret.
I grant I am a woman; but withal
A woman that Lord Brutus took to wife.
I grant I am a woman; but withal
295   A woman well reputed, Cato's daughter.
Think you I am no stronger than my sex,
Being so fathered and so husbanded?
Tell me your counsels, I will not disclose 'em.
I have made strong proof of my constancy,
300   Giving myself a voluntary wound
Here in the thigh; can I bear that with patience,
And not my husband's secrets?

BRUTUS   O ye gods,
Render me worthy of this noble wife!   *Knock.*
Hark, hark! One knocks. Portia, go in a while,
305   And by and by thy bosom shall partake
The secrets of my heart.
All my engagements I will construe to thee,
All the charactery of my sad brows.
Leave me with haste.   *Exit Portia.*

---

283 **in sort or limitation** after a fashion or within a certain restriction (legal terms) 285 **suburbs** outlying districts (where the brothels and least respectable taverns were found) 292 **withal** at the same time 295 **Cato's daughter** (Marcus Porcius Cato was famous for his integrity; he joined Pompey against Caesar and killed himself at Utica in 46 B.C. to avoid capture; he was Brutus' uncle as well as father-in-law) 298 **counsels** secrets 299 **proof of my constancy** trial of my resolution 307 **engagements** commitments 307 **construe** explain 308 **charactery** of writing upon, i.e., wrinkles of grief and worry

Enter Lucius and [Caius] Ligarius.

Lucius, who's that knocks?

LUCIUS Here is a sick man that would speak with you. 310

BRUTUS Caius Ligarius, that Metellus spake of.
Boy, stand aside. Caius Ligarius! How?

CAIUS Vouchsafe good morrow from a feeble tongue.

BRUTUS O, what a time have you chose out, brave Caius.
To wear a kerchief! Would you were not sick! 315

CAIUS I am not sick, if Brutus have in hand
Any exploit worthy the name of honor.

BRUTUS Such an exploit have I in hand, Ligarius,
Had you a healthful ear to hear of it.

CAIUS By all the gods that Romans bow before, 320
I here discard my sickness! Soul of Rome,
Brave son, derived from honorable loins,
Thou, like an exorcist, hast conjured up
My mortifièd spirit. Now bid me run,
And I will strive with things impossible, 325
Yea, get the better of them. What's to do?

BRUTUS A piece of work that will make sick men whole.

CAIUS But are not some whole that we must make sick?

BRUTUS That must we also. What it is, my Caius,
I shall unfold to thee, as we are going 330
To whom it must be done.

CAIUS   Set on your foot,
And with a heart new-fired I follow you,

---

312 How how are you 313 Vouchsafe please accept 314 brave noble
315 To wear a kerchief (as a protection against drafts), i.e., to be sick 322 from
honorable loins i.e., descent from Lucius Junius Brutus, founder of the Roman
Republic 323 exorcist conjurer 324 mortifièd deadened 327 whole
healthy 331 To whom to the house of him to whom 331 Set on advance

To do I know not what; but it sufficeth
That Brutus leads me on.   *Thunder.*

BRUTUS   Follow me, then.   *Exeunt.*

[Scene II. *Caesar's house.*]

Thunder and lightning. Enter Julius Caesar in
his nightgown.

CAESAR Nor heaven nor earth have been at peace
    tonight:
  Thrice hath Calphurnia in her sleep cried out,
  "Help, ho! They murder Caesar!" Who's within?

Enter a Servant.

SERVANT My lord?

5   CAESAR Go bid the priests do present sacrifice,
  And bring me their opinions of success.

SERVANT I will, my lord.   *Exit.*

Enter Calphurnia.

CALPHURNIA What mean you, Caesar? Think you to
    walk forth?
  You shall not stir out of your house today.

CAESAR Caesar shall forth. The things that threatened
10   me
  Ne'er looked but on my back; when they shall see
  The face of Caesar, they are vanishèd.

CALPHURNIA Caesar, I never stood on ceremonies,
  Yet now they fright me. There is one within,
15   Besides the things that we have heard and seen,
  Recounts most horrid sights seen by the watch.

II.ii. s.d. **nightgown** dressing gown **5 present** immediate **6 opinions of suc-**
cess judgment as to the future course of events **13 stood on ceremonies** paid
attention to omens **16 watch** nightwatchmen

A lioness hath whelpèd in the streets,
And graves have yawned, and yielded up their dead;
Fierce fiery warriors fought upon the clouds
In ranks and squadrons and right form of war,   20
Which drizzled blood upon the Capitol;
The noise of battle hurtled in the air,
Horses did neigh and dying men did groan,
And ghosts did shriek and squeal about the streets.
O Caesar, these things are beyond all use,   25
And I do fear them.

CAESAR   What can be avoided
Whose end is purposed by the mighty gods?
Yet Caesar shall go forth; for these predictions
Are to the world in general as to Caesar.

CALPHURNIA When beggars die, there are no comets seen;   30
The heavens themselves blaze forth the death of
    princes.

CAESAR Cowards die many times before their deaths;
The valiant never taste of death but once.
Of all the wonders that I yet have heard,
It seems to me most strange that men should fear,   35
Seeing that death, a necessary end,
Will come when it will come.

Enter a Servant.

                                What say the augurers?

SERVANT They would not have you to stir forth today.
Plucking the entrails of an offering forth,
They could not find a heart within the beast.   40

CAESAR The gods do this in shame of cowardice:
Caesar should be a beast without a heart
If he should stay at home today for fear.
No, Caesar shall not; Danger knows full well
That Caesar is more dangerous than he.   45

20 **right form** proper military formation   22 **hurtled** clashed   25 **use** normal
experience   29 **Are to** apply to   31 **blaze forth** i.e., proclaim (by comets and
meteors)   42 **should** would   42 **heart** (the organ of courage)

We are two lions littered in one day,
And I the elder and more terrible,
And Caesar shall go forth.

CALPHURNIA   Alas, my lord,
Your wisdom is consumed in confidence.
50   Do not go forth today. Call it my fear
That keeps you in the house and not your own.
We'll send Mark Antony to the Senate House,
And he shall say you are not well today.
Let me, upon my knee, prevail in this.

55   CAESAR Mark Antony shall say I am not well,
And for thy humor, I will stay at home.

Enter Decius.

Here's Decius Brutus, he shall tell them so.

DECIUS Caesar, all hail! Good morrow, worthy Caesar;
I come to fetch you to the Senate House.

60   CAESAR And you are come in very happy time
To bear my greeting to the senators,
And tell them that I will not come today.
Cannot, is false; and that I dare not, falser:
I will not come today. Tell them so, Decius.

CALPHURNIA Say he is sick.

65   CAESAR   Shall Caesar send a lie?
Have I in conquest stretched mine arm so far
To be afeard to tell graybeards the truth?
Decius, go tell them Caesar will not come.

DECIUS Most mighty Caesar, let me know some cause,
70   Lest I be laughed at when I tell them so.

CAESAR The cause is in my will: I will not come.
That is enough to satisfy the Senate.
But for your private satisfaction,
Because I love you, I will let you know.

49 **consumed in confidence** destroyed by too much confidence   56 **humor**
whim   59 **fetch** escort   60 **happy time** favorable time (i.e., just at the right
moment)

Calphurnia here, my wife, stays me at home.   75
She dreamt tonight she saw my statue,
Which, like a fountain with an hundred spouts,
Did run pure blood, and many lusty Romans
Came smiling and did bathe their hands in it.
And these does she apply for warning and portents   80
And evils imminent, and on her knee
Hath begged that I will stay at home today.

DECIUS This dream is all amiss interpreted;
It was a vision fair and fortunate:
Your statue spouting blood in many pipes,   85
In which so many smiling Romans bathed,
Signifies that from you great Rome shall suck
Reviving blood, and that great men shall press
For tinctures, stains, relics, and cognizance.
This by Calphurnia's dream is signified.   90

CAESAR And this way have you well expounded it.

DECIUS I have, when you have heard what I can say;
And know it now, the Senate have concluded
To give this day a crown to mighty Caesar.
If you shall send them word you will not come,   95
Their minds may change. Besides, it were a mock
Apt to be rendered, for someone to say
"Break up the Senate till another time,
When Caesar's wife shall meet with better dreams."
If Caesar hide himself, shall they not whisper   100
"Lo, Caesar is afraid"?
Pardon me, Caesar, for my dear dear love
To your proceeding bids me tell you this,
And reason to my love is liable.

75 stays keeps   76 tonight i.e., last night   76 statue (trisyllabic; pronounced "stat-u-a")   80 apply for explain as   80 portents (accent on last syllable)   89 tinctures ... cognizance (Samuel Johnson paraphrases the line: "The Romans, says Decius, all come to you, as to a saint, for relics; as to a prince, for honors")   tinctures (1) alchemical elixirs (2) colors, metals, etc. used in heraldry   stains colors in a coat of arms   relics venerated property of a martyr   cognizance mark of identification worn by a nobleman's followers   96–97 mock ... rendered jeering remark likely to be made   103 proceeding advancement   104 reason ... liable i.e., my affection proves stronger than my judgment (of impropriety) in telling you this (liable = subordinate)

CAESAR How foolish do your fears seem now,
105   Calphurnia!
          I am ashamèd I did yield to them.
          Give me my robe, for I will go.

                *Enter Brutus, Ligarius, Metellus [Cimber], Casca,
                Trebonius, Cinna, and Publius.*

          And look where Publius is come to fetch me.

PUBLIUS Good morrow, Caesar.

CAESAR   Welcome, Publius.
110   What, Brutus, are you stirred so early too?
          Good morrow, Casca. Caius Ligarius,
          Caesar was ne'er so much your enemy
          As that same ague which hath made you lean.
          What is't o'clock?

BRUTUS   Caesar, 'tis strucken eight.

115 CAESAR I thank you for your pains and courtesy.

                        Enter Antony.

          See! Antony, that revels long a-nights,
          Is notwithstanding up. Good morrow, Antony.

ANTONY So to most noble Caesar.

CAESAR   Bid them prepare within.
          I am to blame to be thus waited for.
120   Now, Cinna; now, Metellus; what, Trebonius,
          I have an hour's talk in store for you;
          Remember that you call on me today;
          Be near me, that I may remember you.

TREBONIUS Caesar, I will [*aside*] and so near will I be,
125   That your best friends shall wish I had been further.

---

107 **robe** toga   112 **enemy** (Ligarius had supported Pompey against Caesar in
the Civil War and had recently been pardoned by Caesar)   118 **prepare** i.e., set
out the wine mentioned in line 126

CAESAR Good friends, go in and taste some wine with
    me,
And we (like friends) will straightway go together.

BRUTUS [*Aside*] That every like is not the same, O Caesar,
The heart of Brutus earns to think upon.   *Exeunt*.

[Scene III. *A street near the Capitol, close to
            Brutus' house.*]

Enter Artemidorus [reading a paper].

[ARTEMIDORUS] "Caesar, beware of Brutus; take heed
of Cassius; come not near Casca; have an eye to
Cinna; trust not Trebonius; mark well Metellus
Cimber; Decius Brutus loves thee not; thou hast
wronged Caius Ligarius. There is but one mind in   5
all these men, and it is bent against Caesar. If thou
beest not immortal, look about you: security gives
way to conspiracy. The mighty gods defend thee!
                    Thy lover, ARTEMIDORUS."
Here will I stand till Caesar pass along,   10
And as a suitor will I give him this.
My heart laments that virtue cannot live
Out of the teeth of emulation.
If thou read this, O Caesar, thou mayest live;
If not, the Fates with traitors do contrive.   *Exit*.   15

128 That every like is not the same i.e., what a pity that those who appear
like friends may actually be enemies   129 earns grieves   II.iii.6 bent directed
7-8 security gives way to conspiracy overconfidence gives conspiracy its
opportunity   9 lover devoted friend   11 as a suitor like a petitioner   13 Out of
the teeth of emulation beyond the reach of envious rivalry   15 contrive
conspire

[Scene IV. *Another part of the street.*]

Enter Portia and Lucius.

PORTIA I prithee, boy, run to the Senate House;
Stay not to answer me, but get thee gone.
Why dost thou stay?

LUCIUS   To know my errand, madam.

PORTIA I would have had thee there and here again
5   Ere I can tell thee what thou shouldst do there.
O constancy, be strong upon my side;
Set a huge mountain 'tween my heart and tongue!
I have a man's mind, but a woman's might.
How hard it is for women to keep counsel!
Art thou here yet?

10 LUCIUS   Madam, what should I do?
Run to the Capitol, and nothing else?
And so return to you, and nothing else?

PORTIA Yes, bring me word, boy, if thy lord look well,
For he went sickly forth; and take good note
15   What Caesar doth, what suitors press to him.
Hark, boy, what noise is that?

LUCIUS I hear none, madam.

PORTIA   Prithee, listen well.
I heard a bustling rumor like a fray,
And the wind brings it from the Capitol.

20 LUCIUS Sooth, madam, I hear nothing.

II.iv.6 **constancy** resolution 8 **might** physical strength 9 **counsel** secret
(Brutus has obviously told her of the conspiracy, though "stage time" has allowed
no opportunity for this; the inconsistency is not noticeable during a
performance) 18 **bustling rumor like a fray** confused noise as of battle
20 **Sooth** truly

Enter the Soothsayer.

PORTIA Come hither, fellow. Which way hast thou been?

SOOTHSAYER At mine own house, good lady.

PORTIA What is't o'clock?

SOOTHSAYER   About the ninth hour, lady.

PORTIA Is Caesar yet gone to the Capitol?

SOOTHSAYER Madam, not yet; I go to take my stand,   25
To see him pass on to the Capitol.

PORTIA Thou hast some suit to Caesar, hast thou not?

SOOTHSAYER That I have, lady; if it will please Caesar
To be so good to Caesar as to hear me,
I shall beseech him to befriend himself.   30

PORTIA Why, know'st thou any harm's intended towards
him?

SOOTHSAYER None that I know will be, much that I
fear may chance.
Good morrow to you. Here the street is narrow;
The throng that follows Caesar at the heels,
Of senators, of praetors, common suitors,   35
Will crowd a feeble man almost to death.
I'll get me to a place more void, and there
Speak to great Caesar as he comes along.   *Exit.*

PORTIA I must go in. Ay me, how weak a thing
The heart of woman is! O Brutus,   40
The heavens speed thee in thine enterprise!
Sure, the boy heard me—Brutus hath a suit
That Caesar will not grant—O, I grow faint.
Run, Lucius, and commend me to my lord;
Say I am merry; come to me again,   45
And bring me word what he doth say to thee.
                              Exeunt [*severally*].

32 chance happen   37 more void more empty (less crowded)   41 speed
prosper   44 commend me give my love   45 merry cheerful

ACT III

[Scene I. *Rome. Before the Capitol.*]

Flourish. Enter Caesar, Brutus, Cassius, Casca, Decius,
Metellus [Cimber], Trebonius, Cinna, Antony, Lepidus,
Artemidorus, Publius, [Popilius,] and the Soothsayer.

CAESAR The ides of March are come.

SOOTHSAYER Ay, Caesar, but not gone.

ARTEMIDORUS Hail, Caesar! Read this schedule.

DECIUS Trebonius doth desire you to o'er-read,
5   At your best leisure, this his humble suit.

ARTEMIDORUS O Caesar, read mine first; for mine's a suit
    That touches Caesar nearer. Read it, great Caesar.

CAESAR What touches us ourself shall be last served.

ARTEMIDORUS Delay not, Caesar; read it instantly.

CAESAR What, is the fellow mad?

10 PUBLIUS   Sirrah, give place.

CASSIUS What, urge you your petitions in the street?
    Come to the Capitol.

    [*Caesar goes to the Capitol, the rest following.*]

III.i.3 **schedule** scroll   7 **touches** concerns   10 **Sirrah, give place** fellow, get
out of the way

292

JULIUS CAESAR

JULIUS CAESAR III.i.

POPILIUS I wish your enterprise today may thrive.

CASSIUS What enterprise, Popilius?

POPILIUS   Fare you well.
                    [*Advances to Caesar.*]

BRUTUS What said Popilius Lena?   15

CASSIUS He wished today our enterprise might thrive.
I fear our purpose is discoverèd.

BRUTUS Look how he makes to Caesar; mark him.

CASSIUS Casca, be sudden, for we fear prevention.
Brutus, what shall be done? If this be known,   20
Cassius or Caesar never shall turn back,
For I will slay myself.

BRUTUS   Cassius, be constant.
Popilius Lena speaks not of our purposes;
For look, he smiles, and Caesar doth not change.

CASSIUS Trebonius knows his time; for look you,
    Brutus,   25
He draws Mark Antony out of the way.
                    [*Exeunt Antony and Trebonius.*]

DECIUS Where is Metellus Cimber? Let him go
And presently prefer his suit to Caesar.

BRUTUS He is addressed. Press near and second him.

CINNA Casca, you are the first that rears your hand. 30

CAESAR Are we all ready? What is now amiss
That Caesar and his Senate must redress?

METELLUS Most high, most mighty, and most puissant
    Caesar,
Metellus Cimber throws before thy seat
An humble heart.   [*Kneeling.*]

18 **makes to** heads for 19 **sudden** swift 19 **prevention** being forestalled 21 **turn back** i.e., return alive 22 **constant** calm 24 **change** change his expression 28 **presently prefer** immediately present 29 **addressed** ready 33 **puissant** powerful

293

35 CAESAR   I must prevent thee, Cimber.
     These couchings and these lowly courtesies
     Might fire the blood of ordinary men,
     And turn preordinance and first decree
     Into the law of children. Be not fond
40   To think that Caesar bears such rebel blood
     That will be thawed from the true quality
     With that which melteth fools—I mean sweet words,
     Low-crookèd curtsies, and base spaniel fawning.
     Thy brother by decree is banishèd.
45   If thou dost bend and pray and fawn for him,
     I spurn thee like a cur out of my way.
     Know, Caesar doth not wrong, nor without cause
     Will he be satisfied.

     METELLUS Is there no voice more worthy than my own,
50   To sound more sweetly in great Caesar's ear
     For the repealing of my banished brother?

     BRUTUS I kiss thy hand, but not in flattery, Caesar,
     Desiring thee that Publius Cimber may
     Have an immediate freedom of repeal.

     CAESAR What, Brutus?

55 CASSIUS   Pardon, Caesar; Caesar, pardon!
     As low as to thy foot doth Cassius fall
     To beg enfranchisement for Publius Cimber.

     CAESAR I could be well moved, if I were as you;
     If I could pray to move, prayers would move me;
60   But I am constant as the Northern Star,
     Of whose true-fixed and resting quality

36 **couchings** low bowings   36 **lowly courtesies** humble obeisances   38 **preordinance and first decree** customs and laws established from antiquity   39 **fond** so foolish as   40 **bears such rebel blood** has such uncontrolled emotions   41 **true quality** proper quality (i.e., firmness)   42 **With that** by those things   43 **spaniel** doglike, cringing   51 **repealing** recalling   54 **freedom of repeal** permission to be recalled from exile   57 **enfranchisement** recall, freedom   59 **pray to move** i.e., beg others to change their minds   60 **constant as the Northern Star** unchanging as the pole-star   61 **resting** changeless

There is no fellow in the firmament.
The skies are painted with unnumb'red sparks,
They are all fire and every one doth shine;
But there's but one in all doth hold his place. 65
So in the world; 'tis furnished well with men,
And men are flesh and blood, and apprehensive;
Yet in the number I do know but one
That unassailable holds on his rank,
Unshaked of motion; and that I am he, 70
Let me a little show it, even in this—
That I was constant Cimber should be banished,
And constant do remain to keep him so.

CINNA O Caesar——

CAESAR   Hence! Wilt thou lift up Olympus?

DECIUS Great Caesar——

CAESAR   Doth not Brutus bootless kneel? 75

CASCA Speak hands for me!   *They stab Caesar.*

CAESAR *Et tu, Brutè?* Then fall Caesar.   *Dies.*

CINNA Liberty! Freedom! Tyranny is dead!
    Run hence, proclaim, cry it about the streets.

CASSIUS Some to the common pulpits, and cry out 80
    "Liberty, freedom, and enfranchisement!"

BRUTUS People, and senators, be not affrighted.
    Fly not; stand still; ambition's debt is paid.

CASCA Go to the pulpit, Brutus.

DECIUS   And Cassius too.

---

62 fellow equal 63 unnumb'red innumerable 65 hold keep 67 apprehensive capable of reason 69 holds on his rank maintains his position 70 Unshaked of motion i.e., unmoved by internal or external forces 72 constant firmly determined 74 Olympus a mountain in Greece where the gods lived and held court 75 bootless in vain 77 Et tu, Brutè and you (too), Brutus 80 pulpits platforms for public speakers 83 ambition's debt is paid ambition has received what was due to it

85   BRUTUS Where's Publius?

CINNA Here, quite confounded with this mutiny.

METELLUS Stand fast together, lest some friend of
    Caesar's
Should chance——

BRUTUS Talk not of standing. Publius, good cheer;
90   There is no harm intended to your person,
    Nor to no Roman else. So tell them, Publius.

CASSIUS And leave us, Publius, lest that the people
    Rushing on us should do your age some mischief.

BRUTUS Do so; and let no man abide this deed
95   But we the doers.

Enter Trebonius.

CASSIUS Where is Antony?

TREBONIUS   Fled to his house amazed.
    Men, wives, and children stare, cry out and run,
    As it were doomsday.

BRUTUS   Fates, we will know your pleasures.
    That we shall die, we know; 'tis but the time,
100   And drawing days out, that men stand upon.

CASCA Why, he that cuts off twenty years of life
    Cuts off so many years of fearing death.

BRUTUS Grant that, and then is death a benefit.
    So are we Caesar's friends, that have abridged
105   His time of fearing death. Stoop, Romans, stoop,
    And let us bathe our hands in Caesar's blood
    Up to the elbows, and besmear our swords.
    Then walk we forth, even to the market place,

---

85 **Publius** an old senator, too infirm to flee   86 **confounded with this mutiny** overwhelmed by this uproar   89 **Talk not of standing** i.e., don't worry about making a stand, organizing resistance   94 **abide** bear the consequences of   96 **amazed** utterly confused   98 **As** as if   100 **drawing ... upon** (hope of) prolonging life, that men are concerned about   108 **the market place** the Roman Forum, center of business and public affairs

And waving our red weapons o'er our heads,
Let's all cry "Peace, freedom, and liberty!"   110

CASSIUS Stoop then, and wash. How many ages hence
Shall this our lofty scene be acted over
In states unborn and accents yet unknown!

BRUTUS How many times shall Caesar bleed in sport,
That now on Pompey's basis lies along   115
No worthier than the dust!

CASSIUS   So oft as that shall be,
So often shall the knot of us be called
The men that gave their country liberty.

DECIUS What, shall we forth?

CASSIUS   Ay, every man away.
Brutus shall lead, and we will grace his heels   120
With the most boldest and best hearts of Rome.

Enter a Servant.

BRUTUS Soft, who comes here? A friend of Antony's.

SERVANT Thus, Brutus, did my master bid me kneel;
Thus did Mark Antony bid me fall down;
And, being prostrate, thus he bade me say: 125
Brutus is noble, wise, valiant, and honest;
Caesar was mighty, bold, royal, and loving.
Say I love Brutus and I honor him;
Say I feared Caesar, honored him, and loved him.
If Brutus will vouchsafe that Antony   130
May safely come to him and be resolved
How Caesar hath deserved to lie in death,
Mark Antony shall not love Caesar dead
So well as Brutus living; but will follow
The fortunes and affairs of noble Brutus   135
Thorough the hazards of this untrod state

114 **in sport** for entertainment, i.e., as part of a play   115 **basis** pedestal of statue   115 **along** stretched out   117 **knot** closely bound group   120 **grace** do honor to   122 **Soft** wait a moment   126 **honest** honorable   127 **royal** of princely generosity   131 **be resolved** have it explained to his satisfaction 136 **Thorough** through   136 **untrod state** new and uncertain state of affairs

With all true faith. So says my master Antony.

BRUTUS Thy master is a wise and valiant Roman;
I never thought him worse.
140 Tell him, so please him come unto this place,
He shall be satisfied and, by my honor,
Depart untouched.

SERVANT   I'll fetch him presently.
                                        Exit Servant.

BRUTUS I know that we shall have him well to friend.

CASSIUS I wish we may. But yet have I a mind
145 That fears him much; and my misgiving still
Falls shrewdly to the purpose.

                        Enter Antony.

BRUTUS But here comes Antony. Welcome, Mark
Antony.

ANTONY O mighty Caesar! Dost thou lie so low?
Are all thy conquests, glories, triumphs, spoils,
150 Shrunk to this little measure? Fare thee well.
I know not, gentlemen, what you intend,
Who else must be let blood, who else is rank.
If I myself, there is no hour so fit
As Caesar's death's hour, nor no instrument
155 Of half that worth as those your swords, made rich
With the most noble blood of all this world.
I do beseech ye, if you bear me hard,
Now, whilst your purpled hands do reek and smoke,
Fulfill your pleasure. Live a thousand years,
160 I shall not find myself so apt to die;

140 so if it should 142 **presently** immediately 143 **well to friend** as a good
friend 145–46 **misgiving ... purpose** my forebodings always turn out to be
justified 152 **let blood** (1) bled, purged (common Elizabethan practice of
drawing blood to cure those swollen with disease) (2) put to death 152 **rank**
(1) swollen with disease (2) overgrown, i.e., too powerful 157 **bear me hard**
have a grudge against me 158 **purpled** (1) made scarlet (with blood) (2) made
royal (?) 158 **reek and smoke** i.e., steam (with freshly shed warm blood) 159
Live though I live 160 **apt** prepared

JULIUS CAESAR III.i.

No place will please me so, no mean of death,
As here by Caesar, and by you cut off,
The choice and master spirits of this age.

BRUTUS O Antony, beg not your death of us!
Though now we must appear bloody and cruel,   165
As by our hands and this our present act
You see we do, yet see you but our hands
And this the bleeding business they have done.
Our hearts you see not; they are pitiful;
A pity to the general wrong of Rome—   170
As fire drives out fire, so pity pity—
Hath done this deed on Caesar. For your part,
To you our swords have leaden points, Mark
   Antony:
Our arms in strength of malice, and our hearts
Of brothers' temper, do receive you in   175
With all kind love, good thoughts, and reverence.

CASSIUS Your voice shall be as strong as any man's
In the disposing of new dignities.

BRUTUS Only be patient till we have appeased
The multitude, beside themselves with fear,   180
And then we will deliver you the cause
Why I, that did love Caesar when I struck him,
Have thus proceeded.

ANTONY   I doubt not of your wisdom.
Let each man render me his bloody hand.
First, Marcus Brutus, will I shake with you;   185
Next, Caius Cassius, do I take your hand;
Now, Decius Brutus, yours; now yours, Metellus;
Yours, Cinna; and, my valiant Casca, yours;
Though last, not least in love, yours, good Trebonius.
Gentlemen all—alas, what shall I say?   190
My credit now stands on such slippery ground

161 mean manner 169 pitiful full of pity 171 pity pity pity for Rome's
subjection drove out pity for Caesar 173 leaden blunt 174-75 Our arms ...
temper our arms, strong with the might inspired by enmity, and our hearts, full
of brotherly feeling 177 voice vote 178 dignities offices 181 deliver communicate to 191 credit reputation

299

That one of two bad ways you must conceit me,
Either a coward or a flatterer.
That I did love thee, Caesar, O, 'tis true!
195   If then thy spirit look upon us now,
Shall it not grieve thee dearer than thy death
To see thy Antony making his peace,
Shaking the bloody fingers of thy foes,
Most noble, in the presence of thy corse?
200   Had I as many eyes as thou hast wounds,
Weeping as fast as they stream forth thy blood,
It would become me better than to close
In terms of friendship with thine enemies.
Pardon me, Julius! Here wast thou bayed, brave
        hart;
205   Here didst thou fall, and here thy hunters stand,
Signed in thy spoil and crimsoned in thy lethe.
O world, thou wast the forest to this hart;
And this indeed, O world, the heart of thee.
How like a deer, stroken by many princes,
210   Dost thou here lie!

CASSIUS Mark Antony——

ANTONY   Pardon me, Caius Cassius.
The enemies of Caesar shall say this;
Then, in a friend, it is cold modesty.

CASSIUS I blame you not for praising Caesar so;
215   But what compact mean you to have with us?
Will you be pricked in number of our friends,
Or shall we on, and not depend on you?

ANTONY Therefore I took your hands, but was indeed
Swayed from the point by looking down on Caesar.

192 conceit judge 196 dearer more deeply 199 corse corpse 202 close
make an agreement 204 bayed brought to bay 204 hart (1) deer (2) heart
206 Signed in thy spoil marked with the signs of your slaughter
206 lethe (dissyllabic; the river of oblivion from which the dead drank in Hades;
here, by extension, "stream of death," or "lifeblood") 209 stroken struck
down 213 modesty moderation 216 pricked in number marked down (the
modern "ticks off names"; the Roman made small holes in his wax-covered
tablets) 217 on proceed

Friends am I with you all, and love you all,   220
Upon this hope, that you shall give me reasons
Why, and wherein, Caesar was dangerous.

BRUTUS Or else were this a savage spectacle.
Our reasons are so full of good regard
That were you, Antony, the son of Caesar,   225
You should be satisfied.

ANTONY   That's all I seek;
And am moreover suitor that I may
Produce his body to the market place,
And in the pulpit, as becomes a friend,
Speak in the order of his funeral.   230

BRUTUS You shall, Mark Antony.

CASSIUS   Brutus, a word with you.
[Aside to Brutus] You know not what you do; do not
    consent
That Antony speak in his funeral.
Know you how much the people may be moved
By that which he will utter?

BRUTUS   By your pardon: 235
I will myself into the pulpit first,
And show the reason of our Caesar's death.
What Antony shall speak, I will protest
He speaks by leave and by permission,
And that we are contented Caesar shall   240
Have all true rites and lawful ceremonies.
It shall advantage more than do us wrong.

CASSIUS I know not what may fall; I like it not.

BRUTUS Mark Antony, here, take you Caesar's body.
You shall not in your funeral speech blame us,   245
But speak all good you can devise of Caesar,
And say you do't by our permission;

224 good regard sound considerations 228 Produce bring forth 230 order
course of ceremonies 238 protest declare 241 true proper 242 advantage
benefit 242 wrong harm 243 fall happen

Else shall you not have any hand at all
About his funeral. And you shall speak
250   In the same pulpit whereto I am going,
After my speech is ended.

ANTONY   Be it so;
I do desire no more.

BRUTUS Prepare the body then, and follow us.
                                                Exeunt. Manet Antony.

ANTONY O pardon me, thou bleeding piece of earth,
255   That I am meek and gentle with these butchers!
Thou art the ruins of the noblest man
That ever livèd in the tide of times.
Woe to the hand that shed this costly blood!
Over thy wounds now do I prophesy
260   (Which like dumb mouths do ope their ruby lips
To beg the voice and utterance of my tongue),
A curse shall light upon the limbs of men;
Domestic fury and fierce civil strife
Shall cumber all the parts of Italy;
265   Blood and destruction shall be so in use,
And dreadful objects so familiar,
That mothers shall but smile when they behold
Their infants quartered with the hands of war,
All pity choked with custom of fell deeds;
270   And Caesar's spirit, ranging for revenge,
With Atè by his side come hot from hell,
Shall in these confines with a monarch's voice
Cry "Havoc," and let slip the dogs of war,
That this foul deed shall smell above the earth
275   With carrion men, groaning for burial.

                        Enter Octavius' Servant.

You serve Octavius Caesar, do you not?

257 **tide of times** course (ebb and flow) of history 264 **cumber** burden,
oppress 265 **in use** customary 269 **custom of fell deeds** habituation to cruel
acts 270 **ranging** roving widely in search of prey 271 **Atè** Greek goddess of
discord and vengeance 272 **confines** boundaries, regions 273 **Cry "Havoc"**
give the signal for unrestricted slaughter and looting 273 **let slip** unleash
275 **carrion** dead and rotting

SERVANT I do, Mark Antony.

ANTONY Caesar did write for him to come to Rome.

SERVANT He did receive his letters and is coming,
And bid me say to you by word of mouth— 280
O Caesar!   [*Seeing the body.*]

ANTONY Thy heart is big; get thee apart and weep.
Passion, I see, is catching, for mine eyes,
Seeing those beads of sorrow stand in thine,
Began to water. Is thy master coming? 285

SERVANT He lies tonight within seven leagues of Rome.

ANTONY Post back with speed, and tell him what hath
    chanced.
Here is a mourning Rome, a dangerous Rome,
No Rome of safety for Octavius yet.
Hie hence and tell him so. Yet stay awhile; 290
Thou shalt not back till I have borne this corse
Into the market place; there shall I try
In my oration how the people take
The cruel issue of these bloody men;
According to the which, thou shalt discourse 295
To young Octavius of the state of things.
Lend me your hand.   *Exeunt.*

282 **big** swollen (with grief) 283 **Passion** intense emotion, grief 287 **Post** ride
(with relays of horses), hasten 287 **chanced** happened 289 **Rome** (another
play on the pronunciation "room"; cf. I.ii.156) 290 **Hie** hurry 292 **try**
test 294 **cruel issue** outcome of the cruelty

[Scene II. *The Forum.*]

Enter Brutus and goes into the pulpit, and Cassius,
with the Plebeians.

PLEBEIANS We will be satisfied! Let us be satisfied!

BRUTUS Then follow me, and give me audience, friends.
Cassius, go you into the other street
And part the numbers.
5 Those that will hear me speak, let 'em stay here;
Those that will follow Cassius, go with him;
And public reasons shall be renderèd
Of Caesar's death.

FIRST PLEBEIAN   I will hear Brutus speak.

SECOND PLEBEIAN I will hear Cassius, and compare their
reasons,
10 When severally we hear them renderèd.
[*Exit Cassius, with some of the Plebeians.*]

THIRD PLEBEIAN The noble Brutus is ascended. Silence!

BRUTUS Be patient till the last.
Romans, countrymen, and lovers, hear me for my
cause, and be silent, that you may hear. Believe me
15 for mine honor, and have respect to mine honor, that
you may believe. Censure me in your wisdom, and
awake your senses, that you may the better judge. If
there be any in this assembly, any dear friend of
Caesar's, to him I say that Brutus' love to Caesar
20 was no less than his. If then that friend demand why

III.ii.1 **will be satisfied** want a full explanation   4 **part the numbers** divide the
crowd   10 **severally** separately   12 **last** conclusion (of my speech)   13 **lovers**
dear friends   15 **respect** regard   16 **Censure** judge   17 **senses** powers of
understanding, reason

Brutus rose against Caesar, this is my answer: Not
that I love Caesar less, but that I loved Rome more.
Have you rather Caesar were living, and die all slaves,
than that Caesar were dead, to live all free men? As
Caesar loved me, I weep for him; as he was fortunate,   25
I rejoice at it; as he was valiant, I honor him; but as
he was ambitious, I slew him. There is tears, for his
love; joy, for his fortune; honor, for his valor; and
death, for his ambition. Who is here so base, that
would be a bondman? If any, speak; for him have   30
I offended. Who is here so rude, that would not be
a Roman? If any, speak; for him have I offended.
Who is here so vile, that will not love his country? If
any, speak; for him have I offended. I pause for a
reply.   35

ALL None, Brutus, none!

BRUTUS Then none have I offended. I have done no
more to Caesar than you shall do to Brutus. The
question of his death is enrolled in the Capitol; his
glory not extenuated, wherein he was worthy, nor   40
his offenses enforced, for which he suffered death.

Enter Mark Antony, with Caesar's body.

Here comes his body, mourned by Mark Antony,
who, though he had no hand in his death, shall receive
the benefit of his dying, a place in the commonwealth, as which of you shall not? With this I depart,   45
that, as I slew my best lover for the good of Rome, I
have the same dagger for myself, when it shall please
my country to need my death.

ALL Live, Brutus! Live, live!

FIRST PLEBEIAN Bring him with triumph home unto his
house   50

30 bondman slave   31 rude barbarous   38 shall do i.e., if I should become
equally tyrannical   38-39 The question ... enrolled the considerations that
made necessary his death are recorded   40 extenuated depreciated
41 enforced exaggerated   44 place i.e., as a free citizen   46 lover friend

SECOND PLEBEIAN Give him a statue with his ancestors.

THIRD PLEBEIAN Let him be Caesar.

FOURTH PLEBEIAN   Caesar's better parts
    Shall be crowned in Brutus.

FIRST PLEBEIAN We'll bring him to his house with
    shouts and clamors.

BRUTUS My countrymen——

55   SECOND PLEBEIAN   Peace! Silence! Brutus speaks.

FIRST PLEBEIAN Peace, ho!

BRUTUS Good countrymen, let me depart alone,
    And, for my sake, stay here with Antony.
    Do grace to Caesar's corpse, and grace his speech
60   Tending to Caesar's glories, which Mark Antony
    By our permission, is allowed to make.
    I do entreat you, not a man depart,
    Save I alone, till Antony have spoke.   *Exit*.

FIRST PLEBEIAN Stay, ho! And let us hear Mark Antony.

65   THIRD PLEBEIAN Let him go up into the public chair;
    We'll hear him. Noble Antony, go up.

ANTONY For Brutus' sake, I am beholding to you.

FOURTH PLEBEIAN What does he say of Brutus?

THIRD PLEBEIAN   He says, for Brutus' sake,
    He finds himself beholding to us all.

FOURTH PLEBEIAN 'Twere best he speak no harm of
70   Brutus here!

FIRST PLEBEIAN This Caesar was a tyrant.

THIRD PLEBEIAN   Nay, that's certain.
    We are blest that Rome is rid of him.

---

52 **parts** qualities   59 **Do ... speech** show respect to dead Caesar and listen
respectfully to Antony's speech   60 **Tending** relating   65 **public chair** pulpit,
rostrum   67 **beholding** beholden, indebted

SECOND PLEBEIAN Peace! Let us hear what Antony can
    say.

ANTONY You gentle Romans——

ALL   Peace, ho! Let us hear him.

ANTONY Friends, Romans, countrymen, lend me your
    ears;   75
    I come to bury Caesar, not to praise him.
    The evil that men do lives after them,
    The good is oft interrèd with their bones;
    So let it be with Caesar. The noble Brutus
    Hath told you Caesar was ambitious.   80
    If it were so, it was a grievous fault,
    And grievously hath Caesar answered it.
    Here, under leave of Brutus and the rest
    (For Brutus is an honorable man,
    So are they all, all honorable men),   85
    Come I to speak in Caesar's funeral.
    He was my friend, faithful and just to me;
    But Brutus says he was ambitious,
    And Brutus is an honorable man.
    He hath brought many captives home to Rome,   90
    Whose ransoms did the general coffers fill;
    Did this in Caesar seem ambitious?
    When that the poor have cried, Caesar hath wept;
    Ambition should be made of sterner stuff.
    Yet Brutus says he was ambitious;   95
    And Brutus is an honorable man.
    You all did see that on the Lupercal
    I thrice presented him a kingly crown,
    Which he did thrice refuse. Was this ambition?
    Yet Brutus says he was ambitious;   100
    And sure he is an honorable man.
    I speak not to disprove what Brutus spoke,
    But here I am to speak what I do know.
    You all did love him once, not without cause;
    What cause withholds you then to mourn for him?   105
    O judgment, thou art fled to brutish beasts,

82 **answered** paid the penalty for   91 **general coffers** public treasury

And men have lost their reason! Bear with me;
My heart is in the coffin there with Caesar,
And I must pause till it come back to me.

FIRST PLEBEIAN Methinks there is much reason in his
110   sayings.

SECOND PLEBEIAN If thou consider rightly of the matter,
Caesar has had great wrong.

THIRD PLEBEIAN   Has he, masters?
I fear there will a worse come in his place.

FOURTH PLEBEIAN Marked ye his words? He would not
take the crown,
115   Therefore 'tis certain he was not ambitious.

FIRST PLEBEIAN If it be found so, some will dear abide it.

SECOND PLEBEIAN Poor soul, his eyes are red as fire
with weeping.

THIRD PLEBEIAN There's not a nobler man in Rome
than Antony.

FOURTH PLEBEIAN Now mark him, he begins again to
speak.

120 ANTONY But yesterday the word of Caesar might
Have stood against the world; now lies he there,
And none so poor to do him reverence.
O masters! If I were disposed to stir
Your hearts and minds to mutiny and rage,
125   I should do Brutus wrong and Cassius wrong,
Who, you all know, are honorable men.
I will not do them wrong; I rather choose
To wrong the dead, to wrong myself and you,
Than I will wrong such honorable men.
130   But here's a parchment with the seal of Caesar;
I found it in his closet; 'tis his will.
Let but the commons hear this testament,
Which, pardon me, I do not mean to read,

116 **dear abide it** pay dearly for it   122 **so poor** to so low in rank as to
131 **closet** study (?) desk (?)   132 **commons** plebeians

And they would go and kiss dead Caesar's wounds,
And dip their napkins in his sacred blood;   135
Yea, beg a hair of him for memory,
And dying, mention it within their wills,
Bequeathing it as a rich legacy
Unto their issue.

FOURTH PLEBEIAN We'll hear the will; read it, Mark
    Antony.   140

ALL The will, the will! We will hear Caesar's will!

ANTONY Have patience, gentle friends, I must not read it.
    It is not meet you know how Caesar loved you.
    You are not wood, you are not stones, but men;
    And being men, hearing the will of Caesar,   145
    It will inflame you, it will make you mad.
    'Tis good you know not that you are his heirs;
    For if you should, O, what would come of it?

FOURTH PLEBEIAN Read the will! We'll hear it, Antony!
    You shall read us the will, Caesar's will!   150

ANTONY Will you be patient? Will you stay awhile?
    I have o'ershot myself to tell you of it.
    I fear I wrong the honorable men
    Whose daggers have stabbed Caesar; I do fear it.

FOURTH PLEBEIAN They were traitors. Honorable men!   155

ALL The will! The testament!

SECOND PLEBEIAN They were villains, murderers! The
    will! Read the will!

ANTONY You will compel me then to read the will?
    Then make a ring about the corpse of Caesar,   160
    And let me show you him that made the will.
    Shall I descend? And will you give me leave?

ALL Come down.

SECOND PLEBEIAN Descend.   [*Antony comes down.*]

135 napkins handkerchiefs 139 issue heirs 143 meet fitting 151 stay
wait 152 o'ershot myself gone further than I intended

165 THIRD PLEBEIAN You shall have leave.

FOURTH PLEBEIAN A ring! Stand round.

FIRST PLEBEIAN Stand from the hearse, stand from the
body!

SECOND PLEBEIAN Room for Antony, most noble Antony!

ANTONY Nay, press not so upon me; stand far off.

170 ALL Stand back! Room! Bear back.

ANTONY If you have tears, prepare to shed them now.
You all do know this mantle; I remember
The first time ever Caesar put it on:
'Twas on a summer's evening, in his tent,
175 That day he overcame the Nervii.
Look, in this place ran Cassius' dagger through;
See what a rent the envious Casca made;
Through this the well-belovèd Brutus stabbed,
And as he plucked his cursèd steel away,
180 Mark how the blood of Caesar followed it,
As rushing out of doors, to be resolved
If Brutus so unkindly knocked, or no;
For Brutus, as you know, was Caesar's angel.
Judge, O you gods, how dearly Caesar loved him!
185 This was the most unkindest cut of all;
For when the noble Caesar saw him stab,
Ingratitude, more strong than traitors' arms,
Quite vanquished him. Then burst his mighty heart;
And, in his mantle muffling up his face,
190 Even at the base of Pompey's statue
(Which all the while ran blood) great Caesar fell.
O, what a fall was there, my countrymen!
Then I, and you, and all of us fell down,
Whilst bloody treason flourished over us.

169 **far** farther   172 **mantle** cloak (here, the toga)   175 **Nervii** (a fierce tribe decisively conquered by Caesar in 57 B.C.)   177 **envious** spiteful   181 **As** as though   181 **to be resolved** to learn for certain   182 **unkindly** (1) cruelly (2) unnaturally   183 **angel** favorite (i.e., considered incapable of evil)   185 **most unkindest** most cruel and unnatural   190 **base** pedestal   190 **statue** (pronounced "stat-u-a")   194 **flourished** (1) swaggered (2) brandished a sword in triumph

310

O, now you weep, and I perceive you feel 195
The dint of pity; these are gracious drops.
Kind souls, what weep you when you but behold
Our Caesar's vesture wounded? Look you here,
Here is himself, marred as you see with traitors.

FIRST PLEBEIAN O piteous spectacle! 200

SECOND PLEBEIAN O noble Caesar!

THIRD PLEBEIAN O woeful day!

FOURTH PLEBEIAN O traitors, villains!

FIRST PLEBEIAN O most bloody sight!

SECOND PLEBEIAN We will be revenged. 205

[ALL] Revenge! About! Seek! Burn! Fire! Kill! Slay!
Let not a traitor live!

ANTONY Stay, countrymen.

FIRST PLEBEIAN Peace there! Hear the noble Antony.

SECOND PLEBEIAN We'll hear him, we'll follow him, we'll 210
die with him!

ANTONY Good friends, sweet friends, let me not stir
you up
To such a sudden flood of mutiny.
They that have done this deed are honorable.
What private griefs they have, alas, I know not, 215
That made them do it. They are wise and honorable,
And will, no doubt, with reasons answer you.
I come not, friends, to steal away your hearts;
I am no orator, as Brutus is;
But (as you know me all) a plain blunt man 220
That love my friend, and that they know full well
That gave me public leave to speak of him.
For I have neither writ, nor words, nor worth,

196 dint stroke 197 what why 198 vesture clothing 199 marred
mangled 199 with by 206 About let's go 215 private griefs personal
grievances 222 public leave to speak permission to speak in public

311

Action, nor utterance, nor the power of speech
225   To stir men's blood; I only speak right on.
I tell you that which you yourselves do know,
Show you sweet Caesar's wounds, poor poor dumb
    mouths,
And bid them speak for me. But were I Brutus,
And Brutus Antony, there were an Antony
230   Would ruffle up your spirits, and put a tongue
In every wound of Caesar that should move
The stones of Rome to rise and mutiny.

ALL We'll mutiny.

FIRST PLEBEIAN   We'll burn the house of Brutus.

THIRD PLEBEIAN Away, then! Come, seek the
    conspirators.

235 ANTONY Yet hear me, countrymen. Yet hear me speak.

ALL Peace, ho! Hear Antony, most noble Antony!

ANTONY Why, friends, you go to you know not what:
Wherein hath Caesar thus deserved your loves?
Alas, you know not; I must tell you then:
240   You have forgot the will I told you of.

ALL Most true, the will! Let's stay and hear the will.

ANTONY Here is the will, and under Caesar's seal.
To every Roman citizen he gives,
To every several man, seventy-five drachmas.

SECOND PLEBEIAN Most noble Caesar! We'll revenge his
245   death!

THIRD PLEBEIAN O royal Caesar!

ANTONY Hear me with patience.

ALL Peace, ho!

223–24 neither ... utterance neither a written speech, nor fluency, nor reputation, nor (an orator's) gestures, nor good delivery (perhaps writ should be
emended to wit, "intellectual cleverness") 225 right on directly, without
premeditation 230 ruffle up incite to rage 244 several individual 246 royal
nobly generous

ANTONY Moreover, he hath left you all his walks,
His private arbors, and new-planted orchards, 250
On this side Tiber; he hath left them you,
And to your heirs forever: common pleasures,
To walk abroad and recreate yourselves.
Here was a Caesar! When comes such another?

FIRST PLEBEIAN Never, never! Come, away, away! 255
We'll burn his body in the holy place,
And with the brands fire the traitors' houses.
Take up the body.

SECOND PLEBEIAN Go fetch fire.

THIRD PLEBEIAN Pluck down benches. 260

FOURTH PLEBEIAN Pluck down forms, windows, anything!   *Exeunt Plebeians [with the body].*

ANTONY Now let it work: Mischief, thou art afoot,
Take thou what course thou wilt.

                    Enter Servant.

                              How now, fellow?

SERVANT Sir, Octavius is already come to Rome. 265

ANTONY Where is he?

SERVANT He and Lepidus are at Caesar's house.

ANTONY And thither will I straight to visit him;
He comes upon a wish. Fortune is merry,
And in this mood will give us anything. 270

SERVANT I heard him say, Brutus and Cassius
Are rid like madmen through the gates of Rome.

ANTONY Belike they had some notice of the people,
How I had moved them. Bring me to Octavius.
                                        Exeunt.

249 **walks** parks 250 **orchards** gardens 252 **common pleasures** public places
of recreation 261 **forms, windows** long benches (and) shutters 263 **work**
(1) ferment (as yeast) (2) work itself out 268 **will I straight** will I (go) at once
269 **upon a wish** just as I wished 272 **Are rid** have ridden 273 **Belike**
probably 273 **notice of** news about

[Scene III. *A street*.]

Enter Cinna the Poet, and after him the Plebeians.

CINNA I dreamt tonight that I did feast with Caesar,
　　And things unluckily charge my fantasy.
　　I have no will to wander forth of doors,
　　Yet something leads me forth.

5　FIRST PLEBEIAN What is your name?

　　SECOND PLEBEIAN Whither are you going?

　　THIRD PLEBEIAN Where do you dwell?

　　FOURTH PLEBEIAN Are you a married man or a
　　　bachelor?

　　SECOND PLEBEIAN Answer every man directly.

10　FIRST PLEBEIAN Ay, and briefly.

　　FOURTH PLEBEIAN Ay, and wisely.

　　THIRD PLEBEIAN Ay, and truly, you were best.

　　CINNA What is my name? Whither am I going? Where
　　do I dwell? Am I a married man or a bachelor? Then,
15　to answer every man directly and briefly, wisely and
　　truly: wisely I say, I am a bachelor.

　　SECOND PLEBEIAN That's as much as to say, they are
　　fools that marry: you'll bear me a bang for that, I
　　fear. Proceed directly.

20　CINNA Directly, I am going to Caesar's funeral.

　　FIRST PLEBEIAN As a friend or an enemy?

III.iii.1 **tonight** last night 2 **things ... fantasy** events give ominous weight to
my imaginings 3 **forth** out 9 **directly** straightforwardly 18 **bear me a bang**
get a blow from me

CINNA As a friend.

SECOND PLEBEIAN That matter is answered directly.

FOURTH PLEBEIAN For your dwelling, briefly.

CINNA Briefly, I dwell by the Capitol.   25

THIRD PLEBEIAN Your name, sir, truly.

CINNA Truly, my name is Cinna.

FIRST PLEBEIAN Tear him to pieces! He's a conspirator.

CINNA I am Cinna the poet! I am Cinna the poet!

FOURTH PLEBEIAN Tear him for his bad verses! Tear him   30
for his bad verses!

CINNA I am not Cinna the conspirator.

FOURTH PLEBEIAN It is no matter, his name's Cinna;
pluck but his name out of his heart, and turn him
going.   35

THIRD PLEBEIAN Tear him, tear him! [*They attack him.*]
Come, brands, ho! Firebrands! To Brutus', to Cas-
sius'! Burn all! Some to Decius' house, and some to
Casca's; some to Ligarius'! Away, go!
                    Exeunt all the Plebeians [with Cinna].

34–35 **turn him going** dispatch him

ACT IV

[Scene I. *A house in Rome*.]

Enter Antony, Octavius, and Lepidus.

ANTONY These many then shall die; their names are
    pricked.

OCTAVIUS Your brother too must die; consent you,
    Lepidus?

LEPIDUS I do consent——

OCTAVIUS   Prick him down, Antony.

LEPIDUS Upon condition Publius shall not live,
5   Who is your sister's son, Mark Antony.

ANTONY He shall not live; look, with a spot I damn him.
    But, Lepidus, go you to Caesar's house;
    Fetch the will hither, and we shall determine
    How to cut off some charge in legacies.

10 LEPIDUS What, shall I find you here?

OCTAVIUS Or here or at the Capitol.   *Exit Lepidus.*

IV.i.1 **pricked** ticked off, marked on the list   6 **with a spot I damn him** with a dot (on the wax tablet) I condemn him   9 **cut off some charge** reduce expenses (by altering the amount left in bequests)   11 **Or** either

ANTONY This is a slight unmeritable man,
    Meet to be sent on errands; is it fit,
    The threefold world divided, he should stand
    One of the three to share it?

OCTAVIUS   So you thought him,   15
    And took his voice who should be pricked to die
    In our black sentence and proscription.

ANTONY Octavius, I have seen more days than you;
    And though we lay these honors on this man,
    To ease ourselves of divers sland'rous loads,   20
    He shall but bear them as the ass bears gold,
    To groan and sweat under the business,
    Either led or driven, as we point the way;
    And having brought our treasure where we will,
    Then take we down his load, and turn him off,   25
    (Like to the empty ass) to shake his ears
    And graze in commons.

OCTAVIUS   You may do your will;
    But he's a tried and valiant soldier.

ANTONY So is my horse, Octavius, and for that
    I do appoint him store of provender.   30
    It is a creature that I teach to fight,
    To wind, to stop, to run directly on,
    His corporal motion governed by my spirit.
    And, in some taste, is Lepidus but so.
    He must be taught, and trained, and bid go forth.   35
    A barren-spirited fellow; one that feeds

12 **slight unmeritable** insignificant and undeserving 13 **Meet** fit 14 **three-fold world** three areas of the Roman empire, Europe, Asia, and Africa 16 **voice** vote 17 **black sentence** sentence of death 17 **proscription** condemnation to death or exile 18 **have seen more days** am older (and more experienced) 20 **divers sland'rous loads** blame which will be laid upon us for our various actions 22 **business** hard labor 25 **turn him off** drive him away 26 **empty** unburdened 27 **in commons** on public pasture 28 **soldier** (trisyllabic) 30 **appoint him store** allot him a supply 32 **wind** turn 33 **corporal** physical 33 **spirit** mind 34 **taste** measure 34 **so** the same 36 **barren-spirited** lacking initiative or ideas of his own

On objects, arts, and imitations,
Which, out of use and staled by other men,
Begin his fashion. Do not talk of him
40 But as a property. And now, Octavius,
Listen great things. Brutus and Cassius
Are levying powers; we must straight make head.
Therefore let your alliance be combined,
Our best friends made, our means stretched;
45 And let us presently go sit in council
How covert matters may be best disclosed,
And open perils surest answerèd.

OCTAVIUS Let us do so; for we are at the stake,
And bayed about with many enemies;
50 And some that smile have in their hearts, I fear,
Millions of mischiefs.   *Exeunt.*

[Scene II. *Camp near Sardis.*]

Drum. Enter Brutus, Lucilius, [Lucius,] and the Army.
Titinius and Pindarus meet them.

BRUTUS Stand ho!

LUCILIUS Give the word, ho! and stand.

BRUTUS What now, Lucilius, is Cassius near?

---

37 **objects, arts, and imitations** curiosities, artifices, and fashions (or styles)
38 **staled** made common   39 **Begin his fashion** i.e., he is always far behind
the times 40 **property** mere tool (a thing rather than a person)
42 **powers** armed forces   42 **straight make head** immediately gather troops
44 **Our best friends made** let our closest allies be selected   44 **stretched** be
used to the fullest advantage   45 **presently** immediately   46-47 **How ...
answerèd** to decide how hidden dangers may best be discovered and open dangers
most safely encountered   48 **at the stake** (metaphor derived from Elizabethan
sport of bearbaiting) i.e., like a bear tied to a stake and set upon by many dogs
51 **mischiefs** plans to injure us

LUCILIUS He is at hand, and Pindarus is come
  To do you salutation from his master. 5

BRUTUS He greets me well. Your master, Pindarus,
  In his own change, or by ill officers,
  Hath given me some worthy cause to wish
  Things done undone; but if he be at hand,
  I shall be satisfied.

PINDARUS   I do not doubt 10
  But that my noble master will appear
  Such as he is, full of regard and honor.

BRUTUS He is not doubted. A word, Lucilius,
  How he received you; let me be resolved.

LUCILIUS With courtesy and with respect enough, 15
  But not with such familiar instances,
  Nor with such free and friendly conference
  As he hath used of old.

BRUTUS   Thou has described
  A hot friend cooling. Ever note, Lucilius,
  When love begins to sicken and decay 20
  It useth an enforcèd ceremony.
  There are no tricks in plain and simple faith;
  But hollow men, like horses hot at hand,
  Make gallant show and promise of their mettle;
                      Low march within.
  But when they should endure the bloody spur, 25
  They fall their crests, and like deceitful jades
  Sink in the trial. Comes his army on?

LUCILIUS They mean this night in Sardis to be
  quartered;

IV.ii.6 **He greets me well** he sends greetings by a very good man 7 **In his ...
officers** either from a change in his feelings toward me or through the actions
of bad subordinates 8 **worthy** substantial 10 **be satisfied** receive a satisfactory
explanation 12 **full of regard** worthy of respect 14 **resolved** fully
informed 16 **familiar instances** marks of friendship 17 **conference**
conversation 21 **enforcèd ceremony** strained formality 23 **hollow**
insincere 23 **hot at hand** overspirited at the start 24 **mettle** quality,
courage 26 **fall their crests** let fall the ridges of their necks 26 **jades** nags
27 **Sink in the trial** fail when put to the test

The greater part, the horse in general,
Are come with Cassius.

Enter Cassius and his Powers.

30 BRUTUS   Hark! He is arrived.
March gently on to meet him.

CASSIUS Stand, ho!

BRUTUS Stand, ho! Speak the word along.

[FIRST SOLDIER] Stand!

35 [SECOND SOLDIER] Stand!

[THIRD SOLDIER] Stand!

CASSIUS Most noble brother, you have done me wrong.

BRUTUS Judge me, you gods! Wrong I mine enemies?
And if not so, how should I wrong a brother?

40 CASSIUS Brutus, this sober form of yours hides wrongs;
And when you do them——

BRUTUS   Cassius, be content.
Speak your griefs softly; I do know you well.
Before the eyes of both our armies here
(Which should perceive nothing but love from us)
45 Let us not wrangle. Bid them move away;
Then in my tent, Cassius, enlarge your griefs,
And I will give you audience.

CASSIUS   Pindarus,
Bid our commanders lead their charges off
A little from this ground.

50 BRUTUS Lucilius, do you the like, and let no man
Come to our tent till we have done our conference.
Let Lucius and Titinius guard our door.
                    Exeunt. Mane[n]t Brutus and Cassius.

---

29 **the horse in general** all the cavalry   31 **gently** slowly   40 **sober form** staid
manner   41 **be content** keep calm   42 **griefs** grievances   46 **enlarge** freely
express   48 **charges** troops

[Scene III. *Brutus' tent.*]

CASSIUS That you have wronged me doth appear in this:
You have condemned and noted Lucius Pella
For taking bribes here of the Sardians;
Wherein my letters, praying on his side,
Because I knew the man, was slighted off.   5

BRUTUS You wronged yourself to write in such a case.

CASSIUS In such a time as this it is not meet
That every nice offense should bear his comment.

BRUTUS Let me tell you, Cassius, you yourself
Are much condemned to have an itching palm,   10
To sell and mart your offices for gold
To undeservers.

CASSIUS   I an itching palm?
You know that you are Brutus that speaks this,
Or, by the gods, this speech were else your last.

BRUTUS The name of Cassius honors this corruption,   15
And chastisement doth therefore hide his head.

CASSIUS Chastisement!

BRUTUS Remember March, the ides of March
remember.
Did not great Julius bleed for justice' sake?
What villain touched his body, that did stab,   20
And not for justice? What, shall one of us,
That struck the foremost man of all this world

IV.iii.2. **noted** publicly disgraced   4 **praying on his side** appealing on his
behalf   5 **was slighted off** was contemptuously disregarded ("letters" takes a
singular verb because of its singular meaning)   8 **nice ... comment** trivial fault
should receive criticism (**his**=its)   10 **condemned ... palm** accused of being
mercenary   11 **mart** traffic in   15 **honors** lends an air of respectability   21 **And not**
except

But for supporting robbers, shall we now
Contaminate our fingers with base bribes,
25   And sell the mighty space of our large honors
For so much trash as may be graspèd thus?
I had rather be a dog, and bay the moon,
Than such a Roman.

CASSIUS   Brutus, bait not me;
I'll not endure it. You forget yourself
30   To hedge me in. I am a soldier, I,
Older in practice, abler than yourself
To make conditions.

BRUTUS   Go to! You are not, Cassius.

CASSIUS I am.

BRUTUS I say you are not.

35   CASSIUS Urge me no more, I shall forget myself;
Have mind upon your health; tempt me no farther.

BRUTUS Away, slight man!

CASSIUS Is't possible?

BRUTUS   Hear me, for I will speak.
Must I give way and room to your rash choler?
40   Shall I be frighted when a madman stares?

CASSIUS O ye gods, ye gods! Must I endure all this?

23 **supporting robbers** i.e., protecting dishonest officials (a point made by Plutarch but mentioned only now by Shakespeare)   25 **mighty ... honors** vast capacity to be honorable and magnanimous (with suggestion of potentiality for making other men free, and honorable in office)   26 **trash** rubbish, i.e., money   26 **graspèd thus** (the small confined area of the closed fist contrasts with the "mighty space" gained by their honorable deeds in abolishing injustice and corruption)   27 **bay** howl at   28 **bait** harass and worry (as a bear tied to a stake is baited by dogs)   30 **hedge me in** limit my freedom of action   32 **make conditions** manage practical matters   35 **Urge** drive, bully   36 **health** safety   36 **tempt** provoke   37 **slight** insignificant   39 **give ... choler** let your hasty temper have free vent and run its course unchecked   40 **stares** glares

BRUTUS All this? Ay, more: fret till your proud heart
    break.
  Go show your slaves how choleric you are,
  And make your bondmen tremble. Must I budge?
  Must I observe you? Must I stand and crouch   45
  Under your testy humor? By the gods,
  You shall digest the venom of your spleen,
  Though it do split you; for, from this day forth,
  I'll use you for my mirth, yea, for my laughter,
  When you are waspish.

CASSIUS   Is it come to this?   50

BRUTUS You say you are a better soldier:
  Let it appear so; make your vaunting true,
  And it shall please me well. For mine own part,
  I shall be glad to learn of noble men.

CASSIUS You wrong me every way; you wrong me, Brutus; 55
  I said, an elder soldier, not a better.
  Did I say, better?

BRUTUS   If you did, I care not.

CASSIUS When Caesar lived, he durst not thus have
  moved me.

BRUTUS Peace, peace, you durst not so have tempted
  him.

CASSIUS I durst not?   60

BRUTUS No.

CASSIUS What? Durst not tempt him?

BRUTUS   For your life you durst not.

---

44 budge defer to it 45 observe wait on 45 crouch bow 46 testy humor
irritability 47 digest the venom swallow the poison 47 spleen (considered
the source of sudden passions) i.e., fiery temper 52 vaunting boasting 54
learn of (1) hear about the exploits of (2) take lessons from 58 moved
exasperated 59 tempted provoked

CASSIUS Do not presume too much upon my love;
    I may do that I shall be sorry for.

65 BRUTUS You have done that you should be sorry for.
    There is no terror, Cassius, in your threats;
    For I am armed so strong in honesty
    That they pass by me as the idle wind,
    Which I respect not. I did send to you
70 For certain sums of gold, which you denied me;
    For I can raise no money by vile means.
    By heaven, I had rather coin my heart
    And drop my blood for drachmas than to wring
    From the hard hands of peasants their vile trash
75 By any indirection. I did send
    To you for gold to pay my legions,
    Which you denied me. Was that done like Cassius?
    Should I have answered Caius Cassius so?
    When Marcus Brutus grows so covetous
80 To lock such rascal counters from his friends,
    Be ready, gods, with all your thunderbolts,
    Dash him to pieces!

CASSIUS   I denied you not.

BRUTUS You did.

CASSIUS   I did not. He was but a fool
    That brought my answer back. Brutus hath rived my
    heart.
85 A friend should bear his friend's infirmities;
    But Brutus makes mine greater than they are.

BRUTUS I do not, till you practice them on me.

CASSIUS You love me not.

BRUTUS   I do not like your faults.

CASSIUS A friendly eye could never see such faults.

67 **honesty** integrity 69 **respect** heed 75 **indirection** irregular methods
80 **rascal counters** base (and worthless) coins 84 **rived** broken

324

BRUTUS A flatterer's would not, though they do appear   90
    As huge as high Olympus.

CASSIUS Come, Antony, and young Octavius, come,
    Revenge yourselves alone on Cassius,
    For Cassius is aweary of the world:
    Hated by one he loves; braved by his brother;   95
    Checked like a bondman; all his faults observed,
    Set in a notebook, learned and conned by rote
    To cast into my teeth. O, I could weep
    My spirit from mine eyes! There is my dagger,
    And here my naked breast; within, a heart   100
    Dearer than Pluto's mine, richer than gold;
    If that thou be'st a Roman, take it forth.
    I, that denied thee gold, will give my heart.
    Strike as thou didst at Caesar; for I know,
    When thou didst hate him worst, thou lovedst him
       better   105
    Than ever thou lovedst Cassius.

BRUTUS   Sheathe your dagger.
    Be angry when you will, it shall have scope.
    Do what you will, dishonor shall be humor.
    O Cassius, you are yokèd with a lamb
    That carries anger as the flint bears fire,   110
    Who, much enforcèd, shows a hasty spark,
    And straight is cold again.

CASSIUS   Hath Cassius lived
    To be but mirth and laughter to his Brutus
    When grief and blood ill-tempered vexeth him?

BRUTUS When I spoke that, I was ill-tempered too.   115

---

93 **alone** only   95 **braved** defied   96 **Checked** rebuked   97 **conned by rote** learned by heart   98 **cast into my teeth** i.e., throw in my face   101 **Dearer than Pluto's mine** more precious than all the riches in the earth (Pluto, god of the underworld, and Plutus, god of riches, were frequently confused)   107 **shall have scope** (your anger) shall have free play   108 **dishonor shall be humor** insults shall be regarded as quirks of temperament   111 **much enforcèd** greatly provoked   112 **straight** immediately   114 **blood ill-tempered** i.e., a "black mood"

CASSIUS Do you confess so much? Give me your hand.

BRUTUS And my heart too.

CASSIUS   O Brutus!

BRUTUS   What's the matter?

CASSIUS Have not you love enough to bear with me
    When that rash humor which my mother gave me
    Makes me forgetful?

120 BRUTUS   Yes, Cassius, and from henceforth,
    When you are over-earnest with your Brutus,
    He'll think your mother chides, and leave you so.

Enter a Poet, [followed by Lucilius, Titinius, and Lucius].

POET Let me go in to see the generals;
    There is some grudge between 'em; 'tis not meet
125   They be alone.

LUCILIUS You shall not come to them.

POET Nothing but death shall stay me.

CASSIUS How now. What's the matter?

POET For shame, you generals! What do you mean?
130   Love, and be friends, as two such men should be;
    For I have seen more years, I'm sure, than ye.

CASSIUS Ha, ha! How vilely doth this cynic rhyme!

BRUTUS Get you hence, sirrah! Saucy fellow, hence!

CASSIUS Bear with him, Brutus, 'tis his fashion.

135 BRUTUS I'll know his humor when he knows his time.
    What should the wars do with these jigging fools?
    Companion, hence!

---

119 **rash humor** hasty temperament   122 **your mother** i.e., your inherited
temperament   122 **leave you so** leave it at that   124 **grudge** bad feeling
132 **cynic** rude fellow   133 **Saucy** impertinent   135 **I'll ...time** I'll accept his
eccentricity when he can judge the suitable time for it   136 **jigging** doggerel-
writing, rhyming   137 **Companion** base fellow

CASSIUS   Away, away, be gone!

Exit Poet.

BRUTUS Lucilius and Titinius, bid the commanders
Prepare to lodge their companies tonight.

CASSIUS And come yourselves, and bring Messala with
    you   140
Immediately to us.   [*Exeunt Liucilius and Titinius.*]

BRUTUS   Lucius, a bowl of wine.

[*Exit Lucius.*]

CASSIUS I did not think you could have been so angry.

BRUTUS O Cassius, I am sick of many griefs.

CASSIUS Of your philosophy you make no use,
    If you give place to accidental evils.   145

BRUTUS No man bears sorrow better. Portia is dead.

CASSIUS Ha? Portia?

BRUTUS She is dead.

CASSIUS How scaped I killing when I crossed you so?
    O insupportable and touching loss!   150
    Upon what sickness?

BRUTUS   Impatient of my absence,
    And grief that young Octavius with Mark Antony
    Have made themselves so strong—for with her death
    That tidings came—with this she fell distract,
    And (her attendants absent) swallowed fire.   155

CASSIUS And died so?

BRUTUS   Even so.

---

145 **place** way   145 **accidental evils** misfortunes brought on by chance (Brutus
seems not to be behaving as a Stoic philosopher should)   149 **crossed**
contradicted   150 **touching** wounding, grievous   151 **Upon** as a result of
151 **Impatient of** unable to endure   153-54 **for ... came** i.e., news of her death
came at the same time as news of their strength   154 **fell distract** became
distraught   155 **swallowed fire** (according to Plutarch she choked herself by
putting hot coals into her mouth)

CASSIUS   O ye immortal gods!

Enter Boy [Lucius], with wine and tapers.

BRUTUS Speak no more of her. Give me a bowl of wine.
In this I bury all unkindness, Cassius.   *Drinks.*

CASSIUS My heart is thirsty for that noble pledge.
160   Fill, Lucius, till the wine o'erswell the cup;
I cannot drink too much of Brutus' love.

                              [Drinks. Exit Lucius.]

Enter Titinius and Messala.

BRUTUS Come in, Titinius! Welcome, good Messala.
Now sit we close about this taper here,
And call in question our necessities.

CASSIUS Portia, art thou gone?

165   BRUTUS   No more, I pray you.
Messala, I have here receivèd letters
That young Octavius and Mark Antony
Come down upon us with a mighty power,
Bending their expedition toward Philippi.

170   MESSALA Myself have letters of the selfsame tenure.

BRUTUS With what addition?

MESSALA That by proscription and bills of outlawry
Octavius, Antony, and Lepidus
Have put to death an hundred senators.

175   BRUTUS Therein our letters do not well agree.
Mine speak of seventy senators that died
By their proscriptions, Cicero being one.

CASSIUS Cicero one?

MESSALA   Cicero is dead,
And by that order of proscription.
180   Had you your letters from your wife, my lord?

164 **call in question** consider 168 **power** army 169 **Bending their expedi-**
tion directing their rapid march 170 **tenure** tenor, general meaning
172 **proscription** proclamation of the death sentence 172 **bills of outlawry**
lists of those proscribed

BRUTUS No, Messala.

MESSALA Nor nothing in your letters writ of her?

BRUTUS Nothing, Messala.

MESSALA   That methinks is strange.

BRUTUS Why ask you? Hear you aught of her in yours?

MESSALA No, my lord.   185

BRUTUS Now as you are a Roman, tell me true.

MESSALA Then like a Roman bear the truth I tell,
  For certain she is dead, and by strange manner.

BRUTUS Why, farewell, Portia. We must die, Messala.
  With meditating that she must die once,   190
  I have the patience to endure it now.

MESSALA Even so great men great losses should endure.

CASSIUS I have as much of this in art as you,
  But yet my nature could not bear it so.

BRUTUS Well, to our work alive. What do you think   195
  Of marching to Philippi presently?

CASSIUS I do not think it good.

BRUTUS   Your reason?

CASSIUS   This it is:
  'Tis better that the enemy seek us;
  So shall he waste his means, weary his soldiers,
  Doing himself offense, whilst we, lying still,   200
  Are full of rest, defense, and nimbleness.

BRUTUS Good reasons must of force give place to better.
  The people 'twixt Philippi and this ground

---

190 once at some time   193 this in art i.e., this Stoicism in theory
180–94 Had ... so (some editors suggest that this was the original version of
Shakespeare's account of Portia's death and that he later deleted this and wrote in
lines 142–57, preferring to demonstrate Brutus' humanity rather than his Stoicism; the Folio printer then set up both versions by mistake. Line 158 would follow
141—as 195 would follow 179—neatly enough to make this an attractive
theory)   195 alive as men still living   196 presently immediately   200 offense
harm   202 force necessity

Do stand but in a forced affection;
205   For they have grudged us contribution.
The enemy, marching along by them,
By them shall make a fuller number up,
Come on refreshed, new-added and encouraged;
From which advantage shall we cut him off
210   If at Philippi we do face him there,
These people at our back.

CASSIUS   Hear me, good brother.

BRUTUS Under your pardon. You must note beside
That we have tried the utmost of our friends,
Our legions are brimful, our cause is ripe.
215   The enemy increaseth every day;
We, at the height, are ready to decline.
There is a tide in the affairs of men
Which, taken at the flood, leads on to fortune;
Omitted, all the voyage of their life
220   Is bound in shallows and in miseries.
On such a full sea are we now afloat,
And we must take the current when it serves,
Or lose our ventures.

CASSIUS   Then, with your will, go on;
We'll along ourselves and meet them at Philippi.

225   BRUTUS The deep of night is crept upon our talk,
And nature must obey necessity,
Which we will niggard with a little rest.
There is no more to say?

CASSIUS   No more. Good night.
Early tomorrow will we rise and hence.

Enter Lucius.

---

204 **Do ... affection** i.e., support us only under compulsion   208 **new-added**
reinforced   212 **Under your pardon** excuse me   219 **Omitted** neglected
220 **bound in** limited to   223 **ventures** shipping trade, i.e., risks   223 **with
your will** as you wish   227 **niggard with a little rest** i.e., put off with the
shortest possible sleep   229 **hence** leave this place

BRUTUS Lucius, my gown.   *Exit Lucius.*

               Farewell, good Messala.   230
  Good night, Titinius. Noble, noble Cassius,
  Good night, and good repose.

CASSIUS   O my dear brother,
  This was an ill beginning of the night.
  Never come such division 'tween our souls!
  Let it not, Brutus.

Enter Lucius, with the gown.

BRUTUS   Everything is well.   235

CASSIUS Good night, my lord.

BRUTUS   Good night, good brother.

TITINIUS, MESSALA Good night, Lord Brutus.

BRUTUS   Farewell, every one.
                         Exeunt.
  Give me the gown. Where is thy instrument?

LUCIUS Here in the tent.

BRUTUS   What, thou speak'st drowsily?
  Poor knave, I blame thee not; thou art o'erwatched.   240
  Call Claudius and some other of my men;
  I'll have them sleep on cushions in my tent.

LUCIUS Varro and Claudius!

Enter Varro and Claudius.

VARRO Calls my lord?

BRUTUS I pray you, sirs, lie in my tent and sleep.   245
  It may be I shall raise you by and by
  On business to my brother Cassius.

VARRO So please you, we will stand and watch your
    pleasure.

230 **gown** dressing gown   234 **Never come** may there never again come
238 **instrument** (probably a lute)   240 **knave** boy   240 **o'erwatched** tired out
from lack of sleep   246 **raise** rouse   248 **watch your pleasure** be on the watch
for your command

BRUTUS I will not have it so; lie down, good sirs;
250   It may be I shall otherwise bethink me.

                            [Varro and Claudius lie down.]
      Look, Lucius, here's the book I sought for so;
      I put it in the pocket of my gown.

LUCIUS I was sure your lordship did not give it me.

BRUTUS Bear with me, good boy, I am much forgetful.
255   Canst thou hold up thy heavy eyes awhile,
      And touch thy instrument a strain or two?

LUCIUS Ay, my lord, an't please you.

BRUTUS   It does, my boy.
      I trouble thee too much, but thou art willing.

LUCIUS It is my duty, sir.

260 BRUTUS I should not urge thy duty past thy might;
      I know young bloods look for a time of rest.

LUCIUS I have slept, my lord, already.

BRUTUS It was well done, and thou shalt sleep again;
      I will not hold thee long. If I do live,
265   I will be good to thee.

                     Music, and a song.

      This is a sleepy tune. O murd'rous slumber!
      Layest thou thy leaden mace upon my boy,
      That plays thee music? Gentle knave, good night;
      I will not do thee so much wrong to wake thee.
270   If thou dost nod, thou break'st thy instrument;
      I'll take it from thee; and, good boy, good night.
      Let me see, let me see; is not the leaf turned down
      Where I left reading? Here it is, I think.

               Enter the Ghost of Caesar.

250 **otherwise bethink me** change my mind   256 **touch** play on   256 **strain** tune   257 **an't** if it   261 **young bloods** youthful constitutions   266 **murd'rous** deathlike   267 **leaden** heavy (association also with death, for lead was used in coffin-making)   267 **mace** staff of office (with which a man was touched on the shoulder when arrested)

JULIUS CAESAR IV.iii.

How ill this taper burns. Ha! Who comes here?
I think it is the weakness of mine eyes 275
That shapes this monstrous apparition.
It comes upon me. Art thou anything?
Art thou some god, some angel, or some devil,
That mak'st my blood cold, and my hair to stare?
Speak to me what thou art. 280

GHOST Thy evil spirit, Brutus.

BRUTUS   Why com'st thou?

GHOST To tell thee thou shalt see me at Philippi.

BRUTUS Well; then I shall see thee again?

GHOST Ay, at Philippi.

BRUTUS Why, I will see thee at Philippi then. 285
                              [*Exit Ghost.*]
Now I have taken heart thou vanishest.
Ill spirit, I would hold more talk with thee.
Boy! Lucius! Varro! Claudius! Sirs, awake!
Claudius!

LUCIUS The strings, my lord, are false. 290

BRUTUS He thinks he still is at his instrument.
Lucius, awake!

LUCIUS My lord?

BRUTUS Didst thou dream, Lucius, that thou so criedst
out?

LUCIUS My lord, I do not know that I did cry. 295

BRUTUS Yes, that thou didst. Didst thou see anything?

LUCIUS Nothing, my lord.

BRUTUS Sleep again, Lucius. Sirrah Claudius!
[*To Varro*] Fellow thou, awake!

274 **How ... burns** (lights allegedly burned dimly or blue in the presence of a
supernatural being) 277 **upon** toward 279 **stare** stand on end 290 **false** out
of tune

333

300 VARRO My lord?

CLAUDIUS My lord?

BRUTUS Why did you so cry out, sirs, in your sleep?

BOTH Did we, my lord?

BRUTUS   Ay. Saw you anything?

VARRO No, my lord, I saw nothing.

CLAUDIUS   Nor I, my lord.

305 BRUTUS Go and commend me to my brother Cassius;
        Bid him set on his pow'rs betimes before,
        And we will follow.

BOTH   It shall be done, my lord.
                                        Exeunt.

305 **commend me** give my greetings   306 **set ... before** advance his forces
early in the morning before me

334

ACT V

[Scene I. *The plains of Philippi.*]

Enter Octavius, Antony, and their Army.

OCTAVIUS Now, Antony, our hopes are answerèd;
 You said the enemy would not come down,
 But keep the hills and upper regions.
 It proves not so; their battles are at hand;
 They mean to warn us at Philippi here,   5
 Answering before we do demand of them.

ANTONY Tut, I am in their bosoms, and I know
 Wherefore they do it. They could be content
 To visit other places, and come down
 With fearful bravery, thinking by this face   10
 To fasten in our thoughts that they have courage;
 But 'tis not so.

Enter a Messenger.

MESSENGER   Prepare you, generals,
 The enemy comes on in gallant show;
 Their bloody sign of battle is hung out,

V.i.4 battles armies 5 warn challenge 6 Answering ... demand appearing in
opposition before we force a meeting 7 I am in their bosoms I understand
their inmost thoughts 8–9 They could ... places they would prefer to be
somewhere else 10 fearful (1) frightened (2) awe-inspiring 10 bravery bra-
vado (and show of splendor) 10 face appearance 11 fasten in our thoughts
persuade us 14 bloody sign red flag

335

15   And something to be done immediately.

ANTONY Octavius, lead your battle softly on
        Upon the left hand of the even field.

OCTAVIUS Upon the right hand I; keep thou the left.

ANTONY Why do you cross me in this exigent?

20 OCTAVIUS I do not cross you; but I will do so.   *March.*

        Drum. Enter Brutus, Cassius, and their Army;
        [*Lucilius, Titinius, Messala, and others*].

BRUTUS They stand, and would have parley.

CASSIUS Stand fast, Titinius, we must out and talk.

OCTAVIUS Mark Antony, shall we give sign of battle?

ANTONY No, Caesar, we will answer on their charge.
25   Make forth; the generals would have some words.

OCTAVIUS Stir not until the signal.

BRUTUS Words before blows; is it so, countrymen?

OCTAVIUS Not that we love words better, as you do.

BRUTUS Good words are better than bad strokes,
        Octavius.

ANTONY In your bad strokes, Brutus, you give good
30   words;
        Witness the hole you made in Caesar's heart,
        Crying "Long live! Hail, Caesar!"

CASSIUS   Antony,
        The posture of your blows are yet unknown;
        But for your words, they rob the Hybla bees,
        And leave them honeyless.

35 ANTONY   Not stingless too.

---

16 **battle** softly army slowly   17 **even** level   19 **cross** oppose, contradict
19 **exigent** crisis   24 **answer on their charge** meet them when they attack
25 **Make forth** go forward   33 **posture** nature, quality   34 **Hybla** a Sicilian
town famous for its sweet honey

BRUTUS O, yes, and soundless too;
   For you have stol'n their buzzing, Antony,
   And very wisely threat before you sting.

ANTONY Villains! You did not so, when your vile daggers
   Hacked one another in the sides of Caesar.   40
   You showed your teeth like apes, and fawned like
     hounds,
   And bowed like bondmen, kissing Caesar's feet;
   Whilst damnèd Casca, like a cur, behind
   Struck Caesar on the neck. O you flatterers!

CASSIUS Flatterers! Now, Brutus, thank yourself;   45
   This tongue had not offended so today,
   If Cassius might have ruled.

OCTAVIUS Come, come, the cause. If arguing make us
    sweat,
   The proof of it will turn to redder drops.
   Look,   50
   I draw a sword against conspirators.
   When think you that the sword goes up again?
   Never, till Caesar's three and thirty wounds
   Be well avenged; or till another Caesar
   Have added slaughter to the sword of traitors.   55

BRUTUS Caesar, thou canst not die by traitors' hands,
   Unless thou bring'st them with thee.

OCTAVIUS   So I hope.
   I was not born to die on Brutus' sword.

BRUTUS O, if thou wert the noblest of thy strain,
   Young man, thou couldst not die more honorable.   60

41 **showed your teeth** grinned 47 **ruled** had his way (i.e., in urging that
Antony be slain) 48 **cause** business at hand 49 **proof** test 52 **up** into the
sheath 54 **another Caesar** i.e., Octavius himself 55 **Have added slaughter to**
has also been killed by 59 **strain** family, line of descent

CASSIUS A peevish schoolboy, worthless of such honor,
Joined with a masker and a reveler.

ANTONY Old Cassius still!

OCTAVIUS   Come, Antony; away!
Defiance, traitors, hurl we in your teeth.
65   If you dare fight today, come to the field;
If not, when you have stomachs.
                          Exit Octavius, Antony, and Army.

CASSIUS Why, now blow wind, swell billow, and swim
bark!
The storm is up, and all is on the hazard.

BRUTUS Ho, Lucilius, hark, a word with you.
                    Lucilius and Messala stand forth.

LUCILIUS   My lord?
            [*Brutus and Lucilius converse apart.*]

CASSIUS Messala.

MESSALA   What says my general?

70   CASSIUS   Messala,
This is my birthday; as this very day
Was Cassius born. Give me thy hand, Messala:
Be thou my witness that against my will
(As Pompey was) am I compelled to set
75   Upon one battle all our liberties.
You know that I held Epicurus strong,
And his opinion; now I change my mind,
And partly credit things that do presage.
Coming from Sardis, on our former ensign

---

61 **peevish** childish (Octavius was 21)   61 **worthless** unworthy   62 **masker and a reveler** i.e., the dissipated Antony, who loved participating in masques and wild parties (cf. I.ii.203–04, II.i.189, II.ii.116)   66 **stomachs** inclination, appetite   68 **on the hazard** at stake   74 **As Pompey was** (at Pharsalus where, having been persuaded to give battle against his will, he was decisively defeated and later murdered)   74 **set** stake   76 **held Epicurus strong** believed strongly in the philosophy of Epicurus (a materialist who believed that because the gods were not interested in human affairs omens were to be discounted)   78 **presage** foretell the future   79 **former** foremost

Two mighty eagles fell, and there they perched,   80
Gorging and feeding from our soldiers' hands,
Who to Philippi here consorted us.
This morning are they fled away and gone,
And in their stead do ravens, crows, and kites
Fly o'er our heads and downward look on us   85
As we were sickly prey; their shadows seem
A canopy most fatal, under which
Our army lies, ready to give up the ghost.

MESSALA Believe not so.

CASSIUS   I but believe it partly,
For I am fresh of spirit and resolved   90
To meet all perils very constantly.

BRUTUS Even so, Lucilius.

CASSIUS   Now, most noble Brutus,
The gods today stand friendly, that we may,
Lovers in peace, lead on our days to age!
But since the affairs of men rests still incertain,   95
Let's reason with the worst that may befall.
If we do lose this battle, then is this
The very last time we shall speak together.
What are you then determinèd to do?

BRUTUS Even by the rule of that philosophy   100
By which I did blame Cato for the death
Which he did give himself; I know not how,
But I do find it cowardly and vile,
For fear of what might fall, so to prevent
The time of life, arming myself with patience   105
To stay the providence of some high powers
That govern us below.

80 **fell** swooped down   82 **consorted** accompanied   84 **ravens, crows, and kites** (scavengers; traditionally, they know when a battle is pending and accompany the armies)   86 **sickly** ready for death   87 **fatal** presaging death   91 **constantly** resolutely   94 **Lovers** devoted friends   95 **rests still incertain** always stand in doubt   96 **reason ... befall** consider what must be done if the worst happens   100 **that philosophy** i.e., Stoicism   104 **fall** befall   104 **prevent** anticipate   105 **time** term, natural end   106 **stay the providence** await the ordained fate

CASSIUS   Then, if we lose this battle,
You are contented to be led in triumph
Thorough the streets of Rome?

110 BRUTUS No, Cassius, no; think not, thou noble Roman,
That ever Brutus will go bound to Rome;
He bears too great a mind. But this same day
Must end that work the ides of March begun;
And whether we shall meet again I know not.
115 Therefore our everlasting farewell take.
Forever, and forever, farewell, Cassius!
If we do meet again, why, we shall smile;
If not, why then this parting was well made.

CASSIUS Forever, and forever, farewell, Brutus!
120 If we do meet again, we'll smile indeed;
If not, 'tis true this parting was well made.

BRUTUS Why then, lead on. O, that a man might know
The end of this day's business ere it come!
But it sufficeth that the day will end,
125 And then the end is known. Come, ho! Away!
                                        Exeunt.

[Scene II. *The field of battle.*]

Alarum. Enter Brutus and Messala.

BRUTUS Ride, ride, Messala, ride, and give these bills
Unto the legions on the other side.   *Loud alarum.*
Let them set on at once; for I perceive
But cold demeanor in Octavius' wing,
5 And sudden push gives them the overthrow.
Ride, ride, Messala! Let them all come down. *Exeunt.*

108 in triumph (as a captive) in the victor's procession   V.ii.1 s.d. Alarum call
to arms (drums or trumpets)   1 bills written orders   2 side wing (commanded
by Cassius)   4 But cold demeanor marked lack of spirit in fighting   5 push
attack

340

[Scene III. *The field of battle*.]

Alarums. Enter Cassius and Titinius.

CASSIUS O, look, Titinius, look, the villains fly!
Myself have to mine own turned enemy.
This ensign here of mine was turning back;
I slew the coward, and did take it from him.

TITINIUS O Cassius, Brutus gave the word too early, 5
Who, having some advantage on Octavius,
Took it too eagerly; his soldiers fell to spoil,
Whilst we by Antony are all enclosed.

Enter Pindarus.

PINDARUS Fly further off, my lord, fly further off!
Mark Antony is in your tents, my lord. 10
Fly, therefore, noble Cassius, fly far off!

CASSIUS This hill is far enough. Look, look, Titinius!
Are those my tents where I perceive the fire?

TITINIUS They are, my lord.

CASSIUS   Titinius, if thou lovest me,
Mount thou my horse and hide thy spurs in him 15
Till he have brought thee up to yonder troops
And here again, that I may rest assured
Whether yond troops are friend or enemy.

TITINIUS I will be here again even with a thought.
Exit.

CASSIUS Go, Pindarus, get higher on that hill; 20

V.iii.1 villains i.e., cowardly soldiers of his own side 2 mine own my own
men 3 ensign standard-bearer 4 it i.e., the standard 7 spoil looting 11 far
farther 19 even with a thought as quickly as thought

My sight was ever thick. Regard Titinius,
And tell me what thou not'st about the field.

[*Exit Pindarus.*]

This day I breathèd first. Time is come round,
And where I did begin, there shall I end.

25   My life is run his compass. Sirrah, what news?

PINDARUS (*Above*) O my lord!

CASSIUS What news?

PINDARUS [*Above*] Titinius is enclosèd round about
With horsemen that make to him on the spur;

30   Yet he spurs on. Now they are almost on him.
Now, Titinius! Now some light. O, he lights too!
He's ta'en! (*Shout.*) And, hark! They shout for joy.

CASSIUS Come down; behold no more.
O, coward that I am, to live so long,

35   To see my best friend ta'en before my face!

Enter Pindarus.

Come hither, sirrah.
In Parthia did I take thee prisoner;
And then I swore thee, saving of thy life,
That whatsoever I did bid thee do,

40   Thou shouldst attempt it. Come now, keep thine oath.
Now be a freeman, and with this good sword,
That ran through Caesar's bowels, search this bosom.
Stand not to answer. Here, take thou the hilts,
And when my face is covered, as 'tis now,

45   Guide thou the sword—Caesar, thou art revenged,
Even with the sword that killed thee.   [*Dies.*]

PINDARUS So, I am free; yet would not so have been,
Durst I have done my will. O Cassius!
Far from this country Pindarus shall run,

50   Where never Roman shall take note of him.   [*Exit.*]

21 **My ... thick** I have always been nearsighted   25 **is run his compass** has
completed its circuit   26 s.d. **Above** on the upper stage   29 **make ... spur** ride
toward him at top speed   31 **light** dismount   32 **ta'en** taken, captured
38 **swore ... of** made you swear, when I spared   42 **search** penetrate   43 **Stand**
delay

Enter Titinius and Messala.

MESSALA It is but change, Titinius; for Octavius
  Is overthrown by noble Brutus' power,
  As Cassius' legions are by Antony.

TITINIUS These tidings will well comfort Cassius.

MESSALA Where did you leave him?

TITINIUS   All disconsolate,   55
  With Pindarus his bondman, on this hill.

MESSALA Is not that he that lies upon the ground?

TITINIUS He lies not like the living. O my heart!

MESSALA Is not that he?

TITINIUS   No, this was he, Messala,
  But Cassius is no more. O setting sun,   60
  As in thy red rays thou dost sink to night,
  So in his red blood Cassius' day is set.
  The sun of Rome is set. Our day is gone;
  Clouds, dews, and dangers come; our deeds are done!
  Mistrust of my success hath done this deed.   65

MESSALA Mistrust of good success hath done this deed.
  O hateful Error, Melancholy's child,
  Why dost thou show to the apt thoughts of men
  The things that are not? O Error, soon conceived,
  Thou never com'st unto a happy birth,   70
  But kill'st the mother that engend'red thee!

TITINIUS What, Pindarus! Where art thou, Pindarus?

MESSALA Seek him, Titinius, whilst I go to meet
  The noble Brutus, thrusting this report
  Into his ears. I may say "thrusting" it;   75

---

51 **change** exchange (of fortune)   64 **dews** (considered unwholesome)   65 **Mistrust of** lack of confidence in   67 **Melancholy's child** (i.e., those of despondent temperament are liable to be introspective and full of imaginary fears)   68 **apt** easily impressed   71 **mother** i.e., the melancholy person, Cassius, who conceived the error

For piercing steel and darts envenomèd
Shall be as welcome to the ears of Brutus
As tidings of this sight.

TITINIUS　　　　　　　　　Hie you, Messala,
And I will seek for Pindarus the while.

　　　　　　　　　　　　　　　　　　[*Exit Messala.*]

80　　Why didst thou send me forth, brave Cassius?
Did I not meet thy friends, and did not they
Put on my brows this wreath of victory,
And bid me give it thee? Didst thou not hear their
　　shouts?
Alas, thou hast misconstrued everything!
85　　But hold thee, take this garland on thy brow;
Thy Brutus bid me give it thee, and I
Will do his bidding. Brutus, come apace,
And see how I regarded Caius Cassius.
By your leave, gods. This is a Roman's part:
90　　Come, Cassius' sword, and find Titinius' heart. *Dies.*

Alarum. Enter Brutus, Messala, young Cato, Strato,
Volumnius, and Lucilius.

BRUTUS　Where, where, Messala, doth his body lie?

MESSALA　Lo, yonder, and Titinius mourning it.

BRUTUS　Titinius' face is upward.

CATO　　　　　　　　　　　　　He is slain.

BRUTUS　O Julius Caesar, thou art mighty yet!
95　　Thy spirit walks abroad, and turns our swords
In our own proper entrails.　　　　*Low alarums.*

CATO　　　　　　　　　　　Brave Titinius!
Look, whe'r he have not crowned dead Cassius.

BRUTUS　Are yet two Romans living such as these?
The last of all the Romans, fare thee well!

78 **Hie** hasten　80 **brave** noble　85 **hold thee** wait a moment　87 **apace**
quickly　88 **regarded** honored　89 **By your leave** with your permission (because he is ending his life before the time appointed by the gods)　89 **part** role,
duty　96 **own proper** (emphatic) very own　96 **Brave** noble　97 **whe'r** whether

It is impossible that ever Rome   100
Should breed thy fellow. Friends, I owe moe tears
To this dead man than you shall see me pay.
I shall find time, Cassius; I shall find time.
Come, therefore, and to Thasos send his body;
His funerals shall not be in our camp,   105
Lest it discomfort us. Lucilius, come,
And come, young Cato; let us to the field.
Labeo and Flavius set our battles on.
'Tis three o'clock; and, Romans, yet ere night
We shall try fortune in a second fight.   *Exeunt.*   110

[Scene IV. *The field of battle.*]

Alarum. Enter Brutus, Messala, [young] Cato,
Lucilius, and Flavius.

BRUTUS Yet, countrymen, O, yet hold up your heads!
                              [*Exit, with followers.*]
CATO What bastard doth not? Who will go with me?
I will proclaim my name about the field.
I am the son of Marcus Cato, ho!
A foe to tyrants, and my country's friend.   5
I am the son of Marcus Cato, ho!

Enter Soldiers and fight.

LUCILIUS And I am Brutus, Marcus Brutus, I;
Brutus, my country's friend; know me for Brutus!
                              [*Young Cato falls.*]

101 **fellow** equal 101 **moe** more 104 **Thasos** an island near Philippi
106 **discomfort us** dishearten our troops 108 **battles** armies V.iv.2 **What
bastard** who is such a low fellow that he 4 **son of Marcus Cato** son of Cato of
Utica, hence, brother of Brutus' wife 7 **Lucilius** (the Folio fails to provide a
speech prefix for lines 7–8, but because it is clear from Plutarch and from line 14
that Lucilius impersonates Brutus it is plausible to attribute 7–8 to Lucilius)

O young and noble Cato, art thou down?
10 Why, now thou diest as bravely as Titinius,
And mayst be honored, being Cato's son.

[FIRST] SOLDIER Yield, or thou diest.

LUCILIUS   Only I yield to die.
There is so much that thou wilt kill me straight;
Kill Brutus, and be honored in his death.

15 [FIRST] SOLDIER We must not. A noble prisoner!

Enter Antony.

SECOND SOLDIER Room, ho! Tell Antony, Brutus is ta'en.

FIRST SOLDIER I'll tell thee news. Here comes the
 general.
Brutus is ta'en, Brutus is ta'en, my lord.

ANTONY Where is he?

20 LUCILIUS Safe, Antony; Brutus is safe enough.
I dare assure thee that no enemy
Shall ever take alive the noble Brutus.
The gods defend him from so great a shame!
When you do find him, or alive or dead,
25 He will be found like Brutus, like himself.

ANTONY This is not Brutus, friend, but, I assure you,
A prize no less in worth. Keep this man safe;
Give him all kindness. I had rather have
Such men my friends than enemies. Go on,
30 And see whe'r Brutus be alive or dead,
And bring us word unto Octavius' tent
How everything is chanced.   *Exeunt.*

---

12 **Only I yield to die** I yield only to die 13 **so much** so great an inducement,
i.e., gaining great honor by killing Brutus (?), so much to be blamed for (?), a sum
of money (offered to the soldier) (?) 13 **straight** immediately 25 **like himself**
i.e., behaving in accordance with his noble nature 32 **is chanced** has turned out

[Scene V. *The field of battle*.]

Enter Brutus, Dardanius, Clitus, Strato, and Volumnius.

BRUTUS Come, poor remains of friends, rest on this
   rock.

CLITUS Statilius showed the torchlight, but, my lord,
   He came not back; he is or ta'en or slain.

BRUTUS Sit thee down, Clitus. Slaying is the word;
   It is a deed in fashion. Hark thee, Clitus.   5
                                  [Whispers.]

CLITUS What, I, my lord? No, not for all the world!

BRUTUS Peace then, no words.

CLITUS   I'll rather kill myself.

BRUTUS Hark thee, Dardanius.   *[Whispers.]*

DARDANIUS   Shall I do such a deed?

CLITUS O Dardanius!

DARDANIUS O Clitus!   10

CLITUS What ill request did Brutus make to thee?

DARDANIUS To kill him, Clitus. Look, he meditates.

CLITUS Now is that noble vessel full of grief,
   That it runs over even at his eyes.

V.v. 1 **poor remains** wretched survivors   2 **showed the torchlight** (Statilius
had volunteered to see if Cassius' camp was occupied by the enemy; he signaled on
arrival there but was obviously captured thereafter)   13 **vessel** (figurative for
"human being." Also an allusion to the small jars of tears offered to the dead)

15   BRUTUS Come hither, good Volumnius; list a word.

      VOLUMNIUS What says my lord?

      BRUTUS   Why, this, Volumnius:
          The ghost of Caesar hath appeared to me
          Two several times by night; at Sardis once,
          And this last night here in Philippi fields.
          I know my hour is come.

20   VOLUMNIUS   Not so, my lord.

      BRUTUS Nay, I am sure it is, Volumnius.
          Thou seest the world, Volumnius, how it goes;
          Our enemies have beat us to the pit.   *Low alarums*.
          It is more worthy to leap in ourselves
25   Than tarry till they push us. Good Volumnius,
          Thou know'st that we two went to school together;
          Even for that our love of old, I prithee
          Hold thou my sword-hilts whilst I run on it.

      VOLUMNIUS That's not an office for a friend, my lord.
                                              Alarum still.

30   CLITUS Fly, fly, my lord, there is no tarrying here.

      BRUTUS Farewell to you; and you; and you, Volumnius.
          Strato, thou hast been all this while asleep;
          Farewell to thee too, Strato. Countrymen,
          My heart doth joy that yet in all my life
35   I found no man but he was true to me.
          I shall have glory by this losing day
          More than Octavius and Mark Antony
          By this vile conquest shall attain unto.
          So fare you well at once, for Brutus' tongue
40   Hath almost ended his life's history.
          Night hangs upon mine eyes; my bones would rest,

---

15 **list** hear   18 **several** separate   23 **pit** (1) trap for capturing wild animals
(2) grave   29 s.d. **still** continuing   38 **vile conquest** i.e., overthrow of the
revolution against tyranny   39 **at once** without further delay

348

That have but labored to attain this hour.
Alarum. Cry within, "Fly, fly, fly!"

CLITUS Fly, my lord, fly!

BRUTUS   Hence! I will follow.
    [*Exeunt Clitus, Dardanius, and Volumnius.*]
I prithee, Strato, stay thou by thy lord,
Thou art a fellow of a good respect.   45
Thy life hath had some smatch of honor in it;
Hold then my sword, and turn away thy face,
While I do run upon it. Wilt thou, Strato?

STRATO Give me your hand first. Fare you well, my lord.

BRUTUS Farewell, good Strato—Caesar, now be still;   50
I killed not thee with half so good a will.   *Dies.*

*Alarum. Retreat. Enter Antony, Octavius, Messala,
Lucilius, and the Army.*

OCTAVIUS What man is that?

MESSALA My master's man. Strato, where is thy master?

STRATO Free from the bondage you are in, Messala;
The conquerors can but make a fire of him.   55
For Brutus only overcame himself,
And no man else hath honor by his death.

LUCILIUS So Brutus should be found. I thank thee,
    Brutus,
That thou hast proved Lucilius' saying true.

OCTAVIUS All that served Brutus, I will entertain them.   60
Fellow, wilt thou bestow thy time with me?

STRATO Ay, if Messala will prefer me to you.

OCTAVIUS Do so, good Messala.

---

42 **but ... hour** i.e., worked hard only to reach this goal of death (which brings,
for a Stoic, rest from life's trials)   45 **respect** reputation   46 **smatch** smack,
taste   53 **man** servant   56 **Brutus only overcame himself** only Brutus overcame Brutus   59 **saying** (see V.iv.21–25)   60 **entertain** take into service
61 **bestow** spend   62 **prefer** recommend

MESSALA How died my master, Strato?

65 STRATO I held the sword, and he did run on it.

MESSALA Octavius, then take him to follow thee,
That did the latest service to my master.

ANTONY This was the noblest Roman of them all.
All the conspirators save only he
70 Did that they did in envy of great Caesar;
He, only in a general honest thought
And common good to all, made one of them.
His life was gentle, and the elements
So mixed in him that Nature might stand up
75 And say to all the world, "This was a man!"

OCTAVIUS According to his virtue, let us use him
With all respect and rites of burial.
Within my tent his bones tonight shall lie,
Most like a soldier ordered honorably.
80 So call the field to rest, and let's away
To part the glories of this happy day. *Exeunt omnes.*

FINIS

67 **latest** last 71-72 **He only ... them** he, moved only by impersonal motives
directed to the good of the community, joined the conspirators 73 **gentle**
noble 73 **elements** (the four opposed elements, of which all nature was thought
to be composed, were represented in the human body by the four liquids, bile,
phlegm, blood, and choler; the dominance of one of these determined a man's
temperament—melancholic, phlegmatic, sanguine, or choleric) 74 **So mixed**
i.e., so well-balanced 76 **virtue** excellence 76 **use** treat 79 **ordered honorably** arrayed (and treated) with all honor 80 **field** army 81 **part** divide

Textual Note

THE FIRST FOLIO of 1623 provides us with the text for *Julius Caesar*; there are no early quarto editions. In setting this play for the press, the printer's compositors probably worked from the playhouse promptbook, for the Folio text contains remarkably few misprints, serious errors in punctuation, or misattribution of speeches. The stage directions, unusually numerous and detailed, also suggest a stage manager's prompt copy; stage directions like "Alarum still" and "Enter Boy with wine and tapers" are obviously closely connected with actual performance.

In the present edition, the names of characters have been normalized so that *Marullus* appears for the Folio Murellus (and Murrellus), *Casca* for Caska, *Lucilius* for Lucillius. Occasionally the Folio uses the forms "Antonio" (I.ii.3, 4, 6, 190; I.iii.37), "Claudio" (IV.iii.241, 243 s.d., 288), "Flavio," "Labio" (V.iii.108), "Octavio" (III.i.275 s.d., V.ii.4), "Varrus" (IV.iii.243, 243 s.d., 288); these are standardized, appearing as *Antonius*, *Claudius*, *Flavius*, *Labeo*, *Octavius*, and *Varro*. The present edition modernizes spelling and punctuation, corrects a few obvious misprints, translates the act divisions from Latin into English, expands the speech prefixes, and alters the lineation of a few passages. The only other substantial departures from the Folio are listed below, the present reading in bold and then the Folio's reading in roman.

I.iii.129 **In favor's** Is Fauors

II.i.40 **ides** first   213 **eighth** eight

II.ii. 19 **fought** fight   23 **did neigh** do neigh   46 **are** heare

III.i.39 **law** lane   113 **states** State   115 **lies** lye   283 **for** from

III.ii.106 **art** are

IV.iii.253 **not** it not

V.i.41 **teeth** teethes

V.iii.104 **Thasos** Tharsus

V.iv.7 **Lucilius** [F omits, and prints "Lucilius" as the prefix to line 9]

351

WILLIAM SHAKESPEARE

—

THE TRAGEDY OF ANTONY AND CLEOPATRA

Edited by Barbara Everett

[*Dramatis Personae*

MARK ANTONY
OCTAVIUS CAESAR } triumvirs
M. AEMILIUS LEPIDUS

SEXTUS POMPEIUS
DOMITIUS ENOBARBUS
VENTIDIUS
EROS
SCARUS } friends to Antony
DECRETAS
DEMETRIUS
PHILO

CANIDIUS, lieutenant general to Antony
SILIUS, an officer in Ventidius' army

MAECENAS
AGRIPPA
DOLABELLA
PROCULEIUS } friends to Caesar
THIDIAS
GALLUS

TAURUS, lieutenant general to Caesar

MENAS
MENECRATES } friends to Pompey
VARRIUS

ROMAN OFFICER under Ventidius
AN AMBASSADOR from Antony to Caesar

ALEXAS
MARDIAN
SELEUCUS } attendants on Cleopatra
DIOMEDES

A SOOTHSAYER
A CLOWN
CLEOPATRA, Queen of Egypt
OCTAVIA, sister to Caesar and wife to Antony

CHARMIAN } attendants on Cleopatra
IRAS

OFFICERS, SOLDIERS, MESSENGERS, ATTENDANTS
Scene: several parts of the Roman Empire]

354

THE TRAGEDY OF
ANTONY AND
CLEOPATRA

ACT I

Scene I. [*Alexandria. Cleopatra's palace.*]

Enter Demetrius and Philo.

PHILO Nay, but this dotage of our general's
    O'erflows the measure. Those his goodly eyes
    That o'er the files and musters of the war
    Have glowed like plated Mars, now bend, now turn
    The office and devotion of their view   5
    Upon a tawny front. His captain's heart,
    Which in the scuffles of great fights hath burst
    The buckles on his breast, reneges all temper
    And is become the bellows and the fan
    To cool a gypsy's lust.

Flourish. Enter Antony, Cleopatra, her Ladies,
the Train, with Eunuchs fanning her.

                       Look where they come: 10

A footnote is keyed to the text by line number. Text references are printed in **bold** type; the annotation follows in roman type.
I.i.4 **plated** armored   5 **office** service   6 **tawny front** dark face (with a pun on the military sense of **front**, "first line of battle")   8 **reneges all temper** gives up all self-control   10 **gypsy's** (gypsies were believed to have come from Egypt, hence "'gyptians"; they had a reputation for trickery, sorcery, and lechery)   10 s.d. **Flourish** fanfare of trumpets

Take but good note, and you shall see in him
The triple pillar of the world transformed
Into a strumpet's fool. Behold and see.

CLEOPATRA If it be love indeed, tell me how much.

ANTONY There's beggary in the love that can be
15   reckoned.

CLEOPATRA I'll set a bourn how far to be beloved.

ANTONY Then must thou needs find out new heaven,
new earth.

Enter a Messenger.

MESSENGER News, my good lord, from Rome.

ANTONY   Grates me! The sum.

CLEOPATRA Nay, hear them, Antony.
20   Fulvia perchance is angry; or who knows
If the scarce-bearded Caesar have not sent
His pow'rful mandate to you, "Do this, or this;
Take in that kingdom, and enfranchise that.
Perform't, or else we damn thee."

ANTONY   How, my love?

25 CLEOPATRA Perchance? Nay, and most like:
You must not stay here longer, your dismission
Is come from Caesar; therefore hear it, Antony.
Where's Fulvia's process? Caesar's I would say?
Both?
Call in the messengers. As I am Egypt's Queen,
30   Thou blushest, Antony, and that blood of thine
Is Caesar's homager: else so thy cheek pays shame
When shrill-tongued Fulvia scolds. The messengers!

12 **The triple pillar** i.e., one of the triumvirs who ruled the world   16 **bourn**
limit   18 **Grates me! The sum** It's irritating! Be brief   20 **Fulvia** Antony's
wife   21 **scarce-bearded Caesar** (Octavius, then twenty-three, was some twenty
years younger than Antony)   23 **Take in** occupy   23 **enfranchise** set free from
slavery   24 **How** (a common exclamation, like "What!")   26 **dismission**
dismissal   28 **process** summons (i.e., to appear in court)   31 **homager** vassal
31 **else so** or else

ANTONY Let Rome in Tiber melt, and the wide arch
  Of the ranged empire fall! Here is my space,
  Kingdoms are clay: our dungy earth alike   35
  Feeds beast as man. The nobleness of life
  Is to do thus; when such a mutual pair
  And such a twain can do't, in which I bind,
  On pain of punishment, the world to weet
  We stand up peerless.

CLEOPATRA   Excellent falsehood!   40
  Why did he marry Fulvia, and not love her?
  I'll seem the fool I am not. Antony
  Will be—himself.

ANTONY   But stirred by Cleopatra.
  Now for the love of Love and her soft hours,
  Let's not confound the time with conference harsh.   45
  There's not a minute of our lives should stretch
  Without some pleasure now. What sport tonight?

CLEOPATRA Hear the ambassadors.

ANTONY   Fie, wrangling queen!
  Whom everything becomes—to chide, to laugh,
  To weep; whose every passion fully strives   50
  To make itself, in thee, fair and admired.
  No messenger but thine; and all alone
  Tonight we'll wander through the streets and note
  The qualities of people. Come, my queen;
  Last night you did desire it. [*To Attendants*] Speak
    not to us.   55
        Exeunt [Antony and Cleopatra] with the Train.

DEMETRIUS Is Caesar with Antonius prized so slight?

PHILO Sir, sometimes, when he is not Antony,
  He comes too short of that great property
  Which still should go with Antony.

37 **thus** (perhaps they embrace, but perhaps **thus** alludes to their way of life)
39 **weet** know   43 **himself** (1) the peerless Antony (2) the fool he is   43 **stirred**
(1) angered (2) inspired, inflamed   45 **confound** waste   50 **fully** absolutely and
successfully   56 **with** by   58 **property** quality   59 **still** always

DEMETRIUS   I am full sorry
60   That he approves the common liar, who
      Thus speaks of him at Rome; but I will hope
      Of better deeds tomorrow. Rest you happy! *Exeunt*.

[Scene II. *Alexandria. Cleopatra's palace.*]

*Enter Enobarbus, Lamprius, a Soothsayer, Rannius,
Lucillius, Charmian, Iras, Mardian the Eunuch, and
Alexas.*

CHARMIAN Lord Alexas, sweet Alexas, most anything
      Alexas, almost most absolute Alexas, where's the
      soothsayer that you praised so to th' Queen? O, that
      I knew this husband, which, you say, must charge
5   his horns with garlands!

ALEXAS Soothsayer!

SOOTHSAYER Your will?

CHARMIAN Is this the man? Is't you, sir, that know
      things?

SOOTHSAYER In Nature's infinite book of secrecy
      A little I can read.

10 ALEXAS   Show him your hand.

ENOBARBUS Bring in the banquet quickly: wine enough
      Cleopatra's health to drink.

CHARMIAN Good sir, give me good fortune.

60 **approves** corroborates   I.ii.4–5 **charge his horns with garlands** be a blindly happy cuckold of a husband (**charge**=load; **horns**=symbol of a cuckold; **garlands**=bridegroom's chaplet, and sign of happy prosperity)   11 **banquet** light refreshment of fruit and wine

358

SOOTHSAYER I make not, but foresee.

CHARMIAN Pray then, foresee me one.   15

SOOTHSAYER You shall be yet far fairer than you are.

CHARMIAN He means in flesh.

IRAS No, you shall paint when you are old.

CHARMIAN Wrinkles forbid!

ALEXAS Vex not his prescience; be attentive.   20

CHARMIAN Hush!

SOOTHSAYER You shall be more beloving than beloved.

CHARMIAN I had rather heat my liver with drinking.

ALEXAS Nay, hear him.

CHARMIAN Good now, some excellent fortune! Let me   25
    be married to three kings in a forenoon and widow
    them all; let me have a child at fifty, to whom Herod
    of Jewry may do homage; find me to marry me
    with Octavius Caesar, and companion me with my
    mistress.   30

SOOTHSAYER You shall outlive the lady whom you
    serve.

CHARMIAN O excellent! I love long life better than
    figs.

SOOTHSAYER You have seen and proved a fairer former
    fortune
    Than that which is to approach.   35

CHARMIAN Then belike my children shall have no
    names. Prithee, how many boys and wenches must
    I have?

16 **fairer** more beautiful (though in the next line Charmian pretends to take it another way, "plumper") 23 **liver** (believed to be the seat of sexual desire) 27-28 **Herod of Jewry** i.e., even that blustering tyrant who slaughtered the innocents of Judea 33 **figs** (phallic allusion) 36-37 **have no names** be bastards

SOOTHSAYER If every of your wishes had a womb,
40   And fertile every wish, a million.

CHARMIAN Out, fool! I forgive thee for a witch.

ALEXAS You think none but your sheets are privy to your wishes.

CHARMIAN Nay, come, tell Iras hers.

45 ALEXAS We'll know all our fortunes.

ENOBARBUS Mine, and most of our fortunes, tonight, shall be—drunk to bed.

IRAS There's a palm presages chastity, if nothing else.

CHARMIAN E'en as the o'erflowing Nilus presageth
50   famine.

IRAS Go, you wild bedfellow, you cannot soothsay.

CHARMIAN Nay, if an oily palm be not a fruitful prognostication, I cannot scratch mine ear. Prithee, tell her but a workyday fortune.

55 SOOTHSAYER Your fortunes are alike.

IRAS But how, but how? Give me particulars.

SOOTHSAYER I have said.

IRAS Am I not an inch of fortune better than she?

CHARMIAN Well, if you were but an inch of fortune
60   better than I, where would you choose it?

IRAS Not in my husband's nose.

CHARMIAN Our worser thoughts Heavens mend! Alexas—come, his fortune, his fortune! O, let him marry a woman that cannot go, sweet Isis, I

41 **I forgive thee for a witch** (1) you have no power of prophecy, so I absolve you from the charge of being a witch (2) a sorcerer like you is allowed to be outspoken   52 **oily palm** (sign of a lascivious nature)   52–53 **fruitful prognostication** omen of fertility   54 **workyday** commonplace   61 **husband's nose** (bawdy, hence **worser thoughts** in next line)   64 **go** satisfactorily copulate (?) bear children (?)   64 **Isis** goddess of fertility and the moon

beseech thee, and let her die too, and give him a   65
worse, and let worse follow worse till the worst of
all follow him laughing to his grave, fiftyfold a
cuckold! Good Isis, hear me this prayer, though
thou deny me a matter of more weight: good Isis,
I beseech thee!   70

IRAS Amen. Dear goddess, hear that prayer of the
people! For, as it is a heartbreaking to see a handsome man loose-wived, so it is a deadly sorrow to
behold a foul knave uncuckolded. Therefore, dear
Isis, keep decorum, and fortune him accordingly!   75

CHARMIAN Amen.

ALEXAS Lo, now, if it lay in their hands to make me a
cuckold, they would make themselves whores but
they'd do't.

ENOBARBUS Hush, here comes Antony.

CHARMIAN   Not he, the Queen.   80

Enter Cleopatra.

CLEOPATRA Saw you my lord?

ENOBARBUS   No, lady.

CLEOPATRA   Was he not here?

CHARMIAN No, madam.

CLEOPATRA He was disposed to mirth; but on the sudden
A Roman thought hath struck him. Enobarbus!

ENOBARBUS Madam?   85

CLEOPATRA Seek him, and bring him hither. Where's
Alexas?

ALEXAS Here at your service. My lord approaches.

Enter Antony with a Messenger [and Attendants].

73 **loose-wived** with a faithless, lecherous wife   74 **foul** ugly   75 **keep decorum** i.e., act like a just goddess   84 **Roman thought** (1) thought of Rome (2) serious reflection

CLEOPATRA We will not look upon him. Go with us.
                    Exeunt [all but Antony, Messenger, and
                                        Attendants].

MESSENGER Fulvia thy wife first came into the field.

90 ANTONY Against my brother Lucius?

MESSENGER Ay.
But soon that war had end, and the time's state
Made friends of them, jointing their force 'gainst
    Caesar,
Whose better issue in the war, from Italy
Upon the first encounter drave them.

95 ANTONY   Well, what worst?

MESSENGER The nature of bad news infects the teller.

ANTONY When it concerns the fool or coward. On.
Things that are past are done, with me. 'Tis thus:
Who tells me true, though in his tale lie death,
I hear him as he flattered.

100 MESSENGER   Labienus—
This is stiff news—hath with his Parthian force
Extended Asia: from Euphrates
His conquering banner shook, from Syria
To Lydia and to Ionia,
Whilst——

ANTONY   Antony, thou wouldst say——

105 MESSENGER   O, my lord.

ANTONY Speak to me home, mince not the general
    tongue:
Name Cleopatra as she is called in Rome;
Rail thou in Fulvia's phrase, and taunt my faults
With such full license as both truth and malice
110 Have power to utter. O, then we bring forth weeds

94 better issue greater success 100 as as if 102 Extended seized upon
102 Euphrates (accented on first syllable) 106 Speak . . . tongue be blunt, don't
diminish what everyone is saying

When our quick winds lie still, and our ills told us
Is as our earing. Fare thee well awhile.

MESSENGER   At your noble pleasure.   *Exit Messenger.*

ANTONY   From Sicyon, ho, the news! Speak there!

FIRST ATTENDANT   The man from Sicyon—is there such
    an one?   115

SECOND ATTENDANT   He stays upon your will.

ANTONY   Let him appear.
These strong Egyptian fetters I must break
Or lose myself in dotage.

        Enter another Messenger, with a letter.

                        What are you?

MESSENGER   Fulvia thy wife is dead.

ANTONY   Where died she?

MESSENGER   In Sicyon.   120
Her length of sickness, with what else more serious
Importeth thee to know, this bears.   [*Gives a letter.*]

ANTONY   Forbear me.   [*Exit Messenger.*]
There's a great spirit gone! Thus did I desire it:
What our contempts doth often hurl from us,
We wish it ours again. The present pleasure,   125
By revolution low'ring, does become
The opposite of itself: she's good, being gone;
The hand could pluck her back that shoved her on.
I must from this enchanting queen break off:
Ten thousand harms, more than the ills I know,   130
My idleness doth hatch. Ho now, Enobarbus!

---

111 **quick winds** lively winds (that ventilate the soil)   111–12 **our ills ...
earing** i.e., when our faults are told to us, it is like plowing (that makes the ground
fertile)   116 **stays upon your will** awaits your pleasure   122 **Forbear me** leave
me   126 **By revolution low'ring** sinking in our estimation (as the wheel of time
turns and spins the present moment downward)   128 **could** would like to
129 **enchanting** spellbinding

Enter Enobarbus.

ENOBARBUS What's your pleasure, sir?

ANTONY I must with haste from hence.

ENOBARBUS Why, then we kill all our women. We see
135   how mortal an unkindness is to them. If they suffer
our departure, death's the word.

ANTONY I must be gone.

ENOBARBUS Under a compelling occasion let women
die. It were pity to cast them away for nothing,
140   though between them and a great cause they should
be esteemed nothing. Cleopatra, catching but the
least noise of this, dies instantly; I have seen her
die twenty times upon far poorer moment. I do
think there is mettle in death, which commits some
145   loving act upon her, she hath such a celerity in
dying.

ANTONY She is cunning past man's thought.

ENOBARBUS Alack, sir, no; her passions are made of
nothing but the finest part of pure love. We cannot
150   call her winds and waters sighs and tears; they are
greater storms and tempests than almanacs can report. This cannot be cunning in her; if it be, she
makes a show'r of rain as well as Jove.

ANTONY Would I had never seen her!

155   ENOBARBUS O, sir, you had then left unseen a wonderful piece of work, which not to have been blest
withal would have discredited your travel.

ANTONY Fulvia is dead.

ENOBARBUS Sir?

160   ANTONY Fulvia is dead.

ENOBARBUS Fulvia?

139 die (throughout this speech Enobarbus puns on a second meaning of die, "to
experience sexual orgasm")   143 moment cause   144 mettle strength

ANTONY AND CLEOPATRA   I.ii.

ANTONY Dead.

ENOBARBUS Why, sir, give the gods a thankful sacrifice. When it pleaseth their deities to take the wife
of a man from him, it shows to man the tailors of   165
the earth; comforting therein, that when old robes
are worn out, there are members to make new. If
there were no more women but Fulvia, then had
you indeed a cut, and the case to be lamented.
This grief is crowned with consolation: your old   170
smock brings forth a new petticoat, and indeed the
tears live in an onion that should water this sorrow.

ANTONY The business she hath broachèd in the state
Cannot endure my absence.

ENOBARBUS And the business you have broached here   175
cannot be without you; especially that of Cleopatra's, which wholly depends on your abode.

ANTONY No more light answers. Let our officers
Have notice what we purpose. I shall break
The cause of our expedience to the Queen   180
And get her leave to part. For not alone
The death of Fulvia, with more urgent touches,
Do strongly speak to us, but the letters too
Of many our contriving friends in Rome
Petition us at home. Sextus Pompeius   185
Hath given the dare to Caesar and commands
The empire of the sea. Our slippery people,
Whose love is never linked to the deserver
Till his deserts are past, begin to throw
Pompey the Great and all his dignities   190
Upon his son; who, high in name and power,

169 cut (1) severe blow (2) pudendum (the entire speech infuses bawdy meanings
[e.g., of tailors and members] into the conceit of the world as a tailor's shop,
with the gods as tailors cutting new clothes out of old, replacing old people with
new; the tailor's shop is where men make love and breed) 175-77 And the
business ... abode (bawdy again) 178 light indecent 178 our (royal
plural) 179 break tell 180 expedience (1) haste (2) expedition 182 more
urgent touches more pressing reasons 184 many our contriving friends
many who plot on my behalf 189-91 throw ... /Upon transfer ... to

365

Higher than both in blood and life, stands up
For the main soldier; whose quality, going on,
The sides o' th' world may danger. Much is breed-
  ing,
195 Which, like the courser's hair, hath yet but life
And not a serpent's poison. Say our pleasure,
To such whose places under us require,
Our quick remove from hence.

ENOBARBUS I shall do't.   [*Exeunt.*]

[Scene III. *Alexandria. Cleopatra's palace.*]

Enter Cleopatra, Charmian, Alexas, and Iras.

CLEOPATRA Where is he?

CHARMIAN   I did not see him since.

CLEOPATRA See where he is, who's with him, what he
  does:
I did not send you. If you find him sad,
Say I am dancing; if in mirth, report
5 That I am sudden sick. Quick, and return.
                                    [*Exit Alexas.*]

CHARMIAN Madam, methinks, if you did love him
  dearly,
You do not hold the method to enforce
The like from him.

CLEOPATRA   What should I do, I do not?

192 **blood and life** courage and energy   192–93 **stands ... soldier** sets himself
up as the greatest soldier in the world   193–94 **whose quality ... danger** whose
character may, if his fortunes prosper, threaten the structure of the world
195 **courser's hair** (a horse's hair placed in water was thought to turn into a
serpent)   I.iii.1 **since** recently   3 **sad** serious

CHARMIAN In each thing give him way, cross him in
    nothing.

CLEOPATRA Thou teachest like a fool: the way to lose
    him!   10

CHARMIAN Tempt him not so too far. I wish, forbear.
In time we hate that which we often fear.

Enter Antony.

But here comes Antony.

CLEOPATRA   I am sick and sullen.

ANTONY I am sorry to give breathing to my purpose—

CLEOPATRA Help me away, dear Charmian! I shall fall.   15
It cannot be thus long; the sides of nature
Will not sustain it.

ANTONY   Now, my dearest queen——

CLEOPATRA Pray you, stand farther from me.

ANTONY   What's the matter?

CLEOPATRA I know by that same eye there's some good
    news.
What, says the married woman you may go?   20
Would she had never given you leave to come!
Let her not say 'tis I that keep you here.
I have no power upon you; hers you are.

ANTONY The gods best know——

CLEOPATRA   O, never was there queen
So mightily betrayed! Yet at the first   25
I saw the treasons planted.

ANTONY   Cleopatra——

CLEOPATRA Why should I think you can be mine, and
    true

11 Tempt try 14 breathing utterance 16–17 the sides ... it the human
frame will not stand it 26 planted (like seeds, and like mines)

367

(Though you in swearing shake the thronèd gods)
Who have been false to Fulvia? Riotous madness,
30   To be entangled with those mouth-made vows
Which break themselves in swearing.

ANTONY   Most sweet queen——

CLEOPATRA Nay, pray you seek no color for your
    going,
But bid farewell, and go. When you sued staying,
Then was the time for words: no going then;
35   Eternity was in our lips and eyes,
Bliss in our brows' bent, none our parts so poor
But was a race of heaven; they are so still,
Or thou, the greatest soldier of the world,
Art turned the greatest liar.

ANTONY   How now, lady?

CLEOPATRA I would I had thy inches; thou shouldst
40   know
There were a heart in Egypt.

ANTONY   Hear me, Queen:
The strong necessity of time commands
Our services awhile; but my full heart
Remains in use with you. Our Italy
45   Shines o'er with civil swords; Sextus Pompeius
Makes his approaches to the port of Rome;
Equality of two domestic powers
Breed scrupulous faction; the hated, grown to
    strength,
Are newly grown to love; the condemned Pompey,
50   Rich in his father's honor, creeps apace

31 **Which ... swearing** which are broken the second they are uttered   32 **color** pretext   33 **sued staying** pleaded to stay   36 **brows' bent** eyebrows' arch   37 **a race of heaven** (1) of heavenly flavor (2) of heavenly origin, rooted in heaven   41 **Egypt** (here, as elsewhere, Cleopatra as well as the country)   44 **in use with you** for you to possess   45 **civil swords** swords drawn in civil war   47–48 **Equality ... faction** where the rule at home is equally divided between two, parties grow up, quarreling over tiny points   48–49 **the hated ... to love** the hated begin to be loved as they gain power

Into the hearts of such as have not thrived
Upon the present state, whose numbers threaten;
And quietness, grown sick of rest, would purge
By any desperate change. My more particular,
And that which most with you should safe my
    going,   55
Is Fulvia's death.

CLEOPATRA Though age from folly could not give me
    freedom,
It does from childishness. Can Fulvia die?

ANTONY She's dead, my queen.
Look here, and at thy sovereign leisure read   60
The garboils she awaked. At the last, best,
See when and where she died.

CLEOPATRA   O most false love!
Where be the sacred vials thou shouldst fill
With sorrowful water? Now I see, I see,
In Fulvia's death, how mine received shall be.   65

ANTONY Quarrel no more, but be prepared to know
The purposes I bear; which are, or cease,
As you shall give th' advice. By the fire
That quickens Nilus' slime, I go from hence
Thy soldier-servant, making peace or war   70
As thou affects.

CLEOPATRA   Cut my lace, Charmian, come—
But let it be: I am quickly ill, and well,
So Antony loves.

ANTONY   My precious queen, forbear,

53–54 **quietness ... change** i.e., a long peace has developed disease in the body politic, which demands to be made well by the blood-letting of war and revolution   54 **My more particular** my own more personal reason   61 **garboils** commotion   61 **best** i.e., best news of all   63 **sacred vials** (the bottles of tears supposedly placed by Romans in friends' tombs)   68–69 **By the fire ... slime** by the sun that generates life in the Nile's mud   71 **affects** choosest   71 **Cut my lace** (of her tight bodice, i.e., "Give me air")   73 **So Antony loves** (1) if Antony loves me (2) in just such a changeable way does Antony love me

And give true evidence to his love, which stands
An honorable trial.

75 CLEOPATRA   So Fulvia told me.
I prithee turn aside and weep for her;
Then bid adieu to me, and say the tears
Belong to Egypt. Good now, play one scene
Of excellent dissembling, and let it look
Like perfect honor.

80 ANTONY   You'll heat my blood: no more.

CLEOPATRA You can do better yet; but this is meetly.

ANTONY Now by my sword——

CLEOPATRA   And target. Still he mends.
But this is not the best. Look, prithee, Charmian,
How this Herculean Roman does become
The carriage of his chafe.

85 ANTONY   I'll leave you, lady.

CLEOPATRA Courteous lord, one word.
Sir, you and I must part, but that's not it:
Sir, you and I have loved, but there's not it:
That you know well. Something it is I would—
90 O, my oblivion is a very Antony,
And I am all forgotten.

ANTONY   But that your royalty
Holds idleness your subject, I should take you
For idleness itself.

CLEOPATRA   'Tis sweating labor
To bear such idleness so near the heart
95 As Cleopatra this. But, sir, forgive me,
Since my becomings kill me when they do not

74 **stands** sustains 81 **meetly** suitable 82 **target** small shield 84–85 **How this … his chafe** how gracefully this descendant of Hercules acts out his rage 90–91 **my oblivion … forgotten** (1) my forgetful memory is like Antony and has deserted me (2) my forgetfulness even, like my memory, is consumed by the image of Antony, and my mind is empty of all else 91–92 **But that … subject** if you were not queen over trifling 93–94 **labor/To bear** (pun on childbirth) 96 **becomings** graces

Eye well to you. Your honor calls you hence;
Therefore be deaf to my unpitied folly,
And all the gods go with you. Upon your sword
Sit laurel victory, and smooth success   100
Be strewed before your feet!

ANTONY   Let us go. Come:
Our separation so abides and flies
That thou residing here goes yet with me,
And I hence fleeting here remain with thee.
Away!   *Exeunt.*   105

[Scene IV. *Rome. Caesar's house.*]

Enter Octavius [Caesar], reading a letter,
Lepidus, and their Train.

CAESAR You may see, Lepidus, and henceforth know
It is not Caesar's natural vice to hate
Our great competitor. From Alexandria
This is the news: he fishes, drinks, and wastes
The lamps of night in revel; is not more manlike   5
Than Cleopatra, nor the queen of Ptolemy
More womanly than he; hardly gave audience, or
Vouchsafed to think he had partners. You shall
    find there
A man who is th' abstract of all faults
That all men follow.

LEPIDUS   I must not think there are   10
Evils enow to darken all his goodness;
His faults, in him, seem as the spots of heaven,
More fiery by night's blackness, hereditary

I.iv.3 **competitor** partner 6 **queen of Ptolemy** (Cleopatra had nominally
married her brother Ptolemy, who was only a child, at the command of Julius
Caesar) 9–10 **abstract ... follow** symbol of universal weakness 11 **enow**
enough

371

Rather than purchased, what he cannot change
15   Than what he chooses.

CAESAR You are too indulgent. Let's grant it is not
        Amiss to tumble on the bed of Ptolemy,
        To give a kingdom for a mirth, to sit
        And keep the turn of tippling with a slave,
20   To reel the streets at noon, and stand the buffet
        With knaves that smells of sweat. Say this becomes
            him
        (As his composure must be rare indeed
        Whom these things cannot blemish); yet must
            Antony
        No way excuse his foils when we do bear
25   So great weight in his lightness. If he filled
        His vacancy with his voluptuousness,
        Full surfeits and the dryness of his bones
        Call on him for't. But to confound such time
        That drums him from his sport and speaks as loud
30   As his own state and ours, 'tis to be chid
        As we rate boys who, being mature in knowledge,
        Pawn their experience to their present pleasure
        And so rebel to judgment.

                    Enter a Messenger.

LEPIDUS   Here's more news.

MESSENGER Thy biddings have been done, and every
            hour,
35   Most noble Caesar, shalt thou have report
        How 'tis abroad. Pompey is strong at sea,
        And it appears he is beloved of those
        That only have feared Caesar: to the ports

14 purchased acquired 19 keep the turn of tippling exchange toasts
22 composure character 24 foils stains 24–25 when we ... lightness when
his triviality throws such a burden on us 26 vacancy leisure 27–28 Full ...
for't let him pay the price in sickness and syphilis 28 confound waste
30–33 'tis to be ... judgment deserves the considered rebuke we give to boys
who, though old enough to know better, give up all the wisdom they have learned
in exchange for a moment's pleasure

The discontents repair, and men's reports
Give him much wronged.

CAESAR   I should have known no less. 40
It hath been taught us from the primal state
That he which is was wished until he were;
And the ebbed man, ne'er loved till ne'er worth
  love,
Comes deared by being lacked. This common
  body,
Like to a vagabond flag upon the stream,   45
Goes to and back, lackeying the varying tide,
To rot itself with motion.

MESSENGER   Caesar, I bring thee word
Menecrates and Menas, famous pirates,
Makes the sea serve them, which they ear and
  wound
With keels of every kind. Many hot inroads   50
They make in Italy; the borders maritime
Lack blood to think on't, and flush youth revolt.
No vessel can peep forth but 'tis as soon
Taken as seen; for Pompey's name strikes more
Than could his war resisted.

CAESAR   Antony,   55
Leave thy lascivious wassails. When thou once
Was beaten from Modena, where thou slew'st
Hirtius and Pansa, consuls, at thy heel
Did famine follow, whom thou fought'st against
(Though daintily brought up) with patience more   60
Than savages could suffer. Thou didst drink
The stale of horses and the gilded puddle
Which beasts would cough at. Thy palate then did
  deign

39 **discontents** malcontents 40 **Give him** say he is 41 **from the primal
state** since government began 42 **That he ... were** that a man in power had
supporters until he gained power 44 **common body** populace 45 **vagabond
flag** aimlessly drifting iris 49 **ear** plow 52 **flush** vigorous, lusty 56 **wassails**
revelry 57 **Modena** (accented on second syllable) 61 **suffer** summon up
62 **stale** urine 62 **gilded** i.e., yellow with scum 63 **deign** not disdain

The roughest berry on the rudest hedge.
65   Yea, like the stag when snow the pasture sheets,
The barks of trees thou browsed. On the Alps
It is reported thou didst eat strange flesh,
Which some did die to look on. And all this
(It wounds thine honor that I speak it now)
70   Was borne so like a soldier that thy cheek
So much as lanked not.

LEPIDUS   'Tis pity of him.

CAESAR Let his shames quickly
Drive him to Rome. 'Tis time we twain
Did show ourselves i' th' field; and to that end
75   Assemble we immediate council. Pompey
Thrives in our idleness.

LEPIDUS   Tomorrow, Caesar,
I shall be furnished to inform you rightly
Both what by sea and land I can be able
To front this present time.

CAESAR   Till which encounter,
80   It is my business too. Farewell.

LEPIDUS Farewell, my lord. What you shall know
meantime
Of stirs abroad, I shall beseech you, sir,
To let me be partaker.

CAESAR   Doubt not, sir;
I knew it for my bond   *Exeunt.*

---

71 **lanked** thinned   78 **I can be able** my powers can be   79 **front** confront
84 **bond** duty

[Scene V. *Alexandria. Cleopatra's palace*.]

Enter Cleopatra, Charmian, Iras, and Mardian.

CLEOPATRA Charmian!

CHARMIAN Madam?

CLEOPATRA [*Yawning*] Ha, ha.
  Give me to drink mandragora.

CHARMIAN   Why, madam?

CLEOPATRA That I might sleep out this great gap of time   5
  My Antony is away.

CHARMIAN   You think of him too much.

CLEOPATRA O, 'tis treason!

CHARMIAN   Madam, I trust, not so.

CLEOPATRA Thou, eunuch Mardian!

MARDIAN   What's your Highness' pleasure?

CLEOPATRA Not now to hear thee sing. I take no
  pleasure
  In aught an eunuch has: 'tis well for thee   10
  That, being unseminared, thy freer thoughts
  May not fly forth of Egypt. Hast thou affections?

MARDIAN Yes, gracious madam.

CLEOPATRA Indeed?

MARDIAN Not in deed, madam; for I can do nothing   15
  But what indeed is honest to be done:

I.v.4 **mandragora** mandrake (a strong narcotic) 11 **unseminared** unsexed
12 **affections** passions 16 **honest** chaste

Yet have I fierce affections, and think
What Venus did with Mars.

CLEOPATRA   O, Charmian,
Where think'st thou he is now? Stands he, or sits he?
20 Or does he walk? Or is he on his horse?
O happy horse, to bear the weight of Antony!
Do bravely, horse, for wot'st thou whom thou
          mov'st?
The demi-Atlas of this earth, the arm
And burgonet of men. He's speaking now,
25 Or murmuring, "Where's my serpent of old Nile?"
(For so he calls me.) Now I feed myself
With most delicious poison. Think on me,
That am with Phoebus' amorous pinches black
And wrinkled deep in time. Broad-fronted Caesar,
30 When thou wast here above the ground, I was
A morsel for a monarch; and great Pompey
Would stand and make his eyes grow in my brow;
There would he anchor his aspect, and die
With looking on his life.

Enter Alexas from Antony.

ALEXAS   Sovereign of Egypt, hail!

35 CLEOPATRA How much unlike art thou Mark Antony!
Yet, coming from him, that great med'cine hath
With his tinct gilded thee.
How goes it with my brave Mark Antony?

ALEXAS Last thing he did, dear Queen,
40 He kissed—the last of many doubled kisses—
This orient pearl. His speech sticks in my heart.

18 **Venus ... Mars** (Venus, goddess of love, and Mars, god of war, were
lovers) 22 **wot'st** knowest 23 **demi-Atlas** (the Titan Atlas supported the
heavens on his shoulders) 24 **burgonet** visored helmet 28 **Phoebus'** the
sun's 29 **Broad-fronted Caesar** wide-browed Caesar (i.e., Julius Caesar, whose
mistress she had been in youth) 31 **great Pompey** Cneius Pompeius (son of
Pompey the Great) 33 **aspect** gaze (accented on second syllable) 36–37 **that
great med'cine ... thee** (alchemists long tried to make or discover the "philosopher's stone" or *elixir vitae*—known as the "great medicine" and the "tincture"—
which had the property of turning base metals to gold, and of restoring youth)
41 **orient** eastern, bright

CLEOPATRA Mine ear must pluck it thence.

ALEXAS   "Good friend," quoth he,
"Say the firm Roman to great Egypt sends
This treasure of an oyster; at whose foot,
To mend the petty present, I will piece   45
Her opulent throne with kingdoms. All the East
(Say thou) shall call her mistress." So he nodded,
And soberly did mount an arm-gaunt steed,
Who neighed so high that what I would have spoke
Was beastly dumbed by him.

CLEOPATRA   What was he, sad or merry? 50

ALEXAS Like to the time o' th' year between the extremes
Of hot and cold, he was nor sad nor merry.

CLEOPATRA O well-divided disposition! Note him,
Note him, good Charmian, 'tis the man; but note
   him.
He was not sad, for he would shine on those   55
That make their looks by his; he was not merry,
Which seemed to tell them his remembrance lay
In Egypt with his joy; but between both.
O heavenly mingle! Be'st thou sad or merry,
The violence of either thee becomes,   60
So does it no man else.—Met'st thou my posts?

ALEXAS Ay, madam, twenty several messengers.
Why do you send so thick?

CLEOPATRA   Who's born that day
When I forget to send to Antony
Shall die a beggar. Ink and paper, Charmian.   65
Welcome, my good Alexas. Did I, Charmian,
Ever love Caesar so?

CHARMIAN   O, that brave Caesar!

43 **firm** constant 45 **piece** add to 48 **arm-gaunt** battle-worn (?) battle-hungry (?) 50 **beastly dumbed** silenced by a beast 53 **disposition** temperament 54 **'tis the man** that's exactly what he is like 61 **posts** messengers 62 **several** separate 67 **brave** splendid, fine

CLEOPATRA Be choked with such another emphasis!
Say "the brave Antony."

CHARMIAN   The valiant Caesar!

70 CLEOPATRA By Isis, I will give thee bloody teeth
If thou with Caesar paragon again
My man of men.

CHARMIAN   By your most gracious pardon,
I sing but after you.

CLEOPATRA   My salad days,
When I was green in judgment, cold in blood,
75 To say as I said then. But come, away,
Get me ink and paper.
He shall have every day a several greeting,
Or I'll unpeople Egypt   *Exeunt.*

---

68 **emphasis** forceful statement   71 **paragon** compare   74 **green** young, silly

[ACT II

Scene I. *Messina. Pompey's house*.]

Enter Pompey, Menecrates, and Menas,
in war-like manner.

POMPEY If the great gods be just, they shall assist
    The deeds of justest men.

MENECRATES   Know, worthy Pompey,
    That what they do delay, they not deny.

POMPEY Whiles we are suitors to their throne, decays
    The thing we sue for.

MENECRATES   We, ignorant of ourselves   5
    Beg often our own harms, which the wise pow'rs
    Deny us for our good; so find we profit
    By losing of our prayers.

POMPEY   I shall do well:
    The people love me, and the sea is mine;
    My powers are crescent, and my auguring hope   10

II.i.1 **shall** surely must   3 **what they … deny** i.e., delay in performing does not
necessarily imply a refusal   5 **sue** beg   10 **crescent** growing (i.e., waxing like the
moon—hence the following image)   10 **auguring** prophesying

Says it will come to th' full. Mark Antony
In Egypt sits at dinner, and will make
No wars without doors. Caesar gets money where
He loses hearts. Lepidus flatters both,
15 Of both is flattered, but he neither loves,
Nor either cares for him.

MENAS   Caesar and Lepidus
Are in the field; a mighty strength they carry.

POMPEY Where have you this? 'Tis false.

MENAS   From Silvius, sir.

POMPEY He dreams: I know they are in Rome to-
gether,
20 Looking for Antony. But all the charms of love,
Salt Cleopatra, soften thy waned lip!
Let witchcraft join with beauty, lust with both!
Tie up the libertine in a field of feasts,
Keep his brain fuming. Epicurean cooks
25 Sharpen with cloyless sauce his appetite,
That sleep and feeding may prorogue his honor
Even till a Lethe'd dullness——

Enter Varrius.

                              How now, Varrius?

VARRIUS This is most certain, that I shall deliver:
Mark Antony is every hour in Rome
30 Expected. Since he went from Egypt 'tis
A space for farther travel.

POMPEY   I could have given less matter
A better ear. Menas, I did not think
This amorous surfeiter would have donned his helm
For such a petty war. His soldiership

13 **without doors** out-of-doors (contrasted with the indoor "wars" of love)
17 **in the field** ready for battle   20 **charms** spells   21 **Salt** lustful   21 **waned**
pale and thin (like the old moon)   26 **prorogue** suspend   27 **Lethe'd** oblivious
(from Lethe, a river in Hades; those who drank of the water forgot all)   30–31 **'tis**
... **travel** there has been time for an even longer journey

Is twice the other twain; but let us rear   35
The higher our opinion, that our stirring
Can from the lap of Egypt's widow pluck
The ne'er-lust-wearied Antony.

MENAS   I cannot hope
Caesar and Antony shall well greet together;
His wife that's dead did trespasses to Caesar;   40
His brother warred upon him—although I think
Not moved by Antony.

POMPEY   I know not, Menas,
How lesser enmities may give way to greater.
Were't not that we stand up against them all,
'Twere pregnant they should square between them-
    selves,
For they have entertainèd cause enough   45
To draw their swords; but how the fear of us
May cement their divisions and bind up
The petty difference, we yet not know.
Be't as our gods will have't! It only stands   ·   50
Our lives upon, to use our strongest hands.
Come, Menas.   *Exeunt*.

[Scene II. *Rome. Lepidus' house.*]

Enter Enobarbus and Lepidus.

LEPIDUS Good Enobarbus, 'tis a worthy deed,
And shall become you well, to entreat your captain
To soft and gentle speech.

ENOBARBUS   I shall entreat him

35–36 let us ... opinion let us think all the better of ourselves   38 hope
believe   39 well greet meet amiably   42 moved encouraged   44–45 Were't
not ... themselves had we not challenged them (and thus united them) they
would probably have quarreled among themselves   48 cement (accented on first
syllable)   50–51 It only ... upon only, it is a matter of life and death to us all

To answer like himself: if Caesar move him,
5   Let Antony look over Caesar's head
And speak as loud as Mars. By Jupiter,
Were I the wearer of Antonio's beard,
I would not shave't today!

LEPIDUS   'Tis not a time
For private stomaching.

ENOBARBUS   Every time
10   Serves for the matter that is then born in't.

LEPIDUS But small to greater matters must give way.

ENOBARBUS Not if the small come first.

LEPIDUS   Your speech is passion;
But pray you stir no embers up. Here comes
The noble Antony.

Enter Antony and Ventidius [in conversation].

ENOBARBUS   And yonder, Caesar.

Enter [from the other side] Caesar, Maecenas,
and Agrippa [in conversation].

15   ANTONY If we compose well here, to Parthia.
Hark, Ventidius.

CAESAR   I do not know,
Maecenas; ask Agrippa.

LEPIDUS   Noble friends,
That which combined us was most great, and let not
A leaner action rend us. What's amiss,
20   May it be gently heard. When we debate
Our trivial difference loud, we do commit
Murder in healing wounds. Then, noble partners,
The rather for I earnestly beseech,

II.ii.4 **move** irritate   8 **I would not shave't today** (1) I would not do him the courtesy of clean-shaving (2) I would not remove the temptation of plucking it (an incitement to fight)   9 **private stomaching** personal resentment   15 **compose** come to an agreement

Touch you the sourest points with sweetest terms,
Nor curstness grow to th' matter.

ANTONY   'Tis spoken well.   25
Were we before our armies, and to fight,
I should do thus.   *Flourish.*

CAESAR Welcome to Rome.

ANTONY Thank you.

CAESAR Sit.   30

ANTONY Sit, sir.

CAESAR Nay then.   [*They sit.*]

ANTONY I learn you take things ill which are not so,
Or being, concern you not.

CAESAR   I must be laughed at
If, or for nothing or a little, I   35
Should say myself offended, and with you
Chiefly i' th' world; more laughed at that I should
Once name you derogately, when to sound your name
It not concerned me.

ANTONY   My being in Egypt, Caesar,
What was't to you?   40

CAESAR No more than my residing here at Rome
Might be to you in Egypt: yet if you there
Did practice on my state, your being in Egypt
Might be my question.

ANTONY   How intend you? Practiced?

CAESAR You may be pleased to catch at mine intent   45
By what did here befall me. Your wife and brother

---

25 **Nor ... matter** and do not let ill temper be added to the problem at hand
27 **thus** (perhaps Antony embraces Caesar, but perhaps he means his words would
be temperate in any circumstance)   35 **or ... or** either ... or   38 **derogately**
disparagingly   43 **practice on my state** plot against my rule

Made wars upon me, and their contestation
Was theme for you; you were the word of war.

ANTONY You do mistake your business: my brother never

50 Did urge me in his act. I did inquire it
And have my learning from some true reports
That drew their swords with you. Did he not rather
Discredit my authority with yours,
And make the wars alike against my stomach,

55 Having alike your cause? Of this, my letters
Before did satisfy you. If you'll patch a quarrel,
As matter whole you have to make it with,
It must not be with this.

CAESAR   You praise yourself
By laying defects of judgment to me, but
You patched up your excuses.

60 ANTONY   Not so, not so:
I know you could not lack, I am certain on't,
Very necessity of this thought, that I,
Your partner in the cause 'gainst which he fought,
Could not with graceful eyes attend those wars

65 Which fronted mine own peace. As for my wife,
I would you had her spirit in such another;
The third o' th' world is yours, which with a snaffle
You may pace easy, but not such a wife.

ENOBARBUS Would we had all such wives, that the men

70 might go to wars with the women.

ANTONY So much uncurbable, her garboils, Caesar,
Made out of her impatience—which not wanted
Shrewdness of policy too—I grieving grant

---

48 **Was theme for you** had you as root cause (?) provided you with a
pretext (?)   48 **you were the word of war** the war was about you   50 **Did urge
me** made use of my name   51 **reports** reporters   54 **stomach** desire   56–57 **If
you'll ... with** if you want to fabricate a quarrel out of odds and ends, though in
fact you have more substantial materials for one   64 **with graceful eyes attend**
look favorably on   65 **fronted** attacked   66 **I would ... another** I wish you
were married to just such a wife   68 **pace** train (used of horses)

384

Did you too much disquiet: for that you must
But say, I could not help it.

CAESAR   I wrote to you;   75
When rioting in Alexandria you
Did pocket up my letters, and with taunts
Did gibe my missive out of audience.

ANTONY   Sir,
He fell upon me, ere admitted, then:
Three kings I had newly feasted, and did want   80
Of what I was i' th' morning; but next day
I told him of myself, which was as much
As to have asked him pardon. Let this fellow
Be nothing of our strife: if we contend,
Out of our question wipe him.

CAESAR   You have broken   85
The article of your oath, which you shall never
Have tongue to charge me with.

LEPIDUS   Soft, Caesar!

ANTONY   No,
Lepidus; let him speak.
The honor is sacred which he talks on now,
Supposing that I lacked it. But on, Caesar,   90
The article of my oath——

CAESAR To lend me arms and aid when I required
    them,
The which you both denied.

ANTONY   Neglected rather:
And then when poisonèd hours had bound me up
From mine own knowledge. As nearly as I may,   95
I'll play the penitent to you: but mine honesty
Shall not make poor my greatness, nor my power
Work without it. Truth is, that Fulvia,
To have me out of Egypt, made wars here,
For which myself, the ignorant motive, do   100

75 But only   78 missive messenger   82 myself my condition   84 Be nothing
of have no place in   86 article precise terms   87 Soft be careful   98 it honesty (?)

So far ask pardon as befits mine honor
To stoop in such a case.

LEPIDUS   'Tis noble spoken.

MAECENAS If it might please you, to enforce no further
The griefs between ye: to forget them quite
105 Were to remember that the present need
Speaks to atone you.

LEPIDUS   Worthily spoken, Maecenas.

ENOBARBUS Or, if you borrow one another's love for
the instant, you may, when you hear no more words
of Pompey, return it again: you shall have time to
110 wrangle in when you have nothing else to do.

ANTONY Thou art a soldier only; speak no more.

ENOBARBUS That truth should be silent I had almost
forgot.

ANTONY You wrong this presence; therefore speak no
more.

115 ENOBARBUS Go to, then; your considerate stone.

CAESAR I do not much dislike the matter, but
The manner of his speech; for't cannot be
We shall remain in friendship, our conditions
So diff'ring in their acts. Yet if I knew
120 What hoop should hold us stanch, from edge to edge
O' th' world I would pursue it.

AGRIPPA   Give me leave, Caesar.

CAESAR Speak, Agrippa.

AGRIPPA Thou hast a sister by the mother's side,
Admired Octavia: great Mark Antony
Is now a widower.

104 **griefs** grievances 106 **Speaks to atone you** demands your
reconciliation 114 **presence** dignified company 115 **your considerate stone** I
will be silent as stone about what I am thinking 118 **conditions**
temperaments 123 **by the mother's side** i.e., half sister (though actually
Octavia was a full sister of Octavius)

CAESAR   Say not so, Agrippa: 125
  If Cleopatra heard you, your reproof
  Were well deserved of rashness.

ANTONY I am not married, Caesar: let me hear
  Agrippa further speak.

AGRIPPA To hold you in perpetual amity,   130
  To make you brothers, and to knit your hearts
  With an unslipping knot, take Antony
  Octavia to his wife; whose beauty claims
  No worse a husband than the best of men;
  Whose virtue and whose general graces speak   135
  That which none else can utter. By this marriage
  All little jealousies, which now seem great,
  And all great fears, which now import their
    dangers,
  Would then be nothing: truths would be tales,
  Where now half-tales be truths: her love to both   140
  Would each to other, and all loves to both,
  Draw after her. Pardon what I have spoke;
  For 'tis a studied, not a present thought,
  By duty ruminated.

ANTONY   Will Caesar speak?

CAESAR Not till he hears how Antony is touched   145
  With what is spoke already.

ANTONY   What power is in Agrippa,
  If I would say, "Agrippa, be it so,"
  To make this good?

CAESAR   The power of Caesar, and
  His power unto Octavia.

ANTONY   May I never
  To this good purpose, that so fairly shows,   150
  Dream of impediment! Let me have thy hand.

126–27 **your reproof ... rashness** you would get a deserved reproof for being
foolhardy 137 **jealousies** suspicions 138 **import** bring 139–40 **truths
would ... truths** things true would be disbelieved, whereas now half-truths are
believed 143 **present** momentary 145 **touched** affected

Further this act of grace, and from this hour
The heart of brothers govern in our loves
And sway our great designs.

CAESAR   There's my hand.
155 A sister I bequeath you, whom no brother
Did ever love so dearly. Let her live
To join our kingdoms and our hearts; and never
Fly off our loves again.

LEPIDUS   Happily, amen.

ANTONY I did not think to draw my sword 'gainst
        Pompey,
160 For he hath laid strange courtesies and great
Of late upon me. I must thank him only,
Lest my remembrance suffer ill report:
At heel of that, defy him.

LEPIDUS   Time calls upon's.
Of us must Pompey presently be sought,
Or else he seeks out us.

165 ANTONY   Where lies he?

CAESAR About the Mount Mesena.

ANTONY What is his strength by land?

CAESAR Great and increasing; but by sea
He is an absolute master.

ANTONY   So is the fame.
170 Would we had spoke together! Haste we for it,
Yet, ere we put ourselves in arms, dispatch we
The business we have talked of.

CAESAR   With most gladness;
And do invite you to my sister's view,
Whither straight I'll lead you.

152 **grace** reconciliation   158 **Fly off our loves** may our love for each other
desert us   162 **remembrance** memory (of kindnesses done)   163 **At heel of
that** immediately after   164 **presently** at once   166 **Mesena** Misenum, an
Italian port   169 **fame** report

ANTONY   Let us, Lepidus,
Not lack your company.

LEPIDUS   Noble Antony,   175
Not sickness should detain me.

> *Flourish. Exit [all but]*
> *Enobarbus, Agrippa, Maecenas.*

MAECENAS Welcome from Egypt, sir.

ENOBARBUS Half the heart of Caesar, worthy Maecenas. My honorable friend, Agrippa.

AGRIPPA Good Enobarbus.   180

MAECENAS We have cause to be glad that matters are
so well disgested. You stayed well by't in Egypt.

ENOBARBUS Ay, sir, we did sleep day out of countenance and made the night light with drinking.

MAECENAS Eight wild boars roasted whole at a break-   185
fast, and but twelve persons there; is this true?

ENOBARBUS This was but as a fly by an eagle: we had
much more monstrous matter of feast, which worthily
deserved noting.

MAECENAS She's a most triumphant lady, if report be   190
square to her.

ENOBARBUS When she first met Mark Antony, she
pursed up his heart, upon the river of Cydnus.

AGRIPPA There she appeared indeed; or my reporter
devised well for her.   195

ENOBARBUS I will tell you.
The barge she sat in, like a burnished throne,
Burned on the water: the poop was beaten gold;
Purple the sails, and so perfumèd that

178 **Half the heart** dear friend (though possibly the idea is that Caesar is equally devoted to Agrippa and to Maecenas) 182 **disgested** digested 182 **stayed well by't** "lived it up" 183–84 **we did … countenance** we disconcerted the day by sleeping through it 187 **by** compared with 191 **square** just, true 193 **pursed up** put in her purse, took possession of 195 **devised** invented

The winds were lovesick with them; the oars were
200   silver,
Which to the tune of flutes kept stroke and made
The water which they beat to follow faster,
As amorous of their strokes. For her own person,
It beggared all description: she did lie
205   In her pavilion, cloth-of-gold of tissue,
O'erpicturing that Venus where we see
The fancy outwork nature: on each side her
Stood pretty dimpled boys, like smiling Cupids,
With divers-colored fans, whose wind did seem
210   To glow the delicate cheeks which they did cool,
And what they undid did.

AGRIPPA   O, rare for Antony.

ENOBARBUS Her gentlewomen, like the Nereides,
So many mermaids, tended her i' th' eyes,
And made their bends adornings. At the helm
215   A seeming mermaid steers: the silken tackle
Swell with the touches of those flower-soft hands,
That yarely frame the office. From the barge
A strange invisible perfume hits the sense
Of the adjacent wharfs. The city cast
220   Her people out upon her; and Antony,
Enthroned i' th' marketplace, did sit alone,
Whistling to th' air; which, but for vacancy,
Had gone to gaze on Cleopatra too,
And made a gap in nature.

AGRIPPA   Rare Egyptian!

225   ENOBARBUS Upon her landing, Antony sent to her,
Invited her to supper. She replied,

---

205 **cloth-of-gold of tissue** a rich fabric interwoven with gold threads
206–07 **O'erpicturing ... nature** surpassing that painting of Venus where we can
see the imagination excelling nature itself in creative ability   211 **And ... did** i.e.,
and seemed to produce the warm color they were cooling   212 **Nereides** sea
nymphs   213–14 **tended ... adornings** stood before her and waited on her, their
bowing movements being works of art in themselves   217 **yarely frame the
office** deftly perform the task   219 **wharfs** banks   222 **but for vacancy** i.e., but
for the law that nature abhors a vacuum

It should be better he became her guest;
Which she entreated. Our courteous Antony,
Whom ne'er the word of "No" woman heard speak,
Being barbered ten times o'er, goes to the feast,   230
And, for his ordinary, pays his heart
For what his eyes eat only.

AGRIPPA   Royal wench!
She made great Caesar lay his sword to bed;
He plowed her, and she cropped.

ENOBARBUS   I saw her once
Hop forty paces through the public street;   235
And having lost her breath, she spoke, and panted,
That she did make defect perfection,
And, breathless, pow'r breathe forth.

MAECENAS Now Antony must leave her utterly.

ENOBARBUS Never; he will not: 240
Age cannot wither her, nor custom stale
Her infinite variety: other women cloy
The appetites they feed, but she makes hungry
Where most she satisfies; for vilest things
Become themselves in her, that the holy priests   245
Bless her when she is riggish.

MAECENAS If beauty, wisdom, modesty, can settle
The heart of Antony, Octavia is
A blessèd lottery to him.

AGRIPPA   Let us go.
Good Enobarbus, make yourself my guest   250
Whilst you abide here.

ENOBARBUS   Humbly, sir, I thank you. *Exeunt*.

---

231 **ordinary** public dinner in a tavern   234 **she cropped** i.e., had a child
(Caesarion)   237 **That** so that   245 **Become themselves** are becoming
246 **riggish** wanton   249 **lottery** allotment

[Scene III. *Rome. Caesar's house.*]

Enter Antony, Caesar, Octavia between them.

ANTONY The world and my great office will sometimes
　　Divide me from your bosom.

OCTAVIA　　　　　　　　　　All which time
　　Before the gods my knee shall bow my prayers
　　To them for you.

ANTONY　　　　　　　Good night, sir. My Octavia,
5　　Read not my blemishes in the world's report:
　　I have not kept my square, but that to come
　　Shall all be done by th' rule. Good night, dear lady.
　　Good night, sir.

CAESAR Good night.　　　　　　*Exit [with Octavia].*

Enter Soothsayer.

10 ANTONY Now, sirrah: you do wish yourself in Egypt?

SOOTHSAYER Would I had never come from thence, nor
　　you thither.

ANTONY If you can, your reason?

SOOTHSAYER I see it in my motion, have it not in my
15　　tongue, but yet hie you to Egypt again.

ANTONY Say to me, whose fortunes shall rise higher,
　　Caesar's, or mine?

SOOTHSAYER Caesar's.
　　Therefore, O Antony, stay not by his side.

II.iii.6 **kept my square** kept straight　**14 motion** mind

Thy daemon, that thy spirit which keeps thee, is   20
Noble, courageous, high, unmatchable,
Where Caesar's is not. But near him thy angel
Becomes afeard, as being o'erpow'red: therefore
Make space enough between you.

ANTONY   Speak this no more.

SOOTHSAYER To none but thee; no more but when to
    thee.   25
If thou dost play with him at any game,
Thou art sure to lose; and of that natural luck
He beats thee 'gainst the odds. Thy luster thickens
When he shines by: I say again, thy spirit
Is all afraid to govern thee near him;   30
But he away, 'tis noble.

ANTONY   Get thee gone.
Say to Ventidius I would speak with him.

                        Exit [Soothsayer].
He shall to Parthia. Be it art or hap,
He hath spoken true. The very dice obey him,
And in our sports my better cunning faints   35
Under his chance: if we draw lots, he speeds;
His cocks do win the battle still of mine
When it is all to naught, and his quails ever
Beat mine, inhooped, at odds. I will to Egypt:
And though I make this marriage for my peace,   40
I' th' East my pleasure lies.

                    Enter Ventidius.
                        O, come, Ventidius,
You must to Parthia. Your commission's ready:
Follow me, and receive't.   *Exeunt.*

---

20 **daemon** guardian angel   27 **of** by   28 **thickens** dims   33 **art or hap** skill or chance   36 **chance** luck   36 **speeds** is successful   37 **still** always   38 **it is all to naught** the odds are all to nothing (against him)   39 **inhooped** confined within a ring

[Scene IV. *Rome. A street.*]

Enter Lepidus, Maecenas, and Agrippa.

LEPIDUS Trouble yourselves no further: pray you, hasten
Your generals after.

AGRIPPA   Sir, Mark Antony
Will e'en but kiss Octavia, and we'll follow.

LEPIDUS Till I shall see you in your soldier's dress,
Which will become you both, farewell.

5   MAECENAS   We shall,
As I conceive the journey, be at Mount
Before you, Lepidus.

LEPIDUS   Your way is shorter;
My purposes do draw me much about:
You'll win two days upon me.

BOTH   Sir, good success.

10   LEPIDUS Farewell.   *Exeunt.*

II.iv.6 **conceive** understand   6 **Mount** i.e., Misenum   8 **My purposes** ...
about my plans take me the long way around

ANTONY AND CLEOPATRA   II.v.

[Scene V. *Alexandria. Cleopatra's palace.*]

Enter Cleopatra, Charmian, Iras, and Alexas.

CLEOPATRA Give me some music: music, moody food
Of us that trade in love.

OMNES   The music, ho!

Enter Mardian the Eunuch.

CLEOPATRA Let it alone, let's to billiards: come, Charmian.

CHARMIAN My arm is sore; best play with Mardian.

CLEOPATRA As well a woman with an eunuch played   5
As with a woman. Come, you'll play with me, sir?

MARDIAN As well as I can, madam.

CLEOPATRA And when good will is showed, though't
come too short,
The actor may plead pardon. I'll none now.
Give me mine angle, we'll to th' river: there,   10
My music playing far off, I will betray
Tawny-finned fishes. My bended hook shall pierce
Their slimy jaws; and as I draw them up,
I'll think them every one an Antony,
And say, "Ah, ha! y' are caught!"

CHARMIAN   'Twas merry when   15
You wagered on your angling, when your diver
Did hang a salt fish on his hook, which he
With fervency drew up.

II.v.1 **moody** melancholy (with pun on musical "mood" or key)   2 **Omnes** all
(Latin)   10 **angle** fishing tackle   17 **salt** dried

395

CLEOPATRA   That time—O times!—
I laughed him out of patience; and that night
20   I laughed him into patience; and next morn,
Ere the ninth hour, I drunk him to his bed;
Then put my tires and mantles on him, whilst
I wore his sword Philippan.

Enter a Messenger.

O, from Italy!
Ram thou thy fruitful tidings in mine ears,
That long time have been barren.

25   MESSENGER   Madam, madam——

CLEOPATRA Antonio's dead! If thou say so, villain,
Thou kill'st thy mistress: but well and free,
If thou so yield him. There is gold and here
My bluest veins to kiss, a hand that kings
30   Have lipped, and trembled kissing.

MESSENGER First, madam, he is well.

CLEOPATRA   Why, there's more gold.
But, sirrah, mark, we use
To say the dead are well: bring it to that,
The gold I give thee will I melt and pour
35   Down thy ill-uttering throat.

MESSENGER Good madam, hear me.

CLEOPATRA   Well, go to, I will:
But there's no goodness in thy face if Antony
Be free and healthful; so tart a favor
To trumpet such good tidings? If not well,
Thou shouldst come like a Fury crowned with
40   snakes,
Not like a formal man.

MESSENGER   Will't please you hear me?

22 **tires** headdresses   23 **Philippan** (Antony's sword is named after Philippi,
where he conquered Brutus and Cassius)   33 **well** i.e., in having gone to
heaven   38 **tart a favor** sour an expression   41 **formal** (1) sane (2) normally
shaped

CLEOPATRA I have a mind to strike thee ere thou
    speak'st:
  Yet, if thou say Antony lives, is well,
  Or friends with Caesar, or not captive to him,
  I'll set thee in a shower of gold, and hail   45
  Rich pearls upon thee.

MESSENGER   Madam, he's well.

CLEOPATRA   Well said.

MESSENGER And friends with Caesar.

CLEOPATRA   Th'art an honest man.

MESSENGER Caesar and he are greater friends than
  ever.

CLEOPATRA Make thee a fortune from me.

MESSENGER   But yet, madam——

CLEOPATRA I do not like "But yet"; it does allay   50
  The good precedence: fie upon "But yet";
  "But yet" is as a jailer to bring forth
  Some monstrous malefactor. Prithee, friend,
  Pour out the pack of matter to mine ear,
  The good and bad together: he's friends with
    Caesar,
  In state of health, thou say'st, and thou say'st, free.   55

MESSENGER Free, madam, no: I made no such report;
  He's bound unto Octavia.

CLEOPATRA   For what good turn?

MESSENGER For the best turn i' th' bed.

CLEOPATRA   I am pale, Charmian.

MESSENGER Madam, he's married to Octavia.   60

CLEOPATRA The most infectious pestilence upon thee!
                      Strikes him down.

50–51 allay/The good precedence qualify the good news before it   58 For
what good turn (she takes his *bound* in the sense "indebted to"; he then takes up
her *turn*, or "act," in a sexual sense)

MESSENGER Good madam, patience.

CLEOPATRA   What say you?
                                                    Strikes him.
                                                    Hence,
Horrible villain! Or I'll spurn thine eyes
Like balls before me: I'll unhair thy head,
                          She hales him up and down.
65 Thou shalt be whipped with wire and stewed in
       brine,
Smarting in ling'ring pickle.

MESSENGER   Gracious madam,
I that do bring the news made not the match.

CLEOPATRA Say 'tis not so, a province I will give thee,
And make thy fortunes proud: the blow thou hadst
70 Shall make thy peace for moving me to rage,
And I will boot thee with what gift beside
Thy modesty can beg.

MESSENGER   He's married, madam.

CLEOPATRA Rogue, thou hast lived too long.
                                              Draws a knife.

MESSENGER   Nay, then I'll run.
What mean you, madam? I have made no fault.
                                                    Exit.

CHARMIAN Good madam, keep yourself within your-
75   self,
The man is innocent.

CLEOPATRA Some innocents 'scape not the thunderbolt.
Melt Egypt into Nile, and kindly creatures
Turn all to serpents! Call the slave again:
80 Though I am mad, I will not bite him. Call!

CHARMIAN He is afeard to come.

CLEOPATRA   I will not hurt him.
                                         [*Exit Charmian.*]

63 **spurn** kick   66 **pickle** pickling solution (of painful salt or acid)   71 **boot
thee** compensate you   72 **modesty** humble rank

These hands do lack nobility, that they strike
A meaner than myself; since I myself
Have given myself the cause.

Enter [Charmian and] the Messenger again.
                    Come hither, sir.
Though it be honest, it is never good   85
To bring bad news: give to a gracious message
An host of tongues, but let ill tidings tell
Themselves, when they be felt.

MESSENGER   I have done my duty.

CLEOPATRA Is he married?
I cannot hate thee worser than I do   90
If thou again say "Yes."

MESSENGER   He's married, madam.

CLEOPATRA The gods confound thee! Dost thou hold
    there still?

MESSENGER Should I lie, madam?

CLEOPATRA   O, I would thou didst,
So half my Egypt were submerged and made
A cistern for scaled snakes! Go get thee hence;   95
Hadst thou Narcissus in thy face, to me
Thou wouldst appear most ugly. He is married?

MESSENGER I crave your Highness' pardon.

CLEOPATRA   He is married?

MESSENGER Take no offense that I would not offend
    you:
To punish me for what you make me do   100
Seems much unequal: he's married to Octavia.

CLEOPATRA O, that his fault should make a knave of
    thee,

84 the cause i.e., by loving Antony   92 confound destroy   94 So even if
96 Hadst ... face even if you were as handsome as Narcissus (Greek youth of
great beauty)   99 Take ... offend you do not be angry at me for hesitating to tell
you what I know will anger you   101 unequal unjust

That art not what th' art sure of! Get thee hence,
The merchandise which thou hast brought from
   Rome
105 Are all too dear for me. Lie they upon thy hand,
And be undone by 'em!   [*Exit Messenger.*]

CHARMIAN   Good your Highness, patience.

CLEOPATRA In praising Antony I have dispraised
   Caesar.

CHARMIAN Many times, madam.

CLEOPATRA   I am paid for't now.
Lead me from hence;
110 I faint. O, Iras, Charmian! 'Tis no matter.
Go to the fellow, good Alexas; bid him
Report the feature of Octavia: her years,
Her inclination, let him not leave out
The color of her hair. Bring me word quickly.
           [*Exit Alexas.*]
115 Let him forever go!—let him not!—Charmian,
Though he be painted one way like a Gorgon,
The other way's a Mars. [*To Mardian*] Bid you
   Alexas
Bring me word how tall she is.—Pity me,
   Charmian,
But do not speak to me. Lead me to my chamber.
           Exeunt.

103 **That art ... sure of** who are not really as wicked as the news you insist on 106 **undone** bankrupted 112 **feature** appearance (not limited to facial characteristics) 113 **inclination** character 116–17 **Though he ... Mars** (alluding to "perspective" pictures, trick paintings that showed contrasted figures – here a monstrous woman and the god of war—when looked at from opposite sides)

[Scene VI. *Near Misenum.*]

Flourish. Enter Pompey [and Menas] at one door,
with Drum and Trumpet: at another, Caesar,
Lepidus, Antony, Enobarbus, Maecenas, Agrippa,
with Soldiers marching.

POMPEY Your hostages I have, so have you mine;
And we shall talk before we fight.

CAESAR   Most meet
That first we come to words, and therefore have we
Our written purposes before us sent;
Which, if thou hast considered, let us know   5
If 'twill tie up thy discontented sword
And carry back to Sicily much tall youth
That else must perish here.

POMPEY   To you all three,
The senators alone of this great world,
Chief factors for the gods: I do not know   10
Wherefore my father should revengers want,
Having a son and friends, since Julius Caesar,
Who at Philippi the good Brutus ghosted,
There saw you laboring for him. What was't
That moved pale Cassius to conspire? And what   15
Made all-honored, honest, Roman Brutus,
With the armed rest, courtiers of beauteous free-
    dom,
To drench the Capitol—but that they would
Have one man but a man? And that is it
Hath made me rig my navy, at whose burden   20

II.vi.2 **meet** fit   7 **tall** brave   10 **factors** agents   11 **want** lack   13 **ghosted**
haunted   19 **but a man** merely a man (and not a king or demigod)

The angered ocean foams; with which I meant
To scourge th' ingratitude that despiteful Rome
Cast on my noble father.

CAESAR   Take your time.

ANTONY Thou canst not fear us, Pompey, with thy
        sails.
25 We'll speak with thee at sea. At land thou know'st
    How much we do o'ercount thee.

POMPEY   At land indeed
    Thou dost o'ercount me of my father's house:
    But since the cuckoo builds not for himself,
    Remain in't as thou mayst.

LEPIDUS   Be pleased to tell us
30 (For this is from the present) how you take
    The offers we have sent you.

CAESAR   There's the point.

ANTONY Which do not be entreated to, but weigh
    What it is worth embraced.

CAESAR   And what may follow,
    To try a larger fortune.

POMPEY   You have made me offer
35 Of Sicily, Sardinia; and I must
    Rid all the sea of pirates; then, to send
    Measures of wheat to Rome; this 'greed upon,
    To part with unhacked edges and bear back
    Our targes undinted.

---

24 **fear** frighten   25 **speak with thee** meet you   27 **o'ercount** cheat (Antony
had used it in the sense of "outnumber," but Pompey punningly alludes to a house
Antony bought from the elder Pompey but did not pay for)   28–29 **But since ...
mayst** but since cuckoos can't build (and therefore have to steal other birds'
nests), keep it if you can hold on to it. (Pompey includes in this sentence a jeering
suggestion that Antony is a cuckold, a lover of a faithless woman)   30 **from the
present** beside the point   33 **embraced** if accepted   33–34 **And what ...
fortune** (1) and what the result may be, if you try to do better for yourself (i.e.,
risk war) (2) and the even greater things you may gain, if you join us and our
affairs prosper   38 **edges** swords   39 **targes** shields

OMNES   That's our offer.

POMPEY   Know then
  I came before you here a man prepared   40
  To take this offer. But Mark Antony
  Put me to some impatience. Though I lose
  The praise of it by telling, you must know,
  When Caesar and your brother were at blows,
  Your mother came to Sicily and did find   45
  Her welcome friendly.

ANTONY   I have heard it, Pompey,
  And am well studied for a liberal thanks,
  Which I do owe you.

POMPEY   Let me have your hand:
  I did not think, sir, to have met you here.

ANTONY The beds i' th' East are soft; and thanks to
    you,
  That called me timelier than my purpose hither;   50
  For I have gained by't.

CAESAR   Since I saw you last
  There's a change upon you.

POMPEY   Well, I know not
  What counts harsh fortune casts upon my face,
  But in my bosom shall she never come   55
  To make my heart her vassal.

LEPIDUS   Well met here.

POMPEY I hope so, Lepidus. Thus we are agreed.
  I crave our composition may be written,
  And sealed between us.

CAESAR   That's the next to do.

---

39 **Omnes** i.e., Caesar, Antony, Lepidus   47–48 **am well ... you** I am ready indeed to give you the free and full thanks that I owe you   51 **timelier** earlier   54 **counts** reckonings   54 **casts** (1) throws (2) sums up (the lines and wrinkles resulting from a hard life are compared to a bill of costs written out by a cruelly precise Fortune)   58 **composition** agreement

60 POMPEY We'll feast each other ere we part, and let's
     Draw lots who shall begin.

ANTONY   That will I, Pompey.

POMPEY No, Antony, take the lot:
     But, first or last, your fine Egyptian cookery
     Shall have the fame. I have heard that Julius Caesar
     Grew fat with feasting there.

65 ANTONY   You have heard much.

POMPEY I have fair meanings, sir.

ANTONY   And fair words to them.

POMPEY Then so much have I heard:
     And I have heard Apollodorus carried——

ENOBARBUS No more of that: he did so.

POMPEY   What, I pray you?

70 ENOBARBUS A certain queen to Caesar in a mattress.

POMPEY I know thee now; how far'st thou, soldier?

ENOBARBUS   Well;
     And well am like to do, for I perceive
     Four feasts are toward.

POMPEY   Let me shake thy hand;
     I never hated thee: I have seen thee fight
     When I have envied thy behavior.

75 ENOBARBUS   Sir,
     I never loved you much; but I ha' praised ye
     When you have well deserved ten times as much
     As I have said you did.

POMPEY   Enjoy thy plainness,
     It nothing ill becomes thee.
80 Aboard my galley I invite you all:
     Will you lead, lords?

ALL   Show's the way, sir.

73 **toward** in the offing (accented "tòward")   79 **It . . . thee** it suits you very well

404

POMPEY   Come.

Exeunt. Manet Enobarbus and Menas.

MENAS [*Aside*] Thy father, Pompey, would ne'er have
made this treaty.—You and I have known, sir.

ENOBARBUS At sea, I think.

MENAS We have, sir.   85

ENOBARBUS You have done well by water.

MENAS And you by land.

ENOBARBUS I will praise any man that will praise me;
though it cannot be denied what I have done by
land.   90

MENAS Nor what I have done by water.

ENOBARBUS Yes, something you can deny for your own
safety: you have been a great thief by sea.

MENAS And you by land.

ENOBARBUS There I deny my land service. But give   95
me your hand, Menas: if our eyes had authority,
here they might take two thieves kissing.

MENAS All men's faces are true, whatsome'er their
hands are.

ENOBARBUS But there is never a fair woman has a true   100
face.

MENAS No slander; they steal hearts.

ENOBARBUS We came hither to fight with you.

MENAS For my part, I am sorry it is turned to a drinking. Pompey doth this day laugh away his fortune.   105

ENOBARBUS If he do, sure he cannot weep't back again.

---

81 s.d. **Manet** (Latin for "remains"; the plural is properly *manent*, but the singular
is often used for the plural, just as "exit" is often used for "exeunt")   83 **known**
met   95 **deny my land service** (a quibble: "I claim exemption from military
service" and "I deny that I have been a thief")   96 **authority** authority to
arrest   97 **two thieves kissing** (1) two crooks fraternizing (2) two thieving hands
clasping   98 **true** (1) honest (2) natural, without make-up

MENAS Y' have said, sir. We looked not for Mark
Antony here. Pray you, is he married to Cleopatra?

ENOBARBUS Caesar's sister is called Octavia.

110 MENAS True, sir, she was the wife of Caius Marcellus.

ENOBARBUS But she is now the wife of Marcus Antonius.

MENAS Pray ye, sir?

ENOBARBUS 'Tis true.

115 MENAS Then is Caesar and he forever knit together.

ENOBARBUS If I were bound to divine of this unity, I
would not prophesy so.

MENAS I think the policy of that purpose made more
in the marriage than the love of the parties.

120 ENOBARBUS I think so too. But you shall find the band
that seems to tie their friendship together will be
the very strangler of their amity: Octavia is of a
holy, cold, and still conversation.

MENAS Who would not have his wife so?

125 ENOBARBUS Not he that himself is not so; which is
Mark Antony. He will to his Egyptian dish again:
then shall the sighs of Octavia blow the fire up in
Caesar, and, as I said before, that which is the
strength of their amity shall prove the immediate
130 author of their variance. Antony will use his affection where it is. He married but his occasion here.

MENAS And thus it may be. Come, sir, will you aboard?
I have a health for you.

ENOBARBUS I shall take it, sir: we have used our throats
135 in Egypt.

MENAS Come, let's away.   *Exeunt*

113 **Pray ye** pardon me (incredulous)   118 **policy** political expediency
123 **still conversation** quiet manner   131 **occasion** convenience

406

[Scene VII. *On board Pompey's galley, off Misenum.*]

*Music plays. Enter two or three Servants,
with a banquet.*

FIRST SERVANT Here they'll be, man. Some o' their
plants are ill-rooted already; the least wind i' th'
world will blow them down.

SECOND SERVANT Lepidus is high-colored.

FIRST SERVANT They have made him drink alms drink.   5

SECOND SERVANT As they pinch one another by the disposition, he cries out "No more"; reconciles them
to his entreaty, and himself to th' drink.

FIRST SERVANT But it raises the greater war between
him and his discretion.   10

SECOND SERVANT Why, this it is to have a name in great
men's fellowship. I had as lief have a reed that will
do me no service, as a partisan I could not heave.

FIRST SERVANT To be called into a huge sphere, and
not to be seen to move in't, are the holes where   15
eyes should be, which pitifully disaster the cheeks.

*A sennet sounded. Enter Caesar, Antony, Pom-
pey, Lepidus, Agrippa, Maecenas, Enobarbus,
Menas, with other Captains.*

II.vii.2 **plants** (pun on foot or sole of foot)   5 **alms drink** (1) remains of liquor
usually saved for alms people (2) drinking done kindly, i.e., toasts given to smooth
over quarrels   7 **No more** (1) no more quarreling (2) no more to drink
13 **partisan** great long-handled spear   14 **sphere** (1) area of influence (2)
revolving circle holding a star or planet, in the old astronomy   15 **move** (1) be
active, influential (2) circle, like a planet   16 **disaster** ruin (with a suggestion of a
star's malignant influence)   16 s.d. **sennet** trumpet call signaling the entrance of a
great man

ANTONY Thus do they, sir: they take the flow o' th'
    Nile
By certain scales i' th' pyramid. They know
By th' height, the lowness, or the mean, if dearth
20 Or foison follow. The higher Nilus swells,
The more it promises; as it ebbs, the seedsman
Upon the slime and ooze scatters his grain,
And shortly comes to harvest.

LEPIDUS Y' have strange serpents there.

25 ANTONY Ay, Lepidus.

LEPIDUS Your serpent of Egypt is bred now of your
    mud by the operation of your sun: so is your croco-
    dile.

ANTONY They are so.

30 POMPEY Sit—and some wine! A health to Lepidus!

LEPIDUS I am not so well as I should be, but I'll ne'er
    out.

ENOBARBUS Not till you have slept; I fear me you'll be
    in till then.

35 LEPIDUS Nay, certainly, I have heard the Ptolemies'
    pyramises are very goodly things; without contra-
    diction I have heard that.

MENAS [Aside to Pompey] Pompey, a word.

POMPEY [Aside to Menas] Say in mine ear: what is't?

MENAS [Aside to Pompey] Forsake thy seat, I do be-
    seech thee, captain,
    And hear me speak a word.

17 take measure 18 scales i' degree marks on 19–20 dearth/Or foison
famine or plenty 26 Your (a colloquialism suggesting casual
knowledgeableness) 31–32 I'll ne'er out I won't give in 34 in (1) in the game
(2) in liquor 36 pyramises (a false plural made up from the Latin singular;
Lepidus is pretentious and drunk)

POMPEY   [*Aside to Menas*] Forbear me till anon.   40
                   [*Menas*] *whispers in's ear.*
  This wine for Lepidus!

LEPIDUS What manner o' thing is your crocodile?

ANTONY It is shaped, sir, like itself, and it is as broad
as it hath breadth; it is just so high as it is, and
moves with it own organs. It lives by that which   45
nourisheth it, and the elements once out of it, it
transmigrates.

LEPIDUS What color is it of?

ANTONY Of it own color too.

LEPIDUS 'Tis a strange serpent.   50

ANTONY 'Tis so; and the tears of it are wet.

CAESAR Will this description satisfy him?

ANTONY With the health that Pompey gives him; else
he is a very epicure.

POMPEY [*Aside to Menas*] Go hang, sir, hang! Tell me
of that? Away!   55
  Do as I bid you.—Where's this cup I called for?

MENAS [*Aside to Pompey*] If for the sake of merit
thou wilt hear me,
  Rise from thy stool.

POMPEY [*Aside to Menas*] I think th' art mad. The
matter?   [*Rises and walks aside.*]

MENAS I have ever held my cap off to thy fortunes.

POMPEY Thou hast served me with much faith. What's
else to say?   60
  Be jolly, lords.

ANTONY   These quicksands, Lepidus,
  Keep off them, for you sink.

40 **Forbear me till anon** leave me alone for a minute   45 **it** its   59 **held my
cap off to** treated respectfully

MENAS Wilt thou be lord of all the world?

POMPEY   What say'st thou?

MENAS Wilt thou be lord of the whole world? That's
twice.

POMPEY How should that be?

65   MENAS   But entertain it,
And though thou think me poor, I am the man
Will give thee all the world.

POMPEY   Hast thou drunk well?

MENAS No, Pompey, I have kept me from the cup.
Thou art, if thou dar'st be, the earthly Jove:
70   Whate'er the ocean pales, or sky inclips,
Is thine, if thou wilt ha't.

POMPEY   Show me which way.

MENAS These three world-sharers, these competitors,
Are in thy vessel. Let me cut the cable;
And when we are put off, fall to their throats.
All there is thine.

75   POMPEY   Ah, this thou shouldst have done,
And not have spoke on't. In me 'tis villainy,
In thee't had been good service. Thou must know,
'Tis not my profit that does lead mine honor;
Mine honor, it. Repent that e'er thy tongue
80   Hath so betrayed thine act. Being done unknown,
I should have found it afterwards well done,
But must condemn it now. Desist, and drink.

MENAS [Aside] For this,
I'll never follow thy palled fortunes more.
85   Who seeks, and will not take when once 'tis offered,
Shall never find it more.

POMPEY   This health to Lepidus!

65 But entertain it only accept it   70 pales fences in   70 inclips embraces
72 competitors partners   84 palled decayed

ANTONY Bear him ashore. I'll pledge it for him, Pompey.

ENOBARBUS Here's to thee, Menas!

MENAS   Enobarbus, welcome.

POMPEY Fill till the cup be hid.

ENOBARBUS There's a strong fellow, Menas.   90
        [*Points to the Servant who carries off Lepidus.*]

MENAS Why?

ENOBARBUS 'A bears the third part of the world, man; seest not?

MENAS The third part then is drunk. Would it were all,
    That it might go on wheels!   95

ENOBARBUS Drink thou: increase the reels.

MENAS Come.

POMPEY This is not yet an Alexandrian feast.

ANTONY It ripens towards it. Strike the vessels, ho!
    Here's to Caesar!

CAESAR   I could well forbear't.   100
    It's monstrous labor when I wash my brain
    And it grows fouler.

ANTONY   Be a child o' th' time.

CAESAR Possess it, I'll make answer;
    But I had rather fast from all, four days,
    Than drink so much in one.

ENOBARBUS   Ha, my brave emperor!   105
    Shall we dance now the Egyptian bacchanals
    And celebrate our drink?

---

92 'A he 95 go on wheels (1) go easily (2) spin wildly 96 reels (1) revels
(2) staggering movements 99 Strike the vessels broach the casks 103 Possess
... answer master the time (rather than be mastered by it) is my answer
106 bacchanals riotous salute to Bacchus, god of wine

POMPEY   Let's ha't, good soldier.

ANTONY Come, let's all take hands
    Till that the conquering wine hath steeped our sense
    In soft and delicate Lethe.

110 ENOBARBUS   All take hands:
    Make battery to our ears with the loud music;
    The while I'll place you; then the boy shall sing.
    The holding every man shall bear as loud
    As his strong sides can volley.

        Music plays. Enobarbus places them hand in hand.

                    The Song
115   Come, thou monarch of the vine,
                Plumpy Bacchus with pink eyne!
                In thy fats our cares be drowned,
                With thy grapes our hairs be crowned.
                    Cup us till the world go round,
120   Cup us till the world go round!

CAESAR What would you more? Pompey, good night.
    Good brother,
    Let me request you off: our graver business
    Frowns at this levity. Gentle lords, let's part;
    You see we have burnt our cheeks: strong Enobarb
125 Is weaker than the wine, and mine own tongue
    Splits what it speaks: the wild disguise hath almost
    Anticked us all. What needs more words? Good
        night.
    Good Antony, your hand.

POMPEY   I'll try you on the shore.

ANTONY And shall, sir. Give's your hand.

---

110 **Lethe** forgetfulness 113 **holding** refrain 116 **pink eyne** half-closed
eyes 117 **fats** vats 122 **request you off** beg you leave the ship with me
126 **disguise** drunken revelry 127 **Anticked** made fools of 128 **try you** test
your power (to hold liquor)

POMPEY   O, Antony,
  You have my father's house. But what, we are
    friends!
  Come down into the boat.   130
                [Exeunt all but Enobarbus and Menas.]

ENOBARBUS [*To Menas*] Take heed you fall not.

MENAS I'll not on shore; no, to my cabin!
  These drums! These trumpets, flutes! What!
  Let Neptune hear we bid a loud farewell
  To these great fellows. Sound and be hanged, sound
    out!   *Sound a flourish, with drums.* 135

ENOBARBUS Hoo, says 'a. There's my cap.
                          [Throws his cap in the air.]

MENAS Hoa! Noble captain, come.   *Exeunt.*

[ACT III

Scene I. *A plain in Syria.*]

Enter Ventidius as it were in triumph, the dead body of Pacorus borne before him; [with Silius and other Romans].

VENTIDIUS Now, darting Parthia, art thou struck; and now
Pleased fortune does of Marcus Crassus' death
Make me revenger. Bear the King's son's body
Before our army. Thy Pacorus, Orodes,
Pays this for Marcus Crassus.

5 SILIUS   Noble Ventidius,
Whilst yet with Parthian blood thy sword is warm,
The fugitive Parthians follow. Spur through Media,
Mesopotamia, and the shelters whither
The routed fly. So thy grand captain, Antony,
10 Shall set thee on triumphant chariots, and
Put garlands on thy head.

III.i.1 **darting** (the Parthians' method of attack was to fling darts and then retreat swiftly, shooting arrows) 2 **Marcus Crassus** (treacherously killed by Orodes, King of Parthia and father of Pacorus)

VENTIDIUS   O Silius, Silius,
   I have done enough: a lower place, note well,
   May make too great an act. For learn this, Silius,
   Better to leave undone, than by our deed
   Acquire too high a fame when him we serve's away.   15
   Caesar and Antony have ever won
   More in their officer than person. Sossius,
   One of my place in Syria, his lieutenant,
   For quick accumulation of renown,
   Which he achieved by th' minute, lost his favor.   20
   Who does i' th' wars more than his captain can
   Becomes his captain's captain; and ambition
   (The soldier's virtue) rather makes choice of loss
   Than gain which darkens him.
   I could do more to do Antonius good,   25
   But 'twould offend him, and in his offense
   Should my performance perish.

SILIUS   Thou hast, Ventidius, that
   Without the which a soldier and his sword
   Grants scarce distinction. Thou wilt write to Antony?

VENTIDIUS I'll humbly signify what in his name,   30
   That magical word of war, we have effected;
   How, with his banners and his well-paid ranks,
   The ne'er-yet-beaten horse of Parthia
   We have jaded out o' th' field.

SILIUS   Where is he now?

VENTIDIUS He purposeth to Athens; whither, with what
      haste
                                                              35
   The weight we must convey with's will permit,
   We shall appear before him.—On, there; pass along.
                                                      Exeunt.

12 **lower place** subordinate   18 **place** rank   18 **his** i.e., Antony's   20 **by th' minute** every minute, incessantly   27 **perish** i.e., lose its value to me   27–29 **that ... distinction** that quality (i.e., discretion) without which it is hard to see any difference between a soldier and his sword   34 **jaded** driven like nags

[Scene II. *Rome. Caesar's house.*]

Enter Agrippa at one door, Enobarbus at another.

AGRIPPA What, are the brothers parted?

ENOBARBUS They have dispatched with Pompey; he is
    gone;
    The other three are sealing. Octavia weeps
    To part from Rome; Caesar is sad, and Lepidus
5   Since Pompey's feast, as Menas says, is troubled
    With the green-sickness.

AGRIPPA   'Tis a noble Lepidus.

ENOBARBUS A very fine one. O, how he loves Caesar!

AGRIPPA Nay, but how dearly he adores Mark Antony!

ENOBARBUS Caesar? Why, he's the Jupiter of men.

10 AGRIPPA What's Antony? The god of Jupiter.

ENOBARBUS Spake you of Caesar? How! The non-
    pareil!

AGRIPPA O Antony! O thou Arabian bird!

ENOBARBUS Would you praise Caesar, say "Caesar":
    go no further.

AGRIPPA Indeed, he plied them both with excellent
    praises.

ENOBARBUS But he loves Caesar best, yet he loves
15   Antony:

III.ii.1 **parted** departed 3 **sealing** making the last arrangements 6 **green-
sickness** anemia supposed to affect lovesick girls (Lepidus' hangover is attributed
to his love of Antony and Octavius) 11 **non-pareil** unequaled thing
12 **Arabian bird** phoenix (unique and immortal)

Hoo! Hearts, tongues, figures, scribes, bards, poets,
  cannot
Think, speak, cast, write, sing, number—hoo!—
His love to Antony. But as for Caesar,
Kneel down, kneel down, and wonder.

AGRIPPA   Both he loves.

ENOBARBUS They are his shards, and he their beetle.
  [*Trumpet within.*] So—   20
This is to horse. Adieu, noble Agrippa.

AGRIPPA Good fortune, worthy soldier, and farewell!

  Enter Caesar, Antony, Lepidus, and Octavia.

ANTONY No further, sir.

CAESAR You take from me a great part of myself;
  Use me well in't. Sister, prove such a wife   25
  As my thoughts make thee, and as my farthest band
  Shall pass on thy approof. Most noble Antony,
  Let not the piece of virtue which is set
  Betwixt us as the cement of our love
  To keep it builded, be the ram to batter   30
  The fortress of it: for better might we
  Have loved without this mean, if on both parts
  This be not cherished.

ANTONY   Make me not offended
  In your distrust.

CAESAR   I have said.

ANTONY   You shall not find,
  Though you be therein curious, the least cause   35
  For what you seem to fear. So the gods keep you
  And make the hearts of Romans serve your ends!
  We will here part.

CAESAR Farewell, my dearest sister, fare thee well.

17 **cast** count   20 **shards** wings   26–27 **As my thoughts … approof** as I
believe you to be, and such as I would give my utmost bond that you will
triumphantly prove to be   28 **piece** masterpiece   29 **cement** (accented on first
syllable)   32 **mean** intermediary   34 **In** by   35 **curious** overscrupulous

40   The elements be kind to thee, and make
        Thy spirits all of comfort. Fare thee well.

OCTAVIA My noble brother!

ANTONY The April's in her eyes: it is love's spring,
        And these the showers to bring it on. Be cheerful.

OCTAVIA Sir, look well to my husband's house; and—

45 CAESAR   What,
        Octavia?

OCTAVIA I'll tell you in your ear.

ANTONY Her tongue will not obey her heart, nor can
        Her heart inform her tongue; the swan's-down
            feather
        That stands upon the swell at the full of tide,
50   And neither way inclines.

ENOBARBUS [*Aside to Agrippa*] Will Caesar weep?

AGRIPPA [*Aside to Enobarbus*] He has a cloud in's face.

ENOBARBUS [*Aside to Agrippa*] He were the worse for
        that, were he a horse;
        So is he, being a man.

AGRIPPA [*Aside to Enobarbus*] Why, Enobarbus,
        When Antony found Julius Caesar dead,
55   He cried almost to roaring; and he wept
        When at Philippi he found Brutus slain.

ENOBARBUS [*Aside to Agrippa*] That year indeed he was
        troubled with a rheum.
        What willingly he did confound he wailed,
        Believe't, till I wept too.

CAESAR   No, sweet Octavia,

48–50 **the swan's ... inclines** (pressure of feeling urges Octavia to speak but
prevents her from finding the words; she hesitates—like a feather held immobile
by cross-currents at the turn of the tide—between husband and brother, love and
sorrow, speech and silence) 52 **horse** (a horse with a dark face, or without a
white star on its face, was less prized) 57 **rheum** watering at the eyes
58 **confound** destroy

You shall hear from me still: the time shall not   60
Outgo my thinking on you.

ANTONY   Come, sir, come,
I'll wrestle with you in my strength of love:
Look, here I have you; thus I let you go,
And give you to the gods.

CAESAR   Adieu; be happy!

LEPIDUS Let all the number of the stars give light   65
To thy fair way!

CAESAR   Farewell, farewell! *Kisses Octavia.*

ANTONY   Farewell!
                    Trumpets sound. Exeunt.

[Scene III. *Alexandria. Cleopatra's palace.*]

Enter Cleopatra, Charmian, Iras, and Alexas.

CLEOPATRA Where is the fellow?

ALEXAS   Half afeard to come.

CLEOPATRA Go to, go to.

                    Enter the Messenger as before.

                    Come hither, sir.

ALEXAS   Good Majesty,
Herod of Jewry dare not look upon you
But when you are well pleased.

CLEOPATRA   That Herod's head
I'll have: but how, when Antony is gone   5
Through whom I might command it? Come thou
    near.

III.iii.2 s.d. **as before** i.e., nervously, as he left her   3 **Herod of Jewry** i.e., even
the fiercest of tyrants

MESSENGER Most gracious Majesty!

CLEOPATRA Didst thou behold Octavia?

MESSENGER Ay, dread queen.

10   CLEOPATRA Where?

MESSENGER Madam, in Rome.
I looked her in the face, and saw her led
Between her brother and Mark Antony.

CLEOPATRA Is she as tall as me?

MESSENGER   She is not, madam.

CLEOPATRA Didst hear her speak? Is she shrill-tongued
15   or low?

MESSENGER Madam, I heard her speak; she is low-
voiced.

CLEOPATRA That's not so good. He cannot like her
long.

CHARMIAN Like her? O Isis! 'Tis impossible.

CLEOPATRA I think so, Charmian. Dull of tongue, and
dwarfish.
20   What majesty is in her gait? Remember,
If e'er thou look'st on majesty.

MESSENGER   She creeps:
Her motion and her station are as one.
She shows a body rather than a life,
A statue than a breather.

CLEOPATRA   Is this certain?

MESSENGER Or I have no observance.

25   CHARMIAN   Three in Egypt
Cannot make better note.

CLEOPATRA   He's very knowing,

17 **That's not so good** (1) that's a nuisance. Nevertheless ... (2) that's a bad
thing to be   22 **Her motion ... one** moving and standing still are the same thing
with her

I do perceive't. There's nothing in her yet.
The fellow has good judgment.

CHARMIAN   Excellent.

CLEOPATRA Guess at her years, I prithee.

MESSENGER   Madam,
    She was a widow——

CLEOPATRA   Widow? Charmian, hark.   30

MESSENGER And I do think she's thirty.

CLEOPATRA Bear'st thou her face in mind? Is't long or
    round?

MESSENGER Round, even to faultiness.

CLEOPATRA For the most part, too, they are foolish that
    are so.
    Her hair, what color?   35

MESSENGER Brown, madam; and her forehead
    As low as she would wish it.

CLEOPATRA   There's gold for thee.
    Thou must not take my former sharpness ill;
    I will employ thee back again: I find thee
    Most fit for business. Go, make thee ready;   40
    Our letters are prepared.   [Exit Messenger.]

CHARMIAN   A proper man.

CLEOPATRA Indeed he is so: I repent me much
    That so I harried him. Why, methinks, by him,
    This creature's no such thing.

CHARMIAN   Nothing, madam.

CLEOPATRA The man hath seen some majesty, and
    should know.   45

CHARMIAN Hath he seen majesty? Isis else defend,
    And serving you so long!

31 thirty (Cleopatra, being thirty-eight, lets this pass) 37 As low ... it
(colloquial phrase: low enough, and I hope she's pleased with it) 41 proper
excellent 44 no such thing nothing very much 46 Isis else defend Isis forbid

CLEOPATRA I have one thing more to ask him yet, good
    Charmian;
    But 'tis no matter, thou shalt bring him to me
50   Where I will write. All may be well enough.

CHARMIAN I warrant you, madam.   *Exeunt.*

[Scene IV. *Athens. Antony's house.*]

Enter Antony and Octavia.

ANTONY Nay, nay, Octavia, not only that,
    That were excusable, that and thousands more
    Of semblable import—but he hath waged
    New wars 'gainst Pompey; made his will, and read it
5   To public ear;
    Spoke scantly of me: when perforce he could not
    But pay me terms of honor, cold and sickly
    He vented them, most narrow measure lent me;
    When the best hint was given him, he not took't,
    Or did it from his teeth.

10 OCTAVIA   O, my good lord,
    Believe not all; or, if you must believe,
    Stomach not all. A more unhappy lady,
    If this division chance, ne'er stood between,
    Praying for both parts.
15   The good gods will mock me presently
    When I shall pray "O, bless my lord and husband!"—
    Undo that prayer by crying out as loud
    "O, bless my brother!" Husband win, win brother,
    Prays, and destroys the prayer; no midway
    'Twixt these extremes at all.

III.iv.3 **semblable import** similar significance 4–5 **made ... ear** i.e., like
Julius Caesar, made a will benefiting the people and so worked up popular
support 8 **narrow measure** little credit 10 **from his teeth** grudgingly
12 **Stomach** resent 15 **presently** immediately

ANTONY   Gentle Octavia,   20
Let your best love draw to that point which seeks
Best to preserve it. If I lose mine honor,
I lose myself: better I were not yours
Than yours so branchless. But, as you requested,
Yourself shall go between's: the meantime, lady,   25
I'll raise the preparation of a war
Shall stain your brother. Make your soonest haste;
So your desires are yours.

OCTAVIA   Thanks to my lord.
The Jove of power make me, most weak, most weak,
Your reconciler! Wars 'twixt you twain would be   30
As if the world should cleave, and that slain men
Should solder up the rift.

ANTONY When it appears to you where this begins,
Turn your displeasure that way, for our faults
Can never be so equal that your love   35
Can equally move with them. Provide your going;
Choose your own company, and command what cost
Your heart has mind to.   *Exeunt.*

[Scene V. *Athens. Antony's house.*]

Enter Enobarbus and Eros.

ENOBARBUS How now, friend Eros?

EROS There's strange news come, sir.

ENOBARBUS What, man?

EROS Caesar and Lepidus have made wars upon
Pompey.   5

ENOBARBUS This is old. What is the success?

24 **branchless** mutilated   27 **stain** eclipse (the reputation of)   III.v.6 **success** sequel

EROS Caesar, having made use of him in the wars
'gainst Pompey, presently denied him rivality,
would not let him partake in the glory of the action;
10   and not resting here, accuses him of letters he had
formerly wrote to Pompey; upon his own appeal,
seizes him; so the poor third is up, till death enlarge
his confine.

ENOBARBUS Then, world, thou hast a pair of chaps,
     no more;
15   And throw between them all the food thou hast,
They'll grind the one the other. Where's Antony?

EROS He's walking in the garden—thus, and spurns
The rush that lies before him; cries "Fool Lepidus!"
And threats the throat of that his officer
That murd'red Pompey.

20 ENOBARBUS   Our great navy's rigged.

EROS For Italy and Caesar. More, Domitius:
My lord desires you presently. My news
I might have told hereafter.

ENOBARBUS   'Twill be naught;
But let it be. Bring me to Antony.

EROS   Come, sir. *Exeunt*.

---

8 **rivality** partnership   11 **upon his own appeal** on his (Caesar's) own
accusation   12 **up** shut up, imprisoned   14 **chaps** jaws   15–16 **And throw ...
other** and feed them with all the victims in the world, they (Caesar and Antony)
will nevertheless meet, and one consume the other   20 **Pompey** (Pompey has by
now been murdered, according to Plutarch by Antony's command; Pompey would
have proved useful to Antony in the coming war)

[Scene VI. *Rome. Caesar's house.*]

Enter Agrippa, Maecenas, and Caesar.

CAESAR Contemning Rome, he has done all this and
　　more
　　In Alexandria. Here's the manner of 't:
　　I' th' marketplace on a tribunal silvered,
　　Cleopatra and himself in chairs of gold
　　Were publicly enthroned; at the feet sat　　　　5
　　Caesarion, whom they call my father's son,
　　And all the unlawful issue that their lust
　　Since then hath made between them. Unto her
　　He gave the stablishment of Egypt; made her
　　Of lower Syria, Cyprus, Lydia,　　　　　　10
　　Absolute queen.

MAECENAS　　　　　This in the public eye?

CAESAR I' th' common showplace, where they exercise.
　　His sons he there proclaimed the kings of kings:
　　Great Media, Parthia, and Armenia
　　He gave to Alexander; to Ptolemy he assigned　　15
　　Syria, Cilicia, and Phoenicia. She
　　In th' habiliments of the goddess Isis
　　That day appeared, and oft before gave audience,
　　As 'tis reported, so.

MAECENAS　　　　　Let Rome be thus informed.

AGRIPPA Who, queasy with his insolence already,　　20
　　Will their good thoughts call from him.

III.vi.1 **Contemning** despising 6 **my father** (Octavius had been adopted by
Julius Caesar) 9 **stablishment** possession 20 **queasy** disgusted

CAESAR The people knows it, and have now received
His accusations.

AGRIPPA   Who does he accuse?

CAESAR Caesar: and that, having in Sicily
25 Sextus Pompeius spoiled, we had not rated him
His part o' th' isle. Then does he say he lent me
Some shipping, unrestored. Lastly, he frets
That Lepidus of the triumvirate
Should be deposed; and, being, that we detain
All his revenue.

30 AGRIPPA   Sir, this should be answered.

CAESAR 'Tis done already, and the messenger gone.
I have told him Lepidus was grown too cruel,
That he his high authority abused
And did deserve his change; for what I have
    conquered,
35 I grant him part; but then in his Armenia,
And other of his conquered kingdoms, I
Demand the like.

MAECENAS   He'll never yield to that.

CAESAR Nor must not then be yielded to in this.

Enter Octavia with her Train.

OCTAVIA Hail, Caesar, and my lord, hail, most dear
Caesar!

40 CAESAR That ever I should call thee castaway!

OCTAVIA You have not called me so, nor have you
cause.

CAESAR Why have you stol'n upon us thus? You come
not
Like Caesar's sister. The wife of Antony
Should have an army for an usher, and
45 The neighs of horse to tell of her approach

25 **spoiled** despoiled 25 **rated** allotted 30 **revenue** (accented on second syllable)

426

Long ere she did appear. The trees by th' way
Should have borne men, and expectation fainted,
Longing for what it had not. Nay, the dust
Should have ascended to the roof of heaven,
Raised by your populous troops. But you are come   50
A market maid to Rome, and have prevented
The ostentation of our love; which, left unshown,
Is often left unloved. We should have met you
By sea and land, supplying every stage
With an augmented greeting.

OCTAVIA   Good my lord,   55
To come thus was I not constrained, but did it
On my free will. My lord, Mark Antony,
Hearing that you prepared for war, acquainted
My grievèd ear withal; whereon I begged
His pardon for return.

CAESAR   Which soon he granted,   60
Being an abstract 'tween his lust and him.

OCTAVIA Do not say so, my lord.

CAESAR   I have eyes upon him,
And his affairs come to me on the wind.
Where is he now?

OCTAVIA   My lord, in Athens.

CAESAR No, my most wrongèd sister, Cleopatra   65
Hath nodded him to her. He hath given his empire
Up to a whore, who now are levying
The kings o' th' earth for war. He hath assembled
Bocchus, the King of Libya; Archelaus,
Of Cappadocia; Philadelphos, King   70
Of Paphlagonia; the Thracian king, Adallas;
King Mauchus of Arabia; King of Pont;
Herod of Jewry; Mithridates, King
Of Comagene; Polemon and Amyntas,

52 ostentation public display   53 left unloved (1) unrequited (2) thought not to
exist   61 abstract (1) immaterial, merely notional thing (2) short cut (3) symbol
(of what prevented him from indulging his lust)   67 who now and they now

75   The Kings of Mede and Lycaonia;
    With a more larger list of scepters.

OCTAVIA   Ay me most wretched,
    That have my heart parted betwixt two friends
    That does afflict each other!

CAESAR   Welcome hither.
    Your letters did withhold our breaking forth,
80   Till we perceived both how you were wrong led
    And we in negligent danger. Cheer your heart:
    Be you not troubled with the time, which drives
    O'er your content these strong necessities;
    But let determined things to destiny
85   Hold unbewailed their way. Welcome to Rome,
    Nothing more dear to me. You are abused
    Beyond the mark of thought: and the high gods,
    To do you justice, makes his ministers
    Of us and those that love you. Best of comfort,
    And ever welcome to us.

90 AGRIPPA   Welcome, lady.

MAECENAS Welcome, dear madam.
    Each heart in Rome does love and pity you.
    Only th' adulterous Antony, most large
    In his abominations, turns you off
95   And gives his potent regiment to a trull
    That noises it against us.

OCTAVIA   Is it so, sir?

CAESAR Most certain. Sister, welcome. Pray you
    Be ever known to patience. My dear'st sister!
                           Exeunt.

---

81 **in negligent danger** endangered by doing nothing   86 **abused** deceived
87 **mark** reach   88–89 **makes ... us** make us their agents of justice   93 **large**
loose, licentious   95 **potent regiment to a trull** powerful authority to a
prostitute   96 **noises it** is clamorous

[Scene VII. *Near Actium. Antony's camp.*]

Enter Cleopatra and Enobarbus.

CLEOPATRA I will be even with thee, doubt it not.

ENOBARBUS But why, why, why?

CLEOPATRA Thou hast forspoke my being in these wars,
    And say'st it is not fit.

ENOBARBUS   Well, is it, is it?

CLEOPATRA Is't not denounced against us? Why should
        not we
    Be there in person?   5

ENOBARBUS   [*Aside*] Well, I could reply:
    If we should serve with horse and mares together,
    The horse were merely lost; the mares would bear
    A soldier and his horse.

CLEOPATRA   What is't you say?

ENOBARBUS Your presence needs must puzzle Antony;   10
    Take from his heart, take from his brain, from's
        time,
    What should not then be spared. He is already
    Traduced for levity; and 'tis said in Rome
    That Photinus an eunuch and your maids
    Manage this war.

CLEOPATRA   Sink Rome, and their tongues rot   15
    That speak against us! A charge we bear i' th' war,

III.vii.3 **forspoke** spoken against 5 **denounced against us** (Caesar had dec-
lared, or denounced—the technical term—war on Cleopatra personally)
8 **merely** utterly 10 **puzzle** bewilder, bring to a standstill

And as the president of my kingdom will
Appear there for a man. Speak not against it,
I will not stay behind.

Enter Antony and Canidius.

ENOBARBUS   Nay, I have done.
Here comes the Emperor.

20   ANTONY   Is it not strange, Canidius,
That from Tarentum and Brundusium
He could so quickly cut the Ionian sea
And take in Toryne?—You have heard on't, sweet?

CLEOPATRA Celerity is never more admired
Than by the negligent.

25   ANTONY   A good rebuke,
Which might have well becomed the best of men
To taunt at slackness. Canidius, we
Will fight with him by sea.

CLEOPATRA   By sea; what else?

CANIDIUS Why will my lord do so?

ANTONY   For that he dares us to't.

30   ENOBARBUS So hath my lord dared him to single fight.

CANIDIUS Ay, and to wage this battle at Pharsalia,
Where Caesar fought with Pompey: but these offers,
Which serve not for his vantage, he shakes off;
And so should you.

ENOBARBUS   Your ships are not well manned;
35   Your mariners are muleters, reapers, people
Ingrossed by swift impress. In Caesar's fleet
Are those that often have 'gainst Pompey fought;
Their ships are yare, yours, heavy: no disgrace
Shall fall you for refusing him at sea,
Being prepared for land.

23 take in conquer 29 For that because 35 muleters mule drivers
36 Ingrossed by swift impress collected by hasty conscription 38 yare swift,
nimble

ANTONY   By sea, by sea.   40

ENOBARBUS Most worthy sir, you therein throw away
  The absolute soldiership you have by land,
  Distract your army, which doth most consist
  Of war-marked footmen, leave unexecuted
  Your own renownèd knowledge, quite forgo   45
  The way which promises assurance, and
  Give up yourself merely to chance and hazard
  From firm security.

ANTONY   I'll fight at sea.

CLEOPATRA I have sixty sails, Caesar none better.

ANTONY Our overplus of shipping will we burn,   50
  And with the rest full-manned, from th' head of
    Actium
  Beat th' approaching Caesar. But if we fail,
  We then can do't at land.

Enter a Messenger.

                Thy business?

MESSENGER The news is true, my lord, he is descried;
  Caesar has taken Toryne.   55

ANTONY Can he be there in person? 'Tis impossible;
  Strange that his power should be. Canidius,
  Our nineteen legions thou shalt hold by land
  And our twelve thousand horse. We'll to our ship.
  Away, my Thetis!

Enter a Soldier.

       How now, worthy soldier?   60

SOLDIER O noble Emperor, do not fight by sea,
  Trust not to rotten planks. Do you misdoubt
  This sword and these my wounds? Let th' Egyptians
  And the Phoenicians go a-ducking: we

---

43 **Distract** (1) divide (2) confuse   57 **power** army   60 **Thetis** sea goddess,
mother of Achilles   64 **a-ducking** (1) swimming like ducks (2) tipped underwater

65   Have used to conquer standing on the earth
      And fighting foot to foot.

ANTONY   Well, well: away!
                    Exit Antony, Cleopatra, and Enobarbus.

SOLDIER By Hercules, I think I am i' th' right.

CANIDIUS Soldier, thou art; but his whole action grows
      Not in the power on't: so our leader's led,
      And we are women's men.

70   SOLDIER   You keep by land
      The legions and the horse whole, do you not?

CANIDIUS Marcus Octavius, Marcus Justeius,
      Publicola, and Caelius are for sea;
      But we keep whole by land. This speed of Caesar's
      Carries beyond belief.

75   SOLDIER   While he was yet in Rome,
      His power went out in such distractions as
      Beguiled all spies.

CANIDIUS   Who's his lieutenant, hear you?

SOLDIER They say, one Taurus.

CANIDIUS   Well I know the man.
                    Enter a Messenger.

MESSENGER The Emperor calls Canidius.

CANIDIUS With news the time's with labor, and throws
80   forth
      Each minute some.   *Exeunt.*

68-69 **his whole ... power on't** his entire plan of action has developed away from
its sources of power   75 **Carries** shoots him forward   76 **distractions**
divisions   80-81 **With news ... some** i.e., more news is born every minute

432

[Scene VIII. *A plain near Actium.*]

Enter Caesar, with his Army, marching.

CAESAR Taurus!

TAURUS My lord?

CAESAR Strike not by land; keep whole, provoke not
  battle
  Till we have done at sea. Do not exceed
  The prescript of this scroll. Our fortune lies   5
  Upon this jump. *Exit [with Taurus and the Army].*

[Scene IX. *Another part of the plain.*]

Enter Antony and Enobarbus.

ANTONY Set we our squadrons on yond side o' th' hill
  In eye of Caesar's battle; from which place
  We may the number of the ships behold,
  And so proceed accordingly.   *Exit [with Enobarbus].*

III.viii.6 **jump** risk   III.ix.2 **battle** battle line

[Scene X. *Another part of the plain*.]

*Canidius marcheth with his land army one way over the
stage, and Taurus, the lieutenant of Caesar, [with his
army,] the other way. After their going in is heard the
noise of a sea fight. Alarum. Enter Enobarbus.*

ENOBARBUS Naught, naught, all naught! I can behold
     no longer.
Th' *Antoniad*, the Egyptian admiral,
With all their sixty, fly and turn the rudder:
To see't mine eyes are blasted.

Enter Scarus.

SCARUS   Gods and goddesses,
     All the whole synod of them!

5   ENOBARBUS   What's thy passion?

SCARUS The greater cantle of the world is lost
     With very ignorance; we have kissed away
     Kingdoms and provinces.

ENOBARBUS   How appears the fight?

SCARUS On our side like the tokened pestilence,
     Where death is sure. Yon ribaudred nag of
10   Egypt—
     Whom leprosy o'ertake!—i' th' midst o' th' fight,
     When vantage like a pair of twins appeared,

III.x.1 **Naught** i.e., all's come to nothing 2 **admiral** flagship 5 **synod**
assembly 6 **cantle** segment of a sphere 7 **With very ignorance** by utter
stupidity 9 **tokened pestilence** first fatal symptoms of the plague
10 **ribaudred** (apparently from "ribald," but of uncertain meaning; probably just
a cursing word; "filthy")

434

Both as the same, or rather ours the elder,
The breese upon her, like a cow in June,
Hoists sails, and flies.

ENOBARBUS   That I beheld: 15
Mine eyes did sicken at the sight, and could not
Endure a further view.

SCARUS   She once being loofed,
The noble ruin of her magic, Antony,
Claps on his sea wing, and (like a doting mallard)
Leaving the fight in height, flies after her.   20
I never saw an action of such shame;
Experience, manhood, honor, ne'er before
Did violate so itself.

ENOBARBUS   Alack, alack!

                 Enter Canidius.

CANIDIUS Our fortune on the sea is out of breath,
And sinks most lamentably. Had our general   25
Been what he knew himself, it had gone well.
O, he has given example for our flight
Most grossly by his own.

ENOBARBUS   Ay, are you thereabouts?
Why then, good night indeed.

CANIDIUS Toward Peloponnesus are they fled.   30

SCARUS 'Tis easy to 't; and there I will attend
What further comes.

CANIDIUS   To Caesar will I render
My legions and my horse; six kings already
Show me the way of yielding.

13 **elder** greater   14 **breese** gadfly (with pun on "breeze," "wind")   17 **loofed**
(1) luffed, i.e., with the head of a ship turned into the wind (2) aloofed, rapidly
departing   19 **mallard** wild duck   26 **Been ... himself** been his true self—and
he knew what that was   28 **are you thereabouts** is that where your thoughts are

ENOBARBUS   I'll yet follow
35   The wounded chance of Antony, though my reason
     Sits in the wind against me.   [*Exeunt.*]

[Scene XI. *Alexandria. Cleopatra's palace.*]

Enter Antony with Attendants.

ANTONY Hark! The land bids me tread no more upon't,
     It is ashamed to bear me. Friends, come hither.
     I am so lated in the world that I
     Have lost my way forever. I have a ship
5   Laden with gold: take that, divide it; fly,
     And make your peace with Caesar.

OMNES   Fly? Not we.

ANTONY I have fled myself, and have instructed cow-
         ards
     To run and show their shoulders. Friends, be gone.
     I have myself resolved upon a course
10   Which has no need of you. Be gone.
     My treasure's in the harbor. Take it. O,
     I followed that I blush to look upon.
     My very hairs do mutiny, for the white
     Reprove the brown for rashness, and they them
15   For fear and doting. Friends, be gone; you shall
     Have letters from me to some friends that will
     Sweep your way for you. Pray you, look not sad,
     Nor make replies of loathness; take the hint
     Which my despair proclaims. Let that be left

35 **wounded chance** broken fortunes 36 **Sits ... me** is opposed to me
III.xi.3 **lated** belated (as of a traveler, caught by the encroaching night)
12 **that** what 14 **rashness** foolishness 18 **hint** opportunity

Which leaves itself. To the seaside straightway!   20
I will possess you of that ship and treasure.
Leave me, I pray, a little: pray you now,
Nay, do so; for indeed I have lost command,
Therefore I pray you. I'll see you by and by.

Sits down.

Enter Cleopatra led by Charmian, [Iras,]
and Eros.

EROS Nay, gentle madam, to him, comfort him.   25

IRAS Do, most dear queen.

CHARMIAN Do: why, what else?

CLEOPATRA Let me sit down. O, Juno!

ANTONY No, no, no, no, no.

EROS See you here, sir?   30

ANTONY O, fie, fie, fie!

CHARMIAN Madam!

IRAS Madam, O, good empress!

EROS Sir, sir!

ANTONY Yes, my lord, yes. He at Philippi kept   35
His sword e'en like a dancer, while I struck
The lean and wrinkled Cassius; and 'twas I
That the mad Brutus ended: he alone
Dealt on lieutenantry, and no practice had
In the brave squares of war: yet now—No matter.   40

CLEOPATRA Ah, stand by.

EROS The Queen, my lord, the Queen.

19-20 **Let that ... itself** leave the man who has taken leave of his senses (?);
leave the man who has given himself up for lost (?)   23 **I have lost command**
(1) my feelings are becoming uncontrollable (2) I have lost the right to order you
35 **He** i.e., Octavius   36 **like a dancer** i.e., for ornament only   39 **Dealt on
lieutenantry** told his subordinates how to fight   40 **squares** squadrons

IRAS Go to him, madam, speak to him;
    He is unqualitied with very shame.

45 CLEOPATRA Well then, sustain me. O!

EROS Most noble sir, arise. The Queen approaches.
    Her head's declined, and death will seize her, but
    Your comfort makes the rescue.

ANTONY I have offended reputation,
    A most unnoble swerving.

50 EROS   Sir, the Queen.

ANTONY O, whither hast thou led me, Egypt? See
    How I convey my shame out of thine eyes
    By looking back what I have left behind
    'Stroyed in dishonor.

CLEOPATRA   O my lord, my lord,
55 Forgive my fearful sails! I little thought
    You would have followed.

ANTONY   Egypt, thou knew'st too well
    My heart was to thy rudder tied by th' strings,
    And thou shouldst tow me after. O'er my spirit
    Thy full supremacy thou knew'st, and that
60 Thy beck might from the bidding of the gods
    Command me.

CLEOPATRA   O, my pardon!

ANTONY   Now I must
    To the young man send humble treaties, dodge
    And palter in the shifts of lowness, who
    With half the bulk o' th' world played as I pleased,
65 Making and marring fortunes. You did know
    How much you were my conqueror, and that
    My sword, made weak by my affection, would
    Obey it on all cause.

---

44 **unqualitied** beside himself 47 **but** unless 49 **reputation** honor 53 **By
looking back** i.e., by averting my eyes and by lonely meditation on 63 **palter
... lowness** employ the tricks of a man brought low 67 **affection** love

CLEOPATRA   Pardon, pardon!

ANTONY Fall not a tear, I say; one of them rates
    All that is won and lost. Give me a kiss;   70
    Even this repays me. We sent our schoolmaster:
    Is 'a come back? Love, I am full of lead.
    Some wine, within there, and our viands! Fortune
        knows
    We scorn her most when most she offers blows.

                                        Exeunt.

[Scene XII. *Egypt. Caesar's camp.*]

*Enter Caesar, Agrippa, Dolabella, [Thidias,]
    with others.*

CAESAR Let him appear that's come from Antony.
    Know you him?

DOLABELLA   Caesar, 'tis his schoolmaster:
    An argument that he is plucked, when hither
    He sends so poor a pinion of his wing,
    Which had superfluous kings for messengers   5
    Not many moons gone by.

            Enter Ambassador from Antony.

CAESAR   Approach and speak.

AMBASSADOR Such as I am, I come from Antony.
    I was of late as petty to his ends
    As is the morn-dew on the myrtle leaf
    To his grand sea.

---

69 **Fall** let fall   69 **rates** (1) is worth (2) berates, rebukes as unimportant   71 **our
schoolmaster** i.e., the tutor of his and Cleopatra's children   III.xii.10 **To his
grand sea** (1) to the great sea that is its source and end (2) to the great sea that is
Antony

10 CAESAR   Be't so. Declare thine office.

AMBASSADOR Lord of his fortunes he salutes thee, and
    Requires to live in Egypt; which not granted,
    He lessons his requests, and to thee sues
    To let him breathe between the heavens and earth,
15 A private man in Athens: this for him.
    Next, Cleopatra does confess thy greatness,
    Submits her to thy might, and of thee craves
    The circle of the Ptolemies for her heirs,
    Now hazarded to thy grace.

CAESAR   For Antony,
20 I have no ears to his request. The Queen
    Of audience nor desire shall fail, so she
    From Egypt drive her all-disgracèd friend
    Or take his life there. This if she perform,
    She shall not sue unheard. So to them both.

AMBASSADOR Fortune pursue thee!

25 CAESAR   Bring him through the bands.
                                [Exit Ambassador.]
    [To Thidias] To try thy eloquence now 'tis time.
        Dispatch.
    From Antony win Cleopatra: promise,
    And in our name, what she requires; add more,
    From thine invention, offers. Women are not
30 In their best fortunes strong, but want will perjure
    The ne'er-touched vestal. Try thy cunning,
        Thidias;
    Make thine own edict for thy pains, which we
    Will answer as a law.

THIDIAS   Caesar, I go.

12 **Requires** requests   13 **lessons** disciplines (though perhaps the word should
be emended to "lessens")   18 **circle** crown   19 **Now hazarded to thy grace**
now dependent for its fate on your favor   21 **so** provided that   27–29 **promise
... offers** (possibly corrupt; rearranges to the much more lucid: "promise/What
she requires; and in our name add more/Offers from thine invention")
30 **perjure** make a perjuror of   31 **ne'er-touched vestal** immaculate virgin
32 **Make thine own edict** decree what you think the right reward

CAESAR Observe how Antony becomes his flaw,
     And what thou think'st his very action speaks   35
     In every power that moves.

THIDIAS   Caesar, I shall. *Exeunt*.

[Scene XIII. *Alexandria. Cleopatra's palace.*]

Enter Cleopatra, Enobarbus, Charmian, and Iras.

CLEOPATRA What shall we do, Enobarbus?

ENOBARBUS   Think, and die.

CLEOPATRA Is Antony, or we, in fault for this?

ENOBARBUS Antony only, that would make his will
     Lord of his reason. What though you fled
     From that great face of war, whose several ranges   5
     Frighted each other? Why should he follow?
     The itch of his affection should not then
     Have nicked his captainship, at such a point,
     When half to half the world opposed, he being
     The merèd question. 'Twas a shame no less   10
     Than was his loss, to course your flying flags
     And leave his navy gazing.

CLEOPATRA   Prithee, peace.

     Enter the Ambassador, with Antony.

ANTONY Is that his answer?

AMBASSADOR Ay, my lord.

ANTONY The Queen shall then have courtesy, so she   15

34 **becomes his flaw** takes his fall III.xiii.3 **will** desire, lust 7 **affection**
passion 8 **nicked** (1) maimed (2) got the better of 10 **merèd question** sole
ground of dispute 11 **course** pursue 15 **so** if

441

Will yield us up.

AMBASSADOR   He says so.

ANTONY   Let her know't.
To the boy Caesar send this grizzled head,
And he will fill thy wishes to the brim
With principalities.

CLEOPATRA   That head, my lord?

20 ANTONY To him again! Tell him he wears the rose
Of youth upon him; from which the world should
    note
Something particular. His coin, ships, legions
May be a coward's, whose ministers would prevail
Under the service of a child as soon
25 As i' th' command of Caesar. I dare him therefore
To lay his gay comparisons apart
And answer me declined, sword against sword,
Ourselves alone. I'll write it: follow me.

                    [Exeunt Antony and Ambassador.]

ENOBARBUS [Aside] Yes, like enough: high-battled
    Caesar will
30 Unstate his happiness and be staged to th' show
Against a sworder! I see men's judgments are
A parcel of their fortunes, and things outward
Do draw the inward quality after them
To suffer all alike. That he should dream,
35 Knowing all measures, the full Caesar will
Answer his emptiness! Caesar, thou hast subdued
His judgment too.

                    Enter a Servant.

SERVANT   A messenger from Caesar.

22 **Something particular** i.e., a fact concerning Caesar 26 **comparisons** i.e.,
the ships, etc., which make him Antony's superior by comparison 27 **declined**
i.e., in years and fortunes 29 **high-battled** elevated high by great
armies 30–31 **Unstate … sworder** strip his good fortune of all its power, and
make a public exhibition of himself against a gladiator 32 **parcel** part
34 **suffer all alike** deteriorate together 35 **knowing all measures** having
experienced every measure of fortune

442

CLEOPATRA What, no more ceremony? See, my women,
    Against the blown rose may they stop their nose
    That kneeled unto the buds. Admit him, sir.   40
                        [*Exit Servant.*]

ENOBARBUS [*Aside*] Mine honesty and I begin to square.
    The loyalty well held to fools does make
    Our faith mere folly: yet he that can endure
    To follow with allegiance a fall'n lord
    Does conquer him that did his master conquer   45
    And earns a place i' th' story.

                Enter Thidias.

CLEOPATRA   Caesar's will?

THIDIAS Hear it apart.

CLEOPATRA   None but friends: say boldly.

THIDIAS So, haply, are they friends to Antony.

ENOBARBUS He needs as many, sir, as Caesar has,
    Or needs not us. If Caesar please, our master   50
    Will leap to be his friend; for us, you know,
    Whose he is we are, and that is Caesar's.

THIDIAS   So.
    Thus then, thou most renowned: Caesar entreats
    Not to consider in what case thou stand'st
    Further than he is Caesar.

CLEOPATRA   Go on: right royal.   55

THIDIAS He knows that you embraced not Antony
    As you did love, but as you feared him.

CLEOPATRA   O!

THIDIAS The scars upon your honor therefore he
    Does pity, as constrainèd blemishes,
    Not as deserved.

CLEOPATRA   He is a god, and knows   60

41 **square** quarrel 43 **faith** faithfulness 48 **haply** perhaps 55 **Caesar** i.e.,
famous for generosity

443

What is most right. Mine honor was not yielded,
But conquered merely.

ENOBARBUS   [*Aside*] To be sure of that,
I will ask Antony. Sir, sir, thou art so leaky
That we must leave thee to thy sinking, for
Thy dearest quit thee.   *Exit Enobarbus.*

65 THIDIAS   Shall I say to Caesar
What you require of him? For he partly begs
To be desired to give. It much would please him
That of his fortunes you should make a staff
To lean upon. But it would warm his spirits
70 To hear from me you had left Antony,
And put yourself under his shroud,
The universal landlord.

CLEOPATRA   What's your name?

THIDIAS My name is Thidias.

CLEOPATRA   Most kind messenger,
Say to great Caesar this: in deputation
75 I kiss his conqu'ring hand; tell him I am prompt
To lay my crown at's feet, and there to kneel.
Tell him, from his all-obeying breath I hear
The doom of Egypt.

THIDIAS   'Tis your noblest course:
Wisdom and fortune combating together,
80 If that the former dare but what it can,
No chance may shake it. Give me grace to lay
My duty on your hand.

CLEOPATRA [*Giving her hand*] Your Caesar's father oft,
When he hath mused of taking kingdoms in,

---

62 **merely** utterly   66 **require** request   71 **shroud** protection   74 **in deputation** by proxy   77 **all-obeying** which all obey   78 **doom of Egypt** judgment of the Queen of Egypt   80 **If that … it can** if a wise man has the courage merely to go on being wise   82 **duty** i.e., a kiss

ANTONY AND CLEOPATRA   III.xiii.

Bestowed his lips on that unworthy place,
As it rained kisses.

Enter Antony and Enobarbus.

ANTONY   Favors, by Jove that thunders!   85
What art thou, fellow?

THIDIAS   One that but performs
The bidding of the fullest man, and worthiest
To have command obeyed.

ENOBARBUS   [*Aside*] You will be whipped.

ANTONY [*Calling for Servants*] Approach there!—Ah,
     you kite! Now, gods and devils!
Authority melts from me. Of late, when I cried
     "Ho!"   90
Like boys unto a muss kings would start forth,
And cry "Your will?" Have you no ears? I am
Antony yet.

Enter a Servant [followed by others].

     Take hence this Jack and whip him.

ENOBARBUS [*Aside*] 'Tis better playing with a lion's
     whelp
Than with an old one dying.

ANTONY   Moon and stars!   95
Whip him! Were't twenty of the greatest tributaries
That do acknowledge Caesar, should I find them
So saucy with the hand of she here—what's her
     name
Since she was Cleopatra? Whip him, fellows,
Till like a boy you see him cringe his face   100
And whine aloud for mercy. Take him hence.

THIDIAS Mark Antony——

ANTONY   Tug him away. Being whipped,

85 As as if   87 fullest greatest (in character and fortunes)   89 kite ignoble bird
of prey   91 muss scramble; fighting heap of bodies   93 Jack fellow, knave

445

Bring him again. The Jack of Caesar's shall
Bear us an errand to him.

Exeunt [Servants] with Thidias.

105 You were half blasted ere I knew you. Ha!
Have I my pillow left unpressed in Rome,
Forborne the getting of a lawful race,
And by a gem of women, to be abused
By one that looks on feeders?

CLEOPATRA   Good my lord——

110 ANTONY You have been a boggler ever:
But when we in our viciousness grow hard
(O misery on't!) the wise gods seel our eyes,
In our own filth drop our clear judgments, make us
Adore our errors, laugh at's while we strut
To our confusion.

115 CLEOPATRA   O, is't come to this?

ANTONY I found you as a morsel cold upon
Dead Caesar's trencher: nay, you were a fragment
Of Gneius Pompey's, besides what hotter hours,
Unregist'red in vulgar fame, you have
120 Luxuriously picked out. For I am sure,
Though you can guess what temperance should be,
You know not what it is.

CLEOPATRA   Wherefore is this?

ANTONY To let a fellow that will take rewards
And say "God quit you!" be familiar with
125 My playfellow, your hand, this kingly seal
And plighter of high hearts. O, that I were
Upon the hill of Basan to outroar

---

105 **blasted** worn out 107 **getting** begetting 109 **feeders** servants, parasites 110 **boggler** waverer 112 **seel** blind (in falconry, a hawk's eyelids are seeled, or sewn up, before it grows used to being hooded) 115 **confusion** destruction 117 **trencher** wooden dish 117 **fragment** leftover 119 **vulgar fame** common knowledge, popular rumor 120 **Luxuriously picked out** lecherously selected 124 **quit** reward

446

The hornèd herd! For I have savage cause,
And to proclaim it civilly were like
A haltered neck which does the hangman thank   130
For being yare about him.

Enter a Servant with Thidias.

Is he whipped?

SERVANT Soundly, my lord.

ANTONY   Cried he? And begged 'a pardon?

SERVANT He did ask favor.

ANTONY If that thy father live, let him repent
Thou wast not made his daughter; and be thou sorry   135
To follow Caesar in his triumph, since
Thou hast been whipped for following him. Hence-
    forth
The white hand of a lady fever thee,
Shake thou to look on't. Get thee back to Caesar,
Tell him thy entertainment: look thou say   140
He makes me angry with him; for he seems
Proud and disdainful, harping on what I am,
Not what he knew I was. He makes me angry,
And at this time most easy 'tis to do't,
When my good stars that were my former guides   145
Have empty left their orbs and shot their fires
Into th' abysm of hell. If he mislike
My speech and what is done, tell him he has
Hipparchus, my enfranchèd bondman, whom
He may at pleasure whip, or hang, or torture,   150
As he shall like, to quit me. Urge it thou.
Hence with thy stripes, be gone!   *Exit Thidias.*

CLEOPATRA Have you done yet?

ANTONY   Alack, our terrene moon

126-28 O that ... hornèd herd i.e., Antony is so well provided with the
cuckold's horns that he should be among the "fat bulls of Basan" of
Psalm 22 131 yare deft 140 entertainment reception 146 orbs spheres
149 enfranchèd freed 153 terrene moon earthly Isis (goddess of the moon)

447

Is now eclipsed, and it portends alone
The fall of Antony.

155 CLEOPATRA   I must stay his time.

ANTONY To flatter Caesar, would you mingle eyes
With one that ties his points?

CLEOPATRA   Not know me yet?

ANTONY Cold-hearted toward me?

CLEOPATRA   Ah, dear, if I be so,
From my cold heart let heaven engender hail,
160 And poison it in the source, and the first stone
Drop in my neck: as it determines, so
Dissolve my life! The next Caesarion smite,
Till by degrees the memory of my womb,
Together with my brave Egyptians all,
165 By the discandying of this pelleted storm,
Lie graveless, till the flies and gnats of Nile
Have buried them for prey!

ANTONY   I am satisfied.
Caesar sits down in Alexandria, where
I will oppose his fate. Our force by land
170 Hath nobly held; our severed navy too
Have knit again, and fleet, threat'ning most sea-like.
Where hast thou been, my heart? Dost thou hear,
    lady?
If from the field I shall return once more
To kiss these lips, I will appear in blood;
175 I and my sword will earn our chronicle.
There's hope in't yet.

CLEOPATRA That's my brave lord!

---

155 **stay his time** i.e., wait till his rage ends 157 **one that ties his points** one
who laces up his clothes, i.e., a valet 161 **determines** comes to an end,
melts 163 **memory** memorials, heirs 165 **discandying** melting 169 **oppose
his fate** challenge his destiny 171 **fleet** float 172 **heart** courage 174 **in
blood** (1) covered with blood (2) in full vigor 175 **chronicle** place in history

ANTONY I will be treble-sinewed, hearted, breathed,
 And fight maliciously; for when mine hours
 Were nice and lucky, men did ransom lives   180
 Of me for jests; but now I'll set my teeth
 And send to darkness all that stop me. Come,
 Let's have one other gaudy night: call to me
 All my sad captains; fill our bowls once more;
 Let's mock the midnight bell.

CLEOPATRA   It is my birthday.   185
 I had thought t' have held it poor. But since my lord
 Is Antony again, I will be Cleopatra.

ANTONY We will yet do well.

CLEOPATRA Call all his noble captains to my lord.

ANTONY Do so, we'll speak to them; and tonight I'll
   force   190
 The wine peep through their scars. Come on, my
   queen,
 There's sap in't yet! The next time I do fight,
 I'll make death love me, for I will contend
 Even with his pestilent scythe.
                         Exeunt [all but Enobarbus].

ENOBARBUS Now he'll outstare the lightning. To be
   furious   195
 Is to be frighted out of fear, and in that mood
 The dove will peck the estridge; and I see still
 A diminution in our captain's brain
 Restores his heart. When valor preys on reason,
 It eats the sword it fights with. I will seek   200
 Some way to leave him.   *Exit.*

178 I will ... breathed I will have the strength, courage, and expertise of three
men   180 nice delicate, wanton   183 gaudy joyful   197 estridge goshawk (?)
ostrich (?)

ACT IV

Scene I. *Before Alexandria. Caesar's camp*.]

Enter Caesar, Agrippa, and Maecenas, with his
Army, Caesar reading a letter.

CAESAR He calls me boy, and chides as he had power
To beat me out of Egypt. My messenger
He hath whipped with rods; dares me to personal
    combat.
Caesar to Antony: let the old ruffian know
5   I have many other ways to die; meantime
Laugh at his challenge.

MAECENAS   Caesar must think,
When one so great begins to rage, he's hunted
Even to falling. Give him no breath, but now
Make boot of his distraction: never anger
Made good guard for itself.

10 CAESAR   Let our best heads
Know that tomorrow the last of many battles
We mean to fight. Within our files there are,
Of those that served Mark Antony but late,
Enough to fetch him in. See it done,

IV.i.7 rage grow mad   9 Make boot of his distraction profit from his rage
12 files ranks   14 fetch him in capture him

450

And feast the army; we have store to do't,   15
And they have earned the waste. Poor Antony!

Exeunt.

[Scene II. *Alexandria. Cleopatra's palace.*]

Enter Antony, Cleopatra, Enobarbus, Charmian,
Iras, Alexas, with others.

ANTONY He will not fight with me, Domitius?

ENOBARBUS   No.

ANTONY Why should he not?

ENOBARBUS He thinks, being twenty times of better
    fortune,
He is twenty men to one.

ANTONY   Tomorrow, soldier,
By sea and land I'll fight: or I will live,   5
Or bathe my dying honor in the blood
Shall make it live again. Woo't thou fight well?

ENOBARBUS I'll strike, and cry "Take all!"

ANTONY   Well said, come on;
Call forth my household servants; let's tonight
Be bounteous at our meal.

Enter three or four Servitors.

                          Give me thy hand,   10
Thou hast been rightly honest—so hast thou—
Thou—and thou—and thou: you have served me
    well,
And kings have been your fellows.

CLEOPATRA   [*Aside to Enobarbus*] What means this?

IV.ii.5 or either   7 Woo't wilt   8 Take all all or nothing   13 kings have been
your fellows kings have served me too, but no better

451

ENOBARBUS [*Aside to Cleopatra*] 'Tis one of those odd
    tricks which sorrow shoots
Out of the mind.

15 ANTONY   And thou art honest too.
    I wish I could be made so many men,
    And all of you clapped up together in
    An Antony, that I might do you service
    So good as you have done.

OMNES   The gods forbid!

20 ANTONY Well, my good fellows, wait on me tonight:
    Scant not my cups, and make as much of me
    As when mine empire was your fellow too
    And suffered my command.

CLEOPATRA [*Aside to Enobarbus*] What does he mean?

ENOBARBUS [*Aside to Cleopatra*] To make his fol-
    lowers weep.

ANTONY   Tend me tonight;
25 May be it is the period of your duty.
    Haply you shall not see me more; or if,
    A mangled shadow. Perchance tomorrow
    You'll serve another master. I look on you
    As one that takes his leave. Mine honest friends,
30 I turn you not away, but like a master
    Married to your good service; stay till death.
    Tend me tonight two hours, I ask no more,
    And the gods yield you for't!

ENOBARBUS   What mean you, sir,
    To give them this discomfort? Look, they weep,
35 And I, an ass, am onion-eyed; for shame,
    Transform us not to women.

ANTONY   Ho, ho, ho!
Now the witch take me if I meant it thus!

23 **suffered my command** served under my authority 25 **period** end
26 **Haply** perhaps 33 **yield** reward 37 **the witch take me** may I be bewitched

Grace grow where those drops fall! My hearty
  friends,
You take me in too dolorous a sense,
For I spake to you for your comfort, did desire you   40
To burn this night with torches. Know, my hearts,
I hope well of tomorrow, and will lead you
Where rather I'll expect victorious life
Than death and honor. Let's to supper, come,
And drown consideration.   *Exeunt.*   45

[Scene III. *Alexandria. Before Cleopatra's palace.*]

Enter a Company of Soldiers.

FIRST SOLDIER Brother, good night: tomorrow is the
  day.

SECOND SOLDIER It will determine one way: fare you
  well.
Heard you of nothing strange about the streets?

FIRST SOLDIER Nothing. What news?

SECOND SOLDIER Belike 'tis but a rumor. Good night
  to you.   5

FIRST SOLDIER Well, sir, good night.

They meet other Soldiers.

SECOND SOLDIER   Soldiers, have careful watch.

THIRD SOLDIER And you. Good night, good night.

They place themselves in every corner of the stage.

SECOND SOLDIER Here we; and if tomorrow

38 Grace (1) God's grace, favor (2) herb of grace, rue   44 death and honor
honorable death   IV.iii.5 Belike probably   8 Here we here is our post

Our navy thrive, I have an absolute hope
Our landmen will stand up.

10 FIRST SOLDIER   'Tis a brave army,
And full of purpose.

Music of the hautboys is under the stage.

SECOND SOLDIER   Peace! What noise?

FIRST SOLDIER   List, list!

SECOND SOLDIER Hark!

FIRST SOLDIER   Music i' th' air.

THIRD SOLDIER   Under the earth.

FOURTH SOLDIER It signs well, does it not?

THIRD SOLDIER   No.

FIRST SOLDIER   Peace, I say!
What should this mean?

SECOND SOLDIER 'Tis the god Hercules, whom Antony
15   loved,
Now leaves him.

FIRST SOLDIER Walk; let's see if other watchmen
Do hear what we do.

SECOND SOLDIER How now, masters?

20 OMNES (*Speak together*) How now? How now? Do you
hear this?

FIRST SOLDIER Ay. Is't not strange?

THIRD SOLDIER Do you hear, masters? Do you hear?

FIRST SOLDIER Follow the noise so far as we have
quarter.
25   Let's see how it will give off.

OMNES Content. 'Tis strange.   *Exeunt.*

---

13 **signs** signifies   25 **give off** cease

454

[Scene IV. *Alexandria. Cleopatra's palace.*]

*Enter Antony and Cleopatra, with [Charmian
and] others [attending].*

ANTONY Eros! Mine armor, Eros!

CLEOPATRA   Sleep a little.

ANTONY No, my chuck. Eros! Come, mine armor,
Eros!

Enter Eros [with armor].

Come, good fellow, put thine iron on.
If fortune be not ours today, it is
Because we brave her. Come.

CLEOPATRA   Nay, I'll help too.   5
What's this for?

ANTONY   Ah, let be, let be! Thou art
The armorer of my heart. False, false; this, this.

CLEOPATRA Sooth, la, I'll help: thus it must be.

ANTONY   Well, well,
We shall thrive now. Seest thou, my good fellow?
Go put on thy defenses.

EROS   Briefly, sir.   10

CLEOPATRA Is not this buckled well?

ANTONY   Rarely, rarely:
He that unbuckles this, till we do please
To daff't for our repose, shall hear a storm.

IV.iv.2 **chuck** chick 3 **thine iron** that armor (of mine) you hold 4–5 **If
fortune ... brave her** (1) if fortune is not friendly to us today, it will be because
we defy her (2) we shall be fortunate today, or we shall defy fortune 7 **False** i.e.,
wrong piece 10 **Briefly** soon 13 **daff't** put it off

Thou fumblest, Eros, and my queen's a squire
15   More tight at this than thou. Dispatch. O, love,
That thou couldst see my wars today, and knew'st
The royal occupation: thou shouldst see
A workman in't.

Enter an armed Soldier.

        Good morrow to thee; welcome:
Thou look'st like him that knows a warlike charge.
20   To business that we love we rise betime
And go to't with delight.

SOLDIER   A thousand, sir,
Early though't be, have on their riveted trim,
And at the port expect you.

*Shout. Trumpets flourish. Enter Captains and
Soldiers.*

CAPTAIN The morn is fair. Good morrow, General.

ALL Good morrow, General.

25 ANTONY   'Tis well blown, lads.
This morning, like the spirit of a youth
That means to be of note, begins betimes.
So, so. Come, give me that: this way; well said.
Fare thee well, dame; whate'er becomes of me,
30   This is a soldier's kiss. Rebukable
And worthy shameful check it were to stand
On more mechanic compliment. I'll leave thee
Now like a man of steel. You that will fight,
Follow me close; I'll bring you to't. Adieu.
                Exeunt [all but Cleopatra and Charmian].

CHARMIAN Please you retire to your chamber?

35 CLEOPATRA   Lead me.
He goes forth gallantly. That he and Caesar might

15 **tight** skilled 17 **royal occupation** kingly trade 18 **workman**
professional 19 **charge** duty 22 **riveted trim** armor 23 **port** gate 25 **well
blown** (1) i.e., on the trumpets (2) in full flower (of the morning) 28 **well said**
well done 31 **shameful check** shaming rebuke 31–32 **to stand ... compliment** to make a business of vulgar civilities

456

Determine this great war in single fight!
Then Antony—but now—Well, on   *Exeunt.*

[Scene V. *Alexandria. Antony's camp.*]

Trumpets sound. Enter Antony and Eros,
      [*a soldier meeting them*].

SOLDIER The gods make this a happy day to Antony!

ANTONY Would thou and those thy scars had once pre-
    vailed
    To make me fight at land!

SOLDIER   Hadst thou done so,
    The kings that have revolted, and the soldier
    That has this morning left thee, would have still   5
    Followèd thy heels.

ANTONY   Who's gone this morning?

SOLDIER   Who?
    One ever near thee: call for Enobarbus,
    He shall not hear thee, or from Caesar's camp
    Say "I am none of thine."

ANTONY   What sayest thou?

SOLDIER   Sir,
    He is with Caesar.

EROS   Sir, his chests and treasure   10
    He has not with him.

ANTONY   Is he gone?

SOLDIER   Most certain.

ANTONY Go, Eros, send his treasure after; do it;
    Detain no jot, I charge thee. Write to him

IV.v.1 **happy** fortunate

(I will subscribe) gentle adieus and greetings;
15   Say that I wish he never find more cause
To change a master. O, my fortunes have
Corrupted honest men! Dispatch. Enobarbus!
                    Exit [*with Eros and Soldier*].

[Scene VI. *Alexandria. Caesar's camp.*]

Flourish. Enter Agrippa, Caesar, with Enobarbus,
and Dolabella.

CAESAR Go forth, Agrippa, and begin the fight.
    Our will is Antony be took alive:
    Make it so known.

AGRIPPA Caesar, I shall.   [*Exit.*]

5   CAESAR The time of universal peace is near.
    Prove this a prosp'rous day, the three-nooked world
    Shall bear the olive freely.

               Enter a Messenger.

MESSENGER   Antony
    Is come into the field.

CAESAR   Go charge Agrippa
    Plant those that have revolted in the vant,
10   That Antony may seem to spend his fury
    Upon himself.   *Exeunt* [*all but Enobarbus*].

ENOBARBUS Alexas did revolt and went to Jewry on
    Affairs of Antony; there did dissuade
    Great Herod to incline himself to Caesar
15   And leave his master Antony. For this pains

14 **subscribe** sign IV.vi.6 **three-nooked** three-cornered (Europe, Asia,
Africa) 9 **vant** first lines 13 **dissuade** i.e., persuade to leave Antony

Caesar hath hanged him. Canidius and the rest
That fell away have entertainment, but
No honorable trust. I have done ill,
Of which I do accuse myself so sorely
That I will joy no more.

Enter a Soldier of Caesar's.

SOLDIER   Enobarbus, Antony   20
Hath after thee sent all thy treasure, with
His bounty overplus. The messenger
Came on my guard, and at thy tent is now
Unloading of his mules.

ENOBARBUS   I give it you.

SOLDIER Mock not, Enobarbus: 25
I tell you true: best you safed the bringer
Out of the host; I must attend mine office
Or would have done't myself. Your emperor
Continues still a Jove.   *Exit.*

ENOBARBUS I am alone the villain of the earth,
And feel I am so most. O, Antony,   30
Thou mine of bounty, how wouldst thou have paid
My better service, when my turpitude
Thou dost so crown with gold! This blows my heart.
If swift thought break it not, a swifter mean   35
Shall outstrike thought; but thought will do't, I feel.
I fight against thee! No, I will go seek
Some ditch wherein to die: the foul'st best fits
My latter part of life.   *Exit.*

26–27 best ... host you had better see that the man who brought them has safe-
conduct through enemy lines   30 alone the the only   31 And feel I am so
most and no one could be more bitterly aware of it   34 blows swells
35 thought sorrow

[Scene VII. *Field of battle between the camps.*]

Alarum. Drums and Trumpets. Enter Agrippa
[and Soldiers].

AGRIPPA Retire; we have engaged ourselves too far:
Caesar himself has work, and our oppression
Exceeds what we expected.   *Exit [with Soldiers].*

Alarums. Enter Antony, and Scarus wounded.

SCARUS O my brave emperor, this is fought indeed!
5   Had we done so at first, we had droven them home
With clouts about their heads.

ANTONY   Thou bleed'st apace.

SCARUS I had a wound here that was like a *T*,
But now 'tis made an *H*. [*Retreat sounded*] *far off.*

ANTONY   They do retire.

SCARUS We'll beat 'em into bench holes. I have yet
10   Room for six scotches more.

Enter Eros.

EROS They are beaten, sir, and our advantage serves
For a fair victory.

SCARUS   Let us score their backs
And snatch 'em up, as we take hares, behind:
'Tis sport to maul a runner.

ANTONY   I will reward thee

IV.vii.2 **has work** is hard-pressed   2 **our oppression** the pressure on us
6 **clouts** (1) blows (2) bandages   8 *H* (pun on "ache," pronounced "aitch")
9 **bench holes** holes in a privy   10 **scotches** gashes   12 **score** slash

Once for thy sprightly comfort, and tenfold   15
For thy good valor. Come thee on.

SCARUS   I'll halt after. *Exeunt.*

[Scene VIII. *Before Alexandria.*]

Alarum. Enter Antony again in a march; Scarus,
with others.

ANTONY We have beat him to his camp. Run one
        before
    And let the Queen know of our gests. Tomorrow,
    Before the sun shall see's, we'll spill the blood
    That has today escaped. I thank you all,
    For doughty-handed are you, and have fought   5
    Not as you served the cause, but as't had been
    Each man's like mine: you have shown all Hectors.
    Enter the city, clip your wives, your friends,
    Tell them your feats, whilst they with joyful tears
    Wash the congealment from your wounds, and kiss   10
    The honored gashes whole.

                    Enter Cleopatra.

                    [*To Scarus*] Give me thy hand;
    To this great fairy I'll commend thy acts,
    Make her thanks bless thee.—O thou day o' th'
        world,
    Chain mine armed neck; leap thou, attire and all,
    Through proof of harness to my heart, and there   15
    Ride on the pants triumphing.

15 **sprightly** high-hearted 16 **halt** limp IV.viii.2 **gests** deeds 8 **clip**
embrace 12 **fairy** enchantress 15 **proof of harness** impenetrable armor

461

CLEOPATRA   Lord of lords!
    O infinite virtue, com'st thou smiling from
    The world's great snare uncaught?

ANTONY   Mine nightingale,
    We have beat them to their beds. What, girl! Though
        gray
    Do something mingle with our younger brown, yet
20   ha' we
    A brain that nourishes our nerves, and can
    Get goal for goal of youth. Behold this man:
    Commend unto his lips thy favoring hand.—
    Kiss it, my warrior.—He hath fought today
25 As if a god in hate of mankind had
    Destroyed in such a shape.

CLEOPATRA   I'll give thee, friend,
    An armor all of gold; it was a king's.

ANTONY He has deserved it, were it carbuncled
    Like holy Phoebus' car. Give me thy hand.
30 Through Alexandria make a jolly march;
    Bear our hacked targets like the men that owe
        them.
    Had our great palace the capacity
    To camp this host, we all would sup together
    And drink carouses to the next day's fate,
35 Which promises royal peril. Trumpeters,
    With brazen din blast you the city's ear,
    Make mingle with our rattling tabourines,
    That heaven and earth may strike their sounds
        together,
    Applauding our approach.   Exeunt.

17 virtue valor   22 Get goal for goal of youth keep pace with every point won
by youth   28 carbuncled jeweled   29 Phoebus' car the sun god's chariot
31 targets shields   31 owe own   37 tabourines small drums

[Scene IX. *Caesar's camp.*]

Enter a Sentry and his Company. Enobarbus
follows.

SENTRY If we be not relieved within this hour,
We must return to th' court of guard. The night
Is shiny, and they say we shall embattle
By th' second hour i' th' morn.

FIRST WATCH   This last day was
A shrewd one to's.

ENOBARBUS   O, bear me witness, night—   5

SECOND WATCH What man is this?

FIRST WATCH   Stand close, and list him.

ENOBARBUS Be witness to me, O, thou blessèd moon,
When men revolted shall upon record
Bear hateful memory, poor Enobarbus did
Before thy face repent!

SENTRY   Enobarbus?

SECOND WATCH   Peace: 10
Hark further.

ENOBARBUS O sovereign mistress of true melancholy,
The poisonous damp of night disponge upon me,
That life, a very rebel to my will,
May hang no longer on me. Throw my heart   15
Against the flint and hardness of my fault,
Which, being dried with grief, will break to powder,
And finish all foul thoughts. O, Antony,
Nobler than my revolt is infamous,

IV.ix.5 **shrewd** curst, bad 12 **mistress** i.e., the moon 13 **disponge** drip

463

20   Forgive me in thine own particular,
        But let the world rank me in register
        A master-leaver and a fugitive.
        O, Antony! O, Antony!   [*Dies.*]

FIRST WATCH   Let's speak to him.

SENTRY Let's hear him, for the things he speaks
        May concern Caesar.

25 SECOND WATCH   Let's do so. But he sleeps.

SENTRY Swoons rather, for so bad a prayer as his
        Was never yet for sleep.

FIRST WATCH   Go we to him.

SECOND WATCH Awake, sir, awake; speak to us.

FIRST WATCH   Hear you, sir?

SENTRY The hand of death hath raught him.
                                Drums afar off.
                                Hark! The drums
30   Demurely wake the sleepers. Let us bear him
        To th' court of guard: he is of note. Our hour
        Is fully out.

SECOND WATCH Come on then; he may recover yet.
                                Exeunt [*with the body*].

[Scene X. *Between the two camps.*]

Enter Antony and Scarus, with their Army.

ANTONY Their preparation is today by sea;
        We please them not by land.

20 **in thine own particular** yourself 21 **in register** in its records 22 **master-leaver** (1) supreme traitor (2) runaway servant 27 **for** a prelude to 29 **raught** reached 30 **Demurely** soberly, with a low sound

SCARUS   For both, my lord.

ANTONY I would they'd fight i' th' fire or i' th' air;
    We'd fight there too. But this it is: our foot
    Upon the hills adjoining to the city   5
    Shall stay with us—order for sea is given;
    They have put forth the haven—
    Where their appointment we may best discover
    And look on their endeavor.   *Exeunt.*

[Scene XI. *Between the two camps.*]

Enter Caesar and his Army.

CAESAR But being charged, we will be still by land—
    Which, as I take't, we shall, for his best force
    Is forth to man his galleys. To the vales,
    And hold our best advantage.   *Exeunt.*

[Scene XII. *Before Alexandria.*]

Enter Antony and Scarus.

ANTONY Yet they are not joined. Where yond pine
        does stand
    I shall discover all. I'll bring thee word
    Straight how 'tis like to go.   *Exit.*

IV.x.3 **i' th' fire or i' th' air** i.e., as well as the other two elements, earth and
water (land and sea)   IV.xi.1 **But being charged** unless we are attacked   **4 hold
our best advantage** take up the best position we can   IV.xii.1 **joined** i.e., in
battle

Alarum afar off, as at a sea fight.

SCARUS   Swallows have built
In Cleopatra's sails their nests. The augurers
Say they know not, they cannot tell, look grimly,
And dare not speak their knowledge. Antony
Is valiant, and dejected, and by starts
His fretted fortunes give him hope and fear
Of what he has, and has not.

Enter Antony.

ANTONY   All is lost!
This foul Egyptian hath betrayèd me:
My fleet hath yielded to the foe, and yonder
They cast their caps up and carouse together
Like friends long lost. Triple-turned whore! 'Tis
   thou
Hast sold me to this novice, and my heart
Makes only wars on thee. Bid them all fly;
For when I am revenged upon my charm,
I have done all. Bid them all fly, be gone.
                              [*Exit Scarus.*]

O sun, thy uprise shall I see no more.
Fortune and Antony part here, even here
Do we shake hands. All come to this? The hearts
That spanieled me at heels, to whom I gave
Their wishes, do discandy, melt their sweets
On blossoming Caesar; and this pine is barked,
That overtopped them all. Betrayed I am.
O this false soul of Egypt! This grave charm,
Whose eye becked forth my wars, and called them
   home,
Whose bosom was my crownet, my chief end,

---

3 s.d. **Alarum ... sea fight** (the Folio prints this direction just before the entrance of Antony and Scarus; if F's placement is correct, the noise fills the otherwise empty stage for a moment and makes ironic Antony's first line, but probably the direction should be placed either in its present position or in the middle of line 9) 8 **fretted** (1) checkered (2) worn, decayed 13 **Triple-turned** i.e., from Pompey, from Julius Caesar, from Antony 16 **charm** witch 22 **discandy** dissolve 23 **barked** stripped bare 25 **grave charm** deadly witch 27 **crownet, my chief end** crown and end of all I did

Like a right gypsy hath at fast and loose
Beguiled me, to the very heart of loss.
What, Eros, Eros!

Enter Cleopatra.

Ah, thou spell! Avaunt!   30

CLEOPATRA Why is my lord enraged against his love?

ANTONY Vanish, or I shall give thee thy deserving
And blemish Caesar's triumph. Let him take thee
And hoist thee up to the shouting plebeians;
Follow his chariot, like the greatest spot   35
Of all thy sex: most monsterlike be shown
For poor'st diminutives, for dolts, and let
Patient Octavia plow thy visage up
With her preparèd nails.   *Exit Cleopatra.*
                           'Tis well th' art gone,
If it be well to live; but better 'twere   40
Thou fell'st into my fury, for one death
Might have prevented many. Eros, ho!
The shirt of Nessus is upon me; teach me,
Alcides, thou mine ancestor, thy rage.
Let me lodge Lichas on the horns o' th' moon,   45
And with those hands that grasped the heaviest club
Subdue my worthiest self. The witch shall die:
To the young Roman boy she hath sold me, and
   I fall
Under this plot: she dies for't. Eros, ho!   *Exit.*

---

28 **right** true   28 **fast and loose** (a cheating game played by gypsies, in which the dupe inevitably fails to make fast a coiled rope)   30 **Avaunt** begone   34 **plebeians** (accented on first syllable)   35 **spot** blemish   37 **diminutives** little people, i.e., the populace   43-45 **Nessus ... moon** (the death of Antony's ancestor Hercules—called Alcides in line 44—is here recalled. Hercules killed the centaur Nessus with a poisoned arrow, for trying to rape his wife Deianira; the dying Nessus in revenge gave his robe, soaked in poisoned blood, to Deianira, pretending it would act as a love charm. She sent it to her husband for this purpose; in his dying agonies Hercules hurled the bringer of it, Lichas, high in the air)

[Scene XIII. *Alexandria. Cleopatra's palace.*]

Enter Cleopatra, Charmian, Iras, Mardian.

CLEOPATRA Help me, my women! O, he's more mad
Than Telamon for his shield; the boar of Thessaly
Was never so embossed.

CHARMIAN   To th' monument:
There lock yourself, and send him word you are
dead.

5   The soul and body rive not more in parting
Than greatness going off.

CLEOPATRA   To th' monument!
Mardian, go tell him I have slain myself:
Say that the last I spoke was "Antony"
And word it, prithee, piteously. Hence, Mardian,
And bring me how he takes my death. To th' monu-
10   ment!   *Exeunt.*

IV.xiii.2 **Telamon** i.e., Ajax, who went mad and killed himself when he lost the
contest between himself and Odysseus for the arms and shield of Achilles   2 **the
boar of Thessaly** (sent by Artemis to ravage the country of King Oeneus, and
killed by his son Meleager)   3 **embossed** (of a hunted animal) foaming at the
mouth from fury and exhaustion   5 **rive** rend

[Scene XIV. *Alexandria. Cleopatra's palace.*]

Enter Antony and Eros.

ANTONY Eros, thou yet behold'st me?

EROS   Ay, noble lord.

ANTONY Sometime we see a cloud that's dragonish,
    A vapor sometime like a bear or lion,
    A towered citadel, a pendant rock,
    A forkèd mountain, or blue promontory   5
    With trees upon't that nod unto the world
    And mock our eyes with air. Thou hast seen these
      signs:
    They are black vesper's pageants.

EROS   Ay, my lord.

ANTONY That which is now a horse, even with a
    thought
    The rack dislimns, and makes it indistinct   10
    As water is in water.

EROS   It does, my lord.

ANTONY My good knave Eros, now thy captain is
    Even such a body: here I am Antony,
    Yet cannot hold this visible shape, my knave.
    I made these wars for Egypt; and the Queen—   15
    Whose heart I thought I had, for she had mine,
    Which, whilst it was mine, had annexed unto't
    A million moe, now lost—she, Eros, has

IV.xiv.8 **black vesper's pageants** evening's brightly colored but unreal scenery
(**pageants** = floats of the mystery plays, hence plays, masques, etc.)   9–10 **even
... dislimns** as swift as thought the cloud formation (**rack**) obliterates   12 **knave**
boy   18 **moe** more

20   Packed cards with Caesar, and false-played my glory
     Unto an enemy's triumph.
          Nay, weep not, gentle Eros, there is left us
          Ourselves to end ourselves.

                         Enter Mardian.

                              O, thy vile lady!
          She has robbed me of my sword.

     MARDIAN   No, Antony;
          My mistress loved thee, and her fortunes mingled
          With thine entirely.

25   ANTONY   Hence, saucy eunuch, peace!
          She hath betrayed me and shall die the death.

     MARDIAN Death of one person can be paid but once,
          And that she has discharged. What thou wouldst do
          Is done unto thy hand. The last she spake
30   Was "Antony! most noble Antony!"
          Then in the midst a tearing groan did break
          The name of Antony; it was divided
          Between her heart and lips: she rend'red life,
          Thy name so buried in her.

     ANTONY   Dead, then?

     MARDIAN   Dead.

35   ANTONY Unarm, Eros. The long day's task is done,
          And we must sleep. [*To Mardian*] That thou depart'st
               hence safe
          Does pay thy labor richly: go.   *Exit Mardian.*
                         Off, pluck off:
          The sevenfold shield of Ajax cannot keep
          The battery from my heart. O, cleave, my sides!
40   Heart, once be stronger than thy continent,

19–20 **Packed cards … triumph** stacked the cards to favor herself and Caesar,
and so treacherously played her hand as to allow Caesar to trump my glory
23 **sword** i.e., soldiership, masculinity   29 **unto thy hand** already for you
33 **rend'red** surrendered   38 **sevenfold shield of Ajax** (made of brass and lined
with seven layers of oxhide)   39 **battery** bombardment   40 **thy continent** what
holds you in

Crack thy frail case! Apace, Eros, apace.
No more a soldier. Bruisèd pieces, go;
You have been nobly borne.—From me awhile.

Exit Eros.

I will o'ertake thee, Cleopatra, and
Weep for my pardon. So it must be, for now   45
All length is torture: since the torch is out,
Lie down, and stray no farther. Now all labor
Mars what it does; yea, very force entangles
Itself with strength. Seal then, and all is done.
Eros!—I come, my queen.—Eros!—Stay for me.   50
Where souls do couch on flowers, we'll hand in hand,
And with our sprightly port make the ghosts gaze:
Dido and her Aeneas shall want troops,
And all the haunt be ours.—Come, Eros, Eros!

Enter Eros.

EROS What would my lord?

ANTONY   Since Cleopatra died,   55
I have lived in such dishonor that the gods
Detest my baseness. I, that with my sword
Quartered the world and o'er green Neptune's back
With ships made cities, condemn myself to lack
The courage of a woman; less noble mind   60
Than she which by her death our Caesar tells
"I am conqueror of myself." Thou art sworn, Eros,
That, when the exigent should come, which now
Is come indeed, when I should see behind me
Th' inevitable prosecution of   65
Disgrace and horror, that on my command
Thou then wouldst kill me. Do't, the time is come.

---

42 pieces armor   46 length length of life   48–49 very force ... strength (the
image probably is of a creature caught more tightly in a net by the very violence of
its struggles)   49 Seal then finish then (i.e., the final act of sealing a document,
especially a will)   52 sprightly (1) high-hearted, gay (2) ghostly   52 port
bearing   53 Dido ... Aeneas (the legendary lovers are brought together, though
in Vergil, Dido repulses forever the faithless Aeneas)   53 want troops lack
retinue   58 Quartered (1) covered with troops (2) carved up   59 to lack for
lacking   63 exigent need   65 inevitable prosecution unescapable pursuit

Thou strik'st not me, 'tis Caesar thou defeat'st.
Put color in thy cheek.

EROS   The gods withhold me!
70   Shall I do that which all the Parthian darts,
Though enemy, lost aim and could not?

ANTONY   Eros,
Wouldst thou be windowed in great Rome and see
Thy master thus: with pleached arms, bending down
His corrigible neck, his face subdued
75   To penetrative shame, whilst the wheeled seat
Of fortunate Caesar, drawn before him, branded
His baseness that ensued?

EROS   I would not see't.

ANTONY Come then; for with a wound I must be cured.
Draw that thy honest sword, which thou hast worn
Most useful for thy country.

80   EROS   O, sir, pardon me.

ANTONY When I did make thee free, swor'st thou not
then
To do this when I bade thee? Do it at once,
Or thy precedent services are all
But accidents unpurposed. Draw, and come.

85   EROS Turn from me then that noble countenance
Wherein the worship of the whole world lies.

ANTONY Lo thee!   [Turns from him.]

EROS My sword is drawn.

ANTONY   Then let it do at once
The thing why thou hast drawn it.

EROS   My dear master,

73 **pleached** folded (twisted behind?)   74 **corrigible** submissive
74–75 **subdued/To penetrative shame** filled with the humiliation of deepest
shame   76–77 **branded ... ensued** made as hideously clear as the mark branded
on a criminal or animal the abject nature of the man who followed   83 **precedent**
former   87 **Lo thee** there you are, then

My captain, and my emperor, let me say,   90
Before I strike this bloody stroke, farewell.

ANTONY 'Tis said, man, and farewell.

EROS Farewell, great chief. Shall I strike now?

ANTONY   Now, Eros.

EROS Why, there then! Thus I do escape the sorrow
Of Antony's death.   *Kills himself.*

ANTONY   Thrice-nobler than myself,   95
Thou teachest me, O valiant Eros, what
I should, and thou couldst not. My queen and Eros
Have by their brave instruction got upon me
A nobleness in record. But I will be
A bridegroom in my death, and run into't   100
As to a lover's bed. Come then; and, Eros,
Thy master dies thy scholar. To do thus
                    [*Falls on his sword.*]
I learned of thee. How? Not dead? Not dead?
The guard, ho! O, dispatch me!

   Enter [Decretas and] a [Company of the] Guard.

FIRST GUARD   What's the noise?

ANTONY I have done my work ill, friends. O, make an
   end   105
Of what I have begun.

SECOND GUARD   The star is fall'n.

FIRST GUARD And time is at his period.

ALL   Alas, and woe!

ANTONY Let him that loves me strike me dead.

FIRST GUARD   Not I.

SECOND GUARD Nor I.

THIRD GUARD Nor anyone.   *Exeunt [Guard].* 110

DECRETAS Thy death and fortunes bid thy followers fly.

98–99 got ... record beaten me in achieving a noble place in the story
107 period end

473

This sword but shown to Caesar, with this tidings,
Shall enter me with him.

Enter Diomedes.

DIOMEDES Where's Antony?

DECRETAS   There, Diomed, there.

DIOMEDES   Lives he?
115   Wilt thou not answer, man?   [*Exit Decretas.*]

ANTONY Art thou there, Diomed? Draw thy sword, and
    give me
    Sufficing strokes for death.

DIOMEDES   Most absolute lord,
    My mistress Cleopatra sent me to thee.

ANTONY When did she send thee?

DIOMEDES   Now, my lord.

ANTONY   Where is she?

DIOMEDES Locked in her monument. She had a
120   prophesying fear
    Of what hath come to pass; for when she saw
    (Which never shall be found) you did suspect
    She had disposed with Caesar, and that your rage
    Would not be purged, she sent you word she was
        dead;
125   But, fearing since how it might work, hath sent
    Me to proclaim the truth, and I am come,
    I dread, too late.

ANTONY Too late, good Diomed. Call my guard, I
    prithee.

DIOMEDES What ho! The Emperor's guard! The guard,
    what ho!
130   Come, your lord calls!

Enter four or five of the Guard of Antony.

ANTONY Bear me, good friends, where Cleopatra bides;

113 enter recommend   123 disposed settled things   124 purged cured

'Tis the last service that I shall command you.

FIRST GUARD Woe, woe are we, sir, you may not live
 to wear
All your true followers out.

ALL   Most heavy day!

ANTONY Nay, good my fellows, do not please sharp
 fate   135
To grace it with your sorrows. Bid that welcome
Which comes to punish us, and we punish it,
Seeming to bear it lightly. Take me up:
I have led you oft; carry me now, good friends,
And have my thanks for all.   140
      Exit [the Guard,] bearing Antony.

[Scene XV. *Alexandria. The monument*.]

Enter Cleopatra and her Maids aloft, with
Charmian and Iras.

CLEOPATRA O, Charmian, I will never go from hence.

CHARMIAN Be comforted, dear madam.

CLEOPATRA   No, I will not.
All strange and terrible events are welcome,
But comforts we despise. Our size of sorrow,
Proportioned to our cause, must be as great 5
As that which makes it.

     Enter Diomed [below].

        How now? Is he dead?

DIOMEDES His death's upon him, but not dead.

133–34 live ... out outlive all your faithful men IV.xv.s.d. aloft (presumably on
the upper stage at the back of the main stage)

Look out o' th' other side your monument;
His guard have brought him thither.

*Enter, [below,] Antony, and the Guard [bearing
him].*

CLEOPATRA   O sun,
Burn the great sphere thou mov'st in: darkling
10   stand
The varying shore o' th' world! O Antony,
Antony, Antony! Help, Charmian, help, Iras, help:
Help, friends below, let's draw him hither.

ANTONY   Peace!
Not Caesar's valor hath o'erthrown Antony,
15   But Antony's hath triumphed on itself.

CLEOPATRA So it should be, that none but Antony
Should conquer Antony, but woe 'tis so!

ANTONY I am dying, Egypt, dying; only
I here importune death awhile, until
20   Of many thousand kisses the poor last
I lay upon thy lips.

CLEOPATRA   I dare not, dear;
Dear my lord, pardon: I dare not,
Lest I be taken. Not th' imperious show
Of the full-fortuned Caesar ever shall
25   Be brooched with me, if knife, drugs, serpents have
Edge, sting, or operation. I am safe:
Your wife Octavia, with her modest eyes
And still conclusion, shall acquire no honor
Demuring upon me. But come, come, Antony—
30   Help me, my women—we must draw thee up:
Assist, good friends.

ANTONY   O, quick, or I am gone.

---

10 **darkling** in darkness 12–13 **Help ... hither** (Shakespeare appears to have made a false start, afterwards left uncanceled, in lines 12–13, or even to line 29; Cleopatra's plan for getting Antony in is passed over, then repeated, in a curious way; and Antony's "I am dying" is also repeated) 19 **importune** beg 21 **dare not** i.e., dare not descend, or open the gates 25 **Be brooched with me** have me as its ornament 28 **still conclusion** (1) silent judgment (2) impassive finality 29 **Demuring** looking soberly

CLEOPATRA Here's sport indeed! How heavy weighs my
   lord!
  Our strength is all gone into heaviness,
  That makes the weight. Had I great Juno's power,
  The strong-winged Mercury should fetch thee up   35
  And set thee by Jove's side. Yet come a little,
  Wishers were ever fools. O, come, come, come.
            They heave Antony aloft to Cleopatra.
  And welcome, welcome! Die when thou hast lived,
  Quicken with kissing. Had my lips that power,
  Thus would I wear them out.

ALL   A heavy sight!   40

ANTONY I am dying, Egypt, dying.
  Give me some wine, and let me speak a little.

CLEOPATRA No, let me speak, and let me rail so high
  That the false housewife Fortune break her wheel,
  Provoked by my offense.

ANTONY   One word, sweet queen.   45
  Of Caesar seek your honor, with your safety. O!

CLEOPATRA They do not go together.

ANTONY   Gentle, hear me:
  None about Caesar trust but Proculeius.

CLEOPATRA My resolution and my hands I'll trust,
  None about Caesar.   50

ANTONY The miserable change now at my end
  Lament nor sorrow at, but please your thoughts
  In feeding them with those my former fortunes,
  Wherein I lived; the greatest prince o' th' world,
  The noblest; and do now not basely die,   55
  Not cowardly put off my helmet to
  My countryman; a Roman, by a Roman

---

33 **heaviness** (1) weight (2) sorrow 39 **Quicken** come to life 44 **false
housewife** treacherous hussy, strumpet 44 **wheel** (1) spinning wheel (the
especial property of a "housewife") (2) wheel of Fortune, whose turns govern the
affairs of men 45 **offense** insults

Valiantly vanquished. Now my spirit is going,
I can no more.

CLEOPATRA   Noblest of men, woo't die?
60 Hast thou no care of me? Shall I abide
In this dull world, which in thy absence is
No better than a sty? O, see, my women,

                                    [*Antony dies.*]

The crown o' th' earth doth melt. My lord!
O, withered is the garland of the war,
65 The soldier's pole is fall'n: young boys and girls
Are level now with men. The odds is gone,
And there is nothing left remarkable
Beneath the visiting moon.   [*Faints.*]

CHARMIAN   O, quietness, lady!

IRAS She's dead too, our sovereign.

CHARMIAN   Lady!

IRAS   Madam!

70 CHARMIAN O madam, madam, madam!

IRAS Royal Egypt! Empress!

CHARMIAN   Peace, peace, Iras!

CLEOPATRA No more but e'en a woman, and commanded
By such poor passion as the maid that milks
And does the meanest chares. It were for me
75 To throw my scepter at the injurious gods,
To tell them that this world did equal theirs
Till they had stol'n our jewel. All's but naught.
Patience is sottish, and impatience does
Become a dog that's mad: then is it sin
80 To rush into the secret house of death
Ere death dare come to us? How do you, women?
What, what, good cheer! Why, how now, Charmian?
My noble girls! Ah, women, women, look,

64 **garland** flower, crown 65 **pole** (1) standard (2) polestar (3) Maypole
(suggested by "garland") 66 **odds** measure, distinctive value 67 **remarkable**
wonderful 74 **chares** chores 78 **sottish** dully stupid

Our lamp is spent, it's out. Good sirs, take heart:
We'll bury him; and then, what's brave, what's noble,   85
Let's do't after the high Roman fashion,
And make death proud to take us. Come, away.
This case of that huge spirit now is cold.
Ah, women, women! Come; we have no friend
But resolution, and the briefest end.   90

Exeunt, bearing off Antony's body.

84 sirs (used of women, as of men)   90 briefest swiftest

[ACT V

Scene I. *Alexandria. Caesar's camp*.]

Enter Caesar, Agrippa, Dolabella, Maecenas,
[Gallus, Proculeius,] with his Council of War.

CAESAR Go to him, Dolabella, bid him yield:
　　Being so frustrate, tell him, he mocks
　　The pauses that he makes.

DOLABELLA 　　　　　　　Caesar, I shall.　　[*Exit*.]

　　Enter Decretas, with the sword of Antony.

CAESAR Wherefore is that? And what art thou that
　　dar'st
　　Appear thus to us?

5　DECRETAS 　　　　　I am called Decretas.
　　Mark Antony I served, who best was worthy
　　Best to be served. Whilst he stood up and spoke,
　　He was my master, and I wore my life
　　To spend upon his haters. If thou please
10　To take me to thee, as I was to him
　　I'll be to Caesar; if thou pleasest not,
　　I yield thee up my life.

CAESAR 　　　　　　　What is't thou say'st?

V.i.2–3 **Being so … he makes** tell him that, since he is truly defeated, these
delays are a mere mockery　5 **thus** i.e., holding a naked sword

DECRETAS I say, O Caesar, Antony is dead.

CAESAR The breaking of so great a thing should make
  A greater crack. The round world   15
  Should have shook lions into civil streets
  And citizens to their dens. The death of Antony
  Is not a single doom; in the name lay
  A moiety of the world.

DECRETAS   He is dead, Caesar,
  Not by a public minister of justice   20
  Nor by a hirèd knife; but that self hand
  Which writ his honor in the acts it did
  Hath, with the courage which the heart did lend it,
  Splitted the heart. This is his sword,
  I robbed his wound of it: behold it stained   25
  With his most noble blood.

CAESAR   [*Weeping*] Look you, sad friends.
  The gods rebuke me, but it is tidings
  To wash the eyes of kings.

AGRIPPA   And strange it is
  That nature must compel us to lament
  Our most persisted deeds.

MAECENAS   His taints and honors   30
  Waged equal with him.

AGRIPPA   A rarer spirit never
  Did steer humanity; but you gods will give us
  Some faults to make us men. Caesar is touched.

MAECENAS When such a spacious mirror's set before
    him,
  He needs must see himself.

---

14 **breaking** (1) destruction (2) disclosure, report 15 **crack** (1) breach
(2) explosive sound 16 **civil** city 19 **moiety** half 21 **self** selfsame
30 **persisted** persisted in 31 **Waged equal with** were equally matched in

35 CAESAR   O Antony,
     I have followed thee to this. But we do launch
     Diseases in our bodies. I must perforce
     Have shown to thee such a declining day
     Or look on thine: we could not stall together
40   In the whole world. But yet let me lament
     With tears as sovereign as the blood of hearts
     That thou, my brother, my competitor
     In top of all design, my mate in empire,
     Friend and companion in the front of war,
45   The arm of mine own body, and the heart
     Where mine his thoughts did kindle—that our
         stars,
     Unreconciliable, should divide
     Our equalness to this. Hear me, good friends—

                Enter an Egyptian.

     But I will tell you at some meeter season.
50   The business of this man looks out of him;
     We'll hear him what he says. Whence are you?

     EGYPTIAN A poor Egyptian yet. The Queen my
         mistress,
     Confined in all she has, her monument,
     Of thy intents desires instruction,
55   That she preparèdly may frame herself
     To th' way she's forced to.

     CAESAR   Bid her have good heart:
     She soon shall know of us, by some of ours,
     How honorable and how kindly we
     Determine for her. For Caesar cannot live
     To be ungentle.

60   EGYPTIAN   So the gods preserve thee!   *Exit.*

     CAESAR Come hither, Proculeius. Go and say
     We purpose her no shame: give her what comforts
     The quality of her passion shall require,

36 **followed** pursued 36 **launch** lance 39 **stall** dwell 41 **sovereign**
potent 42–43 **my competitor … design** my partner in noblest enterprise
46 **his** its 52 **yet** still (though Egypt will soon be Roman) 63 **passion** strong
emotion (here, grief)

Lest, in her greatness, by some mortal stroke
She do defeat us. For her life in Rome   65
Would be eternal in our triumph. Go,
And with your speediest bring us what she says
And how you find of her.

PROCULEIUS   Caesar, I shall.
                                        Exit Proculeius.

CAESAR Gallus, go you along. [*Exit Gallus.*] Where's
    Dolabella,
    To second Proculeius?

ALL   Dolabella!   70

CAESAR Let him alone, for I remember now
    How he's employed. He shall in time be ready.
    Go with me to my tent, where you shall see
    How hardly I was drawn into this war,
    How calm and gentle I proceeded still   75
    In all my writings. Go with me, and see
    What I can show in this.   *Exeunt.*

[Scene II. *Alexandria. The monument.*]

Enter Cleopatra, Charmian, Iras, and Mardian.

CLEOPATRA My desolation does begin to make
    A better life. 'Tis paltry to be Caesar:
    Not being Fortune, he's but Fortune's knave,
    A minister of her will. And it is great
    To do that thing that ends all other deeds,   5
    Which shackles accidents and bolts up change;

65–66 For her ... our triumph alive, in Rome, walking in my triumphal
procession, she would manifest my power to the end of time 74 **hardly**
reluctantly V.ii.3 **knave** servant

Which sleeps, and never palates more the dung,
The beggar's nurse and Caesar's.

Enter, [*to the gates of the monument,*] *Proculeius*,
[*Gallus, and Soldiers*].

PROCULEIUS Caesar sends greeting to the Queen of
Egypt,
10   And bids thee study on what fair demands
Thou mean'st to have him grant thee.

CLEOPATRA   What's thy name?

PROCULEIUS My name is Proculeius.

CLEOPATRA   Antony
Did tell me of you, bade me trust you, but
I do not greatly care to be deceived,
15   That have no use for trusting. If your master
Would have a queen his beggar, you must tell him
That majesty, to keep decorum, must
No less beg than a kingdom: if he please
To give me conquered Egypt for my son,
20   He gives me so much of mine own as I
Will kneel to him with thanks.

PROCULEIUS   Be of good cheer:
Y' are fall'n into a princely hand, fear nothing.
Make your full reference freely to my lord,
Who is so full of grace that it flows over
25   On all that need. Let me report to him
Your sweet dependency, and you shall find
A conqueror that will pray in aid for kindness,
Where he for grace is kneeled to.

CLEOPATRA   Pray you, tell him
I am his fortune's vassal, and I send him
30   The greatness he has got. I hourly learn
A doctrine of obedience, and would gladly
Look him i' th' face.

7 **palates** tastes   7–8 **the dung … Caesar's** the dungy earth, whose fruits are the
source of life to beggar and to emperor   14 **to be deceived** whether or not I am
deceived   23 **Make … freely** hand your affairs fully   27 **pray in aid for
kindness** beg you to assist him to be kind to you

484

PROCULEIUS   This I'll report, dear lady.
Have comfort, for I know your plight is pitied
Of him that caused it.

[*Enter Gallus and Soldiers behind.*]

You see how easily she may be surprised.   35
[*They seize Cleopatra.*]
Guard her till Caesar come.

IRAS Royal Queen!

CHARMIAN O, Cleopatra! Thou art taken, Queen.

CLEOPATRA Quick, quick, good hands!
[*Draws a dagger.*]

PROCULEIUS   Hold, worthy lady, hold!
[*Disarms her.*]
Do not yourself such wrong, who are in this   40
Relieved, but not betrayed.

CLEOPATRA   What, of death too,
That rids our dogs of languish?

PROCULEIUS   Cleopatra,
Do not abuse my master's bounty by
Th' undoing of yourself: let the world see
His nobleness well acted, which your death   45
Will never let come forth.

CLEOPATRA   Where art thou, death?
Come hither, come! Come, come, and take a queen
Worth many babes and beggars!

PROCULEIUS   O, temperance, lady!

CLEOPATRA Sir, I will eat no meat, I'll not drink, sir—
If idle talk will once be necessary—   50
I'll not sleep neither. This mortal house I'll ruin,
Do Caesar what he can. Know, sir, that I
Will not wait pinioned at your master's court

34 s.d. (the Folio gives no stage direction here; it was presumably left to the stage
performance to decide on the procedure by which the Romans capture the
tomb) 41 **Relieved** rescued 42 **languish** lingering illness 46 **let come forth**
allow to be revealed 53 **pinioned** with clipped wings

Nor once be chastised with the sober eye
55   Of dull Octavia. Shall they hoist me up
And show me to the shouting varletry
Of censuring Rome? Rather a ditch in Egypt
Be gentle grave unto me! Rather on Nilus' mud
Lay me stark nak'd and let the waterflies
60   Blow me into abhorring! Rather make
My country's high pyramides my gibbet
And hang me up in chains!

PROCULEIUS   You do extend
These thoughts of horror further than you shall
Find cause in Caesar.

Enter Dolabella.

DOLABELLA   Proculeius,
65   What thou hast done, thy master Caesar knows,
And he hath sent for thee. For the Queen,
I'll take her to my guard.

PROCULEIUS   So, Dolabella,
It shall content me best: be gentle to her.
[*To Cleopatra*] To Caesar I will speak what you
      shall please,
If you'll employ me to him.

70   CLEOPATRA   Say, I would die.
                              Exit Proculeius [*with Soldiers*].

DOLABELLA Most noble Empress, you have heard
      of me.

CLEOPATRA I cannot tell.

DOLABELLA   Assuredly you know me.

CLEOPATRA No matter, sir, what I have heard or known.
You laugh when boys or women tell their dreams;
Is't not your trick?

75   DOLABELLA   I understand not, madam.

CLEOPATRA I dreamt there was an Emperor Antony.

56 **varletry** mob   60 **Blow** swell   61 **pyramides** (four syllables, accented on
second)   75 **trick** way

486

O, such another sleep, that I might see
But such another man.

DOLABELLA   If it might please ye——

CLEOPATRA His face was as the heav'ns, and therein
    stuck
    A sun and moon, which kept their course and lighted   80
    The little *O*, th' earth.

DOLABELLA   Most sovereign creature——

CLEOPATRA His legs bestrid the ocean: his reared arm
    Crested the world: his voice was propertied
    As all the tunèd spheres, and that to friends;
    But when he meant to quail and shake the orb,   85
    He was as rattling thunder. For his bounty,
    There was no winter in't: an autumn 'twas
    That grew the more by reaping. His delights
    Were dolphinlike, they showed his back above
    The element they lived in. In his livery   90
    Walked crowns and crownets: realms and islands
        were
    As plates dropped from his pocket.

DOLABELLA   Cleopatra——

CLEOPATRA Think you there was or might be such a man
    As this I dreamt of?

DOLABELLA   Gentle madam, no.

CLEOPATRA You lie, up to the hearing of the gods.
    But if there be nor ever were one such,
    It's past the size of dreaming; nature wants stuff
    To vie strange forms with fancy, yet t' imagine   95

83–84 **propertied ... spheres** musical as the spheres (referring to the belief in the music of the spheres, made by the harmonious blend of each planet's "note" and normally too fine for human ears to catch) 85 **quail** make quail 90 **livery** (1) service (2) possession, guardianship (legal term) 91 **crowns and crownets** i.e., kings and princes 92 **plates** silver coins 96–97 **But if ... dreaming** but suppose you were right, and no such man exists, and never did exist, how can I have imagined such a man, for no mere dreaming fantasy could make something so great

An Antony were nature's piece 'gainst fancy,
Condemning shadows quite.

100 DOLABELLA   Hear me, good madam.
Your loss is as yourself, great; and you bear it
As answering to the weight. Would I might never
O'ertake pursued success, but I do feel,
By the rebound of yours, a grief that smites
My very heart at root.

105 CLEOPATRA   I thank you, sir.
Know you what Caesar means to do with me?

DOLABELLA I am loath to tell you what I would you
    knew.

CLEOPATRA Nay, pray you, sir.

DOLABELLA   Though he be honorable——

CLEOPATRA He'll lead me, then, in triumph?

110 DOLABELLA Madam, he will. I know't.

Flourish. Enter Proculeius, Caesar, Gallus,
Maecenas, and others of his Train.

ALL Make way there! Caesar!

CAESAR Which is the Queen of Egypt?

DOLABELLA It is the Emperor, madam.

Cleopatra kneels.

CAESAR Arise! You shall not kneel:
I pray you rise; rise, Egypt.

115 CLEOPATRA   Sir, the gods
Will have it thus. My master and my lord
I must obey.

CAESAR   Take to you no hard thoughts.
The record of what injuries you did us,

97–100 **nature ... quite** reality lacks the material to compete with imagination in the creation of strange forms, yet the creation of an Antony would be a masterpiece of conception on the part of reality, surpassing and discrediting all the illusions of imagination   103 **but I do** if I do not

Though written in our flesh, we shall remember
As things but done by chance.

CLEOPATRA   Sole sir o' th' world,   120
I cannot project mine own cause so well
To make it clear, but do confess I have
Been laden with like frailties which before
Have often shamed our sex.

CAESAR   Cleopatra, know,
We will extenuate rather than enforce.   125
If you apply yourself to our intents,
Which towards you are most gentle, you shall find
A benefit in this change; but if you seek
To lay on me a cruelty by taking
Antony's course, you shall bereave yourself   130
Of my good purposes, and put your children
To that destruction which I'll guard them from
If thereon you rely. I'll take my leave.

CLEOPATRA And may, through all the world: 'tis yours,
    and we,
Your scutcheons and your signs of conquest, shall   135
Hang in what place you please. Here, my good lord.
                                              [*Hands him a paper.*]

CAESAR You shall advise me in all for Cleopatra.

CLEOPATRA This is the brief of money, plate, and jewels
I am possessed of. 'Tis exactly valued,
Not petty things admitted. [*Calling*] Where's
    Seleucus?   140

                          [*Enter Seleucus.*]

SELEUCUS Here, madam.

CLEOPATRA This is my treasurer; let him speak, my lord,
Upon his peril, that I have reserved
To myself nothing. Speak the truth, Seleucus.

---

121 **project** set forth (accented on first syllable) 122 **clear** innocent
125 **enforce** emphasize 126 **apply** conform 135 **scutcheons** armorial bearings
(alluding to the captured shields displayed by a conqueror) 138 **brief** summary

145 SELEUCUS Madam,
        I had rather seel my lips than to my peril
        Speak that which is not.

     CLEOPATRA   What have I kept back?

     SELEUCUS Enough to purchase what you have made
        known.

     CAESAR Nay, blush not, Cleopatra, I approve
        Your wisdom in the deed.

150 CLEOPATRA   See, Caesar: O, behold,
        How pomp is followed! Mine will now be yours,
        And should we shift estates, yours would be mine.
        The ingratitude of this Seleucus does
        Even make me wild. O slave, of no more trust
        Than love that's hired! What, goest thou back? Thou
155   shalt
        Go back, I warrant thee; but I'll catch thine eyes,
        Though they had wings. Slave, soulless villain, dog!
        O rarely base!

     CAESAR   Good Queen, let us entreat you.

     CLEOPATRA O Caesar, what a wounding shame is this,
160   That thou vouchsafing here to visit me,
        Doing the honor of thy lordliness
        To one so meek, that mine own servant should
        Parcel the sum of my disgraces by
        Addition of his envy. Say, good Caesar,
165   That I some lady trifles have reserved,
        Immoment toys, things of such dignity
        As we greet modern friends withal; and say
        Some nobler token I have kept apart
        For Livia and Octavia, to induce
170   Their mediation—must I be unfolded
        With one that I have bred? The gods! it smites me

---

146 seel sew up   151 Mine i.e., my followers   158 rarely exceptionally
163 Parcel piece out   164 envy malice   165 lady lady's   166 Immoment
unimportant   167   modern   ordinary   169   Livia   Caesar's   wife
170–71 unfolded/With exposed by

Beneath the fall I have. [*To Seleucus*] Prithee go
    hence,
Or I shall show the cinders of my spirits
Through th' ashes of my chance. Wert thou a man,
Thou wouldst have mercy on me.

CAESAR   Forbear, Seleucus.   175
                            [*Exit Seleucus.*]

CLEOPATRA Be it known that we, the greatest, are mis-
    thought
For things that others do, and when we fall,
We answer others' merits in our name,
Are therefore to be pitied.

CAESAR   Cleopatra,
Not what you have reserved, nor what acknowledged,   180
Put we i' th' roll of conquest: still be't yours,
Bestow it at your pleasure, and believe
Caesar's no merchant, to make prize with you
Of things that merchants sold. Therefore be cheered,
Make not your thoughts your prisons: no, dear
    Queen,   185
For we intend so to dispose you as
Yourself shall give us counsel. Feed and sleep:
Our care and pity is so much upon you
That we remain your friend; and so adieu.

CLEOPATRA My master, and my lord!

CAESAR   Not so. Adieu.   190
        Flourish. Exeunt Caesar and his Train.

CLEOPATRA He words me, girls, he words me, that I
    should not
Be noble to myself! But hark thee, Charmian.
                        [*Whispers to Charmian.*]

IRAS Finish, good lady, the bright day is done,
    And we are for the dark.

173 **cinders** burning coals 174 **chance** fortune 176 **misthought**
misjudged 178 **We ... name** (1) we have to be responsible for faults committed
in our name (merits = deserts, acts deserving punishment) (2) our name is used to
validate the actions of others 183 **make prize** haggle

CLEOPATRA   Hie thee again:
195   I have spoke already, and it is provided;
      Go put it to the haste.

CHARMIAN   Madam, I will.
                    Enter Dolabella.

DOLABELLA Where is the Queen?

CHARMIAN   Behold, sir.   [*Exit.*]

CLEOPATRA   Dolabella!

DOLABELLA Madam, as thereto sworn, by your command
      (Which my love makes religion to obey)
200   I tell you this: Caesar through Syria
      Intends his journey, and within three days
      You with your children will he send before.
      Make your best use of this. I have performed
      Your pleasure, and my promise.

CLEOPATRA   Dolabella,
      I shall remain your debtor.

205   DOLABELLA   I, your servant.
      Adieu, good Queen; I must attend on Caesar.

CLEOPATRA Farewell, and thanks.   *Exit* [*Dolabella*].
                        Now, Iras, what think'st thou?
      Thou, an Egyptian puppet, shall be shown
      In Rome as well as I: mechanic slaves
210   With greasy aprons, rules, and hammers shall
      Uplift us to the view. In their thick breaths,
      Rank of gross diet, shall we be enclouded,
      And forced to drink their vapor.

IRAS   The gods forbid!

CLEOPATRA Nay, 'tis most certain, Iras. Saucy lictors
215   Will catch at us like strumpets, and scald rhymers
      Ballad us out o' tune. The quick comedians

208 **puppet** (she envisages Iras as a doll manipulated by the puppeteer, Octavius—
i.e., a figure posed on a float following Caesar in the triumphal procession)
209 **mechanic slaves** vulgar workmen   212 **Rank of gross diet** stinking of bad
food   214 **Saucy lictors** insolent officers   215 **scald** scurvy

ANTONY AND CLEOPATRA   V.ii.

Extemporally will stage us, and present
Our Alexandrian revels: Antony
Shall be brought drunken forth, and I shall see
Some squeaking Cleopatra boy my greatness   220
I' th' posture of a whore.

IRAS   O, the good gods!

CLEOPATRA Nay, that's certain.

IRAS I'll never see't! For I am sure mine nails
Are stronger than mine eyes.

CLEOPATRA   Why, that's the way
To fool their preparation, and to conquer   225
Their most absurd intents.

                    Enter Charmian.

                         Now, Charmian!
Show me, my women, like a queen: go fetch
My best attires. I am again for Cydnus,
To meet Mark Antony. Sirrah Iras, go.
Now, noble Charmian, we'll dispatch indeed,   230
And when thou hast done this chare, I'll give thee
     leave
To play till doomsday.—Bring our crown and all.
                    [*Exit Iras.*] *A noise within.*
Wherefore's this noise?

                    Enter a Guardsman.

GUARDSMAN   Here is a rural fellow
That will not be denied your Highness' presence:
He brings you figs.   235

CLEOPATRA Let him come in.   *Exit Guardsman.*
                    What poor an instrument
May do a noble deed! He brings me liberty.
My resolution's placed, and I have nothing

220 **boy my greatness** reduce my greatness to the crude imitation that a boy can
manage (in England women's parts were acted by boys or young men)
229 **Sirrah** (an address to inferiors, used equally of men or women)   231 **chare**
chore   236 **What poor an** what a poor   238 **placed** fixed

493

Of woman in me: now from head to foot
240 I am marble-constant: now the fleeting moon
No planet is of mine.

Enter Guardsman and Clown [with basket].

GUARDSMAN   This is the man.

CLEOPATRA Avoid, and leave him.   *Exit Guardsman.*
Hast thou the pretty worm of Nilus there,
That kills and pains not?

245 CLOWN Truly I have him; but I would not be the party
that should desire you to touch him, for his biting is
immortal: those that do die of it do seldom or never
recover.

CLEOPATRA Remember'st thou any that have died on't?

250 CLOWN Very many, men and women too. I heard of
one of them no longer than yesterday; a very honest
woman, but something given to lie, as a woman
should not do but in the way of honesty; how she
died of the biting of it, what pain she felt; truly, she
255 makes a very good report o' th' worm; but he that
will believe all that they say shall never be saved
by half that they do; but this is most falliable, the
worm's an odd worm.

CLEOPATRA Get thee hence, farewell.

260 CLOWN I wish you all joy of the worm.

[*Sets down his basket.*]

CLEOPATRA Farewell.

CLOWN You must think this, look you, that the worm
will do his kind.

CLEOPATRA Ay, ay, farewell.

---

240 **fleeting moon** (a symbol of fickleness, especially in women; and Cleopatra's
special symbol, as being Isis or moon goddess) 241 s.d. **Clown** rustic
242 **Avoid** depart   243 **worm of Nilus** serpent of Nile, i.e., asp or small viper
247 **immortal** (his blunder for "mortal") 250 **heard of** heard from
251 **honest** (1) chaste (2) truthful (similar innuendoes fill the speech, with puns on
"lie" and "die")   263 **do his kind** act according to his nature

CLOWN Look you, the worm is not to be trusted but in   265
the keeping of wise people: for indeed there is no
goodness in the worm.

CLEOPATRA Take thou no care; it shall be heeded.

CLOWN Very good. Give it nothing, I pray you, for it
is not worth the feeding.   270

CLEOPATRA Will it eat me?

CLOWN You must not think I am so simple but I know
the devil himself will not eat a woman. I know that
a woman is a dish for the gods, if the devil dress
her not. But truly, these same whoreson devils do   275
the gods great harm in their women; for in every
ten that they make, the devils mar five.

CLEOPATRA Well, get thee gone, farewell.

CLOWN Yes, forsooth. I wish you joy o' th' worm. *Exit*.

[*Enter Iras with a robe, crown, etc.*]

CLEOPATRA Give me my robe, put on my crown, I have   280
Immortal longings in me. Now no more
The juice of Egypt's grape shall moist this lip.
Yare, yare, good Iras; quick: methinks I hear
Antony call: I see him rouse himself
To praise my noble act. I hear him mock   285
The luck of Caesar, which the gods give men
To excuse their after wrath. Husband, I come:
Now to that name my courage prove my title!
I am fire, and air; my other elements
I give to baser life. So, have you done?   290
Come then, and take the last warmth of my lips.
Farewell, kind Charmian, Iras, long farewell.
                    [*Kisses them. Iras falls and dies.*]

274 **dress** (1) prepare (i.e., of food) (2) clothe, equip   281 **Immortal longings**
(1) the desires of a goddess (2) longings for immortality   283 **Yare** quickly
287 **their after wrath** the retributive punishments heaped by the gods on those
who have been too proud of their good fortune   289-90 **I am fire ... life** (man
was believed to be made up of four elements, two higher—fire and air—and two
lower or baser—earth and water)

Have I the aspic in my lips? Dost fall?
If thou and nature can so gently part,
295   The stroke of death is as a lover's pinch,
Which hurts, and is desired. Dost thou lie still?
If thus thou vanishest, thou tell'st the world
It is not worth leave-taking.

CHARMIAN   Dissolve, thick cloud, and rain, that I may
     say
The gods themselves do weep.

300 CLEOPATRA   This proves me base:
If she first meet the curlèd Antony,
He'll make demand of her, and spend that kiss
Which is my heaven to have. Come, thou mortal
     wretch,
         [*To an asp, which she applies to her breast.*]
With thy sharp teeth this knot intrinsicate
305   Of life at once untie. Poor venomous fool,
Be angry, and dispatch. O, couldst thou speak,
That I might hear thee call great Caesar ass
Unpolicied!

CHARMIAN   O eastern star!

CLEOPATRA   Peace, peace!
Dost thou not see my baby at my breast,
That sucks the nurse asleep?

310 CHARMIAN   O, break! O, break!

CLEOPATRA   As sweet as balm, as soft as air, as gentle—
O, Antony! Nay, I will take thee too:
         [*Applies another asp to her arm.*]
What should I stay——   *Dies.*

---

293 **aspic** asp   301 **curlèd** freshly barbered   303 **thou mortal wretch** you deadly little object (**wretch**, like **fool** in line 305, is often an affectionate term, used especially of children)   304 **intrinsicate** intricate   306 **dispatch** quickly end it   308 **Unpolicied** lacking statecraft   308 **eastern star** morning star, Venus   313 **What** why   313 s.d. **Dies** (modern actresses prefer to die upright, seated regally, but Caesar's penultimate and final speeches suggest that Cleopatra dies—as in Plutarch—"upon a bed")

CHARMIAN In this wild world? So, fare thee well.
  Now boast thee, death, in thy possession lies   315
  A lass unparalleled. Downy windows, close;
  And golden Phoebus never be beheld
  Of eyes again so royal! Your crown's awry;
  I'll mend it, and then play——

Enter the Guard, rustling in.

FIRST GUARD Where's the Queen?

CHARMIAN   Speak softly, wake her not. 320

FIRST GUARD Caesar hath sent——

CHARMIAN   Too slow a messenger.
                        [Applies an asp.]
  O, come apace, dispatch; I partly feel thee.

FIRST GUARD Approach, ho! All's not well: Caesar's
  beguiled.

SECOND GUARD There's Dolabella sent from Caesar;
  call him.

FIRST GUARD What work is here! Charmian, is this well
  done?   325

CHARMIAN It is well done, and fitting for a princess
  Descended of so many royal kings.
  Ah, soldier!   *Charmian dies.*

Enter Dolabella.

DOLABELLA How goes it here?   330

SECOND GUARD   All dead.

DOLABELLA   Caesar, thy thoughts
  Touch their effects in this: thyself art coming
  To see performed the dreaded act which thou
  So sought'st to hinder.

Enter Caesar and all his Train, marching.

ALL   A way there, a way for Caesar!

317 **Phoebus** sun god   330 **Touch their effects** meet with realization

DOLABELLA O, sir, you are too sure an augurer:
That you did fear is done.

CAESAR   Bravest at the last,
335 She leveled at our purposes, and being royal,
Took her own way. The manner of their deaths?
I do not see them bleed.

DOLABELLA   Who was last with them?

FIRST GUARD A simple countryman, that brought her
figs.
This was his basket.

CAESAR   Poisoned, then.

FIRST GUARD   O, Caesar,
340 This Charmian lived but now, she stood and spake;
I found her trimming up the diadem
On her dead mistress; tremblingly she stood,
And on the sudden dropped.

CAESAR   O, noble weakness!
If they had swallowed poison, 'twould appear
345 By external swelling; but she looks like sleep,
As she would catch another Antony
In her strong toil of grace.

DOLABELLA   Here, on her breast,
There is a vent of blood, and something blown;
The like is on her arm.

350 FIRST GUARD This is an aspic's trail; and these fig leaves
Have slime upon them, such as th' aspic leaves
Upon the caves of Nile.

CAESAR   Most probable
That so she died: for her physician tells me
She hath pursued conclusions infinite
355 Of easy ways to die. Take up her bed,
And bear her women from the monument.
She shall be buried by her Antony.

335 **leveled at** (1) guessed (2) fought against 347 **toil** snare 348 **vent**
discharge 348 **blown** swollen 354 **conclusions** experiments

No grave upon the earth shall clip in it
A pair so famous. High events as these
Strike those that make them; and their story is   360
No less in pity, than his glory which
Brought them to be lamented. Our army shall
In solemn show attend this funeral,
And then to Rome. Come, Dolabella, see
High order in this great solemnity.   *Exeunt omnes.*   365

                              FINIS

358 clip clasp   360 Strike touch

Textual Note

Antony and Cleopatra was entered in the Stationers' Register in May, 1608. Though this procedure normally suggested that publication would follow shortly, the play remained, in fact, unprinted until 1623, when it appeared in the "Tragedies" section of the First Folio. This First Folio text of the play is therefore the single authoritative one, and all succeeding editions—including of course the present one—derive from it.

It is widely agreed that the Folio text of *Antony and Cleopatra* was almost certainly printed direct from Shakespeare's own manuscript, and not from a transcript or prompter's copy. The features of the Folio text that suggest a source in Shakespearean manuscript may be briefly summarized as follows. First, it contains unusual spellings and word usages, some of which seem to be peculiar to Shakespeare, and some of which were, at any rate, archaic by the time the Folio was printed. Secondly, many of the Folio misprints are of the kind (occurring also in other texts of the plays) that would seem to arise from the individual character of Shakespeare's own handwriting. Thirdly, it lacks all act and scene divisions, except for the opening "Actus Primus, Scoena Prima"; a lack which indicates copy prepared primarily for the theater. Fourthly, its stage directions are unusually full and detailed, and are often of the nature of an author's "notes on the text"; for example, "Alarum afar off, as at a sea fight." And lastly, the Folio text contains a passage in the first Monument scene (IV.xv.12–29) that suggests the direct carrying over of the author's deletions and rewritings. (See relevant footnote to text.) None of this is absolutely conclusive, but taken together the evidence leaves little doubt that the Folio text was printed direct from Shakespeare's manuscript.

As a text, it is relatively good: it contains many slips but few real difficulties. Its major flaw is the occurrence of very frequent mislineation. This has been silently adjusted in the present edition, as the "correct" lineation is either clear, or, where doubtful, immaterial. The present edition also adds a list of dramatis personae, which is lacking in the Folio; and it adds act and scene divisions, and indications of locality, except for the Folio's opening "Actus Primus, Scoena Prima" which is here translated. It also supplements the existing stage directions. All such additions and supplementations are indicated by square brackets. The positions of a few stage directions have been slightly altered; speech prefixes and other abbreviations are expanded, punctuation and spelling are modernized. The spelling of proper names is regularized: for example, "Cleopatra" is given, though in F "Cleopater" also appears; again, "Decretas" is given though in F "Decretus" also appears; "Canidius" is given for F's "Camidius," "Camidias," and "Camindius"; and so forth. (In a few instances, where the change is more marked, the reading is listed below.) All other departures from the Folio text are listed below, and utilize earlier editorial emendations; the adopted reading is given in bold, and then the original reading in roman. As in the footnotes to the text, a line number followed by "s.d." indicates the stage direction which follows the given line, or which interrupts it.

I.i.39 **On** One   50 **whose** who

I.ii.4 **Charge** change   40 **fertile** foretell   63 **Alexas** [F treats "Alexas" as a speech prefix and gives him the rest of the speech here given to Charmian] 81 **Saw** Saue   113 [F adds s.d.: Enter another Messenger]   114 **ho, the news! how the newes?**   115 **First Attendant** 1 Mes   116 **Second Attendant** 2 Mes 119 **Messenger** 3 Mes   131 **Ho now, Enobarbus!** How now Enobarbus. 138 **occasion** an occasion   181 **leave** loue   186 **Hath** Haue   195 **hair** heire

I.iii.25 **first** fitst   43 **services** Seruicles   82 **by my sword** by Sword

I.iv.3 **Our** One   8 **Vouchsafed** vouchsafe   9 **abstract** abstracts   44 **deared** fear'd   46 **lackeying** lacking   56 **wassails** Vassailes   58 **Pansa** Pausa   75 **we** me

I.v.34 s.d. **Antony** Caesar   50 **dumbed** dumbe   61 **man** mans

501

TEXTUAL NOTE

II.i.16,18,38 [F's speech prefix here, as for all speeches in the scene other than those of Pompey and Varrius, is "**Mene.**" But the context clearly indicates that Menas as well as Menecrates speaks in the scene] 21 **waned** wand 41 **warred** wan'd

II.ii.125 **not so** not, say 126 **reproof** proofe 176 s.d. **Exit** Exit omnes. Manet 210 **glow** gloue 212 **gentlewomen** Gentlewoman 229 **heard** hard 238 **pow'r breathe** powr breath

II.iii.23 **afeard** a feare 31 **away** alway

II.v.12 **Tawny-finned** Tawny fine 43 **is** 'tis

II.vi.s.d. **Agrippa, with** Agrippa, Menas with 19 **is** his 52 **jailer** Iaylor 58 **composition** composion 66 **meanings** meaning 69 **more of** more

II.vii.1 **their** th' their 4 **high-colored** high Conlord 12 **lief** liue 36 **pyramises** Pyramisis 94 **then** then he 102 **grows** grow 113 **bear** beate 126 **Splits** Spleet's 130 **father's** Father 131–35 **Take heed ... sound out** [F gives all to Enobarbus, mistaking (?) speech prefix "Menas" for vocative]

III.i.5 **Silius** Romaine [so throughout scene] 8 **whither** whether

III.ii.10 **Agrippa** Ant 16 **figures** Figure 59 **wept** weepe

III.iv.9 **took't** look't 24 **yours** your 30 **Your** You 38 **has** he's

III.v.14 **world, thou hast** would thou hadst 16 **the one** the other the other

III.vi.13 **he there** hither 13 **kings of kings** King of Kings 74 **Comagene** Comageat

III.vii.4 **it is** it it 5 **Is't** If 23 **Toryne** Troine 35 **muleters** Militers 51 **Actium** Action 69 **led** leade 72 **Canidius** Ven

III.x.s.d. **Enobarbus** Enobarbus and Scarus 14 **June** Inne 27 **he** his

III.xi.19 **that** them 44 **He is** Hee's 47 **seize** cease 51 **whither** whether 58 **tow** stowe 59 **Thy** The

III.xiii.10 **mered** meered 55 **Caesar** Caesars 56 **embraced** embrace 74 **deputation** disputation 104 **errand** arrant 162 **smite** smile 165 **discandying** discandering 168 **sits** sets 199 **preys on** prayes in 201 s.d. **Exit** Exeunt

IV.ii.1 **Domitius** Domitian

IV.iii.7 **Third Soldier** 1
IV.iv.5–8 **Nay, I'll help ... must be** [F gives all to Cleopatra, mistaking (?) speech prefix "Antony" for vocative, and misplacing (?) it after "help too"] 8 **Sooth, la** Sooth-law 13 **daff't** daft 24 **Captain** Alex

IV.v.1,3,6 **Soldier** Eros

IV.viii.2 **gests** guests 23 **favoring** sauoring

IV.xii.4 **augurers** Auguries 21 **spanieled** pannelled

502

TEXTUAL NOTE

IV.xiv.4 towered toward   10 dislimns dislimes   19 Caesar Caesars   104 ho! how?

IV.xv.72 e'en in   90 s.d. off of

V.i.s.d. Maecenas Menas   28,31 Agrippa Dol   59 live leaue

V.ii.56 varletry Varlotarie   81 little O, th' earth little o' th' earth   87 autumn 'twas Antony it was   104 smites suites   216 Ballad Ballads   216 o' tune a Tune   228 Cydnus Cidrus   318 awry away   319 s.d. rustling in rustling in and Dolabella

WILLIAM SHAKESPEARE

THE LIFE OF TIMON OF ATHENS

Edited by Maurice Charney

The Actors' Names

TIMON OF ATHENS
LUCIUS, and ⎫
LUCULLUS ⎭ two flattering lords
SEMPRONIUS, another flattering lord
VENTIDIUS, one of Timon's false friends
APEMANTUS, a churlish philosopher
ALCIBIADES, an Athenian captain
POET
PAINTER
JEWELER
MERCHANT
[FLAVIUS, steward to Timon]
FLAMINIUS, one of Timon's servants
SERVILIUS, another
[LUCILIUS, another]
CAPHIS
PHILOTUS
TITUS
HORTENSIUS ⎬ several servants to usurers
[SERVANT TO] VARRO
[SERVANT TO] LUCIUS
[SERVANT TO ISIDORE]
[AN OLD ATHENIAN]
[THREE STRANGERS]
[A PAGE]
[A FOOL]
[PHRYNIA ⎫
[TIMANDRA ⎭ mistresses to Alcibiades]
CERTAIN MASKERS [AS] CUPID [AND AMAZONS]
CERTAIN SENATORS, CERTAIN THIEVES, WITH DIVERS OTHER
  SERVANTS AND ATTENDANTS, [LORDS, OFFICERS, SOLDIERS]

[*Scene*: Athens and the neighboring woods]

THE TRAGEDY OF
TIMON OF
ATHENS

ACT 1

Scene I. [*Athens. Timon's house.*]

*Enter Poet, Painter, Jeweler, Merchant
at several doors.*

POET Good day, sir.

PAINTER   I am glad y'are well.

POET I have not seen you long; how goes the world?

PAINTER It wears, sir, as it grows.

POET   Ay that's well known.
But what particular rarity? What strange,
Which manifold record not matches? See,   5
Magic of bounty, all these spirits thy power
Hath conjured to attend. I know the merchant.

PAINTER I know them both; th' other's a jeweler.

A footnote is keyed to the text by line number. Text references are printed in **bold**
type; the annotation follows in roman type.
I.i.s.d. **several** separate (the Poet and Painter enter at one door, the Jeweler and
Merchant at another)   3 **wears** wears out   5 **manifold record** many and varied
records, history ("record" accented on second syllable)   6 **bounty** generosity

MERCHANT O 'tis a worthy lord.

JEWELER   Nay that's most fixed.

MERCHANT A most incomparable man, breathed, as it
10   were,
      To an untirable and continuate goodness.
      He passes.

JEWELER   I have a jewel here——

MERCHANT O pray let's see't. For the Lord Timon, sir?

JEWELER If he will touch the estimate. But for that——

POET [*Aside to Painter*] When we for recompense
15   have praised the vild,
      It stains the glory in that happy verse
      Which aptly sings the good.

MERCHANT [*Looking at the jewel*] 'Tis a good form.

JEWELER And rich. Here is a water, look ye.

PAINTER You are rapt, sir, in some work, some dedica-
      tion
      To the great lord.

20 POET   A thing slipped idly from me.
      Our poesy is as a gum, which oozes
      From whence 'tis nourished. The fire i' th' flint
      Shows not till it be struck; our gentle flame
      Provokes itself, and like the current flies
25   Each bound it chases. What have you there?

PAINTER A picture, sir. When comes your book forth?

POET Upon the heels of my presentment, sir.
      Let's see your piece.

---

9 **fixed** certain 10 **breathed** exercised, trained 11 **continuate**
uninterrupted 12 **passes** surpasses 14 **touch the estimate** offer the expected
price 15 **vild** vile 16 **happy** fortunate 18 **water** luster (of a jewel)
23–24 **our gentle flame/Provokes itself** i.e., the inspiration of poets is sponta-
neous, not externally provoked like the "fire i' th' flint" 25 **Each bound it
chases** i.e., the stream flows towards the shore but rebounds upon contact
27 **presentment** presentation (to Timon)

PAINTER 'Tis a good piece.

POET So 'tis; this comes off well and excellent.

PAINTER Indifferent.

POET Admirable. How this grace 30
Speaks his own standing! What a mental power
This eye shoots forth! How big imagination
Moves in this lip! To th' dumbness of the gesture
One might interpret.

PAINTER It is a pretty mocking of the life. 35
Here is a touch—is't good?

POET I will say of it,
It tutors nature; artificial strife
Lives in these touches, livelier than life.

*Enter certain Senators, [who pass over the
stage and exeunt].*

PAINTER How this lord is followed!

POET The senators of Athens, happy men! 40

PAINTER Look, moe!

POET You see this confluence, this great flood of
visitors:
I have in this rough work shaped out a man
Whom this beneath world doth embrace and hug
With amplest entertainment. My free drift 45
Halts not particularly, but moves itself
In a wide sea of wax; no leveled malice

---

30 **Indifferent** neither good nor bad   31 **standing** dignity, social status   32 **big** (adverb)   33 **dumbness** silence (as in a dumb show)   34 **interpret** supply words   35 **mocking** imitation   37 **artificial strife** the striving of art to outdo nature   41 **moe** more   44 **beneath world** sublunary world (Timon as the moon)   46 **particularly** at individuals   47 **sea of wax** (either a sea of inspiration as easily molded as wax—not limited to a mere writing tablet of wax—or perhaps a waxing sea swelling with inspiration)   47 **leveled** aimed (at one person)

Infects one comma in the course I hold,
But flies an eagle flight, bold and forth on,
50 Leaving no tract behind.

PAINTER How shall I understand you?

POET   I will unbolt to you.
You see how all conditions, how all minds,
As well of glib and slipp'ry creatures as
Of grave and austere quality, tender down
55 Their services to Lord Timon. His large fortune,
Upon his good and gracious nature hanging,
Subdues and properties to his love and tendance
All sorts of hearts; yea, from the glass-faced
    flatterer
To Apemantus, that few things loves better
60 Than to abhor himself—even he drops down
The knee before him, and returns in peace
Most rich in Timon's nod.

PAINTER   I saw them speak together.

POET Sir, I have upon a high and pleasant hill
Feigned Fortune to be throned. The base o' th'
    mount
65 Is ranked with all deserts, all kind of natures
That labor on the bosom of this sphere
To propagate their states. Amongst them all,
Whose eyes are on this sovereign lady fixed,
One do I personate of Lord Timon's frame,
70 Whom Fortune with her ivory hand wafts to her,

50 **tract** (either "trace" or "track") 52 **conditions** (1) social classes
(2) temperaments 54 **tender down** offer (as one offers money) 57 **properties**
appropriates 57 **tendance** attendance 58 **glass-faced** mirror-faced
64 **Feigned** imagined 65 **deserts** degrees of worth 67 **propagate their states**
increase their possessions 69 **frame** (1) disposition (2) physical stature
70 **ivory hand** hand white and smooth as ivory (this is the right hand of Fortune,
with which she distributes her favors; with the left or dark hand she takes them
away)

Whose present grace to present slaves and servants
Translates his rivals.

PAINTER   'Tis conceived to scope.
This throne, this Fortune, and this hill, methinks,
With one man beckoned from the rest below,
Bowing his head against the steepy mount   75
To climb his happiness, would be well expressed
In our condition.

POET   Nay, sir, but hear me on.
All those which were his fellows but of late,
Some better than his value, on the moment
Follow his strides, his lobbies fill with tendance,   80
Rain sacrificial whisperings in his ear,
Make sacred even his stirrup, and through him
Drink the free air.

PAINTER   Ay marry, what of these?

POET When Fortune in her shift and change of mood
Spurns down her late beloved, all his dependants   85
Which labored after him to the mountain's top,
Even on their knees and hands, let him slip down,
Not one accompanying his declining foot.

PAINTER 'Tis common.
A thousand moral paintings I can show   90
That shall demonstrate these quick blows of
    Fortune's
More pregnantly than words. Yet you do well
To show Lord Timon that mean eyes have seen
The foot above the head.

71 **present** (1) existing now (2) immediate   71 **grace** graciousness,
generosity   72 **Translates** transforms   72 **to scope** to the purpose, just
right   81 **sacrificial whisperings** (lines 81–83 suggest the hieratic atmosphere
surrounding Timon, now high in Fortune's favor)   83 **Drink** breathe   83 **marry**
indeed (originally "By Mary")   90 **moral paintings** allegorical pictures (especially wall hangings)   91 **demonstrate** (accented on second syllable)
91 **quick** (1) swift (2) full of life   93 **mean** lowly   94 **The foot above the head**
i.e., in the quick changes that Fortune brings, the foot of the lowliest may suddenly
appear above the head of the highest

Trumpets sound. Enter Lord Timon, addressing him-
self courteously to every suitor; [a Messenger from
Ventidius talking with him; Lucilius and other servants
following].

TIMON   Imprisoned is he, say you?

95   MESSENGER Ay, my good lord; five talents is his debt,
     His means most short, his creditors most strait.
     Your honorable letter he desires
     To those have shut him up, which failing,
     Periods his comfort.

TIMON   Noble Ventidius—well.
100 I am not of that feather to shake off
     My friend when he must need me. I do know him
     A gentleman that well deserves a help,
     Which he shall have. I'll pay the debt and free him.

MESSENGER Your lordship ever binds him.

105 TIMON Commend me to him; I will send his ransom,
     And being enfranchised bid him come to me.
     'Tis not enough to help the feeble up,
     But to support him after. Fare you well.

MESSENGER All happiness to your honor.   *Exit.*

               Enter an Old Athenian.

OLD ATHENIAN Lord Timon, hear me speak.

110 TIMON   Freely, good father.

OLD ATHENIAN Thou hast a servant named Lucilius.

TIMON I have so. What of him?

OLD ATHENIAN Most noble Timon, call the man before
     thee.

TIMON Attends he here or no? Lucilius!

115 LUCILIUS Here at your lordship's service.

---

96 **strait** strict   99 **Periods** puts an end to   100 **feather** character   104 **binds**
attaches by ties of gratitude (with play on "free" in line 103)

OLD ATHENIAN This fellow here, Lord Timon, this thy
    creature,
  By night frequents my house. I am a man
  That from my first have been inclined to thrift,
  And my estate deserves an heir more raised
  Than one which holds a trencher.

TIMON   Well; what further? 120

OLD ATHENIAN One only daughter have I, no kin else,
  On whom I may confer what I have got.
  The maid is fair, a th' youngest for a bride,
  And I have bred her at my dearest cost
  In qualities of the best. This man of thine   125
  Attempts her love. I prithee, noble lord,
  Join with me to forbid him her resort;
  Myself have spoke in vain.

TIMON   The man is honest.

OLD ATHENIAN Therefore he will be, Timon.
  His honesty rewards him in itself;   130
  It must not bear my daughter.

TIMON   Does she love him?

OLD ATHENIAN She is young and apt.
  Our own precedent passions do instruct us
  What levity's in youth.

TIMON   Love you the maid?

LUCILIUS Ay, my good lord, and she accepts of it.   135

OLD ATHENIAN If in her marriage my consent be miss-
    ing,
  I call the gods to witness, I will choose

---

116 **fellow, creature** (terms of contempt) 120 **trencher** wooden plate or
shallow dish on which meat is served (a servant who waits on tables would hold a
trencher) 123 **a** (a worn down form for "of") 127 **her resort** resort or access
to her 129 **Therefore he will be** i.e., since Lucilius *is* honest (or honorable), he
will therefore show his honesty by not pursuing the Old Athenian's daughter
131 **bear** carry away 133 **precedent** former (accented on second syllable)

Mine heir from forth the beggars of the world,
And dispossess her all.

TIMON   How shall she be endowed,
140   If she be mated with an equal husband?

OLD ATHENIAN Three talents on the present; in future,
        all.

TIMON This gentleman of mine hath served me long.
        To build his fortune I will strain a little,
        For 'tis a bond in men. Give him thy daughter;
145   What you bestow, in him I'll counterpoise,
        And make him weigh with her.

OLD ATHENIAN   Most noble lord,
        Pawn me to this your honor, she is his.

TIMON My hand to thee, mine honor on my promise.

LUCILIUS Humbly I thank your lordship; never may
150   That state or fortune fall into my keeping,
        Which is not owed to you.
                           Exit [Lucilius, with Old Athenian].

POET Vouchsafe my labor, and long live your lord-
        ship.

TIMON I thank you; you shall hear from me anon.
        Go not away. What have you there, my friend?

155 PAINTER A piece of painting, which I do beseech
        Your lordship to accept.

TIMON   Painting is welcome.
        The painting is almost the natural man;
        For since dishonor traffics with man's nature,
        He is but outside. These penciled figures are

---

139 **all** completely 140 **equal** (either socially or financially) 141 **on the
present** at once 144 **bond** obligation 145 **counterpoise** counterbalance
151 **owed** (1) acknowledged to you as the cause of it (2) due to you as a debt
152 **Vouchsafe** deign to accept 158 **traffics** deals (pejorative sense) 159 **but
outside** merely external, a false semblance 159 **penciled** painted

Even such as they give out. I like your work,   160
And you shall find I like it. Wait attendance
Till you hear further from me.

PAINTER   The gods preserve ye.

TIMON Well fare you, gentleman. Give me your hand;
We must needs dine together. Sir, your jewel
Hath suffered under praise.

JEWELER   What, my lord, dispraise?   165

TIMON A mere satiety of commendations.
If I should pay you for't as 'tis extolled,
It would unclew me quite.

JEWELER   My lord, 'tis rated
As those which sell would give. But you well know,
Things of like value, differing in the owners,   170
Are prizèd by their masters. Believe't, dear lord,
You mend the jewel by the wearing it.

TIMON Well mocked.

MERCHANT No, my good lord; he speaks the common
tongue
Which all men speak with him.   175

Enter Apemantus.

TIMON Look who comes here; will you be chid?

JEWELER We'll bear with your lordship.

MERCHANT   He'll spare none.

---

160 **Even such as they give out** i.e., painting, in contrast with human nature, is honest; it makes no pretense to be something other than what it appears to be 165 **under praise** in being praised, since the jewel is beyond praise (but the Jeweler takes it in the sense of "dispraise") 166 **mere absolute** 168 **unclew** undo 169 **As those which sell would give** i.e., at the wholesale price 171 **Are prizèd by their masters** are valued according to the social status of their owners 172 **mend** improve 173 **mocked** simulated (i.e., I know your flattery is only part of your sales talk) 174 **speaks the common tongue** says what everyone is saying

TIMON Good morrow to thee, gentle Apemantus.

APEMANTUS Till I be gentle, stay thou for thy good
morrow——

180 When thou art Timon's dog, and these knaves honest.

TIMON Why dost thou call them knaves, thou know'st
them not?

APEMANTUS Are they not Athenians?

TIMON Yes.

185 APEMANTUS Then I repent not.

JEWELER You know me, Apemantus?

APEMANTUS Thou know'st I do, I called thee by thy
name.

TIMON Thou art proud, Apemantus.

190 APEMANTUS Of nothing so much as that I am not like
Timon.

TIMON Whither art going?

APEMANTUS To knock out an honest Athenian's brains.

TIMON That's a deed thou't die for.

195 APEMANTUS Right, if doing nothing be death by th'
law.

TIMON How lik'st thou this picture, Apemantus?

APEMANTUS The best, for the innocence.

TIMON Wrought he not well that painted it?

200 APEMANTUS He wrought better that made the painter,
and yet he's but a filthy piece of work.

---

178 **gentle** (1) well-born (a conventional complimentary epithet) (2) mild
198 **innocence** (1) harmlessness (2) foolishness   201 **filthy** contemptible

PAINTER Y'are a dog.

APEMANTUS Thy mother's of my generation. What's she, if I be a dog?

TIMON Wilt dine with me, Apemantus?   205

APEMANTUS No. I eat not lords.

TIMON And thou shouldst, thou'dst anger ladies.

APEMANTUS O they eat lords; so they come by great bellies.

TIMON That's a lascivious apprehension.   210

APEMANTUS So, thou apprehend'st it, take it for thy labor.

TIMON How dost thou like this jewel, Apemantus?

APEMANTUS Not so well as plain-dealing, which will not cost a man a doit.   215

TIMON What dost thou think 'tis worth?

APEMANTUS Not worth my thinking. How now, poet?

POET How now, philosopher?

APEMANTUS Thou liest.

POET Art not one?   220

APEMANTUS Yes.

POET Then I lie not.

APEMANTUS Art not a poet?

POET Yes.

---

202 **dog** (Apemantus is a Cynic philosopher; "cynic" is derived from the Greek word for dog)   203 **generation** (1) breed (2) persons born at about the same time   207 **And if**   208–09 **come by great bellies** become pregnant   215 **doit** a small Dutch coin worth less than a farthing (used as a type expression for any very small sum)

225 APEMANTUS Then thou liest. Look in thy last work,
where thou hast feigned him a worthy fellow.

POET That's not feigned, he is so.

APEMANTUS Yes, he is worthy of thee, and to pay thee
for thy labor. He that loves to be flattered is worthy
230 o' th' flatterer. Heavens, that I were a lord!

TIMON What wouldst do then, Apemantus?

APEMANTUS E'en as Apemantus does now: hate a lord
with my heart.

TIMON What, thyself?

235 APEMANTUS Ay.

TIMON Wherefore?

APEMANTUS That I had no angry wit to be a lord.
Art not thou a merchant?

MERCHANT Ay, Apemantus.

240 APEMANTUS Traffic confound thee, if the gods will not.

MERCHANT If traffic do it, the gods do it.

APEMANTUS Traffic's thy god, and thy god confound
thee.

Trumpet sounds. Enter a Messenger.

TIMON What trumpet's that?

245 MESSENGER 'Tis Alcibiades and some twenty horse,
All of companionship.

TIMON Pray entertain them, give them guide to us.
[*Exeunt some Attendants.*]
You must needs dine with me. Go not you hence

---

225 **liest** (a play on the old idea that poetry is a *mimesis*, imitation, mocking, or
feigning of reality and therefore a lie)   226 **him** i.e., Timon   237 **no angry wit
to be a lord** no more wit in my anger than to wish to be a lord (?)   240 **Traffic**
trade, business   245 **horse** horsemen   246 **All of companionship** all of the
same party

Till I have thanked you. When dinner's done
Show me this piece. I am joyful of your sights. 250

Enter Alcibiades with the rest.

Most welcome, sir.

APEMANTUS   So, so.
Their aches contract and starve your supple
    joints!
That there should be small love amongst these
    sweet knaves,
And all this courtesy! The strain of man's bred out 255
Into baboon and monkey.

ALCIBIADES Sir, you have saved my longing, and I
    feed
Most hungerly on your sight.

TIMON   Right welcome, sir.
Ere we depart, we'll share a bounteous time
In different pleasures. Pray you let us in. 260

Exeunt [all but Apemantus].

Enter two Lords.

FIRST LORD What time a day is't, Apemantus?

APEMANTUS Time to be honest.

FIRST LORD That time serves still.

APEMANTUS The most accursèd thou that still omit'st
it. 265

SECOND LORD Thou art going to Lord Timon's feast?

APEMANTUS Ay, to see meat fill knaves and wine heat
fools.

SECOND LORD Fare thee well, fare thee well.

---

250 of your sights at the sight of you 253 Their i.e., of Alcibiades and his
soldiers 253 aches (the reference is probably to venereal disease—"aches" is
dissyllabic, pronounced "aitches") 253 starve destroy 257 saved anticipated
and so prevented 263 still always 264 omit'st neglects

270 APEMANTUS Thou art a fool to bid me farewell twice.

SECOND LORD Why, Apemantus?

APEMANTUS Shouldst have kept one to thyself, for I mean to give thee none.

FIRST LORD Hang thyself!

275 APEMANTUS No, I will do nothing at thy bidding. Make thy requests to thy friend.

SECOND LORD Away, unpeaceable dog, or I'll spurn thee hence.

APEMANTUS I will fly like a dog the heels a th' ass.

[*Exit.*]

FIRST LORD He's opposite to humanity. Come, shall
280   we in
And taste Lord Timon's bounty? He outgoes
The very heart of kindness.

SECOND LORD He pours it out. Plutus, the god of gold,
Is but his steward; no meed but he repays
285   Sevenfold above itself. No gift to him
But breeds the giver a return exceeding
All use of quittance.

FIRST LORD   The noblest mind he carries
That ever governed man.

SECOND LORD   Long may he live
In fortunes. Shall we in?

FIRST LORD   I'll keep you company. *Exeunt*.

---

277 **unpeaceable** quarrelsome 280 **opposite to** (1) hostile to (2) the reverse of 284 **meed** (1) merit, desert (2) gift (?) 287 **All use of quittance** all the customary returns made in repayment of debts (one meaning of "use" is "interest") 287 **carries** bears

[Scene II. *Timon's house.*]

Hautboys playing loud music. A great banquet served in; and then enter Lord Timon, the States, the Athenian Lords, Ventidius (which Timon redeemed from prison), [and Alcibiades. Steward and others attending.] Then comes dropping after all, Apemantus, discontentedly, like himself.

VENTIDIUS Most honored Timon,
It hath pleased the gods to remember my father's
    age,
And call him to long peace.
He is gone happy, and has left me rich.
Then, as in grateful virtue I am bound   5
To your free heart, I do return those talents
Doubled with thanks and service, from whose help
I derived liberty.

TIMON   O by no means,
Honest Ventidius. You mistake my love;
I gave it freely ever, and there's none   10
Can truly say he gives, if he receives.
If our betters play at that game, we must not dare
To imitate them; faults that are rich are fair.

VENTIDIUS A noble spirit.

TIMON Nay, my lords, ceremony was but devised at
    first   15
To set a gloss on faint deeds, hollow welcomes,
Recanting goodness, sorry ere 'tis shown.

I.ii.s.d. **Hautboys** oboes   s.d. **the States** persons of state, the Senators   6 **free**
generous   12 **our betters** those of higher rank   13 **faults that are rich are fair**
i.e., the faults of rich persons are made to seem attractive because of their
wealth   15 **ceremony** ceremonious attitudes

But where there is true friendship, there needs none.
Pray sit; more welcome are ye to my fortunes
20 Than my fortunes to me.

FIRST LORD My lord, we always have confessed it.

APEMANTUS Ho, ho, confessed it? Hanged it, have
you not?

TIMON O Apemantus, you are welcome.

APEMANTUS No, you shall not make me welcome.
25 I come to have thee thrust me out of doors.

TIMON Fie, th'art a churl, y'have got a humor there
Does not become a man; 'tis much to blame.
They say, my lords, *Ira furor brevis est*, but yond
man is ever angry. Go, let him have a table by
30 himself, for he does neither affect company, nor is
he fit for't indeed.

APEMANTUS Let me stay at thine apperil, Timon.
I come to observe, I give thee warning on't.

TIMON I take no heed of thee. Th'art an Athenian,
35 therefore welcome. I myself would have no power;
prithee let my meat make thee silent.

APEMANTUS I scorn thy meat; 'twould choke me, for I
should ne'er flatter thee. O you gods! What a number of men eats Timon, and he sees 'em not! It grieves
40 me to see so many dip their meat in one man's
blood, and all the madness is, he cheers them up
too.
I wonder men dare trust themselves with men.
Methinks they should invite them without knives:

---

22 **confessed it? Hanged it** (an allusion to the proverb "Confess and be
hanged")   26 **humor** temperamental quirk (in the old physiological sense of the
four humors)   28 **Ira furor brevis est** anger is a brief fury or madness (Horace,
Epistles, I.ii.62)   30 **affect** (1) like (2) seek out   32 **apperil** peril   35 **no power**
i.e., to force you to be silent   37–38 **'twould ... thee** i.e., Apemantus would
prefer to choke on Timon's meat than to flatter him   44 **knives** (dinner guests
normally brought their own knives)

Good for their meat, and safer for their lives. 45
There's much example for't; the fellow that sits
next him, now parts bread with him, pledges the
breath of him in a divided draught, is the readiest
man to kill him. 'T'as been proved. If I were a
huge man, I should fear to drink at meals, 50
Lest they should spy my windpipe's dangerous
   notes;
Great men should drink with harness on their
   throats.

TIMON My lord, in heart; and let the health go round.

SECOND LORD Let it flow this way, my good lord.

APEMANTUS Flow this way? A brave fellow. He keeps 55
his tides well. Those healths will make thee and
thy state look ill, Timon.
Here's that which is too weak to be a sinner,
Honest water, which ne'er left man i' th' mire.
This and my food are equals, there's no odds; 60
Feasts are too proud to give thanks to the gods.

Apemantus' Grace.

Immortal gods, I crave no pelf;
I pray for no man but myself.
Grant I may never prove so fond
To trust man on his oath or bond, 65
Or a harlot for her weeping,
Or a dog that seems a-sleeping,
Or a keeper with my freedom,
Or my friends if I should need 'em.
Amen. So fall to't: 70

---

48 **a divided draught** a drink from a cup that is passed around the table
50 **huge** important 51 **Lest ... notes** i.e., lest men should cut my throat when
my head is tilted backward (with additional allusion to the windpipe as a musical
instrument, like a bagpipe) 52 **harness** armor 53 **My lord, in heart** (a
toast) 55 **brave** excellent 56 **tides** times (with play on the usual sense, linked
to "flow") 57 **state** estate, fortune 61 **Feasts** i.e., those who give feasts
62 **pelf** possessions 64 **fond** foolish 68 **keeper** jailer

Rich men sin, and I eat root.   [*Eats and drinks.*]
Much good dich thy good heart, Apemantus.

TIMON Captain Alcibiades, your heart's in the field
now.

75 ALCIBIADES My heart is ever at your service, my lord,

TIMON You had rather be at a breakfast of enemies
than a dinner of friends.

ALCIBIADES So they were bleeding new, my lord,
there's no meat like 'em; I could wish my best
80 friend at such a feast.

APEMANTUS Would all those flatterers were thine enemies then, that then thou mightst kill 'em—and
bid me to 'em.

FIRST LORD Might we but have that happiness, my
85 lord, that you would once use our hearts, whereby
we might express some part of our zeals, we should
think ourselves for ever perfect.

TIMON O no doubt, my good friends, but the gods
themselves have provided that I shall have much
90 help from you: how had you been my friends else?
Why have you that charitable title from thousands, did not you chiefly belong to my heart? I
have told more of you to myself than you can
with modesty speak in your own behalf; and thus
95 far I confirm you. O you gods, think I, what
need we have any friends, if we should ne'er have
need of 'em? They were the most needless creatures
living should we ne'er have use for 'em, and
would most resemble sweet instruments hung up
100 in cases, that keeps their sounds to themselves.
Why I have often wished myself poorer that I

72 dich may it do (?) 76 of consisting of (but later in the sentence it means
"with") 78 So provided that 83 bid invite 85 use our hearts i.e., make trial
of the feelings in our hearts 87 perfect i.e., in our happiness in demonstrating
our love for Timon 91 charitable loving, kindly 91 from from among
95 confirm sanction, corroborate (your claims as friends)

might come nearer to you. We are born to do
benefits; and what better or properer can we call
our own than the riches of our friends? O what a
precious comfort 'tis to have so many like brothers   105
commanding one another's fortunes. O joy's e'en
made away ere't can be born. Mine eyes cannot
hold out water, methinks. To forget their faults,
I drink to you.

APEMANTUS Thou weep'st to make them drink, Timon.   110

SECOND LORD Joy had the like conception in our eyes,
And at that instant like a babe sprung up.

APEMANTUS Ho, ho! I laugh to think that babe a bastard.

THIRD LORD I promise you, my lord, you moved me
much.

APEMANTUS Much.   *Sound tucket.*   115

TIMON What means that trump?

                 Enter Servant.

                                   How now?

SERVANT Please you, my lord, there are certain ladies
most desirous of admittance.

TIMON Ladies? What are their wills?

SERVANT There comes with them a forerunner, my   120
lord, which bears that office to signify their pleasures.

---

102 **nearer** (1) closer to your hearts (2) closer to your financial status
106–07 **e'en ... born** i.e., our weeping for joy seems to destroy joy before it
properly exists   108 **hold out water** keep out tears   108 **faults** defects   110 **to
make them drink** (1) to provide drink for them (they drink up your tears, and
you and your estate, too) (2) to furnish a pretext for their carousing   111 **the
like conception** a similar birth (i.e., accompanied with tears)   112 **like a babe
sprung up** i.e., the sight of Timon's joy immediately caused the birth of a like joy
in the eyes of his friends   115 s.d. **tucket** a flourish on a trumpet
121–22 **pleasures** wishes

525

TIMON I pray let them be admitted.

[*Enter Cupid.*]

CUPID Hail to thee, worthy Timon, and to all
125   That of his bounties taste. The five best senses
Acknowledge thee their patron, and come freely
To gratulate thy plenteous bosom. Th' ear,
Taste, touch, all, pleased from thy table rise;
They only now come but to feast thine eyes.

TIMON They're welcome all; let 'em have kind admit-
130   tance.
Music make their welcome.   [*Exit Cupid.*]

FIRST LORD You see, my lord, how ample y'are beloved.

[*Music.*] *Enter Cupid with the Masque of Ladies* [*as*]
Amazons, with lutes in their hands, dancing and
playing.

APEMANTUS Hoy-day!
What a sweep of vanity comes this way.
135   They dance? They are madwomen.
Like madness is the glory of this life,
As this pomp shows to a little oil and root.
We make ourselves fools to disport ourselves,
And spend our flatteries to drink those men
140   Upon whose age we void it up again
With poisonous spite and envy.
Who lives that's not depravèd or depraves?
Who dies that bears not one spurn to their graves

---

127 **gratulate** (1) greet (2) gratify, please   129 **but to feast thine eyes** i.e., only
to appeal to the sense of sight, whereas at Timon's banquet all the senses were
gratified   131 **Music** i.e., let music   132 s.d. **Masque** an elaborate allegorical
show or entertainment with emphasis on spectacle, music, and dance
132 s.d. **Amazons** legendary female warriors   133 **Hoy-day** (exclamation of
surprise)   134 **sweep** (in reference to the sweeping motion of the dancers)
136 **Like** similar   136 **glory** vainglory   137 **to** compared to   138 **disport**
amuse   139 **drink** drink the health of   140 **void** vomit   141 **envy** malice
142 **depravèd or depraves** slandered or a slanderer   143 **spurn** insult

Of their friends' gift?
I should fear those that dance before me now   145
Would one day stamp upon me. 'T'as been done.
Men shut their doors against a setting sun.

*The Lords rise from table, with much adoring of Timon,
and to show their loves, each single out an Amazon, and
all dance, men with women, a lofty strain or two to the
hautboys, and cease.*

TIMON You have done our pleasures much grace, fair
        ladies,
Set a fair fashion on our entertainment,
Which was not half so beautiful and kind.   150
You have added worth unto't and luster,
And entertained me with mine own device.
I am to thank you for't.

FIRST LADY My lord, you take us even at the best.

APEMANTUS Faith, for the worst is filthy, and would   155
    not hold taking, I doubt me.

TIMON Ladies, there is an idle banquet attends you,
    Please you to dispose yourselves.

ALL LADIES Most thankfully, my lord.
                              Exeunt [Cupid and Ladies].

TIMON Flavius.   160

FLAVIUS My lord.

TIMON   The little casket bring me hither.

FLAVIUS Yes, my lord. [*Aside*] More jewels yet?

144 gift giving 147 s.d. adoring of paying homage to 149 Set a fair fashion
on given a pleasant semblance to 150 kind gracious 152 mine own device
(suggests that Timon designed the masque or at least had the idea for it)
154 take us even at the best judge us in the most favorable and complimentary
way 155–56 would not hold taking i.e., sexual "taking" is not possible because
of rottenness caused by venereal disease 156 doubt me fear, suspect
(reflexive) 157 idle banquet trifling dessert or light collation 158 Please you
to dispose yourselves if you please to take your places

There is no crossing him in's humor,
Else I should tell him well, i' faith I should,
When all's spent, he'd be crossed then, and he
165   could.
'Tis pity bounty had not eyes behind,
That man might ne'er be wretched for his mind.

Exit.

FIRST LORD Where be our men?

SERVANT Here, my lord, in readiness.

170 SECOND LORD Our horses.

Enter Flavius [with the casket].

TIMON O my friends,
I have one word to say to you. Look you, my good
     lord,
I must entreat you honor me so much
As to advance this jewel; accept it and wear it,
175 Kind my lord.

FIRST LORD I am so far already in your gifts—

ALL So are we all.

Enter a Servant.

SERVANT My lord, there are certain nobles of the senate newly alighted, and come to visit you.

180 TIMON They are fairly welcome.

FLAVIUS I beseech your honor, vouchsafe me a word;
it does concern you near.

TIMON Near? Why then another time I'll hear thee. I
prithee let's be provided to show them entertain-
185   ment.

FLAVIUS *[Aside]* I scarce know how.

---

163 **no crossing him in's humor** no thwarting him in his capricious
disposition   165 **crossed** (1) thwarted (2) have his debts canceled ("crossed" off a
list) (3) be given money (have his palm "crossed")   165 **and** if   167 **for his
mind** for his generous inclinations   174 **advance** enhance in value (by your
wearing it)   180 **fairly** courteously

Enter another Servant.

SECOND SERVANT May it please your honor, Lord
Lucius,
Out of his free love, hath presented to you
Four milk-white horses, trapped in silver.

TIMON I shall accept them fairly. Let the presents   190
Be worthily entertained.

Enter a third Servant.

How now? What news?

THIRD SERVANT Please you, my lord, that honorable
gentleman Lord Lucullus entreats your company
tomorrow to hunt with him, and has sent your
honor two brace of greyhounds.   195

TIMON I'll hunt with him, and let them be received
Not without fair reward.

FLAVIUS [*Aside*]   What will this come to?
He commands us to provide, and give great gifts,
And all out of an empty coffer;
Nor will he know his purse, or yield me this,   200
To show him what a beggar his heart is,
Being of no power to make his wishes good.
His promises fly so beyond his state
That what he speaks is all in debt; he owes for
ev'ry word.
He is so kind that he now pays interest for't;   205
His land's put to their books. Well, would I were
Gently put out of office before I were forced out.
Happier is he that has no friend to feed
Than such that do e'en enemies exceed.
I bleed inwardly for my lord.   *Exit.*   210

189 **trapped in silver** with harness coverings adorned in silver 191 **worthily
entertained** appropriately received 195 **two brace** two pairs 200 **yield**
grant 203 **state** estate, possessions 206 **put to their books** mortgaged (entered
on creditors' account books) 209 **Than such that do e'en enemies exceed**
(1) than such a number that surpasses the number of one's enemies (2) than such
sort of friends whose demands go beyond those of one's enemies

TIMON You do yourselves much wrong,
You bate too much of your own merits.
Here, my lord, a trifle of our love.

SECOND LORD With more than common thanks I will
receive it.

215   THIRD LORD O he's the very soul of bounty.

TIMON And now I remember, my lord, you gave good
words the other day of a bay courser I rode on.
'Tis yours because you liked it.

FIRST LORD O I beseech you pardon me, my lord, in
220   that.

TIMON You may take my word, my lord, I know no
man can justly praise but what he does affect. I
weigh my friend's affection with mine own. I'll
tell you true, I'll call to you.

225   ALL LORDS O none so welcome.

TIMON I take all and your several visitations
So kind to heart, 'tis not enough to give.
Methinks I could deal kingdoms to my friends,
And ne'er be weary. Alcibiades,
230   Thou art a soldier, therefore seldom rich;
It comes in charity to thee, for all thy living
Is 'mongst the dead, and all the lands thou hast
Lie in a pitched field.

ALCIBIADES Ay, defiled land, my lord.

235   FIRST LORD We are so virtuously bound——

TIMON And so am I to you.

212 bate abate, undervalue 217 bay courser reddish-brown stallion
219-20 in that in accepting your gift (because I seemed to solicit it) 222 affect
like, desire to possess 223 weigh consider 223 with equal with 223-24 I'll
tell you true, I'll call to you I assure you I will call on you 226 all and your
several the sum total (an intensive form) 227 'tis not enough to give i.e., mere
gifts, no matter how great, cannot truly express the feeling in my heart 228 deal
distribute 231 It what you receive, a gift 231 living (1) existence (2) property
(3) livelihood 233 pitched field field prepared for a battle 234 defiled land (a
quibble on the proverb, "He that toucheth pitch shall be defiled," *Ecclesiasticus*
13:1)

SECOND LORD So infinitely endeared——

TIMON All to you. Lights, more lights!

FIRST LORD The best of happiness, honor, and fortunes
    Keep with you, Lord Timon.   240

TIMON Ready for his friends.   *Exeunt Lords.*

APEMANTUS   What a coil's here,
    Serving of becks and jutting out of bums!
    I doubt whether their legs be worth the sums
    That are given for 'em. Friendship's full of dregs;
    Methinks false hearts should never have sound legs.   245
    Thus honest fools lay out their wealth on curtsies.

TIMON Now Apemantus, if thou wert not sullen,
    I would be good to thee.

APEMANTUS No, I'll nothing; for if I should be bribed
    too, there would be none left to rail upon thee,   250
    and then thou wouldst sin the faster. Thou giv'st so
    long, Timon, I fear me thou wilt give away thy-
    self in paper shortly. What needs these feasts,
    pomps, and vainglories?

TIMON Nay, and you begin to rail on society once, I   255
    am sworn not to give regard to you. Farewell, and
    come with better music.   *Exit.*

APEMANTUS So. Thou wilt not hear me now, thou
    shalt not then.
    I'll lock thy heaven from thee.
    O that men's ears should be   260
    To counsel deaf, but not to flattery.   *Exit.*

---

237 **endeared** indebted   238 **All to you** i.e., I am all of these things to you rather
than vice versa   241 **coil** fuss, bustle, confusion   242 **Serving of becks** offering
of nods or curtsies   242 **bums** posteriors   243 **legs** (1) bows (cf. "to make a
leg") (2) the limbs themselves   245 **sound legs** i.e., legs healthy enough to make
obeisances   246 **curtsies** (1) bows (2) courtesies (a different spelling of the same
word)   250 **rail upon** revile   253 **in paper** i.e., in promissory notes and other
paper records of debts   258 **thou shalt not then** you will not be able to listen to
me later, when you are bankrupt   259 **thy heaven** i.e., the advice by which I
might have saved you from ruin

[ACT II

Scene I. *A Senator's house*.]

Enter a Senator.

SENATOR And late five thousand. To Varro and to
    Isidore
    He owes nine thousand, besides my former sum,
    Which makes it five and twenty. Still in motion
    Of raging waste? It cannot hold, it will not.
5   If I want gold, steal but a beggar's dog
    And give it Timon—why the dog coins gold.
    If I would sell my horse and buy twenty moe
    Better than he—why give my horse to Timon;
    Ask nothing, give it him, it foals me straight,
10   And able horses. No porter at his gate,
    But rather one that smiles, and still invites
    All that pass by. It cannot hold; no reason
    Can sound his state in safety. Caphis, ho!
    Caphis, I say!

II.i.1 **late** lately 3 **Still** always 4 **hold** last 9 **straight** immediately 10 **No porter** (because a porter's function is to keep out undesirable persons) 12–13 **no reason/Can sound his state in safety** i.e., because Timon is insolvent, no reasonable person can safely fathom or test his estate ("sound" in its nautical sense)

Enter Caphis.

CAPHIS   Here, sir, what is your pleasure?

SENATOR   Get on your cloak, and haste you to Lord
    Timon;   15
    Importune him for my moneys; be not ceased
    With slight denial; nor then silenced when
    "Commend me to your master" and the cap
    Plays in the right hand, thus—but tell him,
    My uses cry to me; I must serve my turn   20
    Out of mine own; his days and times are past,
    And my reliances on his fracted dates
    Have smit my credit. I love and honor him,
    But must not break my back to heal his finger.
    Immediate are my needs, and my relief   25
    Must not be tossed and turned to me in words,
    But find supply immediate. Get you gone;
    Put on a most importunate aspect,
    A visage of demand; for I do fear,
    When every feather sticks in his own wing,   30
    Lord Timon will be left a naked gull,
    Which flashes now a phoenix. Get you gone.

CAPHIS   I go, sir.

SENATOR   Ay, go sir! Take the bonds along with you,
    And have the dates in. Come!

CAPHIS   I will, sir.

SENATOR   Go!   35
                                    Exeunt.

18–19 "Commend me ..." ... thus (examples of anticipated ceremonious delays by Timon) 20 uses financial needs 21 mine own i.e., my own money 21 days and times due dates of his debts 22 fracted broken 28 aspect (accented on second syllable) 30 sticks in his own wing is returned to the bird to which it belongs (i.e., when Timon's debts, and the security he has given for them, are settled) 31 gull (1) unfledged bird (2) credulous dupe 32 phoenix a rare legendary bird which immolated itself and was reborn from its own ashes; a unique or matchless person 35 have the dates in put in the exact dates when the bonds fall due

[Scene II. *Timon's house.*]

Enter [Flavius, the] Steward, with many bills in his hand.

FLAVIUS No care, no stop, so senseless of expense
That he will neither know how to maintain it,
Nor cease his flow of riot. Takes no accompt
How things go from him, nor resumes no care
5   Of what is to continue. Never mind
Was to be so unwise to be so kind.
What shall be done he will not hear, till feel.
I must be round with him, now he comes from
hunting.
Fie, fie, fie, fie!

Enter Caphis, [with the Servants of] Isidore and Varro.

CAPHIS Good even, Varro. What, you come for
10   money?

VARRO'S SERVANT Is't not your business too?

CAPHIS It is; and yours too, Isidore?

ISIDORE'S SERVANT It is so.

CAPHIS Would we were all discharged.

15 VARRO'S SERVANT I fear it.

CAPHIS Here comes the lord.

Enter Timon and his Train, [and Alcibiades].

TIMON So soon as dinner's done, we'll forth again,

II.ii.3 **riot** extravagance, irresponsible reveling 4 **resumes no care** has no
concern 6 **to be so kind** (1) as to be so generous (2) in order to be so
generous 8 **round** blunt 14 **discharged** paid (of a debt) 15 **I fear it** I
doubt it

534

My Alcibiades. [*To Caphis*] With me, what is your
   will?

CAPHIS My lord, here is a note of certain dues.

TIMON Dues? Whence are you?

CAPHIS   Of Athens here, my lord.   20

TIMON Go to my steward.

CAPHIS Please it your lordship, he hath put me off
   To the succession of new days this month.
   My master is awaked by great occasion
   To call upon his own, and humbly prays you   25
   That with your other noble parts you'll suit
   In giving him his right.

TIMON   Mine honest friend,
   I prithee but repair to me next morning.

CAPHIS Nay, good my lord——

TIMON   Contain thyself, good friend.

VARRO'S SERVANT One Varro's servant, my good lord—   30

ISIDORE'S SERVANT From Isidore; he humbly prays your
   speedy payment.

CAPHIS If you did know, my lord, my master's
   wants——

VARRO'S SERVANT 'Twas due on forfeiture, my lord, six   35
   weeks and past.

ISIDORE'S SERVANT Your steward puts me off, my lord,
   and I am sent expressly to your lordship.

TIMON Give me breath.
   I do beseech you, good my lords, keep on;   40
   I'll wait upon you instantly.
              [*Exeunt Alcibiades and Lords.*]

23 **To the succession of new days** from one day to the next 26 **That ... suit**
i.e., that you will act in accordance with your other noble qualities 28 **repair**
return 35 **on** on penalty of 40 **keep on** go ahead

[*To Flavius*] Come hither. Pray you,
How goes the world, that I am thus encount'red
With clamorous demands of broken bonds,
And the detention of long since due debts
Against my honor?

45 FLAVIUS   Please you, gentlemen,
The time is unagreeable to this business.
Your importunacy cease till after dinner,
That I may make his lordship understand
Wherefore you are not paid.

50 TIMON Do so, my friends. See them well entertained.
                                                                    Exit.

FLAVIUS Pray draw near.   [*Exit.*]

                    Enter Apemantus and Fool.

CAPHIS Stay, stay, here comes the fool with Ape-
        mantus.
        Let's ha' some sport with 'em.

55 VARRO'S SERVANT Hang him, he'll abuse us.

ISIDORE'S SERVANT A plague upon him, dog!

VARRO'S SERVANT How dost, fool?

APEMANTUS Dost dialogue with thy shadow?

VARRO'S SERVANT I speak not to thee.

60 APEMANTUS No, 'tis to thyself. [*To the Fool*] Come
        away.

ISIDORE'S SERVANT [*To Varro's Servant*] There's the
        fool hangs on your back already.

APEMANTUS No, thou stand'st single, th'art not on
65   him yet.

CAPHIS Where's the fool now?

APEMANTUS He last asked the question. Poor rogues
        and usurers' men, bawds between gold and want.

42 **How goes the world** what is going on 44 **detention** withholding
payment 47 **importunacy** urgent solicitation 64 **single** alone

536

ALL SERVANTS What are we, Apemantus?

APEMANTUS Asses. 70

ALL SERVANTS Why?

APEMANTUS That you ask me what you are, and do
not know yourselves. Speak to 'em, fool.

FOOL How do you, gentlemen?

ALL SERVANTS Gramercies, good fool. How does your 75
mistress?

FOOL She's e'en setting on water to scald such chickens as you are. Would we could see you at Corinth.

APEMANTUS Good, gramercy.

Enter Page.

FOOL Look you, here comes my mistress' page. 80

PAGE [*To the Fool*] Why, how now, captain? What do
you in this wise company? How dost thou, Apemantus?

APEMANTUS Would I had a rod in my mouth, that
I might answer thee profitably. 85

PAGE Prithee, Apemantus, read me the superscription
of these letters. I know not which is which.

APEMANTUS Canst not read?

PAGE No.

APEMANTUS There will little learning die then that 90
day thou art hanged. This is to Lord Timon, this
to Alcibiades. Go, thou wast born a bastard, and
thou'lt die a bawd.

---

75 **Gramercies** thanks   77 **scald** a method of removing feathers from chickens
(with suggestions of loss of hair in venereal disease, and of sweating in a heated
tub, which was one of the treatments of venereal disease)   78 **Corinth** ancient
city noted for licentiousness (hence a cant term for brothel or red-light
district)   84 **rod** stick to beat you   85 **profitably** for your profit or
improvement   86–87 **superscription** address

PAGE Thou wast whelped a dog, and thou shalt fam-
95   ish a dog's death. Answer not, I am gone.   *Exit*.

APEMANTUS E'en so thou outrun'st grace. Fool, I will go
with you to Lord Timon's.

FOOL Will you leave me there?

APEMANTUS If Timon stay at home. You three serve
100   three usurers?

ALL SERVANTS Ay; would they served us.

APEMANTUS So would I—as good a trick as ever hangman served thief.

FOOL Are you three usurers' men?

105 ALL SERVANTS Ay, fool.

FOOL I think no usurer but has a fool to his servant.
My mistress is one, and I am her fool. When men
come to borrow of your masters, they approach
sadly, and go away merry; but they enter my
110   mistress' house merrily, and go away sadly. The
reason of this?

VARRO'S SERVANT I could render one.

APEMANTUS Do it then, that we may account thee a
whoremaster and a knave, which notwithstanding,
115   thou shalt be no less esteemed.

VARRO'S SERVANT What is a whoremaster, fool?

FOOL A fool in good clothes, and something like thee.
'Tis a spirit; sometime't appears like a lord, sometime like a lawyer, sometime like a philosopher,
120   with two stones moe than's artificial one. He is
very often like a knight; and generally, in all shapes

94–95 **famish a dog's death** die by famishing, a mean death appropriate for a
dog   96 **E'en so thou outrun'st grace** i.e., by leaving now and not listening to
my profitable answer, you will never receive grace   109 **sadly** gravely
120 **stones** testicles   120 **artificial one** philosopher's stone (a highly refined
substance which could turn base metals into gold)

that man goes up and down in, from fourscore to
thirteen, this spirit walks in.

VARRO'S SERVANT Thou are not altogether a fool.

FOOL Nor thou altogether a wise man. As much fool-   125
ery as I have, so much wit thou lack'st.

APEMANTUS That answer might have become Apemantus.

Enter Timon and [Flavius, the] Steward.

ALL SERVANTS Aside, aside, here comes Lord Timon.

APEMANTUS Come with me, fool, come.   130

FOOL I do not always follow lover, elder brother, and
woman; sometime the philosopher.

FLAVIUS Pray you, walk near: I'll speak with you anon.
                         Exeunt [Apemantus, Fool, and Servants].

TIMON You make me marvel wherefore ere this time
Had you not fully laid my state before me,   135
That I might so have rated my expense
As I had leave of means.

FLAVIUS   You would not hear me.
At many leisures I proposed——

TIMON   Go to.
Perchance some single vantages you took
When my indisposition put you back,   140
And that unaptness made your minister
Thus to excuse yourself.

FLAVIUS   O my good lord,
At many times I brought in my accompts,

131–32 **lover, elder brother, and woman** (persons who might be expected to be
generous) 133 **anon** soon 135 **state** financial situation 136 **rated**
regulated 137 **As I had leave of means** as my means would allow 138 **At
many leisures** i.e., when you were at leisure 138 **Go to** nonsense (an exclamation of impatience) 139 **vantages** opportunities 140 **indisposition**
disinclination 141 **unaptness** unreadiness to listen 141 **minister** ministration,
prompting

Laid them before you; you would throw them off,
145 And say you found them in mine honesty.
When for some trifling present you have bid me
Return so much, I have shook my head and wept;
Yea 'gainst th' authority of manners, prayed you
To hold your hand more close. I did endure
150 Not seldom, nor no slight checks, when I have
Prompted you in the ebb of your estate
And your great flow of debts. My loved lord,
Though you hear now, too late, yet now's a time:
The greatest of your having lacks a half
To pay your present debts.

155 TIMON   Let all my land be sold.

FLAVIUS 'Tis all engaged, some forfeited and gone,
And what remains will hardly stop the mouth
Of present dues. The future comes apace.
What shall defend the interim? And at length
160 How goes our reck'ning?

TIMON To Lacedaemon did my land extend.

FLAVIUS O my good lord, the world is but a word;
Were it all yours to give it in a breath,
How quickly were it gone!

TIMON   You tell me true.

165 FLAVIUS If you suspect my husbandry or falsehood,
Call me before th' exactest auditors,
And set me on the proof. So the gods bless me,
When all our offices have been oppressed
With riotous feeders, when our vaults have wept
170 With drunken spilth of wine, when every room
Hath blazed with lights and brayed with minstrelsy,

---

148 th' authority of manners the dictates of good manners 150 checks
rebukes 151 Prompted (in its theatrical sense) 154 The greatest of your
having your worth estimated at the highest possible figure 156 engaged
mortgaged 158 apace swiftly 165 suspect my husbandry or falsehood
suspect me of false husbandry or dishonest management 167 on to 168 offices
service rooms of a household 168 oppressed crowded 169 feeders
servants 169 vaults wine cellars 170 spilth spilling

I have retired me to a wasteful cock,
And set mine eyes at flow.

TIMON   Prithee no more.

FLAVIUS Heavens, have I said, the bounty of this lord!
How many prodigal bits have slaves and peasants   175
This night englutted! Who is not Timon's?
What heart, head, sword, force, means, but is
   Lord Timon's?
Great Timon, noble, worthy, royal Timon!
Ah, when the means are gone that buy this praise,
The breath is gone whereof this praise is made.   180
Feast-won, fast-lost; one cloud of winter show'rs,
These flies are couched.

TIMON   Come, sermon me no further.
No villainous bounty yet hath passed my heart;
Unwisely, not ignobly, have I given.
Why dost thou weep? Canst thou the conscience
   lack   185
To think I shall lack friends? Secure thy heart.
If I would broach the vessels of my love,
And try the argument of hearts by borrowing,
Men and men's fortunes could I frankly use
As I can bid thee speak.

FLAVIUS   Assurance bless your thoughts.   190

TIMON And in some sort these wants of mine are
   crowned,
That I account them blessings; for by these

---

172 **wasteful cock** spigot (of a wine cask) that has not been shut off 173 **And set mine eyes at flow** i.e., following the example of the "wasteful cock," I have added my tears to the general riot and superfluity 175 **prodigal bits** wasteful morsels 176 **englutted** gulped down 181 **Feast-won, fast-lost** the friendship that is won by giving feasts is quickly lost (with pun on "fast" as noun and adverb) 182 **couched** lying hidden 183 **villainous bounty** generosity for evil purposes 185 **conscience** reasonableness 186 **Secure** make free from care or apprehension 187 **broach the vessels** tap the casks 188 **try the argument** test the theme or contents 189 **frankly** freely 190 **Assurance** i.e., may assurance 191 **crowned** given a royal dignity

Shall I try friends. You shall perceive how you
Mistake my fortunes; I am wealthy in my friends.
195 Within there! Flaminius! Servilius!

    Enter [Flaminius, Servilius, and Third Servant].

SERVANTS My lord, my lord.

TIMON I will dispatch you severally.   [*To Servilius*]
You to Lord Lucius, [*to Flaminius*] to Lord Lucullus you; I hunted with his honor today. [*To Third*
200 *Servant*] You to Sempronius. Commend me to their
loves; and I am proud, say, that my occasions
have found time to use 'em toward a supply of
money. Let the request be fifty talents.

FLAMINIUS As you have said, my lord.
                        [*Exeunt Servants.*]

205 FLAVIUS [*Aside*] Lord Lucius and Lucullus? Humh!

TIMON Go you, sir, to the senators,
Of whom, even to the state's best health, I have
Deserved this hearing. Bid 'em send o' th' instant
A thousand talents to me.

FLAVIUS   I have been bold,
210 For that I knew it the most general way,
To them to use your signet and your name;
But they do shake their heads, and I am here
No richer in return.

TIMON   Is't true? Can't be?

FLAVIUS They answer in a joint and corporate voice,
215 That now they are at fall, want treasure, cannot
Do what they would, are sorry; you are honorable,
But yet they could have wished—they know not;
Something hath been amiss—a noble nature

197 **severally** separately   201 **occasions** needs   207 **even to the state's best
health** i.e., Timon, because of his own generosity to the state in the past, now
deserves a loan from them to the very outermost limit they can pay (?)
210 **general** usual   211 **signet** signet ring (as sign of authority to act)   215 **at
fall** at ebb tide

May catch a wrench—would all were well—'tis
   pity—
And so, intending other serious matters,   220
After distasteful looks, and these hard fractions,
With certain half-caps and cold-moving nods,
They froze me into silence.

TIMON   You gods reward them!
   Prithee man look cheerly. These old fellows
Have their ingratitude in them hereditary.   225
Their blood is caked, 'tis cold, it seldom flows;
'Tis lack of kindly warmth they are not kind;
And nature, as it grows again toward earth,
Is fashioned for the journey, dull and heavy.
Go to Ventidius. Prithee be not sad;   230
Thou art true and honest; ingeniously I speak,
No blame belongs to thee. Ventidius lately
Buried his father, by whose death he's stepped
Into a great estate. When he was poor,
Imprisoned, and in scarcity of friends,   235
I cleared him with five talents. Greet him from me,
Bid him suppose some good necessity
Touches his friend, which craves to be rememb'red
With those five talents. That had, give't these
   fellows
To whom 'tis instant due. Nev'r speak or think   240
That Timon's fortunes 'mong his friends can sink.

FLAVIUS I would I could not think it; that thought is
   bounty's foe.
Being free itself, it thinks all others so.   *Exeunt.*

---

219 **catch a wrench** accidentally be twisted from its natural bent   220 **intending**
pretending   221 **hard fractions** harsh fragments of speech (conveyed in the
broken syntax)   222 **half-caps** half-courteous salutations   222 **cold-moving**
producing cold, frigid   227 **kindly** (1) natural (2) generous   228 **grows again
toward earth** approaches death and the grave   231 **ingeniously** ingenuously,
candidly   237 **good necessity** valid need   240 **instant** instantly,
immediately   241 **'mong** in the midst of   243 **free** bounteous

[ACT III

Scene I. *Lucullus' house.*]

*Flaminius waiting to speak with Lord [Lucullus]
from his Master, enters a Servant to him.*

SERVANT I have told my lord of you; he is coming
down to you.

FLAMINIUS I thank you, sir.

Enter Lucullus.

SERVANT Here's my lord.

5 LUCULLUS [*Aside*] One of Lord Timon's men? A gift
I warrant. Why this hits right; I dreamt of a silver
basin and ewer tonight.—Flaminius, honest Flaminius, you are very respectively welcome, sir.
Fill me some wine. [*Exit Servant.*] And how does
10 that honorable, complete, free-hearted gentleman
of Athens, thy very bountiful good lord and master?

FLAMINIUS His health is well, sir.

III.i.7 **tonight** last night 8 **respectively** respectfully 10 **complete** fully
equipped or endowed, perfect

544

LUCULLUS I am right glad that his health is well, sir.
And what hast thou there under thy cloak, pretty   15
Flaminius?

FLAMINIUS Faith, nothing but an empty box, sir,
which in my lord's behalf I come to entreat your
honor to supply; who, having great and instant
occasion to use fifty talents, hath sent to your lord-   20
ship to furnish him, nothing doubting your present
assistance therein.

LUCULLUS La, la, la, la! "Nothing doubting," says he?
Alas, good lord, a noble gentleman 'tis, if he would
not keep so good a house. Many a time and often   25
I ha' dined with him, and told him on't, and come
again to supper to him of purpose to have him
spend less, and yet he would embrace no counsel,
take no warning by my coming. Every man has
his fault, and honesty is his. I ha' told him on't,   30
but I could ne'er get him from't.

Enter Servant, with wine.

SERVANT Please your lordship, here is the wine.

LUCULLUS Flaminius, I have noted thee always wise.
Here's to thee.

FLAMINIUS Your lordship speaks your pleasure.   35

LUCULLUS I have observed thee always for a towardly
prompt spirit, give thee thy due, and one that
knows what belongs to reason; and canst use the
time well, if the time use thee well. Good parts
in thee. [*To Servant*] Get you gone, sirrah. [*Exit*   40
Servant.] Draw nearer, honest Flaminius. Thy
lord's a bountiful gentleman, but thou art wise,
and thou know'st well enough, although thou

15 **pretty** (vague epithet of praise)   19 **supply** fill   21 **present** immediate
25 **so good a house** such lavish hospitality   30 **honesty** generosity   35 **speaks
your pleasure** is pleased to say so   36–37 **towardly prompt spirit** well-
disposed and well-inclined person   39 **if the time use thee well** if you strike
good fortune   39 **parts** qualities

545

com'st to me, that this is no time to lend money,
45   especially upon bare friendship without security.
Here's three solidares for thee. Good boy, wink
at me, and say thou saw'st me not. Fare thee well.

FLAMINIUS   Is't possible the world should so much
    differ,
And we alive that lived? Fly, damnèd baseness,
50   To him that worships thee.

                    [*Throws back the money.*]

LUCULLUS   Ha? Now I see thou art a fool, and fit for
thy master.   *Exit.*

FLAMINIUS   May these add to the number that may
    scald thee.
Let molten coin be thy damnation,
55   Thou disease of a friend, and not himself.
Has friendship such a faint and milky heart
It turns in less than two nights? O you gods!
I feel my master's passion. This slave
Unto his honor has my lord's meat in him;
60   Why should it thrive and turn to nutriment
When he is turned to poison?
O may diseases only work upon't,
And when he's sick to death, let not that part of
    nature
Which my lord paid for be of any power
65   To expel sickness, but prolong his hour.   *Exit.*

---

46 **solidares** (perhaps Shakespeare was referring to the Roman "solidus," which
was used in England for a shilling)   46 **wink** shut your eyes   48 **differ**
change   49 **And we alive that lived** i.e., the world changes so swiftly, it is hard
to believe that the same people are still alive   53 **these** (the rejected coins)
53 **scald** i.e., in hell   54 **thy damnation** the torment you will suffer in hell
(perhaps a reference to the pouring of molten gold down the throat of Marcus
Crassus by the Parthians, thought of as a punishment in hell for avarice)
57 **turns** curdles   58 **passion** anger, suffering (trisyllabic)   58–59 **slave/Unto
his honor** (ironical: "this man who claims to be so devoted to honor")   59 **meat**
food (in general, in contradistinction to "drink")   63 **that part of nature** i.e.,
that part of his body nourished by Timon's food   65 **but prolong his hour** i.e.,
may he have a lingering death

[Scene II. *A public place.*]

Enter Lucius, with three Strangers.

LUCIUS Who, the Lord Timon? He is my very good
friend and an honorable gentleman.

FIRST STRANGER We know him for no less, though we
are but strangers to him. But I can tell you one
thing, my lord, and which I hear from common   5
rumors: now Lord Timon's happy hours are done
and past, and his estate shrinks from him.

LUCIUS Fie, no, do not believe it; he cannot want for
money.

SECOND STRANGER But believe you this, my lord, that   10
not long ago, one of his men was with the Lord
Lucullus to borrow so many talents, nay urged
extremely for't, and showed what necessity be-
longed to't, and yet was denied.

LUCIUS How?   15

SECOND STRANGER I tell you, denied, my lord.

LUCIUS What a strange case was that! Now before
the gods I am ashamed on't. Denied that honorable
man? There was very little honor showed in't. For
my own part, I must needs confess, I have received   20
some small kindnesses from him, as money, plate,
jewels, and suchlike trifles, nothing comparing to
his; yet had he mistook him and sent to me, I
should ne'er have denied his occasion so many
talents.   25

III.ii.s.d. **Strangers** foreigners, non-Athenians   12 **so many talents** (an indefi-
nite number probably intended to be replaced, in revision, by a definite
number)   21 **plate** utensils for domestic use, especially of gold or silver   23 **his**
i.e., Lucullus'   23 **mistook him** made a mistake   24 **occasion** need

SERVILIUS See, by good hap, yonder's my lord; I have
sweat to see his honor. My honored lord.

LUCIUS Servilius? You are kindly met, sir. Fare thee
well; commend me to thy honorable virtuous lord,
30   my very exquisite friend.

SERVILIUS May it please your honor, my lord hath
sent——

LUCIUS Ha? What has he sent? I am so much endeared to that lord; he's ever sending. How shall
35   I thank him, think'st thou? And what has he sent
now?

SERVILIUS Has only sent his present occasion now, my
lord, requesting your lordship to supply his instant
use with so many talents.

40   LUCIUS I know his lordship is but merry with me,
He cannot want fifty five hundred talents.

SERVILIUS But in the meantime he wants less, my lord.
If his occasion were not virtuous,
I should not urge it half so faithfully.

45   LUCIUS Dost thou speak seriously, Servilius?

SERVILIUS Upon my soul 'tis true, sir.

LUCIUS What a wicked beast was I to disfurnish myself against such a good time, when I might ha'
shown myself honorable! How unluckily it
50   happ'ned that I should purchase the day before for
a little part, and undo a great deal of honor!
Servilius, now before the gods I am not able to
do—the more beast, I say! I was sending to use

33–34 **endeared** indebted 41 **want** (1) be without, lack (2) need, desire
41 **fifty five hundred talents** a huge sum 47–48 **disfurnish myself against** to
allow myself to be unprovided for 50–51 **for a little part** for a little business
transaction (deliberately vague) 51 **undo a great deal of honor** i.e., lose the
anticipated honor of lending to Timon

Lord Timon myself, these gentlemen can witness;
but I would not for the wealth of Athens I had   55
done't now. Commend me bountifully to his good
lordship, and I hope his honor will conceive the
fairest of me, because I have no power to be kind.
And tell him this from me, I count it one of my
greatest afflictions, say, that I cannot pleasure such   60
an honorable gentleman. Good Servilius, will you
befriend me so far as to use mine own words to
him?

SERVILIUS Yes, sir, I shall.

LUCIUS I'll look you out a good turn, Servilius.   65
                                        Exit Servilius.

True, as you said, Timon is shrunk indeed,
And he that's once denied will hardly speed.   *Exit.*

FIRST STRANGER Do you observe this, Hostilius?

SECOND STRANGER   Ay, too well.

FIRST STRANGER Why this is the world's soul, and just
     of the same piece
Is every flatterer's sport. Who can call him his friend   70
That dips in the same dish? For in my knowing
Timon has been this lord's father,
And kept his credit with his purse;
Supported his estate; nay, Timon's money
Has paid his men their wages. He ne'er drinks   75
But Timon's silver treads upon his lip,
And yet—O see the monstrousness of man
When he looks out in an ungrateful shape—
He does deny him, in respect of his,
What charitable men afford to beggars.   80

THIRD STRANGER Religion groans at it.

57–58 **conceive the fairest** think the best   67 **speed** be successful, prosper
69 **piece** sort, kind   70 **sport** mockery, diversion (as Lucius has just made sport
of Timon)   73 **kept his** sustained Lucius'   73 **his** i.e., Timon's   76 **treads**
presses   78 **shape** form   79 **in respect of his** in relation to what Lucius is worth

FIRST STRANGER   For mine own part,
    I never tasted Timon in my life,
    Nor came any of his bounties over me
    To mark me for his friend. Yet I protest,
85   For his right noble mind, illustrious virtue,
    And honorable carriage,
    Had his necessity made use of me,
    I would have put my wealth into donation,
    And the best half should have returned to him,
90   So much I love his heart. But I perceive
    Men must learn now with pity to dispense,
    For policy sits above conscience.   *Exeunt.*

[Scene III. *Sempronius' house.*]

*Enter a Third Servant [of Timon] with
Sempronius, another of Timon's friends.*

SEMPRONIUS Must he needs trouble me in't—humh!—
    'bove all others?
    He might have tried Lord Lucius or Lucullus,
    And now Ventidius is wealthy too,
    Whom he redeemed from prison. All these
    Owes their estates unto him.

5 THIRD SERVANT   My lord,
    They have all been touched and found base metal,
    For they have all denied him.

SEMPRONIUS   How? Have they denied him?
    Has Ventidius and Lucullus denied him,
    And does he send to me? Three? Humh!

82 **tasted** experienced the qualities of 85 **right** very 86 **carriage** moral
conduct 88 **put my wealth into donation** i.e., treated my fortune as a gift from
Timon 89 **returned** been given back 92 **policy** cunning III.iii.6 **touched**
tested (by being rubbed on a touchstone; unlike base metals, gold and silver
produced the proper colored streak)

It shows but little love or judgment in him.   10
Must I be his last refuge? His friends, like physi-
    cians,
Thrive, give him over. Must I take th' cure upon
    me?
Has much disgraced me in't; I'm angry at him
That might have known my place. I see no sense
    for't,
But his occasions might have wooed me first;   15
For, in my conscience, I was the first man
That e'er received gift from him.
And does he think so backwardly of me now
That I'll requite it last? No.
So it may prove an argument of laughter   20
To th' rest, and I 'mongst lords be thought a fool.
I'd rather than the worth of thrice the sum,
Had sent to me first, but for my mind's sake;
I'd such a courage to do him good. But now return,
And with their faint reply this answer join: 25
Who bates mine honor shall not know my coin.

                                            Exit.

THIRD SERVANT Excellent. Your lordship's a goodly
    villain. The devil knew not what he did when he
    made man politic; he crossed himself by't: and
    I cannot think but in the end the villainies of   30
    man will set him clear. How fairly this lord
    strives to appear foul! Takes virtuous copies to be
    wicked. Like those that under hot ardent zeal

12 **Thrive, give him over** i.e., prosper on his money while they are giving him up for dead (?) 14 **my place** i.e., before Lucullus, Lucius, and Ventidius 15 **occasions** needs 18 **backwardly** (1) poorly (2) near the end, late 20 **argument** occasion, subject 23 **Had** i.e., he had (perhaps "H'ad"?) 23 **but for my mind's sake** if only to express my good will towards him 24 **courage** desire 26 **bates** abates, undervalues 29 **politic** cunning 29 **he crossed himself by't** i.e., the devil thwarted his own purposes by making man his rival in shrewdness and guile 31 **will set him clear** will make the devil appear innocent (when compared with the "villainies of man") 31 **How fairly** with what a beautiful appearance 32 **foul** ugly 32–33 **Takes virtuous copies to be wicked** i.e., models himself on exemplars of virtue to serve as disguise for his wickedness 33 **those** i.e., religious fanatics (perhaps "zeal" suggests an allusion to Puritans)

35
would set whole realms on fire, of such a nature is
his politic love.
This was my lord's best hope; now all are fled
Save only the gods. Now his friends are dead,
Doors that were ne'er acquainted with their wards
Many a bounteous year, must be employed
40
Now to guard sure their master.
And this is all a liberal course allows;
Who cannot keep his wealth must keep his house.

Exit.

[Scene IV. *Timon's house.*]

Enter Varro's [two Servants], meeting others. All [the Servants of] Timon's creditors to wait for his coming out. Then enter [the Servant of] Lucius; [then Titus] and Hortensius.

VARRO'S FIRST SERVANT Well met; good morrow, Titus
and Hortensius.

TITUS The like to you, kind Varro.

HORTENSIUS   Lucius!
What, do we meet together?

LUCIUS' SERVANT   Ay, and I think
One business does command us all;
For mine is money.

5   TITUS   So is theirs and ours.

Enter Philotus.

LUCIUS' SERVANT And, sir, Philotus' too!

PHILOTUS   Good day at once.

38 **wards** locks 40 **sure** securely 41 **liberal** generous 42 **keep his house**
remain at home (for fear of being arrested for debt) III.iv.6 **at once** to you all

552

LUCIUS' SERVANT Welcome, good brother. What do you
   think the hour?

PHILOTUS Laboring for nine.

LUCIUS' SERVANT So much?

PHILOTUS   Is not my lord seen yet?

LUCIUS' SERVANT   Not yet.

PHILOTUS I wonder on't; he was wont to shine at seven.   10

LUCIUS' SERVANT Ay, but the days are waxed shorter
   with him.
  You must consider that a prodigal course
  Is like the sun's,
  But not like his recoverable, I fear.
  'Tis deepest winter in Lord Timon's purse;   15
  That is, one may reach deep enough and yet
  Find little.

PHILOTUS   I am of your fear for that.

TITUS I'll show you how t' observe a strange event.
  Your lord sends now for money?

HORTENSIUS   Most true, he does.

TITUS And he wears jewels now of Timon's gift,   20
  For which I wait for money.

HORTENSIUS It is against my heart.

LUCIUS' SERVANT   Mark how strange it shows,
  Timon in this should pay more than he owes;
  And e'en as if your lord should wear rich jewels
  And send for money for 'em.   25

HORTENSIUS I'm weary of this charge, the gods can
   witness.

---

11 **waxed** grown 12–14 **prodigal course ... recoverable** i.e., the prodigal, like
the sun, declines, but cannot renew himself every day 18 **observe** observe and
interpret 22 **against my heart** contrary to my natural feeling 23 **should pay
more than he owes** i.e., he has given the gifts, and now he is also asked for the
money for them 26 **charge** task

I know my lord hath spent of Timon's wealth,
And now ingratitude makes it worse than stealth.

VARRO'S FIRST SERVANT Yes, mine's three thousand
crowns. What's yours?

30 LUCIUS' SERVANT Five thousand mine.

VARRO'S FIRST SERVANT 'Tis much deep, and it should
seem by th' sum
Your master's confidence was above mine,
Else surely his had equaled.

Enter Flaminius.

TITUS One of Lord Timon's men.

35 LUCIUS' SERVANT Flaminius? Sir, a word. Pray is my
lord ready to come forth?

FLAMINIUS No, indeed he is not.

TITUS We attend his lordship; pray signify so much.

FLAMINIUS I need not tell him that; he knows you are
40 too diligent.   [*Exit.*]

*Enter [Flavius, the] Steward, in a cloak,
muffled.*

LUCIUS' SERVANT Ha! Is not that his steward muffled
so?
He goes away in a cloud. Call him, call him.

TITUS Do you hear, sir?

VARRO'S SECOND SERVANT By your leave, sir.

45 FLAVIUS What do ye ask of me, my friend?

TITUS We wait for certain money here, sir.

FLAVIUS   Ay,
If money were as certain as your waiting,

28 **stealth** stealing 32 **confidence** trust 32 **mine** i.e., my master's
40 s.d. **muffled** wrapped up, especially about the face 42 **in a cloud** (1) in a
state of gloominess and concern (2) covered with a cloud because he is muffled

'Twere sure enough.
Why then preferred you not your sums and bills
When your false masters ate of my lord's meat?   50
Then they could smile, and fawn upon his debts,
And take down th' int'rest into their glutt'nous
    maws.
You do yourselves but wrong to stir me up;
Let me pass quietly.
Believe't, my lord and I have made an end;   55
I have no more to reckon, he to spend.

LUCIUS' SERVANT Ay, but this answer will not serve.

FLAVIUS If 'twill not serve, 'tis not so base as you,
    For you serve knaves   [Exit.]

VARRO'S FIRST SERVANT How? What does his cashiered
    worship mutter?   60

VARRO'S SECOND SERVANT No matter what; he's poor,
and that's revenge enough. Who can speak
broader than he that has no house to put his head
in? Such may rail against great buildings.

Enter Servilius.

TITUS O here's Servilius. Now we shall know some   65
answer.

SERVILIUS If I might beseech you, gentlemen, to repair some other hour, I should derive much
from't. For take't of my soul, my lord leans won-
drously to discontent. His comfortable temper has   70
forsook him, he's much out of health, and keeps
his chamber.

LUCIUS' SERVANT Many do keep their chambers are
    not sick;

49 **preferred** proffered, presented   51 **fawn upon** seek favor by servility (used
especially of dogs)   52 **th' int'rest** i.e., what they ate was equivalent to the
interest due on the money owed them by Timon   56 **reckon** keep account of
60 **cashiered** dismissed from employment   63 **broader** more critically
67–68 **repair** come   69 **tak't of my soul** take it from my heart (i.e., sincerely)
70 **comfortable** cheerful

And if it be so far beyond his health,
75 Methinks he should the sooner pay his debts,
And make a clear way to the gods.

SERVILIUS   Good gods!

TITUS We cannot take this for answer, sir.

FLAMINIUS (*Within*) Servilius, help! My lord, my lord!

Enter Timon in a rage.

TIMON What, are my doors opposed against my
    passage?
80 Have I been ever free, and must my house
Be my retentive enemy? My jail?
The place which I have feasted, does it now,
Like all mankind, show me an iron heart?

LUCIUS' SERVANT Put in now, Titus.

85 TITUS My lord, here is my bill.

LUCIUS' SERVANT Here's mine.

HORTENSIUS And mine, my lord.

BOTH VARRO'S SERVANTS And ours, my lord.

PHILOTUS All our bills.

TIMON Knock me down with 'em, cleave me to the
90   girdle.

LUCIUS' SERVANT Alas, my lord——

TIMON Cut my heart in sums.

TITUS Mine, fifty talents.

---

76 **clear** (1) free from debt (2) innocent, unstained (because he has paid his debts)
(3) untrammeled, without the obstacle of debts 80 **free** (1) generous
(2) unrestrained 81 **retentive** confining 82 **The place which I have feasted**
i.e., the house itself in which I have given feasts 84 **Put in** i.e., put in your claim
for money 90 **Knock ... girdle** (Timon chooses to understand "bills" not as
"accounts of money due," but as "weapons"—a bill had a long wooden handle
with a blade or ax-shaped head at one end, and it was capable of cutting a man
through to the belt) 92 **in sums** into sums of money

TIMON Tell out my blood.

LUCIUS' SERVANT Five thousand crowns, my lord.   95

TIMON Five thousand drops pays that. What yours? And yours?

VARRO'S FIRST SERVANT My lord—

VARRO'S SECOND SERVANT My lord—

TIMON Tear me, take me, and the gods fall upon you.
Exit Timon.

HORTENSIUS Faith, I perceive our masters may throw   100
their caps at their money; these debts may well be
called desperate ones, for a madman owes 'em.
Exeunt.

Enter Timon [and Flavius].

TIMON They have e'en put my breath from me, the
slaves.
Creditors? Devils!

FLAVIUS My dear lord——   105

TIMON What if it should be so?

FLAVIUS My lord——

TIMON I'll have it so. My steward!

FLAVIUS Here, my lord.

TIMON So fitly? Go, bid all my friends again,   110
Lucius, Lucullus, and Sempronius—all.
I'll once more feast the rascals.

FLAVIUS   O my lord,
You only speak from your distracted soul;
There's not so much left to furnish out
A moderate table.

94 Tell out count out   100-01 may throw ... money may give up their money
for lost   102 desperate beyond hope of recovery (cf. "sperate,"
recoverable)   103 put my breath from me put me out of breath   110 fitly
conveniently   110 bid invite

115 TIMON   Be it not in thy care.
       Go, I charge thee, invite them all, let in the tide
       Of knaves once more; my cook and I'll provide.

                                             Exeunt.

              [Scene V. *The Senate House.*]

       *Enter three Senators at one door, Alcibiades meeting
                    them with Attendants.*

   FIRST SENATOR My lord, you have my voice to't. The
       fault's
       Bloody; 'tis necessary he should die.
       Nothing emboldens sin so much as mercy.

   SECOND SENATOR Most true; the law shall bruise 'em.

   ALCIBIADES Honor, health, and compassion to the
5   senate.

   FIRST SENATOR Now, captain?

   ALCIBIADES I am an humble suitor to your virtues;
       For pity is the virtue of the law,
       And none but tyrants use it cruelly.
10   It pleases time and fortune to lie heavy
       Upon a friend of mine, who in hot blood
       Hath stepped into the law; which is past depth
       To those that, without heed, do plunge into't.
       He is a man, setting his fate aside,
15   Of comely virtues;
       Nor did he soil the fact with cowardice
       (An honor in him which buys out his fault),

115 **Be it not in thy care** i.e., let the feast be my concern   III.v.1 **voice** vote
4 **bruise 'em** crush them (possibly sinners or wrongdoers in general?)   8 **virtue**
characteristic excellence   12 **stepped into the law** done something to bring him
within the jurisdiction of the law   12 **past depth** beyond any measurable
depth   14 **his fate** i.e., this one fateful action of his   16 **soil the fact** sully the
deed   17 **buys out** redeems

But with a noble fury and fair spirit,
Seeing his reputation touched to death,
He did oppose his foe;   20
And with such sober and unnoted passion
He did behove his anger, ere 'twas spent,
As if he had but proved an argument.

FIRST SENATOR You undergo too strict a paradox,
Striving to make an ugly deed look fair.   25
Your words have took such pains as if they labored
To bring manslaughter into form, and set
Quarreling upon the head of valor, which indeed
Is valor misbegot, and came into the world
When sects and factions were newly born.   30
He's truly valiant that can wisely suffer
The worst that man can breathe,
And make his wrongs his outsides,
To wear them like his raiment, carelessly,
And ne'er prefer his injuries to his heart,   35
To bring it into danger.
If wrongs be evils and enforce us kill,
What folly 'tis to hazard life for ill.

ALCIBIADES My lord——

FIRST SENATOR You cannot make gross sins look clear.
To revenge is no valor, but to bear.   40

ALCIBIADES My lords, then, under favor, pardon me,
If I speak like a captain.
Why do fond men expose themselves to battle,
And not endure all threats? Sleep upon't,

---

18 **fair** excellent 21 **unnoted** not notable, i.e., calm 22 **behove** control
23 **argument** i.e., a *point d'honneur* rather than a personal passion 24 **undergo
too strict a paradox** i.e., attempt to argue a position that is excessively
paradoxical 27 **form** i.e., a legal and acceptable form 30 **factions**
(trisyllabic) 32 **breathe** utter 33 **outsides** mere externals 35 **prefer**
present 39 **clear** innocent 40 **bear** tolerate (our wrongs) 41 **under favor** by
your leave (a formula of politeness) 43 **fond** foolish

45 And let the foes quietly cut their throats
    Without repugnancy? If there be
    Such valor in the bearing, what make we
    Abroad? Why then, women are more valiant
    That stay at home, if bearing carry it,
50 And the ass more captain than the lion, the fellow
    Loaden with irons wiser than the judge,
    If wisdom be in suffering. O my lords,
    As you are great, be pitifully good.
    Who cannot condemn rashness in cold blood?
55 To kill, I grant, is sin's extremest gust,
    But in defense, by mercy, 'tis most just.
    To be in anger is impiety;
    But who is man that is not angry?
    Weigh but the crime with this.

SECOND SENATOR You breathe in vain.

60 ALCIBIADES   In vain? His service done
    At Lacedaemon and Byzantium
    Were a sufficient briber for his life.

FIRST SENATOR What's that?

    ALCIBIADES   Why say, my lords, h'as
    done fair service,
    And slain in fight many of your enemies.
65 How full of valor did he bear himself
    In the last conflict, and made plenteous wounds!

SECOND SENATOR He has made too much plenty with
    'em.
    He's a sworn rioter; he has a sin that often
    Drowns him and takes his valor prisoner.
70 If there were no foes, that were enough
    To overcome him. In that beastly fury
    He has been known to commit outrages,

46 **repugnancy** resistance, fighting back 48 **Abroad** i.e., away from home, at
battle 49 **bearing** (1) enduring of wrongs (2) childbearing (3) bearing of men in
sexual intercourse 49 **carry it** win the day 53 **be pitifully good** i.e., be good
in showing pity 55 **gust** (1) taste, relish (2) strong wind or storm 56 **by mercy**
in a merciful interpretation 63 **say** let us say, let us admit 68 **rioter**
debauchee 68 **sin** i.e., drunkenness

And cherish factions. 'Tis inferred to us
His days are foul and his drink dangerous.

FIRST SENATOR He dies.

ALCIBIADES   Hard fate. He might have died
  in war.   75
My lords, if not for any parts in him—
Though his right arm might purchase his own time,
And be in debt to none—yet, more to move you,
Take my deserts to his, and join 'em both.
And for I know your reverend ages love   80
Security, I'll pawn my victories, all
My honor to you, upon his good returns.
If by this crime he owes the law his life,
Why, let the war receive't in valiant gore,
For law is strict, and war is nothing more.   85

FIRST SENATOR We are for law. He dies. Urge it no
  more,
On height of our displeasure. Friend or brother,
He forfeits his own blood that spills another.

ALCIBIADES Must it be so? It must not be.
My lords, I do beseech you know me.

SECOND SENATOR   How?   90

ALCIBIADES Call me to your remembrances.

THIRD SENATOR   What?

ALCIBIADES I cannot think but your age has forgot me;
It could not else be I should prove so base
To sue and be denied such common grace.
My wounds ache at you.

FIRST SENATOR   Do you dare our anger?   95
'Tis in few words, but spacious in effect:
We banish thee for ever.

---

73 **cherish factions** foster dissension 73 **inferred** reported 76 **parts** good
qualities 77 **his own time** i.e., his proper time to die 81 **Security** (1) safety,
freedom from care or apprehension (2) collateral for a debt 82 **good returns**
profit on an investment 92 **your age** i.e., you, because of your age 94 **To sue**
to beg

ALCIBIADES   Banish me?
Banish your dotage, banish usury,
That makes the senate ugly.

FIRST SENATOR If after two days' shine Athens contain
100   thee,
Attend our weightier judgment. And, not to swell
our spirit,
He shall be executed presently.

Exeunt [Senators].

ALCIBIADES Now the gods keep you old enough, that
you may live
Only in bone, that none may look on you.
105   I'm worse than mad. I have kept back their foes,
While they have told their money, and let out
Their coin upon large interest, I myself
Rich only in large hurts. All those, for this?
Is this the balsam that the usuring Senate
110   Pours into captains' wounds? Banishment!
It comes not ill. I hate not to be banished;
It is a cause worthy my spleen and fury,
That I may strike at Athens. I'll cheer up
My discontented troops and lay for hearts.
115   'Tis honor with most lands to be at odds;
Soldiers should brook as little wrongs as gods.

Exit.

---

101 **Attend our weightier judgment** expect a more severe sentence from
us 101 **not to swell our spirit** not to allow our anger any further scope
102 **presently** at once 104 **Only in bone** i.e., be mere hideous skeletons
106 **told** counted 109 **balsam** balm 112 **spleen** malice, passionate
hatred 114 **lay for hearts** i.e., try to win their hearts to my cause (or, possibly,
try to win the hearts of new followers) 116 **brook** endure

[Scene VI. *A banqueting hall in Timon's house.*

Music. Tables set out, Servants attending.] *Enter divers Friends* [*of Timon*] *at several doors.*

FIRST LORD The good time of day to you, sir.

SECOND LORD I also wish it to you. I think this honorable lord did but try us this other day.

FIRST LORD Upon that were my thoughts tiring when we encount'red. I hope it is not so low with him as   5
he made it seem in the trial of his several friends.

SECOND LORD It should not be, by the persuasion of his new feasting.

FIRST LORD I should think so. He hath sent me an earnest inviting, which many my near occasions   10
did urge me to put off; but he hath conjured me beyond them, and I must needs appear.

SECOND LORD In like manner was I in debt to my importunate business, but he would not hear my excuse. I am sorry, when he sent to borrow of me,   15
that my provision was out.

FIRST LORD I am sick of that grief too, as I understand how all things go.

SECOND LORD Every man here's so. What would he have borrowed of you?   20

III.vi.4 **tiring** feeding (especially, to tear flesh in feeding as does a bird of prey) 7 **by the persuasion of** on the evidence of 10 **many my near occasions** my many pressing social obligations 16 **provision** supply (of money) 17–18 **as I ... go** i.e., on the evidence of his "new feasting," things seem to be picking up again with Timon

FIRST LORD A thousand pieces.

SECOND LORD A thousand pieces?

FIRST LORD What of you?

SECOND LORD He sent to me, sir——

Enter Timon and Attendants.

Here he comes.

25   TIMON With all my heart, gentlemen both; and how fare you?

FIRST LORD Ever at the best, hearing well of your lordship.

SECOND LORD The swallow follows not summer more
30   willing than we your lordship.

TIMON [*Aside*] Nor more willingly leaves winter, such summer birds are men.—Gentlemen, our dinner will not recompense this long stay. Feast your ears with the music awhile, if they will fare so harshly
35   o' th' trumpet's sound; we shall to't presently.

FIRST LORD I hope it remains not unkindly with your lordship that I returned you an empty messenger.

TIMON O sir, let it not trouble you.

SECOND LORD My noble lord——

40   TIMON Ah my good friend, what cheer?

SECOND LORD My most honorable lord, I am e'en sick of shame that when your lordship this other day sent to me, I was so unfortunate a beggar.

TIMON Think not on't, sir.

45   SECOND LORD If you had sent but two hours before—

---

21 **pieces** gold coins worth about a pound (but probably used vaguely)
29 **swallow** (cf. the proverb: "Swallows, like false friends, fly away upon the approach of winter")   34 **fare so harshly** feed on such rough food   35 **we shall to't presently** we shall sit down to eat immediately

TIMON Let it not cumber your better remembrance.

The banquet brought in.

Come, bring in all together.

SECOND LORD All covered dishes.

FIRST LORD Royal cheer, I warrant you.

THIRD LORD Doubt not that, if money and the season   50
can yield it.

FIRST LORD How do you? What's the news?

THIRD LORD Alcibiades is banished. Hear you of it?

FIRST AND SECOND LORDS Alcibiades banished?

THIRD LORD 'Tis so, be sure of it.   55

FIRST LORD How? How?

SECOND LORD I pray you upon what?

TIMON My worthy friends, will you draw near?

THIRD LORD I'll tell you more anon. Here's a noble
feast toward.   60

SECOND LORD This is the old man still.

THIRD LORD Will't hold? Will't hold?

SECOND LORD It does; but time will—and so—

THIRD LORD I do conceive.

TIMON Each man to his stool, with that spur as he   65
would to the lip of his mistress. Your diet shall be
in all places alike. Make not a city feast of it, to let

---

46 **cumber your better remembrance** burden your good memory   48 **covered dishes** (signifies food of high quality)   49 **Royal cheer** i.e., food fit for a king   57 **upon what** for what cause   59 **anon** soon   60 **toward** forthcoming   61 **still** ever, without change   62 **Will't hold** will it last   63 **time will** (presumably a platitude such as "time will alter all things")   64 **conceive** understand   65 **spur** spurring, speed   66 **diet** food   67 **in all places alike** the same at all places of the table (i.e., no need for seating according to rank)   67 **city feast** a formal London banquet (London is the "City")

the meat cool ere we can agree upon the first place.
Sit, sit. The gods require our thanks.

70   You great benefactors, sprinkle our society with
thankfulness. For your own gifts, make yourselves
praised. But reserve still to give, lest your deities
be despised. Lend to each man enough that one
need not lend to another; for were your godheads to
75 borrow of men, men would forsake the gods. Make
the meat be beloved more than the man that gives
it. Let no assembly of twenty be without a score of
villains. If there sit twelve women at the table, let
a dozen of them be as they are. The rest of your
80 fees, O gods—the senators of Athens, together
with the common leg of people—what is amiss in
them, you gods, make suitable for destruction. For
these my present friends, as they are to me nothing,
so in nothing bless them, and to nothing are they
85 welcome.
Uncover, dogs, and lap.

                              [*The dishes are uncovered
                              and seen to be full of water.*]

SOME SPEAK What does his lordship mean?

SOME OTHER I know not.

TIMON May you a better feast never behold,
90   You knot of mouth-friends. Smoke and lukewarm
            water
        Is your perfection. This is Timon's last,
        Who, stuck and spangled with your flatteries,
        Washes it off and sprinkles in your faces
        Your reeking villainy.   [*Throws the water
                                        in their faces.*]
                    Live loathed and long,

---

72 **reserve** i.e., keep something in reserve   80 **fees** property, possessions   81 **leg**
limb (as a literal part of the body politic)   90 **knot of mouth-friends** pack of
(1) friends merely in speech (2) friends won through feeding, "trencher-friends"
90 **Smoke** (1) insubstantiality (2) mere talk   91 **perfection** highest excellence (?)
perfect likeness of you (?)   92 **stuck and spangled** bespattered and tricked out
(as if with spangles)   94 **reeking** giving off smoke or fumes, stinking

Most smiling, smooth, detested parasites,   95
Courteous destroyers, affable wolves, meek bears,
You fools of fortune, trencher-friends, time's flies,
Cap-and-knee slaves, vapors, and minute-jacks.
Of man and beast the infinite malady
Crust you quite o'er. What, dost thou go?   100
Soft, take thy physic first; thou too, and thou.
Stay, I will lend thee money, borrow none.
                                        [Drives them out.]
What? All in motion? Henceforth be no feast,
Whereat a villain's not a welcome guest.
Burn house, sink Athens, henceforth hated be   105
Of Timon man and all humanity.   Exit.

        Enter the Senators, with other Lords.

FIRST LORD How now, my lords?

SECOND LORD Know you the quality of Lord Timon's
    fury?

THIRD LORD Push, did you see my cap?   110

FOURTH LORD I have lost my gown.

FIRST LORD He's but a mad lord, and naught but
    humors sways him. He gave me a jewel th' other
    day, and now he has beat it out of my hat. Did
    you see my jewel?   115

THIRD LORD Did you see my cap?

SECOND LORD Here 'tis.

FOURTH LORD Here lies my gown.

FIRST LORD Let's make no stay.

---

95 **smooth** flattering 97–98 **You fools ... minute-jacks** you dupes of fortune,
friends won by feeding, insects that appear only in fair weather, servile slaves
always kneeling or removing caps in deference, insubstantial creatures, and figures
who strike the bell of a clock (i.e., opportunistic persons) 99 **infinite**
unlimited 101 **physic** medicine 102 **borrow** i.e., borrow none from others (?)
I will borrow none (?) 106 **Of** by 110 **Push** (an effeminate expression of
impatience) 113 **humors** whims, caprices

SECOND LORD Lord Timon's mad.

120 THIRD LORD   I feel't upon my bones.

FOURTH LORD One day he gives us diamonds, next day stones.

Exeunt the Senators [and others].

[ACT IV

Scene I. *Outside the walls of Athens.*]

Enter Timon.

TIMON Let me look back upon thee. O thou wall
    That girdles in those wolves, dive in the earth,
    And fence not Athens. Matrons, turn incontinent;
    Obedience fail in children. Slaves and fools,
    Pluck the grave wrinkled senate from the bench,   5
    And minister in their steads. To general filths
    Convert o' th' instant green virginity;
    Do't in your parents' eyes. Bankrupts, hold fast
    Rather than render back; out with your knives,
    And cut your trusters' throats. Bound servants,
        steal;   10
    Large-handed robbers your grave masters are,
    And pill by law. Maid, to thy master's bed,
    Thy mistress is o' th' brothel. Son of sixteen,
    Pluck the lined crutch from thy old limping sire,
    With it beat out his brains. Piety, and fear,   15

IV.i.6 **minister** govern 6 **filths** harlots (or, more generally, immoral acts or
corruption) 7 **green** young, inexperienced 9 **render back** repay debts
10 **Bound** under obligation to serve for a stated period 11 **Large-handed**
rapacious (usually means "generous") 12 **pill** steal 14 **lined** padded

569

Religion to the gods, peace, justice, truth,
Domestic awe, night-rest, and neighborhood,
Instruction, manners, mysteries, and trades,
Degrees, observances, customs, and laws,
20 Decline to your confounding contraries,
And let confusion live. Plagues incident to men,
Your potent and infectious fevers heap
On Athens ripe for stroke. Thou cold sciatica,
Cripple our senators, that their limbs may halt
25 As lamely as their manners. Lust and liberty
Creep in the minds and marrows of our youth,
That 'gainst the stream of virtue they may strive,
And drown themselves in riot. Itches, blains,
Sow all th' Athenian bosoms, and their crop
30 Be general leprosy. Breath infect breath,
That their society, as their friendship, may
Be merely poison. Nothing I'll bear from thee
But nakedness, thou detestable town;
Take thou that too, with multiplying bans.
35 Timon will to the woods, where he shall find
Th' unkindest beast more kinder than mankind.
The gods confound—hear me, you good gods all—
Th' Athenians both within and out that wall.
And grant, as Timon grows, his hate may grow
40 To the whole race of mankind, high and low.
Amen.   *Exit.*

16 **Religion to** religious concern for   17 **Domestic awe** the respect appropriate
to domestic relations (to parents, home, etc.)   17 **neighborhood**
neighborliness   18 **mysteries** crafts, callings   19 **Degrees** social classes
20 **confounding contraries** opposites which destroy each other and so bring on
general chaos   21 **confusion** ruin   21 **incident to** natural to   24 **halt** limp
25 **liberty** licentiousness   28 **blains** blisters   32 **merely** utterly   33 **detestable**
(primary accent on first syllable)   34 **multiplying bans** ever-increasing curses (?)
multiple curses (?)   36 **more kinder** (1) more generous, gracious (2) more
natural, closer to the moral law of nature

[Scene II. *Athens. Timon's house.*]

Enter [Flavius, the] Steward, with two or three
Servants.

FIRST SERVANT Hear you, master steward, where's our
    master?
  Are we undone, cast off, nothing remaining?

FLAVIUS Alack, my fellows, what should I say to you?
  Let me be recorded by the righteous gods,
  I am as poor as you.

FIRST SERVANT   Such a house broke?   5
  So noble a master fall'n, all gone, and not
  One friend to take his fortune by the arm,
  And go along with him?

SECOND SERVANT   As we do turn our backs
  From our companion thrown into his grave,
  So his familiars to his buried fortunes   10
  Slink all away, leave their false vows with him,
  Like empty purses picked; and his poor self,
  A dedicated beggar to the air,
  With his disease of all-shunned poverty,
  Walks like contempt alone.

Enter other Servants.

                  More of our fellows.   15

FLAVIUS All broken implements of a ruined house.

THIRD SERVANT Yet do our hearts wear Timon's livery,

IV.ii.4 **Let me be recorded** let it be recorded of me   7 **his fortune** i.e., Timon
in his ill fortune   10 **his familiars to his buried fortunes** those who were the
familiar friends of his now buried fortunes (also suggests "familiar spirit," a
personal servant from the spirit world)   13 **A dedicated beggar to the air** a
beggar vowed or doomed to wander about in the open air

That see I by our faces; we are fellows still,
Serving alike in sorrow. Leaked is our bark,
20   And we poor mates stand on the dying deck,
Hearing the surges threat. We must all part
Into this sea of air.

FLAVIUS   Good fellows all,
The latest of my wealth I'll share amongst you.
Wherever we shall meet, for Timon's sake,
25   Let's yet be fellows. Let's shake our heads and say,
As 'twere a knell unto our master's fortunes,
"We have seen better days." Let each take some.
                                    [*Gives money*.]
Nay, put out all your hands. Not one word more;
Thus part we rich in sorrow, parting poor.
                        Embrace, and part several ways.
30   O the fierce wretchedness that glory brings us!
Who would not wish to be from wealth exempt,
Since riches point to misery and contempt?
Who would be so mocked with glory, or to live
But in a dream of friendship,
35   To have his pomp and all what state compounds
But only painted, like his varnished friends?
Poor honest lord, brought low by his own heart,
Undone by goodness. Strange, unusual blood,
When man's worst sin is, he does too much good.
40   Who then dares to be half so kind again?
For bounty, that makes gods, do still mar men.
My dearest lord, blessed to be most accursed,
Rich only to be wretched, thy great fortunes
Are made thy chief afflictions. Alas, kind lord,
45   He's flung in rage from this ingrateful seat
Of monstrous friends;

18 **fellows** fellow servants   22 **this sea of air** i.e., the open air, which is as comfortless to us as is the sea to sailors on a sinking ship   23 **latest** last   32 **point to** lead to   33 **to live** i.e., who would wish to live   35 **all what state compounds** all that worldly splendor is composed of   36 **painted** illusory   36 **varnished** fair-seeming   38 **blood** disposition   40 **half so kind** i.e., as Timon was, who came to grief because of it   42 **blessed to be** i.e., blessed with wealth only to be   45 **seat** residence

Nor has he with him to supply his life,
Or that which can command it.
I'll follow and inquire him out.
I'll ever serve his mind with my best will;   50
Whilst I have gold, I'll be his steward still.   *Exit*.

[Scene III. *Before Timon's cave*.]

Enter Timon in the woods.

TIMON O blessèd breeding sun, draw from the earth
    Rotten humidity; below thy sister's orb
    Infect the air. Twinned brothers of one womb,
    Whose procreation, residence, and birth,
    Scarce is dividant—touch them with several
        fortunes,   5
    The greater scorns the lesser. Not nature,
    To whom all sores lay siege, can bear great fortune
    But by contempt of nature.
    Raise me this beggar, and deny't that lord,
    The senators shall bear contempt hereditary,   10
    The beggar native honor.
    It is the pasture lards the brother's sides,
    The want that makes him lean. Who dares?
        Who dares

---

47 **to supply his life** i.e., he has no food and drink 48 **that** i.e., money
IV.iii.2 **Rotten humidity** humidity that causes things to rot 2 **below thy
sister's orb** beneath the moon (i.e., in the middle air between earth and moon)
5 **dividant** divisible, separable 5 **touch** test 5 **several** different 6–8 **Not
nature ... nature** i.e., human nature, which is subjected to all sorts of miseries,
when it encounters good fortune rejects its own natural affection and despises
mankind 9 **deny't** i.e., deny to raise 10 **hereditary** i.e., as if they were born
that way and not simply victims of fortune's caprices 11 **native** i.e., as if he were
born with it 12–13 **It is ... lean** i.e., the "twinned brothers" (line 3) are
distinguished by their gifts of fortune; the rich pasture, and not any intrinsic
worth, makes one brother fat and the other lean

573

In purity of manhood stand upright
15   And say, this man's a flatterer? If one be,
So are they all, for every grise of fortune
Is smoothed by that below. The learned pate
Ducks to the golden fool. All's obliquy;
There's nothing level in our cursèd natures
20   But direct villainy. Therefore be abhorred
All feasts, societies, and throngs of men.
His semblable, yea himself, Timon disdains;
Destruction fang mankind. Earth, yield me roots.

                                        [*Digs.*]

Who seeks for better of thee, sauce his palate
25   With thy most operant poison. What is here?
Gold? Yellow, glittering, precious gold?
No, gods, I am no idle votarist.
Roots, you clear heavens! Thus much of this will
       make
Black, white; foul, fair; wrong, right;
30   Base, noble; old, young; coward, valiant.
Ha, you gods! Why this? What this, you gods?
    Why this
Will lug your priests and servants from your sides;
Pluck stout men's pillows from below their heads.
This yellow slave
35   Will knit and break religions, bless th' accursed,
Make the hoar leprosy adored, place thieves,
And give them title, knee, and approbation
With senators on the bench. This is it
That makes the wappened widow wed again;
40   She, whom the spital-house and ulcerous sores

---

16 **grise** step   17 **smoothed** flattered, facilitated by flattery   17 **pate** head
18 **Ducks to the golden fool** inclines in deference to the rich fool   18 **obliquy**
obliquity, moral crookedness   22 **semblable** anything like himself   23 **fang**
(1) seize, as with fangs (2) provide with fangs   24 **sauce** season   25 **operant**
potent   27 **no idle votarist** i.e., I have not sworn my vow in an idle or trifling
way   28 **clear** pure   33 **Pluck ... heads** i.e., kill even strong men by sudden
suffocation   36 **hoar** white   36 **place** elevate to a place or office of dignity
39 **wappened** sexually exhausted   40 **spital-house** hospital (especially for the
lower classes and sufferers from loathsome diseases)   40 **ulcerous sores** i.e.,
those afflicted with ulcerous sores

Would cast the gorge at, this embalms and spices
To th' April day again. Come, damned earth,
Thou common whore of mankind, that puts odds
Among the rout of nations, I will make thee
Do thy right nature.

                                             March afar off.
                    Ha? A drum? Th' art quick,   45
But yet I'll bury thee. Thou't go, strong thief,
When gouty keepers of thee cannot stand.
Nay, stay thou out for earnest.   [*Keeps some gold.*]

            *Enter Alcibiades, with drum and fife, in
            warlike manner; and Phrynia and Timandra.*

ALCIBIADES What art thou there? Speak.

TIMON A beast as thou art. The canker gnaw thy
        heart   50
For showing me again the eyes of man.

ALCIBIADES What is thy name? Is man so hateful to
        thee
    That art thyself a man?

TIMON I am Misanthropos and hate mankind.
    For thy part, I do wish thou wert a dog,   55
    That I might love thee something.

ALCIBIADES   I know thee well,
    But in thy fortunes am unlearned and strange.

TIMON I know thee too, and more than that I know
        thee
    I not desire to know. Follow thy drum,
    With man's blood paint the ground gules, gules.   60

---

41 **cast the gorge** vomit 41–42 **embalms and spices/To th' April day** i.e.,
preserves, perfumes, and generally revivifies to a springlike and youthful
amorousness 43–44 **puts odds/Among the rout of nations** sets the disorderly
mob of nations at strife with each other 45 **Do thy right nature** i.e., cause strife
and dissension 45 **quick** (1) alive (2) speedily had and lost 46 **go** walk,
move 48 **for earnest** as an installment 50 **canker** (1) ulcerous sore
(2) canker-worm 54 **Misanthropos** the man-hater 56 **something** somewhat
57 **strange** ignorant 60 **gules** red (the heraldic term)

Religious canons, civil laws are cruel;
Then what should war be? This fell whore of thine
Hath in her more destruction than thy sword,
For all her cherubin look.

PHRYNIA   Thy lips rot off.

65 TIMON I will not kiss thee; then the rot returns
To thine own lips again.

ALCIBIADES How came the noble Timon to this
change?

TIMON As the moon does, by wanting light to give.
But then renew I could not like the moon;
70   There were no suns to borrow of.

ALCIBIADES Noble Timon, what friendship may I do
thee?

TIMON None, but to maintain my opinion.

ALCIBIADES What is it, Timon?

TIMON Promise me friendship, but perform none.
75   If thou wilt not promise, the gods plague thee,
For thou art a man. If thou dost perform,
Confound thee, for thou art a man.

ALCIBIADES I have heard in some sort of thy miseries.

TIMON Thou saw'st them when I had prosperity.

80 ALCIBIADES I see them now; then was a blessed time.

TIMON As thine is now, held with a brace of harlots.

TIMANDRA Is this th' Athenian minion, whom the
world
Voiced so regardfully?

---

62 **fell** destructive   65 **the rot returns** (based on a prevalent belief that by
transmitting a venereal infection to another, one loses it himself)   68 **wanting**
lacking   69 **renew** (1) to become new (2) to extend a loan (as in the next
line)   72 **maintain my opinion** i.e., be a misanthropist, too   81 **brace** (usually
used for a pair of dogs on a leash)   82 **minion** favorite, darling   83 **Voiced so
regardfully** spoke of with so much regard

TIMON   Art thou Timandra?

TIMANDRA   Yes.

TIMON Be a whore still; they love thee not that use
    thee.
  Give them diseases, leaving with thee their lust.   85
  Make use of thy salt hours. Season the slaves
  For tubs and baths; bring down rose-cheeked
    youth
  To the tub-fast and the diet.

TIMANDRA   Hang thee, monster!

ALCIBIADES Pardon him, sweet Timandra, for his wits
  Are drowned and lost in his calamities.   90
  I have but little gold of late, brave Timon,
  The want whereof doth daily make revolt
  In my penurious band. I have heard, and grieved,
  How cursèd Athens, mindless of thy worth,
  Forgetting thy great deeds, when neighbor states,   95
  But for thy sword and fortune, trod upon them—

TIMON I prithee beat thy drum and get thee gone.

ALCIBIADES I am thy friend and pity thee, dear Timon.

TIMON How dost thou pity him whom thou dost
    trouble?
  I had rather be alone.

ALCIBIADES   Why fare thee well.   100
  Here is some gold for thee.

TIMON   Keep it, I cannot eat it.

ALCIBIADES When I have laid proud Athens on a
  heap——

---

85 **leaving** i.e., while they leave 86 **salt** lustful, salacious 86 **Season** spice
87 **tubs and baths** sweating-tubs and hot baths (used to treat venereal disease)
88 **tub-fast and the diet** (fasting and special diet were treatments for venereal
disease) 91 **brave** excellent 93 **penurious** needy 96 **trod** i.e., would have
trodden 97 **beat thy drum** i.e., let thy drummer give the signal for departure

TIMON War'st thou 'gainst Athens?

ALCIBIADES   Ay, Timon, and have cause.

TIMON The gods confound them all in thy conquest,
105   And thee after when thou hast conquerèd.

ALCIBIADES Why me, Timon?

TIMON   That by killing of villains
       Thou wast born to conquer my country.
       Put up thy gold. Go on, here's gold, go on.
       Be as a planetary plague, when Jove
110   Will o'er some high-viced city hang his poison
       In the sick air. Let not thy sword skip one.
       Pity not honored age for his white beard:
       He is an usurer. Strike me the counterfeit matron:
       It is her habit only that is honest,
115   Herself's a bawd. Let not the virgin's cheek
       Make soft thy trenchant sword: for those milk
             paps,
       That through the window-bars bore at men's eyes,
       Are not within the leaf of pity writ,
       But set them down horrible traitors. Spare not the
             babe
       Whose dimpled smiles from fools exhaust their
120   mercy:
       Think it a bastard, whom the oracle
       Hath doubtfully pronounced thy throat shall cut,
       And mince it sans remorse. Swear against objects.
       Put armor on thine ears and on thine eyes,
125   Whose proof nor yells of mothers, maids, nor babes,

104 **in thy conquest** i.e., in your victory over them   108 **Put up** put away
109 **planetary plague** plague caused by the planets   114 **habit** dress
114 **honest** chaste   116 **trenchant** cutting   117 **window-bars** lattice work of a
window (?) open-work squares of the bodice of a woman's frock (?)   118 **within
the leaf of pity writ** i.e., written down on the page with the names of those who
are to be pitied and spared   120 **exhaust** draw out, elicit   122 **doubtfully**
ambiguously   123 **mince it sans remorse** cut it up without pity   123 **objects**
objections, accusations of cruelty   125 **proof** high quality (of armor),
impenetrability

Nor sight of priests in holy vestments bleeding,
Shall pierce a jot. There's gold to pay thy soldiers.
Make large confusion; and, thy fury spent,
Confounded be thyself. Speak not, begone.

ALCIBIADES Hast thou gold yet, I'll take the gold thou
    givest me,   130
Not all thy counsel.

TIMON Dost thou or dost thou not, heaven's curse
    upon thee.

PHRYNIA AND TIMANDRA Give us some gold, good
    Timon; hast thou more?

TIMON Enough to make a whore forswear her trade,
And to make whores, a bawd. Hold up, you sluts, 135
Your aprons mountant. You are not oathable,
Although I know you'll swear, terribly swear
Into strong shudders and to heavenly agues
Th' immortal gods that hear you. Spare your oaths;
I'll trust to your conditions. Be whores still, 140
And he whose pious breath seeks to convert you,
Be strong in whore, allure him, burn him up;
Let your close fire predominate his smoke,
And be no turncoats. Yet may your pains six months
Be quite contrary. And thatch 145
Your poor thin roofs with burdens of the dead—
Some that were hanged, no matter.
Wear them, betray with them; whore still;

---

128 **confusion** destruction 130 **Hast** i.e., if you have 135 **And to make whores, a bawd** i.e., and enough to make a bawd give up her trade of making whores (or, perhaps, enough to make a whore set herself up as a bawd, making whores instead of being one) 136 **aprons mountant** rising aprons (a mock heraldic phrase with sexual overtones) 136 **oathable** capable of being placed under oath 140 **conditions** dispositions 140 **still** always 143 **Let … smoke** i.e., let the hidden fire of your sexuality or disease dominate over the smoke of idle words of he who "seeks to convert you" 144–45 **Yet … contrary** i.e., may you spend six months of the year in being whores and the other six in repairing the physical damage occasioned by your debaucheries (?) 145–46 **And thatch … dead** i.e., wear wigs (or possibly false pubes) made from loads of hair taken from the dead (venereal disease was thought to cause loss of hair)

Paint till a horse may mire upon your face.
A pox of wrinkles!

150 PHRYNIA AND TIMANDRA Well, more gold. What then?
Believe't that we'll do anything for gold.

TIMON Consumptions sow
In hollow bones of man; strike their sharp shins,
And mar men's spurring. Crack the lawyer's voice,
155 That he may never more false title plead,
Nor sound his quillets shrilly. Hoar the flamen,
That scolds against the quality of flesh
And not believes himself. Down with the nose,
Down with it flat, take the bridge quite away
160 Of him, that his particular to foresee,
Smells from the general weal. Make curled-pate
ruffians bald,
And let the unscarred braggarts of the war
Derive some pain from you. Plague all,
That your activity may defeat and quell
165 The source of all erection. There's more gold.
Do you damn others, and let this damn you,
And ditches grave you all.

PHRYNIA AND TIMANDRA More counsel with more
money, bounteous Timon.

TIMON More whore, more mischief first; I have given
you earnest.

---

149 **mire** sink into the mire or mud (because of the thickness of cosmetics)
150 **A pox of wrinkles** i.e., a pox on wrinkles, away with wrinkles (since they can
be covered with cosmetics)   152 **Consumptions** wasting diseases (here venereal
disease)   153 **hollow ... sharp** i.e., the disease will make the bones hollow and
the shins painful   156 **quillets** subtle verbal distinctions   156 **Hoar the flamen**
whiten the priest with disease, or cause his hair to turn white (possible pun on
"whore")   157 **quality of flesh** the nature of the flesh, sexual pleasure
158 **Down with the nose** (an effect of syphilis)   160–61 **his particular ... weal**
i.e., to provide for his private advantage or profit, he abandons the proper scent
that contributes to the public good or welfare   165 **The source of all erection**
i.e., sexuality itself   167 **grave** be a grave for, bury   169 **earnest** a part payment
to seal a bargain

ALCIBIADES Strike up the drum towards Athens. Farewell, Timon.   170
   If I thrive well, I'll visit thee again.

TIMON If I hope well, I'll never see thee more.

ALCIBIADES I never did thee harm.

TIMON Yes, thou spok'st well of me.

ALCIBIADES   Call'st thou that harm?

TIMON Men daily find it. Get thee away, and take   175
   Thy beagles with thee.

ALCIBIADES   We but offend him. Strike!
       [*Drum beats.*] *Exeunt* [*Alcibiades, Phrynia, and*
                               Timandra].

TIMON That nature, being sick of man's unkindness,
   Should yet be hungry! Common mother, thou,
                           [*Digging*]
   Whose womb unmeasurable and infinite breast
   Teems and feeds all; whose selfsame mettle,   180
   Whereof thy proud child, arrogant man, is puffed,
   Engenders the black toad and adder blue,
   The gilded newt and eyeless venomed worm,
   With all th' abhorrèd births below crisp heaven
   Whereon Hyperion's quick'ning fire doth shine;   185
   Yield him, who all the human sons do hate,
   From forth thy plenteous bosom, one poor root.
   Ensear thy fertile and conceptious womb;
   Let it no more bring out ingrateful man.
   Go great with tigers, dragons, wolves, and bears,   190
   Teem with new monsters, whom thy upward face
   Hath to the marbled mansion all above

---

172 **If I hope well** if my hopes are realized   177 **of** as a result of   180 **Teems** brings forth   180 **mettle** (1) substance (2) vigorous spirit   181 **puffed** puffed up with pride   184 **crisp** with curled clouds (?) shining, clear (?)   185 **Hyperion's quick'ning fire** (the sun was thought to have the power of generating some of the lower forms of insect life)   188 **Ensear** dry up   188 **conceptious** conceiving, prolific   190 **great** pregnant   192 **above** in heaven

Never presented. O, a root, dear thanks!
Dry up thy marrows, vines and plough-torn leas,
195 Whereof ingrateful man, with liquorish draughts
And morsels unctious, greases his pure mind,
That from it all consideration slips——

Enter Apemantus.

More man? Plague, plague!

APEMANTUS I was directed hither. Men report
200 Thou dost affect my manners, and dost use them.

TIMON 'Tis then because thou dost not keep a dog
Whom I would imitate. Consumption catch thee.

APEMANTUS This is in thee a nature but infected,
A poor unmanly melancholy sprung
From change of future. Why this spade? This
205   place?
This slave-like habit and these looks of care?
Thy flatterers yet wear silk, drink wine, lie soft,
Hug their diseased perfumes, and have forgot
That ever Timon was. Shame not these woods
210 By putting on the cunning of a carper.
Be thou a flatterer now, and seek to thrive
By that which has undone thee. Hinge thy knee,
And let his very breath whom thou'lt observe
Blow off thy cap; praise his most vicious strain
215 And call it excellent. Thou wast told thus.

---

194 **marrows** (the type of a rich food, not a necessity of life, produced by the "vines" and "leas") 196 **unctious** (an obsolete variant form of "unctuous") 197 **consideration** ability to consider 200 **affect** imitate 202 **Consumption** any wasting disease 203 **infected** (1) affected, factitious (2) caught like an infection from your changed circumstances 205 **change of future** i.e., change in your material prospects 206 **habit** dress, garb 208 **diseased perfumes** diseased and perfumed mistresses 210 **By ... carper** i.e., by pretending to the profession of a cynic or railer (which any fool can do) 213–14 **let his ... cap** kneel so obsequiously close to the person you are paying court to that his breath may blow off your cap 214 **strain** quality 215 **Thou wast told thus** i.e., in your prosperity others spoke to you in this manner

Thou gav'st thine ears, like tapsters that bade
  welcome,
To knaves and all approachers. 'Tis most just
That thou turn rascal; hadst thou wealth again,
Rascals should have't. Do not assume my likeness.

TIMON Were I like thee, I'd throw away myself.   220

APEMANTUS Thou hast cast away thyself, being like
    thyself:
  A madman so long, now a fool. What, think'st
  That the bleak air, thy boisterous chamberlain,
  Will put thy shirt on warm? Will these moist trees,
  That have outlived the eagle, page thy heels   225
  And skip when thou point'st out? Will the cold
    brook,
  Candied with ice, caudle thy morning taste
  To cure thy o'er-night's surfeit? Call the creatures
  Whose naked natures live in all the spite
  Of wreakful heaven, whose bare unhousèd trunks,   230
  To the conflicting elements exposed,
  Answer mere nature. Bid them flatter thee.
  O thou shalt find——

TIMON   A fool of thee. Depart.

APEMANTUS I love thee better now than e'er I did.

TIMON I hate thee worse.

APEMANTUS   Why?

TIMON   Thou flatter'st misery.   235

APEMANTUS I flatter not, but say thou art a caitiff.

216 **tapsters** (tavern-keepers or bartenders are proverbial for their indiscriminate hospitality) 223 **chamberlain** one who waits on a king or lord in his bedchamber 224 **moist** damp 226 **point'st out** indicate your desires 227 **Candied** congealed, encrusted 227 **caudle** offer a caudle (a warm, spiced, mildly alcoholic drink given to the sick) 228 **o'er-night's surfeit** previous night's indulgence in drink 230 **wreakful** vengeful 232 **Answer mere nature** correspond to or reflect nature in its barest and most rigorous form 236 **caitiff** wretch

TIMON Why dost thou seek me out?

APEMANTUS   To vex thee.

TIMON Always a villain's office or a fool's.
    Dost please thyself in't?

APEMANTUS   Ay.

TIMON   What, a knave too?

240 APEMANTUS If thou didst put this sour cold habit on
        To castigate thy pride, 'twere well; but thou
        Dost it enforcedly. Thou'dst courtier be again
        Wert thou not beggar. Willing misery
        Outlives incertain pomp, is crowned before.
245   The one is filling still, never complete;
        The other, at high wish. Best state, contentless,
        Hath a distracted and most wretched being,
        Worse than the worst, content.
        Thou shouldst desire to die, being miserable.

250 TIMON Not by his breath that is more miserable.
        Thou art a slave, whom Fortune's tender arm
        With favor never clasped, but bred a dog.
        Hadst thou, like us, from our first swath proceeded
        The sweet degrees that this brief world affords
255   To such as may the passive drudges of it
        Freely command, thou wouldst have plunged thyself
        In general riot, melted down thy youth
        In different beds of lust, and never learned

238 **office** duty 240 **habit** (1) garment (2) outward manner, bearing
242 **enforcedly** i.e., as if you were being forced to do it 243 **Willing misery**
voluntary poverty 244 **is crowned before** comes earlier to the fulfillment of its
desires and wishes 245 **The one is filling still** i.e., pomp, like a leaky vessel, can
never be filled (or fulfilled) 246 **The other, at high wish** i.e., "willing misery,"
because it wishes little, can easily arrive at the height of its wishes 246–48 **Best
state ... content** i.e., a man in even the best material condition, if he is without
content or happiness, is confused and wretched, worse than a man in the poorest
condition who is contented 250 **breath** voice 253 **swath** swaddling
clothes 253–54 **proceeded/The sweet degrees** advanced from one stage to the
next above it (in sense of academic "degrees") 255 **passive drudges** submissive
menial servants 257 **riot** debauchery

The icy precepts of respect, but followed
The sug'red game before thee. But myself—   260
Who had the world as my confectionary,
The mouths, the tongues, the eyes, and hearts of
    men
At duty, more than I could frame employment;
That numberless upon me stuck, as leaves
Do on the oak, have with one winter's brush   265
Fell from their boughs, and left me open, bare
For every storm that blows—I to bear this,
That never knew but better, is some burden.
Thy nature did commence in sufferance, time
Hath made thee hard in't. Why shouldst thou hate
    men?   270
They never flattered thee. What hast thou given?
If thou wilt curse, thy father, that poor rogue,
Must be thy subject; who in spite put stuff
To some she-beggar and compounded thee
Poor rogue hereditary. Hence, begone.   275
If thou hadst not been born the worst of men,
Thou hadst been a knave and flatterer.

APEMANTUS   Art thou proud yet?

TIMON Ay, that I am not thee.

APEMANTUS   I, that I was
    No prodigal.

TIMON   I, that I am one now.
    Were all the wealth I have shut up in thee,   280
    I'd give thee leave to hang it. Get thee gone.
    That the whole life of Athens were in this!
    Thus would I eat it.   [*Eats a root*.]

259 **icy precepts of respect** i.e., the chilling rules of reason which constitute
proper social conduct 260 **sug'red game** outwardly sweet quarry (probably
whores) 261 **confectionary** a place where sweetmeats or candy are made
263 **frame employment** invent work for 265 **winter's brush** i.e., brush of a
wintry wind 266 **Fell** fallen 269 **sufferance** suffering 273–74 **put stuff/To**
i.e., made pregnant (contemptuous) 276 **worst** i.e., in social and financial
position 282 **That** i.e., would that

APEMANTUS   Here, I will mend thy feast.
                             [*Offers him food.*]

TIMON First mend my company, take away thyself.

APEMANTUS So I shall mend mine own, by th' lack of
285   thine.

TIMON 'Tis not well mended so, it is but botched;
       If not, I would it were.

APEMANTUS What wouldst thou have to Athens?

TIMON Thee thither in a whirlwind. If thou wilt,
290   Tell them there I have gold; look, so I have.

APEMANTUS Here is no use for gold.

TIMON   The best and truest;
       For here it sleeps and does no hirèd harm.

APEMANTUS Where liest a nights, Timon?

TIMON   Under that's above me.
       Where feed'st thou a days, Apemantus?

295 APEMANTUS Where my stomach finds meat, or rather
       where I eat it.

TIMON Would poison were obedient and knew my
       mind!

APEMANTUS Where wouldst thou send it?

300 TIMON To sauce thy dishes.

APEMANTUS The middle of humanity thou never
       knewest, but the extremity of both ends. When thou
       wast in thy gilt and thy perfume, they mocked thee
       for too much curiosity; in thy rags thou know'st
305   none, but art despised for the contrary. There's a
       medlar for thee; eat it.

283 **mend** improve   286 **botched** clumsily repaired (because Apemantus is still
present—with himself)   288 **to** in   293 **that's above me** i.e., that which is
above me, the sky   304 **curiosity** carefulness, fastidiousness   306 **medlar** a fruit
like a small brown-skinned apple, not ready to be eaten until in the early stages of
decay

586

TIMON On what I hate I feed not.

APEMANTUS Dost hate a medlar?

TIMON Ay, though it look like thee.

APEMANTUS And th'hadst hated meddlers sooner, 310
thou shouldst have loved thyself better now. What
man didst thou ever know unthrift that was beloved after his means?

TIMON Who, without those means thou talk'st of, didst
thou ever know beloved?   315

APEMANTUS Myself.

TIMON I understand thee; thou hadst some means to
keep a dog.

APEMANTUS What things in the world canst thou nearest compare to thy flatterers?   320

TIMON Women nearest, but men—men are the
things themselves. What wouldst thou do with the
world, Apemantus, if it lay in thy power?

APEMANTUS Give it the beasts, to be rid of the men.

TIMON Wouldst thou have thyself fall in the confu- 325
sion of men, and remain a beast with the beasts?

APEMANTUS Ay, Timon.

TIMON A beastly ambition, which the gods grant
thee t' attain to. If thou wert the lion, the fox
would beguile thee. If thou wert the lamb, the   330
fox would eat thee. If thou wert the fox, the lion
would suspect thee, when peradventure thou wert
accused by the ass. If thou wert the ass, thy

308 hate ("eat" and "hate" were pronounced alike in Elizabethan English)
310 And if   310 meddlers (1) the fruit (2) busybodies, intriguers (3) those who
overindulge in sexual intercourse   312 unthrift prodigal, spendthrift   313 after
in accordance with (i.e., the true love for an "unthrift" is not in proportion with
his bounty)   318 a dog i.e., you had just enough to keep a dog so that something
might love you   325-26 the confusion of men i.e., the original Fall in the
Garden of Eden   330 beguile trick   332 peradventure perchance

dullness would torment thee, and still thou liv'dst
335 but as a breakfast to the wolf. If thou wert the
wolf, thy greediness would afflict thee, and oft
thou shouldst hazard thy life for thy dinner. Wert
thou the unicorn, pride and wrath would confound
thee, and make thine own self the conquest of thy
340 fury. Wert thou a bear, thou wouldst be killed by
the horse. Wert thou a horse, thou wouldst be
seized by the leopard. Wert thou a leopard, thou
wert german to the lion, and the spots of thy
kindred were jurors on thy life. All thy safety
345 were remotion, and thy defense absence. What
beast couldst thou be that were not subject to a
beast? And what a beast art thou already, that
seest not thy loss in transformation!

APEMANTUS If thou couldst please me with speaking
350 to me, thou mightst have hit upon it here. The
commonwealth of Athens is become a forest of
beasts.

TIMON How has the ass broke the wall, that thou art
out of the city?

355 APEMANTUS Yonder comes a poet and a painter. The
plague of company light upon thee! I will fear to
catch it, and give way. When I know not what
else to do, I'll see thee again.

TIMON When there is nothing living but thee, thou
360 shalt be welcome. I had rather be a beggar's dog
than Apemantus.

APEMANTUS Thou art the cap of all the fools alive.

---

338 **unicorn** (an untamable beast, who, in his fury to attack the treed lion, runs
his horn into the tree and puts himself at the mercy of the lion) 338 **confound**
destroy 343 **german** akin 343 **spots** (1) markings (2) moral stains, vices
344 **jurors** witnesses (especially false ones) 345 **remotion** removal of yourself
(to a distance), remoteness 348 **in transformation** i.e., in seeking to be
transformed into a beast 355 **a poet and a painter** (they do not actually enter
until the beginning of Act V) 357 **give way** retire 362 **cap** chief, summit

TIMON Would thou wert clean enough to spit upon.

APEMANTUS A plague on thee, thou art too bad to curse.

TIMON All villains that do stand by thee are pure.   365

APEMANTUS There is no leprosy but what thou speak'st.

TIMON If I name thee.
I'll beat thee, but I should infect my hands.

APEMANTUS I would my tongue could rot them off.

TIMON Away, thou issue of a mangy dog.   370
Choler does kill me that thou art alive;
I swound to see thee.

APEMANTUS Would thou wouldst burst.

TIMON Away, thou tedious rogue, I am sorry I shall
lose a stone by thee.   [*Throws a stone at him.*]   375

APEMANTUS Beast!

TIMON Slave!

APEMANTUS Toad!

TIMON Rogue, rogue, rogue!
I am sick of this false world, and will love naught   380
But even the mere necessities upon't.
Then, Timon, presently prepare thy grave.
Lie where the light foam of the sea may beat
Thy gravestone daily. Make thine epitaph,
That death in me at others' lives may laugh.   385
[*To the gold*] O thou sweet king-killer, and dear divorce
'Twixt natural son and sire, thou bright defiler
Of Hymen's purest bed, thou valiant Mars,

---

365 **that do stand by thee** compared to you   371 **Choler** anger   372 **swound**
swoon   381 **But even ... upon't** i.e., except the bare necessities of life
382 **presently** immediately   385 **in me** by my example   387 **natural** son by
birth (does not mean "illegitimate")   382 **Hymen** Greek god of marriage

Thou ever young, fresh, loved, and delicate wooer,
390   Whose blush doth thaw the consecrated snow
That lies on Dian's lap. Thou visible god,
That sold'rest close impossibilities
And mak'st them kiss; that speak'st with every
      tongue
To every purpose. O thou touch of hearts,
395   Think thy slave man rebels, and by thy virtue
Set them into confounding odds, that beasts
May have the world in empire.

APEMANTUS   Would 'twere so,
But not till I am dead. I'll say th'hast gold.
Thou wilt be thronged to shortly.

TIMON   Thronged to?

APEMANTUS   Ay.

TIMON Thy back, I prithee.

400   APEMANTUS   Live, and love thy misery.

TIMON Long live so, and so die. I am quit.

Enter the Banditti.

APEMANTUS Moe things like men! Eat, Timon, and
abhor them.   *Exit Apemantus.*

FIRST BANDIT Where should he have this gold? It is
some poor fragment, some slender ort of his re-
405   mainder. The mere want of gold, and the falling-
from of his friends, drove him into this melancholy.

SECOND BANDIT It is noised he hath a mass of treasure.

410   THIRD BANDIT Let us make the assay upon him. If

390 **blush** glow   391 **Dian** Diana, the virgin huntress, Greek goddess of
chastity   392 **sold'rest close impossibilities** joins closely together things
thought to be irreconcilable   394 **touch** touchstone   396 **into confounding
odds** at ruinous strife   401 **quit** rid (of Apemantus)   404 **ort** leftover bit
405 **mere** sheer   405–06 **falling-from** falling-off   408 **noised** rumored
410 **make the assay** put it to the test

he care not for't, he will supply us easily; if he covetously reserve it, how shall's get it?

SECOND BANDIT True, for he bears it not about him; 'tis hid.

FIRST BANDIT Is not this he? 415

ALL Where?

SECOND BANDIT 'Tis his description.

THIRD BANDIT He? I know him.

ALL Save thee, Timon.

TIMON Now, thieves? 420

ALL Soldiers, not thieves.

TIMON Both too, and women's sons.

ALL We are not thieves, but men that much do want.

TIMON Your greatest want is, you want much of
    meat.
  Why should you want? Behold, the earth hath
    roots;
  Within this mile break forth a hundred springs; 425
  The oaks bear mast, the briers scarlet hips;
  The bounteous huswife nature on each bush
  Lays her full mess before you. Want? Why want?

FIRST BANDIT We cannot live on grass, on berries,
    water,
  As beasts and birds and fishes. 430

TIMON Nor on the beasts themselves, the birds and
    fishes;
  You must eat men. Yet thanks I must you con
  That you are thieves professed, that you work not
  In holier shapes; for there is boundless theft

419 **Save thee** God save thee (a conventional salutation) 422 **want** need, lack 423 **you want much of meat** you desire (or lack) a good deal of food (i.e., if you didn't eat so much your wants would be smaller) 426 **mast** acorns (generally fed to swine) 426 **hips** fruit of the rose 427 **huswife** housewife 428 **mess** meal 432 **con** offer

435   In limited professions. Rascal thieves,
        Here's gold. Go, suck the subtle blood o' th' grape,
        Till the high fever seethe your blood to froth,
        And so 'scape hanging. Trust not the physician;
        His antidotes are poison, and he slays
440   Moe than you rob. Take wealth and lives together,
        Do, villain, do, since you protest to do't.
        Like workmen, I'll example you with thievery:
        The sun's a thief, and with his great attraction
        Robs the vast sea. The moon's an arrant thief,
445   And her pale fire she snatches from the sun.
        The sea's a thief, whose liquid surge resolves
        The moon into salt tears. The earth's a thief,
        That feeds and breeds by a composture stol'n
        From gen'ral excrement. Each thing's a thief.
450   The laws, your curb and whip, in their rough power
        Has unchecked theft. Love not yourselves; away,
        Rob one another. There's more gold; cut throats,
        All that you meet are thieves. To Athens go,
        Break open shops; nothing can you steal
455   But thieves do lose it. Steal less for this I give you,
        And gold confound you howsoe'er. Amen.

        THIRD BANDIT Has almost charmed me from my pro-
        fession by persuading me to it.

        FIRST BANDIT 'Tis in the malice of mankind that he
460   thus advises us, not to have us thrive in our
        mystery.

---

435 **limited** limited in numbers, restricted (as a guild) 436 **subtle**
treacherous 437 **high fever** i.e., of drunkenness 440 **Moe** more 441 **protest**
profess 442 **Like ... thievery** i.e., as one instructs workmen by practical
example, so I will give you some precedents for your line of work, thievery
443 **attraction** drawing power 446–47 **whose ... tears** (the idea is that the sea's
tides are stolen from the moon's precipitation) 448 **composture** compost,
manure 455 **Steal less for this I give you** i.e., even if you steal less because of
the gold I am giving you 456 **howsoe'er** nevertheless 459 **in the malice of
mankind** i.e., because of the malice Timon bears to all mankind 461 **mystery**
trade, profession

SECOND BANDIT I'll believe him as an enemy, and give
over my trade.

FIRST BANDIT Let us first see peace in Athens; there
is no time so miserable but a man may be true.   465

Exit Thieves.

Enter [Flavius,] the Steward to Timon.

FLAVIUS O you gods!
Is yond despised and ruinous man my lord?
Full of decay and failing? O monument
And wonder of good deeds evilly bestowed!
What an alteration of honor has desp'rate want
made!   470
What vilder thing upon the earth than friends,
Who can bring noblest minds to basest ends!
How rarely does it meet with this time's guise,
When man was wished to love his enemies!
Grant I may ever love, and rather woo   475
Those that would mischief me than those that do.
Has caught me in his eye; I will present
My honest grief unto him, and as my lord
Still serve him with my life. My dearest master.

TIMON Away! What art thou?

FLAVIUS   Have you forgot me, sir?   480

TIMON Why dost ask that? I have forgot all men.
Then, if thou grunt'st th'art a man,
I have forgot thee.

---

462 **I'll believe him as an enemy** i.e., since he is an enemy, I'll do the opposite
of what he advises   463 **give over** give up   464-65 **there is ... true** i.e., you
can become an honest man any time you choose (therefore, why do it now?)
467 **ruinous** ruined   468-69 **monument/And wonder** i.e., wonderful monument (memorial or tombstone)   470 **alteration of honor** change (for the worse)
in honor   471 **vilder** viler   473 **How ... guise** i.e., how excellently does
Timon's example fit in with the moral tone of these times (spoken ironically)
474 **wished** desired (by God)   476 **Those ... do** i.e., I will love those enemies
who are direct and open in their desire to harm me better than those who harm me
under the guise of friendship   482 **grunt'st** i.e., even your claim to be a man is
delivered in an animal grunt (since all men are bestial)

FLAVIUS An honest poor servant of yours.

485 TIMON Then I know thee not.
I never had honest man about me, I; all
I kept were knaves, to serve in meat to villains.

FLAVIUS The gods are witness,
Nev'r did poor steward wear a truer grief
490 For his undone lord than mine eyes for you.

TIMON What, dost thou weep? Come nearer. Then
I love thee
Because thou art a woman, and disclaim'st
Flinty mankind, whose eyes do never give
But thorough lust and laughter. Pity's sleeping.
Strange times, that weep with laughing, not with
495   weeping!

FLAVIUS I beg of you to know me, good my lord,
T' accept my grief, and whilst this poor wealth lasts,
To entertain me as your steward still.

TIMON Had I a steward
500 So true, so just, and now so comfortable?
It almost turns my dangerous nature mild.
Let me behold thy face. Surely, this man
Was born of woman.
Forgive my general and exceptless rashness,
505 You perpetual-sober gods. I do proclaim
One honest man. Mistake me not, but one.
No more I pray—and he's a steward.
How fain would I have hated all mankind,
And thou redeem'st thyself. But all save thee
510 I fell with curses.
Methinks thou art more honest now than wise;
For, by oppressing and betraying me,

487 **knaves** (1) servants (2) villains 493 **Flinty** hardhearted 493 **give weep** 494 **But thorough** except through 498 **entertain** receive into service 500 **comfortable** comforting 504 **exceptless** making no exceptions 510 **fell** cause to fall, strike down 512 **oppressing** distressing

594

Thou might'st have sooner got another service.
For many so arrive at second masters
Upon their first lord's neck. But tell me true—   515
For I must ever doubt, though ne'er so sure—
Is not thy kindness subtle, covetous,
A usuring kindness, as rich men deal gifts,
Expecting in return twenty for one?

FLAVIUS No, my most worthy master, in whose breast   520
Doubt and suspect, alas, are placed too late.
You should have feared false times when you did
     feast.
Suspect still comes where an estate is least.
That which I show, heaven knows, is merely love,
Duty and zeal to your unmatchèd mind,   525
Care of your food and living; and believe it,
My most honored lord,
For any benefit that points to me,
Either in hope or present, I'd exchange
For this one wish, that you had power and wealth   530
To requite me by making rich yourself.

TIMON Look thee, 'tis so. Thou singly honest man,
Here, take. The gods out of my misery
Has sent thee treasure. Go, live rich and happy,
But thus conditioned: thou shalt build from men;   535
Hate all, curse all, show charity to none,
But let the famished flesh slide from the bone
Ere thou relieve the beggar. Give to dogs
What thou deniest to men. Let prisons swallow 'em,
Debts wither 'em to nothing; be men like blasted
     woods,   540
And may diseases lick up their false bloods.
And so farewell, and thrive.

---

513 **service** position as a servant   515 **Upon their first lord's neck** i.e., by
treading down their first master and mounting on his neck (or shoulders)
516 **doubt suspect,** fear   518 **deal** distribute   521 **suspect** suspicion   523 **still**
always   524 **merely** entirely   528 **points** might accrue   532 **singly**
(1) uniquely (2) truly   535 **But thus conditioned** with this condition
535 **from** away from   540 **blasted** blighted

FLAVIUS O let me stay and comfort you, my master.

TIMON If thou hat'st curses

545   Stay not; fly, whilst thou art blessed and free.
         Ne'er see thou man, and let me ne'er see thee.

                    Exit [Flavius; and exit Timon into his cave].

[ACT V

Scene I. *Before Timon's cave*.]

Enter Poet and Painter; [*Timon listens from his cave, unseen*].

PAINTER As I took note of the place, it cannot be far where he abides.

POET What's to be thought of him? Does the rumor hold for true that he's so full of gold?

PAINTER Certain. Alcibiades reports it. Phrynia and 5
Timandra had gold of him. He likewise enriched poor straggling soldiers with great quantity. 'Tis said he gave unto his steward a mighty sum.

POET Then this breaking of his has been but a try for his friends? 10

PAINTER Nothing else. You shall see him a palm in Athens again, and flourish with the highest. There-fore 'tis not amiss we tender our loves to him in this supposed distress of his. It will show honestly in us, and is very likely to load our purposes with 15
what they travail for, if it be a just and true re-port that goes of his having.

V.i.7 **soldiers** i.e., the banditti, who claimed to be soldiers   9 **breaking** going bankrupt   9 **try** test   11 **palm** (cf. Psalm 92:11 "The righteous shall flourish like the palm-tree")   13 **tender** offer   14 **honestly** honorably   16 **travail** (1) labor (2) travel   17 **having** wealth

POET What have you now to present unto him?

PAINTER Nothing at this time but my visitation; only
20   I will promise him an excellent piece.

POET I must serve him so too, tell him of an intent
      that's coming toward him.

PAINTER Good as the best. Promising is the very air
      o' th' time; it opens the eyes of expectation. Per-
25   formance is ever the duller for his act, and but
      in the plainer and simpler kind of people, the deed
      of saying is quite out of use. To promise is most
      courtly and fashionable; performance is a kind of
      will or testament, which argues a great sickness in
30   his judgment that makes it.

Enter Timon from his cave.

TIMON [*Aside*] Excellent workman, thou canst not
      paint a man so bad as is thyself.

POET I am thinking what I shall say I have provided
      for him. It must be a personating of himself; a
35   satire against the softness of prosperity, with a
      discovery of the infinite flatteries that follow youth
      and opulency.

TIMON [*Aside*] Must thou needs stand for a villain
      in thine own work? Wilt thou whip thine own faults
40   in other men? Do so, I have gold for thee.

POET Nay, let's seek him.
      Then do we sin against our own estate,
      When we may profit meet, and come too late.

PAINTER True.
45   When the day serves, before black-cornered night,

25 **his act** its act, its having been put into action   26–27 **the deed of saying** i.e.,
the doing of what a person says he will do   34 **personating of himself**
representation of Timon and his situation   35 **softness** weakness, flabbiness
36 **discovery** revelation (a theatrical term)   38 **stand for** serve as a model for
42 **estate** fortune, material possessions   45 **black-cornered night** i.e., night
which creates dark corners and is obscure like them

Find what thou want'st by free and offered light.
Come.

TIMON [*Aside*] I'll meet you at the turn.
  What a god's gold, that he is worshiped
  In a baser temple than where swine feed!   50
  'Tis thou that rig'st the bark and plough'st the
     foam,
  Settlest admirèd reverence in a slave.
  To thee be worshiped and thy saints for aye;
  Be crowned with plagues that thee alone obey.
  Fit I meet them.   [*Comes forward.*]   55

POET Hail, worthy Timon.

PAINTER   Our late noble master.

TIMON Have I once lived to see two honest men?

POET Sir,
  Having often of your open bounty tasted,
  Hearing you were retired, your friends fall'n off,   60
  Whose thankless natures, O abhorrèd spirits,
  Not all the whips of heaven are large enough—
  What, to you,
  Whose star-like nobleness gave life and influence
  To their whole being! I am rapt, and cannot cover   65
  The monstrous bulk of this ingratitude
  With any size of words.

TIMON   Let it go;
  Naked, men may see't the better.
  You that are honest, by being what you are,
  Make them best seen and known.

PAINTER   He and myself   70

---

48 **I'll meet you at the turn** i.e., I will match your tricks with better ones of my own 50 **baser temple** i.e., the human body 52 **Settlest admirèd reverence** establishes a wondering awe (of his master) 53 **for aye** forever 54 **Be** i.e., may they be 57 **once** indeed (an intensive) 60 **retired** withdrawn 64 **influence** i.e., astrological influence 65 **rapt** carried away with emotion 67 **size** (1) magnitude (2) starch-like glue used on cloth, especially before painting on it 70 **them** i.e., the thankless natures of his fair-weather friends

Have traveled in the great show'r of your gifts,
And sweetly felt it.

TIMON   Ay, you are honest men.

PAINTER We are hither come to offer you our service.

TIMON Most honest men. Why, how shall I requite you?
75   Can you eat roots and drink cold water? No?

BOTH What we can do, we'll do to do you service.

TIMON Y'are honest men. Y'have heard that I have gold,
        I am sure you have. Speak truth, y'are honest men.

PAINTER So it is said, my noble lord, but therefore
80   Came not my friend nor I.

TIMON Good honest men. Thou draw'st a counterfeit
        Best in all Athens. Th'art indeed the best;
        Thou counterfeit'st most lively.

PAINTER   So-so, my lord.

TIMON E'en so, sir, as I say. And for thy fiction,
85   Why thy verse swells with stuff so fine and smooth
        That thou art even natural in thine art.
        But for all this, my honest-natured friends,
        I must needs say you have a little fault;
        Marry, 'tis not monstrous in you, neither wish I
        You take much pains to mend.

90 BOTH   Beseech your honor
        To make it known to us.

TIMON   You'll take it ill.

BOTH Most thankfully, my lord.

---

81 **counterfeit** (1) representation, picture (2) false representation   83 **most
lively** in a most lifelike manner   84 **fiction** imaginative feigning   85 **smooth**
polished (with implication of flattery)   86 **thou ... art** (1) your writings represent
a triumph of nature over art; your art conceals itself (2) you show your evil natural
self in your artful dissimulation   89 **Marry** indeed

TIMON   Will you indeed?

BOTH Doubt it not, worthy lord.

TIMON There's never a one of you but trusts a knave
    That mightily deceives you.

BOTH   Do we, my lord?   95

TIMON Ay, and you hear him cog, see him dissemble,
    Know his gross patchery, love him, feed him,
    Keep in your bosom, yet remain assured
    That he's a made-up villain.

PAINTER I know none such, my lord.

POET   Nor I.   100

TIMON Look you, I love you well; I'll give you gold:
    Rid me these villains from your companies.
    Hang them, or stab them, drown them in a draught,
    Confound them by some course, and come to me,
    I'll give you gold enough.   105

BOTH Name them, my lord, let's know them.

TIMON You that way, and you this; but two in com-
        pany.
    Each man apart, all single and alone,
    Yet an arch-villain keeps him company.
    [To one] If where thou art, two villains shall not be,   110
    Come not near him. [To the other] If thou wouldst
        not reside
    But where one villain is, then him abandon.
    Hence, pack, there's gold; you came for gold, ye
        slaves.
    [To one] You have work for me, there's payment.
        Hence!

---

96 cog cheat   97 patchery roguery   98 Keep i.e., let him dwell   99 made-up
complete   103 draught privy, sink   104 Confound destroy   107 but two in
company i.e., wherever either of them is, there is both a poet (or painter) and a
villain   112 But except   113 pack be off

[*To the other*] You are an alchemist, make gold
115   of that.
Out, rascal dogs!
                    [*Beats them out, then retires into his cave.*]

    Enter [Flavius, the] Steward, and two Senators.

FLAVIUS It is vain that you would speak with Timon,
For he is set so only to himself
That nothing but himself, which looks like man,
Is friendly with him.

120   FIRST SENATOR   Bring us to his cave.
It is our part and promise to th' Athenians
To speak with Timon.

SECOND SENATOR   At all times alike
Men are not still the same; 'twas time and griefs
That framed him thus. Time with his fairer hand
125   Offering the fortunes of his former days,
The former man may make him. Bring us to him,
And chance it as it may.

FLAVIUS   Here is his cave.
Peace and content be here. Lord Timon! Timon!
Look out, and speak to friends. Th' Athenians
130   By two of their most reverend senate greet thee.
Speak to them, noble Timon.

    Enter Timon out of his cave.

TIMON Thou sun that comforts, burn! Speak and be
    hanged.
For each true word a blister, and each false
Be as a cauterizing to the root o' th' tongue,
Consuming it with speaking.

135   FIRST SENATOR   Worthy Timon——

TIMON Of none but such as you, and you of Timon.

118 **is set so only to himself** is so completely preoccupied with himself
121 **our part and promise** the role we promised to play   127 **chance it** may it
turn out   133 **For each true word a blister** (an ironic reversal of the proverbial
belief that a lie causes a blister on the tongue)

FIRST SENATOR The senators of Athens greet thee,
    Timon.

TIMON I thank them, and would send them back the
    plague,
  Could I but catch it for them.

FIRST SENATOR   O forget
  What we are sorry for ourselves in thee.   140
  The senators, with one consent of love,
  Entreat thee back to Athens, who have thought
  On special dignities, which vacant lie
  For thy best use and wearing.

SECOND SENATOR   They confess
  Toward thee forgetfulness too general gross;   145
  Which now the public body, which doth seldom
  Play the recanter, feeling in itself
  A lack of Timon's aid, hath sense withal
  Of it own fall, restraining aid to Timon;
  And send forth us to make their sorrowed render, 150
  Together with a recompense more fruitful
  Than their offense can weigh down by the dram—
  Ay, even such heaps and sums of love and wealth
  As shall to thee blot out what wrongs were theirs,
  And write in thee the figures of their love,   155
  Ever to read them thine.

TIMON   You witch me in it;
  Surprise me to the very brink of tears.

---

140 **in thee** i.e., in the wrongs we have caused you 141 **consent of love**
harmonious voice of affection 144 **For thy best use and wearing** i.e., only you
are suited to fill these dignities with the proper distinction 145 **general**
universally 146 **the public body** the senate as representative of the body
politic 148 **withal** at the same time 149 **it own fall** its own fall from
grace 149 **restraining** keeping back 150 **sorrowed render** sorrowful rendering of an account 151 **fruitful** abundant 152 **weigh down by the dram** i.e.,
balance in weight even if measured to the last tiny unit 155 **figures** (1) written
characters (2) numerals (as in counting money) (3) images, representations
156 **them** i.e., the Athenians as represented in the "figures of their love"
156 **witch** bewitch

Lend me a fool's heart and a woman's eyes,
And I'll beweep these comforts, worthy senators.

FIRST SENATOR Therefore so please thee to return with
160 us,
And of our Athens, thine and ours, to take
The captainship, thou shalt be met with thanks,
Allowed with absolute power, and thy good name
Live with authority. So soon we shall drive back
165 Of Alcibiades th' approaches wild,
Who like a boar too savage doth root up
His country's peace.

SECOND SENATOR And shakes his threat'ning sword
Against the walls of Athens.

FIRST SENATOR   Therefore, Timon——

TIMON Well, sir, I will; therefore I will, sir, thus:
170 If Alcibiades kill my countrymen,
Let Alcibiades know this of Timon,
That Timon cares not. But if he sack fair Athens,
And take our goodly agèd men by th' beards,
Giving our holy virgins to the stain
175 Of contumelious, beastly, mad-brained war,
Then let him know, and tell him Timon speaks it,
In pity of our agèd and our youth,
I cannot choose but tell him that I care not,
And let him take't at worst. For their knives care not
180 While you have throats to answer. For myself,
There's not a whittle in th' unruly camp
But I do prize it at my love before
The reverend'st throat in Athens. So I leave you

---

159 **comforts** pleasures 163 **Allowed** endowed 175 **contumelious**
insolent 179 **take't at worst** put the worst interpretation he wishes on it
180 **throats to answer** i.e., throats to be cut by the knives of Alcibiades' soldiers
(and voices to protest for yourselves) 181 **whittle** small knife 181 **th' unruly
camp** (1) the party of those revolting against Athens (2) the disorderly, turbulent
army (of Alcibiades) 182 **prize it at my love** value it in my esteem

To the protection of the prosperous gods,
As thieves to keepers.

FLAVIUS   Stay not, all's in vain.   185

TIMON Why I was writing of my epitaph;
It will be seen tomorrow. My long sickness
Of health and living now begins to mend,
And nothing brings me all things. Go, live still;
Be Alcibiades your plague, you his,   190
And last so long enough.

FIRST SENATOR   We speak in vain.

TIMON But yet I love my country, and am not
One that rejoices in the common wrack,
As common bruit doth put it.

FIRST SENATOR   That's well spoke.

TIMON Commend me to my loving countrymen.   195

FIRST SENATOR These words become your lips as they
pass thorough them.

SECOND SENATOR And enter in our ears like great triumphers
In their applauding gates.

TIMON   Commend me to them,
And tell them that to ease them of their griefs,
Their fears of hostile strokes, their aches, losses,   200
Their pangs of love, with other incident throes
That nature's fragile vessel doth sustain
In life's uncertain voyage, I will some kindness do
them;
I'll teach them to prevent wild Alcibiades' wrath.

184 **prosperous** propitious 185 **As thieves to keepers** i.e., as I would leave
thieves to the protection of their jailers 189 **nothing** nothingness, oblivion
191 **last** endure 193 **wrack** destruction 194 **bruit** rumor 196 **become**
befit 197 **triumphers** triumphant marchers 198 **applauding gates** i.e., city
gates thronged with those applauding the triumph 200 **aches** (two syllables,
pronounced "aitches") 201 **incident throes** agonies likely to occur 204 **prevent** anticipate (but First Senator interprets "to keep from occurring")

205   FIRST SENATOR I like this well; he will return again.

TIMON I have a tree which grows here in my close,
       That mine own use invites me to cut down,
       And shortly must I fell it. Tell my friends,
       Tell Athens, in the sequence of degree,
210   From high to low throughout, that whoso please
       To stop affliction, let him take his haste;
       Come hither ere my tree hath felt the ax,
       And hang himself. I pray you do my greeting.

FLAVIUS Trouble him no further; thus you still shall
         find him.

215   TIMON Come not to me again, but say to Athens,
       Timon hath made his everlasting mansion
       Upon the beachèd verge of the salt flood,
       Who once a day with his embossèd froth
       The turbulent surge shall cover. Thither come,
220   And let my gravestone be your oracle.
       Lips, let four words go by and language end.
       What is amiss, plague and infection mend.
       Graves only be men's works and death their gain.
       Sun, hide thy beams; Timon hath done his reign.
                                                    Exit Timon.

225   FIRST SENATOR His discontents are unremovably
       Coupled to nature.

SECOND SENATOR Our hope in him is dead. Let us
                return,

---

206 **close** enclosure 209 **sequence of degree** proper order of the social hierarchy 214 **still** always 217 **beachèd verge of the salt flood** edge of the sea that forms a beach 218 **Who** i.e., "the beachèd verge" 218 **embossèd** covered with foam (usually from the mouth of a hunted animal) 220 **be your oracle** i.e., be consulted by you as if it were an oracle (a place where divine pronouncements are made, or the god making such pronouncements) 221 **let four words go by and language end** i.e., speak only a few more words ("four" is used indefinitely) and then not speak any further 226 **Coupled to nature** a part of his nature

And strain what other means is left unto us
In our dear peril.

FIRST SENATOR   It requires swift foot.   *Exeunt*.

[Scene II. *Before the walls of Athens*.]

Enter two other Senators with a Messenger.

THIRD SENATOR Thou hast painfully discovered. Are
    his files
As full as thy report?

MESSENGER   I have spoke the least.
    Besides, his expedition promises
    Present approach.

FOURTH SENATOR We stand much hazard if they bring
    not Timon.   5

MESSENGER I met a courier, one mine ancient friend,
    Whom though in general part we were opposed,
    Yet our old love made a particular force,
    And made us speak like friends. This man was
      riding
    From Alcibiades to Timon's cave   10
    With letters of entreaty, which imported
    His fellowship i' th' cause against your city,
    In part for his sake moved.

---

228 **strain** exert to the utmost   229 **dear** grievous, dire   V.ii.1 **Thou hast
painfully discovered** (1) your revelation was painful to us (2) you have made
your revelation in painstaking detail   1 **files** ranks   2 **spoke the least** reported
the minimum   3 **expedition** speed   4 **Present** immediate   6 **ancient**
former   7 **in general part** i.e., in matters of general or public interest
8 **particular** personal   11 **imported** bore as their message (with additional
suggestion of "importuned" or urged)   13 **moved** instigated

Enter the other Senators [from Timon].

THIRD SENATOR   Here come our brothers.

FIRST SENATOR No talk of Timon, nothing of him
    expect.
15   The enemy's drum is heard, and fearful scouring
       Doth choke the air with dust. In, and prepare.
       Ours is the fall, I fear, our foes the snare.   *Exeunt.*

[Scene III. *Before Timon's cave.*]

Enter a Soldier in the woods, seeking Timon.

SOLDIER By all description this should be the place.
       Who's here? Speak, ho! No answer? What is this?
       "Timon is dead, who hath outstretched his span.
       Some beast read this; there does not live a man."
5   Dead, sure, and this his grave. What's on this tomb
       I cannot read. The character I'll take with wax;
       Our captain hath in every figure skill,
       An aged interpreter, though young in days.
       Before proud Athens he's set down by this,
10   Whose fall the mark of his ambition is.   *Exit.*

14 **No talk** i.e., let us not talk   15 **scouring** scurrying about (in preparation for
battle)   17 **our foes the snare** i.e., our foes are the snare or trap which will cause
the downfall of Athens   V.iii.2 **What is this** (presumably the Soldier finds an
inscription or trial epitaph composed by Timon in English, which the Soldier can
read, whereas the epitaph on Timon's tomb is in Latin, which the Soldier cannot
read)   3 **outstretched his span** lived beyond his allotted or desired life span
4 **there does not live a man** i.e., all men left alive are merely beasts   6 **The
character I'll take with wax** I will take a wax impression of the letters   7 **figure**
written character   8 **aged** experienced   9 **set down** i.e., in a siege   10 **mark**
goal

[Scene IV. *Before the walls of Athens*.]

*Trumpets sound. Enter Alcibiades with his
powers before Athens.*

ALCIBIADES Sound to this coward and lascivious town
   Our terrible approach.   *Sounds a parley*.

The Senators appear upon the walls.

Till now you have gone on, and filled the time
With all licentious measure, making your wills
The scope of justice. Till now, myself and such   5
As slept within the shadow of your power,
Have wandered with our traversed arms and
   breathed
Our sufferance vainly. Now the time is flush,
When crouching marrow in the bearer strong
Cries, of itself, "No more." Now breathless wrong 10
Shall sit and pant in your great chairs of ease,
And pursy insolence shall break his wind
With fear and horrid flight.

FIRST SENATOR   Noble and young,
When thy first griefs were but a mere conceit,

V.iv.2 **terrible** terrifying 2 s.d. **Sounds a parley** i.e., by a special signal on drum or trumpet, Alcibiades calls for a conference with the enemy to try to make peace 2 s.d. **upon the walls** i.e., upon the upper stage 4 **With all licentious measure** with all kinds of unbridled conduct 5 **scope** extent 6 **slept** (1) were asleep, inactive (2) lived 7 **traversed** folded across (in resignation) 7–8 **breathed/Our sufferance vainly** spoke in vain about our sufferings 8 **flush** ripe 9 **When … strong** i.e., when the resolute man's courage is aroused 10 **breathless wrong** wrongdoers breathless through fear 11 **great chairs of ease** comfortably upholstered chairs of state 12 **pursy** short-winded 13 **horrid** horrible 14 **griefs** grievances 14 **conceit** idea

15   Ere thou hadst power or we had cause of fear,
        We sent to thee to give thy rages balm,
        To wipe out our ingratitude with loves
        Above their quantity.

        SECOND SENATOR   So did we woo
        Transformèd Timon to our city's love
20   By humble message and by promised means.
        We were not all unkind, nor all deserve
        The common stroke of war.

        FIRST SENATOR   These walls of ours
        Were not erected by their hands from whom
        You have received your grief; nor are they such
        That these great tow'rs, trophies, and schools
25   should fall
        For private faults in them.

        SECOND SENATOR   Nor are they living
        Who were the motives that you first went out
        Shame that they wanted, cunning in excess
        Hath broke their hearts. March, noble lord,
30   Into our city with thy banners spread.
        By decimation and a tithèd death,
        If thy revenges hunger for that food
        Which nature loathes, take thou the destined tenth,
        And by the hazard of the spotted die,
        Let die the spotted.

35   FIRST SENATOR   All have not offended.
        For those that were, it is not square to take

---

18 **their** (the antecedent is either "griefs" or "rages" or both) 20 **means**
conditions of peace (or possibly "riches") 25 **trophies, and schools** monuments, and public buildings 27 **motives** that you first went out instigators or
movers of your original banishment 28–29 **Shame ... hearts** i.e., their hearts
were broken with remorse for two common moral failings: lack of a sense of
disgrace for their wrongdoing and excess of crafty deceit 31 **decimation and a
tithèd death** the killing of one person in ten 34 **by the hazard of the spotted
die** by chance, as in dice ("die" is the singular of "dice") 35 **spotted** (1) guilty
(2) those selected by the "spots" on the dice 36 **square** honest

On those that are, revenge. Crimes, like lands,
Are not inherited. Then, dear countryman,
Bring in thy ranks, but leave without thy rage.
Spare thy Athenian cradle and those kin   40
Which in the bluster of thy wrath must fall
With those that have offended. Like a shepherd,
Approach the fold and cull th' infected forth,
But kill not all together.

SECOND SENATOR   What thou wilt,
Thou rather shalt enforce it with thy smile   45
Than hew to't with thy sword.

FIRST SENATOR   Set but thy foot
Against our rampired gates, and they shall ope,
So thou wilt send thy gentle heart before
To say thou't enter friendly.

SECOND SENATOR   Throw thy glove,
Or any token of thine honor else,   50
That thou wilt use the wars as thy redress
And not as our confusion. All thy powers
Shall make their harbor in our town till we
Have sealed thy full desire.

ALCIBIADES   Then there's my glove.
Descend and open your unchargèd ports.   55
Those enemies of Timon's and mine own
Whom you yourselves shall set out for reproof,
Fall, and no more. And to atone your fears
With my more noble meaning, not a man
Shall pass his quarter, or offend the stream   60
Of regular justice in your city's bounds,

39 **without** outside   41 **bluster** tempest   43 **fold** enclosure for sheep or the
flock itself   46 **hew to't** cut thy way to it   47 **rampired** fortified   48 **So**
provided that   52 **confusion** destruction   52 **powers** armed forces   53 **make
their harbor** be billeted   54 **sealed** solemnly ratified (by fulfilling)
55 **unchargèd ports** unassailed gates   57 **reproof** shame   58 **atone** appease
59 **meaning** intention   60 **quarter** billet (?) area of duty (?)

But shall be remedied to your public laws
At heaviest answer.

BOTH SENATORS   'Tis most nobly spoken.

ALCIBIADES Descend, and keep your words.
[*The Senators descend, and open the gates.*]

Enter a Soldier.

65   SOLDIER My noble general, Timon is dead,
Entombed upon the very hem o' th' sea,
And on his gravestone this insculpture which
With wax I brought away, whose soft impression
Interprets for my poor ignorance.

Alcibiades reads the epitaph.

ALCIBIADES "Here lies a wretched corse, of wretched
70   soul bereft.
Seek not my name. A plague consume you, wicked
caitiffs left.
Here lie I, Timon, who alive all living men did
hate.
Pass by and curse thy fill, but pass, and stay not
here thy gait."
These well express in thee thy latter spirits.
75   Though thou abhorr'dst in us our human griefs,
Scorn'dst our brains' flow, and those our droplets
which
From niggard nature fall; yet rich conceit
Taught thee to make vast Neptune weep for aye
On thy low grave, on faults forgiven. Dead
80   Is noble Timon, of whose memory
Hereafter more. Bring me into your city,

---

62 **remedied** turned over for remedy   63 **At heaviest answer** for the maximum
punishment   66 **hem** edge (the "beachèd verge" of V.i.217)   67 **insculpture**
inscription   69 **Interprets** acts as an interpreter   69 s.d. **epitaph** (there are two
epitaphs here, both from North's *Plutarch*, and it seems very likely that one of
them—probably the first—was intended to be omitted)   70 **corse** corpse
71 **caitiffs** wretches   74 **latter** later, more recent   76 **brains' flow** tears
77 **niggard** stingy   77 **rich conceit** fanciful imagination   78 **for aye** forever

And I will use the olive with my sword,
Make war breed peace, make peace stint war, make each
Prescribe to other, as each other's leech.
Let our drums strike.   *Exeunt.*   85

FINIS

82 **use the olive with my sword** i.e., combine the olive branch of peace with the sword of war, show mercy even though I enter your city as a conqueror   83 **stint** cause to stop   84 **leech** physician

Textual Note

Our sole authority for the text of *Timon of Athens* is the First Folio of Shakespeare, published in 1623. It may only be the result of a lucky accident that the play was printed at all, since *Troilus and Cressida* was intended to follow *Romeo and Juliet* in the section of Tragedies, and three pages of *Troilus* were actually set up and printed. But difficulties over the copyright of *Troilus* probably forced Jaggard to stop work on it. He allowed a sufficient number of blank pages for it, and then went on to set up and print *Julius Caesar*. Contrary to Jaggard's expectations, the difficulties with *Troilus* were not quickly resolved. Something had to fill the space left for *Troilus*, and *Timon* was decided on. It is a relatively short play, so that it only partially fills the allotted pages. Signature ii is omitted and there is an awkward gap between pages 98 and 109 (beginning of *Julius Caesar*), despite the blown-up and elaborately decorated list of actors' names that has a page to itself at the end of *Timon*.

Whether *Timon* would have been printed at all if the difficulties with *Troilus* had not occurred is a teasing question, but the condition of its text strongly confirms its role as an afterthought or stopgap. *Timon* is full of the kind of inconsistencies and roughnesses that suggest a play that has not received any final revision. There is no record of a performance of the play during Shakespeare's lifetime, and the possibility seems unlikely. It is obviously not the sort of play that a business-minded publisher would be eager to include in an expensive and speculative venture like the Shakespeare Folio. The text of *Timon* was set up either directly from Shakespeare's "foul papers" (rough draft), or from a transcript of them made by a scribe.

The state of the text has an important bearing on the editing of the play. If *Timon* is indeed a play that has not received that final revision and polishing necessary to put it into actable (or printable) form, it is not the job of a modern editor to undertake this task for Shakespeare. It is not up to a modern editor, for example, to make the lines scan by piecing them out differently (a formidable task here), or to distribute specific roles to the First, Second, Third, and Fourth Lords, or to make other changes of an essentially "improving" nature. I assume that the present-day reader would like to have the play in a modernized form, but as close as possible to the way Shakespeare left it. I have therefore made very few changes in the Folio text, even at the expense of leaving loose ends or inconsistencies. (It would be wonderfully satisfying to know whom Alcibiades is pleading for in Act III, Scene v.)

Two matters of special interest are related to the nature of the text: lineation and stage directions. In the text of *Timon* there is either serious mislineation (the printing of blank verse lines in some other form, either broken in two or run together as prose), or a failure in a number of places to write regular, five-beat, iambic lines. That is, either the compositor took wide liberties with the metrics, or the author himself made errors or allowed himself a great deal of freedom. Considering the unrevised state of the text, one is forced to conclude that the printed version is probably an accurate rendering of the copy. "Mislineation" is, therefore, a misleading term. I have generally followed the lineation of the Folio, except where lines are obviously broken into two to fill up the "cast off" space (that is, the amount of space estimated to be needed for a certain quantity of copy), or run together as prose where not enough space was allowed. The Folio lineation usually makes for good speech rhythm, with important pauses at the ends of lines. To run these lines through the blank verse meat grinder would distort their quality as dramatic speech.

How one treats the Folio stage directions of *Timon* also depends upon one's attitude to the text. The indications of action in this play are of the permissive and literary sort characteristic of an author's manuscript. For example, the final part of the stage direction that opens Act I, Scene ii, reads: "*Then comes dropping after all, Apemantus, discontentedly, like himself.*" This is a descriptive stage direction, which would have been put into a more practical form in a promptbook prepared by the stage manager. To change this direction to "*Then enter Apemantus, alone and at a distance*" (as Sisson does in his fine text) is to throw away a significant Shakespearean line for the sake of some imagined modern production. In an unrevised play such as *Timon* there is a special sanction for retaining the obviously authorial stage directions of the Folio, which bring us closer to the original manuscript of the play than do the colorless, clarified directions of a modern editor. I have also avoided one other type of correction in the stage directions. When it is not clear who is being addressed, I have not seen fit to supply a name. In Act V, Scene i, for example, Timon is upbraiding Poet and Painter in turn, but the text never specifies which one. I have simply indicated *To one* and *To the other*, although in a production it would obviously have to be either to Poet or Painter. Perhaps these two characters are meant to have a Rosencrantz and Guildenstern interchangeability.

In the present text spelling has been modernized, except that certain older forms have been retained when they are essentially different from their modern counterparts, for example, "vild" (for "vile"), "huswife" (for "housewife"), "a th'" (for "o' th'"). The punctuation has been modernized within limits, but I have generally been wary of introducing changes where the Folio pointing makes good sense. Even editors scrupulous about the language of the Folio seem not to feel bound by the punctuation. Capitalization has been modernized, and contractions not affecting pronunciation have been eliminated (especially in the verb forms). For stylistic reasons, I have omitted many traditional exclamation marks. The speech prefixes have been expanded and somewhat clarified. The list of actors' names is taken from the Folio, where it is printed (with one name given twice, and with the names in a slightly different order) at the end of the play.

Typographical errors have been corrected, and some stage directions have been slightly moved. Many traditional stage directions, not in the Folio, have been supplied

TEXTUAL NOTE

in square brackets. The traditional act and scene divisions and scene locations have been indicated for convenience, but the reader should recall that the action of the play was continuous and the scenes often unlocalized. The Folio indicates only "Actus Primus, Scœna Prima."

Other departures from the Folio are listed below. The reading of the present text is given first, in bold, and then the reading of the Folio (F) in roman.

I.i.s.d. **Enter Poet, Painter, Jeweler, Merchant** [F adds "and Mercer"] 21 **gum, which oozes** Gowne, which vses 87 **hands** hand 87 **slip** sit 166 **satiety** society 215 **cost** cast 280 **Come** Comes 289 **I'll keep you company** [in F part of speech of Second Lord]

I.ii.29 **ever** verie 115 s.d. **Sound tucket** [F follows this with another s.d., "Enter the Maskers of Amazons, with Lutes in their hands, dauncing and playing," incorrectly anticipating the entry at line 132; the necessary part of this s.d. is therefore added to that of line 132] 127 **Th'ear** There 132 **First Lord** First Lord Luc. 154 **First Lady** I Lord

II.ii.4 **resumes** resume 43 **of broken** of debt, broken 80 **mistress'** Masters 110 **mistress'** Masters 138 **proposed** propose 195 **Flaminius** Flauius 195 s.d. **Enter Flaminius, Servilius, and Third Servant** Enter three Seruants

III.i.s.d. **with** with a

III.iii.21 **and I** and

III.iv.s.d. **two Servants** man 50 **ate** eate 87 **Hortensius** 1. Var. 111 **Sempronius—all** Sempronius Vllorxa

III.v.17 **An** And 67 **'em** him

III.vi.92 **with your** you with 116–17 [speech prefixes reversed]

IV.i.13 **Son** Some 21 **let** yet

IV.iii.12 **pasture** Pastour 13 **lean** leaue 88 **tub-fast** fubfast 117 **window-bars** window Barne 122 **thy** the 157 **scolds** scold'st 255 **drudges** drugges 256 **command** command'st 272 **rogue** ragge 284 **my** thy 402 **them** then 501 **mild** wilde 518 **A usuring kindness, as** If not a Vsuring kindnesse, and as

V.i.5–6 **Phrynia and Timandra** Phrinica and Timandylo 72 **men** man 116 s.d. **Beats ... cave** Exeunt 127 **chance** chanc'd 134 **cauterizing** Cantherizing 148 **sense** since 183 **reverend'st** reuerends

V.iv.55 **Descend** Defend 64 s.d. **Soldier** Messenger

618

WILLIAM SHAKESPEARE

THE TRAGEDY

OF

CORIOLANUS

Edited by Reuben Brower

CAIUS MARCIUS, afterwards Caius Marcius Coriolanus

TITUS LARTIUS
COMINIUS } generals against the Volscians

MENENIUS AGRIPPA, friend to Coriolanus

SICINIUS VELUTUS
JUNIUS BRUTUS } tribunes of the people

YOUNG MARCIUS, son to Coriolanus

A ROMAN HERALD

A ROMAN, named Nicanor

TULLUS AUFIDIUS, general of the Volscians

LIEUTENANT TO AUFIDIUS

CONSPIRATORS WITH AUFIDIUS

A VOLSCIAN, named Adrian

A CITIZEN OF ANTIUM

TWO VOLSCIAN GUARDS

VOLUMNIA, mother to Coriolanus

VIRGILIA, wife to Coriolanus

VALERIA, friend to Virgilia

GENTLEWOMAN ATTENDING ON VIRGILIA

USHER ATTENDING ON VALERIA

ROMAN AND VOLSCIAN SENATORS, PATRICIANS, AEDILES, LICTORS, SOLDIERS, CITIZENS, MESSENGERS, SERVANTS TO AUFIDIUS, AND OTHER ATTENDANTS

Scene: Rome and the neighborhood; Corioli and the neighborhood; Antium]

THE TRAGEDY OF CORIOLANUS

ACT I

Scene I. [*Rome. A street.*]

Enter a company of mutinous Citizens, with staves,
clubs, and other weapons.

FIRST CITIZEN Before we proceed any further, hear me
speak.

ALL Speak, speak.

FIRST CITIZEN You are all resolved rather to die than
to famish?   5

ALL Resolved, resolved.

FIRST CITIZEN First you know, Caius Marcius is chief
enemy to the people.

ALL We know't, we know't.

FIRST CITIZEN Let us kill him, and we'll have corn at   10
our own price. Is't a verdict?

ALL No more talking on't; let it be done. Away, away!

A footnote is keyed to the text by line number. Text references are printed in
boldface type; the annotation follows in roman type. I.i.10 **corn** grain (wheat,
barley, etc., not Indian corn)

SECOND CITIZEN One word, good citizens.

15 FIRST CITIZEN We are accounted poor citizens, the patricians good. What authority surfeits on would relieve us. If they would yield us but the superfluity while it were wholesome, we might guess they relieved us humanely; but they think we are too
20 dear; the leanness that afflicts us, the object of our misery, is as an inventory to particularize their abundance; our sufferance is a gain to them. Let us revenge this with our pikes ere we become rakes. For the gods know I speak this in hunger
25 for bread, not in thirst for revenge.

SECOND CITIZEN Would you proceed especially against Caius Marcius?

FIRST CITIZEN Against him first: he's a very dog to the commonalty.

30 SECOND CITIZEN Consider you what services he has done for his country?

FIRST CITIZEN Very well, and could be content to give him good report for't, but that he pays himself with being proud.

35 SECOND CITIZEN Nay, but speak not maliciously.

FIRST CITIZEN I say unto you, what he hath done famously he did it to that end; though soft-con-scienced men can be content to say it was for his country, he did it to please his mother and to be
40 partly proud, which he is, even to the altitude of his virtue.

SECOND CITIZEN What he cannot help in his nature you account a vice in him. You must in no way say he is covetous.

16 **good** well-off 18 **guess** think 20 **dear** expensive 20 **object** sight 21–22 **inventory to particularize their abundance** list in which to read a detailed account of their wealth as compared with our poverty 23 **pikes** pitchforks 24 **rakes** cf. "lean as a rake" 29 **commonalty** common people 39–40 **to be partly proud** in part from pride 41 **virtue** valor (Latin sense)

FIRST CITIZEN If I must not, I need not be barren of   45
accusations. He hath faults (with surplus) to tire in
repetition. (*Shouts within.*) What shouts are these?
The other side o' th' city is risen. Why stay we
prating here? To th' Capitol!

ALL Come, come.   50

FIRST CITIZEN Soft, who comes here?

Enter Menenius Agrippa

SECOND CITIZEN Worthy Menenius Agrippa, one that
hath always loved the people.

FIRST CITIZEN He's one honest enough; would all the
rest were so!   55

MENENIUS What work's, my countrymen, in hand?
    Where go you
With bats and clubs? The matter? Speak, I pray you.

FIRST CITIZEN Our business is not unknown to th'
Senate; they have had inkling this fortnight what
we intend to do, which now we'll show 'em in   60
deeds. They say poor suitors have strong breaths;
they shall know we have strong arms too.

MENENIUS Why, masters, my good friends, mine
    honest neighbors,
Will you undo yourselves?

FIRST CITIZEN We cannot, sir; we are undone already.   65

MENENIUS I tell you, friends, most charitable care
Have the patricians of you. For your wants,
Your suffering in this dearth, you may as well
Strike at the heaven with your staves as lift them
Against the Roman state, whose course will on   70
The way it takes, cracking ten thousand curbs
Of more strong link asunder than can ever

---

49 **Capitol** Capitoline Hill, on which the Temple of Jupiter stood (here and often,
for the Senate House nearby)   51 **Soft** stop (an interjection)   68 **dearth**
famine   71 **curbs** restraints

Appear in your impediment. For the dearth,
The gods, not the patricians, make it, and
75   Your knees to them (not arms) must help. Alack,
You are transported by calamity
Thither where more attends you; and you slander
The helms o' th' state, who care for you like
    fathers,
When you curse them as enemies.

80 FIRST CITIZEN Care for us! True, indeed! They ne'er
cared for us yet. Suffer us to famish, and their store-
houses crammed with grain; make edicts for usury,
to support usurers; repeal daily any wholesome act
established against the rich, and provide more
85 piercing statutes daily to chain up and restrain the
poor. If the wars eat us not up, they will; and
there's all the love they bear us.

MENENIUS Either you must
Confess yourselves wondrous malicious,
90   Or be accused of folly. I shall tell you
A pretty tale; it may be you have heard it;
But since it serves my purpose, I will venture
To stale't a little more.

FIRST CITIZEN Well, I'll hear it, sir. Yet you must not
95 think to fob off our disgrace with a tale. But,
and't please you, deliver.

MENENIUS There was a time when all the body's mem-
    bers
Rebelled against the Belly; thus accused it:
That only like a gulf it did remain
100 I' th' midst o' th' body, idle and unactive,
Still cupboarding the viand, never bearing
Like labor with the rest; where th' other instruments

---

73 **in your impediment** in any hindrance you make 76 **transported** carried
out of your minds 78 **helms** helmsmen 93 **stale't** make it stale 95 **fob off** set
aside with a trick 95 **disgrace** misfortune 96 **and't** if it 99 **gulf**
whirlpool 101 **viand** food 102 **instruments** organs

Did see and hear, devise, instruct, walk, feel,
And, mutually participate, did minister
Unto the appetite and affection common   105
Of the whole body. The Belly answered——

FIRST CITIZEN Well, sir, what answer made the Belly?

MENENIUS Sir, I shall tell you. With a kind of smile,
Which ne'er came from the lungs, but even thus—
For, look you, I may make the Belly smile   110
As well as speak—it tauntingly replied
To th' discontented members, the mutinous parts
That envied his receipt; even so most fitly
As you malign our senators for that
They are not such as you.

FIRST CITIZEN   Your Belly's answer—What?   115
The kingly crownèd head, the vigilant eye,
The counselor heart, the arm our soldier,
Our steed the leg, the tongue our trumpeter,
With other muniments and petty helps
In this our fabric, if that they—

MENENIUS   What then?   120
'Fore me, this fellow speaks! What then? What then?

FIRST CITIZEN Should by the cormorant Belly be re-
    strained,
Who is the sink o' th' body——

MENENIUS   Well, what then?

FIRST CITIZEN The former agents, if they did complain,
What could the Belly answer?

MENENIUS   I will tell you;   125
If you'll bestow a small (of what you have little)
Patience awhile, you'st hear the Belly's answer.

FIRST CITIZEN Y'are long about it.

---

104 **mutually participate** taking part in common 105 **affection**
inclination 133 **his receipt** what he received 119 **muniments** furnishings
(fortifications) 121 **'Fore me** by my soul 123 **sink** sewer 127 **you'st** you'll
(for "you shalt") 128 **Y'are** you're

MENENIUS　　　　　　　　　Note me this, good friend;
　　　　Your most grave Belly was deliberate,
130　　Not rash like his accusers, and thus answered:
　　　　"True is it, my incorporate friends," quoth he,
　　　　"That I receive the general food at first,
　　　　Which you do live upon; and fit it is,
　　　　Because I am the storehouse and the shop
135　　Of the whole body. But, if you do remember,
　　　　I send it through the rivers of your blood,
　　　　Even to the court, the heart, to th' seat o' th' brain;
　　　　And, through the cranks and offices of man,
　　　　The strongest nerves and small inferior veins
140　　From me receive that natural competency
　　　　Whereby they live; and though that all at once"—
　　　　You, my good friends, this says the Belly, mark
　　　　　me—

FIRST CITIZEN Ay, sir; well, well.

MENENIUS　　　　　　　　　"Though all at once cannot
　　　　See what I do deliver out to each,
145　　Yet I can make my audit up, that all
　　　　From me do back receive the flour of all,
　　　　And leave me but the bran." What say you to't?

FIRST CITIZEN It was an answer. How apply you this?

MENENIUS The senators of Rome are this good Belly,
150　　And you the mutinous members. For examine
　　　　Their counsels and their cares, digest things rightly
　　　　Touching the weal o' th' common, you shall find
　　　　No public benefit which you receive
　　　　But it proceeds or comes from them to you,
155　　And no way from yourselves. What do you think,
　　　　You, the great toe of this assembly?

129 **Your most grave Belly** this most grave belly we speak of　134 **Shop**
factory　138 **cranks** winding paths　138 **offices** parts of a house where household work is done, e.g., kitchen　139 **nerves** tendons　140 **natural competency**
supply adequate to their nature　151 **disgest** digest　152 **weal o' th' common**
welfare of the people

626

FIRST CITIZEN I the great toe! Why the great toe?

MENENIUS For that, being one o' th' lowest, basest, poorest,
Of this most wise rebellion, thou goest foremost.
Thou rascal, that are worst in blood to run,   160
Lead'st first to win some vantage.
But make you ready your stiff bats and clubs;
Rome and her rats are at the point of battle;
The one side must have bale.

Enter Caius Marcius.

                                Hail, noble Marcius!

MARCIUS Thanks. What's the matter, you dissentious
rogues   165
That, rubbing the poor itch of your opinion,
Make yourselves scabs?

FIRST CITIZEN   We have ever your good word.

MARCIUS He that will give good words to thee will
flatter
Beneath abhorring. What would you have, you curs,
That like nor peace nor war? The one affrights you,   170
The other makes you proud. He that trusts to you,
Where he should find you lions, finds you hares;
Where foxes, geese. You are no surer, no,
Than is the coal of fire upon the ice,
Or hailstone in the sun. Your virtue is   175
To make him worthy whose offense subdues him
And curse that justice did it. Who deserves great-
ness
Deserves your hate; and your affections are
A sick man's appetite, who desires most that
Which would increase his evil. He that depends   180
Upon your favors swims with fins of lead

160 **rascal** a lean deer, or a hound 160 **blood** condition 161 **vantage** advantage 162 **stiff** stout 164 **bale** harm 167 **Make yourselves scabs** make scabs for yourselves (also, "make yourselves into loathsome fellows") 176 **subdues him** lays him low 177 **that justice did it** the justice that punished him 178 **affections** desires

And hews down oaks with rushes. Hang ye! Trust
  ye?
With every minute you do change a mind,
And call him noble that was now your hate,
185   Him vile that was your garland. What's the matter
That in these several places of the city
You cry against the noble Senate, who
(Under the gods) keep you in awe, which else
Would feed on one another? What's their seeking?

MENENIUS   For corn at their own rates, whereof they
190   say
The city is well stored.

MARCIUS   Hang 'em! They say!
They'll sit by th' fire, and presume to know
What's done i' th' Capitol: who's like to rise,
Who thrives and who declines; side factions and
  give out
195   Conjectural marriages, making parties strong,
And feebling such as stand not in their liking
Below their cobbled shoes. They say there's grain
  enough!
Would the nobility lay aside their ruth,
And let me use my sword, I'd make a quarry
200   With thousands of these quartered slaves, as high
As I could pick my lance.

MENENIUS   Nay, these are almost thoroughly persuaded;
For though abundantly they lack discretion,
Yet are they passing cowardly. But, I beseech you,
What says the other troop?

205   MARCIUS   They are dissolved. Hang 'em!
They said they were an-hungry; sighed forth
  proverbs——

194 **side factions** take sides (form parties) 196 **feebling** weakening (bringing
down) 198 **ruth** compassion 199 **quarry** heap of dead (usually of game
animals) 204 **passing** exceedingly 206 **an-hungry** hungry 206 **sighed
forth proverbs** (implying that they talk like rustics)

628

That hunger broke stone walls, that dogs must eat,
That meat was made for mouths, that the gods sent
  not
Corn for the rich men only. With these shreds
They vented their complainings, which being
  answered,   210
And a petition granted them, a strange one,
To break the heart of generosity
And make bold power look pale, they threw their
  caps
As they would hang them on the horns o' th' moon,
Shouting their emulation.

MENENIUS   What is granted them?   215

MARCIUS Five tribunes to defend their vulgar wisdoms,
Of their own choice. One's Junius Brutus—
Sicinius Velutus, and—I know not. 'Sdeath!
The rabble should have first unroofed the city,
Ere so prevailed with me; it will in time   220
Win upon power and throw forth greater themes
For insurrection's arguing.

MENENIUS   This is strange.
MARCIUS Go, get you home, you fragments!

       Enter a Messenger, hastily.

MESSENGER Where's Caius Marcius?

MARCIUS   Here: what's the matter?

MESSENGER The news is, sir, the Volsces are in arms.   225

MARCIUS I am glad on't: then we shall ha' means to
  vent
Our musty superfluity. See, our best elders.

---

212 **break the heart of generosity** give the deathblow to the nobility
215 **Shouting their emulation** expressing envious joy 216 **vulgar** common,
plebeian 221 **Win upon power** get the better of authority 222 **For insurrection's arguing** for rebels to debate in action (abstract for concrete, as often in
Coriolanus) 226 **vent** get rid of

Enter Sicinius Velutus, Junius Brutus, Cominius,
Titus Lartius, with other Senators.

FIRST SENATOR Marcius, 'tis true that you have lately
    told us;
    The Volsces are in arms.

MARCIUS   They have a leader,
230   Tullus Aufidius, that will put you to't.
    I sin in envying his nobility;
    And were I anything but what I am,
    I would wish me only he.

COMINIUS   You have fought together.

MARCIUS Were half to half the world by th' ears, and
    he
235   Upon my party, I'd revolt, to make
    Only my wars with him. He is a lion
    That I am proud to hunt.

FIRST SENATOR   Then, worthy Marcius,
    Attend upon Cominius to these wars.

COMINIUS It is your former promise.

MARCIUS   Sir, it is,
240   And I am constant. Titus Lartius, thou
    Shalt see me once more strike at Tullus' face.
    What, art thou stiff? Stand'st out?

TITUS   No, Caius Marcius;
    I'll lean upon one crutch and fight with t'other
    Ere stay behind this business.

MENENIUS   O, true-bred!

FIRST SENATOR Your company to th' Capitol; where I
245   know
    Our greatest friends attend us.

TITUS   [*To Cominius*] Lead you on.

230 **put you to't** test you severely   240 **constant** faithful   242 **stiff** obstinate,
set (on not fighting)   242 **Stand'st out** you're staying out of it?

[*To Marcius*] Follow Cominius; we must follow
   you;
Right worthy you priority.

COMINIUS   Noble Marcius!

FIRST SENATOR [*To the Citizens*] Hence to your homes;
   begone!

MARCIUS   Nay, let them follow.
The Volsces have much corn; take these rats
   thither   250
To gnaw their garners. Worshipful mutineers,
Your valor puts well forth. Pray, follow.   *Exeunt*.

   Citizens steal away. Manet Sicinius and Brutus.

SICINIUS Was ever man so proud as is this Marcius?

BRUTUS He has no equal.

SICINIUS When we were chosen tribunes for the people— 255

BRUTUS Marked you his lip and eyes?

SICINIUS   Nay, but his taunts.

BRUTUS Being moved, he will not spare to gird the
   gods.

SICINIUS Bemock the modest moon.

BRUTUS The present wars devour him; he is grown
   Too proud to be so valiant.

SICINIUS   Such a nature,   260
Tickled with good success, disdains the shadow
Which he treads on at noon. But I do wonder
His insolence can brook to be commanded
Under Cominius.

---

248 **Right worthy you priority** you well deserve first place 252 **puts well
forth** gives fair promise (literally, buds) 252 s.d. **Manet** remains (Latin;
although the subject is plural, this form, the third person singular, commonly
appears in Elizabeth stage directions) 257 **gird** taunt 259–60 **grown/Too
proud to be so valiant** i.e., such pride is not permissible in one so warlike
(because dangerous) 261 **success** outcome

BRUTUS   Fame, at the which he aims,
265 In whom already he's well graced, can not
Better be held, nor more attained, than by
A place below the first. For what miscarries
Shall be the general's fault, though he perform
To th' utmost of a man; and giddy censure
270 Will then cry out of Marcius "O, if he
Had borne the business!"

SICINIUS   Besides, if things go well,
Opinion, that so sticks on Marcius, shall
Of his demerits rob Cominius.

BRUTUS   Come:
Half all Cominius' honors are to Marcius,
275 Though Marcius earned them not; and all his faults
To Marcius shall be honors, though indeed
In aught he merit not.

SICINIUS   Let's hence, and hear
How the dispatch is made; and in what fashion,
More than his singularity, he goes
Upon this present action.

280 BRUTUS   Let's along.   *Exeunt.*

[Scene II. *Corioli. The Senate House.*]

Enter Tullus Aufidius, with Senators of Corioles.

FIRST SENATOR So, your opinion is, Aufidius,
That they of Rome are ent'red in our counsels,
And know how we proceed.

AUFIDIUS   Is it not yours?

273 **demerits** deserts   278 **dispatch** execution of the business   279 **More than
his singularity** apart from his usual peculiarity of manner   I.ii.2 **ent'red in**
initiated into (familiar with)

What ever have been thought on in this state
That could be brought to bodily act ere Rome   5
Had circumvention? 'Tis not four days gone
Since I heard thence—these are the words—I think
I have the letter here. Yes, here it is:
"They have pressed a power, but it is not known
Whether for east or west. The dearth is great;   10
The people mutinous; and it is rumored,
Cominius, Marcius your old enemy
(Who is of Rome worse hated than of you),
And Titus Lartius, a most valiant Roman,
These three lead on this preparation   15
Whither 'tis bent—most likely 'tis for you.
Consider of it."

FIRST SENATOR   Our army's in the field.
We never yet made doubt but Rome was ready
To answer us.

AUFIDIUS   Nor did you think it folly
To keep your great pretenses veiled till when   20
They needs must show themselves; which in the
     hatching,
It seemed, appeared to Rome. By the discovery
We shall be short'ned in our aim, which was
To take in many towns ere almost Rome
Should know we were afoot.

SECOND SENATOR   Noble Aufidius,   25
Take your commission; hie you to your bands:
Let us alone to guard Corioles.
If they set down before's, for the remove
Bring up your army; but I think you'll find
They've not prepared for us.

AUFIDIUS   O, doubt not that;   30
I speak from certainties. Nay, more,

4 **What** (plural, i.e., "counsels," line 2) 6 **circumvention** means to circumvent 9 **pressed a power** collected troops 15 **preparation** force that has been prepared 20 **great pretenses** main intentions (cf. "grand design") 24 **take in** capture 28 **set down before's** lay siege to us 28 **remove** raising of the siege

Some parcels of their power are forth already,
And only hitherward. I leave your honors.
If we and Caius Marcius chance to meet,
35 'Tis sworn between us we shall ever strike
Till one can do no more.

ALL   The gods assist you!

AUFIDIUS And keep your honors safe!

FIRST SENATOR   Farewell.

SECOND SENATOR   Farewell.

ALL Farewell.   *Exeunt omnes.*

[Scene III. *Rome. A room in Marcius' house.*]

*Enter Volumnia and Virgilia, mother and wife to Marcius.
They set them down on two low stools, and sew.*

VOLUMNIA I pray you, daughter, sing, or express yourself in a more comfortable sort. If my son were
my husband, I should freelier rejoice in that absence wherein he won honor than in the embrace-
5 ments of his bed where he would show most love.
When yet he was but tender-bodied, and the only
son of my womb; when youth with comeliness
plucked all gaze his way; when, for a day of kings'
entreaties, a mother should not sell him an hour
10 from her beholding; I, considering how honor
would become such a person—that it was no
better than picture-like to hang by th' wall, if renown made it not stir—was pleased to let him seek

32 **parcels** portions   33 **hitherward** i.e., to attack Rome   38 s.d. **omnes** all
(Latin)   I.iii.2 **Comfortable** cheerful   8 **plucked all gaze** drew the eyes of
all   11 **person** handsome figure

danger where he was like to find fame. To a cruel
war I sent him, from whence he returned, his brows 15
bound with oak. I tell thee, daughter, I sprang not
more in joy at first hearing he was a man-child than
now in first seeing he had proved himself a man.

VIRGILIA But had he died in the business, madam,
how then? 20

VOLUMNIA Then his good report should have been my
son; I therein would have found issue. Hear me
profess sincerely: had I a dozen sons, each in my
love alike, and none less dear than thine and my
good Marcius, I had rather had eleven die nobly 25
for their country than one voluptuously surfeit out
of action.

Enter a Gentlewoman.

GENTLEWOMAN Madam, the Lady Valeria is come to
visit you.

VIRGILIA Beseech you give me leave to retire myself. 30

VOLUMNIA Indeed, you shall not.
Methinks I hear hither your husband's drum;
See him pluck Aufidius down by th' hair;
As children from a bear, the Volsces shunning him.
Methinks I see him stamp thus, and call thus: 35
"Come on, you cowards, you were got in fear,
Though you were born in Rome." His bloody brow
With his mailed hand then wiping, forth he goes,
Like to a harvest-man that's tasked to mow
Or all or lose his hire. 40

VIRGILIA His bloody brow? O Jupiter, no blood!

VOLUMNIA Away, you fool! It more becomes a man
Than gilt his trophy. The breasts of Hecuba,
When she did suckle Hector, looked not lovelier
Than Hector's forehead when it spit forth blood 45

16 oak ("garland" of honor for saving a fellow Roman in battle) 23 **profess**
declare 30 **Beseech** I beg 36 **got** begotten 40 **Or** either 43 **trophy**
monument 43 **Hecuba** (Queen of Troy and mother of Hector, who defended the
city from the Greeks)

At Grecian sword, contemning. Tell Valeria
We are fit to bid her welcome.　　*Exit Gentlewoman.*

VIRGILIA Heavens bless my lord from fell Aufidius!

VOLUMNIA He'll beat Aufidius' head below his knee,
50　　And tread upon his neck.

Enter Valeria with an Usher and a Gentlewoman.

VALERIA My ladies both, good day to you.

VOLUMNIA Sweet madam!

VIRGILIA I am glad to see your ladyship.

VALERIA How do you both? You are manifest house-
55　　keepers. What are you sewing here? A fine spot,
in good faith. How does your little son?

VIRGILIA I thank your ladyship; well, good madam.

VOLUMNIA He had rather see the swords and hear a
drum than look upon his schoolmaster.

60　VALERIA O' my word, the father's son! I'll swear 'tis
a very pretty boy. O' my troth, I looked upon him
o' Wednesday half an hour together; has such a
confirmed countenance! I saw him run after a
gilded butterfly; and when he caught it, he let it go
65　　again; and after it again; and over and over he
comes, and up again; catched it again; or whether
his fall enraged him, or how 'twas, he did so set
his teeth, and tear it. O, I warrant, how he mammocked it!

70　VOLUMNIA One on's father's moods.

VALERIA Indeed, la, 'tis a noble child.

VIRGILIA A crack, madam.

46 **contemning** in scorn 47 **fit** ready 48 **bless** guard 48 **fell** savage
50 **s.d. Usher** servant accompanying a lady 54–55 **manifest housekeepers**
clearly stay-at-homes 55 **spot** pattern in embroidery 63 **confirmed**
determined 68–69 **mammocked** tore to pieces 70 **on's** of his 72 **crack**
rascal

VALERIA Come, lay aside your stitchery; I must have you play the idle huswife with me this afternoon.

VIRGILIA No, good madam; I will not out of doors. 75

VALERIA Not out of doors!

VOLUMNIA She shall, she shall.

VIRGILIA Indeed, no, by your patience; I'll not over the threshold till my lord return from the wars.

VALERIA Fie, you confine yourself most unreasonably; 80 come, you must go visit the good lady that lies in.

VIRGILIA I will wish her speedy strength, and visit her with my prayers; but I cannot go thither.

VOLUMNIA Why I pray you?

VIRGILIA 'Tis not to save labor, nor that I want love. 85

VALERIA You would be another Penelope; yet, they say, all the yarn she spun in Ulysses' absence did but fill Ithaca full of moths. Come; I would your cambric were sensible as your finger, that you might leave pricking it for pity.Come, you shall go 90 with us.

VIRGILIA No, good madam, pardon me; indeed, I will not forth.

VALERIA In truth, la, go with me, and I'll tell you excellent news of your husband. 95

VIRGILIA O, good madam, there can be none yet.

VALERIA Verily, I do not jest with you; there came news from him last night.

VIRGILIA Indeed, madam?

VALERIA In earnest, it's true; I heard a senator speak 100 it. Thus it is: the Volsces have an army forth;

78 patience leave   85 want am lacking in   86 Penelope (Ulysses' faithful wife, who by using her weaving as an excuse, postponed her answer to offers of marriage)   88 Ithaca (Ulysses' home city)   89 sensible sensitive

against whom Cominius the general is gone, with
one part of our Roman power. Your lord and Titus
Lartius are set down before their city Corioles; they
105 nothing doubt prevailing, and to make it brief wars.
This is true, on mine honor; and so, I pray, go
with us.

VIRGILIA Give me excuse, good madam; I will obey
you in everything hereafter.

110 VOLUMNIA Let her alone, lady; as she is now, she will
but disease our better mirth.

VALERIA In troth, I think she would. Fare you well,
then. Come, good sweet lady. Prithee, Virgilia, turn
thy solemness out o'door, and go along with us.

115 VIRGILIA No, at a word, madam; indeed, I must not.
I wish you much mirth.

VALERIA Well then, farewell.

Exeunt Ladies.

[Scene IV. *Before Corioli.*]

*Enter Marcius, Titus Lartius, with drum and colors,
with Captains and Soldiers, as before the city Corioles.
To them a Messenger.*

MARCIUS Yonder comes news: a wager they have met.

LARTIUS My horse to yours, no.

MARCIUS   'Tis done.

LARTIUS   Agreed.

MARCIUS Say, has our general met the enemy?

---

111 **disease our better mirth** spoil our fun, which would be better (without
her)   115 **at a word** to put it briefly

CORIOLANUS I.iv.

MESSENGER They lie in view, but have not spoke as yet.

LARTIUS So, the good horse is mine.

MARCIUS   I'll buy him of you.   5

LARTIUS No, I'll nor sell nor give him; lend you him I will
For half a hundred years. Summon the town.

MARCIUS How far off lie these armies?

MESSENGER   Within this mile and half.

MARCIUS Then shall we hear their 'larum, and they ours.
Now, Mars, I prithee, make us quick in work,   10
That we with smoking swords may march from hence
To help our fielded friends! Come, blow thy blast.
They sound a parley. Enter two Senators
with others, on the walls of Corioles.
Tullus Aufidius, is he within your walls?

FIRST SENATOR No, nor a man that fears you less than he;
That's lesser than a little. (*Drum afar off.*) Hark, our drums   15
Are bringing forth our youth. We'll break our walls
Rather than they shall pound us up. Our gates,
Which yet seem shut, we have but pinned with rushes;
They'll open of themselves. (*Alarum far off.*) Hark you, far off!
There is Aufidius. List what work he makes   20
Amongst your cloven army.

MARCIUS   O, they are at it!

I.iv.4 **spoke** engaged   9 **'larum** alarum, call to arms   11 **smoking** reeking (with blood)   12 **fielded** in the field of battle   17 **pound us up** shut us in (cf. "dog pound")   21 **Cloven** divided

639

LARTIUS Their noise be our instruction. Ladders, ho!

Enter the Army of the Volsces.

MARCIUS They fear us not, but issue forth their city.
Now put your shields before your hearts, and fight
With hearts more proof than shields. Advance,
25   brave Titus.
They do disdain us much beyond our thoughts,
Which makes me sweat with wrath. Come on, my
    fellows.
He that retires, I'll take him for a Volsce,
And he shall feel mine edge.

*Alarum. The Romans are beat back
to their trenches. Enter Marcius, cursing.*

30 MARCIUS All the contagion of the south light on you,
You shames of Rome! You herd of—boils and
    plagues
Plaster you o'er, that you may be abhorred
Farther than seen, and one infect another
Against the wind a mile! You souls of geese
35 That bear the shapes of men, how have you run
From slaves that apes would beat! Pluto and hell!
All hurt behind, backs red, and faces pale
With flight and agued fear! Mend and charge
    home,
Or, by the fires of heaven, I'll leave the foe,
40 And make my wars on you. Look to't. Come on;
If you'll stand fast, we'll beat them to their wives,
As they us to our trenches. Follow's.

---

22 **be our instruction** be a lesson to us 25 **proof** tested (and so
impenetrable) 30 **South** south wind (pestilential) 34 **Against the wind a mile**
i.e., the infection carrying a mile in the face of a contrary wind 38 **agued** i.e.,
shaking as if from an ague-fit (*Ague* = malarial fever) 38 **Mend** do better (pun
on the hygienic sense) 38 **Home** i.e., into the heart of the enemy's forces
42 **Follow's** follow us, i.e., follow me (the Folio gives "trenches followes." The
adopted reading makes sense out of the Folio reading, but it is ugly and
anticlimactic. Perhaps "followes" is a misplaced stage direction)

Another alarum; and Marcius follows them to
[the] gates and is shut in.

So, now the gates are ope. Now prove good
   seconds!
'Tis for the followers Fortune widens them,
Not for the fliers. Mark me, and do the like.   45
                     Enters the gates.

FIRST SOLDIER Foolhardiness; not I.

SECOND SOLDIER Nor I.

FIRST SOLDIER See, they have shut him in.
                     Alarum continues.

ALL   To th' pot, I warrant him.

Enter Titus Lartius.

LARTIUS What is become of Marcius?

ALL   Slain, sir, doubtless.

FIRST SOLDIER Following the fliers at the very heels,   50
With them he enters; who, upon the sudden,
Clapped to their gates. He is himself alone,
To answer all the city.

LARTIUS   O noble fellow!
Who sensibly outdares his senseless sword,
And when it bows stand'st up! Thou art left,
   Marcius!   55
A carbuncle entire, as big as thou art,
Were not so rich a jewel. Thou wast a soldier
Even to Cato's wish, not fierce and terrible
Only in strokes; but with thy grim looks and
The thunder-like percussion of thy sounds   60
Thou mad'st thine enemies shake, as if the world
Were feverous and did tremble.

---

42 s.d. **is shut in** i.e., at the end of this speech Marcius enters the gates and is shut
in   43 **seconds** helpers   44 **followers** pursuers   48 **to th' pot** to destruction
(cf. "gone to pot")   54 **sensibly** though subject to feeling   56 **A carbuncle** a red
precious stone   58 **Cato** (the Censor, stern upholder of old Roman virtues).

Enter Marcius, bleeding, assaulted
by the enemy.

FIRST SOLDIER   Look, sir.

LARTIUS   O, 'tis Marcius!
Let's fetch him off, or make remain alike.
           They fight, and all enter the city.

[Scene V. *Within Corioli.*]

Enter certain Romans, with spoils.

FIRST ROMAN This will I carry to Rome.

SECOND ROMAN And I this.

THIRD ROMAN A murrain on't! I took this for silver.
                    Exeunt.
         Alarum continues still afar off.

Enter Marcius and Titus Lartius
with a Trumpet.

MARCIUS See here these movers that do prize their
      hours
5   At a cracked drachma! Cushions, leaden spoons,
     Irons of a doit, doublets that hangmen would
     Bury with those that wore them, these base slaves,
     Ere yet the fight be done, pack up. Down with
      them!
     And hark, what noise the general makes! To him!
10   There is the man of my soul's hate, Aufidius,
     Piercing our Romans. Then, valiant Titus, take
     Convenient numbers to make good the city;

63 **make remain alike** stay like him (*remain*, a noun, means "a stay")
I.v.3 **murrain on't** plague on it   3 s.d. **Trumpet** trumpeter   4 **movers** active
fellows (ironical)   5 **drachma** Greek coin   6 **of a doit** worth a doit (coin of little
value)   12 **make good** make sure of

Whilst I, with those that have the spirit, will haste
To help Cominius.

LARTIUS   Worthy sir, thou bleed'st;
Thy exercise hath been too violent   15
For a second course of fight.

MARCIUS   Sir, praise me not;
My work hath yet not warmed me. Fare you well.
The blood I drop is rather physical
Than dangerous to me. To Aufidius thus
I will appear, and fight.

LARTIUS   Now the fair goddess, Fortune,   20
Fall deep in love with thee; and her great charms
Misguide thy opposers' swords! Bold gentleman,
Prosperity be thy page!

MARCIUS   Thy friend no less
Than those she placeth highest! So farewell.

LARTIUS Thou worthiest Marcius!

                                    [Exit Marcius.]   25
Go, sound thy trumpet in the marketplace;
Call thither all the officers o' th' town,
Where they shall know our mind. Away!   Exeunt.

[Scene VI. Near the camp of Cominius.]

Enter Cominius, as it were in retire, with soldiers.

COMINIUS Breathe you, my friends; well fought; we
    are come off
Like Romans, neither foolish in our stands
Nor cowardly in retire. Believe me, sirs,
We shall be charged again. Whiles we have struck,

16 course bout 18 physical beneficial 23 page attendant I.vi.1 Breathe
rest 1 are come off leave the field 3 retire retreat

5   By interims and conveying gusts we have heard
           The charges of our friends. The Roman gods,
           Lead their successes as we wish our own,
           That both our powers, with smiling fronts
               encount'ring,
           May give you thankful sacrifice!

                              Enter a Messenger.

                                          Thy news?

10   MESSENGER   The citizens of Corioles have issued,
           And given to Lartius and to Marcius battle.
           I saw our party to their trenches driven,
           And then I came away.

     COMINIUS   Though thou speakest truth,
           Methinks thou speak'st not well. How long is't
               since?

15   MESSENGER   Above an hour, my lord.

     COMINIUS   'Tis not a mile; briefly we heard their
               drums.
           How couldst thou in a mile confound an hour,
           And bring thy news so late?

     MESSENGER   Spies of the Volsces
           Held me in chase, that I was forced to wheel
20   Three or four miles about; else had I, sir,
           Half an hour since brought my report.

                              Enter Marcius.

     COMINIUS   Who's yonder
           That does appear as he were flayed? O gods!
           He has the stamp of Marcius, and I have
           Before-time seen him thus.

     MARCIUS   Come I too late?

---

5 **By interims and conveying gusts** at intervals, by gusts of wind carrying (the
sound)   7 **successes** outcomes   8 **fronts** first lines (also, "faces")   16 **briefly** a
short time ago   17 **confound** waste   23 **stamp** characteristic features (metaphor
from coining)

COMINIUS The shepherd knows not thunder from a
    tabor   25
  More than I know the sound of Marcius' tongue
  From every meaner man.

MARCIUS   Come I too late?

COMINIUS Ay, if you come not in the blood of others,
  But mantled in your own.

MARCIUS   O, let me clip ye
  In arms as sound as when I wooed; in heart   30
  As merry as when our nuptial day was done,
  And tapers burned to bedward!

COMINIUS   Flower of warriors!
  How is't with Titus Lartius?

MARCIUS As with a man busied about decrees:
  Condemning some to death and some to exile;   35
  Ransoming him, or pitying, threat'ning th' other;
  Holding Corioles in the name of Rome,
  Even like a fawning greyhound in the leash,
  To let him slip at will.

COMINIUS   Where is that slave
  Which told me they had beat you to your trenches?   40
  Where is he? Call him hither.

MARCIUS   Let him alone;
  He did inform the truth. But for our gentlemen,
  The common file—a plague! tribunes for them!—
  The mouse ne'er shunned the cat as they did budge
  From rascals worse than they.

COMINIUS   But how prevailed you?   45

MARCIUS Will the time serve to tell? I do not think.
  Where is the enemy? Are you lords o' th' field?
  If not, why cease you till you are so?

COMINIUS   Marcius,

25 tabor small drum   29 clip embrace   32 burned to bedward burned low,
announcing the time for bed   39 let him slip unleash him   42 inform
report   42 gentlemen (ironically)   43 common file i.e., the plebeian soldiers

We have at disadvantage fought and did
50   Retire to win our purpose.

MARCIUS How lies their battle? Know you on which
    side
They have placed their men of trust?

COMINIUS   As I guess, Marcius,
    Their bands i' th' vaward are the Antiates,
    Of their best trust; o'er them Aufidius,
    Their very heart of hope.

55 MARCIUS   I do beseech you,
    By all the battles wherein we have fought,
    By th' blood we have shed together, by th' vows
    We have made to endure friends, that you directly
    Set me against Aufidius and his Antiates;
60   And that you not delay the present, but,
    Filling the air with swords advanced and darts,
    We prove this very hour.

COMINIUS   Though I could wish
    You were conducted to a gentle bath,
    And balms applied to you, yet dare I never
65   Deny your asking. Take your choice of those
    That best can aid your action.

MARCIUS   Those are they
    That most are willing. If any such be here—
    As it were sin to doubt—that love this painting
    Wherein you see me smeared; if any fear
70   Lesser his person than an ill report;
    If any think brave death outweighs bad life,
    And that his country's dearer than himself;
    Let him alone, or so many so minded,
    Wave thus, to express his disposition,
75   And follow Marcius.

            They all shout, and wave their swords; take
            him up in their arms, and cast up their caps.

---

53 **vaward** vanguard, advance troops 60 **delay the present** put off the present
occasion 62 **prove** make trial of 69–70 **fear/Lesser his person** fear less for his
body 74 **disposition** inclination

O me alone! Make you a sword of me?
If these shows be not outward, which of you
But is four Volsces? None of you but is
Able to bear against the great Aufidius
A shield as hard as his. A certain number,   80
Though thanks to all, must I select from all. The
    rest
Shall bear the business in some other fight,
As cause will be obeyed. Please you to march;
And four shall quickly draw out my command,
Which men are best inclined.

COMINIUS   March on, my fellows: 85
Make good this ostentation, and you shall
Divide in all with us.   *Exeunt.*

[Scene VII. *The gates of Corioli.*]

*Titus Lartius, having set a guard upon Corioles, going
with drum and trumpet toward Cominius and Caius
Marcius, enters with a Lieutenant, other Soldiers, and
a Scout.*

LARTIUS So, let the ports be guarded; keep your
    duties
As I have set them down. If I do send, dispatch
Those centuries to our aid; the rest will serve
For a short holding. If we lose the field,
We cannot keep the town.

LIEUTENANT   Fear not our care, sir.   5

LARTIUS Hence, and shut your gates upon's.
Our guider, come; to th' Roman camp conduct us.
                              Exit [*with the rest*].

83 **cause will be obeyed** occasion shall demand   86 **ostentation** display
I.vii.1 **ports** gates   3 **centuries** companies (smallest units of Roman legion)

[Scene VIII. *A field of battle.*]

Alarum as in battle. Enter Marcius and Aufidius,
at several doors.

MARCIUS I'll fight with none but thee, for I do hate
        thee
    Worse than a promise-breaker.

AUFIDIUS   We hate alike:
    Not Afric owns a serpent I abhor
    More than thy fame and envy. Fix thy foot.

5   MARCIUS Let the first budger die the other's slave,
    And the gods doom him after!

AUFIDIUS   If I fly, Marcius,
    Holloa me like a hare.

MARCIUS   Within these hours, Tullus,
    Alone I fought in your Corioles walls,
    And made what work I pleased. 'Tis not my blood
10 Wherein thou seest me masked. For thy revenge
    Wrench up thy power to th' highest.

AUFIDIUS   Wert thou the Hector
    That was the whip of your bragged progeny,
    Thou shouldst not scape me here.
                    Here they fight, and certain Volsces come in
                    the aid of Aufidius. Marcius fights till they
                    be driven in breathless.
    Officious, and not valiant, you have shamed me
15 In your condemnèd seconds.

I.viii.s.d. **at several doors** from different entrances   3 **Afric** Africa   5 **budger**
one who moves   7 **Holloa** shout "halloo" after (in hunting)   12 **whip of your**
bragged progeny the whip used by your boasted ancestors, the Trojans, against
the Greeks   15 **In your condemnèd seconds** by your damnable help (cf.
I.iv.43)

[Scene IX. *The Roman camp*.]

*Flourish. Alarum. A retreat is sounded. Enter at one
door, Cominius with the Romans; at another door,
Marcius, with his arm in a scarf.*

COMINIUS If I should tell thee o'er this thy day's work,
Thou't not believe thy deeds. But I'll report it
Where senators shall mingle tears with smiles;
Where great patricians shall attend, and shrug,
I' th' end admire; where ladies shall be frighted,   5
And, gladly quaked, hear more; where the dull
    tribunes,
That with the fusty plebeians hate thine honors,
Shall say against their hearts "We thank the gods
Our Rome hath such a soldier."
Yet cam'st thou to a morsel of this feast,   10
Having fully dined before.

            *Enter Titus [Lartius], with his power,
                    from the pursuit.*

LARTIUS   O general,
Here is the steed, we the caparison!
Hadst thou beheld—

MARCIUS   Pray now, no more. My mother,
Who has a charter to extol her blood,
When she does praise me grieves me. I have done   15
As you have done, that's what I can; induced
As you have been, that's for my country.

I.ix.2 **Thou't** thou wouldst 4 **shrug** i.e., in disbelief 6 **quaked** made to
shake 7 **fusty** moldy 10 **cam'st thou to a morsel of this feast** (refers to
Marcius' coming to support Cominius in the latter part of the battle just
ended) 12 **caparison** the (mere) trappings 14 **charter** privilege granted her

He that has but effected his good will
Hath overta'en mine act.

COMINIUS　　　　　　　　　You shall not be
20　　The grave of your deserving; Rome must know
The value of her own. 'Twere a concealment
Worse than a theft, no less than a traducement,
To hide your doings; and to silence that
Which, to the spire and top of praises vouched,
25　　Would seem but modest. Therefore, I beseech you,
In sign of what you are, not to reward
What you have done, before our army hear me.

MARCIUS　I have some wounds upon me, and they
　　　　smart
To hear themselves rememb'red.

COMINIUS　　　　　　　　　　　Should they not,
30　　Well might they fester 'gainst ingratitude,
And tent themselves with death. Of all the
　　　horses—
Whereof we have ta'en good, and good store—
　　　of all
The treasure in this field achieved and city,
We render you the tenth; to be ta'en forth
35　　Before the common distribution at
Your only choice.

MARCIUS　　　　　　I thank you, general;
But cannot make my heart consent to take
A bribe to pay my sword. I do refuse it,
And stand upon my common part with those
40　　That have beheld the doing.
　　　　　　　　　A long flourish. They all cry "Marcius!
　　　　　　　　　Marcius!" cast up their caps and lances.
　　　　　　　　　Cominius and Lartius stand bare.

18 **good will** firm intention　19 **overta'en** surpassed　22 **traducement**
slander　24 **To the spire and top of praises vouched** though attested in the
highest terms of praise　30 **'gainst** against, in the face of　31 **tent themselves**
be cleansed (refers to cleaning a wound with a linen roll, a "tent")　31 **death** (the
"tent" being "death," the wounds would prove fatal)　32 **good store** plenty

MARCIUS May these same instruments, which you
    profane,
  Never sound more! When drums and trumpets shall
  I' th' field prove flatterers, let courts and cities be
  Made all of false-faced soothing!
  When steel grows soft as the parasite's silk,   45
  Let him be made a coverture for th' wars!
  No more, I say! For that I have not washed
  My nose that bled, or foiled some debile wretch,
  Which without note here's many else have done,
  You shout me forth   50
  In acclamations hyperbolical;
  As if I loved my little should be dieted
  In praises sauced with lies.

COMINIUS   Too modest are you;
  More cruel to your good report than grateful
  To us that give you truly. By your patience,   55
  If 'gainst yourself you be incensed, we'll put you
  (Like one that means his proper harm) in manacles,
  Then reason safely with you. Therefore, be it known,
  As to us, to all the world, that Caius Marcius
  Wears this war's garland: in token of the which,   60
  My noble steed, known to the camp, I give him,
  With all his trim belonging; and from this time,
  For what he did before Corioles, call him,
  With all th' applause and clamor of the host,
  Caius Marcius Coriolanus.   65
  Bear th' addition nobly ever!
                Flourish. Trumpets sound, and drums.

OMNES Caius Marcius Coriolanus!

CORIOLANUS I will go wash:
  And when my face is fair, you shall perceive
  Whether I blush, or no. Howbeit, I thank you.   70

---

44 **soothing** flattery   46 **coverture** clothing   47 **For that** because   48 **foiled**
defeated   48 **debile** weak   52-53 **dieted/In** fed by   55 **give** report
57 **proper** own   62 **his trim belonging** the equipment that goes with it
66 **addition** title   67 **Omnes** all (Latin)

I mean to stride your steed, and at all times
To undercrest your good addition
To th' fairness of my power.

COMINIUS   So, to our tent;
Where, ere we do repose us, we will write
75   To Rome of our success. You, Titus Lartius,
Must to Corioles back; send us to Rome
The best, with whom we may articulate
For their own good and ours.

LARTIUS   I shall, my lord.

CORIOLANUS The gods begin to mock me. I, that now
80   Refused most princely gifts, am bound to beg
Of my lord general.

COMINIUS   Take't; 'tis yours. What is't?

CORIOLANUS I sometime lay here in Corioles
At a poor man's house; he used me kindly.
He cried to me; I saw him prisoner;
85   But then Aufidius was within my view,
And wrath o'erwhelmed my pity. I request you
To give my poor host freedom.

COMINIUS   O, well begged!
Were he the butcher of my son, he should
Be free as is the wind. Deliver him, Titus.

LARTIUS Marcius, his name?

90   CORIOLANUS   By Jupiter, forgot!
I am weary; yea, my memory is tired.
Have we no wine here?

COMINIUS   Go we to our tent.
The blood upon your visage dries; 'tis time
It should be looked to. Come.   *Exeunt.*

---

72 **undercrest your good addition** support the fine title you give (a "crest" in
heraldry is a figure above a shield; the suggested image is of a shield with a man on
horseback [line 71], beneath a crest [the "addition"])   73 **To th' fairness** to the
exact measure   77 **best** chief men   77 **articulate** make terms

[Scene X. *The camp of the Volsces.*]

*A flourish. Cornets. Enter Tullus Aufidius,
    bloody, with two or three soldiers.*

AUFIDIUS The town is ta'en!

FIRST SOLDIER 'Twill be delivered back on good con-
    dition.

AUFIDIUS Condition!
  I would I were a Roman; for I cannot,
  Being a Volsce, be that I am. Condition!   5
  What good condition can a treaty find
  I' th' part that is at mercy? Five times, Marcius,
  I have fought with thee; so often hast thou beat me;
  And wouldst do so, I think, should we encounter
  As often as we eat. By th' elements,   10
  If e'er again I meet him beard to beard,
  He's mine or I am his. Mine emulation
  Hath not that honor in't it had; for where
  I thought to crush him in an equal force,
  True sword to sword, I'll potch at him some way,   15
  Or wrath or craft may get him.

FIRST SOLDIER   He's the devil.

AUFIDIUS Bolder, though not so subtle. My valor's
    poisoned
  With only suff'ring stain by him; for him
  Shall fly out of itself. Nor sleep nor sanctuary,
  Being naked, sick, nor fane nor Capitol,   20
  The prayers of priests nor times of sacrifice,

I.x.2 **condition** terms   6 **condition** (with pun on sense of "quality")   7 **I' th'
part that is at mercy** on the side that is vanquished (at the mercy of the
victor)   15 **potch** poke (thrust, in fencing)   18 **stain** darkening   19 **fly out of
itself** go out of its natural course   20 **naked** unarmed   20 **fane** shrine

Embarquements all of fury, shall lift up
Their rotten privilege and custom 'gainst
My hate to Marcius. Where I find him, were it

25 At home, upon my brother's guard, even there,
Against the hospitable canon, would I
Wash my fierce hand in's heart. Go you to th' city;
Learn how 'tis held, and what they are that must
Be hostages for Rome.

FIRST SOLDIER   Will not you go?

AUFIDIUS I am attended at the cypress grove. I pray

30   you—
'Tis south the city mills—bring me word thither
How the world goes, that to the pace of it
I may spur on my journey.

FIRST SOLDIER   I shall, sir.   [*Exeunt.*]

---

22 **Embarquements** restraints   25 **upon my brother's guard** with my brother
on guard (over him)   26 **hospitable canon** law of hospitality   30 **attended**
awaited

[ACT II

Scene I. *Rome. A public place.*]

*Enter Menenius, with the two Tribunes of the
people, Sicinius, and Brutus.*

MENENIUS The augurer tells me we shall have news
tonight.

BRUTUS Good or bad?

MENENIUS Not according to the prayer of the people,
for they love not Marcius.   5

SICINIUS Nature teaches beasts to know their friends.

MENENIUS Pray you, who does the wolf love?

SICINIUS The lamb.

MENENIUS Ay, to devour him, as the hungry plebeians   10
would the noble Marcius.

BRUTUS He's a lamb indeed, that baas like a bear.

MENENIUS He's a bear indeed, that lives like a lamb.
You two are old men: tell me one thing that I shall
ask you.

BOTH Well, sir.   15

MENENIUS In what enormity is Marcius poor in, that
you two have not in abundance?

II.i.1 **augurer** (more correctly "augur," Roman official who foretold the
future)   16 **enormity** fault

BRUTUS He's poor in no one fault, but stored with all.

SICINIUS Especially in pride.

20 BRUTUS And topping all others in boasting.

MENENIUS This is strange now. Do you two know how you are censured here in the city—I mean of us o' th' right-hand file? Do you?

BOTH Why, how are we censured?

25 MENENIUS Because you talk of pride now—will you not be angry?

BOTH Well, well, sir, well.

MENENIUS Why 'tis no great matter; for a very little thief of occasion will rob you of a great deal of 30 patience. Give your dispositions the reins, and be angry at your pleasures; at the least, if you take it as a pleasure to you in being so. You blame Marcius for being proud?

BRUTUS We do it not alone, sir.

35 MENENIUS I know you can do very little alone; for your helps are many, or else your actions would grow wondrous single: your abilities are too infantlike for doing much alone. You talk of pride: O that you could turn your eyes toward the napes of 40 your necks, and make but an interior survey of your good selves! O that you could!

BOTH What then, sir?

MENENIUS Why, then you should discover a brace of unmeriting, proud, violent, testy magistrates (alias 45 fools) as any in Rome.

SICINIUS Menenius, you are known well enough too.

21–22 **how you are censured** the opinion held of you   23 **o' th' right-hand file** of the upper classes, patricians   28–29 **a very little thief of occasion** i.e., a very little occasion is a thief who   37 **single** weak, slight   44 **testy** snappish   46 **known well enough** i.e., notorious

MENENIUS I am known to be a humorous patrician,
and one that loves a cup of hot wine with not a
drop of allaying Tiber in't; said to be something
imperfect in favoring the first complaint, hasty and   50
tinderlike upon too trivial motion; one that converses more with the buttock of the night than
with the forehead of the morning. What I think I
utter, and spend my malice in my breath. Meeting
two such wealsmen as you are—I cannot call   55
you Lycurguses—if the drink you give me touch
my palate adversely, I make a crooked face at it.
I cannot say your worships have delivered the
matter well, when I find the ass in compound with
the major part of your syllables; and though I   60
must be content to bear with those that say you
are reverend grave men, yet they lie deadly that
tell you you have good faces. If you see this in the
map of my microcosm, follows it that I am
known well enough too? What harm can your   65
bisson conspectuities glean out of this character,
if I be known well enough too?

BRUTUS Come, sir, come, we know you well enough.

MENENIUS You know neither me, yourselves, nor any
thing. You are ambitious for poor knaves' caps and   70
legs. You wear out a good wholesome forenoon in
hearing a cause between an orange-wife and a
forset-seller, and then rejourn the controversy of
threepence to a second day of audience. When you
are hearing a matter between party and party, if   75
you chance to be pinched with the colic, you make

47 humorous whimsical   49 allaying diluting   49–50 something imperfect
in favoring the first complaint somewhat at fault in siding with the party who
first puts his case   51 motion impulse   51–52 Converses associates   55 wealsmen statesmen   56 Lycurgus (a Greek lawgiver)   59–60 ass in compound
with the major part of your syllables (pun on over-use of "as-es" in legal
expressions, e.g., "whereas")   64 map i.e., face   64 microcosm little world,
i.e., body   66 bisson conspectuities blind visual powers   70–71 caps and legs
salutes and bows   72 cause case   73 forset-seller seller of taps for wine
kegs   73 rejourn adjourn

faces like mummers, set up the bloody flag
against all patience, and, in roaring for a chamber
pot, dismiss the controversy bleeding, the more en-
80   tangled by your hearing. All the peace you make
in their cause is calling both the parties knaves.
You are a pair of strange ones.

BRUTUS Come, come, you are well understood to be
a perfecter giber for the table than a necessary
85   bencher in the Capitol.

MENENIUS Our very priests must become mockers, if
they shall encounter such ridiculous subjects as you
are. When you speak best unto the purpose, it is
not worth the wagging of your beards; and your
90   beards deserve not so honorable a grave as to stuff
a botcher's cushion or to be entombed in an ass's
packsaddle. Yet you must be saying Marcius is
proud; who, in a cheap estimation, is worth all
your predecessors since Deucalion; though per-
95   adventure some of the best of 'em were hereditary
hangmen. Good-e'en to your worships. More of
your conversation would infect my brain, being
the herdsmen of the beastly plebeians. I will be
bold to take my leave of you.

                           Brutus and Sicinius [step] aside.

            Enter Volumnia, Virgilia, and Valeria.

100   How now, my as fair as noble ladies—and the
moon, were she earthly, no nobler—whither do
you follow your eyes so fast?

VOLUMNIA Honorable Menenius, my boy Marcius approaches; for the love of Juno, let's go.

105   MENENIUS Ha? Marcius coming home?

---

77 **mummers** Christmas masquers, who act impromptu plays   77 **bloody flag**
war flag   84 **giber** joker   84–85 **necessary bencher in the Capitol** indispensable judge in the Senate (cf. "the bench" for "court")   91 **botcher** mender of old
clothes   94 **Deucalion** (the Noah of Greek myth)   97 **conversation** cf. lines
51–52

VOLUMNIA Ay, worthy Menenius; and with most prosperous approbation.

MENENIUS Take my cap, Jupiter, and I thank thee.
Hoo! Marcius coming home!

TWO LADIES Nay, 'tis true.   110

VOLUMNIA Look, here's a letter from him; the state
hath another, his wife another; and, I think, there's
one at home for you.

MENENIUS I will make my very house reel tonight.
A letter for me?   115

VIRGILIA Yes, certain, there's a letter for you; I saw't.

MENENIUS A letter for me? It gives me an estate of
seven years' health; in which time I will make a
lip at the physician. The most sovereign prescrip-
tion in Galen is but empiricutic, and, to this pre-   120
servative, of no better report than a horse-drench.
Is he not wounded? He was wont to come home
wounded.

VIRGILIA O, no, no, no.

VOLUMNIA O, he is wounded; I thank the gods for't.   125

MENENIUS So do I too, if it be not too much. Brings
'a victory in his pocket? The wounds become him.

VOLUMNIA On's brows, Menenius. He comes the third
time home with the oaken garland.

MENENIUS Has he disciplined Aufidius soundly?   130

VOLUMNIA Titus Lartius writes they fought together,
but Aufidius got off.

MENENIUS And 'twas time for him too, I'll warrant
him that. And he had stayed by him, I would

106–07 with most prosperous approbation with signs of the greatest
success   108 Jupiter (god of the sky and upper air)   117 estate state (fortune?)
118–19 make a lip make a face   120 Galen Greek physician   120 empiricutic
quackish   121 report reputation   121 horse-drench drink of horse-
medicine   127 'a he   134 And if

135   not have been so fidiused for all the chests in
Corioles, and the gold that's in them. Is the Senate
possessed of this?

VOLUMNIA Good ladies, let's go. Yes, yes, yes. The
Senate has letters from the General, wherein he
140   gives my son the whole name of the war. He hath
in this action outdone his former deeds doubly.

VALERIA In troth, there's wondrous things spoke of
him.

MENENIUS Wondrous! Ay, I warrant you, and not
145   without his true purchasing.

VIRGILIA The gods grant them true!

VOLUMNIA True? Pow waw!

MENENIUS True! I'll be sworn they are true. Where
is he wounded?—[*To the Tribunes*] God save your
150   good worships! Marcius is coming home. He has
more cause to be proud.—Where is he wounded?

VOLUMNIA I' th' shoulder and i' th' left arm. There
will be large cicatrices to show the people, when
he shall stand for his place. He received in the
155   repulse of Tarquin seven hurts i' th' body.

MENENIUS One i' th' neck, and two i' th' thigh—
there's nine that I know.

VOLUMNIA He had before this last expedition twenty-
five wounds upon him.

160 MENENIUS Now it's twenty-seven: every gash was an
enemy's grave. (*A shout and flourish.*) Hark! the
trumpets.

VOLUMNIA These are the ushers of Marcius. Before

---

135 **fidiused** "Aufidius-ed" (cf. line 130 "disciplined Aufidius soundly")
137 **possessed** duly informed   140 **name of credit** for   145 **true purchasing**
really earning (the praise)   147 **Pow waw** (a Volumnian "pooh-pooh")
153 **cicatrices** scars (Latin)   154 **place** i.e., the consulship

him he carries noise, and behind him he leaves
tears.   165
Death, that dark spirit, in's nervy arm doth lie,
Which, being advanced, declines, and then men die.

> *A sennet. Trumpets sound. Enter Cominius the*
> *general and Titus Lartius; between them, Corio-*
> *lanus, crowned with an oaken garland; with*
> *Captains and Soldiers, and a Herald.*

HERALD Know, Rome, that all alone Marcius did fight
Within Corioles gates, where he hath won,
With fame, a name to Caius Marcius; these   170
In honor follows Coriolanus.
Welcome to Rome, renownèd Coriolanus!

> *Sound. Flourish.*

ALL Welcome to Rome, renownèd Coriolanus!

CORIOLANUS No more of this, it does offend my heart;
Pray now, no more.

COMINIUS   Look, sir, your mother!

CORIOLANUS   O,   175
You have, I know, petitioned all the gods
For my prosperity!   *Kneels.*

VOLUMNIA   Nay, my good soldier, up;
My gentle Marcius, worthy Caius, and
By deed-achieving honor newly named—
What is it?—Coriolanus must I call thee?—   180
But, O, thy wife!

CORIOLANUS   My gracious silence, hail!
Wouldst thou have laughed had I come coffined
   home,
That weep'st to see me triumph? Ah, my dear,
Such eyes the widows in Corioles wear,
And mothers that lack sons.

166 **nervy** sinewy   167 s.d. **sennet** (set of notes for trumpet or cornet to herald
an important person, differing from a "flourish" or "fanfare"; cf. s.d. line
161)   179 **deed-achieving** achieved by deeds (cf. "the deeds of Coriolanus,"
II.ii.83)

185 MENENIUS   Now, the gods crown thee!

CORIOLANUS And live you yet? [*To Valeria*] O my
    sweet lady, pardon.

VOLUMNIA I know not where to turn. O, welcome
    home!
  And welcome, General: and y'are welcome all.

MENENIUS A hundred thousand welcomes. I could
    weep,
190 And I could laugh, I am light and heavy. Welcome!
  A curse begin at very root on's heart
  That is not glad to see thee! You are three
  That Rome should dote on. Yet, by the faith of
    men,
  We have some old crab-trees here at home that
    will not
195 Be grafted to your relish. Yet welcome, warriors.
  We call a nettle but a nettle, and
  The faults of fools but folly.

COMINIUS   Ever right.

CORIOLANUS Menenius, ever, ever.

HERALD Give way there, and go on.

CORIOLANUS [*To Volumnia and Virgilia*] Your hand,
200   and yours!
  Ere in our own house I do shade my head,
  The good patricians must be visited;
  From whom I have received not only greetings,
  But with them change of honors.

VOLUMNIA   I have lived
205 To see inherited my very wishes
  And the buildings of my fancy. Only
  There's one thing wanting, which I doubt not but
  Our Rome will cast upon thee.

190 **light and heavy** both merry and sad   195 **grafted** i.e., improved
204 **change of honors** fresh honors   205 **inherited** in my possession

CORIOLANUS   Know, good mother,
  I had rather be their servant in my way
  Than sway with them in theirs.

COMINIUS   On, to the Capitol!   210
     Flourish. Cornets. Exeunt in state, as before.
       Brutus and Sicinius [come forward].

BRUTUS All tongues speak of him, and the blearèd
    sights
  Are spectacled to see him. Your prattling nurse
  Into a rapture lets her baby cry
  While she chats him; the kitchen malkin pins
  Her richest lockram 'bout her reechy neck,   215
  Clamb'ring the walls to eye him. Stalls, bulks,
    windows,
  Are smothered up, leads filled and ridges horsed
  With variable complexions, all agreeing
  In earnestness to see him. Seld-shown flamens
  Do press among the popular throngs, and puff   220
  To win a vulgar station. Our veiled dames
  Commit the war of white and damask in
  Their nicely gawded cheeks to th' wanton spoil
  Of Phoebus' burning kisses. Such a pother,
  As if that whatsoever god who leads him   225
  Were slyly crept into his human powers,
  And gave him graceful posture.

SICINIUS   On the sudden,
  I warrant him consul.

BRUTUS   Then our office may,
  During his power, go sleep.

SICINIUS He cannot temp'rately transport his honors   230

213 **rapture** fit   214 **chats** gossips about   214 **malkin** slut   215 **lockram**
coarse linen   215 **reechy** dirty   216 **bulks** stalls (stands for goods to be
sold)   217 **leads** roofs (leaded)   217 **horsed** "ridden" by viewers   218 **variable
complexions** different physical types   219 **Seld-shown flamens** priests rarely
seen in public (each flamen was in charge of the cult of a particular deity)
221 **vulgar station** place with the common people   223 **gawded** adorned
224 **Phoebus** sun-god   224 **pother** commotion

From where he should begin and end, but will
Lose those he hath won.

BRUTUS   In that there's comfort.

SICINIUS   Doubt not
The commoners, for whom we stand, but they
Upon their ancient malice will forget
235   With the least cause these his new honors; which
That he will give them make I as little question
As he is proud to do't.

BRUTUS   I heard him swear,
Were he to stand for consul, never would he
Appear i' th' marketplace, nor on him put
240   The napless vesture of humility;
Nor, showing, as the manner is, his wounds
To th' people, beg their stinking breaths.

SICINIUS   'Tis right.

BRUTUS It was his word. O, he would miss it rather
Than carry it but by the suit of the gentry to him
And the desire of the nobles.

245   SICINIUS   I wish no better
Than have him hold that purpose and to put it
In execution.

BRUTUS   'Tis most like he will.

SICINIUS It shall be to him then as our good wills:
A sure destruction.

BRUTUS   So it must fall out
250   To him or our authorities. For an end,
We must suggest the people in what hatred
He still hath held them; that to's power he would
Have made them mules, silenced their pleaders and

231 and end i.e., to where he should end   234 Upon on account of   235 which
i.e., "cause"   237 As as that   240 napless threadbare   244 carry win   248 as
our good wills as we strongly desire   250 For an end to force the issue (?)
finally (?)   251 suggest insinuate into the minds of   252 still ever

Dispropertied their freedoms; holding them,
In human action and capacity,   255
Of no more soul nor fitness for the world
Than camels in their war, who have their provand
Only for bearing burdens, and sore blows
For sinking under them.

SICINIUS   This, as you say, suggested
At some time when his soaring insolence   260
Shall touch the people—which time shall not want,
If he be put upon't, and that's as easy
As to set dogs on sheep—will be his fire
To kindle their dry stubble; and their blaze
Shall darken him forever.

Enter a Messenger.

BRUTUS   What's the matter?   265

MESSENGER You are sent for to the Capitol. 'Tis
    thought
That Marcius shall be consul.
I have seen the dumb men throng to see him and
The blind to hear him speak. Matrons flung gloves,
Ladies and maids their scarfs and handkerchers,   270
Upon him as he passed; the nobles bended,
As to Jove's statue, and the commons made
A shower and thunder with their caps and shouts.
I never saw the like.

BRUTUS   Let's to the Capitol,
And carry with us ears and eyes for th' time,   275
But hearts for the event.

SICINIUS   Have with you.   *Exeunt.*

---

254 **Dispropertied** dispossessed them of   257 **provand** provisions   261 **want**
be lacking   262 **put upon't** provoked to it   276 **event** outcome   276 **Have
with you** coming with you!

[Scene II. *Rome. The Senate House.*]

Enter two Officers, to lay cushions, as it were,
in the Capitol.

FIRST OFFICER Come, come, they are almost here. How
many stand for consulships?

SECOND OFFICER Three, they say; but 'tis thought of
everyone Coriolanus will carry it.

5   FIRST OFFICER That's a brave fellow; but he's vengeance proud, and loves not the common people.

SECOND OFFICER Faith, there hath been many great
men that have flattered the people, who ne'er loved
them; and there be many that they have loved,
10   they know not wherefore; so that, if they love they
know not why, they hate upon no better a ground.
Therefore, for Coriolanus neither to care whether
they love or hate him manifests the true knowledge
he has in their disposition, and out of his noble
15   carelessness lets them plainly see't.

FIRST OFFICER If he did not care whether he had their
love or no, he waved indifferently 'twixt doing
them neither good nor harm. But he seeks their
hate with greater devotion than they can render it
20   him, and leaves nothing undone that may fully discover him their opposite. Now, to seem to affect
the malice and displeasure of the people is as bad
as that which he dislikes, to flatter them for their
love.

II.ii.s.d. **cushions** i.e., seats for dignitaries   5–6 **vengeance** frightfully (cf. "with
a vengeance"   14 **in their disposition** of their mood   17 **waved** would
waver   20–21 **discover** show   21 **opposite** opponent   21 **affect** aim at
22 **malice** ill will

SECOND OFFICER He hath deserved worthily of his   25
    country; and his ascent is not by such easy degrees
    as those who, having been supple and courteous
    to the people, bonneted, without any further deed
    to have them at all into their estimation and re-
    port. But he hath so planted his honors in their   30
    eyes and his actions in their hearts that for their
    tongues to be silent and not confess so much were
    a kind of ingrateful injury; to report otherwise were
    a malice that, giving itself the lie, would pluck
    reproof and rebuke from every ear that heard it.   35

FIRST OFFICER No more of him; he's a worthy man.
    Make way, they are coming.

    *A sennet. Enter the Patricians and the Tribunes of the
    People, Lictors before them; Coriolanus, Menenius, Com-
    inius the Consul. Sicinius and Brutus take their places by
    themselves. Coriolanus stands.*

MENENIUS Having determined of the Volsces, and
    To send for Titus Lartius, it remains,
    As the main point of this our after-meeting,   40
    To gratify his noble service that
    Hath thus stood for his country. Therefore, please
      you
    Most reverend and grave elders, to desire
    The present consul and last general
    In our well-found successes, to report   45
    A little of that worthy work performed
    By Caius Marcius Coriolanus; whom
    We met here both to thank and to remember
    With honors like himself.

FIRST SENATOR   Speak, good Cominius:

28 **bonneted** took off their caps (in flattery)   29–30 **to have them at all into
their estimation and report** to get themselves at all into, win their way into,
their esteem   34 **malice** act of ill will   37 s.d. **Lictors** (attendants who preceded
Roman officials to announce their approach)   38 **determined of** decided
concerning   41 **gratify** reward   42 **stood for** defended   44 **last** late   45 **well-
found** fortunately met with   48 **remember** distinguish

50   Leave nothing out for length, and make us think
        Rather our state's defective for requital
        Than we to stretch it out. [*To the Tribunes*] Mas-
            ters o' th' people,
        We do request your kindest ears; and, after,
        Your loving motion toward the common body,
        To yield what passes here.

55 SICINIUS   We are convented
        Upon a pleasing treaty, and have hearts
        Inclinable to honor and advance
        The theme of our assembly.

    BRUTUS   Which the rather
        We shall be blessed to do, if he remember
60   A kinder value of the people than
        He hath hereto prized them at.

    MENENIUS   That's off, that's off;
        I would you rather had been silent. Please you
        To hear Cominius speak?

    BRUTUS   Most willingly.
        But yet my caution was more pertinent
        Than the rebuke you gave it.

65 MENENIUS   He loves your people;
        But tie him not to be their bedfellow.
        Worthy Cominius, speak.
                            Coriolanus rises and offers to go away.
                            Nay, keep your place.

    FIRST SENATOR Sit, Coriolanus; never shame to hear
        What you have nobly done.

    CORIOLANUS   Your honors' pardon:
70   I had rather have my wounds to heal again
        Than hear say how I got them.

51–52 **our state's ... out** our government (the Senate) is lacking in the resources
for reward rather than we in our effort to extend it   54 **motion toward the
common body** influence with the common people   55 **yield** approve
55 **convented** convened   56 **treaty** proposal for discussion   58 **rather** sooner
59 **blessed** happy   60 **value** estimate   61 **off** not to the point

BRUTUS   Sir, I hope
  My words disbenched you not.

CORIOLANUS   No, sir. Yet oft,
  When blows have made me stay, I fled from words.
  You soothed not, therefore hurt not; but your
      people,
  I love them as they weigh——

MENENIUS   Pray now, sit down.   75

CORIOLANUS I had rather have one scratch my head
      i' th' sun
  When the alarum were struck than idly sit
  To hear my nothings monstered.   *Exit Coriolanus.*

MENENIUS   Masters of the people,
  Your multiplying spawn how can he flatter—
  That's thousand to one good one—when you now
      see   80
  He had rather venture all his limbs for honor
  Than one on's ears to hear it? Proceed, Cominius.

COMINIUS I shall lack voice: the deeds of Coriolanus
  Should not be uttered feebly. It is held
  That valor is the chiefest virtue and   85
  Most dignifies the haver. If it be,
  The man I speak of cannot in the world
  Be singly counterpoised. At sixteen years,
  When Tarquin made a head for Rome, he fought
  Beyond the mark of others. Our then dictator,   90
  Whom with all praise I point at, saw him fight,
  When with his Amazonian chin he drove
  The bristled lips before him. He bestrid
  An o'erpressed Roman, and i' th' consul's view
  Slew three opposers; Tarquin's self he met,   95

72 **disbenched** unseated   74 **soothed** flattered   78 **monstered** turned into
marvels   82 **Than one on's ears** than venture one of his ears   85 **virtue** (cf.
Latin *virtus*, manly strength)   88 **singly counterpoised** matched in value (literally, in weight) by one man   89 **Tarquin** (early king of Rome, expelled from the
city)   89 **made a head for** raised a force against   92 **Amazonian** i.e., beardless

And struck him on his knee. In that day's feats,
When he might act the woman in the scene,
He proved best man i' th' field, and for his meed
Was brow-bound with the oak. His pupil age
100   Man-ent'red thus, he waxèd like a sea;
And, in the brunt of seventeen battles since,
He lurched all swords of the garland. For this last,
Before and in Corioles, let me say,
I cannot speak him home. He stopped the fliers,
105   And by his rare example made the coward
Turn terror into sport; as weeds before
A vessel under sail, so men obeyed
And fell below his stem. His sword, death's stamp,
Where it did mark, it took; from face to foot
110   He was a thing of blood, whose every motion
Was timed with dying cries. Alone he ent'red
The mortal gate of th' city, which he painted
With shunless destiny; aidless came off,
And with a sudden reinforcement struck
115   Corioles like a planet. Now all's his,
When by and by the din of war 'gan pierce
His ready sense, then straight his doubled spirit
Requick'ned what in flesh was fatigate,
And to the battle came he; where he did
120   Run reeking o'er the lives of men, as if
'Twere a perpetual spoil; and till we called
Both field and city ours, he never stood
To ease his breast with panting.

MENENIUS   Worthy man!

96 **on his knee** to his knees 97 **in the scene** on that stage 98 **meed** reward 99 **His pupil age** the years when he was learning (the art of war) 100 **Man-ent'red** having been initiated into manhood 102 **lurched** robbed 104 **speak him home** find words to match his merit 108 **stem** bow 108 **stamp** a die for stamping a coin or medal 109 **took** made its mark; killed (perhaps also, "infected fatally," cf. "struck," line 114) 112–13 **painted/With shunless destiny** smeared with blood of dying men, who could not shun their fate 114–15 **struck/Corioles like a planet** (planets supposedly had power to "strike," i.e., infect with disease) 116 **'gan** began to 117 **ready** responsive 117 **doubled** renewed 118 **fatigate** fatigued 121 **spoil** slaughter

FIRST SENATOR He cannot but with measure fit the
 honors
 Which we devise him.

COMINIUS   Our spoils he kicked at,   125
 And looked upon things precious as they were
 The common muck of the world. He covets less
 Than misery itself would give, rewards
 His deeds with doing them, and is content
 To spend the time to end it.

MENENIUS   He's right noble.   130
 Let him be called for.

FIRST SENATOR   Call Coriolanus.

OFFICER He doth appear.

Enter Coriolanus.

MENENIUS The Senate, Coriolanus, are well pleased
 To make thee consul.

CORIOLANUS   I do owe them still
 My life and services.

MENENIUS   It then remains   135
 That you do speak to the people.

CORIOLANUS   I do beseech you
 Let me o'erleap that custom, for I cannot
 Put on the gown, stand naked, and entreat them,
 For my wounds' sake, to give their suffrage. Please you
 That I may pass this doing.

SICINIUS   Sir, the people   140
 Must have their voices; neither will they bate
 One jot of ceremony.

---

124 **with measure fit** measure up to; or, "bear with self-control" (?)
128 **misery** poverty 130 **To spend the time to end it** to kill it in action ("to
live it up in action") 134 **still** always 138 **gown** "vesture of humility" (cf.
II.i.240) 138 **naked** i.e., "without any coat underneath" (North) 140 **pass**
pass over 141 **voices** votes 141 **bate** deduct

MENENIUS   Put them not to't.
Pray you, go fit you to the custom, and
Take to you, as your predecessors have,
Your honor with your form.

145 CORIOLANUS   It is a part
That I shall blush in acting, and might well
Be taken from the people.

BRUTUS. [TO SICINIUS]   Mark you that.

CORIOLANUS To brag unto them, "Thus I did, and
        thus!"
Show them th' unaching scars which I should hide,
150 As if I had received them for the hire
Of their breath only!

MENENIUS   Do not stand upon't.
We recommend to you, tribunes of the people,
Our purpose to them; and to our noble consul
Wish we all joy and honor.

155 SENATORS To Coriolanus come all joy and honor!
                    Flourish cornets. Then exeunt. Manet
                    Sicinius and Brutus.

BRUTUS You see how he intends to use the people.

SICINIUS May they perceive's intent! He will require
        them,
As if he did contemn what he requested
Should be in them to give.

BRUTUS   Come, we'll inform them
160 Of our proceedings here. On th' marketplace,
I know, they do attend us.   [*Exeunt.*]

---

142 **Put them not to't** don't test them (by omitting any part of the
ceremony) 145 **Your honor with your form** the honor with the ceremony it
imposes on you 151 **stand upon't** make an issue of it 153 **purpose**
proposal 157 **require** ask

[Scene III. *Rome. The Forum.*]

Enter seven or eight Citizens.

FIRST CITIZEN Once if he do require our voices, we
ought not to deny him

SECOND CITIZEN We may, sir, if we will.

THIRD CITIZEN We have power in ourselves to do it,
but it is a power that we have no power to do; for   5
if he show us his wounds and tell us his deeds, we
are to put our tongues into those wounds and speak
for them; so, if he tell us his noble deeds, we must
also tell him our noble acceptance of them. Ingratitude is monstrous; and for the multitude to be   10
ingrateful, were to make a monster of the multitude; of the which we being members, should bring
ourselves to be monstrous members.

FIRST CITIZEN And to make us no better thought of, a
little help will serve; for once we stood up about   15
the corn, he himself stuck not to call us the many-
headed multitude.

THIRD CITIZEN We have been called so of many; not
that our heads are some brown, some black, some
abram, some bald, but that our wits are so di-   20
versely colored. And truly I think, if all our wits
were to issue out of one skull, they would fly east,
west, north, south, and their consent of one direct
way should be at once to all the points o' th'
compass.   25

SECOND CITIZEN Think you so? Which way do you
judge my wit would fly?

II.iii.1 **Once if he** if he once   15 **once we stood up** when we took a stand
20 **abram** auburn   23 **consent of** agreement on

THIRD CITIZEN Nay, your wit will not so soon out as
　　another man's will; 'tis strongly wedged up in a
30　blockhead; but if it were at liberty, 'twould, sure,
　　southward.

SECOND CITIZEN Why that way?

THIRD CITIZEN To lose itself in a fog; where being
　　three parts melted away with rotten dews, the
35　fourth would return for conscience sake, to help
　　to get thee a wife.

SECOND CITIZEN You are never without your tricks.
　　You may, you may.

THIRD CITIZEN Are you all resolved to give your
40　voices? But that's no matter, the greater part car-
　　ries it. I say, if he would incline to the people, there
　　was never a worthier man.

　　　　　Enter Coriolanus in a gown of humility,
　　　　　　　　with Menenius.

　　Here he comes, and in the gown of humility. Mark
　　his behavior. We are not to stay all together, but to
45　come by him where he stands, by ones, by twos,
　　and by threes. He's to make his requests by par-
　　ticulars; wherein every one of us has a single
　　honor, in giving him our own voices with our own
　　tongues. Therefore follow me, and I'll direct you
50　how you shall go by him.

ALL Content, content.　　　　　　[*Exeunt Citizens.*]

MENENIUS O sir, you are not right. Have you not
　　　known
　　The worthiest men have done't?

CORIOLANUS　　　　　　　　　What must I say?—
　　"I pray, sir"—Plague upon't! I cannot bring
55　My tongue to such a pace. "Look, sir, my wounds!

---

34 **rotten** unhealthy　35–36 **for conscience ... wife** i.e., because of the bastards
he had fathered (?)　38 **You may, you may** cf. "O.K., O.K."
40 **greater part** majority　46–47 **by particulars** to each in turn

I got them in my country's service, when
Some certain of your brethren roared and ran
From th' noise of our own drums."

MENENIUS   O me, the gods!
You must not speak of that. You must desire them
To think upon you.

CORIOLANUS   Think upon me! Hang 'em!   60
I would they would forget me, like the virtues
Which our divines lose by 'em.

MENENIUS   You'll mar all.
I'll leave you. Pray you, speak to 'em, I pray you,
In wholesome manner.   *Exit*.

Enter three of the Citizens.

CORIOLANUS   Bid them wash their faces,
And keep their teeth clean. So, here comes a
    brace.   65
You know the cause, sir, of my standing here.

THIRD CITIZEN We do, sir; tell us what hath brought
    you to't.

CORIOLANUS Mine own desert.

SECOND CITIZEN Your own desert?   70

CORIOLANUS Ay, not mine own desire.

THIRD CITIZEN How not your own desire?

CORIOLANUS No, sir, 'twas never my desire yet to
    trouble the poor with begging.

THIRD CITIZEN You must think, if we give you any-   75
    thing, we hope to gain by you.

CORIOLANUS Well then, I pray, your price o' th' con-
    sulship?

FIRST CITIZEN The price is, to ask it kindly.

60 **think upon** think well of   62 **lose by 'em** waste on them in preaching
("pearls before swine")   64 **wholesome** reasonable   65 **brace** pair (of dogs)

675

80   CORIOLANUS Kindly sir, I pray let me ha't. I have
     wounds to show you, which shall be yours in pri-
     vate. Your good voice, sir; what say you?

     SECOND CITIZEN You shall ha't, worthy sir.

     CORIOLANUS A match, sir. There's in all two worthy
85   voices begged. I have your alms. Adieu.

     THIRD CITIZEN But this is something odd.

     SECOND CITIZEN And 'twere to give again—but 'tis no
     matter.   *Exeunt.*

     Enter two other Citizens.

     CORIOLANUS Pray you now, if it may stand with the
90   tune of your voices that I may be consul, I have
     here the customary gown.

     FIRST CITIZEN You have deserved nobly of your coun-
     try, and you have not deserved nobly.

     CORIOLANUS Your enigma?

95   FIRST CITIZEN You have been a scourge to her enemies,
     you have been a rod to her friends. You have not
     indeed loved the common people.

     CORIOLANUS You should account me the more virtuous,
     that I have not been common in my love. I will, sir,
100 flatter my sworn brother, the people, to earn a
     dearer estimation of them; 'tis a condition they
     account gentle; and since the wisdom of their choice
     is rather to have my hat than my heart, I will prac-
     tice the insinuating nod, and be off to them most
105 counterfeitly; that is, sir, I will counterfeit the be-
     witchment of some popular man, and give it boun-
     tiful to the desirers. Therefore, beseech you I may
     be consul.

---

84 **A match** agreed   86 **something** somewhat   89 **stand** agree   101 **dearer
estimation of** higher valuation from   101 **condition** quality   104 **be off** take
my hat off   106 **popular man** ("friend of the people")

SECOND CITIZEN We hope to find you our friend; and
    therefore give you our voices heartily.   110

FIRST CITIZEN You have received many wounds for
    your country.

CORIOLANUS I will not seal your knowledge with
    showing them. I will make much of your voices
    and so trouble you no farther.   115

BOTH The gods give you joy, sir, heartily!   [*Exeunt.*]

CORIOLANUS Most sweet voices!
    Better it is to die, better to starve,
    Than crave the hire which first we do deserve.
    Why in this woolvish toge should I stand here,   120
    To beg of Hob and Dick that does appear
    Their needless vouches? Custom calls me to't.
    What custom wills, in all things should we do't,
    The dust on antique time would lie unswept,
    And mountainous error be too highly heaped   125
    For truth to o'erpeer. Rather than fool it so,
    Let the high office and the honor go
    To one that would do thus. I am half through:
    The one part suffered, the other will I do.

Enter three Citizens more.

    Here come moe voices.   130
    Your voices! For your voices I have fought;
    Watched for your voices; for your voices bear
    Of wounds two dozen odd; battles thrice six
    I have seen, and heard of; for your voices have
    Done many things, some less, some more. Your
        voices!   135
    Indeed, I would be consul.

---

113 **seal** make authentic (legal sense)   120 **in this woolvish toge** i.e., disguising
myself (a backhand reference to "wolf in sheep's clothing"; note that Coriolanus
"lives like a lamb," according to II.i.12)   121 **Hob** (nickname of "Robert"; a
country fellow)   121 **that does appear** i.e., as they come, one by one
122 **vouches** confirmations   126 **o'erpeer** rise above   130 **moe** more
132 **Watched** kept watch

FIRST CITIZEN He has done nobly, and cannot go without any honest man's voice.

SECOND CITIZEN Therefore let him be consul. The gods
140   give him joy, and make him good friend to the
people!

ALL Amen, amen. God save thee, noble consul!
[*Exeunt Citizens.*]

CORIOLANUS Worthy voices!

Enter Menenius, with Brutus and Sicinius.

MENENIUS You have stood your limitation; and the
tribunes
145   Endue you with the people's voice. Remains
That in th' official marks invested you
Anon do meet the Senate.

CORIOLANUS   Is this done?

SICINIUS The custom of request you have discharged:
The people do admit you, and are summoned
150   To meet anon upon your approbation.

CORIOLANUS Where? At the Senate House?

SICINIUS   There, Coriolanus.

CORIOLANUS May I change these garments?

SICINIUS   You may, sir.

CORIOLANUS That I'll straight do, and, knowing myself
again,
Repair to th' Senate House.

155 MENENIUS I'll keep you company. Will you along?

BRUTUS We stay here for the people.

SICINIUS   Fare you well.
Exeunt Coriolanus and Menenius.

144 **limitation** time set for requesting votes   146 **Marks** insignia   150 **anon**
upon your approbation at once to confirm your appointment (as consul)
154 **Repair** return   155 **along** come too

He has it now; and, by his looks, methinks
'Tis warm at's heart.

BRUTUS   With a proud heart he wore
His humble weeds. Will you dismiss the people?

Enter the Plebeians.

SICINIUS How now, my masters, have you chose this
    man?   160

FIRST CITIZEN He has our voices, sir.

BRUTUS We pray the gods he may deserve your loves.

SECOND CITIZEN Amen, sir. To my poor unworthy
    notice,
He mocked us when he begged our voices.

THIRD CITIZEN   Certainly;
He flouted us downright.   165

FIRST CITIZEN No, 'tis his kind of speech—he did not
    mock us.

SECOND CITIZEN Not one amongst us, save yourself,
    but says
He used us scornfully. He should have showed us
His marks of merit, wounds received for's country.

SICINIUS Why, so he did, I am sure.   170

ALL No, no; no man saw 'em.

THIRD CITIZEN He said he had wounds which he could
    show in private;
And with his hat, thus waving it in scorn,
"I would be consul," says he. "Agèd custom,
But by your voices, will not so permit me;   175
Your voices therefore." When we granted that,
Here was "I thank you for your voices. Thank you,
Your most sweet voices. Now you have left your
    voices,

157 it (the emotion that "warms his heart," either the satisfaction of success, or
the irritation of offended pride; cf. "his fire," II.i.263)   158 at's his   160 my
masters gentlemen

679

I have no further with you." Was not this mockery?

180 SICINIUS Why either were you ignorant to see't,
Or, seeing it, of such childish friendliness
To yield your voices?

BRUTUS   Could you not have told him
As you were lessoned: when he had no power,
But was a petty servant to the state,
185 He was your enemy, ever spake against
Your liberties and the charters that you bear
I' th' body of the weal; and now, arriving
A place of potency and sway o' th' state,
If he should still malignantly remain
190 Fast foe to th' plebeii, your voices might
Be curses to yourselves? You should have said
That as his worthy deeds did claim no less
Than what he stood for, so his gracious nature
Would think upon you for your voices, and
195 Translate his malice towards you into love,
Standing your friendly lord.

SICINIUS   Thus to have said,
As you were fore-advised, had touched his spirit
And tried his inclination; from him plucked
Either his gracious promise, which you might,
200 As cause had called you up, have held him to;
Or else it would have galled his surly nature,
Which easily endures not article
Tying him to aught. So, putting him to rage,
You should have ta'en th' advantage of his choler,
And passed him unelected.

205 BRUTUS   Did you perceive
He did solicit you in free contempt

179 **no further** no more to do 180 **ignorant** too dull 182 **yield** give
183 **lessoned** instructed 186 **charters** privileges 187 **weal** commonwealth
188 **A place** (direct object of "arriving," i.e., "reaching") 188 **potency and
sway o' th' state** power in managing the state 190 **plebeii** (Latin for
"plebeians") 193 **what he stood for** the office he ran for 194 **think upon you**
think well of you 195 **Translate** transform 197 **touched** tested 200 **As
cause had called you up** as an occasion (emergency) would have roused
you 202 **article** condition 204 **choler** anger 206 **free** open

When he did need your loves; and do you think
That his contempt shall not be bruising to you
When he hath power to crush? Why, had your
    bodies
No heart among you? Or had you tongues to cry   210
Against the rectorship of judgment?

SICINIUS   Have you
Ere now denied the asker, and now again,
Of him that did not ask but mock, bestow
Your sued-for tongues?

THIRD CITIZEN He's not confirmed; we may deny him
    yet.   215

SECOND CITIZEN And will deny him.
I'll have five hundred voices of that sound.

FIRST CITIZEN I twice five hundred, and their friends
    to piece 'em.

BRUTUS Get you hence instantly, and tell those friends
They have chose a consul that will from them take   220
Their liberties, make them of no more voice
Than dogs that are as often beat for barking
As therefor kept to do so.

SICINIUS   Let them assemble;
And, on a safer judgment, all revoke
Your ignorant election. Enforce his pride   225
And his old hate unto you; besides, forget not
With what contempt he wore the humble weed,
How in his suit he scorned you; but your loves,
Thinking upon his services, took from you
Th' apprehension of his present portance,   230
Which most gibingly, ungravely, he did fashion
After the inveterate hate he bears you.

BRUTUS   Lay

210 heart spirit 210 cry give your voices 211 rectorship rule 213 Of
on 218 piece 'em add to them (cf. "piece out") 223 therefore for that
reason 224 safer sounder 225 ignorant election choice made in
ignorance 225 Enforce urge, insist on 230 apprehension perception
230 portance bearing

A fault on us, your tribunes, that we labored,
No impediment between, but that you must
Cast your election on him.

235 SICINIUS   Say you chose him
More after our commandment than as guided
By your own true affections; and that your minds,
Preoccupied with what you rather must do
Than what you should, made you against the grain
240 To voice him consul. Lay the fault on us.

BRUTUS Ay, spare us not. Say we read lectures to you,
How youngly he began to serve his country,
How long continued; and what stock he springs of,
The noble house o' th' Marcians, from whence came
245 That Ancus Marcius, Numa's daughter's son,
Who after great Hostilius here was king;
Of the same house Publius and Quintus were,
That our best water brought by conduits hither;
[And Censorinus that was so surnamed]
250 And nobly namèd so, twice being censor,
Was his great ancestor.

SICINIUS   One thus descended,
That hath beside well in his person wrought
To be set high in place, we did commend
To your remembrances: but you have found,
255 Scaling his present bearing with his past,
That he's your fixèd enemy, and revoke
Your sudden approbation.

BRUTUS   Say you ne'er had done't
(Harp on that still) but by our putting on;
And presently, when you have drawn your number,
Repair to th' Capitol.

234 **No impediment between** putting no obstacle in your way (i.e., we have made the way free for you to choose him)   236 **after** following   237 **Affections** desires   240 **voice him consul** make him consul by your votes   245 **Numa** (second king of Rome)   249 **And ... surnamed** (see Textual note, p. 769)   255 **Scaling** weighing   257 **sudden** hasty   258 **putting on** urging   259 **drawn your number** gathered your crowd (of supporters)

CITIZENS   We will so. Almost all   260
  Repent in their election.   *Exeunt Plebeians*.

BRUTUS   Let them go on;
  This mutiny were better put in hazard
  Than stay, past doubt, for greater.
  If, as his nature is, he fall in rage
  With their refusal, both observe and answer   265
  The vantage of his anger.

SICINIUS   To th' Capitol, come.
  We will be there before the stream o' th' people;
  And this shall seem, as partly 'tis, their own,
  Which we have goaded onward.   *Exeunt*.

262 **This ... hazard** i.e., it would be better to run the risk of this minor
disorder   265–66 **answer/The vantage of his anger** take advantage of the
opportunity his anger affords

ACT III

[Scene I. *Rome. A street.*]

Cornets. Enter Coriolanus, Menenius, all the Gentry, Cominius, Titus Lartius, and other Senators.

CORIOLANUS Tullus Aufidius then had made new head?

LARTIUS He had, my lord; and that it was which caused
   Our swifter composition.

CORIOLANUS So then the Volsces stand but as at first;
5   Ready, when time shall prompt them, to make road
   Upon's again.

COMINIUS   They are worn, Lord Consul, so
   That we shall hardly in our ages see
   Their banners wave again.

CORIOLANUS   Saw you Aufidius?

LARTIUS On safeguard he came to me; and did curse
10   Against the Volsces, for they had so vilely
   Yielded the town. He is retired to Antium.

CORIOLANUS Spoke he of me?

LARTIUS   He did, my lord.

CORIOLANUS   How? What?

III.i.1 **made new head** raised a new force   3 **swifter composition** coming to terms sooner   5–6 **make road/Upon's** invade us   6 **worn** worn out   7 **ages** lifetime   9 **On safeguard** under safe-conduct

LARTIUS How often he had met you, sword to sword;
  That of all things upon the earth he hated
  Your person most; that he would pawn his fortunes   15
  To hopeless restitution, so he might
  Be called your vanquisher.

CORIOLANUS   At Antium lives he?

LARTIUS At Antium.

CORIOLANUS I wish I had a cause to seek him there,
  To oppose his hatred fully. Welcome home.   20

Enter Sicinius and Brutus.

  Behold, these are the tribunes of the people,
  The tongues o' th' common mouth. I do despise
    them;
  For they do prank them in authority,
  Against all noble sufferance.

SICINIUS   Pass no further.

CORIOLANUS Ha? What is that?   25

BRUTUS It will be dangerous to go on—no further.

CORIOLANUS What makes this change?

MENENIUS The matter?

COMINIUS Hath he not passed the noble and the
  common?

BRUTUS Cominius, no.

CORIOLANUS   Have I had children's voices?   30

FIRST SENATOR Tribunes, give way; he shall to th'
  marketplace.

BRUTUS The people are incensed against him.

16 **To hopeless restitution** without hope of their being redeemed   23 **prank them** dress themselves up   24 **Against all noble sufferance** so that no noble can endure it   29 **the noble and the common** the patricians and the plebeians

SICINIUS   Stop,
Or all will fall in broil.

CORIOLANUS   Are these your herd?
Must these have voices, that can yield them now,
And straight disclaim their tongues? What are
35   your offices?
You being their mouths, why rule you not their
      teeth?
Have you not set them on?

MENENIUS   Be calm, be calm.

CORIOLANUS It is a purposed thing, and grows by plot,
To curb the will of the nobility.
40 Suffer't, and live with such as cannot rule,
Nor ever will be ruled.

BRUTUS   Call't not a plot.
The people cry you mocked them; and of late,
When corn was given them gratis, you repined,
Scandaled the suppliants for the people, called
      them
45 Time-pleasers, flatterers, foes to nobleness.

CORIOLANUS Why, this was known before.

BRUTUS   Not to them all.

CORIOLANUS Have you informed them sithence?

BRUTUS   How! I inform them!

CORIOLANUS You are like to do such business.

BRUTUS   Not unlike
Each way to better yours.

CORIOLANUS Why then should I be consul? By yond
50   clouds,

33 in broil into a riot 34 now at one time 35 disclaim disown 38 purposed
thing premeditated affair 43 repined regretted it 44 Scandaled
slandered 47 informed instructed 47 sithence since 48-49 Not unlike/
Each way to better yours likely in every way to do your business better

Let me deserve so ill as you, and make me
Your fellow tribune.

SICINIUS   You show too much of that
For which the people stir. If you will pass
To where you are bound, you must inquire your way,
Which you are out of, with a gentler spirit,   55
Or never be so noble as a consul,
Nor yoke with him for tribune.

MENENIUS   Let's be calm.

COMINIUS The people are abused; set on. This
     palt'ring
Becomes not Rome; nor has Coriolanus
Deserved this so dishonored rub, laid falsely   60
I' th' plain way of his merit.

CORIOLANUS   Tell me of corn!
This was my speech, and I will speak't again——

MENENIUS Not now, not now.

FIRST SENATOR   Not in this heat, sir, now.

CORIOLANUS Now, as I live, I will.
My nobler friends, I crave their pardons.   65
For the mutable, rank-scented meiny, let them
Regard me as I do not flatter, and
Therein behold themselves. I say again,
In soothing them, we nourish 'gainst our Senate
The cockle of rebellion, insolence, sedition,   70
Which we ourselves have ploughed for, sowed,
     and scattered,
By mingling them with us, the honored number;
Who lack not virtue, no, nor power, but that
Which they have given to beggars.

MENENIUS   Well, no more.

53 **stir** are rebelling 55 **are out of** are straying from 57 **for** as 58 **abused**
deceived 58 **set on** incited 58 **palt'ring** cheating 60 **rub** hindrance (in
bowling on the green, any roughness of ground) 60 **falsely** treacherously
66 **meiny** crowd 70 **cockle** weed

FIRST SENATOR No more words, we beseech you.

75 CORIOLANUS   How! No more!
    As for my country I have shed my blood,
    Not fearing outward force, so shall my lungs
    Coin words till their decay against those measles,
    Which we disdain should tetter us, yet sought
    The very way to catch them.

80 BRUTUS   You speak o' th' people,
    As if you were a god, to punish, not
    A man of their infirmity.

    SICINIUS   'Twere well
    We let the people know't.

    MENENIUS   What, what? His choler?

    CORIOLANUS Choler?
85 Were I as patient as the midnight sleep,
    By Jove, 'twould be my mind!

    SICINIUS   It is a mind
    That shall remain a poison where it is,
    Not poison any further.

    CORIOLANUS   Shall remain!
    Hear you this Triton of the minnows? Mark you
    His absolute "shall"?

    CORIOLANUS   'Twas from the canon.

90 CORIOLANUS   "Shall"!
    O good but most unwise patricians! Why,
    You grave but reckless senators, have you thus
    Given Hydra here to choose an officer,
    That with his peremptory "shall," being but
95 The horn and noise o' th' monster's, wants not spirit
    To say he'll turn your current in a ditch,

78 decay death 78 measles (the disease; and "foul wretches," from *mesel*,
"leper") 79 tetter infect with leprous eruption 82 of their infirmity having
the same weaknesses as they 89 Triton sea-god, trumpeter of Neptune (cf.
"horn," line 95) 90 from the canon against the law 93 Given Hydra here
permitted this many-headed beast 96 in (aside) into

And make your channel his? If he have power,
Then vail your ignorance; if none, awake
Your dangerous lenity. If you are learned,
Be not as common fools; if you are not,   100
Let them have cushions by you. You are plebeians,
If they be senators; and they are no less,
When, both your voices blended, the great'st taste
Most palates theirs. They choose their magistrate;
And such a one as he, who puts his "shall,"   105
His popular "shall," against a graver bench
Than ever frowned in Greece. By Jove himself,
It makes the consuls base; and my soul aches
To know, when two authorities are up,
Neither supreme, how soon confusion   110
May enter 'twixt the gap of both and take
The one by th' other.

COMINIUS   Well, on to th' marketplace.

CORIOLANUS Whoever gave that counsel to give forth
The corn o' th' storehouse gratis, as 'twas used
Sometime in Greece—

MENENIUS   Well, well, no more of that.   115

CORIOLANUS Though there the people had more abso-
lute pow'r,
I say they nourished disobedience, fed
The ruin of the state.

BRUTUS   Why shall the people give
One that speaks thus their voice?

CORIOLANUS   I'll give my reasons,
More worthier than their voices. They know the
corn   120

98 **vail your ignorance** let your ignorance (that gave the power) bow (to
him) 99 **learned** wise 101 **cushions** (symbol of senatorial rank; cf.
II.ii.s.d.) 102 **no less** i.e., no less than senators 103–04 **the great'st taste/
Most palates theirs** the dominant flavor tastes most of them (they have the most
votes) 106 **bench** court 109 **up** active 110 **confusion** violent disorder (in a
revolution) 111–12 **take/The one by th' other** seize and overthrow one by
means of the other

Was not our recompense, resting well assured
They ne'er did service for't. Being pressed to th' war,
Even when the navel of the state was touched,
They would not thread the gates; this kind of
    service
125 Did not deserve corn gratis. Being i' th' war,
Their mutinies and revolts, wherein they showed
Most valor, spoke not for them. Th' accusation
Which they have often made against the Senate,
All cause unborn, could never be the native
130 Of our so frank donation. Well, what then?
How shall this bosom multiplied digest
The Senate's courtesy? Let deeds express
What's like to be their words: "We did request it;
We are the greater poll, and in true fear
135 They gave us our demands." Thus we debase
The nature of our seats, and make the rabble
Call our cares fears; which will in time
Break ope the locks o' th' Senate and bring in
The crows to peck the eagles.

MENENIUS   Come, enough.

BRUTUS Enough, with over measure.

140 CORIOLANUS   No, take more.
What may be sworn by, both divine and human,
Seal what I end withal! This double worship,
Where one part does disdain with cause, the other
Insult without all reason; where gentry, title,
    wisdom,
145 Cannot conclude but by the yea and no

---

121 **recompense** reward for past services   122 **pressed to** conscripted for
123 **navel** center (cf. Menenius' fable, I.i)   124 **thread** pass through   129 **All
cause unborn** with no cause in existence   129 **native** original, parent (i.e., their
accusation not the origin of our gift)   130 **frank** unsolicited   131 **bosom
multiplied** many-bosomed beast ("Hydra," line 93)   131 **digest** (1) digest
(2) understand ("bosom" can mean both "cavity of the stomach" and "heart," i.e.,
"mind")   134 **poll** number   137 **cares** (concern for the state)   142 **withal** with
144 **without** beyond   144 **gentry** gentle birth   145 **conclude** decide

Of general ignorance—it must omit
Real necessities, and give way the while
To unstable slightness. Purpose so barred, it
      follows
Nothing is done to purpose. Therefore, beseech
      you—
You that will be less fearful than discreet;   150
That love the fundamental part of state
More than you doubt the change on't; that prefer
A noble life before a long, and wish
To jump a body with a dangerous physic
That's sure of death without it—at once pluck out 155
The multitudinous tongue; let them not lick
The sweet which is their poison. Your dishonor
Mangles true judgment, and bereaves the state
Of that integrity which should become't;
Not having the power to do the good it would,   160
For th' ill which doth control't.

BRUTUS   'Has said enough.

SICINIUS Has spoken like a traitor and shall answer
As traitors do.

CORIOLANUS   Thou wretch, despite o'erwhelm thee!
What should the people do with these bald tribunes,
On whom depending, their obedience fails   165
To th' greater bench? In a rebellion,
When what's not meet, but what must be, was law,
Then were they chosen; in a better hour

---

146 omit overlook   148 unstable slightness unsteady trifling   148 Purpose so
barred when the intention (of charting a policy in advance) is so thwarted
150 less fearful than discreet i.e., more prudent than fearful   151 fundamental part of state basic constitution of the government   152 doubt fear
154 jump risk harming   154 physic medicine, treatment   156 multitudinous
tongue (the voice of the "Hydra," the tribuneship)   159 integrity
wholeness   161 control't overpower it   162 answer i.e., in court, be brought to
trial; cf. lines 176, 323   164 bald trivial (pun)   166 th' greater bench i.e., the
senate

Let what is meet be said it must be meet,
170   And throw their power i' th' dust.

BRUTUS Manifest treason!

SICINIUS   This a consul? No.

BRUTUS The aediles, ho!

Enter an Aedile.

Let him be apprehended.

SICINIUS Go, call the people, [*exit Aedile*] in whose
    name myself
    Attach thee as a traitorous innovator,
175   A foe to th' public weal. Obey, I charge thee,
    And follow to thine answer.

CORIOLANUS   Hence, old goat!

ALL [PATRICIANS] We'll surety him.

COMINIUS   Aged sir, hands off.

CORIOLANUS Hence, rotten thing, or I shall shake thy
    bones
    Out of thy garments.

SICINIUS   Help, ye citizens!

Enter a rabble of Plebeians, with the Aediles.

180 MENENIUS On both sides more respect.

SICINIUS Here's he that would take from you all your
    power.

BRUTUS Seize him, aediles!

ALL [CITIZENS] Down with him, down with him!

SECOND SENATOR Weapons, weapons, weapons!
                          They all bustle about Coriolanus.

169 **it must be meet** that it *must* be fitting   172 **aediles** officers attached to the
tribunes   174 **Attach** arrest   176 **answer** (legal term for "meeting a
charge")   176 **goat** (the tribunes are evidently bearded; cf. II.i.89)   177 **surety**
stand surety for

[ALL] Tribunes!—Patricians!—Citizens!—What,
   ho!— 185
  Sicinius!—Brutus!—Coriolanus!—Citizens!—
  Peace, peace, peace!—Stay! Hold! Peace!

MENENIUS What is about to be? I am out of breath.
  Confusion's near. I cannot speak. You, tribunes
  To th' people! Coriolanus, patience! 190
  Speak, good Sicinius.

SICINIUS   Hear me, people; peace!

ALL [CITIZENS] Let's hear our tribune. Peace!—Speak,
  speak, speak.

SICINIUS You are at point to lose your liberties:
  Marcius would have all from you; Marcius,
  Whom late you have named for consul.

MENENIUS   Fie, fie, fie! 195
  This is the way to kindle, not to quench.

FIRST SENATOR To unbuild the city, and to lay all flat.

SICINIUS What is the city but the people?

ALL [CITIZENS]   True,
  The people are the city.

BRUTUS By the consent of all, we were established 200
  The people's magistrates.

ALL [CITIZENS]   You so remain.

MENENIUS And so are like to do.

COMINIUS That is the way to lay the city flat,
  To bring the roof to the foundation,
  And bury all which yet distinctly ranges, 205
  In heaps and piles of ruin.

SICINIUS   This deserves death.

189 **Confusion** ruin (resulting from civil disorder, cf. line 110) 193 **at point to lose** on point of losing 205 **distinctly ranges** extends in separate orderly rows (of buildings)

BRUTUS Or let us stand to our authority,
　　　Or let us lose it. We do here pronounce,
　　　Upon the part o' th' people, in whose power
210　　We were elected theirs, Marcius is worthy
　　　Of present death.

SICINIUS　　　　　　Therefore lay hold of him;
　　　Bear him to th' rock Tarpeian, and from thence
　　　Into destruction cast him.

BRUTUS　　　　　　　　　Aediles, seize him!

ALL [CITIZENS] Yield, Marcius, yield!

MENENIUS　　　　　　　　Hear me one word;
215　　Beseech you, tribunes, hear me but a word.

AEDILES Peace, peace!

MENENIUS [To Brutus] Be that you seem, truly your
　　　country's friend,
　　　And temp'rately proceed to what you would
　　　Thus violently redress.

BRUTUS　　　　　　　Sir, those cold ways,
220　　That seem like prudent helps, are very poisonous
　　　Where the disease is violent. Lay hands upon him,
　　　And bear him to the rock.

　　　　　　　　　　　　　Coriolanus draws his sword.

CORIOLANUS　　　　　No, I'll die here.
　　　There's some among you have beheld me fighting;
　　　Come, try upon yourselves what you have seen me.

MENENIUS Down with that sword! Tribunes, withdraw
225　　awhile.

BRUTUS Lay hands upon him.

MENENIUS　　　　　　Help Marcius, help,
　　　You that be noble; help him, young and old!

---

207 **Or** either　207 **stand to** stand by　209 **in** by　210 **theirs** i.e., their
representatives　212 **rock Tarpeian** (from which criminals were thrown)

ALL [CITIZENS] Down with him, down with him!
> *In this mutiny, the Tribunes, the Aediles, and*
> *the people are beat in.*

MENENIUS Go, get you to your house; begone, away!
    All will be naught else.

SECOND SENATOR   Get you gone.

CORIOLANUS   Stand fast;   230
    We have as many friends as enemies.

MENENIUS Shall it be put to that?

FIRST SENATOR   The gods forbid!
    I prithee, noble friend, home to thy house;
    Leave us to cure this cause.

MENENIUS   For 'tis a sore upon us
    You cannot tent yourself. Begone, beseech you.   235

COMINIUS Come, sir, along with us.

CORIOLANUS I would they were barbarians, as they are,
    Though in Rome littered; not Romans, as they are
        not,
    Though calved i' th' porch o' th' Capitol.

MENENIUS   Begone.
    Put not your worthy rage into your tongue: 240
    One time will owe another.

CORIOLANUS   On fair ground
    I could beat forty of them.

MENENIUS   I could myself
    Take up a brace o' th' best of them; yea, the two
        tribunes.

---

228 s.d. **mutiny** riot 229 **naught** ruined 232 **put to that** driven to that
extremity 234 **cause** dispute 235 **tent** treat (cf. I.ix.31) 239 **porch o' th'**
Capitol (portico of the temple of Jupiter on the Capitoline Hill) 240 **worthy**
justifiable (?) noble (?) 241 **One time will owe another** one time (the present,
when the people are in revolt) will be compensated by another (when the people
are checked) 243 **Take up a brace** take on a couple ("brace" often of dogs)

COMINIUS But now 'tis odds beyond arithmetic;
245   And manhood is called foolery when it stands
       Against a falling fabric. Will you hence
       Before the tag return? Whose rage doth rend
       Like interrupted waters, and o'erbear
       What they are used to bear.

MENENIUS   Pray you, begone.
250   I'll try whether my old wit be in request
       With those that have but little. This must be
         patched
       With cloth of any color.

COMINIUS   Nay, come away.
                     Exeunt Coriolanus and Cominius.

PATRICIAN This man has marred his fortune.

MENENIUS His nature is too noble for the world:
255   He would not flatter Neptune for his trident,
       Or Jove for's power to thunder. His heart's his
         mouth:
       What his breast forges, that his tongue must vent;
       And, being angry, does forget that ever
       He heard the name of death.   *A noise within.*
       Here's goodly work!

260 PATRICIAN   I would they were abed!

MENENIUS I would they were in Tiber! What the
         vengeance!
       Could he not speak 'em fair?

       Enter Brutus and Sicinius, with the rabble again.

SICINIUS   Where is this viper
       That would depopulate the city and
       Be every man himself?

MENENIUS   You worthy tribunes——

244 **beyond arithmetic** beyond number 246 **fabric** building 247 **tag** riffraff
("tag and rag") 248 **o'erbear** overcome 261 **What the vengeance** (an emphatic "What!"; cf. "What the devil!") 262 **speak 'em fair** talk civilly to them (and
so flatter)

SICINIUS He shall be thrown down the Tarpeian rock   265
   With rigorous hands. He hath resisted law,
   And therefore law shall scorn him further trial
   Than the severity of the public power,
   Which he so sets at nought.

FIRST CITIZEN   He shall well know
   The noble tribunes are the people's mouths,   270
   And we their hands.

ALL [CITIZENS] He shall, sure on't.

MENENIUS   Sir, sir——

SICINIUS Peace!

MENENIUS Do not cry havoc, where you should but
    hunt
   With modest warrant.

SICINIUS   Sir, how comes't that you
   Have holp to make this rescue?

MENENIUS   Hear me speak: 275
   As I do know the consul's worthiness,
   So can I name his faults.

SICINIUS   Consul! What consul?

MENENIUS The consul Coriolanus.

BRUTUS   He consul!

ALL [CITIZENS] No, no, no, no, no.

MENENIUS If, by the tribunes' leave, and yours, good
    people,   280
   I may be heard, I would crave a word or two;
   The which shall turn you to no further harm
   Than so much loss of time.

SICINIUS   Speak briefly then;
   For we are peremptory to dispatch

268 **the public power** i.e., the power derived from the people   273 **cry havoc** call for general slaughter ("total war")   274 **With modest warrant** with moderate justification   275 **holp** helped   284 **peremptory** resolved

285   This viperous traitor. To eject him hence
        Were but our danger, and to keep him here
        Our certain death. Therefore it is decreed
        He dies tonight.

MENENIUS   Now the good gods forbid
        That our renownèd Rome, whose gratitude
290   Towards her deservèd children is enrolled
        In Jove's own book, like an unnatural dam
        Should now eat up her own!

SICINIUS He's a disease that must be cut away.

MENENIUS O, he's a limb that has but a disease;
295   Mortal, to cut it off; to cure it, easy.
        What has he done to Rome that's worthy death?
        Killing our enemies, the blood he hath lost—
        Which I dare vouch is more than that he hath
        By many an ounce—he dropped it for his country;
300   And what is left, to lose it by his country
        Were to us all that do't and suffer it
        A brand to th' end o' th' world.

SICINIUS   This is clean kam.

BRUTUS Merely awry. When he did love his country,
        It honored him.

MENENIUS   The service of the foot
305   Being once gangrened, is not then respected
        For what before it was.

BRUTUS   We'll hear no more.
        Pursue him to his house and pluck him thence,
        Lest his infection, being of catching nature,
        Spread further.

MENENIUS   One word more, one word!
310   This tiger-footed rage, when it shall find
        The harm of unscanned swiftness, will, too late,

286 **but our danger** only the risk we now run 290 **deservèd** deserving
295 **Mortal** deadly 302 **brand** mark of disgrace 302 **clean kam** completely
wrong (literally *kam*=crooked) 303 **Merely** absolutely 307 **pluck** take
311 **unscanned** thoughtless

Tie leaden pounds to's heels. Proceed by process;
Lest parties (as he is beloved) break out,
And sack great Rome with Romans.

BRUTUS   If it were so—

SICINIUS What do ye talk?   315
Have we not had a taste of his obedience?
Our aediles smote? Ourselves resisted? Come!

MENENIUS Consider this: he has been bred i' th' wars
Since 'a could draw a sword, and is ill schooled
In bolted language; meal and bran together   320
He throws without distinction. Give me leave,
I'll go to him, and undertake to bring him
Where he shall answer, by a lawful form,
In peace, to his utmost peril.

FIRST SENATOR   Noble tribunes,
It is the humane way. The other course   325
Will prove too bloody, and the end of it
Unknown to the beginning.

SICINIUS   Noble Menenius,
Be you then as the people's officer.
Masters, lay down your weapons.

BRUTUS   Go not home.

SICINIUS Meet on the marketplace. We'll attend you
there,   330
Where, if you bring not Marcius, we'll proceed
In our first way.

MENENIUS   I'll bring him to you.
[*To the Senators*] Let me desire your company. He
must come,
Or what is worst will follow.

SENATORS   Pray you, let's to him.
                        Exeunt omnes.

312 **pounds** pound-weights 312 **to's** to his 312 **process** due process of
law 315 **What** why 320 **bolted** refined (literally, sifted) 323 **answer, by a
lawful form** meet the charges according to the forms of law 324 **to his utmost
peril** at the risk of the severest penalty 334 s.d. **omnes** all (Latin)

[Scene II. *Rome. The house of Coriolanus.*]

Enter Coriolanus with Nobles.

CORIOLANUS Let them pull all about mine ears; present
      me
      Death on the wheel or at wild horses' heels;
      Or pile ten hills on the Tarpeian rock,
      That the precipitation might down stretch
5   Below the beam of sight; yet will I still
      Be thus to them.

A NOBLE   You do the nobler.

CORIOLANUS I muse my mother
      Does not approve me further, who was wont
      To call them woolen vassals, things created
10   To buy and sell with groats; to show bare heads
      In congregations, to yawn, be still and wonder,
      When one but of my ordinance stood up
      To speak of peace or war.

Enter Volumnia.

                    I talk of you:
      Why did you wish me milder—Would you have me
15   False to my nature? Rather say I play
      The man I am.

VOLUMNIA   O, sir, sir, sir,
      I would have had you put your power well on,
      Before you had worn it out.

III.ii.2 **the wheel** (by being bound to a wheel and beaten to death; an Elizabethan,
not Roman, penalty) 4 **precipitation** steepness 5 **Below the beam of sight**
i.e., beyond the range of sight (*beam* = a ray passing from the object to the eye)
7 **muse** wonder 9 **woolen vassals** i.e., rough-dressed members of the lowest
class 10 **groats** four-penny coins 12 **ordinance** rank

CORIOLANUS   Let go.

VOLUMNIA You might have been enough the man you
    are,
  With striving less to be so. Lesser had been   20
  The thwartings of your dispositions, if
  You had not showed them how ye were disposed
  Ere they lacked power to cross you.

CORIOLANUS   Let them hang.

VOLUMNIA Ay, and burn too.

     Enter Menenius with the Senators.

MENENIUS Come, come, you have been too rough,
    something too rough;   25
  You must return and mend it.

SENATOR   There's no remedy,
  Unless, by not so doing, our good city
  Cleave in the midst and perish.

VOLUMNIA   Pray be counseled;
  I have a heart as little apt as yours,
  But yet a brain that leads my use of anger   30
  To better vantage.

MENENIUS   Well said, noble woman!
  Before he should thus stoop to th' herd, but that
  The violent fit o' th' time craves it as physic
  For the whole state, I would put mine armor on,
  Which I can scarcely bear.

CORIOLANUS   What must I do?   35

MENENIUS Return to th' tribunes.

CORIOLANUS   Well, what then? What then?

MENENIUS Repent what you have spoke.

---

18 Let go enough of that 21 dispositions inclinations 25 **something**
somewhat 26–28 **There's ... midst** there's no help for it; (you must compromise;) else, because of your failure to do so, our good city may be split in
two 29 apt compliant 33 physic medical treatment

CORIOLANUS For them! I cannot do it to the gods;
　　　　Must I then do't to them?

VOLUMNIA   You are too absolute;
40　　Though therein you can never be too noble
　　　But when extremities speak. I have heard you say,
　　　Honor and policy, like unsevered friends,
　　　I' th' war do grow together. Grant that, and tell me
　　　In peace what each of them by th' other lose
　　　That they combine not there.

CORIOLANUS   Tush, tush!

45　MENENIUS   A good demand.

VOLUMNIA If it be honor in your wars to seem
　　　The same you are not, which for your best ends
　　　You adopt your policy, how is it less or worse
　　　That it shall hold companionship in peace
50　　With honor as in war; since that to both
　　　It stands in like request?

CORIOLANUS   Why force you this?

VOLUMNIA Because that now it lies you on to speak
　　　To th' people, not by your own instruction,
　　　Nor by th' matter which your heart prompts you,
55　　But with such words that are but roted in
　　　Your tongue, though but bastards and syllables
　　　Of no allowance to your bosom's truth.
　　　Now, this no more dishonors you at all
　　　Than to take in a town with gentle words,
60　　Which else would put you to your fortune and
　　　The hazard of much blood.
　　　I would dissemble with my nature, where
　　　My fortunes and my friends at stake required

41 **when extremities speak** when the most critical situations demand.
42 **unsevered** inseparable 48 **adopt** adopt as 49 **it** (pretense, "to seem/The same you are not") 51 **stands in like request** is equally in demand 51 **force** urge 52 **it lies you on** it is your duty 55 **roted** learned by rote 56–57 **but ... truth** only false expressions of your heart's true understanding wholly unacceptable to it 59 **take in** capture 60 **put you to your fortune** force you to take your chances (in war)

I should do so in honor. I am in this
Your wife, your son, these senators, the nobles;   65
And you will rather show our general louts
How you can frown than spend a fawn upon 'em
For the inheritance of their loves and safeguard
Of what that want might ruin.

MENENIUS   Noble lady!
Come, go with us; speak fair; you may salve so,   70
Not what is dangerous present, but the loss
Of what is past.

VOLUMNIA   I prithee now, my son,
Go to them with this bonnet in thy hand;
And thus far having stretched it (here be with
  them),
Thy knee bussing the stones (for in such business   75
Action is eloquence, and the eyes of th' ignorant
More learnèd than the ears), waving thy head,
Which often thus correcting thy stout heart,
Now humble as the ripest mulberry
That will not hold the handling; or say to them,   80
Thou art their soldier, and being bred in broils
Hast not the soft way which, thou dost confess,
Were fit for thee to use, as they to claim,
In asking their good loves; but thou wilt frame
Thyself, forsooth, hereafter theirs, so far   85
As thou hast power and person.

MENENIUS   This but done,
Even as she speaks, why, their hearts were yours;
For they have pardons, being asked, as free
As words to little purpose.

---

64 **in honor** in honor bound (*not* Coriolanus' understanding of "Honor") 64 **I
am in this** I speak in this for (implying also, "I stand in place of") 66 **general**
common 68 **inheritance** possession 69 **that want** (of their loves) 74–80 (the
text may be corrupt) 75 **bussing** kissing (touching) 77 **waving** bowing up and
down 78 **Which** (subject of "correcting" in a nominative absolute; the sentence
is urgent; the syntax, sketchy) 78 **stout** proud 80 **or** (marks the turn from
"action" to "eloquence," line 76) 85 **forsooth** in truth 88 **free** liberal (to
grant)

VOLUMNIA   Prithee now,
Go, and be ruled; although I know thou hadst
90   rather
Follow thine enemy in a fiery gulf
Than flatter him in a bower.

                    Enter Cominius.

                          Here is Cominius.

COMINIUS I have been i' th' marketplace; and, sir,
    'tis fit
You make strong party, or defend yourself
95   By calmness or by absence. All's in anger.

MENENIUS Only fair speech.

COMINIUS   I think 'twill serve, if he
Can thereto frame his spirit.

VOLUMNIA   He must, and will.
Prithee now, say you will, and go about it.

CORIOLANUS Must I go show them my unbarbed
    sconce? Must I
100   With my base tongue give to my noble heart
A lie that it must bear? Well, I will do't.
Yet, were there but this single plot to lose,
This mold of Marcius, they to dust should grind it,
And throw't against the wind. To th' marketplace!
105   You have put me now to such a part which never
I shall discharge to th' life.

COMINIUS   Come, come, we'll prompt you.

VOLUMNIA I prithee now, sweet son, as thou has said
My praises made thee first a soldier, so,
To have my praise for this, perform a part
Thou hast not done before.

110   CORIOLANUS   Well, I must do't.

91 **in a fiery gulf** into an abyss of flame   92 **bower** ladies' chamber
93 **marketplace** i.e., Forum of ancient Rome   94 **make strong party** maintain
your side strongly   99 **unbarbed sconce** unarmed head ("sconce" often used in
comic contexts)   102 **plot** (of earth)   103 **mold** (both "frame" and "earth"; cf.
V.iii.22)   105 **part** (in a play)   106 **discharge** perform

Away, my disposition, and possess me
Some harlot's spirit! My throat of war be turned,
Which quired with my drum, into a pipe
Small as an eunuch or the virgin voice
That babies lulls asleep! The smiles of knaves   115
Tent in my cheeks, and schoolboys' tears take up
The glasses of my sight! A beggar's tongue
Make motion through my lips, and my armed
    knees,
Who bowed but in my stirrup, bend like his
That hath received an alms! I will not do't;   120
Lest I surcease to honor mine own truth,
And by my body's action teach my mind
A most inherent baseness.

VOLUMNIA   At thy choice then.
To beg of thee, it is my more dishonor
Than thou of them. Come all to ruin! Let   125
Thy mother rather feel they pride than fear
Thy dangerous stoutness, for I mock at death
With as big heart as thou. Do as thou list.
Thy valiantness was mine, thou suck'st it from me,
But owe thy pride thyself.

CORIOLANUS   Pray, be content: 130
Mother, I am going to the marketplace;
Chide me no more. I'll mountebank their loves,
Cog their hearts from them, and come home be-
    loved
Of all the trades in Rome. Look, I am going.
Commend me to my wife. I'll return consul;   135
Or never trust to what my tongue can do
I' th' way of flattery further.

---

112 **harlot** rascal (used of both sexes) 113 **quired** sang harmoniously
113 **pipe** i.e., voice 116 **take up** possess 117 **The glasses of my sight** my
eyeballs 121 **surcease** cease 123 **inherent** firmly settled 126–27 **feel …
stoutness** suffer the effects of thy pride, but not fear the danger of it (*stoutness* =
obstinacy, as in North, nearly equal to "pride"; cf. line 78) 127 **thou list** you
please 130 **owe** own, have 132 **mountebank** win their loves by tricky actions
(cf. a "mountebank," a quack doctor, who puts on an act to sell his wares)
133 **Cog** cheat

VOLUMNIA   Do your will. *Exit Volumnia.*

COMINIUS Away, the tribunes do attend you. Arm
    yourself
    To answer mildly; for they are prepared
140   With accusations, as I hear, more strong
    Than are upon you yet.

CORIOLANUS The word is "mildly." Pray you, let
    us go.
    Let them accuse me by invention, I
    Will answer in mine honor.

MENENIUS   Ay, but mildly.

145 CORIOLANUS Well, mildly be it then—mildly. *Exeunt.*

[Scene III. *Rome. The Forum.*]

Enter Sicinius and Brutus.

BRUTUS In this point charge him home, that he
    affects
    Tyrannical power. If he evade us there,
    Enforce him with his envy to the people,
    And that the spoil got on the Antiates
    Was ne'er distributed.

Enter an Aedile.

5   What, will he come?

AEDILE He's coming.

BRUTUS   How accompanied?

142 **word** password   143 **accuse me by invention** invent accusations against
me   144 **in** in a way consistent with   III.iii.1 **charge him home** press your
accusations against him to the limit   1 **affects** aims at   3 **Enforce him** press him
hard   3 **envy** ill-will   4 **got on** won from

AEDILE With old Menenius and those senators
  That always favored him.

SICINIUS   Have you a catalog
  Of all the voices that we have procured,
  Set down by th' poll?

AEDILE   I have; 'tis ready.   10

SICINIUS Have you collected them by tribes?

AEDILE   I have.

SICINIUS Assemble presently the people hither:
  And when they hear me say "It shall be so
  I' th' right and strength o' th' commons," be it
    either
  For death, for fine, or banishment, then let them,   15
  If I say "Fine," cry "Fine!"—if "Death," cry
    "Death!"
  Insisting on the old prerogative
  And power i' th' truth o' th' cause.

AEDILE   I shall inform them.

BRUTUS And when such time they have begun to
    cry,
  Let them not cease, but with a din confused   20
  Enforce the present execution
  Of what we chance to sentence.

AEDILE   Very well.

SICINIUS Make them be strong, and ready for this
    hint,
  When we shall hap to give't them.

BRUTUS   Go about it. [*Exit Aedile.*]
  Put him to choler straight. He hath been used   25
  Ever to conquer and to have his worth

10 **by th' poll** by counting heads 12 **presently** at once (cf. line 21) 18 **i' th' truth o' th' cause** resting in the justice of the case 19 **when such time** at such time when 21 **Enforce** press for 23 **hint** opportunity 25 **Put him to** drive him to 26 **his worth** his pennyworth, i.e., his fill

Of contradiction. Being once chafed, he cannot
Be reined again to temperance; then he speaks
What's in his heart, and that is there which looks
With us to break his neck.

Enter Coriolanus, Menenius, and Cominius,
with others.

30 SICINIUS   Well, here he comes.

MENENIUS Calmly, I do beseech you.

CORIOLANUS Ay, as an ostler, that for th' poorest piece
    Will bear the knave by th' volume. Th' honored
        gods
    Keep Rome in safety, and the chairs of justice
35 Supplied with worthy men! Plant love among's!
    Throng our large temples with the shows of peace,
    And not our streets with war!

FIRST SENATOR   Amen, amen.

MENENIUS A noble wish.

Enter the Aedile, with the Plebeians.

SICINIUS Draw near, ye people.

40 AEDILE List to your tribunes. Audience! peace, I say!

CORIOLANUS First, hear me speak.

BOTH TRIBUNES   Well, say. Peace, ho!

CORIOLANUS Shall I be charged no further than this
        present?
    Must all determine here?

SICINIUS   I do demand,
    If you submit you to the people's voices,
45 Allow their officers, and are content

29–30 **looks/With us** promises in harmony with our intent   32 **piece** coin
33 **bear the knave by th' volume** endure being called knave enough times to fill
a book   40 **Audience** give ear   42 **this present** this immediate occasion
43 **determine** reach a conclusion   43 **demand** ask   45 **Allow** acknowledge

To suffer lawful censure for such faults
As shall be proved upon you.

CORIOLANUS   I am content.

MENENIUS Lo, citizens, he says he is content.
The warlike service he has done, consider; think
Upon the wounds his body bears, which show   50
Like graves i' th' holy churchyard.

CORIOLANUS   Scratches with briers,
Scars to move laughter only.

MENENIUS   Consider further,
That when he speaks not like a citizen,
You find him like a soldier. Do not take
His rougher accents for malicious sounds,   55
But, as I say, such as become a soldier
Rather than envy you.

COMINIUS   Well, well, no more.

CORIOLANUS What is the matter
That, being passed for consul with full voice,
I am so dishonored that the very hour   60
You take it off again?

SICINIUS   Answer to us.

CORIOLANUS Say, then. 'Tis true, I ought so.

SICINIUS We charge you, that you have contrived to take
From Rome all seasoned office, and to wind
Yourself into a power tyrannical,   65
For which you are a traitor to the people.

CORIOLANUS How! Traitor!

MENENIUS   Nay, temperately! Your promise.

---

54 like a soldier   57 envy express malice towards   64 seasoned established (or "moderate," "well moderated")   64–65 wind/Yourself into make your way by indirect and crooked means

CORIOLANUS The fires i' th' lowest hell fold in the
          people!
      Call me their traitor, thou injurious tribune!
70   Within thine eyes sat twenty thousand deaths,
      In thy hands clutched as many millions, in
      Thy lying tongue both numbers, I would say
      "Thou liest" unto thee with a voice as free
      As I do pray the gods.

SICINIUS   Mark you this, people?

ALL [CITIZENS] To th' rock, to th' rock with him!

75   SICINIUS   Peace!
      We need not put new matter to his charge.
      What you have seen him do and heard him speak,
      Beating your officers, cursing yourselves,
      Opposing laws with strokes, and here defying
80   Those whose great power must try him—even this,
      So criminal and in such capital kind,
      Deserves th' extremest death.

BRUTUS   But since he hath
      Served well for Rome——

CORIOLANUS   What do you prate of service?

BRUTUS I talk of that that know it.

85   CORIOLANUS You!

MENENIUS Is this the promise that you made your
          mother?

COMINIUS Know, I pray you——

CORIOLANUS   I'll know no further.
      Let them pronounce the steep Tarpeian death,
      Vagabond exile, flaying, pent to linger
90   But with a grain a day, I would not buy
      Their mercy at the price of one fair word,

69 **injurious** insulting 70 **Within** if within 73 **free** unrestrained 81 **capital**
(defined by line 82) 88 **steep Tarpeian death** cf. line 103 89 **pent** i.e., "Let
them pronounce" the sentence of being "pent," imprisoned

Nor check my courage for what they can give,
To have't with saying "Good morrow."

SICINIUS   For that he has
    (As much as in him lies) from time to time
    Envied against the people, seeking means   95
    To pluck away their power, as now at last
    Given hostile strokes, and that not in the presence
    Of dreaded justice, but on the ministers
    That do distribute it—in the name o' th' people,
    And in the power of us the tribunes, we,   100
    Even from this instant, banish him our city,
    In peril of precipitation
    From off the rock Tarpeian, never more
    To enter our Rome gates. I' th' people's name,
    I say it shall be so.   105

ALL [CITIZENS] It shall be so, it shall be so! Let him
        away!
    He's banished, and it shall be so.

COMINIUS Hear me, my masters and my common
        friends——

SICINIUS He's sentenced; no more hearing.

COMINIUS   Let me speak.
    I have been consul, and can show for Rome   110
    Her enemies' marks upon me. I do love
    My country's good with a respect more tender,
    More holy and profound, than mine own life,
    My dear wife's estimate, her womb's increase
    And treasure of my loins; then if I would   115
    Speak that—

SICINIUS   We know your drift. Speak what?

BRUTUS There's no more to be said, but he is banished
    As enemy to the people and his country.
    It shall be so.

92 courage spirit   94 as in him lies as lies in his power   95 Envied against
shown malice towards   96 as now with respect to this occasion (or, "now," "as"
being redundant)   97 not not only   114 estimate worth

ALL [CITIZENS] It shall be so, it shall be so.

CORIOLANUS You common cry of curs, whose breath
120   I hate
      As reek o' th' rotten fens, whose loves I prize
      As the dead carcasses of unburied men
      That do corrupt my air, I banish you.
      And here remain with your uncertainty!
125   Let every feeble rumor shake your hearts!
      Your enemies, with nodding of their plumes,
      Fan you into despair! Have the power still
      To banish your defenders, till at length
      Your ignorance (which finds not till it feels,
130   Making but reservation of yourselves,
      Still your own foes) deliver you as most
      Abated captives to some nation
      That won you without blows! Despising
      For you the city, thus I turn my back.
135   There is a world elsewhere.

Exeunt Coriolanus, Cominius, [Menenius,]
with the other Senators.

AEDILE The people's enemy is gone, is gone!

ALL [CITIZENS] Our enemy is banished, he is gone!
      Hoo—oo!

They all shout, and throw up their caps.

SICINIUS Go see him out at gates, and follow him,
      As he hath followed you, with all despite;
140   Give him deserved vexation. Let a guard
      Attend us through the city.

ALL [CITIZENS] Come, come, let's see him out at gates;
      come!
      The gods preserve our noble tribunes! Come.

Exeunt.

120 cry pack 121 reek mist 129 finds not till it feels does not understand
until it suffers the consequences 130 Making ... yourselves saving only
yourselves 131 Still ever 132 Abated beaten down 139 despite
contempt 140 Give him deserved vexation torment him as he deserves

ACT IV

[Scene I. *Rome. Before a gate of the city*.]

Enter Coriolanus, Volumnia, Virgilia, Menenius,
Cominius, with the young Nobility of Rome.

CORIOLANUS Come, leave your tears; a brief farewell.
  The beast
With many heads butts me away. Nay, mother,
Where is your ancient courage? You were used
To say extremities was the trier of spirits;
That common chances common men could bear;   5
That when the sea was calm all boats alike
Showed mastership in floating; fortune's blows
When most struck home, being gentle wounded
  craves
A noble cunning. You were used to load me
With precepts that would make invincible   10
The heart that conned them.

VIRGILIA O heavens! O heavens!

CORIOLANUS   Nay, I prithee, woman—

IV.i.4 **extremities was** (plural subject permissible in Elizabethan usage)
7 **fortune's blows** (supply introductory "that") 7–9 **fortune's ... cunning**
(when fortune's blows strike hardest, to act the gentleman though wounded
demands a noble use of intelligence) 11 **conned** studied

VOLUMNIA Now the red pestilence strike all trades in
    Rome,
    And occupations perish!

CORIOLANUS   What, what, what!
15 I shall be loved when I am lacked. Nay, mother,
    Resume that spirit when you were wont to say,
    If you had been the wife of Hercules,
    Six of his labors you'd have done, and saved
    Your husband so much sweat. Cominius,
20 Droop not; adieu. Farewell, my wife, my mother.
    I'll do well yet. Thou old and true Menenius,
    Thy tears are salter than a younger man's,
    And venomous to thine eyes. My sometime
        general,
    I have seen thee stern, and thou hast oft beheld
25 Heart-hard'ning spectacles; tell these sad women
    'Tis fond to wail inevitable strokes,
    As 'tis to laugh at 'em. My mother, you wot well
    My hazards still have been your solace, and
    Believe't not lightly—though I go alone,
30 Like to a lonely dragon, that his fen
    Makes feared and talked of more than seen—your
        son
    Will or exceed the common or be caught
    With cautelous baits and practice.

VOLUMNIA   My first son,
    Whither wilt thou go? Take good Cominius
35 With thee awhile. Determine on some course
    More than a wild exposture to each chance
    That starts i' th' way before thee.

CORIOLANUS   O the gods!

COMINIUS I'll follow thee a month, devise with thee
    Where thou shalt rest, that thou mayst hear of us

23 **sometime** former 26 **fond** foolish 27 **wot** know 28 **solace** interest
32 **or exceed the common** either surpass the usual achievements of men
33 **cautelous** crafty 33 **practice** treachery 36 **exposture** exposure

714

And we of thee. So, if the time thrust forth   40
A cause for thy repeal, we shall not send
O'er the vast world to seek a single man,
And lose advantage, which doth ever cool
I' th' absence of the needer.

CORIOLANUS   Fare ye well!
Thou hast years upon thee; and thou art too full   45
Of the wars' surfeits to go rove with one
That's yet unbruised. Bring me but out at gate.
Come, my sweet wife, my dearest mother, and
My friends of noble touch; when I am forth,
Bid me farewell, and smile. I pray you, come.   50
While I remain above the ground you shall
Hear from me still, and never of me aught
But what is like me formerly.

MENENIUS   That's worthily
As any ear can hear. Come, let's not weep.
If I could shake off but one seven years   55
From these old arms and legs, by the good gods,
I'd with thee every foot.

CORIOLANUS   Give me thy hand.
Come.   *Exeunt.*

[Scene II. *Rome. Near the gate.*]

Enter the two Tribunes, Sicinius and Brutus,
with the Aedile.

SICINIUS Bid them all home; he's gone, and we'll no
    further.

---

41 **repeal** recall 43 **advantage** the opportune moment 44 **needer** (of
"advantage") 47 **Bring** conduct 49 **noble touch** tested nobility (cf.
"touchstone") 57 **I'd** I would (go) IV.ii.1 **them all** (the plebeians)

The nobility are vexed, whom we see have sided
In his behalf.

BRUTUS   Now we have shown our power,
Let us seem humbler after it is done
Than when it was a–doing.

5   SICINIUS   Bid them home.
Say their great enemy is gone, and they
Stand in their ancient strength.

BRUTUS   Dismiss them home. [*Exit Aedile.*]
Here comes his mother.

Enter Volumnia, Virgilia, and Menenius.

SICINIUS   Let's not meet her.

BRUTUS   Why?

SICINIUS They say she's mad.

10 BRUTUS They have ta'en note of us. Keep on your way.

VOLUMNIA O, y'are well met. Th' hoarded plague o'
th' gods
Requite your love!

MENENIUS   Peace, peace, be not so loud.

VOLUMNIA If that I could for weeping, you should
hear—
Nay, and you shall hear some. [*To Brutus*] Will you
be gone?

VIRGILIA. [*To Sicinius*] You shall stay too. I would I
15   had the power
To say so to my husband.

SICINIUS   Are you mankind?

VOLUMNIA Ay, fool; is that a shame? Note but this,
fool.
Was not a man my father? Hadst thou foxship

---

11 **hoarded** stored up (for punishment) 16 **mankind** mad, of manlike violence
(Sicinius' meaning; but Volumnia takes it in the sense of "human") 18 **foxship**
cunning

To banish him that struck more blows for Rome
Than thou hast spoken words?

SICINIUS   O blessed heavens!   20

VOLUMNIA Moe noble blows than ever thou wise
    words;
And for Rome's good. I'll tell thee what—yet go!
Nay, but thou shalt stay too. I would my son
Were in Arabia, and thy tribe before him,
His good sword in his hand.

SICINIUS   What then?

VIRGILIA   What then!   25
He'd make an end of thy posterity.

VOLUMNIA Bastards and all.
Good man, the wounds that he does bear for Rome!

MENENIUS Come, come, peace.

SICINIUS I would he had continued to his country   30
As he began, and not unknit himself
The noble knot he made.

BRUTUS   I would he had.

VOLUMNIA "I would he had!" 'Twas you incensed the
    rabble;
Cats, that can judge as fitly of his worth
As I can of those mysteries which heaven   35
Will not have earth to know.

BRUTUS   Pray, let's go.

VOLUMNIA Now, pray, sir, get you gone;
You have done a brave deed. Ere you go, hear this:
As far as doth the Capitol exceed
The meanest house in Rome, so far my son—   40
This lady's husband here, this, do you see?
Whom you have banished—does exceed you all.

BRUTUS Well, well, we'll leave you.

21 Moe more   24 Arabia a desert (outside Roman law and order)   32 noble
knot he made (bond to Rome made by his heroic deeds)

SICINIUS   Why stay we to be baited
With one that wants her wits?   *Exit Tribunes.*

VOLUMNIA   Take my prayers with you.
45   I would the gods had nothing else to do
        But to confirm my curses! Could I meet 'em
        But once a day, it would unclog my heart
        Of what lies heavy to't.

MENENIUS   You have told them home,
        And by my troth you have cause. You'll sup with
        me?
50 VOLUMNIA Anger's my meat; I sup upon myself,
        And so shall starve with feeding. Come, let's go.
        Leave this faint puling, and lament as I do,
        In anger, Juno-like. Come, come, come.
                          Exeunt [Volumnia and Virgilia].

MENENIUS Fie, fie, fie!   *Exit.*

            [Scene III. *Between Rome and Antium.*]

                Enter a Roman and a Volsce.

ROMAN I know you well, sir, and you know me: your
    name, I think, is Adrian.

VOLSCE It is so, sir. Truly, I have forgot you.

ROMAN I am a Roman; and my services are, as you
5   are, against 'em. Know you me yet?

VOLSCE Nicanor? No!

ROMAN The same, sir.

VOLSCE You had more beard when I last saw you; but

44 With by 48 told them home ("hit them where it hurts") 52 puling
whining IV.iii.5 'em the Romans

your favor is well appeared by your tongue.
What's the news in Rome? I have a note from the   10
Volscian state to find you out there. You have well
saved me a day's journey.

ROMAN There hath been in Rome strange insurrec-
tions; the people against the senators, patricians,
and nobles.   15

VOLSCE Hath been! Is it ended then? Our state thinks
not so; they are in a most warlike preparation, and
hope to come upon them in the heat of their
division.

ROMAN The main blaze of it is past, but a small thing   20
would make it flame again; for the nobles receive
so to heart the banishment of that worthy Coriolanus, that they are in a ripe aptness to take all
power from the people and to pluck from them
their tribunes forever. This lies glowing, I can tell   25
you, and is almost mature for the violent breaking
out.

VOLSCE Coriolanus banished!

ROMAN Banished, sir.

VOLSCE You will be welcome with this intelligence,   30
Nicanor.

ROMAN The day serves well for them now. I have
heard it said the fittest time to corrupt a man's wife
is when she's fall'n out with her husband. Your
noble Tullus Aufidius will appear well in these   35
wars, his great opposer, Coriolanus, being now in
no request of his country.

VOLSCE He cannot choose. I am most fortunate thus
accidentally to encounter you. You have ended my
business, and I will merrily accompany you home.   40

9 favor face   9 appeared made to appear   10 a note instructions   21 receive
take   32 them (the Volscians)   36–37 in no request of in no demand by
38 cannot choose (but appear well)

ROMAN I shall, between this and supper, tell you
most strange things from Rome, all tending to the
good of their adversaries. Have you an army ready,
say you?

45 VOLSCE A most royal one; the centurions and their
charges, distinctly billeted, already in th' entertainment, and to be on foot at an hour's warning.

ROMAN I am joyful to hear of their readiness, and am
the man, I think, that shall set them in present
50 action. So, sir, heartily well met, and most glad of
your company.

VOLSCE You take my part from me, sir. I have the
most cause to be glad of yours.

ROMAN Well, let us go together.   *Exeunt.*

[Scene IV. *Antium. Before Aufidius' house.*]

*Enter Coriolanus in mean apparel, disguised
and muffled.*

CORIOLANUS A goodly city is this Antium. City,
'Tis I that made thy widows: many an heir
Of these fair edifices 'fore my wars
Have I heard groan and drop. Then know me not,
5 Lest that thy wives with spits and boys with stones
In puny battle slay me.

Enter a Citizen.

Save you, sir.

41 **this** this time   45 **centurions** commanders of smallest unit (century) of a
Roman legion   46 **charges** men under them   46 **distinctly billeted** separately
enrolled   46–47 **in th' entertainment** in service (maintained by the
army)   IV.iv.3 **'fore my wars** before my attacks   6 **Save you** God save you

CITIZEN And you.

CORIOLANUS   Direct me, if it be your will,
Where great Aufidius lies. Is he in Antium?

CITIZEN He is, and feasts the nobles of the state
At his house this night.

CORIOLANUS   Which is his house, beseech you?   10

CITIZEN This here before you.

CORIOLANUS   Thank you, sir: farewell.
                                Exit Citizen.
O world, thy slippery turns! Friends now fast sworn,
Whose double bosoms seems to wear one heart,
Whose hours, whose bed, whose meal and exercise
Are still together, who twin, as 'twere, in love   15
Unseparable, shall within this hour,
On a dissension of a doit, break out
To bitterest enmity. So fellest foes,
Whose passions and whose plots have broke their
    sleep
To take the one the other, by some chance,   20
Some trick not worth an egg, shall grow dear
    friends
And interjoin their issues. So with me:
My birthplace hate I, and my love's upon
This enemy town. I'll enter. If he slay me,
He does fair justice; if he give me way,   25
I'll do his country service.   *Exit.*

8 lies lives 13 seems (perhaps an old plural in -s) 17 of a doit worth a doit
(coin of little value; cf. I.v.6) 18 fellest fiercest 21 trick trifle 22 interjoin
their issues let their children intermarry; become close partners in action
("issues" in sense of "deeds"?)

[Scene V. *Antium. A hall in Aufidius' house.*]

Music plays. Enter a Servingman.

FIRST SERVINGMAN Wine, wine, wine! What service is
here! I think our fellows are asleep.　　　[*Exit.*]

Enter another Servingman.

SECOND SERVINGMAN Where's Cotus? My master calls
for him. Cotus!　　　　　　　　　　　　*Exit.*

Enter Coriolanus.

CORIOLANUS A goodly house. The feast smells well,
but I

5 Appear not like a guest.

Enter the First Servingman.

FIRST SERVINGMAN What would you have, friend?
Whence are you? Here's no place for you: pray go
to the door!　　　　　　　　　　　　　*Exit.*

10 CORIOLANUS I have deserved no better entertainment,
In being Coriolanus.

Enter Second Servingman.

SECOND SERVINGMAN Whence are you, sir? Has the
porter his eyes in his head that he gives entrance to
such companions? Pray get you out.

15 CORIOLANUS Away!

SECOND SERVINGMAN "Away!" Get you away.

CORIOLANUS Now thou'rt troublesome.

IV.v.9 **to the door** out of doors　14 **companions** fellows (in bad sense)

SECOND SERVINGMAN Are you so brave? I'll have you talked with anon.

Enter Third Servingman; the first meets him.

THIRD SERVINGMAN What fellow's this?   20

FIRST SERVINGMAN A strange one as ever I looked on! I cannot get him out o' th' house. Prithee call my master to him.

THIRD SERVINGMAN What have you to do here, fellow? Pray you avoid the house.   25

CORIOLANUS Let me but stand; I will not hurt your hearth.

THIRD SERVINGMAN What are you?

CORIOLANUS A gentleman.

THIRD SERVINGMAN A marv'lous poor one.   30

CORIOLANUS True, so I am.

THIRD SERVINGMAN Pray you, poor gentleman, take up some other station; here's no place for you. Pray you avoid. Come.

CORIOLANUS Follow your function, go and batten on   35 cold bits.
                    Pushes him away from him.

THIRD SERVINGMAN What, you will not? Prithee, tell my master what a strange guest he has here.

SECOND SERVINGMAN And I shall.
                    Exit Second Servingman.

THIRD SERVINGMAN Where dwell'st thou?   40

CORIOLANUS Under the canopy.

THIRD SERVINGMAN Under the canopy!

CORIOLANUS Ay.

18 **brave** impudent 19 **anon** soon 25 **avoid** leave 30 **marv'lous** strangely 35 **Follow your function** do your regular work 35 **batten** grow fat 41 **canopy** sky (cf. "canopy" over a throne)

723

THIRD SERVINGMAN　Where's that?

45　CORIOLANUS　I' th' city of kites and crows.

THIRD SERVINGMAN　I' th' city of kites and crows! What
an ass it is! Then thou dwell'st with daws too?

CORIOLANUS　No, I serve not thy master.

THIRD SERVINGMAN　How, sir! Do you meddle with my
50　master?

CORIOLANUS　Ay; 'tis an honester service than to meddle with thy mistress. Thou prat'st, and prat'st;
serve with thy trencher. Hence!

Beats him away.

Enter Aufidius with the [Second] Servingman.

AUFIDIUS　Where is this fellow?

55　SECOND SERVINGMAN　Here, sir. I'd have beaten him
like a dog, but for disturbing the lords within.

AUFIDIUS　Whence com'st thou? What wouldst thou?
Thy name?
Why speak'st not? Speak, man. What's thy name?

CORIOLANUS　[*Unmuffling*]　　　　　If, Tullus,
Not yet thou know'st me, and, seeing me, dost not
60　Think me for the man I am, necessity
Commands me name myself.

AUFIDIUS　　　　　　What is thy name?

CORIOLANUS　A name unmusical to the Volscians' ears,
And harsh in sound to thine.

AUFIDIUS　　　　　　　Say, what's thy name?
Thou hast a grim appearance, and thy face
65　Bears a command in't. Though thy tackle's torn,
Thou show'st a noble vessel. What's thy name?

---

47 **daws** (foolish birds)　53 **trencher** wooden plate　60 **Think me** i.e., take
me　65 **a command** i.e., a look of authority　66 **show'st** appear'st

CORIOLANUS Prepare thy brow to frown. Know'st thou
  me yet?

AUFIDIUS I know thee not. Thy name!

CORIOLANUS My name is Caius Marcius, who hath done
  To thee particularly, and to all the Volsces,   70
  Great hurt and mischief; thereto witness may
  My surname, Coriolanus. The painful service,
  The extreme dangers, and the drops of blood
  Shed for my thankless country, are requited
  But with that surname—a good memory   75
  And witness of the malice and displeasure
  Which thou shouldst bear me. Only that name
    remains.
  The cruelty and envy of the people,
  Permitted by our dastard nobles, who
  Have all forsook me, hath devoured the rest;   80
  And suffered me by th' voice of slaves to be
  Whooped out of Rome. Now, this extremity
  Hath brought me to thy hearth; not out of hope
  (Mistake me not) to save my life; for if
  I had feared death, of all the men i' th' world   85
  I would have 'voided thee; but in mere spite,
  To be full quit of those my banishers,
  Stand I before thee here. Then if thou hast
  A heart of wreak in thee, that wilt revenge
  Thine own particular wrongs and stop those maims   90
  Of shame seen through thy country, speed thee
    straight
  And make my misery serve thy turn. So use it
  That my revengeful services may prove
  As benefits to thee; for I will fight
  Against my cank'red country with the spleen   95
  Of all the under fiends. But if so be

71 **mischief** serious harm 72 **painful** laborious 75 **memory** memorial
78 **envy** ill-will 87 **full quit of** fully revenged on (cf. "quits with") 89 **heart
of wreak** vengeful heart 90–91 **maims/Of shame** shameful wounds (e.g., the
Roman occupation of Corioli) 95 **cank'red** corrupted (by ingratitude and
envy) 95 **spleen** rage 96 **under fiends** devils in hell

Thou dar'st not this and that to prove more for-
    tunes
Thou'rt tired, then, in a word, I also am
Longer to live most weary, and present
100   My throat to thee and to thy ancient malice;
Which not to cut would show thee but a fool,
Since I have ever followed thee with hate,
Drawn tuns of blood out of thy country's breast,
And cannot live but to thy shame, unless
It be to do thee service.

105 AUFIDIUS   O Marcius, Marcius!
Each work thou hast spoke hath weeded from my
    heart
A root of ancient envy. If Jupiter
Should from yond cloud speak divine things,
And say " 'Tis true," I'd not believe them more
110   Than thee, all noble Marcius. Let me twine
Mine arms about that body, where against
My grainèd ash an hundred times hath broke
And scarred the moon with splinters. Here I clip
The anvil of my sword, and do contest
115   As hotly and as nobly with thy love
As ever in ambitious strength I did
Contend against thy valor. Know thou first,
I loved the maid I married; never man
Sighed truer breath. But that I see thee here,
120   Thou noble thing, more dances my rapt heart
Than when I first my wedded mistress saw
Bestride my threshold. Why, thou Mars, I tell thee,
We have a power on foot, and I had purpose
Once more to hew thy target from thy brawn,
125   Or lose mine arm for't. Thou hast beat me out
Twelve several times, and I have nightly since
Dreamt of encounters 'twixt thyself and me.
We have been down together in my sleep,

97 **prove more fortunes** try the chances of fortune further 103 **tuns**
casks 112 **grainèd ash** spear of ash, the grain showing 113 **clip** embrace
119 **that** because 120 **rapt** enraptured 123 **power on foot** force in the field
124 **target** shield 124 **brawn** brawny arm 125 **out** completely

Unbuckling helms, fisting each other's throat,
And waked half dead with nothing. Worthy
    Marcius,   130
Had we no other quarrel else to Rome but that
Thou art thence banished, we would muster all
From twelve to seventy, and pouring war
Into the bowels of ungrateful Rome,
Like a bold flood o'erbeat. O, come, go in,   135
And take our friendly senators by th' hands,
Who now are here, taking their leaves of me
Who am prepared against your territories,
Though not for Rome itself.

CORIOLANUS   You bless me, gods!

AUFIDIUS Therefore, most absolute sir, if thou wilt
    have   140
The leading of thine own revenges, take
Th' one half of my commission, and set down—
As best thou art experienced, since thou know'st
Thy country's strength and weakness—thine own
    ways,
Whether to knock against the gates of Rome,   145
Or rudely visit them in parts remote
To fright them ere destroy. But come in.
Let me commend thee first to those that shall
Say yea to thy desires. A thousand welcomes!
And more a friend than e'er an enemy;   150
Yet, Marcius, that was much. Your hand:
    most welcome!   *Exeunt*.

                Enter two of the Servingmen.

FIRST SERVINGMAN Here's a strange alteration!

SECOND SERVINGMAN By my hand, I had thought to
    have strucken him with a cudgel; and yet my mind
    gave me his clothes made a false report of him.   155

130 **waked** (I have) awakened   135 **o'erbeat** surge over (the land)   140 **absolute** perfect   142 **my commission** the forces under me   142 **set down** determine   151 s.d **Enter** (perhaps they come forward from backstage, since neither has been assigned an "*Exit*")   154–55 **my mind gave me** I had an idea

FIRST SERVINGMAN What an arm he has! He turned me about with his finger and his thumb, as one would set up a top.

SECOND SERVINGMAN Nay, I knew by his face that there
160   was something in him; he had, sir, a kind of face, methought—I cannot tell how to term it.

FIRST SERVINGMAN He had so, looking as it were— would I were hanged, but I thought there was more in him than I could think.

165   SECOND SERVINGMAN So did I, I'll be sworn. He is simply the rarest man i' th' world.

FIRST SERVINGMAN I think he is; but a greater soldier than he, you wot one.

SECOND SERVINGMAN Who, my master?

170   FIRST SERVINGMAN Nay, it's no matter for that.

SECOND SERVINGMAN Worth six on him.

FIRST SERVINGMAN Nay, not so neither. But I take him to be the greater soldier.

SECOND SERVINGMAN Faith, look you, one cannot tell
175   how to say that. For the defense of a town our general is excellent.

FIRST SERVINGMAN Ay, and for an assault too.

Enter the Third Servingman.

THIRD SERVINGMAN O slaves, I can tell you news— news, you rascals!

180   BOTH [FIRST AND SECOND SERVINGMEN] What, what, what? Let's partake.

THIRD SERVINGMAN I would not be a Roman, of all nations; I had as lief be a condemned man.

168–77 (the *First Servingman* is cautiously and cunningly vague in his references to the "greater soldier")   168 wot know   183 lief willingly

BOTH Wherefore? Wherefore?

THIRD SERVINGMAN Why here's he that was wont to 185
thwack our general—Caius Marcius.

FIRST SERVINGMAN Why do you say "thwack our
general"?

THIRD SERVINGMAN I do not say "thwack our general,"
but he was always good enough for him. 190

SECOND SERVINGMAN Come, we are fellows and
friends. He was ever too hard for him; I have heard
him say so himself.

FIRST SERVINGMAN He was too hard for him directly,
to say the troth on't. Before Corioles he scotched 195
him and notched him like a carbonado.

SECOND SERVINGMAN And he had been cannibally
given, he might have boiled and eaten him too.

FIRST SERVINGMAN But more of thy news?

THIRD SERVINGMAN Why, he is so made on here within 200
as if he were son and heir to Mars; set at upper end
o' th' table; no question asked him by any of the
senators but they stand bald before him. Our general
himself makes a mistress of him; sanctifies himself
with's hand, and turns up the white o' th' eye to his 205
discourse. But the bottom of the news is, our general
is cut i' th' middle and but one half of what he was
yesterday, for the other has half by the entreaty and
grant of the whole table. He'll go, he says, and sowl
the porter of Rome gates by th' ears. He will mow all 210
down before him, and leave his passage polled.

191 fellows comrades   194 directly plainly   195 scotched slashed   196 carbonado meat scored with knife, for broiling   200 so made on made so much
of   203 bald bareheaded   205 sanctifies himself with's hand touches his hand
as if it were a holy relic   205–06 turns up the white o' th' eye (in pious
wonder)   206 bottom last (jokingly for "the climax")   209–10 has ... table i.e.,
has half because all at the table beg him to take it, and give it to him   210 sowl
drag   212 polled cleared (used of cutting hair)

SECOND SERVINGMAN And he's as like to do't as any man I can imagine.

215 THIRD SERVINGMAN Do't! He will do't; for look you, sir, he has as many friends as enemies; which friends, sir, as it were, durst not (look you, sir) show themselves (as we term it) his friends whilst he's in directitude.

220 FIRST SERVINGMAN Directitude! What's that?

THIRD SERVINGMAN But when they shall see, sir, his crest up again and the man in blood, they will out of their burrows (like conies after rain) and revel all with him.

225 FIRST SERVINGMAN But when goes this forward?

THIRD SERVINGMAN Tomorrow, today, presently. You shall have the drum struck up this afternoon. 'Tis as it were a parcel of their feast, and to be executed ere they wipe their lips.

230 SECOND SERVINGMAN Why, then we shall have a stirring world again. This peace is nothing but to rust iron, increase tailors, and breed ballad-makers.

FIRST SERVINGMAN Let me have war, say I; it exceeds peace as far as day does night; it's sprightly walk-
235 ing, audible, and full of vent. Peace is a very apoplexy, lethargy; mulled, deaf, sleepy, insensi-ble; a getter of more bastard children than war's a destroyer of men.

SECOND SERVINGMAN 'Tis so; and as wars in some sort
240 may be said to be a ravisher, so it cannot be denied but peace is a great maker of cuckolds.

FIRST SERVINGMAN Ay, and it makes men hate one another.

219 directitude (comic mistake for "discredit"?)   222 crest up (like an animal aroused)   222 in blood in top condition   223 conies rabbits   226 presently now   228 parcel part   235 audible of good hearing   235 full of vent with plenty of outlets for energy (?: cf. I.i.226)   236 mulled dulled (like wine sweetened and heated)

THIRD SERVINGMAN Reason: because they then less
   need one another. The wars for my money. I hope   245
   to see Romans as cheap as Volscians. They are
   rising, they are rising.

BOTH [FIRST AND SECOND SERVINGMEN] In, in, in, in!
                                       Exeunt.

[Scene VI. *Rome. A public place*.]

Enter the two Tribunes, Sicinius and Brutus.

SICINIUS We hear not of him, neither need we fear
   him;
   His remedies are tame. The present peace
   And quietness of the people, which before
   Were in wild hurry, here do make his friends
   Blush that the world goes well; who rather had,   5
   Though they themselves did suffer by't, behold
   Dissentious numbers pest'ring streets than see
   Our tradesmen singing in their shops, and going
   About their functions friendly.

BRUTUS We stood to't in good time.   10

               Enter Menenius.

                           Is this Menenius?

SICINIUS 'Tis he, 'tis he. O, he is grown most kind
   Of late. Hail, sir!

MENENIUS   Hail to you both!

SICINIUS Your Coriolanus is not much missed

247 **rising** getting up from table   **IV.vi.2 His remedies are tame** his attempts
to "cure" the state are (now) harmless (cf. "dangerous physic," III.i.154)
4 hurry commotion   **7 pest'ring** filling with disturbance   **10 stood to't** made
an issue of it

But with his friends. The commonwealth doth
  stand,
And so would do, were he more angry at it.

MENENIUS All's well; and might have been much
    better, if
He could have temporized.

SICINIUS   Where is he, hear you?

MENENIUS Nay, I hear nothing. His mother and his
    wife
Hear nothing from him.

Enter three or four Citizens.

ALL [CITIZENS] The gods preserve you both!

SICINIUS   Good-e'en, our neighbors.

BRUTUS Good-e'en to you all, good-e'en to you all.

FIRST CITIZEN Ourselves, our wives, and children, on
    our knees,
Are bound to pray for you both.

SICINIUS   Live, and thrive!

BRUTUS Farewell, kind neighbors. We wished
    Coriolanus
Had loved you as we did.

ALL [CITIZENS]   Now the gods keep you!

BOTH TRIBUNES Farewell, farewell.

Exeunt Citizens.

SICINIUS This is a happier and more comely time
Than when these fellows ran about the streets
Crying confusion.

BRUTUS   Caius Marcius was
A worthy officer i' th' war, but insolent,
O'ercome with pride, ambitious past all thinking,
Self-loving——

20 **Good-e'en** good evening 27 **comely** respectable 29 **Crying confusion**
calling for disorder

SICINIUS   And affecting one sole throne,
Without assistance.

MENENIUS   I think not so.

SICINIUS We should by this, to all our lamentation,
  If he had gone forth consul, found it so.   35

BRUTUS The gods have well prevented it, and Rome
  Sits safe and still without him.

Enter an Aedile.

AEDILE   Worthy tribunes,
  There is a slave, whom we have put in prison,
  Reports the Volsces with two several powers
  Are ent'red in the Roman territories,   40
  And with the deepest malice of the war
  Destroy what lies before 'em.

MENENIUS   'Tis Aufidius,
  Who, hearing of our Marcius' banishment,
  Thrusts forth his horns again into the world,
  Which were inshelled when Marcius stood for
    Rome,   45
  And durst not once peep out.

SICINIUS   Come, what talk you
  Of Marcius?

BRUTUS Go see this rumorer whipped. It cannot be
  The Volsces dare break with us.

MENENIUS   Cannot be!
  We have record that very well it can;   50
  And three examples of the like hath been
  Within my age. But reason with the fellow,
  Before you punish him, where he heard this,
  Lest you shall chance to whip your information
  And beat the messenger who bids beware   55
  Of what is to be dreaded.

32 **affecting** aiming at   33 **Without assistance** not sharing his powers with
others   35 **found** have found   39 **several powers** separate forces   44 **horns**
(like a snail)   52 **reason with** talk with

SICINIUS   Tell not me:
I know this cannot be.

BRUTUS   Not possible.

Enter a Messenger.

MESSENGER The nobles in great earnestness are going
All to the Senate House. Some news is coming
60   That turns their countenances.

SICINIUS   'Tis this slave—
Go whip him 'fore the people's eyes—his raising,
Nothing but his report.

MESSENGER   Yes, worthy sir,
The slave's report is seconded; and more,
More fearful, is delivered.

SICINIUS   What more fearful?

65   MESSENGER It is spoke freely out of many mouths,
How probable I do not know, that Marcius,
Joined with Aufidius, leads a power 'gainst Rome,
And vows revenge as spacious as between
The young'st and oldest thing.

SICINIUS   This is most likely!

70   BRUTUS Raised only that the weaker sort may wish
Good Marcius home again.

SICINIUS   The very trick on't.

MENENIUS This is unlikely:
He and Aufidius can no more atone
Than violent'st contrariety.

Enter [a second] Messenger.

75   SECOND MESSENGER You are sent for to the Senate.
A fearful army, led by Caius Marcius

---

60 **turns** changes   61 **his raising** his starting (i.e., the rumor; note comma and the following explanatory phrase)   63 **seconded** confirmed (by further reports)   68–69 **as spacious ... thing** covering the span between youngest and oldest, i.e., the whole population   73 **atone** be reconciled

Associated with Aufidius, rages
Upon our territories, and have already
O'erborne their way, consumed with fire, and took
What lay before them.   80

Enter Cominius.

COMINIUS O, you have made good work!

MENENIUS   What news? What news?

COMINIUS You have holp to ravish your own daugh-
    ters and
To melt the city leads upon your pates,
To see your wives dishonored to your noses——

MENENIUS What's the news? What's the news?   85

COMINIUS Your temples burnèd in their cement, and
Your franchises, whereon you stood, confined
Into an auger's bore.

MENENIUS   Pray now, your news?——
You have made fair work, I fear me.—Pray, your
    news?——
If Marcius should be joined wi' th' Volscians——

COMINIUS   If!   90
He is their god; he leads them like a thing
Made by some other deity than Nature,
That shapes man better; and they follow him
Against us brats with no less confidence
Than boys pursuing summer butterflies,   95
Or butchers killing flies.

MENENIUS   You have made good work,
You and your apron-men; you that stood so much
Upon the voice of occupation and
The breath of garlic-eaters!

COMINIUS   He'll shake
Your Rome about your ears.

79 **O'erborne their way** (like a stream) overflowed everything in their way
83 **leads** roofs 84 **to** before 87 **franchises, whereon you stood** rights on
which you insisted 97 **apron-men** artisans 98 **occupation** manual workers

100 MENENIUS   As Hercules
    Did shake down mellow fruit. You have made fair
        work!

BRUTUS But is this true, sir?

COMINIUS   Ay; and you'll look pale
    Before you find it other. All the regions
    Do smilingly revolt, and who resists
105 Are mocked for valiant ignorance,
    And perish constant fools. Who is't can blame him?
    Your enemies and his find something in him.

MENENIUS We are all undone, unless
    The noble man have mercy.

COMINIUS   Who shall ask it?
110 The tribunes cannot do't for shame; the people
    Deserve such pity of him as the wolf
    Does of the shepherds. For his best friends, if they
    Should say "Be good to Rome," they charged him
        even
    As those should do that had deserved his hate,
    And therein showed like enemies.

115 MENENIUS   'Tis true:
    If he were putting to my house the brand
    That should consume it, I have not the face
    To say "Beseech you, cease." You have made fair
        hands,
    You and your crafts! You have crafted fair!

COMINIUS   You have brought
120 A trembling upon Rome, such as was never
    S' incapable of help.

TRIBUNES   Say not we brought it.

106 constant loyal   113 charged would attack, urge (both senses relevant)
115 showed would show   118 made fair hands handled matters finely
119 crafted fair plied your trade (of cunning) beautifully   121 S' incapable so
unsusceptible

MENENIUS How! Was't we? We loved him, but, like
  beasts
  And cowardly nobles, gave way unto your clusters,
  Who did hoot him out o' th' city.

COMINIUS   But I fear
  They'll roar him in again. Tullus Aufidius,   125
  The second name of men, obeys his points
  As if he were his officer. Desperation
  Is all the policy, strength, and defense,
  That Rome can make against them.

                    Enter a troop of Citizens.

MENENIUS   Here come the clusters.
  And is Aufidius with him? You are they   130
  That made the air unwholesome when you cast
  Your stinking greasy caps in hooting at
  Coriolanus' exile. Now he's coming,
  And not a hair upon a soldier's head
  Which will not prove a whip. As many coxcombs   135
  As you threw caps up will he tumble down,
  And pay you for your voices. 'Tis no matter;
  If he could burn us all into one coal,
  We have deserved it.

OMNES Faith, we hear fearful news.

FIRST CITIZEN   For mine own part,   140
  When I said banish him, I said 'twas pity.

SECOND CITIZEN And so did I.

THIRD CITIZEN And so did I; and, to say the truth, so
  did very many of us. That we did, we did for the
  best; and though we willingly consented to his ban-   145
  ishment, yet it was against our will.

COMINIUS Y'are goodly things, you voices!

---

123 **clusters** crowds 126 **second name of men** second in renown (to
Coriolanus) 126 **points** directions (?) 135 **coxcombs** fools' heads (cf. costume
of a fool) 137 **voices** votes 138 **coal** piece of burned fuel (cf. charcoal)

MENENIUS   You have made
  Good work, you and your cry! Shall's to the
      Capitol?

COMINIUS O, ay, what else?   *Exeunt both*.

150 SICINIUS Go masters, get you home; be not dismayed;
  These are a side that would be glad to have
  This true which they so seem to fear. Go home,
  And show no sign of fear.

FIRST CITIZEN The gods be good to us! Come, masters,
155 let's home. I ever said we were i' th' wrong when we
  banished him.

SECOND CITIZEN So did we all. But come, let's home.
                                      Exit Citizens.

BRUTUS I do not like this news.

SICINIUS Nor I.

160 BRUTUS Let's to the Capitol. Would half my wealth
  Would buy this for a lie!

SICINIUS   Pray, let's go.
                                  Exeunt Tribunes.

[Scene VII. *A camp not far from Rome*.]

Enter Aufidius with his Lieutenant.

AUFIDIUS Do they still fly to th' Roman?

LIEUTENANT I do not know what witchcraft's in him,
      but
  Your soldiers use him as the grace 'fore meat,
  Their talk at table and their thanks at end;
5   And you are dark'ned in this action sir,
  Even by your own.

148 **cry** pack   148 **Shall's** shall us (we)   151 **side** faction   IV.vii.5 **dark'ned**
put in the shade   6 **your own** your own men

AUFIDIUS   I cannot help it now,
Unless by using means I lame the foot
Of our design. He bears himself more proudlier,
Even to my person, than I thought he would
When first I did embrace him; yet his nature   10
In that's no changeling, and I must excuse
What cannot be amended.

LIEUTENANT   Yet I wish, sir—
I mean for your particular—you had not
Joined in commission with him, but either
Have borne the action of yourself, or else   15
To him had left it solely.

AUFIDIUS I understand thee well; and be thou sure,
When he shall come to his account, he knows not
What I can urge against him. Although it seems,
And so he thinks, and is no less apparent   20
To th' vulgar eye, that he bears all things fairly,
And shows good husbandry for the Volscian state,
Fights dragon-like, and does achieve as soon
As draw his sword. Yet he hath left undone
That which shall break his neck or hazard mine,   25
Whene'er we come to our account.

LIEUTENANT Sir, I beseech you, think you he'll carry
    Rome?

AUFIDIUS All places yields to him ere he sits down,
And the nobility of Rome are his;
The senators and patricians love him too.   30
The tribunes are no soldiers, and their people
Will be as rash in the repeal, as hasty
To expel him thence. I think he'll be to Rome
As is the osprey to the fish, who takes it
By sovereignty of nature. First he was   35
A noble servant to them, but he could not

7 **using means** taking steps   11 **no changeling** i.e., he is the self-same man
13 **your particular** your own sake   14 **Joined in commission** shared the
command   22 **husbandry** management   28 **sits down** lays siege   34 **osprey**
fish hawk   35 **By sovereignty of nature** (refers to the osprey's supposed power
of subduing its prey before touching it)

Carry his honors even. Whether 'twas pride,
Which out of daily fortune ever taints
The happy man; whether defect of judgment,
40 To fail in the disposing of those chances
Which he was lord of; or whether nature,
Not to be other than one thing, not moving
From th' casque to th' cushion, but commanding
      peace
Even with the same austerity and garb
45 As he controlled the war; but one of these—
As he hath spices of them all—not all,
For I dare so far free him—made him feared,
So hated, and so banished. But he has a merit
To choke it in the utt'rance. So our virtues
50 Lie in th' interpretation of the time;
And power, unto itself most commendable,
Hath not a tomb so evident as a chair
T' extol what it hath done.
One fire drives out one fire; one nail, one nail;
Rights by rights founder, strengths by strengths do
55   fail.
Come, let's away. When, Caius, Rome is thine,
Thou art poor'st of all; then shortly art thou mine.
                                                      Exeunt.

37 **even** (and keep his balance)   38 **daily fortune ever taints** success coming
day after day always infects   39 **happy** lucky   43 **casque** helmet, i.e., military
life   43 **cushion** i.e., position of authority in civil life; cf. III.i.101   46 **spices**
flavors, i.e., traces   48–49 **a merit/To choke it in the utt'rance** a merit that is
nullified in the very act of being expressed (because of faults inseparable from the
particular virtues being praised)   50 **the time** the age (our contemporaries)
52 **chair** (of the speaker who praises the achievements made possible by "power,"
line 51; probably with reference to the Roman rostrum, or speakers' platform)
54–55 **One fire ... fail** (examples of the self-destructive process described in lines
48–53)

ACT V

[Scene I. *Rome. A public place.*]

Enter Menenius, Cominius, Sicinius, Brutus,
the two Tribunes, with others.

MENENIUS No, I'll not go. You hear what he hath
    said
  Which was sometime his general, who loved him
  In a most dear particular. He called me father;
  But what o' that? Go you that banished him,
  A mile before his tent fall down, and knee   5
  The way into his mercy. Nay, if he coyed
  To hear Cominius speak, I'll keep at home.

COMINIUS He would not seem to know me.

MENENIUS   Do you hear?

COMINIUS Yet one time he did call me by my name.
  I urged our old acquaintance, and the drops   10
  That we have bled together. Coriolanus
  He would not answer to; forbad all names;
  He was a kind of nothing, titleless,
  Till he had forged himself a name o' th' fire
  Of burning Rome.

V.i.2 *sometime* formerly 3 *a most dear particular* a most precious
intimacy 5–6 *knee/The way* make your way on your knees 6 *coyed* showed
reluctance

741

15 MENENIUS   Why, so! You have made good work!
    A pair of tribunes that have wracked fair Rome
    To make coals cheap! A noble memory!

    COMINIUS I minded him how royal 'twas to pardon
    When it was less expected; he replied,
20 It was a bare petition of a state
    To one whom they had punished.

    MENENIUS   Very well.
    Could he say less?

    COMINIUS I offered to awaken his regard
    For's private friends. His answer to me was,
25 He could not stay to pick them in a pile
    Of noisome musty chaff. He said 'twas folly,
    For one poor grain or two, to leave unburnt
    And still to nose th' offense.

    MENENIUS   For one poor grain or two!
    I am one of those; his mother, wife, his child,
30 And this brave fellow too, we are the grains;
    You are the musty chaff, and you are smelt
    Above the moon. We must be burnt for you.

    SICINIUS Nay, pray, be patient; if you refuse your aid
    In this so never-needed help, yet do not
35 Upbraid's with our distress. But, sure, if you
    Would be your country's pleader, your good tongue,
    More than the instant army we can make,
    Might stop our countryman.

    MENENIUS   No, I'll not meddle.

    SICINIUS Pray you, go to him.

    MENENIUS   What should I do?

40 BRUTUS Only make trial what your love can do
    For Rome, towards Marcius.

16 **wracked** ruined   17 **coals** charcoal   18 **minded** reminded   20 **bare**
mere   23 **offered** tried   28 **nose th' offense** smell the offensive stuff   34 **so
never-needed** never so needed (as now)   37 **the instant army we can make**
the army we can raise at this time   41 **towards** in relation to

742

MENENIUS   Well, and say that Marcius
Return me, as Cominius is returned,
Unheard—what then?
But as a discontented friend, grief-shot
With his unkindness? Say't be so?

SICINIUS   Yet your good will   45
Must have that thanks from Rome after the measure
As you intended well.

MENENIUS   I'll undertake't:
I think he'll hear me. Yet to bite his lip
And hum at good Cominius much unhearts me.
He was not taken well; he had not dined.   50
The veins unfilled, our blood is cold, and then
We pout upon the morning, are unapt
To give or to forgive; but when we have stuffed
These pipes and these conveyances of our blood
With wine and feeding, we have suppler souls   55
Than in our priestlike fasts. Therefore I'll watch
   him
Till he be dieted to my request,
And then I'll set upon him.

BRUTUS You know the very road into his kindness,
And cannot lose your way.

MENENIUS   Good faith, I'll prove him,   60
Speed how it will. I shall ere long have knowledge
Of my success.   *Exit*.

COMINIUS   He'll never hear him.

SICINIUS   Not?

COMINIUS I tell you he does sit in gold, his eye
Red as 'twould burn Rome, and his injury
The jailer to his pity. I kneeled before him;   65

44 **grief-shot** struck by grief   46–47 **after the measure/As you intended well**
in proportion to your good intentions   49 **unhearts** discourages   50 **taken well**
approached at a good time   54 **conveyances** channels   57 **dieted to** prepared
for by feeding   60 **prove** make trial of   61 **Speed** turn out   64 **injury** sense of
the wrong done to him

'Twas very faintly he said "Rise"; dismissed me
Thus with his speechless hand. What he would do
He sent in writing after me, what he would not,
Bound with an oath to yield to his conditions;
70   So that all hope is vain,
Unless his noble mother and his wife,
Who (as I hear) mean to solicit him
For mercy to his country. Therefore, let's hence,
And with our fair entreaties haste them on.

                         Exeunt.

[Scene II. *Entrance of the Volscian camp
before Rome.*]

Enter Menenius to the Watch on Guard.

FIRST WATCH   Stay. Whence are you?

SECOND WATCH   Stand, and go back.

MENENIUS   You guard like men, 'tis well; but, by your
     leave,
   I am an officer of state, and come
   To speak with Coriolanus.

FIRST WATCH   From whence?

MENENIUS   From Rome.

FIRST WATCH   You may not pass, you must return: our
5   general
   Will no more hear from thence.

67–69 **What ... yield** i.e., he sent a written message saying what he would do and
what he would not, all this (the statement of terms) being bound with an oath that
we should yield (text probably corrupt)   70 **vain** (because the conditions are
ruinous)   71 **Unless** except for (or perhaps "solicit him," line 72, is to be
understood: "unless his noble mother and his wife solicit him")

SECOND WATCH You'll see your Rome embraced with
   fire, before
   You'll speak with Coriolanus.

MENENIUS   Good my friends,
   If you have heard your general talk of Rome
   And of his friends there, it is lots to blanks   10
   My name hath touched your ears: it is Menenius.

FIRST WATCH Be it so; go back. The virtue of your
   name
   Is not here passable.

MENENIUS   I tell thee, fellow,
   Thy general is my lover. I have been
   The book of his good acts whence men have read   15
   His fame unparalleled—haply amplified;
   For I have ever verified my friends
   (Of whom he's chief) with all the size that verity
   Would without lapsing suffer. Nay, sometimes,
   Like to a bowl upon a subtle ground,   20
   I have tumbled past the throw, and in his praise
   Have almost stamped the leasing. Therefore,
   fellow,
   I must have leave to pass.

FIRST WATCH Faith, sir, if you had told as many lies
   in his behalf as you have uttered words in your   25
   own, you should not pass here; no, though it were
   as virtuous to lie as to live chastely. Therefore go
   back.

MENENIUS Prithee, fellow, remember my name is
   Menenius, always factionary on the party of your   30
   general.

V.ii.10 **lots to blanks** (more than an even chance; "lots" refers to tickets in a
lottery taking prizes; "blanks," to those not taking prizes)   13 **passable** current
(of money, but with a pun on "password")   17 **verified** testified to the merit
of   19 **lapsing** slipping (into error)   20 **subtle** deceptive   21 **tumbled past
the throw** rolled beyond the proper distance   22 **stamped** given currency to (cf.
"stamp" a coin)   22 **leasing** falsehood   30 **factionary** an active worker

SECOND WATCH Howsoever you have been his liar, as you say you have, I am one that, telling true under him, must say you cannot pass. Therefore go back.

35 MENENIUS Has he dined, canst thou tell? For I would not speak with him till after dinner.

FIRST WATCH You are a Roman, are you?

MENENIUS I am, as thy general is.

FIRST WATCH Then you should hate Rome, as he does.
40 Can you, when you have pushed out your gates the very defender of them, and in a violent popular ignorance given your enemy your shield, think to front his revenges with the easy groans of old women, the virginal palms of your daughters, or
45 with the palsied intercession of such a decayed dotant as you seem to be? Can you think to blow out the intended fire your city is ready to flame in, with such weak breath as this? No, you are deceived; therefore, back to Rome, and prepare for
50 your execution. You are condemned; our general has sworn you out of reprieve and pardon.

MENENIUS Sirrah, if thy captain knew I were here, he would use me with estimation.

FIRST WATCH Come, my captain knows you not.

55 MENENIUS I mean, thy general.

FIRST WATCH My general cares not for you. Back, I say; go, lest I let forth your half-pint of blood. Back—that's the utmost of your having. Back.

MENENIUS Nay, but, fellow, fellow——

Enter Coriolanus with Aufidius.

60 CORIOLANUS What's the matter?

MENENIUS Now, you companion, I'll say an errand

---

43 front face   46 dotant dotard   53 estimation esteem   58 of your having you can get   61 companion fellow   61 say an errand give a message

for you; you shall know now that I am in estimation; you shall perceive that a Jack guardant cannot office me from my son Coriolanus. Guess but
by my entertainment with him if thou stand'st not   65
i' th' state of hanging, or of some death more long
in spectatorship and crueller in suffering; behold
now presently, and swoon for what's to come upon
thee. [*To Coriolanus*] The glorious gods sit in
hourly synod about thy particular prosperity, and   70
love thee no worse than thy old father Menenius
does! O my son, my son! Thou art preparing fire
for us; look thee, here's water to quench it. I was
hardly moved to come to thee; but being assured
none but myself could move thee, I have been   75
blown out of your gates with sighs; and conjure
thee to pardon Rome and thy petitionary countrymen. The good gods assuage thy wrath, and turn
the dregs of it upon this varlet here; this, who, like
a block, hath denied my access to thee.   80

CORIOLANUS Away!

MENENIUS How! Away!

CORIOLANUS Wife, mother, child, I know not. My
    affairs
Are servanted to others. Though I owe
My revenge properly, my remission lies   85
In Volscian breasts. That we have been familiar,
Ingrate forgetfulness shall poison rather
Than pity note how much. Therefore be gone.
Mine ears against your suits are stronger than
Your gates against my force. Yet, for I loved thee,   90
Take this along; I writ it for thy sake,

63 **Jack guardant** wretch of a sentry 64 **office me** use his office to keep me
65 **entertainment** reception 74 **hardly** with difficulty 76 **your** (of Rome)
77 **petitionary** who are asking for mercy 80 **block** blockhead 84 **servanted**
subject (servant-like) 84–85 **I owe/My revenge properly** my revenge belongs
to me alone 85 **remission** power to pardon 86 **That we have been familiar**
our intimacy in the past 87 **Ingrate forgetfulness** my ungrateful
forgetfulness 88 **how much** (how much "we have been familiar," how great the
intimacy was) 90 **for** because

And would have sent it. Another word, Menenius,
I will not hear thee speak. This man, Aufidius,
Was my beloved in Rome; yet thou behold'st.

95 AUFIDIUS You keep a constant temper.

> *Exeunt [Coriolanus and Aufidius].*
> *Manet the Guard and Menenius.*

FIRST WATCH Now, sir, is your name Menenius?

SECOND WATCH 'Tis a spell, you see, of much power.
You know the way home again.

FIRST WATCH Do you hear how we are shent for
100 keeping your greatness back?

SECOND WATCH What cause, do you think, I have to
swoon?

MENENIUS I neither care for th' world nor your general. For such things as you, I can scarce think
105 there's any, y'are so slight. He that hath a will to
die by himself fears it not from another. Let your
general do his worst. For you, be that you are,
long; and your misery increase with your age! I
say to you, as I was said to, Away!   *Exit.*

110 FIRST WATCH A noble fellow, I warrant him.

SECOND WATCH The worthy fellow is our general. He's
the rock, the oak not to be wind-shaken.

> *Exit Watch.*

---

95 **constant** loyal, true   99 **shent** scolded   106 **by himself** by his own hand

[Scene III. *The tent of Coriolanus.*]

Enter Coriolanus and Aufidius [with others].

CORIOLANUS We will before the walls of Rome to-
    morrow
Set down our host. My partner in this action,
You must report to th' Volscian lords how plainly
I have borne this business.

AUFIDIUS   Only their ends
You have respected; stopped your ears against   5
The general suit of Rome; never admitted
A private whisper—no, not with such friends
That thought them sure of you.

CORIOLANUS   This last old man,
Whom with a cracked heart I have sent to Rome,
Loved me above the measure of a father,   10
Nay, godded me indeed. Their latest refuge
Was to send him; for whose old love I have
(Though I showed sourly to him) once more
    offered
The first conditions, which they did refuse
And cannot now accept; to grace him only   15
That thought he could do more, a very little
I have yielded to. Fresh embassies and suits,
Nor from the state nor private friends, hereafter
Will I lend ear to. (*Shout within.*) Ha! What shout
    is this?
Shall I be tempted to infringe my vow   20
In the same time 'tis made? I will not.

V.iii.2 **Set down** i.e., in a siege 3 **plainly** openly 4 **borne** conducted
11 **godded me** made me a god 11 **latest refuge** last resource 13 **showed**
appeared 15 **grace** honor 18 **Nor** neither

Enter Virgilia, Volumnia, Valeria, young Marcius,
with Attendants.

My wife comes foremost; then the honored mold
Wherein this trunk was framed, and in her hand
The grandchild to her blood. But out, affection!
25   All bond and privilege of nature, break!
Let it be virtuous to be obstinate.
What is that curtsy worth? Or those doves' eyes,
Which can make gods forsworn? I melt, and am not
Of stronger earth than others. My mother bows,
30   As if Olympus to a molehill should
In supplication nod; and my young boy
Hath an aspect of intercession which
Great Nature cries "Deny not." Let the Volsces
Plough Rome, and harrow Italy! I'll never
35   Be such a gosling to obey instinct, but stand
As if a man were author of himself
And knew no other kin.

VIRGILIA   My lord and husband!

CORIOLANUS These eyes are not the same I wore in
        Rome.

VIRGILIA The sorrow that delivers us thus changed
        Makes you think so.

40   CORIOLANUS   Like a dull actor now,
I have forgot my part and I am out,
Even to a full disgrace.—Best of my flesh,
Forgive my tyranny; but do not say,
For that, "Forgive our Romans." O, a kiss
45   Long as my exile, sweet as my revenge!
Now, by the jealous queen of heaven, that kiss
I carried from thee, dear, and my true lip
Hath virgined it e'er since. You gods! I prate,
And the most noble mother of the world

22 **mold** form (also "earth")   23 **trunk** body   28–29 **not/Of stronger earth** cf.
"our common clay"   30 **Olympus** a mountain, home of the Greek gods   35 **to**
as to   39 **delivers** presents   41 **out** speechless ("stuck")   43 **tyranny**
cruelty   46 **queen of heaven** Juno, guardian of marriage   48 **prate** babble

Leave unsaluted. Sink, my knee, i' th' earth; [*Kneels.*]   50
Of thy deep duty more impression show
Than that of common sons.

VOLUMNIA   O, stand up blest!
Whilst with no softer cushion than the flint
I kneel before thee, and unproperly
Show duty, as mistaken all this while   55
Between the child and parent.   [*Kneels.*]

CORIOLANUS   What's this?
Your knees to me? To your corrected son?
Then let the pebbles on the hungry beach
Fillip the stars! Then let the mutinous winds
Strike the proud cedars 'gainst the fiery sun,   60
Murd'ring impossibility, to make
What cannot be, slight work.

VOLUMNIA   Thou art my warrior;
I holp to frame thee. Do you know this lady?

CORIOLANUS The noble sister of Publicola,
The moon of Rome, chaste as the icicle   65
That's curdied by the frost from purest snow
And hangs on Dian's temple—dear Valeria!

VOLUMNIA This is a poor epitome of yours,
Which by th' interpretation of full time
May show like all yourself.

CORIOLANUS   The god of soldiers,   70
With the consent of supreme Jove, inform
Thy thoughts with nobleness, that thou mayst
    prove
To shame unvulnerable, and stick i' th' wars

51 **duty** reverence   51 **impression** i.e., "i' th' earth"   54 **unproperly** (defined by lines 55–56: in a way that does not belong to me, as though I had always misunderstood the relation between child and parent)   57 **corrected** who is corrected (by your kneeling)   58 **hungry** barren   59 **Fillip** strike   66 **curdied** congealed   68 **epitome** brief but comprehensive version of a larger work   68 **of yours** belonging to you, of you   69 **time** ("time" is compared to a commentator on a text)   70 **show** appear   70 **god of soldiers** Mars, Coriolanus' special divinity   71 **inform** imbue (give an inner form or character to)   73 **stick** stand out

Like a great sea-mark, standing every flaw,
And saving those that eye thee!

75 VOLUMNIA   Your knee, sirrah.

CORIOLANUS That's my brave boy!

VOLUMNIA Even he, your wife, this lady, and myself
Are suitors to you.

CORIOLANUS   I beseech you, peace!
Or, if you'd ask, remember this before:
80   The thing I have forsworn to grant may never
Be held by you denials. Do not bid me
Dismiss my soldiers, or capitulate
Again with Rome's mechanics. Tell me not
Wherein I seem unnatural. Desire not
85   T' allay my rages and revenges with
Your colder reasons.

VOLUMNIA   O, no more, no more!
You have said you will not grant us anything;
For we have nothing else to ask but that
Which you deny already. Yet we will ask,
90   That, if you fail in our request, the blame
May hang upon your hardness. Therefore hear us.

CORIOLANUS Aufidius, and you Volsces, mark; for
we'll
Hear nought from Rome in private. Your request?

VOLUMNIA Should we be silent and not speak, our
raiment
95   And state of bodies would bewray what life
We have led since thy exile. Think with thyself
How more unfortunate than all living women
Are we come hither; since that thy sight, which
should

74 a great sea-mark some prominent object that guides mariners (cf. "land-mark," the common modern term) 74 flaw gust of wind 75 sirrah sir (affectionately) 80 forsworn sworn not to 81 denials i.e., refusals to all of you (therefore, plural) 82 capitulate arrange terms 83 mechanics manual laborers 90 fall in fail to grant 95 bewray reveal

Make our eyes flow with joy, hearts dance with
    comforts,
Constrains them weep and shake with fear and
    sorrow,   100
Making the mother, wife, and child, to see
The son, the husband, and the father, tearing
His country's bowels out. And to poor we
Thine enmity's most capital: thou barr'st us
Our prayers to the gods, which is a comfort   105
That all but we enjoy. For how can we,
Alas, how can we for our country pray,
Whereto we are bound, together with thy victory,
Whereto we are bound? Alack, or we must lose
The country, our dear nurse, or else thy person,   110
Our comfort in the country. We must find
An evident calamity, though we had
Our wish, which side should win; for either thou
Must as a foreign recreant be led
With manacles through our streets, or else   115
Triumphantly tread on thy country's ruin,
And bear the palm for having bravely shed
Thy wife and children's blood. For myself, son,
I purpose not to wait on fortune till
These wars determine. If I can not persuade thee 120
Rather to show a noble grace to both parts
Than seek the end of one, thou shalt no sooner
March to assault thy country than to tread
(Trust to't, thou shalt not) on thy mother's womb
That brought thee to this world.

VIRGILIA.   Ay, and mine,   125
That brought you forth this boy, to keep your name
Living to time.

BOY   'A shall not tread on me;
I'll run away till I am bigger, but then I'll fight.

103 we (for "us") 104 capital deadly 109 or either 112 evident
certain 114 recreant traitor 120 determine come to an end 121 grace
consideration, favor 121 parts sides (parties) 126–27 keep your name/
Living to time perpetuate your name (keep living as long as time lasts)
127 'A he

CORIOLANUS Not of a woman's tenderness to be,
130   Requires nor child nor woman's face to see.
        I have sat too long.

VOLUMNIA   Nay, go not from us thus.
                                              [*Rises.*]
        If it were so that our request did tend
        To save the Romans, thereby to destroy
        The Volsces whom you serve, you might condemn
            us,
135   As poisonous of your honor. No, our suit
        Is that you reconcile them; while the Volsces
        May say "This mercy we have showed," the
            Romans,
        "This we received"; and each in either side
        Give the all-hail to thee, and cry "Be blest
        For making up this peace!" Thou know'st, great
140   son,
        The end of war's uncertain; but this certain,
        That, if thou conquer Rome, the benefit
        Which thou shalt thereby reap is such a name
        Whose repetition will be dogged with curses,
145   Whose chronicle thus writ, "The man was noble,
        But with his last attempt he wiped it out,
        Destroyed his country, and his name remains
        To th' ensuing age abhorred." Speak to me, son.
        Thou hast affected the fine strains of honor,
150   To imitate the graces of the gods,
        To tear with thunder the wide cheeks o' th' air,
        And yet to charge thy sulphur with a bolt
        That should but rive an oak. Why dost not speak?
        Think'st thou it honorable for a noble man
155   Still to remember wrongs? Daughter, speak you:
        He cares not for your weeping. Speak thou, boy:
        Perhaps thy childishness will move him more

145 **writ** will be written 146 **attempt** undertaking 146 **it** (his nobility)
149 **affected the fine strains** aimed at the refinements 150 **graces of the gods**
(qualities that give the gods splendor and power; illustrated with irony, lines
151–53) 152 **charge** load (make heavy, or "load," as of a gun) 152 **sulphur**
lightning

Than can our reasons. There's no man in the world
More bound to's mother, yet here he lets me prate
Like one i' th' stocks. Thou hast never in thy life   160
Showed thy dear mother any courtesy,
When she (poor hen) fond of no second brood,
Has clocked thee to the wars, and safely home
Loaden with honor. Say my request's unjust,
And spurn me back. But if it be not so,   165
Thou art not honest, and the gods will plague thee,
That thou restrain'st from me the duty which
To a mother's part belongs. He turns away.
Down, ladies! Let us shame him with our knees.
To his surname Coriolanus 'longs more pride   170
Than pity to our prayers. Down! An end;
This is the last. So we will home to Rome,
And die among our neighbors. Nay, behold's!
This boy, that cannot tell what he would have,
But kneels and holds up hands for fellowship,   175
Does reason our petition with more strength
Than thou hast to deny't. Come, let us go.
This fellow had a Volscian to his mother;
His wife is in Corioles, and his child
Like him by chance. Yet give us our dispatch.   180
I am hushed until our city be a-fire,
And then I'll speak a little.

                        Holds her by the hand, silent.

CORIOLANUS   O mother, mother!
What have you done? Behold, the heavens do ope,
The gods look down, and this unnatural scene
They laugh at. O my mother, mother! O!   185
You have won a happy victory to Rome;
But, for your son—believe it, O, believe it!—
Most dangerously you have with him prevailed,
If not most mortal to him. But let it come.
Aufidius, though I cannot make true wars,   190
I'll frame convenient peace. Now, good Aufidius,

162 **fond of** eager for   163 **clocked** clucked   164 **Loaden** laden   166 **honest**
honorable   173 **behold's** behold us   176 **reason** plead for   180 **dispatch**
dismissal   189 **mortal to** with deadly results for   191 **convenient** fitting

Were you in my stead, would you have heard
A mother less? Or granted less, Aufidius?

AUFIDIUS I was moved withal.

CORIOLANUS   I dare be sworn you were!
195 And, sir, it is no little thing to make
Mine eyes to sweat compassion. But, good sir,
What peace you'll make, advise me. For my part,
I'll not to Rome, I'll back with you; and pray you
Stand to me in this cause. O mother! Wife!

AUFIDIUS [*Aside*] I am glad thou hast set thy mercy
200   and thy honor
At difference in thee. Out of that I'll work
Myself a former fortune.

CORIOLANUS [*To Volumnia and Virgilia*] Ay, by and
      by;
But we will drink together; and you shall bear
A better witness back than words, which we
205 On like conditions will have countersealed.
Come, enter with us. Ladies, you deserve
To have a temple built you. All the swords
In Italy, and her confederate arms,
Could not have made this peace.   *Exeunt.*

[Scene IV. *Rome. A public place.*]

Enter Menenius and Sicinius.

MENENIUS See you yond coign o' th' Capitol, yond
cornerstone?

194 **withal** by it (thereby) 199 **Stand** to stand by 201–02 **work/Myself a
former fortune** regain my former position and power 204 **which** i.e., the
written document 207 **temple** (of the Fortune of Women; see Plutarch,
p. 246) 208 **confederate arms** allied powers. V.iv.1 **coign** corner

SICINIUS Why, what of that?

MENENIUS If it be possible for you to displace it with
your little finger, there is some hope the ladies of   5
Rome, especially his mother, may prevail with him.
But I say there is no hope in't; our throats are sentenced, and stay upon execution.

SICINIUS Is't possible that so short a time can alter the
condition of a man?   10

MENENIUS There is difference between a grub and a
butterfly; yet your butterfly was a grub. This Marcius is grown from man to dragon: he has wings;
he's more than a creeping thing.

SICINIUS He loved his mother dearly.   15

MENENIUS So did he me; and he no more remembers
his mother now than an eight-year-old horse. The
tartness of his face sours ripe grapes. When he
walks, he moves like an engine and the ground
shrinks before his treading. He is able to pierce a   20
corslet with his eye, talks like a knell, and his
hum is a battery. He sits in his state as a thing
made for Alexander. What he bids be done is finished with his bidding. He wants nothing of a god
but eternity and a heaven to throne in.   25

SICINIUS Yes, mercy, if you report him truly.

MENENIUS I paint him in the character. Mark what
mercy his mother shall bring from him . There is no
more mercy in him than there is milk in a male
tiger; that shall our poor city find. And all this is   30
'long of you.

SICINIUS The gods be good unto us!

MENENIUS No, in such a case the gods will not be

8 stay upon wait for   19 engine machine of war   21 corslet body armor
21–22 his hum i.e., his saying "Hum!"   22 battery beating of drums for an
attack   22 state chair of state   22–23 thing made for Alexander image of
Alexander the Great   31 'long of along of, because of

757

good unto us. When we banished him, we respected
35   not them; and, he returning to break our necks,
they respect not us.

Enter a Messenger.

MESSENGER Sir, if you'd save your life, fly to your
house.
The plebeians have got your fellow-tribune,
And hale him up and down; all swearing if
40   The Roman ladies bring not comfort home
They'll give him death by inches.

Enter another Messenger.

SICINIUS   What's the news?

SECOND MESSENGER Good news, good news! The ladies
have prevailed,
The Volscians are dislodged, and Marcius gone.
A merrier day did never yet greet Rome,
No, not th' expulsion of the Tarquins.

45   SICINIUS   Friend,
Art thou certain this is true? Is't most certain?

SECOND MESSENGER As certain as I know the sun is
fire.
Where have you lurked, that you make doubt of it?
Ne'er through an arch so hurried the blown tide,
50   As the recomforted through th' gates. Why, hark you!
Trumpets, hautboys; drums beat; all together.
The trumpets, sackbuts, psalteries, and fifes,
Tabors and cymbals, and the shouting Romans,
Make the sun dance. Hark you! (*A shout within.*)

MENENIUS   This is good news.
I will go meet the ladies. This Volumnia
55   Is worth of consuls, senators, patricians,

---

39 **hale** haul 43 **are dislodged** have broken up camp 48 **lurked** been
hiding 49 **blown** swollen (by wind) 50 s.d. **hautboy** (original of the modern
oboe) 51 **sackbuts** trombones 51 **psalteries** harp-like stringed
instruments 52 **Tabors** small drums

A city full; of tribunes such as you,
A sea and land full. You have prayed well today.
This morning for ten thousand of your throats
I'd not have given a doit. Hark, how they joy!

Sound still with the shouts.

SICINIUS First, the gods bless you for your tidings;
next,   60
Accept my thankfulness.

SECOND MESSENGER   Sir, we have all
Great cause to give great thanks.

SICINIUS   They are near the city!

SECOND MESSENGER Almost at point to enter.

SICINIUS   We'll meet them,
And help the joy.   *Exeunt.*

[Scene V. *Rome. Near the gate.*]

*Enter two Senators, with Ladies, passing over the
Stage, with other Lords.*

FIRST SENATOR Behold our patroness, the life of Rome!
Call all your tribes together, praise the gods,
And make triumphant fires; strew flowers before
them.
Unshout the noise that banished Marcius,
Repeal him with the welcome of his mother.   5
Cry "Welcome, ladies, welcome!"

ALL   Welcome, ladies,
Welcome!

A flourish with drums and trumpets.

V.v.5 **Repeal** recall

[Scene VI. *Corioli. A public place.*]

Enter Tullus Aufidius, with Attendants.

AUFIDIUS Go tell the lords o' th' city I am here.
Deliver them this paper. Having read it,
Bid them repair to th' marketplace, where I,
Even in theirs and in the commons' ears,
5   Will vouch the truth of it. Him I accuse
The city ports by this hath entered, and
Intends t' appear before the people, hoping
To purge himself with words. Dispatch.
                              [*Exeunt Attendants.*]

Enter three or four Conspirators of Aufidius' faction.

Most welcome!

FIRST CONSPIRATOR How is it with our general?

10   AUFIDIUS   Even so
As with a man by his own alms empoisoned,
And with his charity slain.

SECOND CONSPIRATOR   Most noble sir,
If you do hold the same intent wherein
You wished us parties, we'll deliver you
Of your great danger.

15   AUFIDIUS   Sir, I cannot tell;
We must proceed as we do find the people.

THIRD CONSPIRATOR The people will remain uncertain
whilst
'Twixt you there's difference; but the fall of either
Makes the survivor heir of all.

V.vi.5 **Him** he whom 6 **ports** gates 11 **empoisoned** destroyed 12 **with** by 14 **parties** partisans

AUFIDIUS   I know it,
  And my pretext to strike at him admits   20
  A good construction. I raised him, and I pawned
  Mine honor for his truth; who being so heightened,
  He watered his new plants with dews of flattery,
  Seducing so my friends; and, to this end,
  He bowed his nature, never known before   25
  But to be rough, unswayable, and free.

THIRD CONSPIRATOR Sir, his stoutness
  When he did stand for consul, which he lost
  By lack of stooping——

AUFIDIUS   That I would have spoke of.
  Being banished for't, he came unto my hearth,   30
  Presented to my knife his throat. I took him,
  Made him joint-servant with me; gave him way
  In all his own desires; nay, let him choose
  Out of my files, his projects to accomplish,
  My best and freshest men; served his designments   35
  In mine own person; holp to reap the fame
  Which he did end all his; and took some pride
  To do myself this wrong; till at the last
  I seemed his follower, not partner; and
  He waged me with his countenance, as if   40
  I had been mercenary.

FIRST CONSPIRATOR   So he did, my lord.
  The army marveled at it; and, in the last,
  When he had carried Rome and that we looked
  For no less spoil than glory——

AUFIDIUS   There was it;
  For which my sinews shall be stretched upon him.   45
  At a few drops of women's rheum, which are

21 **pawned** staked   22 **truth** loyalty   27 **stoutness** proud obstinacy   32 **joint-servant with me** sharer of my service (to the state)   32 **gave him way** humored him   34 **files** ranks   35 **designments** designs   37 **end** get in (of crops)   40 **waged me with his countenance** for wages gave me patronizing looks   41 **mercenary** serving for pay   42 **in the last** in the last place, finally   43 **carried** won   44 **There was it** that was the crucial thing   45 **sinews** i.e., strength   45 **upon** against   46 **At** at the price of   46 **rheum** tears

As cheap as lies, he sold the blood and labor
Of our great action. Therefore shall he die,
And I'll renew me in his fall. But hark!

Drums and trumpets sounds, with great shouts
of the people.

FIRST CONSPIRATOR Your native town you entered like
50   a post,
And had no welcomes home; but he returns,
Splitting the air with noise.

SECOND CONSPIRATOR   And patient fools,
Whose children he hath slain, their base throats tear
With giving him glory.

THIRD CONSPIRATOR   Therefore, at your vantage,
55   Ere he express himself or move the people
With what he would say, let him feel your sword,
Which we will second. When he lies along,
After your way his tale pronounced shall bury
His reasons with his body.

AUFIDIUS   Say no more:
60   Here come the lords.

Enter the Lords of the city.

ALL LORDS You are most welcome home.

AUFIDIUS   I have not deserved it.
But, worthy lords, have you with heed perused
What I have written to you?

ALL [LORDS]   We have.

FIRST LORD   And grieve to hear't.
What faults he made before the last, I think
65   Might have found easy fines; but there to end
Where he was to begin, and give away

50 **post** messenger 54 **at your vantage** at a moment opportune for you
57 **second** support (with our swords) 57 **along** stretched at full length
58 **After your way his tale pronounced** his story told in your version 65 **fines**
penalties

The benefit of our levies, answering us
With our own charge, making a treaty where
There was a yielding—this admits no excuse.

AUFIDIUS He approaches. You shall hear him.   70

Enter Coriolanus, marching with drum and colors,
the commoners being with him.

CORIOLANUS Hail, lords! I am returned your soldier;
No more infected with my country's love
Than when I parted hence, but still subsisting
Under your great command. You are to know
That prosperously I have attempted, and   75
With bloody passage led your wars even to
The gates of Rome. Our spoils we have brought
    home
Doth more than counterpoise a full third part
The charges of the action. We have made peace
With no less honor to the Antiates   80
Than shame to th' Romans; and we here deliver,
Subscribed by th' consuls and patricians,
Together with the seal o' th' senate, what
We have compounded on.

AUFIDIUS   Read it not, noble lords;
But tell the traitor in the highest degree   85
He hath abused your powers.

CORIOLANUS Traitor! How now!

AUFIDIUS   Ay, traitor, Marcius!

CORIOLANUS   Marcius!

AUFIDIUS Ay, Marcius, Caius Marcius! Dost thou
    think
I'll grace thee with that robbery, thy stol'n name
Coriolanus, in Corioles?   90

---

67 **our levies** the armies we raised 67–68 **answering us/With our own charge**
paying us (only) with our own expenditure 73 **parted** departed 73 **subsisting**
remaining 76 **passage** action 78–79 **more ... charges** exceed the costs by a
whole third (cf. line 68) 82 **Subscribed** signed 84 **compounded** agreed
89 **grace** honor

You lords and heads o' th' state, perfidiously
He has betrayed your business and given up,
For certain drops of salt, your city Rome,
I say "your city," to his wife and mother;
95   Breaking his oath and resolution, like
A twist of rotten silk; never admitting
Counsel o' th' war; but at his nurse's tears
He whined and roared away your victory;
That pages blushed at him, and men of heart
Looked wond'ring each at others.

100 CORIOLANUS   Hear'st thou, Mars?

AUFIDIUS Name not the god, thou boy of tears!

CORIOLANUS   Ha!

AUFIDIUS No more.

CORIOLANUS Measureless liar, thou hast made my
    heart
Too great for what contains it. "Boy"! O slave!
105   Pardon me, lords, 'tis the first time that ever
I was forced to scold. Your judgments, my grave
    lords,
Must give this cur the lie; and his own notion—
Who wears my stripes impressed upon him, that
Must bear my beating to his grave—shall join
110   To thrust the lie unto him.

FIRST LORD Peace, both, and hear me speak.

CORIOLANUS Cut me to pieces, Volsces, men and lads,
Stain all your edges on me. "Boy"! False hound!
If you have writ your annals true, 'tis there,
115   That, like an eagle in a dovecote, I
Fluttered your Volscians in Corioles.
Alone I did it. "Boy"?

AUFIDIUS   Why, noble lords,

96 **twist** thread (made of more than one strand)   99 **That** so that   99 **of heart** of
spirit   107 **notion** understanding   114 **there** (written) there

Will you be put in mind of his blind fortune,
Which was your shame, by this unholy braggart,
'Fore your own eyes and ears?

ALL CONSPIRATORS   Let him die for't.   120

ALL PEOPLE Tear him to pieces!—Do it presently!—
He killed my son!—My daughter!—He killed my
cousin Marcius!—He killed my father!

SECOND LORD Peace, ho! no outrage, peace!
The man is noble, and his fame folds in   125
This orb o' th' earth. His last offenses to us
Shall have judicious hearing. Stand, Aufidius,
And trouble not the peace.

CORIOLANUS   O that I had him,
With six Aufidiuses or more—his tribe,
To use my lawful sword!

AUFIDIUS   Insolent villain!   130

ALL CONSPIRATORS Kill, kill, kill, kill, kill him!
Draw the Conspirators and kills Marcius, who falls.
Aufidius stands on him.

LORDS   Hold, hold, hold, hold!

AUFIDIUS My noble masters, hear me speak.

FIRST LORD   O Tullus!

SECOND LORD Thou hast done a deed whereat valor
will weep.

THIRD LORD Tread not upon him. Masters all, be
quiet;
Put up your swords.   135

AUFIDIUS My lords, when you shall know—as in this
rage
Provoked by him, you cannot—the great danger
Which this man's life did owe you, you'll rejoice

---

118 blind fortune mere good luck (Fortune is a blind goddess)   121 presently
at once   125 folds in embraces   127 judicious judicial   127 Stand stop
138 did owe you held in payment for you

That he is thus cut off. Please it your honors
140 To call me to your senate, I'll deliver
Myself your loyal servant, or endure
Your heaviest censure.

FIRST LORD   Bear from hence his body,
And mourn you for him. Let him be regarded
As the most noble corse that ever herald
Did follow to his urn.

145 SECOND LORD   His own impatience
Takes from Aufidius a great part of blame.
Let's make the best of it.

AUFIDIUS   My rage is gone,
And I am struck with sorrow. Take him up.
Help, three o' th' chiefest soldiers; I'll be one.
150 Beat thou the drum, that it speak mournfully;
Trail your steel pikes. Though in this city he
Hath widowed and unchilded many a one,
Which to this hour bewail the injury,
Yet he shall have a noble memory.
155 Assist.

Exeunt bearing the body of Marcius.
A dead march sounded.

FINIS

140 **deliver** prove 142 **censure** sentence 144 **corse** corpse 154 **memory**
memorial

Textual Note

The text of *Coriolanus* has survived only in the First
Folio (1623), on which the present edition is based.
There are no records of performances earlier than 1623,
but there is a mocking imitation of the curious phrase,
"lurched all swords of the garland" (II.ii.102), in Ben
Jonson's *Epicoene, or The Silent Woman* (1609). It is
therefore almost certain that the play was written and
performed not later than 1609. The use in Menenius'
fable of the body and its members of expressions from
William Camden's *Remains* of 1605 and the probable
allusion to the Midlands revolt of 1607, point to a date
of 1607 or later. There is also the possible reference
to the Great Frost of 1607-08 in the phrase "the coal
of fire upon the ice" (I.i.174). It seems safe to assume
that *Coriolanus* was written after *Antony and Cleopatra*,
somewhere between 1607 and 1609.

The Folio text of *Coriolanus* might be described, like
that of *The Tempest*, as a distinguished one; it was prepared with great care and is especially remarkable for its
elaborate stage directions. W. W. Greg's assertion that the
text was printed from the author's manuscript is now
widely accepted. The stage directions, presumably Shakespeare's own, are those of a man of the theater who has
his eye on the stage and the actors. For example: "*Enter
Marcius and Aufidius, at several doors*" (I.viii); "*They
all bustle about Coriolanus*" (III.i.184); and the most
telling gesture of the play, "*Holds her by the hand, silent*"
(V.iii.182).

But though the text brings us so close to the practicing
hand of the poet-playwright, it was edited and printed
by mortal men. It has a fairly high number of errors, and
emendations have been found necessary in at least twenty
to twenty-five places. One line has been omitted (II.iii.
249), and in two passages the style is so cryptic as to
seem almost surely corrupt (III.ii.74-80; V.i.67-69).
The most disturbing defect of the Folio text of *Coriolanus*

TEXTUAL NOTE

is the widespread mislineation. There are many lines that are either too short or too long, as measured by the usual blank-verse norm, and it is often very hard to determine where the line division should occur. Most of these abnormalities, it has been pointed out, come in short speeches, or at the end or beginning of speeches in rapid dialogue. There are a relatively few instances in which speeches are assigned to seemingly inappropriate speakers. There are also variations in the names of speakers, most of them of little significance, and usually in names of minor persons. The town that gives the hero his honorific title is usually called "Corioles," though "Coriolus" and "Corialus" also occur. There is considerable uncertainty as to how both "Corioles" and "Coriolanus" are to be accented. The common reader, like the learned editor, is free to follow his rhythmic sense in particular lines: "Coríoles" or "Corióles"? "Coriolānus" (the usual pronunciation) or "Coríolanus"?

The present edition follows the Folio text closely, but spelling and punctuation are modernized, abbreviations are amplified, names of speakers regularized, and some stage directions are moved slightly. The act divisions (translated from Latin) are those of the Folio; no scenes, except the first, are indicated in the Folio text. All other scene divisions printed here (in square brackets) are those of the Globe edition. The list of readings given in the following table includes only those words in the Folio that have been omitted or emended. The reading adopted in this edition is printed in bold, followed by the original reading in roman.

I.i.7 **Marcius** Martius (throughout the play) 16 **on one** 28 **First Citizen** All 35 **Second Citizen** All 58 **First Citizen** 2 Cit. (throughout the rest of Scene i) 93 **stale't** scale't 111 **tauntingly** taintingly 215 **Shouting** Shooting 219 **unroofed** vnroo'st 227 s.d. **Junius** Annius 240 **Lartius** Lucius

I.ii. s.d. **Corioles** Coriolus 4 **on one** 30 **They've** Th'haue

I.iii.39 **that's** that 46 **sword, contemming. Tell** sword. Contenning, tell 85 **Virgilia** Vlug. 87 **yarn** yearne 88 **Ithaca** Athica 102 **whom** who

TEXTUAL NOTE

I.iv. s.d., 12s.d. **Corioles** Corialus 31 **herd of**—**boils** Heard of Byles 42 **trenches. Follow's** Trenches followes 45 s.d. **Enters the gates** Enter the Gati 57 **Were** Weare 58 **Cato's** Calues

I.vi.21 **Who's** Whose 22 **flayed** Flead 53 **Antiates** Antients 70 **Lesser** Lessen

I.viii.7 **Holloa** hollow

I.ix.46 **coverture** Ouerture 50 **shout** shoot 65 **Caius Marcius** Marcus Caius (in this order throughout)

I.x.30 **cypress** Cyprus

II.i.24 **how are** ho ware 58 **cannot** can 63 **you** you you 66 **bisson** beesome 171 **Coriolanus** Martius Caius Coriolanus 184 **wear** were 186 **Coriolanus** Com. 192 **you** yon 210 s.d. **Brutus** Enter Brutus 219 **flamens** Plamins 240 **napless** Naples 261 **touch** teach

II.ii.26 **ascent** assent 51 **state's** states 82 **one on's** on ones 92 **chin** Shinne 93 **bristled** brizled

II.iii.29 **wedged** wadg'd 44 **all together** altogether 71 **Ay, not I, but** 119 **hire** higher 120 **toge** tongue 249 **And Censorinus that was so surnamed** [F omits. This line, invented by N. Delius in his edition of 1872, is indebted to Plutarch. 260 **Citizens** All

III.i.33 **herd** Heard 48 **Coriolanus** Com. 91 **good God!** 92 **reckless** wreaklesse 126 **Their** There 143 **Where one** Whereon 185 **All** [F has no speech prefix here, but gives "All" before line 187] 214 **All [Citizens]** All Ple. 228 **him!** him. Exeunt. 229 **your** our 230 **Coriolanus** Com. 236 **Cominius** Corio. 237 **Coriolanus** Mene. [speech assigned to Menenius through line 241] 239 **Menenius** [see preceding note] 286 **our** one 322 **bring him** bring him in peace

III.ii.21 **thwartings** things 32 **herd** heart 55 **roted** roated 115 **lulls** lull

III.iii.32 **for th'** fourth 36 **Throng** Through 55 **accents** Actions 89 **flaying** Fleaing 99 **do** doth 110 **for** from 135 s.d. **The other Senators** Cumalijs

IV.i.24 **thee** the 34 **Whither wilt** Whether will

IV.iii.35 **will** well

IV.iv.23 **hate** haue

IV.v.3 **master** M. 82 **Whooped** Hoop'd 98 **Thou'rt** Th'art 113 **clip** cleep 183 **lief** liue 236 **sleepy** sleepe

IV.vi.4 **do** do we 34 **lamentation** Lamention 90 **wi' th'**

IV.vii.34 **osprey** Aspray 37 **'twas** 'was 39 **defect** detect 49 **virtues** Vertue 55 **founder** fouler

V.i.16 **wracked fair** Wrack'd for with 138 **one** oue

769

TEXTUAL NOTE

V.ii.s.d. **on** or   16 **haply** happely   61 **errand** arrant   64–65 **but by me but my**   102 **swoon** swoond

V.iii.48 **prate** pray   63 **holp** hope   104 **enmity's** enmities   141 **war's** Warres   149 **fine** fiue   152 **charge** change   169 **him with** him with him with   192 **stead** steed

V.iv.50 s.d. **all together** altogether

V.v.4 **Unshout** Vnshoot

V.vi.116 **Fluttered** Flatter'd   131 s.d. **the Conspirators** both the Conspirators

770

This book is set in EHRHARDT. The precise origin
of the typeface is unclear. Most of the founts were
probably cut by the Hungarian punch-cutter
Nicholas Kis for the Ehrhardt foundry
in Leipzig, where they were left
for sale in 1689. In 1938 the
Monotype foundry pro-
duced the modern
version.